INTERNATIONAL CRIMINAL PROCEDURE

Volume III of the International Criminal Law Practitioner Library completes the review of international criminal law begun in Volumes I and II, which analyse the forms of responsibility and the elements of the core crimes. This volume reviews the procedural law and practices of the international criminal tribunals from investigation to trial, appeal, and punishment, and examines the framework within which the substantive law operates. The authors present a critical study of those procedures that are essential to effective investigations and fair trials, and explore how the ICC, ICTY, and ICTR – as well as the SCSL and other internationalised tribunals, where relevant – have shaped the evolution of international criminal procedure in order to meet new challenges and changing circumstances. The key jurisprudence and rule amendments up to 1 December 2009 have been surveyed, making this a highly relevant and timely work.

GIDEON BOAS is a Senior Lecturer in Law at Monash University Law Faculty and an international law consultant.

JAMES L. BISCHOFF is an Attorney-Adviser in the Office of the Legal Adviser of the United States Department of State. He participated in this series in his personal capacity, and the views expressed are his and his coauthors' own. They do not necessarily reflect the views of the United States Department of State or the United States Government.

NATALIE L. REID is an Associate with Debevoise & Plimpton LLP, New York.

B. DON TAYLOR III is an Instructor in Law at Washington University in St. Louis School of Law.

INTERNATIONAL CRIMINAL PROCEDURE

International Criminal Law Practitioner Library Series

Volume III

GIDEON BOAS

JAMES L. BISCHOFF

NATALIE L. REID

B. DON TAYLOR III

The views expressed in this book are those of the authors alone. They do not necessarily reflect the views or official positions of the International Criminal Tribunal for the former Yugoslavia, the United Nations in general, the United States Department of State, or the United States government.

CAMBRIDGE
UNIVERSITY PRESS

CAMBRIDGE UNIVERSITY PRESS
Cambridge, New York, Melbourne, Madrid, Cape Town, Singapore,
São Paulo, Delhi, Dubai, Tokyo, Mexico City

Cambridge University Press
The Edinburgh Building, Cambridge CB2 8RU, UK

Published in the United States of America by Cambridge University Press, New York

www.cambridge.org
Information on this title: www.cambridge.org/9780521116305

First published 2011

Printed in the United Kingdom at the University Press, Cambridge

A catalogue record for this publication is available from the British Library

Library of Congress Cataloguing in Publication data
International criminal procedure / Gideon Boas ... [et al.].
p. cm. – (International criminal law practitioner library ; vol. 3)
Includes bibliographical references and index.
ISBN 978-0-521-11630-5 (hardback)
1. International criminal courts–Rules and practice. 2. Criminal procedure
(International law) 3. Criminal justice, Administration of. I. Boas, Gideon.
KZ6304.I579 2010
345′.05–dc22
2010040916

ISBN 978-0-521-11630-5 Hardback

Contents

Foreword

This is the third volume in the *International Criminal Law Practitioner Library Series*. Volumes I and II dealt with substantive international criminal law, particularly forms of individual criminal responsibility and the core crimes of genocide, crimes against humanity and war crimes. The present volume is devoted to international criminal procedure, the most controversial and most important aspect of international criminal law.

While substantive international criminal law is accepted as a branch of international law, doubts have been raised as to whether there is a body of law that can legitimately be called international criminal procedure. In large measure these doubts arise from the fact that international criminal procedure embraces both the accusatorial system of the common law and the inquisitorial system of the civil law. The argument is made that it lacks coherence and certainty because these two systems are as yet still engaged in a struggle for supremacy. The present careful and comprehensive study of the rules and principles of international criminal procedure refutes this argument and shows convincingly that international criminal procedure is a *sui generis* system, with a common foundational source – international human rights law and the basic norm of the right to a fair trial.

The authors accept that different international criminal courts are governed by different rules under their different founding Statutes. Indeed, much of the study is dedicated to comparing and contrasting these differences. Significant differences are the judge-made rules of the *ad hoc* criminal tribunals for the former Yugoslavia (ICTY) and Rwanda (ICTR) and the detailed Rules of Procedure and Evidence prepared by the Preparatory Commission following the Conference at which the Rome Statute of the International Criminal Court (ICC) was adopted; the different jurisdictional rules which confer primacy of jurisdiction upon the ICTY and ICTR but upon national courts rather than the ICC under the principle of complementarity; and the different approaches of the *ad hoc* tribunals and the ICC to victim participation in the proceedings. Such differences, however, are no greater than the differences between different members of the accusatorial system (the United States and England) or inquisitorial system (Germany and France) and do not undermine the inherent unity of the system of international criminal procedure.

The authors correctly show that the *sui generis* system of international criminal procedure accommodates both the accusatorial and inquisitorial systems. Certainly there is an accusatorial or adversarial slant to the proceedings before international criminal tribunals, but at the same time there are many features of the proceedings which are foreign to the common law, such as active judicial intervention, victim participation, flexible rules of admissibility of evidence which know few exclusionary rules, the discouragement of plea bargaining and the rejection of 'witness proofing'.

Treatises on national systems of criminal procedure tend to take the more basic features of the proceedings for granted and to plunge immediately into legal technicalities. Not so the present work. The authors trace the law governing proceedings before international criminal courts in a readable manner which provides a clear picture of the whole process. Thus the reader is given a complete account of the investigation, arrest, charging, pre-trial, trial, appeal, and sentencing. Broad principle is not sacrificed on the altar of detail but nevertheless the detailed rules are thoroughly examined, analysed and, where necessary, criticised. Problems particularly relevant to international criminal tribunals receive special attention. These include the privileged position of the International Committee of the Red Cross to giving evidence; special rules relating to the admissibility of evidence in cases involving sexual violence; and the problem of self-representation in the trials of Milošević, Šešelj and Krajišnik in which the accused sought to use the court as a political platform.

Some aspects of international criminal procedure are novel and receive particular attention. Victim participation is unknown to common law systems but features prominently in the Rome Statute of the ICC. At present the rules governing this participation are in their infancy. On the one hand it is fair that victims should be given greater recognition in criminal proceedings, but there is a real danger that the participation of several hundred witnesses in proceedings will unduly prejudice the accused and add substantially to the length of proceedings. The principle of complementarity, which allows national courts to deal with prosecutions in the first instance, is, like victim participation, a hallmark of the ICC. Yet to date few states have initiated proceedings in national courts, largely because most states have either failed to incorporate the Rome Statute into domestic law or because states lack the political will to prosecute international crimes. Consequently the judges of the ICC have readily accepted cases referred to the ICC by states parties – self-referrals – despite the fact that the Rome Statute makes no provision for self-referrals. As the authors correctly state, the judges have so watered down the principle of complementarity that it is beginning to resemble the primacy of jurisdiction practised by the *ad hoc* tribunals.

The *ad hoc* tribunals for the former Yugoslavia and Rwanda have been in existence for over fifteen years while the ICC is yet to celebrate its tenth anniversary. Consequently, the practice and jurisprudence of the former far exceeds that of the latter in substance. Despite this, the authors have endeavoured to strike a balance in the attention they give to different tribunals. Certainly the study is not, as might be expected, weighted in favour of the *ad hoc* tribunals. This is wise as it supports the principal thesis of the authors that there is a common system of international criminal procedure. Reports that the ICC does not pay particular attention to the jurisprudence of the *ad hoc* tribunals are disturbing. The ICC has much to learn from the *ad hoc* tribunals and should not hesitate to seek guidance from this jurisprudence. Indeed while the ICTY and ICC co-exist in the same city – The Hague – one would expect joint judicial seminars to enable the ICC to learn from the experience of the *ad hoc* tribunals. Judges in all tribunals have asserted their power and expanded the law contained in their founding Statutes. While judicial creativity is to be welcomed, judges of the ICC should learn from the experience of their forerunner. Certainly the present study will assist them in this task.

In recent years justice has come to compete with peace as a foundational value of the international order. International courts have become an indispensable part of the pursuit for justice. Consequently it is important that such courts should be fair, transparent, and effective. This will not be achieved if international courts are allowed to operate in a cocoon, free from comment and critical assessment. It is essential that the practices and decisions of the prosecutor, defence counsel, registrar, officers of the courts, and particularly judges be subjected to close scrutiny for without such scrutiny, the goal of international justice will not be achieved. Suggestions that international courts, particularly the ICC, are still too young and too fragile to be exposed to the kind of criticism directed at national courts in democratic countries are without substance. Only incisive and robust, but fair and constructive, criticism will ensure that courts – particularly the ICC – will meet the expectations that the international community has placed on them. The authors, all young international criminal lawyers who have seen and experienced international criminal courts from within, are to be congratulated on a study that accurately portrays and analyses the law and practice of international courts; that compares and contrasts the jurisprudence of different courts; and, above all, that does not hesitate to criticise where criticism is needed and which proposes ways in which weaknesses in the practice and jurisprudence of the courts may be remedied. This is more than a book about international criminal procedure. It is at the same time a timely evaluation of the performance of international criminal courts.

John Dugard
The Hague

Table of authorities

Court and tribunal statutes

Court and tribunal rules

Court and tribunal codes, directives, and regulations

International Criminal Court

International Criminal Tribunal for the former Yugoslavia

International Criminal Tribunal for Rwanda

Internationalised tribunals

Court and tribunal practice directions

International Criminal Tribunal for the former Yugoslavia

International Criminal Tribunal for Rwanda

Special Court for Sierra Leone

International Criminal Court situations and cases

International Criminal Tribunal for the former Yugoslavia (ICTY) cases

International Criminal Tribunal for Rwanda (ICTR) Cases

Special Court for Sierra Leone (SCSL) cases

Other internationalised criminal tribunal cases

Other international cases

Other international and United Nations materials

Treaties and other international agreements

National cases and legislation

Secondary sources

Amoury Combs, Nancy, 'Copping a Plea to Genocide: The Plea Bargaining of International Crimes', (2002) 151 *University of Pennsylvania Law Review* 1, 215

Amoury Combs, Nancy, *Guilty Pleas in International Criminal Law: Constructing a Restorative Justice Approach* (2007), 214, 221, 224, 226

Amoury Combs, Nancy, 'Procuring Guilty Pleas for International Crimes: The Limited Influence of Sentence Discounts', (2006) 59 *Vanderbilt Law Review* 69, 213, 224

Aptel, Cécile, 'Closing the U.N. International Criminal Tribunal for Rwanda: Completion Strategy and Residual Issues', (2008) 14 *New England Journal of International and Comparative Law* 169, 58, 63

Aptel, Cécile, 'Some Innovations in the Statute of the Special Tribunal for Lebanon', (2005) 5 *Journal of International Criminal Justice* 1107, 148

Arsanjani, Mahnoush H. and W. Michael Reisman, 'The Law-in-Action of the International Criminal Court', (2005) 99 *American Journal International Law* 385, 94

Baig, Laurel, 'International Criminal Law and Legal Ethics: The Need for Shared Expectations', in (2009) *Proceedings of the103rd Annual Meeting of the American Society of International Law*, 148

Bartholomeusz, Lance, 'The *Amicus Curiae* before the International Courts and Tribunals', (2005) 5 *Non-State Actors and International Law* 211, 166, 168, 169

Bassiouni, M. Cherif and Peter Manikas, *The Law of the International Criminal Tribunal for the Former Yugoslavia* (1996), 139

Behrens, Hans-Jörg, 'Article 52 Regulations of the Court', in Otto Triffterer (ed.), *Commentary on the Rome Statute of the International Criminal Court: Observers' Notes, Article by Article* (1999), 42

Bell, John, *French Legal Cultures* (2001), 429

Bibas, Stephanos and William W. Burke-White, 'International Idealism Meets Domestic-Criminal-Procedure Realism', (2010) 59 *Duke Law Journal* 637, 254

Bierbauer, Erik and Rebecca Jenkin, 'A Growing Distance Between The Hague and Strasbourg?: An International Criminal Tribunal and the European Court of Human Rights Reach Different Results in Two Reporter's Privilege Cases', *MLRC MediaLawLetter*, September 2009, 371

Blumenstock, Tilman and Wayde Pittman, 'The Transfer of Cases Before the International Criminal Tribunal for the Former Yugoslavia to Competent National Jurisdictions', (2008) 21(2) *Journal of International Law of Peace and Armed Conflict (Humanitäres Völkerrecht-Informationsschriften)* 106, 58, 59, 60, 61, 63

Boas, Gideon, 'Admissibility of Evidence Under the Rules of Procedure and Evidence of the ICTY: Development of the "Flexibility Principle"', in Richard May *et al.* (eds.), *Essays on ICTY Procedure and Evidence in Honour of Gabrielle Kirk McDonald* (2001), 336

Boas, Gideon, 'The Case for a New Appellate Jurisdiction for International Criminal Law', in Göran Sluiter and Sergey Vasiliev (eds.), *International Criminal Procedure: Towards a Coherent Body of Law* (2008), 36, 254, 384, 429, 430, 440, 460, 461

Boas, Gideon, 'A Code of Evidence and Procedure for International Criminal Law? The Rules of the ICTY', in Gideon Boas and William A. Schabas (eds.), *International Criminal Law Developments in the Case Law of the ICTY* (2002), 15, 17, 21, 24, 30, 35, 36, 37

Boas, Gideon, 'Comparing the ICTY and the ICC: Some Procedural and Substantive Issues', (2000) 47 *Netherlands International Law Review* 267, 15, 26

Boas, Gideon, *The Milošević Trial: Lessons for the Conduct of Complex International Criminal Proceedings* (2007), 15, 16, 35, 36, 37, 138, 139, 156, 159, 198, 203, 242, 247, 265, 277, 289, 300, 365, 440

Boas, Gideon, James L. Bischoff, and Natalie L. Reid, *Elements of Crimes in International Criminal Law* (2008), 14, 15, 37, 51, 64, 74, 84, 100, 185, 187, 199, 200, 219, 296, 340, 352, 362, 376, 386, 387, 390, 393, 394, 397, 410, 422, 432, 448, 472

Boas, Gideon, James L. Bischoff, and Natalie L. Reid, *Forms of Responsibility in International Criminal Law* (2007), 1, 36, 100, 181, 193, 198, 202, 347, 352, 356, 389, 390, 398, 399, 421, 429, 430, 431, 446, 464

Boas, Gideon and Gabriel Oosthuizen, International Criminal Law Services, 'Suggestions for Future Lessons-Learned Studies: The Experience of Other International and Hybrid Criminal Courts of Relevance to the International Criminal Court', January 2010, 147, 148

Bohlander, Michael, 'The Defence', in Gideon Boas and William A. Schabas, *International Criminal Law Developments in the Case Law of the ICTY* (2003), 141

Bohlander, Michael, 'Plea-Bargaining Before the ICTY', in Richard May, David Tolbert, John Hocking, Ken Roberts, Bing Bing Jia, Daryl Mundis, and Gabriel Oosthuizen (eds.), *Essays on ICTY Procedure and Evidence in Honour of Gabrielle Kirk McDonald* (2001), 214

Bohlander, Michael, 'Referring an Indictment from the ICTY and ICTR to Another Court: Rule 11 *bis* and the Consequences for the Law of Extradition', (2006) 55 *International and Comparative Law Quarterly* 219, 62

Bonomy, Iain, 'The Reality of Conducting a War Crimes Trial', (2007) 5 *Journal of International Criminal Justice* 348, 421

Bosly, Henri D., 'Admission of Guilt Before the ICC and in Continental Systems' (2004) 2 *Journal of International Criminal Justice* 1040, 214

Broomhall, Bruce, 'Article 51 Rules of Procedure and Evidence', in Otto Triffterer (ed.), *Commentary on the Rome Statute of the International Criminal Court* (2nd edn 2008), 39

Broun, Kenneth S. *et al.*, *McCormick on Evidence*, Vol. II (6th edn 2006), 347

Brown, Bartram S., 'Primacy or Complementarity: Reconciling the Jurisdiction of National Courts and International Criminal Tribunals', (1998) 23 *Yale Journal of International Law* 383, 51, 52, 53, 55

Burke-White, William W., 'Complementarity in Practice: The International Criminal Court as Part of a System of Multi-Level Global Governance in the Democratic Republic of Congo', (2005) 18 *Leiden Journal of International Law* 557, 94

Burke-White, William W., 'The Domestic Influence of International Criminal Tribunals: The International Criminal Tribunal for the Former Yugoslavia and the Creation of the State Court of Bosnia & Herzegovina', (2008) 46 *Columbia Journal of Transnational Law* 279, 47, 99

Burke-White, William W., 'The International Criminal Court and the Future of Legal Accountability', (2003) *ILSA Journal of International and Comparative Law* 195, 67, 68, 99, 471, 472

Butt, Peter (ed.), *Butterworths Concise Australian Legal Dictionary* (2nd edn 2001), 452

Carroll, Christina M., 'An Assessment of the Role and Effectiveness of the International Criminal Tribunal for Rwanda and the Rwandan National Justice System in Dealing with Mass Atrocities of 1994' (2000) 18 *Boston University International Law Journal* 163, 251

Cassese, Antonio, 'The ICTY: A Living and Vital Reality', (2004) 2 *Journal of International Criminal Justice* 585, 59

Cassese, Antonio, *International Criminal Law* (2nd edn 2008), 1, 4, 8, 10, 11, 13, 98, 424, 464

Cassese, Antonio, 'Opinion: The ICTY and Human Rights', (1997) *European Human Rights Law Review* 329, 12

Cassese, Antonio, 'Statement by the President at a Briefing to Members of Diplomatic Missions Concerning the Adoption of the Rules of Procedure and Evidence of the ICTY', UN Doc. IT/29, 11 February 1994, 337

Cassese, Antonio, 'The Statute of the International Criminal Court: Some Preliminary Reflections', (1999) 10 *European Journal of International law* 144, 43, 429

Charney, Jonathan, 'Universal International Law', (1993) 87 *American Journal of International Law* 529, 3

Chinkin, Christine M., 'Due Process and Witness Anonymity', (1997) 91 *American Journal of International Law* 75, 269

Chung, Christine, 'Victims' Participation at the International Criminal Court: Are Concessions of the Court Clouding the Promise?', (2008) 6 *Northwestern University Journal of International Human Rights* 459, 311, 321, 323

Cockayne, James, 'Special Court for Sierra Leone: Decisions on the Recusal of Judges Robertson and Winter', (2004) 2 *Journal of International Criminal Justice* 1154, 257

Cogan, Jacob Katz, 'International Criminal Courts and Fair Trials: Difficulties and Prospects', (2002) 27 *Yale Journal of International Law* 134, 35, 49

Cogan, Jacob Katz, 'The Problem of Obtaining Evidence for International Criminal Courts', (2000) 22 *Human Rights Quarterly* 404, 66

Condorelli, Luigi and Annalisa Ciampi, 'Comments on the Security Council Referral of the Situation in Darfur to the ICC', (2005) 3 *Journal of International Criminal Justice* 590, 70

Cook, III, Julian A., 'Plea Bargaining at The Hague', (2005) 30 *Yale Journal of International Law* 473, 214, 220, 221

Corrie, Karen, American NGO Coalition for the International Criminal Court, 'Questions & Answers on Defense Counsel at the International Criminal Court', 30 June 2008, 145

Cryer, Robert, *Prosecuting International Crimes: Selectivity and the International Criminal Law Regime* (2005), 53, 55, 66, 96

Cryer, Robert, Håkan Friman, Darryl Robinson, and Elizabeth Wilmshurst, *An Introduction to International Criminal Law and Procedure* (2007)., 1, 15, 104, 106, 114, 123, 226, 311, 330, 350

Czajkowski, Steve 'ICTY Delays Seselj Trial over Witness Intimidation Concerns', *Jurist*, 12 February 2009, 354, 357

Damaška, Mirjan, 'Negotiated Justice in International Criminal Courts', (2004) 2 *Journal of International Criminal Justice* 1018, 214

Damaška, Mirjan, 'The Uncertain Fate of Evidentiary Transplants: Anglo-American and Contemporary Experiments', (1997) 45 *American Journal of Comparative Law* 839, 14, 15, 25

Danner, Allison Marston, 'Constructing a Hierarchy of Crimes in International Criminal Law Sentencing', (2001) 87 *Virginia Law Review* 415, 397
Danner, Allison Marston, 'When Courts Make Law: How the International Criminal Tribunals Recast the Laws of War', (2006) 59 *Vanderbilt Law Review* 1, 470
de Bertodano, Sylvia, 'What Price Defence? Resourcing the Defence at the ICTY', (2004) 2 *Journal of International Criminal Justice* 503, 145
Dechênes, Jules, 'Excusing and Disqualification of Judges', in Otto Triffterer (ed.), Commentary on the Rome Statute of the International Criminal Court: Observers' Notes, Article by Article (1999), 258
De Guzman, Margaret M., 'Gravity and the Legitimacy of the International Criminal Court', (2009) 32 *Fordham International Law Journal* 1400, 82, 85
de Hemptinne, Jérôme and Francesco Rindi, 'ICC Pre-Trial Chamber Allows Victims to Participate in the Investigation Phase of Proceedings' (2006) 4 *Journal of International Criminal Justice* 342, 308, 321
Dixon, Rodney and Alexis Demirdjian, 'Advising Defendants About Guilty Pleas Before International Courts' (2005) 3 *Journal of International Criminal Justice* 680, 220
Dixon, Rodney, Aga Khan, and Richard May (eds.), *Archbold International Criminal Courts: Practice, Procedure and Evidence* (2003), 1, 166, 167
Drumbl, Mark A., *Atrocity, Punishment, and International Law* (2007), 304
Drumbl, Mark A. and Kenneth S. Gallant, 'Appeals in the *Ad hoc* International Criminal Tribunals: Structure, Procedure, and Recent Cases', (2001) 3 *The Journal of Appellate Practice and Process* 589, 429
Ega-Musa, Nasser, 'Another Failure of Justice in Africa', *Washington Post*, 6 March 1997, 267
Elberling, Björn, 'The Next Step in History-Writing Through Criminal Law: Exactly How Tailor-Made Is the Special Tribunal for Lebanon?' (2008) 21 *Leiden Journal of International Law* 529, 272
El Zeidy, Mohamed M., 'The Principle of Complementarity: A New Machinery to Implement International Criminal Law', (2002) 23 *Michigan Journal of International Law* 869, 99, 472
Fairlie, Megan, 'Rulemaking from the Bench: A Place for Minimalism at the ICTY', (2004) 39 *Texas International Law Journal* 257, 27
Fairlie, Megan, 'The Marriage Between Common and Continental Law at the ICTY and Its Progeny: Due Process Deficit', (2004) 4 *International Criminal Law Review* 243, 14, 24
Farquhar, Michael, Global Policy Forum, 'Witness Intimidation Is a Serious Problem in Kosovo', 1 April 2005, 267
Feldman, David J. 'England and Wales', in Craig M. Bradley (ed.), *Criminal Procedure: A Worldwide Study* (2nd edn 2007), 306
Fernández de Gurmendi, Silvia A., 'International Criminal Law Procedures', in Roy S. Lee (ed.), *The International Criminal Court: The Making of the Rome Statute* (1999), 225
Fernández de Gurmendi, Silvia A., 'The Role of the International Prosecutor', in Roy S. Lee (ed.), *The International Criminal Court: The Making of the Rome Statute* (1999), 71
Fernández de Gurmendi, Silvia A., and Håkan Friman, 'The Rules of Procedure and Evidence of the International Criminal Court', (2000) 3 *Yearbook of International Humanitarian Law* 289, 39

Fernández de Gurmendi, Silvia A., and Håkan Friman, 'The Rules of Procedure and Evidence and the Regulations of the Court', in José Doria, Hans-Peter Gasser, and M. Cherif Bassiouni (eds.), *The Legal Regime of the International Criminal Court* (2009), 39

Fife, Rolf Einar, 'Applicable Penalties', in Otto Triffterer (ed.), *Commentary on the Rome Statute of the International Criminal Court: Observers' Notes, Article by Article* (1999), 392, 412

Fife, Rolf Einar, 'Penalties', in Roy S. Lee (ed.), *The International Criminal Court: Elements of Crimes and Rules of Procedure and Evidence* (2001), 411, 412

Finlay, Lorraine, 'Does the International Criminal Court Protect Against Double Jeopardy: An Analysis of Article 20 of the Rome Statute', (2009) 15 *U.C. Davis Journal of International Law and Policy* 221, 82, 92

Fitzgerald, Kate, 'Problems of Prosecution and Adjudication of Rape and Other Sexual Assaults Under International Law,' (1997) 8 *European Journal of International Law* 638, 350

Fritz, Nicole, and Alison Smith, 'Current Apathy for Coming Anarchy: Building the Special Court for Sierra Leone', (2001) 25 *Fordham International Law Journal* 391, 50

Frulli, Micaela, 'The Special Court for Sierra Leone: Some Preliminary Comments', (2000) 11 *European Journal of International Law* 857, 50

Gaeta, Paola, 'Is the Practice of "Self-Referrals" a Sound Start for the ICC?', (2004) 2 *Journal of International Criminal Justice* 949, 64, 93

Gaparayi, Idi, 'The Milošević Trial at the Halfway Stage: Judgement on the Motion for Acquittal', (2004) 17 *Leiden Journal of International Law* 737, 289

Garner, Bryan A. (ed.), *Black's Law Dictionary* (7th edn 1999), 428

Garner, Bryan A., *Legal Writing in Plain English* (2001), 419

Gowlland-Debbas, Vera, 'Security Council Enforcement Action and Issues of State Responsibility', (1994) 43 *International Criminal Law Quarterly* 55, 23

Green, Jennifer, Rhonda Copelon, Patrick Cotter, and Beth Stephens, 'Affecting the Rules for the Prosecution of Rape and Other Gender-Based Violence Before the International Criminal Tribunal for the Former Yugoslavia: A Feminist Proposal and Critique', (1994) 5 *Hastings Women's Law Journal* 171, 350

Guariglia, Fabricio, 'Article 65', in Otto Triffterer (ed.), Commentary on the Rome Statute of the International Criminal Court: Observers' Notes, Article by Article (1999), 225, 226

Guariglia, Fabricio, 'The Rules of Procedure and Evidence for the International Criminal Court: A New Development in International Adjudication of Individual Criminal Responsibility', in Antonio Cassese, Paola Gaeta, and John R.W.D. Jones (eds.), *The Rome Statute of the International Criminal Court: A Commentary* (2002), Vol. ii, 31

Hafner, Gerhard, Kristen Boon, Anne Rübesame, and Jonathan Huston, 'A Response to the American View as Presented by Ruth Wedgwood', (1999) 10 *European Journal of International Law* 108, 473

Halley, Janet, 'Rape at Rome: Feminist Interventions in the Criminalization of Sex-Related Violence in Positive International Criminal Law', (2008) 30 *Michigan Journal of International Law* 1, 350

Happold, Matthew, 'Prosecutor v. Thomas Lubanga, Decision of Pre-Trial Chamber I of the International Criminal Court, 29 January 2007', (2007) 56 *International and Comparative Law Quarterly* 713, 473

Harmon, Mark B. 'The Pre-Trial Process at the ICTY as a Means of Ensuring Expeditious Trials: A Potential Unrealized', (2007) 5 *Journal of International Criminal Justice* 377, 251, 300

Harmon, Mark B. and Fergal Gaynor, 'Ordinary Sentences for Extraordinary Crimes', (2007) 5 *Journal of International Criminal Justice* 683, 393, 405, 421

Harmon, Mark B. and Fergal Gaynor, 'Prosecuting Massive Crimes with Primitive Tools: Three Difficulties Encountered by Prosecutors in International Criminal Proceedings', (2004) 2 *Journal of International Criminal Justice* 403, 64, 66, 210

Hart, H.L.A., *The Concept of Law* (1961), 3

Heller, Kevin Jon, '"Recharacterizing" Facts in Lubanga', 10 August 2009 http://opiniojuris.org/, 191

Heller, Kevin Jon, 'Situational Gravity Under the Rome Statute', in Carsten Stahn and Larissa van den Herik (eds.), *Future Perspectives on International Criminal Justice* (2010), 83, 84, 85

Heller, Kevin Jon, 'What Happens to the Acquitted?', (2008) 21 *Leiden Journal of International Law* 663, 416

Henham, Ralph and Mark Dumbl, 'Plea Bargaining at the International Criminal Tribunal for the Former Yugoslavia', (2005) 16 *Criminal Law Forum* 49, 221

Henry, Benoit, 'The Acquitted Accused, a Forgotten Party of the ICTR', (2005) 12 *New England Journal of International and Comparative Law* 81, 416

Hervé, Ascensio, 'L'*amicus curiae* devant les juridictions internationales', (2001) 105 *Revue générale de droit international public* 4, 166

Higgins, Gillian, 'Fair and Expeditious Pre-Trial Proceedings: The Future of International Criminal Trials', (2007) 5 *Journal of International Criminal Justice* 394, 174

Holmes, John T., 'Complementarity: National Courts Versus the ICC', in Antonio Cassese, Paola Gaeta, and John R.W.D. Jones (eds.), *The Rome Statute of the International Criminal Court: A Commentary*, Vol. i (2002), 53, 67, 78, 79, 80, 81

Holmes, John T., 'The Principle of Complementarity', in Roy S. Lee (ed.), *The International Criminal Court: The Making of the Rome Statute* (1999), 80

Human Rights Watch, *World Report 2008*, January 2008, 63

Hunt, David, Address at the Conference of the Australian and New Zealand Society of International Law, Canberra, 19 June 2004, 337

Hunt, David, 'The International Criminal Court: High Hopes, "Creative Ambiguity" and an Unfortunate Mistrust of International Judges', (2004) 2 *Journal of International Criminal Justice* 56, 97, 471, 472, 473

Institute For War and Peace Reporting, 'Prosecution, Judges in Karadzic Case Stand-Off', 25 September 2009, 246

International Bar Association, 'First Challenges: An Examination of Recent Landmark Developments at the International Criminal Court', June 2009, 311

Jackson, John, 'Creating Evidentiary Processes in the International Criminal Tribunals that Are Fit for Purpose: Beyond the Common Law–Civil Law Divide', (2009) *Journal of International Criminal Justice* 17, 12, 15, 16, 17

Jeannet, Stéphane, 'Testimony of ICRC Delegates Before the International Criminal Court', *International Review of the Red Cross*, No. 840 December 2000, 372

Jennings, Robert Y. and Arthur Watts (eds.), *Oppenheim's International Law* (9th edn 1992), 138

Kreß, Claus, 'The Procedural Law of the International Criminal Court in Outline: Anatomy of a Unique Compromise', (2003) 1 *Journal of International Criminal Justice* 603, 97, 301

Kreß, Claus, 'The Procedural Texts of the International Criminal Court', (2007) 5 *Journal of International Criminal Justice* 537, 7, 15, 38, 42, 44

Kreß, Claus, '"Self-Referrals" and "Waivers of Complementarity": Some Considerations in Law and Policy', (2004) 2 *Journal of International Criminal Justice* 944, 94

Kwon, O-Gon, 'The Challenge of an International Criminal Trial as Seen from the Bench', (2007) 5 *Journal of International Criminal Justice* 360, 31, 251, 265, 300, 301, 337, 353, 354, 357, 468

La Rosa, Ann-Marie, 'Revision Procedure under the Rome Statute', in Antonio Cassese, Paola Gaeta, and John R.W.D. Jones, (eds.), *The Rome Statute of the International Criminal Court: A Commentary* (2002), Vol. ii, 426, 428, 458, 459

Laughland, John, 'The Anomalies of the International Criminal Tribunal are Legion', *The Times*, 17 June 1999, 30

Leigh, Monroe, 'The Yugoslav Tribunal: Use of Unnamed Witnesses Against Accused', (1996) 90 *American Journal of International Law* 235, 269

Leigh, Monroe, 'Witness Anonymity Is Inconsistent with Due Process', (1997) 91 *American Journal of International Law* 80, 269

Lombardi, Gregory P. 'Legitimacy and the Expanding Power of the ICTY', (2003) 37 *New England Law Review* 887, 300, 471, 473

MacCormick, D. Neil, and Robert S. Summers, 'Introduction', in D. Neil MacCormick and Robert S. Summers (eds.), *Interpreting Precedents: A Comparative Study* (1997), 460

Martin, Francisco F., Stephen J. Schnably, Richard Wilson, Jonathan S. Simon, and Mark V. Tushnet, *International Human Rights and Humanitarian Law: Treaties, Cases, and Analysis* (2006), 138, 139

Massidda, Paolina, and Sarah Pellet, 'Role and Practice of the Office of Public Counsel for Victims', in Carsten Stahn and Göran Sluiter (eds.), *The Emerging Practice of the International Criminal Court* (2009), 318

May, Richard, and Marieke Wierda, 'Trends in International Criminal Evidence: Nuremberg, Tokyo, The Hague, and Arusha', (1999) 37 *Columbia Journal of Transnational Law* 725, 336

McCormack, Timothy L.H. and Gerry Simpson, 'Achieving the Promise of Nuremberg: A New International Criminal Law Regime', in Timothy L.H. McCormack and Gerry Simpson (eds.), *The Law of War Crimes, National and International Approaches* (1997), 40

McGonigle, Brianne N., 'Bridging the Divides in International Criminal Proceedings: An Examination into the Victim Participation Endeavor of the International Criminal Court, (2009) 21 *Florida Journal of International Law* 93, 315, 324

McIntyre, Gabrielle, 'Defining Human Rights in the Arena of International Humanitarian Law: Human Rights in the Jurisprudence of the ICTY', in Gideon Boas and William A. Schabas (eds.), *International Criminal Law Developments in the Case Law of the ICTY* (2002), 139

Meernik, James, and Kimi King, 'The Sentencing Determinants of the International Criminal Tribunal for the Former Yugoslavia: An Empirical and Doctrinal Analysis', (2003) 16 *Leiden Journal of International Law* 717, 395

Megret, Frédéric, 'In Defense of Hybridity: Towards a Representational Theory of International Criminal Justice', (2005) 38 *Cornell International Law Journal* 725, 99

Meijer, Ernestine E., 'The Extraordinary Chambers in the Courts of Cambodia for Prosecuting Crimes Committed by the Khmer Rouge: Jurisdiction, Organization, and Procedure of an Internationalized National Tribunal', in Cesare P.R. Romano, André Nollkaemper, and Jann K. Kleffner (eds.), *Internationalized Criminal Courts and Tribunals: Sierra Leone, East Timor, Kosovo, and Cambodia* (2004), 7

Mendelson, Maurice H., 'Formation of Customary International Law', (1998) 272 *Recueil des Cours* 165, 3

Meron, Theodor, 'Editorial Comment: Revival of Customary Humanitarian law', (2005) 99 *American Journal of International Law* 817, 10

Meron, Theodor, 'Judicial Independence and Impartiality in International Criminal Tribunals', (2005) 99 *American Journal of International Law* 359, 255

Meron, Theodor, 'Procedural Evolution in the ICTY', (2004) 2 *Journal of International Criminal Justice* 520, 300, 301

Meron, Theodor, 'Reflections on the Prosecution of War Crimes by International Tribunals', (2006) 100 *American Journal of International Law* 551, 66

Mettraux, Guénaël, *International Crimes and the Ad Hoc Tribunals* (2005), 416

Miraglia, Michela, 'Admissibility of Evidence, Standard of Proof, and Nature of the Decision in the ICC Confirmation of Charges in Lubanga', (2008) 6 *Journal of International Criminal Justice* 489, 186

Mochochoko, Phakiso, 'International Cooperation and Judicial Assistance', in Roy S. Lee (ed.), *The International Criminal Court: The Making of the Rome Statute* (1999), 96

Moranchek, Laura, 'Protecting National Security Evidence While Prosecuting War Crimes: Problems and Lessons for International Justice from the ICTY', (2006) 31 *Yale Journal of International Law* 477, 212

Moreno-Ocampo, Luis, Prosecutor of the International Criminal Court, *Address to the Assembly of States Parties*, 14 November 2008, 71, 85, 95

Morris, Madeline H., 'The Trials of Concurrent Jurisdiction: The Case of Rwanda', (1997) 7 *Duke Journal of Comparative and International Law* 349, 53

Morris, Virginia and Michael P. Scharf, *An Insider's Guide to the International Criminal Tribunal for the Former Yugoslavia: A Documentary History and Analysis* (1995), 24

Møse, Erik, 'The ICTR's Completion Strategy – Challenges and Possible Solutions', (2008) 6 *Journal of International Criminal Justice* 667, 58

Mundis, Daryl A., 'From "Common Law" Towards "Civil Law": The Evolution of the ICTY Rules of Procedure and Evidence', (2001) 14 *Leiden Journal of International Law* 367, 15, 24, 300

Mundis, Daryl A., 'The Judicial Effects of the "Completion Strategies" on the Ad Hoc International Criminal Tribunals', (2005) 99 *American Journal of International Law* 142, 58

Mundis, Daryl A., 'The Legal Character and Status of the Rules of Procedure and Evidence of the ad hoc International Criminal Tribunals', (2001) 1 *International Criminal Law Review* 191, 30, 33, 35

Mundis, Daryl A., 'Reporting Non-Compliance: Rule 7 *bis*', in Richard May, David Tolbert, and John Hocking (eds.), *Essays on ICTY Procedure and Evidence in Honour of Gabrielle Kirk McDonald* (2001), 66

Murphy, Ray, 'Gravity Issues and the International Criminal Court', (2006) 17 *Criminal Law Forum* 281, 82

Murphy, Sean D., 'Progress and Jurisprudence of the International Criminal Tribunal for the Former Yugoslavia', (1999) 93 *American Journal of International Law* 57, 57

Ntanda Nsereko, Daniel D., 'Article 18: Preliminary Rulings Regarding Admissibility', in Otto Triffterer (ed.), *Commentary on the Rome Statute of the International Criminal Court: Observers' Notes, Article by Article* (1999), 89

Nowak, Manfred, U.N. Covenant on Civil and Political Rights: CCPR Commentary (1993), 156

Olásolo, Héctor, *The Triggering Procedure of the International Criminal Court* (2003), 69, 81, 88

Oosthuizen, Gabriël H., 'Playing Devil's Advocate: The United Nations Security Council Is Unbound by Law', (1999) 12 *Leiden Journal of International Law* 549, 23

Open Society Justice Initiative, 'Briefing Paper: Residual Functions of the UN International Criminal Tribunals for the Former Yugoslavia and Rwanda and the Special Court for Sierra Leone and Potential Mechanisms to Address Them', January 2008, 455

Orie, Alphons, 'Accusatorial v. Inquisitorial Approach in International Criminal Proceedings Prior to the Establishment of the ICC and in the Proceedings Before the ICC', in Antonio Cassese, Paola Gaeta, and John R.W.D. Jones (eds.), *The Rome Statute of the International Criminal Court: A Commentary*, Vol. II (2002), 291, 302

O'Sullivan, Eugene, and Deirdre Montgomery, 'The Erosion of the Right to Confrontation under the Cloak of Fairness at the ICTY', (2010) 8 *Journal of International Criminal Justice* 511, 353, 355, 357, 365

Pejić, Jelena, 'The Tribunal and the ICC: Do Precedents Matter?', (1997) 60 *Albany Law Review* 841, 208

Penrose, Mary Margaret, 'Lest We Fail: The Importance of Enforcement in International Criminal Law,' (1999–2000) 15 *American University International Law Review* 321, 208

Pickard, Daniel B., 'Proposed Sentencing Guidelines for the International Criminal Court', (1997) 20 *Loyola of Los Angeles International and Comparative Law Journal* 123, 422

Piragoff, Donald K., 'Evidence', in Roy S. Lee (ed.), *The International Criminal Court: Elements of Crimes and Rules of Procedure and Evidence* (2001), 350, 351, 368

Pizzi, William T. and Walter Perron, 'Crime Victims in German Courtrooms: A Comparative Perspective on American Problems', (1996) *32 Stanford Journal of International Law* 37, 467

Privacy International, 'Silencing Sources: An International Survey of Protections and Threats to Journalists' Sources', November 2007, 371

Purvis, Andrew, 'Dead Witnesses Tell No Tales: Rwandan Genocide Survivors Are the Latest Targets of Hutu Killer Gangs', *Time* (International Edition), 23 September 1996, 267

Rapp, Stephen J., 'Achieving Accountability for the Greatest Crimes: The Legacy of the International Tribunals', (2007) 55 *Drake Law Review* 259, 60

Rapp, Stephen J., 'The Compact Model in International Criminal Justice: The Special Court for Sierra Leone', (2008) 57 *Drake Law Review* 11, 263

Ratner, Steven R., Jason S. Abrams, and James L. Bischoff, *Accountability for Human Rights Atrocities in International Law: Beyond the Nuremberg Legacy* (3rd edn 2008), 15, 17, 32, 38, 47, 49, 53, 56, 59, 68, 99, 224, 239, 251, 349, 353, 357, 402, 406

Rearick, Daniel J., 'Innocent Until Alleged Guilty: Provisional Release at the ICTR,' (2003) 44 *Harvard International Law Journal* 577, 251

Reid, Karen, *A Practitioner's Guide to the European Convention on Human Rights* (1998), 428

Restatement (Third) of the Law Governing Lawyers (2009), 367

Reydams, Luc, 'The ICTR Ten Years On: Back to the Nuremberg Paradigm?', (2005) 3 *Journal of International Criminal Justice* 977, 95

Roach, Kent, 'Canada', in Craig M. Bradley (ed.), *Criminal Procedure: A Worldwide Study* (2nd edn 2007), 306

Robinson, Patrick L., 'Ensuring Fair and Expeditious Trials at the International Criminal Tribunal for the Former Yugoslavia', (2000) 11 *European Journal of International Law* 569, 14, 15, 24, 139

Robinson, Patrick L., 'Fair but Expeditious Trials', in Hirad Abtahi and Gideon Boas (eds.), *The Dynamics of International Criminal Justice: Essays in Honour of Sir Richard May* (2005), 14, 15

Robinson, Patrick L., 'Rough Edges in the Alignment of Legal Systems in the Proceedings at the ICTY', (2005) 3 *Journal of International Criminal Justice* 1, 14

Rona, Gabor, 'The ICRC Privilege Not to Testify: Confidentiality in Action', 28 February 2004, 371, 373

Rosenne, Shabtai, *The Law and Practice of the International Court* (1985), 427

Roth, Robert and Marc Henzelin, 'The Appeal Procedure of the ICC', in Antonio Cassese, Paola Gaeta, and John R.W.D. Jones, (eds.), *The Rome Statute of the International Criminal Court: A Commentary* (2002), Vol. II, 436

Rozakis, Christos L., *The Concept of Jus Cogens in the Law of Treaties* (1976), 138

Sadat, Leila Nadya, *The International Criminal Court and the Transformation of International Law: Justice for the New Millennium* (2002), 89

Safferling, Christoph, *Towards an International Criminal Procedure* (2001), 12, 139, 214, 225

Sautenet, Vincent, 'The International Criminal Tribunal for the Former Yugoslavia: Activities in 2004', (2005) 4 *Chinese Journal of International Law* 515, 58

Schabas, William A., 'Barayagwiza v. Prosecutor', (2000) 94 *American Journal of International Law* 563, 114

Schabas, William A., 'International Criminal Tribunals: A Review of 2007', (2008) 6 *Northwestern University Journal of International Human Rights* 382, 181

Schabas, William A., *An Introduction to the International Criminal Court* (3rd edn 2009), 25, 58, 70, 71, 76, 94, 253, 306, 307, 309, 311, 334, 377

Schabas, William A., 'Penalties', in Cassese, Gaeta, and Jones (eds.), in Antonio Cassese, Paola Gaeta, and John R.W.D. Jones (eds.), *The Rome Statute of the International Criminal Court: A Commentary*, Vol. II (2002), 392, 394, 407, 411, 412

Schabas, William A., 'Presumption of Innocence', in Triffterer (ed.), Otto Triffterer (ed.), *Commentary on the Rome Statute of the International Criminal Court: Observers' Notes, Article by Article* (1999), 385

Schabas, William A., 'Prosecutorial Discretion v. Judicial Activism at the International Criminal Court', (2008) 6 *Journal of International Criminal Justice* 731, 85, 473

Schabas, William A., 'United States Hostility to the International Criminal Court: It's All About the Security Council', (2004) *European Journal of International Law* 701, 68

Schabas, William A., *The UN International Criminal Tribunals: The Former Yugoslavia, Rwanda and Sierra Leone* (2006), 55, 254, 269

Scharf, Michael P., *Balkan Justice* (1997), 269

Scharf, Michael P. and Christopher M. Rassi, 'Do Former Rogue Leaders Have an International Right to Act as Their Own Lawyers in War Crimes Trials?', (2004) 20 *Ohio State Journal on Dispute Resolution* 1, 156, 158

Scheffer, David, 'A Review of the Experiences of the Pre-Trial and Appeals Chambers of the International Criminal Court Regarding the Disclosure of Evidence', in Carsten Stahn and Göran Sluiter (eds.), *The Emerging Practice of the International Criminal Court* (2009), 232, 248

Scheffer, David J., 'The United States and the International Criminal Court', (1999) 93 *American Journal of International Law* 12, 273

Schwarzenberger, Georg, *The Inductive Approach to International Law* (1965), 9

Schwarzenberger, Georg, 'The Problem of an International Criminal Law', (1950) 3 *Current Legal Problems* 263, 4, 11

Schwarzenberger, Georg, 'The Province of International Judicial Law', (1983) 21 *Notre Dame International Law Journal* 21, 4, 11

Shahabuddeen, Mohammed, *Precedent in the World Court* (1996), 428

Shraga, Daphna, 'Politics and Justice: The Role of the Security Council', in Antonio Cassese (ed.), *The Oxford Companion to International Criminal Justice* (2009) 66

Sloane, Robert D., 'Sentencing for the "Crime of Crimes": The Evolving "Common Law" of Sentencing of the International Criminal Tribunal for Rwanda', (2007) 5 *Journal of International Criminal Justice* 713, 392, 421

Sluiter, Göran, 'Compromising the Authority of International Criminal Justice: How Vojislav Šešelj Runs His Trial', (2007) 5 *Journal of International Criminal Justice* 529, 160

Sluiter, Göran, 'Cooperation of States with International Criminal Tribunals', in Antonio Cassese (ed.), *The Oxford Companion to International Criminal Justice* (2009), 67

Sluiter, Göran, 'Due Process and Criminal Procedure in the Cambodian Extraordinary Chambers', (2006) *Journal of International Criminal Justice* 314, 6

Sluiter, Göran, 'The ICTY and Offences against the Administration of Justice', (2004) 2 *Journal of International Criminal Justice* 631, 295

Sluiter, Göran, 'The Law of International Criminal Procedure and Domestic War Crimes Trials', (2006) 6 *International Criminal Law Review* 605, 5, 11, 464

Smidt, Michael L., 'The International Criminal Court: An Effective Means of Deterrence?', (2001) 167 *Military Law Review* 156, 393

Stahn, Carsten, 'The Ambiguities of Security Council Resolution 1422 (2002)', (2003) 14 *European Journal of International Law* 85, 96

Stahn, Carsten, 'Judicial Review of Prosecutorial Discretion: Five Years On', in Carsten Stahn and Göran Sluiter (eds.), *The Emerging Practice of the International Criminal Court* (2009), 105

Stahn, Carsten, 'Modification of the Legal Characterization of Facts in the ICC System: A Portrayal of Regulation 55', (2005) 1 *Criminal Law Forum* 31, 42, 190

Stahn, Carsten, Héctor Olásolo, and Kate Gibson, 'Participation of Victims in Pre-Trial Proceedings of the ICC', (2006) 4 *Journal of International Criminal Justice* 219, 306, 319, 320

Stromseth, Jane E., 'Pursuing Accountability for Atrocities After Conflict: What Impact on Building the Rule of Law?', (2007) 38 *Georgetown Journal of International Law* 251, 99

Swart, Bert, 'Cooperation Challenges for the Special Tribunal for Lebanon', (2007) 5 *Journal of International Criminal Justice* 1153, 148

Swart, Bert, 'General Problems', in Antonio Cassese, Paola Gaeta, and John R.W.D. Jones (eds.), *The Rome Statute of the International Criminal Court: A Commentary*, Vol. I (2002), 96

Swart, Mia, 'Ad Hoc Rules for Ad Hoc Tribunals? The Rule-Making Power of the Judges of the ICTY and ICTR', (2002) 18 *South African Journal of Human Rights* 570, 25, 30, 31, 32, 35, 36

Tallgren, Immi, 'Article 20: Ne Bis in Idem', in Otto Triffterer (ed.), *Commentary on the Rome Statute of the International Criminal Court: Observers' Notes, Article by Article* (1999), 82

Tavernier, Paul, 'The Experience of the International Criminal Tribunals for the Former Yugoslavia and for Rwanda', (1997) 321 *International Review of the Red Cross* 605, 23

Taylor III, B. Don, 'Demystifying the Procedural Framework of the International Criminal Court: A Modest Proposal for Radical Revision', in Carsten Stahn and Göran Sluiter (eds.), *The Emerging Practice of the International Criminal Court* (2009), 7, 38, 42, 43

Taylor III, B. Don, 'Witness Proofing in International Criminal Law: Is Widening Procedural Divergence in International Criminal Tribunals a Case for Concern?', paper submitted to the 22nd International Conference of the International Society for the Reform of Criminal Law, 11–15 July 2008, 285

Terrier, Frank, 'The Procedure Before the Trial Chamber', in Antonio Cassese, Paola Gaeta, and John R.W.D. Jones (eds.), *The Rome Statute of the International Criminal Court: A Commentary*, Vol. II (2002), 384

Thanki, Bankim, *The Law of Privilege* (2006), 368

Tieger, Alan, and Milbert Shin, 'Plea Agreements at the ICTY' (2005) 3 *Journal of International Criminal Justice* 666, 214

Tochilovsky, Vladimir, 'International Criminal Justice: Strangers in the Foreign System', (2004) 15 *Criminal Law Forum* 319, 16

Tolbert, David, 'The International Criminal Tribunal for the Former Yugoslavia: Unforeseen Successes and Foreseeable Shortcomings', (2002) 26 *Fletcher Forum of World Affairs* 7 , 99

Tracol, Xavier, 'The Precedent of Appeals Chambers Decisions in the International Criminal Tribunals', (2004) 17 *Leiden Journal of International Law* 67, 429

Triffterer, Otto, 'Requirements for the Decision', in Otto Triffterer (ed.), *Commentary on the Rome Statute of the International Criminal Court: Observers' Notes, Article by Article* (1999), 378, 384

Tulkens, Françoise, 'Main Comparable Features of the Different European Criminal Justice Systems', in Mireille Delmas-Marty (ed.), *The Criminal Process and Human Rights: Toward a European Consciousness* (1995), 14, 15, 25

Turner, Jenia Iontcheva, 'International Decision', (2009) 103 *American Journal of International Law* 116, 333

Turone, Giuliano, 'The Denial of the Accused's Right to Make Unsworn Statements in *Delalić*', (2004) 2 *Journal of International Criminal Justice* 455, 280

Turone, Giuliano, 'Powers and Duties of the Prosecutor', in Antonio Cassese, Paola Gaeta, and John R.W.D. Jones (eds.), *The Rome Statute of the International Criminal Court: A Commentary*, Vol. I (2002), 71, 85, 87, 88, 89, 90, 95, 99, 472

Triggs, Gillian D., *International Law: Contemporary Principles and Practices* (2006), 4

Udombana, Nsongurua J., 'Pay Back Time in Sudan? Darfur in the International Criminal Court', (2005) 13 *Tulsa Journal of Comparative and International Law* 1, 70

Vasiliev, Sergey, 'Art. 68(3) and Personal Interests of Victims in the Emerging Practice of the ICC', in Carsten Stahn and Göran Sluiter (eds.), *The Emerging Practice of the International Criminal Court* (2009), 312, 321

Vasiliev, Sergey, 'General Rules and Principles of International Criminal Procedure: Definition, Legal Nature, and Identification', in Göran Sluiter and Sergey Vasiliev (eds.), *International Criminal Procedure: Towards A Coherent Body of Law* (2008), 8, 11

Vasiliev, Sergey, 'Proofing the Ban on "Witness Proofing": Did the ICC Get It Right?', (2009) 20 *Criminal Law Forum* 193, 285

Virally, M., 'The Sources of International Law', in M. Sørensen (ed.), *Manual of Public International Law* (1968), 9

Voeten, Erik, 'The Politics of International Judicial Appointments', (2009) 9 *Chicago Journal of International Law* 387, 254

Wald, Patricia M., 'The International Criminal Tribunal for the Former Yugoslavia Comes of Age: Some Observations on Day-to-Day Dilemmas of an International Court', (2001) 5 *Washington University Journal of Law and Policy* 87, 292, 418

Wald, Patricia M., 'To "Establish Incredible Events by Credible Evidence": The Use of Affidavit Testimony in Yugoslavia War Crimes Tribunal Proceedings', (2001) 42 *Harvard International Law Journal* 535, 352, 353, 355, 360

War Crimes Research Office, 'Victim Participation at the Case Stage of Proceedings', February 2009, 325

War Crimes Research Office, 'Victim Participation Before the International Criminal Court', November 2007, 308

Weissbrodt, David, *The Right to a Fair Trial under the Universal Declaration of Human Rights and the International Covenant on Civil and Political Rights* (2001), 156

Wetzel, Jan Erik and Yvonne Mitri, 'The Special Tribunal for Lebanon: A Court "Off the Shelf" for a Divided Country', (2008) 7 *The Law and Practice of International Courts and Tribunals* 81, 148

Williams, Sarah 'The Completion Strategy of the ICTY and the ICTR', in Michael Bohlander (ed.), *International Criminal Justice: A Critical Analysis of Institutions and Procedures* (2007), 58

Williams, Sarah, 'ICTY Referrals to National Jurisdictions: A Fair Trial or a Fair Price?', (2006) 17 *Criminal Law Forum* 177, 63

Wippman, David, 'The Costs of International Justice,' (2006) 100 *American Journal of International Law* 861, 251

Zacklin, Ralph, 'The Failings of Ad Hoc International Tribunals', (2004) 2 *Journal of International Criminal Justice* 541, 106

Zagaris, Bruce, 'Law of War: A Bomb Kills Croatian Witness Who Was Cooperating with War Crimes Tribunal', (2000) 16 *International Enforcement Law Reporter* 977, 267

Zahar, Alexander 'International Court and Private Citizen', (2009) 12 *New Criminal Law Review* 569, 65, 354, 471

Zahar, Alexander, 'Legal Aid, Self-Representation, and the Crisis at the Hague Tribunal', (2008) 19 *Criminal Law Forum* 241, 160

Zahar, Alexander and Göran Sluiter, *International Criminal Law: A Critical Introduction* (2007), 1, 55, 57, 64, 106, 108, 115, 119, 122, 123, 139, 214, 309

Zappalà, Salvatore, 'Foreword, Symposium: Lubanga Before the ICC', (2008) 6 *Journal of International Criminal Justice* 467, 186

Zappalà, Salvatore, *Human Rights in International Criminal Proceedings* (2003), 12, 14, 139, 241, 306, 307, 311, 330

Zappalà, Salvatore, 'The Prosecutor's Duty to Disclose Exculpatory Materials and the Recent Amendment to Rule 68 ICTY RPE', (2004) 2 *Journal of International Criminal Justice* 620, 106

Zarembo, Alan, 'Rwanda's Genocide Witnesses are Killed as Wheels of Justice Slowly Begin Turning: More than 200 Rwandan Genocide Survivors Were Killed Last Year Before They Could Testify in Court', *Christian Science Monitor*, 23 January 1997, 267

Table of short forms

ACHR	American Convention on Human Rights, 21 November 1969, 1144 UNTS 123
ECCC	Extraordinary Chambers in the Courts of Cambodia
ECCC Agreement	Agreement Between the United Nations and the Royal Government of Cambodia Concerning the Prosecution Under Cambodian Law of Crimes Committed During the Period of Democratic Kampuchea, 6 June 2003, 2329 UNTS 117
ECCC Rules	Internal Rules (Rev. 4), 11 September 2009, available at www.eccc.gov.kh/english/cabinet/fileUpload/121/IRv4-EN.pdf
ECCC Statute (ECCC Law)	Law on the Establishment of the Extraordinary Chambers in the Courts of Cambodia for the Prosecution of Crimes Committed During the Period of Democratic Kampuchea, as amended on 27 October 2004, Doc. No. NS/RKM/1004/006, unofficial translation by the Council of Jurists and the Secretariat of the Task Force, revised on 26 August 2007
ECHR	Convention on Human Rights and Fundamental Freedoms (also known as the European Convention on Human Rights), 4 November 1950, 213 UNTS 222
ICC	International Criminal Court
ICC Code	Code of Professional Conduct for Counsel, Doc. No. ICC-ASP/4/Res.1, 2 December 2005
ICC Court Regulations	Regulations of the Court, Doc. No. ICC-BD/01-02–07 entered into force 18 December 2007
ICC Registry Regulations	Regulations of the Registry, Doc. No. ICC-BD/03-01-06-Rev.1, 6 March 2006
ICC Rules	Rules of Procedure and Evidence of the International Criminal Court, Doc. No. ICC-ASP/1/3, September 2002
ICCPR	International Covenant on Civil and Political Rights, 16 December 1966, 999 UNTS 171
ICTR	International Criminal Tribunal for Rwanda

ICTR Code	Code of Professional Conduct for Defence Counsel, 14 March 2008, http://www.ictrcaselaw.org/docs/20080314-defense%20code%20conduct%20ENFR.pdf
ICTR Directive	Directive on Assignment of Defence Counsel, Directive No. 1/96, 14 March 2008
ICTR Rules	Rules of Procedure and Evidence of the International Criminal Tribunal for Rwanda, Revision 17, 14 March 2008, UN Doc. ITR/3/Rev. 17
ICTR Statute	Statute of the International Criminal Tribunal for Rwanda, UN Doc. S/RES/955 (1994), Annex as amended by SC Res. 1774 (2007)
ICTY	International Criminal Tribunal for the former Yugoslavia
ICTY Code	Code of Professional Conduct for Counsel Appearing Before the International Tribunal, UN Doc. IT/125/Rev.3, 22 July 2009
ICTY Directive	Directive on Assignment of Defence Counsel, UN Doc. IT/73/Rev.11, 11 July 2006
ICTY Rules	Rules of Procedure and Evidence of the International Criminal Tribunal for the former Yugoslavia, Revision 43, 24 July 2009, UN Doc. IT/32/Rev.43
ICTY Statute	Statute of the International Criminal Tribunal for the Prosecution of Persons Responsible for Serious Violations of International Humanitarian Law Committed in the Territory of the former Yugoslavia Since 1991, UN Doc. S/RES/827 (1993), Annex, as amended by SC Res. 1877 (2009)
Rome Statute (ICC Statute)	Rome Statute of the International Criminal Court, Doc. No. A/CONF.183/9, 17 July 1998, entered into force 1 July 2002
SCSL	Special Court for Sierra Leone
SCSL Rules	Rules of Procedure and Evidence of the Special Court for Sierra Leone, as amended on 27 May 2008, available at www.sc-sl.org/LinkClick.aspx?fileticket=yNjqn5TIYKs%3d&tabid=176
SCSL Statute	Statute of the Special Court for Sierra Leone, UN Doc. S/2002/246, Appendix II, 16 January 2002, 2178 UNTS 138

1

The nature of international criminal procedure

CONTENTS

Few today would dispute the existence of substantive international criminal law and its legitimacy under international law. With some noteworthy exceptions, it is well accepted that the core categories of crimes, their underlying offences, and the forms of responsibility listed in the statutes of the international and internationalised criminal courts and tribunals (collectively, 'international criminal tribunals') are established in customary international law, treaty law or general principles of international law.[1] The same cannot be said, however, for the procedural rules that govern the conduct of international criminal proceedings. Despite fifteen years of procedural activity at the international criminal tribunals, generating far more jurisprudence on matters of procedure than on substantive law, considerable scepticism remains about the legitimacy of international criminal procedure as a body of international law in its own right.

[1] See Gideon Boas, James L. Bischoff, and Natalie L. Reid, *Forms of Responsibility in International Criminal Law* (2007), pp. 113–114; Gideon Boas, James L. Bischoff, and Natalie L. Reid, *Elements of Crimes in International Criminal Law* (2008), pp. 5–9 ('Boas, Bischoff, and Reid, *Elements of Crimes*'). See also, e.g., Antonio Cassese, *International Criminal Law* (2nd edn 2008), pp. 13–22; Robert Cryer, Håkan Friman, Darryl Robinson, and Elizabeth Wilmshurst, *An Introduction to International Criminal Law and Procedure* (2007), pp. 6–12; Alexander Zahar and Göran Sluiter, *International Criminal Law: A Critical Introduction* (2007), pp. 79–105; Karim Khan and Rodney Dixon, *Archbold International Criminal Courts: Practice, Procedure, and Evidence* (2nd edn 2005), pp. 7–14.

This third volume of the *International Criminal Law Practitioner Library Series* presents international criminal procedure as a comprehensive and coherent body by describing and explaining the framework within which substantive international criminal law is developed and applied at the tribunals. The first three chapters look at the infrastructure of the international criminal tribunals, including the sources of rules of international criminal procedure and the tribunals' relationship with national courts. The remaining chapters examine the key procedures as defined and elaborated in the governing instruments and jurisprudence of the international criminal tribunals, including those relating to investigations, detention, assignment of defence counsel and self-representation, the pre-trial and trial processes, victim participation, evidence, judgement, sentencing, and appeal.

This chapter proceeds in Section 1.1 with a discussion of the sources of international criminal procedure and its status as a unitary set of rules and principles existing in international law. Section 1.2 examines a persistent challenge facing those constructing rules of international criminal procedure: the difficulty in reconciling, in an international forum, procedures deriving from inquisitorial systems characteristic of civil law countries, and those deriving from accusatorial systems characteristic of common law countries. The section discusses how the debate over the merits of each system too often ignores the reality that international criminal procedure is a *sui generis* system that should be left free to borrow from any existing legal tradition or to invent rules of its own, with the ultimate goal of fairer, more efficient, and more transparent proceedings. Finally, Section 1.3 describes the scope of the subject matter covered in this book, as well as some of the key terms used throughout.

1.1 What is international criminal procedure?

Much has been written about specific rules of international criminal procedure including, most notably, the rules of evidence, the role of the victim, and the relationship between the international criminal tribunals and national jurisdictions. By contrast, little has been thoughtfully written about the more fundamental questions of what international criminal procedure is, the sources from which it is derived, or how it exists and is developed within the international legal framework. Moreover, the little that has been written, in limited scholarship and in some international tribunal case law, provides unclear answers to these questions, which play a fundamental role in understanding the nature and legitimacy of international criminal procedure and the place of international criminal law within the broader regime of international law.

1.1.1 The sources of international criminal procedure

As international criminal procedure is a creature of public international law, its primary legal sources are those enumerated in Article 38 of the Statute of the

International Court of Justice (ICJ): treaties or conventions; customary international law, or the consistent practice of states undertaken in the belief that the conduct is permitted, required, or prohibited by international law; the general principles of law recognised by, and typically derived from the domestic legal systems of, states; and, as a subsidiary source, commentaries in judicial decisions and academic writings of the 'most highly qualified publicists'.[2] Yet there is considerable internal confusion – or disregard – in the decision-making of the international criminal tribunals about what some of the primary sources of law actually are, which of them are applicable, and in what manner they bind courts applying international criminal procedure. Having considered these issues in the broader context of international law and suggested a place for them, this volume seeks in its subsequent chapters to unravel some of the ensuing confusion that occurs in specific areas of procedure.

Before the creation of the ICTY and ICTR (jointly, '*ad hoc* Tribunals'),[3] the idea that international criminal law, including international criminal procedure, constituted a legitimate body of international law was in some doubt. Given the conjecture by some eminent theorists as to whether international law existed at all,[4] it is hardly surprising that international criminal law was considered, a mere ten years before the creation of the ICTY, as an area of international law constituting no more than an idea or aspiration. Georg Schwarzenberger, writing in 1983, considered that the

[2] Statute of the International Court of Justice, 26 June 1945, entered into force 24 October 1945, 3 Bevans 1179, T.S. 993, Art. 38(1). This traditional list of the sources of international law has been criticised as underinclusive and overly focused on the role of states as international actors, as it is now generally accepted that other entities and persons have international legal personality and should therefore play a role in providing the content and shaping the development of international law. See, e.g., Maurice H. Mendelson, 'Formation of Customary International Law', (1998) 272 *Recueil des Cours* 165, 188, 203; Jonathan Charney, 'Universal International Law', (1993) 87 *American Journal of International Law* 529, 543 ('Rather than state practice and *opinio juris*, multilateral forums [where representatives of states and other interested groups come together to address important international problems of mutual concern] often play a central role in the creation and shaping of contemporary [customary] international law'). In particular, the role of international and non-governmental organisations in the field of international criminal law has been especially pronounced in the preparations for, establishment, and initial functioning of the ICC. Furthermore, despite there being no formal system of precedent in international law, the ICJ has increasingly begun to rely upon its own prior decisions respecting statements of the customary international legal status of a proposition, or to simply state that it has reviewed state practice without articulating clearly the sources of such a review. See, e.g., Case Concerning the Arrest Warrant of 11 April 2000 (*Democratic Republic of Congo* v. *Belgium*), (2002) ICJ Rep. 3, para. 58. The ICJ also appears to have begun to relax its previously rigorous requirement that state practice and *opinio juris* be identified before custom can be said to exist, relying more heavily on UN Resolutions. See, e.g., Legal Consequences of the Construction of a Wall in the Occupied Palestinian Territories, Advisory Opinion, (2004) ICJ Rep. 136, paras. 18–23.

[3] As noted in the Table of Short Forms, throughout this volume we call the International Criminal Tribunal for the former Yugoslavia the ICTY, the International Criminal Tribunal for Rwanda the ICTR, the International Criminal Court the ICC, the Special Court for Sierra Leone the SCSL or the 'Special Court', the East Timor Special Panels for Serious Crimes the SPSC or the 'Special Panels', the Extraordinary Chambers in the Courts of Cambodia the ECCC or the 'Extraordinary Chambers', the Supreme Iraqi Criminal Tribunal the SICT, and the Special Tribunal for Lebanon the STL.

[4] See, e.g., H.L.A. Hart, *The Concept of Law* (1961), p. 209 ('[T]he absence of an international legislature, courts with compulsory jurisdiction, and centrally organised sanctions have inspired misgivings, at any rate in the breasts of legal theorists. The absence of these institutions means that the rules for states resemble that

law of international criminal procedure, along with substantive international criminal law, did 'not exist in the international customary law of unorganized international society'.[5] He considered the creation by states of certain organs vested with criminal jurisdiction, along with unspecified supranational institutions, as 'evidence of an incipient international criminal law and procedure'.[6] Interestingly, Schwarzenberger perceived the Charters of the Nuremberg and Tokyo Tribunals as representing no evidence of an international criminal jurisdiction; he believed the Allied states were doing no more in acting as a confederation of states than they could have done individually, exercising an extraordinary jurisdiction against individuals accused of war crimes.[7] Schwarzenberger concluded that international criminal law and procedure could only escape from 'the limbo of *lex ferenda*' by the creation of a 'stronger *de facto* and *de jure* order than confederate unions are able to provide'.[8]

While this scepticism as to the existence of international criminal procedure may have been understandable in 1983, it would be absurd to suggest the same now. The extraordinary development of international criminal tribunals since 1993 has quelled any real debate about the existence of substantive international criminal law, and with it a set of rules of procedure and evidence that underpin the conduct of proceedings. Yet debate persists over whether these rules enjoy sufficient homogeneity and coherency to constitute a discrete and identifiable area of international law.[9] For example, Antonio Cassese argues that, while it may be possible to set out some 'general principles governing international trials'[10] – including certain fundamental due-process rights enshrined in Article 14 of the International Covenant on Civil and Political Rights (ICCPR) and other human rights treaties – '[t]here do not yet exist international general rules on international criminal proceedings'.[11] As explained below, it is in fact the human rights principle of a right to a fair trial that is the foundation of international criminal procedure, providing coherency and legitimacy to it as a body of international law.

simple form of social structure, consisting only of primary rules of obligations ... It is indeed arguable ... that international law not only lacks the secondary rules of change and adjudication which provide for legislature and courts, but also a unifying rule of recognition specifying "sources" of law and providing general criteria for the identification of its rules. These differences are indeed striking and the question "Is international law really law?" can hardly be put aside.'). See also Gillian D. Triggs, *International Law: Contemporary Principles and Practices* (2006), p. 3.

[5] Georg Schwarzenberger, 'The Province of International Judicial Law', (1983) 21 *Notre Dame International Law Journal* 21, 25 ('Schwarzenberger, "International Judicial Law"'). Indeed, Schwarzenberger had maintained such a view since 1950. See generally Georg Schwarzenberger, 'The Problem of an International Criminal Law', (1950) 3 *Current Legal Problems* 263.

[6] Schwarzenberger, 'International Judicial Law', *supra* note 5, p. 25.

[7] *Ibid.* This view raises interesting questions about what Schwarzenberger considered to be the legal status of this 'extraordinary jurisdiction'. Was he suggesting a form of universal jurisdiction? However, no specificity is provided. Cf. Cassese, *supra* note 1, p. 378.

[8] Schwarzenberger, 'International Judicial Law', *supra* note 5, p. 25.

[9] For a discussion of the source and status of substantive international criminal law, see Boas, Bischoff, and Reid, *Elements of Crimes*, *supra* note 1, pp. 5–9.

[10] Cassese, *supra* note 1, p. 378. [11] *Ibid.*

1.1.2 The structure of rulemaking at the international criminal tribunals

The anxiety over declaring the existence of a body of international criminal procedural rules appears to relate to two areas of concern. First, there is a belief that while a myriad of international criminal tribunals have developed and applied rules of international criminal procedure, there remains too much diversity, in both the varying regulatory structure of these institutions and in the apparently divergent application of the same or analogous rules in different tribunals, for these rules to be regarded as a coherent body of international law. Göran Sluiter reasons that the 'growing number of international criminal tribunals, with their own distinctive law of criminal procedure, and numerous amendments to their rules of procedure and evidence may make it difficult to identify *firmly* established rules of international criminal procedure'.[12] Second, there is a concern that international criminal procedure as a coherent body of rules is not rooted to a formal source of international law and, therefore, lacks legitimacy. As we will show, both of these concerns can be assuaged.

It is simple to highlight differences among the tribunals on a variety of issues that arguably make it difficult to identify a unitary, coherent body of procedural law. For a start, the tribunals were each created under different circumstances and with different mandates imbuing them with different jurisdictional parameters and procedural structures.[13] The Security Council created the *ad hoc* Tribunals pursuant to Chapter VII of the United Nations Charter, and they thus derive their constitutional legitimacy from their status as subsidiary bodies of the United Nations, an organisation that was itself created by a treaty (the Charter) with almost universal membership. Yet unlike the Rome Statute of the ICC, the Statutes of the *ad hoc* Tribunals contain very few procedural and evidentiary rules themselves; they instead invest the judges with the authority and duty to elaborate and enforce such rules.[14] At the ICTY, the judges adopted the Rules of Procedure and Evidence in 1993 that they have since amended more than forty times and that now contain more than 150 rules; the ICTR judges based their Rules on those elaborated by the ICTY and have amended them some sixteen times, often to reflect amendments made to the ICTY Rules. The *ad hoc* Tribunal structure, with a skeletal primary instrument created by Security Council resolution and the judges left to elaborate the vast majority of rules and enforce rules they have themselves created, is extraordinary.

[12] Göran Sluiter, 'The Law of International Criminal Procedure and Domestic War Crimes Trials', (2006) 6 *International Criminal Law Review* 605, 606 (emphasis in original).

[13] For a discussion of these issues, see generally Steven R. Ratner, Jason S. Abrams, and James L. Bischoff, *Accountability for Human Rights Atrocities in International Law: Beyond the Nuremberg Legacy* (3rd edn 2008), ch. 9.

[14] See ICTY Statute, Art. 15; ICTR Statute, Art. 14. The structure of the rule creation and amendment process is considered at length later in this volume. See generally Chapter 2.

The internationalised, or hybrid, tribunals, by contrast, were developed under agreements between the relevant host state and the United Nations, and have varying procedural structures. The SCSL, for example, was set up in 2002 following a cessation of hostilities achieved by UN peacekeeping forces.[15] It formally adopted the Rules of the ICTR as being applicable to the conduct of its proceedings *mutatis mutandis*.[16] Furthermore, the SCSL's Statute provides that '[t]he judges of the Appeals Chamber of the Special Court shall be guided by the decisions of the Appeals Chamber of the International Tribunals for the former Yugoslavia and for Rwanda'.[17] This statement has since been held equally applicable to SCSL trial chambers.[18] At the same time, the judges 'may amend the Rules of Procedure and Evidence or adopt additional rules where the applicable Rules do not, or do not adequately, provide for a specific situation' and, in so doing, may be guided by the Criminal Procedure Act 1965 of Sierra Leone.[19] As illustrated on several occasions in the chapters that follow, since the importation of the ICTR Rules for the SCSL, the SCSL's judges have made a number of unique changes to their Rules, and have declined to adopt certain changes implemented by the ICTR's judges, thereby fostering an increasing divergence between these two sets of Rules.

By comparison, the agreement between Cambodia and the United Nations on the establishment of the ECCC provides that proceedings before the Extraordinary Chambers shall be conducted in accordance with Cambodian law.[20] Interestingly, the same provision states that where Cambodian law 'does not deal with a particular matter, or where there is uncertainty regarding the interpretation or application of a relevant rule … or where there is a question regarding the consistency of such a rule with international standards, guidance may also be sought in procedural rules established at the international level'.[21] In this way, the ECCC has created a set of procedural rules that embrace its domestic context but refer it to rules applied at the international level. In a similar vein to the ECCC, the procedural law governing

[15] See Report of the Secretary-General on the Establishment of a Special Court for Sierra Leone, UN Doc. S/2000/915, 4 October 2000. See also Ratner, Abrams, and Bischoff, *supra* note 13, p. 250.

[16] SCSL Statute, Art. 14.

[17] *Ibid.*, Art. 14(1).

[18] *Prosecutor* v. *Brima, Kamara, and Kanu*, Case No. SCSL-04-16-T, Judgement, 20 June 2007, para. 639 n. 1269 ('[T]he Trial Chamber finds that as a matter of course, the provision equally applies to triers of fact at first instance').

[19] SCSL Statute, Art. 14(2).

[20] ECCC Agreement, Art. 12(1).

[21] *Ibid.* ECCC Rules, Rule 2, (providing for any lacunae in the ECCC Internal Rules to be resolved by reference, *inter alia*, to Art. 12 of the ECCC Agreement). For a discussion of these issues, see Göran Sluiter, 'Due Process and Criminal Procedure in the Cambodian Extraordinary Chambers', (2006) *Journal of International Criminal Justice* 314. See also Ernestine E. Meijer, 'The Extraordinary Chambers in the Courts of Cambodia for Prosecuting Crimes Committed by the Khmer Rouge: Jurisdiction, Organization, and Procedure of an Internationalized National Tribunal', in Cesare P.R. Romano, André Nollkaemper, and Jann K. Kleffner (eds.), *Internationalized Criminal Courts and Tribunals: Sierra Leone, East Timor, Kosovo, and Cambodia* (2004), pp. 224–228.

East Timor's now-defunct SPSC set up a deference to international rules. The relevant provision of one of the Special Panels' governing instruments provided that in respect of 'points of criminal procedure not prescribed in the present regulation, internationally recognized principles shall apply'.[22]

The ICC applies a different institutional approach. The Rome Statute and the ICC Rules are negotiated outcomes of a multilateral treaty-making process. Their content, so far as it relates to international criminal procedure, is determined by a broad agreement amongst states parties to the Statute, which currently number at least 110 states,[23] and the Rome Statute has a self-contained provision dealing with sources of law.[24] The procedural structure of the ICC is also characterised by 'architecture … of unprecedented complexity',[25] due to the Regulations of the Court and the Regulations of the Registry. These Regulations, unlike the Statute and Rules of the Court, are not formally created – or subject to amendment by – the Assembly of States Parties, but by the judges. Although they are limited by the Statute to matters 'necessary for [the Court's] routine functioning',[26] these provisions have in some areas developed into rules of international criminal procedure that are quite fundamental to the operation of the Court.[27] To the extent that the ICC's Statute and Rules reflect those of other international criminal tribunals, they may serve as a statement by a considerable body of states as to the content of international criminal procedure.

[22] United Nations Transitional Administration in East Timor, Regulation No. 2000/30 on Transitional Rules of Criminal Procedure, UN Doc. UNTAET/REG/2000/30, 25 September 2000, § 53.5.

[23] See 'ICC at a Glance', at www.icc-cpi.int/Menus/ICC/About+the+Court/ICC+at+a+glance.

[24] Article 21 of the Rome Statute provides for a set of sources similar, but not exactly the same as, Article 38 of the ICJ Statute:

1. The Court shall apply:
   (a) In the first place, this Statute, Elements of Crimes and its Rules of Procedure and Evidence;
   (b) In the second place, where appropriate, applicable treaties and the principles and rules of international law, including the established principles of the international law of armed conflict;
   (c) Failing that, general principles of law derived by the Court from national laws of legal systems of the world including, as appropriate, the national laws of States that would normally exercise jurisdiction over the crime, provided that those principles are not inconsistent with this Statute and with international law and internationally recognized norms and standards.
2. The Court may apply principles and rules of law as interpreted in its previous decisions.
3. The application and interpretation of law pursuant to this article must be consistent with internationally recognized human rights, and be without any adverse distinction founded on grounds such as gender as defined in article 7, paragraph 3, age, race, colour, language, religion or belief, political or other opinion, national, ethnic or social origin, wealth, birth or other status.

It should be noted that the failure of Article 21 to include either the Regulations of the Court or the Regulations of the Registry makes the ICC's sources of law somewhat hierarchically ambiguous. See B. Don Taylor III, 'Demystifying the Procedural Framework of the International Criminal Court: A Modest Proposal for Radical Revision', in Carsten Stahn and Göran Sluiter (eds.), *The Emerging Practice of the International Criminal Court* (2009), p. 756.

[25] Claus Kreß, 'The Procedural Texts of the International Criminal Court', (2007) 5 *Journal of International Criminal Justice* 537, 537.

[26] Rome Statute, Art. 52(1).

[27] Kreß, *supra* note 25, p. 537; Taylor, *supra* note 24, pp. 757–758. For discussions of regulations in the ICC that have proven especially sweeping, see Chapter 2, Section 2.2.3.

Yet caution is necessary in drawing conclusions too hastily as to the transformation of this treaty activity into customary international law. Indeed, the *travaux préparatoires* of the Statute at times reveal intense debate between a variety of international actors over how far a specific requirement or prohibition had developed in customary international law,[28] with the result that the final text represents a partial codification of custom, partial progressive development of the law, and often a compromise between the different participants in the process.[29] Nonetheless, this widespread agreement between a diverse range of states, particularly where it reflects rules applicable in other international criminal tribunals, is further evidence of the development and crystallisation of a body of rules of international criminal procedure.

1.1.3 A coherent body of international rules of procedure?

The debate over whether international criminal procedure is a coherent body of international law appears to revolve around the fact that distinct sets of rules are applied in the different international criminal tribunals. Indeed, it has become fashionable since the 2006 Fragmentation Report of the International Law Commission (ILC)[30] to talk about the differences between international institutions adjudicating or regulating the same or similar issues as fragmenting, and thereby weakening, the status of international law.[31] The thrust of this argument is that different tribunals apply different rules, apply similar but not identical rules, or construe and apply the same or analogous rules in a manner different from that of other tribunals. Much can no doubt be made of the differences between the rules and the tribunals' interpretation of them.[32] Cassese has suggested that, with the closure of the *ad hoc* Tribunals and the ICC becoming the central rule-making court, a set of procedural rules might emerge to create a body of 'general international rules'.[33] He considers there to be some established general principles

[28] See generally Report of the *Ad Hoc* Committee on the Establishment of an International Criminal Court, UN Doc. A/50/22, 6 September 1995 ('1995 *Ad Hoc* Committee Report').

[29] An interesting discussion may revolve around the question of whether the Rome Statute constitutes a 'general multilateral treaty', which the ILC has stated relates to general norms of international law or matters of general interest to states as a whole. See Draft Articles on the Law of Treaties, in First Report on the Law of Treaties by Sir Humphrey Waldock, Special Rapporteur, International Law Commission, UN Doc. A/CN.4/144 and Add.l (1962), Art. 1, para. 1. However, it is difficult to see the relevance of the Rome Statute as a 'general multilateral treaty' beyond its potential reflection of customary rules generated by broad membership.

[30] Report of the Study Group of the ILC on Fragmentation of International Law: Difficulties Arising from the Diversification and Expansion of International Law, UN Doc. A/CN.4/L.702, 18 July 2006.

[31] See, e.g., Sergey Vasiliev, 'General Rules and Principles of International Criminal Procedure: Definition, Legal Nature, and Identification', in Göran Sluiter and Sergey Vasiliev (eds.), *International Criminal Procedure: Towards A Coherent Body of Law* (2008), p. 11.

[32] See, e.g., *ibid.*

[33] Cassese, *supra* note 1, p. 378. It is unclear precisely what Cassese means by this term.

governing international criminal trials: '(i) the requirement that the accused be tried by an independent and impartial court; (ii) the presumption of innocence . . .; (iii) the requirement that the trial be fair and expeditious; and (iv) the right of the accused to be present during trial'.[34] However, he, like others, argues that beyond such fundamental principles, themselves reflected in established human rights treaties and customary law, an accepted body of international rules is some years away.[35]

Yet despite the scepticism of some academic commentators, considerable homogeneity does exist in the content of many rules of international criminal procedure and the tribunals' interpretation of them, even though the rules may differ in certain details, and may be created by significantly different processes. As the subsequent chapters of this volume attest,[36] a great many rules of this nature currently exist. If these rules do not reflect a coherent body, then what do they reflect?

Part of the difficulty in answering this question is the confusion over how these rules are characterised in the literature and jurisprudence of international criminal law. For example, endeavours to identify some higher order of international law norms – usually derived from an over-thinking of language employed by the ICJ[37] – has led to conjecture as to the existence of 'fundamental principles' or principles of international 'constitutional' law that sit somehow above the accepted sources of international law.[38] However, the ILC had clearly resolved this issue as long ago as 1976:

> [I]t is only by erroneously equating the situation under international law with that under internal law that some lawyers have been able to see in the 'constitutional' or 'fundamental' principles of the international legal order an independent and higher 'source' of international obligations, in reality there is, in the international legal order, no special source of law for creating 'constitutional' or 'fundamental' principles. The principles which come to mind when using these terms are themselves customary rules, rules embodied in treaties, or even rules emanating from bodies or procedures which have themselves been established by treaties.[39]

[34] *Ibid.*

[35] *Ibid.* Interestingly, this argument has echoes of the comments made by Schwarzenberger in 1983. See *supra* text accompanying notes 5–8.

[36] See especially Chapter 12, Section 12.1 (giving examples from throughout the chapters of this volume).

[37] See, e.g., Case Concerning Military and Paramilitary Activities in and Against Nicaragua (*Nicaragua* v. *United States*), (1986) ICJ Rep. 14, para. 181 (referring to the use of force); Applicability of the Obligation to Arbitrate Under Section 21 of the United Nations Headquarters Agreement of 28 June 1947, Advisory Opinion, (1988) ICJ Rep. 12, para. 57 (referring to the relationship between municipal and international law).

[38] See, e.g., M. Virally, 'The Sources of International Law', in M. Sørensen (ed.), *Manual of Public International Law* (1968), pp. 144–145; Georg Schwarzenberger, *The Inductive Approach to International Law* (1965), p. 89.

[39] Draft Articles on State Responsibility, in 'Report of the International Law Commission on the Work of Its Twenty-Eighth Session', UN Doc. A/31/10 (1976), Commentary to Article 17, para. 21.

The simple fact is that the primary sources of international law are clear and defined: they are treaty, custom, or general principles of international law. A binding set of international rules must be rooted in one or more of these sources. However, the little international jurisprudence that discusses these issues tends to employ unhelpful nomenclature. Consider the confusing endeavour in one of the earlier ICTY trial judgements:

> [A]ny time the Statute does not regulate a specific matter, and the *Report of the Secretary-General* does not prove to be of any assistance in the interpretation of the Statute, it falls to the International Tribunal to draw upon (i) rules of customary international law or (ii) general principles of international criminal law; or, lacking such principles, (iii) general principles of criminal law common to the major legal systems of the world; or, lacking such principles, (iv) general principles of law consonant with the basic requirements of international justice. It must be assumed that the draftspersons intended the Statute to be based on international law, with the consequence that any possible *lacunae* must be filled by having recourse to that body of law.[40]

The proposition that the ICTY Statute is a primary source for the identification of rules, including those of international criminal procedure, seems clear. A reasonable interpretation of this statement is that these rules may be viewed as a form of subsidiary treaty law, derived from the power of the Security Council to create the ICTY pursuant to the UN Charter.[41] Analogous support for such a proposition may be drawn from the ICTY Appeals Chamber's ruling concerning the jurisdictional legitimacy of that Tribunal, created, as it was, by the Security Council acting under Chapter VII of the UN Charter.[42] The reference to customary international law in the *Kupreškić* extract is also meaningful as a primary source of international law itself.[43] The reference to three further forms of general principles, however, leaves one without any comprehension of their meaning or relationship with the 'general

40 *Prosecutor* v. *Kupreškić, Kupreškić, Kupreškić, Josipović, Papić, and Šantić*, Case No. IT-95-16-T, Judgement, 14 January 2000, para. 591.

41 See, e.g., Cassese, *supra* note 1, pp. 15–16.

42 See *Prosecutor* v. *Tadić*, Case No. IT-94-1-AR72, Decision on Defence Motion for Interlocutory Appeal on Jurisdiction, 2 October 1995 ('*Tadić* Jurisdiction Appeal Decision'), paras. 21, 47 (determining that the ICTY maintained an 'incidental jurisdiction', empowering it to consider and determine jurisdictional questions unrelated to subject-matter jurisdiction, and finding 'that the International Tribunal has been established in accordance with the appropriate procedures under the United Nations Charter and provides all the necessary safeguards of a fair trial' and 'is thus "established by law"') (quotation at para. 47).

43 This is not to say that the international tribunals' application of this source of international law has been unproblematic. Indeed, the identification and use of custom as a source for particular rules of international criminal procedure has, at times, been confusing. This matter will be taken up in detail in relevant places throughout this volume. Furthermore, the myth of these international criminal tribunals conservatively and cautiously applying customary international law does little to clarify the law-creating role of these courts. See, e.g., Theodor Meron, 'Editorial Comment: Revival of Customary Humanitarian Law', (2005) 99 *American Journal of International Law* 817, 818, 821 (in particular arguing that international criminal tribunals have taken an essentially conservative and traditional approach to the identification and application of customary international legal principles – an assertion that is difficult to support in light of the actual practice of these institutions).

principles of law' enshrined as a source of international law in Article 38 of the ICJ Statute.[44]

1.1.4 Principles and rules

It is also important to consider the role of principles and rules when discussing the sources of international criminal procedure, because one should flow from the other. The ICJ has stated:

> [T]he association of the terms 'rules' and 'principles' is no more than the use of a dual expression to convey one and the same idea, since in this context 'principles' clearly means principles of law, that is, it also includes rules of international law in whose case the use of the term 'principles' may be justified because of their more general and more fundamental character.[45]

Sergey Vasiliev refers to Sir Gerald Fitzmaurice's explanation that by principle, or general principle, is meant 'chiefly something which itself is not a rule, but which underlies a rule, and explains or provides the reason for it. A rule answers the question "what": a principle in effect answers the question "why"'.[46]

International criminal procedure is derived from acknowledged international law sources through the various tribunals that create and apply it: by treaty in respect of the ICC and the *ad hoc* Tribunals; and by a more circuitous treaty route in respect of the internationalised tribunals (which are, after all, created by agreement with the ultimate treaty body – the United Nations). This reality leads to the conclusion that international criminal procedure is a form of subsidiary treaty law.[47] In part, therefore, the answer to the fundamental question – 'from where does international criminal procedure obtain its legitimacy?' – may be as simple as saying that it is derived from the treaties that lie behind these legitimately created tribunals. However, this is not the entire answer. As noted above, there seems to be a prevailing suggestion in the literature that international criminal procedure has not attained the status of a coherent and legitimate body of law.[48] If these commentators are correct, then the real challenge facing international criminal procedure

[44] Similar, but less pronounced, confusion occurs in another trial judgement, where the Trial Chamber refers to 'the general principles of international criminal law or, if such principles are of no avail, to the general principles of international law'. *Prosecutor* v. *Furundžija* , Case No. IT-95-17/1-T, Judgement, 10 December 1998, para. 182 For a detailed discussion of these issues, see Sergey Vasiliev, 'General Rules and Principles of International Criminal Procedure: Definition, Legal Nature, and Identification', in Sluiter and Vasiliev, *supra* note 31, pp. 31–42.

[45] Case Concerning Delimitation in the Gulf of Maine Area (*Canada* v. *United States*), (1984) ICJ Rep. 246 ('*Gulf of Maine* Case'), para. 79.

[46] Vasiliev, *supra* note 44, p. 41 (quoting Gerald Fitzmaurice, 'The General Principles of International Law Considered from the Standpoint of the Rule of Law', (1957-II) 2 *Recueil des Cours de l'Academie de Droit International* 1, 7).

[47] See *supra* text accompanying notes 41–42.

[48] See generally, e.g., Cassese, *supra* note 1; Schwarzenberger, *supra* note 5; Sluiter, *supra* note 12.

is the perception that it encompasses a body of rules ostensibly developed by an inversion of international lawmaking: instead of a coherent and stated principle derived from international law leading to an articulated set of rules, international criminal procedure is an evolving set of dynamic rules that may be leading to some form of legitimate international law. As we shall see, that is far from the case.

1.1.5 Human rights: the legal principles behind international criminal procedure

While the treaty roots of the international criminal tribunals satisfy the required link between formal sources of international law and international criminal procedure as a body of international law, they do not provide us with the legal principles that give a philosophical foundation for this body of law. It is tempting to formulate, as some scholars have, these principles in the following terms: to try those most responsible for mass atrocity, to end impunity for leaders of oppressive regimes responsible for such crimes, to facilitate truth finding, to give victims an opportunity for closure, to promote international peace and security.[49] Yet, while these are *moral* principles and practical concerns that have motivated the creation of international criminal tribunals, and which have underpinned their proceedings, they are not themselves legal principles consisting of a 'more general and more fundamental character', in the terminology of the ICJ.[50] We would instead argue that the legal principles which underlie the rules of international criminal procedure can be found in human rights principles which are a foundational part of the construct of international criminal law.

Under this view, the rules of international criminal procedure find their origins not only in the treaties that created the international criminal tribunals, but also in the principles underlying the framework of the human rights regime, and the adherence of these rules to that regime. Thus, while (as noted above) the provisions found in the Statutes, Rules, and other procedural instruments of the international criminal tribunals are a form of subsidiary treaty law, the development and application of these instruments are guided by the fundamental (and legitimising) principle of an individual's right to a fair trial – itself a treaty norm and a *jus cogens* norm of international human rights law.

This relationship is crucial because all international criminal tribunals expressly require adherence to the fair trial rights derived from Article 14 of the ICCPR.[51]

[49] See, e.g., John Jackson, 'Creating Evidentiary Processes in the International Criminal Tribunals that Are Fit for Purpose: Beyond the Common Law–Civil Law Divide', (2009) *Journal of International Criminal Justice* 17; Claude Jorda, 'The Major Hurdles and Accomplishments of the ICTY', (2004) *Journal of International Criminal Justice* 572; Antonio Cassese, 'Opinion: The ICTY and Human Rights', (1997) *European Human Rights Law Review* 329.

[50] See *Gulf of Maine* Case, *supra* note 45, para. 79.

[51] For a discussion of the right to a fair trial, see generally Salvatore Zappalà, *Human Rights in International Criminal Proceedings* (2003); Christoph Safferling, *Towards an International Criminal Procedure* (2001), pp. 21–30.

Early in the ICTY's existence, the Appeals Chamber insisted that the very legitimacy of the Tribunal as being 'established by law' was dependent upon its compliance with fundamental fair trial, or due process, rights, primarily articulated in Article 14 of the ICCPR:

> The important consideration in determining whether a tribunal has been 'established by law' is not whether it was pre-established or established for a specific purpose or situation; what is important is that it be set up by a competent organ in keeping with the relevant legal procedures, and should [*sic*] that it observes the requirements of procedural fairness.
>
> ...
>
> An examination of the Statute of the International Tribunal, and of the Rules of Procedure and Evidence adopted pursuant to that Statute leads to the conclusion that it has been established in accordance with the rule of law. The fair trial guarantees in Article 14 of the International Covenant on Civil and Political Rights have been adopted almost verbatim in Article 21 of the Statute. Other fair trial guarantees appear in the Statute and the Rules of Procedure and Evidence. For example, Article 13, paragraph 1, of the Statute ensures the high moral character, impartiality, integrity and competence of the Judges of the International Tribunal, while various other provisions in the Rules ensure equality of arms and fair trial.[52]

Indeed, no international criminal tribunal renders decisions applying rules of international criminal procedure to any issue in express (or implied) disregard for human rights norms, and international criminal procedure is founded on the legal principles articulated in the human rights regime, whether they are referred to as due process or fair trial rights. Such an understanding also explains Cassese's proposition referred to earlier in this chapter, that there are certain 'general principles governing international trials' – all of which are derived directly from these identified human rights.[53] While Cassese identifies certain articulations of fair trial rights as areas of procedure definable as general principles, we contend that these human rights principles give legitimacy to international criminal procedure. As we argue further in Chapter 12, they are the glue that binds together the entire body of international criminal procedure.[54]

It is beyond dispute that rules of international criminal procedure exist; and that they have and continue to be created, interpreted, and applied. Surely it is an extraordinary proposition to suggest that these rules have no origin in a source of international law – that they are only 'what' and are not rooted in the 'why' of human rights law – and yet are applied to resolve crucial questions involving the determination of guilt or innocence of accused persons, sentencing, and conditions of detention, among many others. Far from being a set of discordant and disembodied rules created and applied

[52] *Tadić* Jurisdiction Appeal Decision, *supra* note 42, paras. 45, 46.

[53] Cassese, *supra* note 1, p. 378. See also *supra* text accompanying notes 10, 33–35.

[54] See Chapter 12, Section 12.1 (reprising these considerations in the light of specific procedures and practices discussed in Chapters 2 through 11 of this volume).

in a haphazard manner, international criminal procedure is a coherent body of rules (albeit with internal variations) that are derived from the traditional sources of international law and legitimised by their adherence to legal principles entrenched in the human rights regime – in particular, the *jus cogens* norm of the right to a fair trial.

1.2 Common law versus civil law: the old debate in a new light

Large amounts of literature and jurisprudence address the well-worn discussion about the differences between the two major systems of law – common law and civil law – and how they are reflected in the international and internationalised criminal tribunals.[55] These two systems of law, especially as applied in the criminal context, differ in some profound respects. In common law adversarial systems of criminal justice, the court tends not to interfere significantly in the preparation or indeed, to a great degree, in the running of the case. In the First Annual Report of the ICTY, President Cassese stated that the Statute of the ICTY had adopted 'a largely adversarial approach to its procedures, rather than the inquisitorial system prevailing in continental Europe and elsewhere'.[56] The truth of this statement is clear from the allocation to the Prosecutor of sole responsibility for inquiring into allegations of crimes under the Statute, submitting indictments for review, and obtaining the necessary evidence to secure a conviction.[57] In contrast, in civil law inquisitorial criminal systems, the court is deeply involved in the process from the investigation phase onward. So in France, for example, an investigating judge directs the investigation and determines whether or not a criminal trial will proceed.[58]

Mirjan Damaška has written extensively on the risks inherent in transplanting rules from different systems of law.[59] Patrick Robinson has similarly argued that 'if not properly resolved, tension between the legal systems may lead to unfairness'.[60] While the structure of the *ad hoc* Tribunals is based ostensibly upon the adversarial

[55] See, e.g., Patrick L. Robinson, 'Fair but Expeditious Trials', in Hirad Abtahi and Gideon Boas (eds.), *The Dynamics of International Criminal Justice: Essays in Honour of Sir Richard May* (2005), p. 169 ('Robinson, "Fair but Expeditious Trials"'); Megan Fairlie, 'The Marriage Between Common and Continental Law at the ICTY and Its Progeny: Due Process Deficit', (2004) 4 *International Criminal Law Review* 243; Zappalà, *supra* note 51; Patrick L. Robinson, 'Ensuring Fair and Expeditious Trials at the International Criminal Tribunal for the Former Yugoslavia', (2000) 11 *European Journal of International Law* 569 ('Robinson, "Ensuring Fair and Expeditious Trials"'); Mirjan Damaška, 'The Uncertain Fate of Evidentiary Transplants: Anglo-American and Contemporary Experiments', (1997) 45 *American Journal of Comparative Law* 839; Françoise Tulkens, 'Main Comparable Features of the Different European Criminal Justice Systems', in Mireille Delmas-Marty (ed.), *The Criminal Process and Human Rights: Toward a European Consciousness* (1995), p. 5.

[56] Report of the International Tribunal for the Prosecution of Persons Responsible for Serious Violations of International Humanitarian Law Committed in the Territory of the Former Yugoslavia Since 1991, UN Doc. A/49/342, 29 August 1994, para. 71.

[57] See ICTY Rules 39–43, 47, 84, 85.

[58] See Code de Procédure Pénale (France), Art. 81(1).

[59] See, e.g., Damaška, *supra* note 55.

[60] Patrick L. Robinson, 'Rough Edges in the Alignment of Legal Systems in the Proceedings at the ICTY', (2005) 3 *Journal of International Criminal Justice* 1, 4.

model, they have incorporated procedural aspects of the civil law system to a considerable degree, as will be seen in the chapters that follow.[61] Meanwhile, the internationalised criminal tribunal models vary depending on the system of criminal justice operative in the host state, with the ECCC having a very strong civil law component to the entire structure of that court including investigating judges, and the SCSL bearing the common law hallmarks of the Sierra Leonean judicial system.[62] The ICC, while based on the adversarial model broadly entrenched in the *ad hoc* Tribunals,[63] contains some significant civil law infrastructure, including a pre-trial chamber and a system of victim representation and compensation.[64] In general, it is fair to say that international criminal law is infrastructurally adversarial but that it has many civil law overlays which can or do impact profoundly on the conduct of proceedings,[65] and that, in the context of the ICC, a larger number of civil law-oriented procedures are taking root than have been seen in the *ad hoc* Tribunals.[66]

Several commentators have suggested that international criminal tribunals should have a unique procedural system which 'would be *sui generis* in the sense that it would depart from any one domestic system or legal tradition … [although] inevitably, it would have elements from the major domestic legal systems of the world',[67] and that we need to look beyond the common law/civil law hybrid system of procedural rules that has evolved in international criminal procedure.[68] The difficulty with such a discussion, however, is determining what it should evolve into.

[61] See *infra* note 65 and sources cited therein. For a brief description of the distinction between the different legal traditions, see Cryer, Friman, Robinson, and Wilmshurst, *supra* note 1, pp. 349–350. See also, e.g., Chapter 9, Sections 9.1, 9.2.1; Chapter 6, Section 6.4.3.

[62] ECCC Statute, Art. 23; SCSL Statute, Art. 1.

[63] See Gideon Boas, 'Comparing the ICTY and the ICC: Some Procedural and Substantive Issues', (2000) 47 *Netherlands International Law Review* 267, 278–287. See also Chapter 6, Section 6.6; Chapter 7, Section 7.9.

[64] See Ratner, Abrams, and Bischoff, *supra* note 13, pp. 240–241; Cryer, Friman, Robinson, and Wilmshurst, *supra* note 1, pp. 351–352; Kreß, *supra* note 25, p. 540.

[65] See generally Robinson, 'Ensuring Fair and Expeditious Trials', *supra* note 55; Robinson, 'Fair but Expeditious Trials', *supra* note 55; Daryl A. Mundis, 'From "Common Law" Towards "Civil Law": The Evolution of the ICTY Rules of Procedure and Evidence', (2001) 14 *Leiden Journal of International Law* 367; Gideon Boas, 'A Code of Evidence and Procedure for International Criminal Law? The Rules of the ICTY', in Gideon Boas and William A. Schabas (eds.), *International Criminal Law Developments in the Case Law of the ICTY* (2002); Damaška, *supra* note 55; Tulkens, *supra* note 55, p. 5.

[66] For a discussion of these issues, see Gideon Boas, *The Milošević Trial: Lessons for the Conduct of Complex International Criminal Proceedings* (2007), pp. 39–41. See also Chapter 12, Section 12.2; but see Chapter 6, Section 6.6; Chapter 7, Section 7.9 (trial proceedings at the ICC remain essentially adversarial).

[67] See, e.g., Cryer, Friman, Robinson, and Wilmshurst, *supra* note 1, p. 349. Cf. Boas, Bischoff, and Reid, *Elements of Crime*, *supra* note 1, p. 8 ('The role that states play in the lawmaking process at the international level is complemented by the contribution that their domestic criminal legal systems make to the growing sophistication of international criminal law. Although relatively few prosecutions for crimes under international law have taken place at the domestic level, the procedural rules of international criminal adjudication are based on – and are in fact an attempt to take the best practices from – the rules in the principal legal systems of the world').

[68] See Jackson, *supra* note 49, pp. 19–24; Boas, *supra* note 66, pp. 286–288. This is a somewhat different argument to the simple (or even simplistic) expression of concern at international criminal tribunals applying a body of procedural rules that lack the foundation that such rules have in domestic criminal justice systems. Compare, e.g., Vladimir Tochilovsky, 'International Criminal Justice: Strangers in the Foreign System', (2004) 15 *Criminal Law Forum* 319.

As John Jackson rightly states, having indicated his belief that international criminal procedure should be oriented towards some of the fundamental goals of international criminal justice, including truth-telling, reconciliation, and establishing a historical record:

> From an evidentiary perspective, it is by no means clear that an adversarial mode of procedure is suited to these wider goals. For one thing, this mode of procedure conceived as it is as a contest between prosecution and defence can serve to exclude the interests of victims and others in the community who need to be included if the aim of reconciliation is to be achieved. When the parties are able to bargain outcomes without the need for oral presentation of evidence at all, the voices of these groups are silenced. Far from leading to a historical record it can instead result in charges which bear little relation to the bargained reality. Even when the contest results in a trial, victims as witnesses are hampered from giving a full version of events in the manner they choose by the constraints of examination and cross-examination. Nor however is it clear that inquisitorial procedures are the answer. These may give victims a voice within the context of a closed inquiry but when it comes to trial there is a heavy reliance on written statements and documents taken from the earlier closed phases of the procedure with the result that there is little opportunity for the transparency needed in order to engage interested communities.[69]

Jackson is not alone in his inability to articulate what it is that international criminal procedure should be evolving into. Nonetheless, the instinct that it is time to move away from this hybrid preoccupation seems well placed. If we accept the proposition, argued in the previous section of this chapter, that international criminal procedure is a legitimate body of international law, then it seems clear that international criminal law should embrace its status as a jurisdiction in its own right. Only then will those who draft and interpret the law be free from preoccupation with the common and civil law approaches to problem-solving in international criminal procedure. Freedom from the perceived constraints of procedure derived from national legal precedent will facilitate a clearer application of principles developed in the context of the international legal system and encourage lawyers and judges to look at these issues in their context, rather than through the lens of their own domestic legal experience. This sense that the legitimacy of rules of international criminal procedure can only be established by reference to their existence in the common law or civil law systems (or both) reveals the uncertain status of this area of law. The hybrid paradigm, and its relationship with the fair trial norm, was critically important in the early years of development of modern international criminal law.[70] But international criminal procedure, as developed in the rules and jurisprudence of international criminal tribunals, has outgrown this

[69] Jackson, *supra* note 49, p. 22 (footnotes omitted).
[70] Boas, *supra* note 66, p. 288.

need; indeed, it threatens to constrain the development of this still-fledgling area of international law.[71]

An opportunity exists to develop a coherent and comprehensive body of international criminal procedure, capable of succeeding in the prosecution of cases of great size and complexity, in an environment at least partially removed from the strictures of long-established domestic criminal law systems (though we do acknowledge the difficulty of weaning lawyers trained in a national system off the tendency to rely too heavily on that system in their search for solutions). The set of rules discussed in this volume reveals an articulated foundation for international criminal procedure as a body of *international* law, drawn in part from domestic criminal justice systems but created and applied as a body of international law intimately intertwined with substantive international criminal law, with many new rules pragmatically conceived to address specific needs facing international criminal practice which have no analogue in the domestic legal systems of either common law or civil law countries. The reader will come across many such rules in the subsequent chapters of this volume.[72]

1.3 Scope of this book and terminology used

In this volume, we consider international criminal procedure as a tangible set of rules created for application in international criminal tribunals. We use the term to refer not only to the rules that apply to the conduct of investigations and court proceedings, but in a much broader sense that encompasses rules of evidence; rules on assignment of defence counsel and *amici curiae*; rules of professional conduct; rules on electing judges and assigning them to cases; principles for deciding the sentence to impose on an accused; rules on pardon and commutation; and many other areas. Yet international criminal procedure comprises a vast corpus of law, and it has not been possible within the scope of this book to discuss every subject falling under its purview. Thus, for example, this book does not discuss minor or technical rules such as those on time and page limits, or rules whose interpretation and application does not arise frequently in the case law, such as those on reparations for malicious prosecution or state requests for review of tribunal decisions.

[71] This is not to suggest that the judges, in their rule-making role, have not evolved rules of procedure and evidence beyond a simple selection of common law or civil law approaches. Examples of such developments include the admission into evidence of written statements in lieu of oral testimony reflected in ICTY Rules 92 *bis* and *ter*, among others. See Chapter 9, Section 9.2.1.1. Such regulatory and jurisprudential evolution will be discussed in the following chapters of this volume. For a discussion of these matters, see generally Ratner, Abrams, and Bischoff, *supra* note 13, ch. 11; Jackson, *supra* note 49; Boas, *supra* note 65.

[72] See especially Chapter 12, Section 12.2 (reprising these considerations and discussing specific examples from Chapters 2 through 11 of this volume).

Furthermore, some areas of international criminal law that were not discussed in Volumes I or II also fall outside the scope of this volume. Most noteworthy among these are defences and immunities.

The rules and jurisprudence discussed in this volume often reveal a misunderstanding and misapplication of the sources of international law. Those who make the rules, or chambers of the tribunals applying them or creating new rules in the case law, too often fail to adequately explain how the rules in question find their origins in customary international law or general principles of law.[73] Of similar concern is the manner in which rules are created, amended, altered, and abrogated in judicial and quasi-legislative contexts.[74] While the primary goal of this volume is to survey the most important rules of procedure at the international criminal tribunals and provide examples of how they operate in practice, we do not simply recount the rules and related case law uncritically, but instead draw attention to aspects that have failed to adequately address the relevant legal or policy basis or to achieve the desired goal, and consider how these procedures may be better developed in the future. As such, although this book is, like the first two volumes of this series, primarily intended for the practitioner of international criminal law, the analysis is also relevant and useful for academics and students.

Throughout this book, we refer jointly to the ICTY and ICTR as the ***ad hoc* Tribunals**. We use the term **international criminal tribunals** as a general label applicable to both these tribunals and the ICC, in addition to the various internationalised courts and tribunals, whatever their precise relationship to a national legal system. We usually refer to the tribunal document entitled the Rules of Procedure and Evidence as the **Rules**, and use the lowercase **rule** to refer generically to any procedural principle, rule, or regulation, whether specifically contained within the **Rules** or deriving from elsewhere. The term **governing instruments** indicates the collectivity of a tribunal's Statute, Rules, Regulations, Practice Directions, Codes, and other legal and quasi-legal documents setting forth rules relevant to procedure.

The international criminal tribunals often differ from one another in the terms they use to denote things or procedures that are the same or roughly analogous. For convenience, we have sometimes opted to use a single, standard term in general discussions, though we may use the tribunal-specific term when focusing on that tribunal's practice. Hence, the person under investigation by the prosecution

[73] Some chambers have used even more confusing nomenclature such as 'general principles of criminal law' and 'general principles of law consonant with the basic requirements of international justice'. See *supra* note 40 and accompanying text.

[74] This issue is discussed in Chapter 2, Sections 2.1.4 and 2.2.3.

is referred to as the **suspect**. The document charging the accused with one or more crimes is generally described as the **indictment** or the **charging** or **accusatory instrument** and the document setting forth the judges' verdict and the reasons behind it is the **judgement**, while decisions on interlocutory matters are **decisions** or **orders**. The prosecution and defence are jointly the **parties**. The first party to question a witness conducts the **examination** or the **direct examination**; the opposing party questioning the same witness conducts a **cross-examination**; and the original party questioning the witness again conducts a **re-examination**. The entity presiding over the pre-trial phase of proceedings is the **pre-trial chamber** and that presiding over the trial is the **trial chamber**; either collectivity of judges, or those on the **Appeals Chamber**, may be referred to as the **chamber** or the **bench**.

As they have in the areas of substantive law discussed in Volumes I and II, the ICTY and ICTR play the most significant role, through their Rules and jurisprudence, in developing and applying rules of international criminal procedure. In contrast to Volumes I and II, which provided a comparative survey of the substantive law of the ICC necessarily limited by that Court's still sparse jurisprudence on crimes and forms of responsibility, the ICC features a complex web of procedural rules in its Statute, Rules, and Regulations, and a rapidly expanding body of case law interpreting these rules. Indeed, the ICC has already established itself as the primary source for certain procedural rules, including those relating to victim participation in proceedings. Considering the ICC's prominence in the field of procedure, most chapters endeavour to give the ICC roughly equal treatment to the *ad hoc* Tribunals, and for some chapters the ICC focus is even greater. Depending on the degree of divergence in procedures between the *ad hoc* Tribunals, on the one hand, and the ICC, on the other, we may discuss the rules of each in separate subsections of a given chapter or in tandem. We assess approaches taken by the internationalised tribunals where they aid the discussion, are especially illustrative of a given procedural mechanism, or helpfully demonstrate a contrasting approach to that taken by the *ad hoc* Tribunals or the ICC. Most significant among these, and most often mentioned in this book, is the SCSL, but occasional reference is made to the SPSC, the ECCC, and others.

Notwithstanding – or perhaps because of – the completion strategies at the two *ad hoc* Tribunals,[75] their chambers remain extremely active, releasing interlocutory decisions relevant to international criminal procedure on an almost daily basis. The

[75] See Security Council Resolution 1534, UN Doc. S/RES/1534 (2004), para. 5; Security Council Resolution 1503, UN Doc. S/RES/1503, (28 August 2003), pp. 1–2.

ICC is likewise very active, and its caseload has steadily increased with each passing year. Readers should note that this analysis is current as of 1 December 2009. They should also keep in mind that the tribunals' governing instruments, and especially the ICTY Rules, are the subject of frequent amendments, and any reference to a tribunal's Rules or other governing instrument pertains to the version of the document in force on 1 December 2009.

2

Creation and amendment of rules of international criminal procedure

CONTENTS

Two of the notable differences among the various international criminal tribunals are the manner in which their respective procedural architectures are created, and the constitutional frameworks for their amendment. Though the legitimacy of international criminal procedure as a body of law has begun to receive more academic attention,[1] an infrastructural issue of considerable significance to the debate remains relatively unexplored: how rules and regulations that bind parties and courts (and indeed, states, international organisations, and individuals through orders of these courts[2]) are created and amended.

The judges of the ICTY and the ICTR (jointly, *ad hoc* Tribunals) have a unique, and now well entrenched, power to create and amend their own rules as 'quasi-legislators'.[3]

[1] See Chapter 1, Section 1.2.

[2] See Chapter 3, text accompanying notes 10–11, 94–96; Chapter 6, Section 6.3.2.

[3] See Gideon Boas, 'A Code of Evidence and Procedure for International Criminal Law? The Rules of the ICTY', in Gideon Boas and William A. Schabas (eds.), *International Criminal Law Developments in the Case Law of the ICTY* (2002), pp. 9–18.

The drafters of the Rome Statute, however, rejected such an approach, opting instead for greater control of the procedural framework by the Assembly of States Parties (ASP) – an approach reflected more in form than in substance, as discussed below. Diversifying further the rule-making frameworks, the internationalised tribunals have opted either for the largely wholesale adoption of the ICTY or ICTR Rules, as in the case of the SCSL; or the application of the rules of domestic courts, in the cases of the Cambodian Extraordinary Chambers and the now-defunct East Timor Special Panels.

This chapter discusses the manner in which rules of procedure and evidence have been created and how they are amended in the different international criminal tribunals. Section 2.1 starts by considering the approach of the *ad hoc* Tribunals, examining the appropriateness and consequences of judges having largely unfettered power both to create and amend their Rules, as well as to adjudicate on their interpretation and application. The section examines the benefits and drawbacks of such a flexible structure, as well as ways in which the Tribunals might increase the transparency of this process in order to improve its actual and perceived legitimacy. Section 2.2 considers the approach of the ICC, an institution which, notwithstanding the rules drafted by the ASP and a procedural framework that appears to require review and amendment by the states parties, has managed to construct a web of procedural provisions that effectively grants judges and administrators *de facto* amendment powers consonant with those of the judges of the *ad hoc* Tribunals. The section considers the impact of this approach in practice and makes recommendations as to how the ICC might be more candid in the construction and application of its rules.[4]

[4] For two reasons, the internationalised tribunals are less significant illustrations of the creation and amendment of rules of procedure in international criminal tribunals. First, for some of these tribunals, their procedural rules are taken directly from those of existing international criminal tribunals, with unique amendments as necessary. See, e.g., SCSL Statute, Art. 14(1) (SCSL to adopt ICTR Rules and amend as necessary); United Nations Transitional Administration in East Timor, Regulation No. 2001/25, UN Doc. UNTAET/REG/2001/25, 14 September 2001, Section 54.5 (providing that '[o]n points of criminal procedure not prescribed in the present regulation, internationally recognized principles shall apply' to proceedings before East Timor's Special Panels for Serious Crimes). Second, some of the internationalised tribunals are required to apply, at least in part, domestic criminal procedure, with a vague reference to the application of international standards of criminal procedure where lacunae or inconsistencies exist. See, e.g., Agreement Between the United Nations and the Royal Government of Cambodia Concerning the Prosecution Under Cambodian Law of Crimes Committed During the Period of Democratic Kampuchea, 17 March 2003, approved by General Assembly Resolution 57/2288 (2003), Art. 12(1), available at www.eccc.gov.kh/english/cabinet/agreement/5/Agreement_between_UN_and_RGC.pdf; Extraordinary Chambers in the Courts of Cambodia, Internal Rules, 12 June 2007, Rule 2, available at www.eccc.gov.kh/english/cabinet/files/irs/ECCC_IRs_English_2007_06_12.pdf. Because the internationalised criminal tribunals have tended to follow the case law of the *ad hoc* Tribunals and more limited jurisprudence of the ICC in construing their rules of procedure and evidence, this aspect of their functioning will not be considered further in this chapter.

2.1 The *ad hoc* Tribunals

2.1.1 Creation of the Rules of Procedure and Evidence

One of the extraordinary features of the ICTY is the manner in which it was created.[5] The UN Security Council, exercising its Chapter VII powers to maintain international peace and security, adopted in Resolution 827 the Report of the Secretary-General[6] and the Statute annexed to that Report as the foundational documents for the Tribunal.[7] The Statute, in turn, empowered the judges of the ICTY to create the Rules of Procedure and Evidence.[8] In doing so, the Security Council also requested the Secretary-General 'to submit to the judges of the International Tribunal, upon their election, any suggestions received from States for the rules of procedure and evidence called for in Article 15 of the Statute of the International Tribunal'.[9] The Secretary-General, for his part, agreed that 'the judges of the International Tribunal as a whole should draft and adopt the rules of procedure and evidence', and set about gathering suggestions from UN member states.[10]

It appears there is little precedent for granting the judges of a court the power to create their own rules of evidence and procedure with no oversight or review by another body, such as a legislature. Certainly in domestic criminal justice systems, while it may be common to allow courts to issue practice directions or regulations relating to procedural conduct within that jurisdiction, it is most often the legislative arm of government that determines the critical procedural and evidentiary rules that will regulate the conduct of investigations, trials, appeals, and sentencing, along with the raft of other aspects of the procedural structure that governs the proper conduct of cases in which serious crime is prosecuted.[11] Even the

[5] For a discussion of the creation and legitimacy of the ICTY, see generally Paul Tavernier, 'The Experience of the International Criminal Tribunals for the Former Yugoslavia and for Rwanda', (1997) 321 *International Review of the Red Cross* 605. Some commentators considered the creation of the ICTY under Chapter VII of the UN Charter to be an unlawful exercise of the Security Council's powers. See, e.g., Vera Gowlland-Debbas, 'Security Council Enforcement Action and Issues of State Responsibility', (1994) 43 *International Criminal Law Quarterly* 55; Gabriël H. Oosthuizen, 'Playing Devil's Advocate: The United Nations Security Council Is Unbound by Law', (1999) 12 *Leiden Journal of International Law* 549.

[6] Report of the Secretary-General Pursuant to Paragraph 2 of Security Council Resolution 808, UN Doc. S/25704, 3 May 1993 ('Secretary-General's ICTY Report').

[7] The Statute of the ICTY has been amended nine times since, most significantly to accommodate the addition of *ad litem* (or temporary) judges to enable the Tribunal to dispose of cases more quickly. Despite these minor changes to the Statute's provisions, it has never been amended in a way that alters the Tribunal's substantive jurisdiction and amendments have always been effected by Security Council resolution.

[8] ICTY Statute, Art. 15 ('The judges of the International Tribunal shall adopt rules of procedure and evidence for the conduct of the pre-trial phase of the proceedings, trials and appeals, the admission of evidence, the protection of victims and witnesses and other appropriate matters').

[9] Security Council Resolution 827, UN Doc. S/RES/827 (1993), para. 3.

[10] See Secretary-General's ICTY Report, *supra* note 6, para. 83.

[11] Exceptions exist in some jurisdictions, however. In certain U.S. states, for example, the state supreme court promulgates and amends procedural and evidentiary rules with no involvement by the state legislature.

Charters of the Nuremberg and Tokyo Tribunals were drawn up and promulgated by a supranational governmental structure of sorts.[12]

In line with the Security Council's request that the Secretary-General submit to the ICTY's judges suggestions for rules by states, a number of states and organisations made proposals, most of which were very general.[13] While the judges rejected the United States' proposal that the Tribunal adopt its rules of procedure and evidence only with the Security Council's approval,[14] it was the U.S. government's draft set of rules that proved most influential in the construction of the first Rules of Procedure and Evidence.[15] This factor goes a long way toward explaining the strong influence of the Anglo-American adversarial system that serves as the basis for the ICTY's regulatory structure and, consequently, that of several subsequent international criminal tribunals, which relied heavily on the ICTY's pioneering Rules in constructing their own rules.[16]

Following its precedent in creating the ICTY the previous year, the Security Council created the ICTR in 1994 through Resolution 995, and annexed the Tribunal's Statute to the resolution. Article 14 of the ICTR Statute explicitly ties the ICTR Rules to those already created by the ICTY judges:

> The judges of the International Tribunal for Rwanda shall adopt, for the purpose of proceedings before the International Tribunal for Rwanda, the rules of procedure and evidence for the conduct of the pre-trial phase of the proceedings, trials and appeals, the admission of evidence, the protection of victims and witnesses and other appropriate matters of the International Tribunal for the Former Yugoslavia with such changes as they deem necessary.

[12] See Agreement for the Prosecution and Punishment of Major War Criminals of the European Axis, and Establishing the Charter of the International Military Tribunal, Annex, 8 August 1945 ('IMT Charter'), 82 UNTS 279; Charter of the International Military Tribunal for the Far East, 19 January 1946 ('IMTFE Charter'), 4 Bevans 20; Control Council Law No. 10, Punishment of Persons Guilty of War Crimes, Crimes Against Peace and Against Humanity, in *Trials of War Criminals Before the Nuernberg Military Tribunals Under Control Council Law No. 10* (1997), Vol. I, pp. xvi–xix. For a discussion of the drafting process relating to the IMT Charter and IMTFE Charter, see Megan Fairlie, 'The Marriage of Common and Continental Law at the ICTY and its Progeny: Due Process Deficit', (2004) 4 *International Criminal Law Review* 243, 260–262.

[13] See, e.g., Letter Dated 16 February 1993 from the Permanent Representative of Italy to the United Nations Addressed to the Secretary-General, UN Doc. S/25300, 17 February 1993; Letter Dated 10 February 1993 from the Permanent Representative of France to the United Nations Addressed to the Secretary-General, UN Doc. S/25266, 10 February 1993; Letter Dated 5 April 1993 from the Permanent Representative of the Russian Federation to the United Nations Addressed to the Secretary-General, UN Doc. S/25537, 6 April 1993; Letter Dated 13 April 1993 from the Permanent Representative of Canada to the United Nations Addressed to the Secretary-General, UN Doc. S/25594, 14 April 1993. See also Boas, *supra* note 3, p. 3; Virginia Morris and Michael P. Scharf, *An Insider's Guide to the International Criminal Tribunal for the Former Yugoslavia: A Documentary History and Analysis* (1995), pp. 211–310.

[14] Letter Dated 5 April 1993 from the Permanent Representative of the United States of America to the United Nations Addressed to the Secretary-General, UN Doc. S/25575, 12 April 1993, Annex II, Art. 6.

[15] The U.S. draft rules are reprinted in Morris and Scharf, *supra* note 13, pp. 509 *et seq.*

[16] See generally Patrick L. Robinson, 'Ensuring Fair and Expeditious Trials at the International Criminal Tribunal for the Former Yugoslavia', (2000) 11 *European Journal of International Law* 569; Fairlie, *supra* note 12, p. 245; Daryl A. Mundis, 'From "Common Law" Towards "Civil Law": The Evolution of the ICTY

William Schabas has described the ICTR as being 'joined at the hip' to the ICTY, sharing almost identical Statutes and Rules and most of the same judges in their respective Appeals Chambers.[17] Certainly, the ICTR has done little to distinguish itself procedurally from the ICTY and, after adopting an almost identical set of Rules at its first plenary session in June 1995, the ICTR judges have tended to adopt the amendments, deletions, and additions to the Rules that have periodically been implemented at the ICTY. However, the ICTR judges have at times disagreed with the changes and opted not to follow the ICTY. The resulting occasional differences between the two sets of Rules are highlighted where pertinent in this volume.[18] Because the two Tribunals' Rules remain largely the same, however, this section of the chapter will focus mainly on the ICTY. The judges of that institution have been much more active in creating rules, analysing and debating existing rules' utility and effectiveness, and codifying important rulings from Appeals Chamber jurisprudence.

2.1.2 Structure of the ICTY and ICTR Rules

The Rules of the *ad hoc* Tribunals follow a structure that has been generally copied in subsequent rules of procedure and evidence of international criminal tribunals. Elaborating on the sparse procedural guidance contained in their Statutes, the ICTY and ICTR Rules follow a linear progression of proceedings, beginning with the investigation phase, and continuing through the pre-trial, trial, sentencing, appeal, and post-appellate review stages.[19] The Rules also define the structure of the Tribunals, divided between the Chambers, the Office of the Prosecutor, and the Registry; this latter body, in turn, regulates the conditions and provision of defence counsel.[20] Unlike the ICC, where the Rome Statute's drafters included in the Statute itself many aspects of the Court's jurisdiction and functioning, the

Rules of Procedure and Evidence', (2001) 14 *Leiden Journal of International Law* 367; Mirjan Damaška, 'The Uncertain Fate of Evidentiary Transplants: Anglo-American and Contemporary Experiments', (1997) 45 *American Journal of Comparative Law* 839; Françoise Tulkens, 'Main Comparable Features of the Different European Criminal Justice Systems', in Mireille Delmas-Marty (ed.), *The Criminal Process and Human Rights: Toward a European Consciousness* (1995), p. 5.

17 William A. Schabas, *An Introduction to the International Criminal Court* (3rd edn 2009), p. 12.

18 See Mia Swart, 'Ad Hoc Rules for Ad Hoc Tribunals? The Rule-Making Power of the Judges of the ICTY and ICTR', (2002) 18 *South African Journal of Human Rights* 570, 576–577. For example, the ICTR judges opted not to adopt Rule 54 *bis*, an important rule in the ICTY governing how a party may obtain documents from states, or Rule 28(A), creating an admissibility test for the ICTY to accept a case; amended the criteria for deferral of a case under Rule 9 so that they are easier to satisfy than those in the ICTY; and opted not to incorporate some important amendments made to ICTY Rule 11 *bis* requiring the referring chamber to examine the gravity of the accused's crimes and his or her level of responsibility. See Chapter 3, Sections 3.1.1–3.1.3.

19 See, respectively, ICTY Rules, Parts IV–VIII; ICTR Rules, Parts IV–VIII. Part Two of each Tribunal's Rules is entitled 'Primacy of the Tribunal', and is discussed in Chapter 3, Section 3.1.1. Part Nine, on pardon and commutation, is discussed in Chapter 10, Section 10.5.

20 See ICTY Rules, Part III; ICTR Rules, Part III. On defence counsel generally, see Chapter 5.

ad hoc Tribunals' judges have used their Rules to fill many of the cavernous gaps left by the ICTY and ICTR Statutes, leading to some dramatic rule-making.[21]

One of the more notable aspects of the Rules is their status as the only governing instruments of the ICTY and ICTR containing any rules of evidence or reference thereto. And even here the evidentiary rules are few in number, particularly when compared with the extensive rules of evidence used in adversarial common law jurisdictions, leaving the interpretation of crucial areas of the criminal trial process to judicial development.[22] Another notable point is the lack of detail in these Tribunals' Rules relating to the appeal and review processes. These provisions state that appellate proceedings will apply the rules designed for the trial and pre-trial phases – which are laid out in detail in the rules – on a *mutatis mutandis* basis. This superficially efficient solution has, in practice, led to imprecision, and has required the judges to interpret these rules out of their initial intended context.

2.1.3 Amending the ICTY and ICTR Rules

With no mention in the *ad hoc* Tribunal Statutes of the process by which rules were to be amended, the Tribunals have assumed an implied power to do so.[23] ICTY Rule 6 (titled 'Amendments to the Rules') sets out the procedures to be followed in this respect:

(A) Proposals for amendment of the Rules may be made by a Judge, the Prosecutor or the Registrar and shall be adopted if agreed to by not less than ten permanent Judges at a plenary meeting of the Tribunal convened with notice of the proposal addressed to all Judges.
(B) An amendment to the Rules may be otherwise adopted, provided it is unanimously approved by the permanent Judges.
(C) Proposals for amendment of the Rules may otherwise be made in accordance with the Practice Direction issued by the President.
(D) An amendment shall enter into force seven days after the date of issue of an official Tribunal document containing the amendment, but shall not operate to prejudice the rights of the accused or of a convicted or acquitted person in any pending case.

There are three ways in which Rules may be created or amended: (1) in an ordinary plenary session;[24] (2) in an extraordinary plenary; and (3) by a unanimous vote

[21] See *infra* Section 2.1.4 (discussing the consequences of this practice).

[22] See ICTY Rules, Part VI, Section 3; ICTR Rules, Part VI, Section 3. On rules of evidence generally, see Chapter 9.

[23] See Gideon Boas, 'Comparing the ICTY and the ICC: Some Procedural and Substantive Issues', (2000) 47 *Netherlands International Law Review* 267, 274.

[24] A 'plenary session' at the *ad hoc* Tribunals is a meeting of all the judges at which the judges elect the President of the Tribunal, create and amend rules, discuss administrative and policy issues that affect the running of the Tribunal, and perform several other administrative and quasi-legislative functions. All such sessions are held *in camera* and no public transcript is made, although the judges issue public statements about some decisions taken, including rule amendments.

outside of plenary.[25] Early on in the Tribunals' existence, an Intersessional Working Group for the Amendment of the Rules was established at the ICTY, consisting of a five-judge panel whose task was to review the first version of the Rules and identify specific amendments that should be made. The Group's work led to forty-one amendments to the original set of Rules on a range of matters, including the rights of suspects and accused and the protection of victims and witnesses.[26] This set the precedent for a process of continual significant amendment to the ICTY Rules over the Tribunal's existence, with the ICTR largely endorsing the changes made in the ICTY.

The ICTY subsequently created a standing Rules Committee 'to investigate the objective of conducting trials more expeditiously without jeopardising respect for the rights of accused persons'.[27] In effect, the Committee serves as a permanent working group for the plenary of judges in respect of changes to the Rules of Procedure and Evidence. It consists of one judicial representative of each of the three Trial Chambers, the Tribunal's President, and the Vice-President; these latter two are also judges, and the President sits on the Appeals Chamber. By virtue of the great diversity of the judges at the ICTY, the backgrounds of the judicial representatives on the Committee tend to reflect the different legal systems of the world. These judges bring to the table proposals for rule creation and amendment, and consider proposals made by other judges, the Registry, the Office of the Prosecutor and, less often, the Association of Defence Counsel. While the Office of the Prosecutor, the Association of Defence Counsel, and the Registry all send representatives to Committee meetings, and may make proposals, they may only observe and comment at meetings, and only the judges may vote on proposals. If the Committee judges vote in favour of a given proposal, they then forward it to the plenary of all judges with comments and recommendations. Rejected proposals might not ever reach the plenary for consideration, although judges are always free to raise a proposal in plenary themselves. The records of the Rules Committee's meetings are not public. The ICTR has no equivalent of the ICTY Rules Committee.

In 1998, the President of the ICTY issued a Practice Direction setting out a procedure for the proposal, consideration, and publication of amendments to the ICTY

[25] ICTY Rule 6(B). See also *infra* text accompanying note 36 (discussing ICTY Rule 6(B)).

[26] See Report of the International Tribunal for the Prosecution of Persons Responsible for Serious Violations of International Humanitarian Law Committed in the Territory of the former Yugoslavia Since 1991, UN Doc. A/50/365-S/1995/728, 23 August 1995, paras. 19–26. See also Megan Fairlie, 'Rulemaking from the Bench: A Place for Minimalism at the ICTY', (2004) 39 *Texas International Law Journal* 257, 261–262.

[27] Report of the International Tribunal for the Prosecution of Persons Responsible for Serious Violations of International Humanitarian Law Committed in the Territory of the former Yugoslavia Since 1991, UN Doc. A/53/219-S/1998/737, 10 August 1998, para. 106.

Rules.[28] Rule 19(B) governs practice directions: in consultation with the Bureau,[29] the Registrar, and the Prosecutor, the President of the Tribunal may issue such directions to address detailed aspects of the conduct of proceedings, so long as they are consistent with the Statute and the Rules. While not strictly dealing with the conduct of proceedings before the Tribunal, this 1998 Practice Direction sought to regulate the manner in which amendments were made to the ICTY Rules. In the 2002 revision of this Practice Direction the President stated that, except in urgent or exceptional cases, all amendments to the Rules shall take place only once during the year, at the final plenary session of judges,[30] a practice not followed at the ICTR.

In fact, the judges of the ICTY have amended the Rules with remarkable frequency. The original Rules were adopted on 11 February 1994 and modified twice in that year. In 1995 and 1996 they were amended four times each year, usually in extraordinary plenary sessions. From then on, the judges have amended the Rules an average of twice per year. With the ICTY surpassing fifteen years of operation, its Rules have been amended no fewer than forty-two times, with the largest number of revisions being made in 2000 and 2001. By any regulatory standard, this is an unusual number of amendments to a set of approximately 153 provisions. The ICTR judges have apparently felt much less compunction to continually fine-tune their Rules, and have amended them about once a year over that Tribunal's lifespan. Section 2.1.4 considers the rule-amending process, how the judges have exercised these powers, and the impact on the conduct of these Tribunals' proceedings. To avoid confusion in light of these extensive and repeated amendments of the Tribunals' Rules, particularly those of the ICTY, references in this volume to specific provisions of the Rules reflect the numbering as of 1 December 2009.

Rule 6(D) of both Tribunals requires that any amendment to the Rules 'shall not operate to prejudice the rights of the accused in any pending case'. Accused have invoked this rule many times to argue that the application of an amended rule would prejudice their rights. Early in the life of the ICTY, the Appeals Chamber in the *Blaškić* case had occasion to consider Rule 6(D) in two decisions triggered by the new Rule 108 *bis*, which allowed a state to request appellate review of a

[28] Practice Direction on Procedure for the Proposal, Consideration of and Publication of Amendments to the Rules of Procedure and Evidence of the International Tribunal, UN Doc. IT/143, 18 December 1998. That Practice Direction was amended to allow *ad litem* judges to have input into the process. See Practice Direction on Procedure for the Proposal, Consideration of and Publication of Amendments to the Rules of Procedure and Evidence of the International Tribunal, UN Doc. IT/143/Rev.1, 4 May 2001. It was further amended to incorporate changes to the composition and structure of the Rules Committee. See Practice Direction on Procedure for the Proposal, Consideration of and Publication of Amendments to the Rules of Procedure and Evidence of the International Tribunal, UN Doc. IT/143/Rev.2, 26 February 2002 ('ICTY Rule Amendments 2002 Practice Direction').

[29] The Bureau is set up under ICTY Rule 23. It is comprised of the President, Vice-President, and presiding judges of the Trial Chambers and discusses 'all major questions relating to the functioning of the Tribunal'. ICTR Rule 23 establishes an identical Bureau for that Tribunal.

[30] ICTY Rule Amendments 2002 Practice Direction, *supra* note 28, para. 3.

trial chamber decision, and concluded that Croatia could seek such review even though the trial decision in question predated the new rule, because granting its request would not prejudice the accused's rights.[31] An early Trial Chamber ruling in *Blaškić* also considered Rule 6(D) in relation to an amendment to Rule 66(A), dealing with disclosure by the Prosecutor. The Trial Chamber held that the amendment in question did not change the sense of Rule 66(A), but merely clarified its 'spirit and meaning', and that there was therefore no violation in applying the new Rule immediately.[32] Another Trial Chamber ruled in 2001 that the application of a new Rule 75(D), concerning requests for access to confidential material produced in another trial before the Tribunal, did not prejudice the accused within the meaning of Rule 6(D).[33] In that case, the Trial Chamber held that 'Rule 75(D) is a procedural provision and that its operation in the current matter would not operate to prejudice the rights of the accused'.[34] Most chambers have followed the lead of these two in dismissing challenges to Rule 6(D) upon finding that a rule amendment did not prejudice the accused's rights.[35]

The process set up under Rule 6(B) of both Tribunals, allowing for amendment of the Rules by unanimous vote outside of plenary sessions, has been little used. The ICTY judges resorted to Rule 6(B) in October 1994 to amend Rule 70(B), in order to remedy an urgent problem encountered by the Prosecutor in obtaining information from non-governmental organisations and other bodies. Prompted by the resignation of Judge Sidhwa, Rule 15 was amended in July 1996 to address the contingency of the sudden resignation of a judge due to ill health.[36] In March 1999, the judges amended Rule 23 in the same way to allow the Bureau to convene in the absence or unavailability of judges ordinarily members of the Bureau, by calling

[31] See *Prosecutor* v. *Blaškić*, Case No. IT-95-14-AR108*bis*, Decision on the Admissibility of the Request for Review by the Republic of Croatia of an Interlocutory Decision of a Trial Chamber (Issuance of Subpoenae Duces Tecum) and Scheduling Order, 29 July 1997, paras. 10–11 (discussing the provision then labelled Rule 6(C)); *Prosecutor* v. *Blaškić*, Case No. IT-95-14-AR108*bis*, Decision on Prosecution Motion to Set Aside the Decision of the Appeals Chamber of 29 July 1997, 12 August 1997, paras. 11–13.

[32] *Prosecutor* v. *Blaškić*, Case No. IT-95-14-T, Decision on the Defence Motion to Compel the Disclosure of Rule 66 and 68 Material Relating to Statements Made by a Person Known as X, 15 July 1998, paras. 7–12 (quotation at para. 8).

[33] See *Prosecutor* v. *Došen and Kolundžija*, Case No. IT-95-8-PT, Order on Motion of Accused Kolundžija for Access to Certain Confidential Materials, 3 February 2000 ('*Došen and Kolundžija* Confidential Materials Order'). The judges later amended Rule 75(D) at the twenty-fifth session of the Plenary. See Amendments to the Rules of Procedure and Evidence, UN Doc. IT/199, 21 December 2001.

[34] *Došen and Kolundžija* Confidential Materials Order, *supra* note 33, para. 3.

[35] See, e.g., *Prosecutor* v. *Milutinović, Šainović, Ojdanić, Pavković, Lazarević, and Lukić*, Case No. IT-05-87-T, Decision on Lukić Defence Alteration of Official Translations of Witness Statements, 22 May 2008; *Prosecutor* v. *Prlić, Stojić, Praljak, Petković, Ćorić, and Pušić*, Case No. IT-04-74-T, Decision on Slobodan Praljak's Motion on the Application of Rule 67(A) of the Rules, 4 April 2008; *Prosecutor* v. *Nyiramasuhuko and Ntahobali*, Case Nos. ICTR-97-21-T, ICTR-97-29A&B-T, ICTR-96-15-T, ICTR-96-8-T, and ICTR-98-42-A15*bis*, Decision in the Matter of Proceedings Under Rule 15 *bis* (D), 24 September 2004; *Prosecutor* v. *Ntakirutimana and Ntakirutimana*, Case Nos. ICTR-96-10-A and ICTR-96-17-A, Reasons for the Decision on Request for Admission of Additional Evidence, 8 September 2004.

[36] On the substitution of a judge who resigns or dies mid-trial, see Chapter 7, Section 7.1.4.

upon the next senior available judge, apparently so that the Bureau could continue to function.[37]

It is clear that the judges of the ICTY and the ICTR have considerable power over their regulatory structure. Yet the Rules of Procedure and Evidence of these institutions are considerably farther-reaching than simple procedural rules. As noted above, these Rules regulate the entire legal process before the Tribunals: investigation, pre-trial, trial, sentencing, appeal, and review of judgements. Moreover, their interpretation by the same judges who create and amend them has a significant impact on the fair trial rights of accused persons. The judges have sometimes used this rule-making power to codify the jurisprudence, amending rules to reflect the clarifications provided in trial and appeals chamber rulings.[38] It has also been used, however, to alter or overrule decisions of trial and appeals chambers, thus raising concerns about the appropriateness of this dual role of the judges.

2.1.4 *Quasi-judicial legislating and the separation of powers in the* ad hoc *Tribunals*

The powers of the judges of the ICTY were deemed 'quasi-legislative' as early as the Tribunal's first annual report, in which the President referred to the 'quasi-legislative task of preparing a code of criminal procedure (its rules of procedure and evidence)'.[39] As noted earlier in this chapter, the power of the judges to make and amend rules, as well as to adjudicate upon their meaning and application, is extraordinary, and has raised intemperate allegations of illegitimacy in the press,[40] as well as arguments by scholars that the rule-making power violates the separation of powers doctrine and may infringe the legality principle.[41] Broadly speaking, the separation of powers doctrine prevents judges in national jurisdictions from legislating and requires that they apply existing law. Even though there are

[37] On the Bureau, see *supra* note 29.

[38] For example, Rule 62 *bis*(ii), requiring that a guilty plea be 'informed', was a partial codification of the Appeals Chamber's holding in *Prosecutor* v. *Erdemović*, Case No. IT-96-22-A, Judgment, 7 October 1999, para. 20. For more on this issue, see *infra* Section 2.1.4; see also Chapter 6, Section 6.4.1.1.2.

[39] See Report of the International Tribunal for the Prosecution of Persons Responsible for Serious Violations of International Humanitarian Law Committed in the Territory of the former Yugoslavia Since 1991, UN Doc. A/49/342-S/1994/1007, 29 August 1994, para. 27. This description of the ICTY's rule-making activity has also been offered in scholarly literature. See, e.g., Fairlie, *supra* note 26, pp. 261–263; Boas, *supra* note 3, pp. 9–18; Daryl A. Mundis, 'The Legal Character and Status of the Rules of Procedure and Evidence of the ad hoc International Criminal Tribunals', (2001) 1 *International Criminal Law Review* 191, 198. See also generally Swart, *supra* note 18.

[40] An oft-cited and not particularly measured example is John Laughland, 'The Anomalies of the International Criminal Tribunal are Legion', *The Times*, 17 June 1999.

[41] On the separation of powers, see *infra* note 65. For arguments on the potential of the Tribunals' rule-making power to violate the principle of legality and, even less convincingly, the rule of law, see Swart, *supra* note 18, pp. 570–571 (arguing that Article 15 of the ICTY Statute, which allows the judges to make and amend rules, 'runs awry of the issue of separation of powers, both mandating and enabling the judiciary to draft the rules they will ultimately apply').

clearly instances in any domestic legal system where the interpretative role of a judge exceeds the simple application of the law and may be perceived as a form of judicial legislating, generally the doctrine prevents any substantial interference of the judiciary in the legislative task.

Public statements by judges and annual reports of the Tribunals evince considerable support both for the existence of the *ad hoc* Tribunals' unusual rule-making power and its application. The first President of the ICTY, Antonio Cassese, argued persuasively that it was 'essential, in the interests of justice, to amend the Rules in light of new problems ... or unanticipated situations'.[42] The Third Annual Report of the ICTY reflected a similar, though vaguer, sentiment: '[S]ince it was not possible at the outset to anticipate every eventuality which would arise, the Rules have been amended from time to time, by a plenary of the judges, to take account of various eventualities'.[43]

The *ad hoc* Tribunals, and especially the ICTY, have used the rule-making and rule-amending powers to respond to an array of different issues that have arisen in practice, and many of these rule changes have been perfectly appropriate. One important motivation for rule creation and amendment has been the effort, noted above, to use the Rules to codify important Appeals Chamber jurisprudence. ICTY Rule 54 *bis*, for example, was inspired by a desire to codify several rulings, most significantly a groundbreaking appeal decision in *Blaškić* setting out a test to be applied to the request by a party for documents from a state that has national security concerns about such disclosure.[44] More recently, Rule 92 *ter* codified a practice that developed in the *Milošević* case for the admission of written statements in lieu of direct examination, while requiring the witness's presence for cross-examination.[45]

[42] Address by President Cassese to the UN General Assembly, 4 November 1997, cited in Swart, *supra* note 18, p. 581.

[43] Report of the International Tribunal for the Prosecution of Persons Responsible for Serious Violations of International Humanitarian Law Committed in the Territory of the former Yugoslavia Since 1991, UN Doc. A/51292-5/1996/665, 16 August 1996, para. 66. See also Fabricio Guariglia, 'The Rules of Procedure and Evidence for the International Criminal Court: A New Development in International Adjudication of Individual Criminal Responsibility', in Antonio Cassese, Paola Gaeta, and John R.W.D. Jones (eds.), *The Rome Statute of the International Criminal Court: A Commentary* (2002), Vol. II, p. 1116.

[44] See *Prosecutor* v. *Blaškić*, Case No. IT-95-14-AR108 *bis*, Judgement on the Request of the Republic of Croatia for Review of the Decision of Trial Chamber II of 18 July 1997, 29 October 1997, paras. 67–69; see also Chapter 6, Section 6.5 (discussing the disclosure regimes at the international tribunals).

[45] See *Prosecutor* v. *Milošević*, Case No. IT-02-54-AR73.4, Decision on Interlocutory Appeal on the Admissibility of Evidence-in-Chief in the Form of Written Statements, 30 September 2003. This practice also led to the creation of Rule 92 *quater* and further amendments to the already existing Rule 92 *bis*. These amended provisions entered into force in 2006. They regulate the circumstances in which evidence in the form of a written statement or transcript of evidence from a prior Tribunal proceeding may be admitted; whether such evidence may describe the accused's own criminal conduct; and whether cross-examination of the declarant is required. See Amendments to the Rules of Procedure and Evidence, UN Doc. No. IT/250, 15 September 2006; see also Chapter 9, Section 9.2.1.1 (discussing these rules). For a discussion of the jurisprudential foundations of these rules, see O-Gon Kwon, 'The Challenge of an International Criminal Trial as Seen from the Bench', (2007) 5 *Journal of International Criminal Justice* 360, 363–368.

A second key motivation behind the creation and amendment of the Rules, especially for the ICTY, has been the *ad hoc* Tribunals' desire to speed up proceedings. In 2000 and 2001 alone, ninety-one rules were amended, seven new rules were adopted and one rule was deleted. In the ICTY, Rule 92 *bis* (concerning the admission of written statements in lieu of oral testimony), Rule 73 *bis* (granting judges extensive powers to regulate the scope and preparation of cases for trial), Rule 28(A) (requiring any new indictments to be approved by a panel of judges as focusing on senior offenders), and Rule 11 *bis* (providing for the transfer of less serious cases to national jurisdictions) all reflect an effort to conclude the Tribunal's work in accordance with the Security Council's call to finish investigations by 2004, trials by 2008, and appeals by 2010.[46] Moreover, many of the significant number of amendments made in 2001 and 2002 were minor changes prompted by the creation of *ad litem* judges to help the Tribunal hear more cases and conclude its work within the completion strategy timeline.[47]

While it has been argued that the rule-making power, and in particular frequent amendments to the Rules, threaten the fundamental criminal law principle of legality[48] – that is, the requirement that an individual be subject to criminal punishment only if and to the extent provided for by law – there appears to be no available evidence that this is in fact the case. Furthermore, the arguments raised along these lines do not clearly articulate why the principle of legality is violated by such a rule-making framework. It is difficult to see how, despite the unusual nature of these powers and the importance of some of the subject-matter of the Rules, the principle of legality is implicated. The substantive crimes and forms of responsibility are not subject to the rule-making powers. If anything, criticism of this nature might be better directed to the judicial expansion of the elements of the core crimes or forms of responsibility – discussed in the first two volumes of this Series – but are not justified in the context of the rules of procedure and evidence.

[46] See Security Council Resolution 1503, UN Doc. S/RES/1503 (2003); Security Council Resolution 1504, UN Doc. S/RES/1534 (2004). For a detailed discussion of Rules 28(A) and 11 *bis*, see Chapter 3, Sections 3.1.2–3.1.3. See also Steven R. Ratner, Jason S. Abrams, and James L. Bischoff, *Accountability for Human Rights Atrocities in International Law: Beyond the Nuremberg Legacy* (3rd edn 2009), p. 221. As of 1 December 2009, all ICTY investigations have been concluded, but trials were anticipated to continue until 2012, and appeals until 2014. See Letter Dated 12 November 2009 from the President of the International Tribunal for the Prosecution of Persons Responsible for Serious Violations of International Humanitarian Law Committed in the Territory of the former Yugoslavia Since 1991, Addressed to the President of the Security Council, UN Doc. S/2009/589, 29 September 2009, paras. 4, 5.

[47] The Security Council appoints *ad litem* judges for the limited duration of a trial, although this term may be and often is extended. *Ad litem* judges' powers under the Statute are more limited than those of permanent judges. For example, they have no vote on the creation or amendment of the Rules under Article 15. However, their involvement in the preparation of cases in the pre-trial phase has increased over time, as the Tribunal's pre-trial workload has increased and efforts to complete its work have intensified. See ICTY Statute, Art. 13 *quater*; see also, e.g., Security Council Resolution 1481 (2003), UN Doc. S/RES/1481, 19 May 2003. The ICTR has a similar system of *ad litem* judges, aimed at facilitating its own completion strategy. See ICTR Statute, Art. 12 *quater*. On the procedures for appointment of *ad litem* judges to particular trials, see Chapter 7, Section 7.1.2.

[48] See, e.g., Swart, *supra* note 18, pp. 579–581. See also *supra* text accompanying note 41.

Setting aside this animated criticism, a third motivation for making and amending the Rules – the creation or amendment of rules intended to overrule judicial rulings of the Tribunal – has given rise to a genuine concern that the judges' employment of these quasi-legislative powers has at times threatened the certainty of the law. This interesting practice warrants in-depth consideration of whether the rule-making and amending authority can be legitimately utilised as a quasi-legislative power to overrule decisions made at a trial or even at the appellate level.

The debate over this question got off to a bad start at the ICTR, where one Trial Chamber incorrectly stated the position:

> Apart from case law that emerges in judicial proceedings as a result of judicial interpretation of the law, judges do not make Rules. As a general principle of law, this Trial Chamber, therefore, does not have the mandate to make Rules in the manner requested by the Defence because according to Article 14 of the Statute [equivalent to Article 15 of the ICTY Statute] and Rule 6 of the Rules, this is a function of the Plenary of the Tribunal.[49]

It is quite true that the judges of the *ad hoc* Tribunals, acting in their judicial capacity in ruling in an individual case, do not have the power to make rules or amend them. However, as one senior prosecution attorney at the ICTY has noted, 'it is precisely the judges, sitting collectively in Plenary and acting in their capacity of quasi-legislators, who do make the Rules'.[50]

On several occasions, the judges of the *ad hoc* Tribunals have acted in plenary to amend the Rules with the effect of overruling or varying decisions of the Appeals Chamber – perhaps most notoriously in the *Kupreškić* case. At the time, Rule 71(A) provided that '[a]t the request of either party, a Trial Chamber may, in exceptional circumstances and in the interests of justice, order that a deposition be taken for use at trial, and appoint, for that purpose, a Presiding Officer'.[51] After one of the judges of the *Kupreškić* Trial Chamber fell ill, the remaining two members of the bench encouraged the prosecution to elicit the evidence of a witness by deposing him in their presence, with one of the judges acting as 'Presiding Officer' for the purposes of Rule 71(A). One of the accused challenged this proposal on the ground that witnesses were going to give evidence on specific facts relating to the charges, and therefore all three judges must be present.[52] The two members of the Chamber,

[49] *Prosecutor* v. *Bagosora*, Case No. ICTR-96-7-T, Decision on the Defence Motion for Pre-Determination of Rules of Evidence, 8 July 1998, Part C.

[50] Mundis, *supra* note 39, p. 198.

[51] International Tribunal for the Prosecution of Persons Responsible for Serious Violations of International Humanitarian Law Committed in the Territory of former Yugoslavia Since 1991, Rules of Procedure and Evidence, UN Doc. IT/32/Rev.13, 25 February 1999, Rule 71(A). Rule 15(E) states that '[i]n case of illness or an unfilled vacancy or in any other circumstances, the President may authorise a Chamber to conduct routine matters, such as the holding of an initial appearance under Rule 62 or the delivery of decisions, in the absence of one or more of its members'.

[52] *Prosecutor* v. *Kupreškić, Kupreškić, Kupreškić, Jošipović, Papić, and Santić*, Case No. IT-95-16-AR73.3, Decision on Appeal by Dragan Papić Against Ruling to Proceed by Deposition, 15 July 1999, para. 5.

having invited the prosecution's application to take a deposition in this manner, held that 'in spite of the opposition of the Defence counsel and the accused, Rule 71 is fully applicable because according to this Rule the request of one party is sufficient, and we feel that we are confronted with exceptional circumstances and that the interests of justice command that a fair and expeditious trial be held'.[53]

The accused appealed this ruling and the Appeals Chamber reversed. The Appeals Chamber noted that Article 12 of the Statute requires Trial Chambers to be composed of three judges and that the two judges in the *Kupreškić* case had acted in the absence of the third judge, without having previously consulted that judge. The only way the two judges could legally have proceeded was to obtain an order from the President under Rule 15(E),[54] which at the time only allowed the Trial Chamber to proceed in the absence of one of its members on 'routine matters'. The Appeals Chamber found that 'no such authorisation had been given by the President, and, in any event, the making of a decision to proceed by way of deposition with regard to the examination of witnesses giving evidence on facts relating to the specific charges ... does not ... constitute "routine matters"'.[55] The Appeals Chamber, therefore, held that the ruling was 'null and void since it was rendered without jurisdiction'.[56]

Ironically, prior to the *Kupreškić* Appeals Chamber decision, ICTY trial chambers had frequently held trial sessions in the absence of one judge pursuant to Rule 71. The judges obviously considered this procedure a convenient way to continue sitting when a judge was absent, for whatever reason, for a short period of time. And, indeed, the judges of the ICTY must have considered it an essential procedure as, a mere four months following the Appeals Chamber ruling, the judges of the ICTY acting in plenary amended Rules 15 and 71 and created a new Rule 15 *bis* which provided, in relevant part, that if:

(i) a judge is, for illness or other urgent personal reasons, or for reasons of authorised Tribunal business, unable to continue sitting in a part-heard case for a period which is likely to be of short duration, and
(ii) the remaining judges of the Chamber are satisfied that it is in the interests of justice to do so, those remaining judges of the Chamber may order that the hearing of the case continue in the absence of that judge for a period of not more than three days.[57]

By this amendment, the judges, acting in a quasi-legislative capacity, removed the requirement that a trial continue in the absence of a judge with respect only to

53 *Ibid.*, para. 6.
54 *Ibid.*, para. 14. For the text of Rule 15(E), see *supra* note 51.
55 *Ibid.* 56 *Ibid.*
57 This amendment was adopted at the twenty-first session of the plenary held 15 to 17 November 1999. The new and amended Rules entered into force on 6 December 2000. See Amendments to the Rules of Procedure and Evidence, UN Doc. IT/161, 30 November 1999.

'routine matters'; they removed the need to establish 'exceptional circumstances'; and they placed the authority to proceed in the absence of a member of the bench exclusively in the hands of the remaining judges.[58] The direct effect of this legislative action was to overrule the *Kupreškić* Appeals Chamber decision. It is impossible to know how the judges voted to achieve this result. As explained above, a two-thirds majority vote is required to achieve an amendment. Because transcripts of plenary meetings are not publicly available documents, no public record exists setting forth the articulated basis for the amendments or, indeed, which judges voted for and against these amendments.

The *Kupreškić* case is but the first of many examples where the judges, sitting in plenary, have created or amended rules to overrule previous trial or appeals rulings. Several other and significant examples exist, often relating to core areas of law, including the procedure for the admission of written statements in lieu of oral evidence;[59] the procedure for the delivery of discrete sentences for each finding of guilt by a trial chamber;[60] amending the provisions on the right to appeal, in an apparent endeavour to avoid the political embarrassment created by an initial decision of the ICTR Appeals Chamber to release the accused Jean-Bosco Barayagwiza;[61] and, a series of amendments designed to expedite proceedings following the recommendations of a UN-appointed expert group set up to review the efficiency of the *ad hoc* Tribunals.[62]

[58] Rule 15 *bis* and examples of its application are discussed in Chapter 7, Section 7.1.4.

[59] In this instance, the judges amended the Rules by deleting then-Rule 94 *ter* and creating Rule 92 *bis*, in order to overrule an Appeals Chamber decision on the requirements of then-Rule 94 *ter*. See *Prosecutor* v. *Kordić and Čerkez*, Case No. IT-95-14/2-AR73.6, Decision on Appeal Regarding the Admission into Evidence of Seven Affidavits and One Formal Statement, 18 September 2000. The amendment was approved at the twenty-third plenary session held 29 November to 1 December 2000, and entered into force on 19 January 2001. See Amendments to the Rules of Procedure and Evidence, UN Doc. IT/183, 12 January 2001. For a detailed discussion, see Boas, *supra* note 3, pp. 12–15.

[60] See *Prosecutor* v. *Blaškić*, Case No. IT-95-14-T, Judgement, 3 March 2000; *Prosecutor* v. *Musema*, Case No. ICTR-96-13-T, Sentence and Judgement, 27 January 2000; *Prosecutor* v. *Jelisić*, Case No. IT-95-10-T, Judgement, 14 December 1999; *Prosecutor* v. *Serushago*, Case No. ICTR-98-39-S, Sentence, 5 February 1999; *Prosecutor* v. *Kambanda*, Case No. ICTR-97-23-S, Sentence and Judgement, 4 September 1998. Amendments were subsequently made at the twenty-third plenary session held on 13 December 2000, and entered into force on 19 January 2001. See Amendments to the Rules of Procedure and Evidence, UN Doc. IT/183, 12 January 2001. For a detailed discussion, see Boas, *supra* note 3, pp. 15–18; Mundis, *supra* note 39, pp. 199–206. The handing-down of sentences is discussed in Chapter 7, Section 7.6.7 and Chapter 10, Section 10.1.7; the factors that go into determining the sentence are discussed in Chapter 10, Section 10.2.2.

[61] The ICTR Appeals Chamber initially attributed Barayagwiza's prolonged pre-trial detention to the ICTR Prosecutor, and ruled that ICTR Rules 40 and 40 *bis* required his release. Although the Appeals Chamber later reversed this ruling, the original decision still prompted amendments to ICTY Rule 72 on 21 February 2000. See *Barayagwiza* v. *Prosecutor*, Case No. ICTR-97-19-AR72, Decision, 3 November 1999. For discussion of this decision, see Chapter 4, Section 4.2.7; see also Swart, *supra* note 18, pp. 581–586; Mundis, *supra* note 39, pp. 196–199; Jacob Katz Cogan, 'International Criminal Courts and Fair Trials: Difficulties and Prospects', (2002) 27 *Yale Journal of International Law* 134, 135.

[62] See Report of the Expert Group to Conduct a Review of the Effective Operation and Functioning of the International Tribunal for the Former Yugoslavia and International Criminal Tribunal for Rwanda, UN Doc. A/54/634, 22 November 1999. For a discussion of some of the implications of the Group's work, see Gideon Boas, *The Milošević Trial: Lessons for the Conduct of International Criminal Proceedings* (2007), pp. 65–69. For a recounting of some arguably inappropriate uses of the rule-making power to expedite proceedings, see

It has been argued that:

A process of codification of case law is not in itself an objectionable process, even where those amending the Rules are the very judges interpreting the provisions in the first place. This is especially so in an institution like the ICTY, which is developing the first comprehensive body of rules of procedure and evidence for the prosecution of international crimes. The need for flexibility in that development process is obvious and efficacious, so long as the rights of the accused are fully respected. Such a codification process can increase clarity and consistency in the application of important procedural and substantive rules, particularly where judges and lawyers come from different jurisdictions with sometimes very different legal systems. Such codification will assist everybody in understanding how to conduct proceedings in an international criminal law jurisdiction.[63]

Difficulty arises, however, where judges, sitting in a quasi-legislative capacity, amend the Rules to overrule decisions made by judges of the same institution exercising their interpretative judicial functions. Such activity can create uncertainty and undermine the *ad hoc* Tribunals' self-styled doctrine of precedent,[64] and it may well be a violation of the requirement that judges act with independence and impartiality.[65]

Where the Appeals Chamber has ruled definitively on a question of law, we find little merit in the judges, sitting afterwards in plenary, overriding such a ruling. It would lend greater certainty to the development and application of the Rules for parties to be able to rely upon their interpretation at an appellate level. By implementing a formal system of precedent in the jurisprudence itself,[66] the Tribunals

Swart, *supra* note 18, pp. 587–588. Extraordinary evidence also exists of the Appeals Chamber exercising its powers to further the completion strategy in violation of the accused's right to a fair trial. On this issue, see Gideon Boas, 'The Case for a New Appellate Jurisdiction for International Criminal Law', in Göran Sluiter and Sergey Vasiliev (eds.), *International Criminal Procedure: Towards A Coherent Body of Law* (2008), pp. 439–442 and cases cited therein.

[63] Boas, *supra* note 3, p. 17.

[64] The ICTY and ICTR Appeals Chambers have held that a formal doctrine of precedent operates at the *ad hoc* Tribunals, whereby decisions of the Appeals Chamber of each Tribunal are binding on the trial chambers of that Tribunal, and are otherwise persuasive precedent. See Gideon Boas, James L. Bischoff, and Natalie L. Reid, *Forms of Responsibility in International Criminal* Law (2007), p. 26 n. 94 and cases cited therein. See also, e.g., *Prosecutor* v. *Delalić, Mucić, Delić, and Landžo*, Case No. IT-96-21-A, Judgement, 20 February 2001 ('*Čelebići* Appeal Judgement'), para. 8; *Prosecutor* v. *Aleksovski*, Judgment, Case No. IT-95-14-1-A, 24 March 2000 ('*Aleksovski* Appeal Judgement'), paras. 112–113. For a discussion of the application and appropriateness of this doctrine in the Tribunals, see Boas, *supra* note 62, pp. 432–436; Chapter 11, Section 11.3.1.

[65] This aspect of judicial legislating may also have tangential relevance to the 'separation of powers' doctrine, as interpreted in the context of the ICTY. The Appeals Chamber has related the doctrine to the question of actual or perceived bias of judges, stating that it is 'beyond question that the principles of judicial independence and impartiality are of a fundamental nature which underpin international as well as national law'. See *Čelebići* Appeal Judgement, *supra* note 64, para. 689. These principles, reflected in human rights law and in the ICTY and ICTR Statutes, may be relevant where judges act in a quasi-legislative capacity to overrule decisions of trial or appeals chambers. See Universal Declaration of Human Rights, UN Doc. A/810, 10 December 1948, Art. 10; International Covenant on Civil and Political Rights, 16 December 1966, entered into force 23 March 1976, UN Doc. A/6316 (1966), 999 UNTS 171, Art. 14; ICTY Statute, Arts. 12–13; ICTR Statute, Arts. 11–12.

[66] On the *ad hoc* Tribunals' doctrine of precedent, see *supra* note 64 and sources cited therein; Chapter 11, Section 11.3.1. The *Aleksovski* formulation of the principle of binding precedent is somewhat confusing and gives rise to a possible interpretation that facts, and not just the *ratio decidendi* of a given decision, may be

have created such an expectation. The Tribunals have further aggravated the effect of this process by declining to produce publicly available records of their plenary debates, and the reasoning proffered for Rule amendments produced in their annual reports is extremely sparse.[67]

2.1.5 ICTY and ICTR Regulations

Of final note, the important rule-making powers given to the *ad hoc* Tribunals are not limited to the Rules of Procedure and Evidence. The judges – as well as the Tribunals' Presidents or Registrars acting either alone or in concert with the plenary – are empowered to create and amend regulations of considerable import to the conduct of fair proceedings.[68] These regulations are created pursuant to relevant Articles of the Statutes or Rules of Procedure and Evidence and are subordinate to them. These instruments include, for example, regulations relating to the detention of accused persons,[69] and the appointment and management of defence counsel.[70] The President may also create practice directions regulating many other aspects of the running of the tribunal including, for example, the conditions for granting a convicted accused early release from prison.[71] As will be seen in the following section, the judges of the ICC have

binding on other chambers. See *Aleksovski* Appeal Judgment, *supra* note 64, paras. 112–113. Several other rulings and opinions have clarified, however, that this is not the case. See, e.g., *Prosecutor* v. *Semanza*, Case No. ICTR-97-20-A, Judgement, 20 May 2005, para. 92; *Čelebići* Appeal Judgement, *supra* note 64, para. 8; *Prosecutor* v. *Brđanin*, Case No. IT-99-36-T, Decision on Application by Momir Talić for the Disqualification and Withdrawal of a Judge, 18 May 2000, para. 6 (Judge Hunt). See also Boas, *supra* note 62; Gideon Boas, James L. Bischoff, and Natalie L. Reid, *Elements of Crimes Under International Law* (2008) ('Boas, Bischoff, and Reid, *Elements of Crimes*'), pp. 344–345.

67 See Boas, *supra* note 3, pp. 31–32 (arguing that '[i]mproved explanatory reporting would enhance transparency and treat this ostensibly legislative function in a more traditional and publicly acceptable manner', and that '[i]t would also give an interpretative basis upon which applications under new and amended Rules could be considered, much in the way that second reading speeches are used as a basis for interpreting legislation').

68 The provisions in the *ad hoc* Tribunals' Statutes and Rules that support the power to create Directives and Codes are those which grant general powers to the chambers and Registry of the Tribunals. See generally ICTY Rules, Part III, Sections 2, 3, 5; ICTR Rules, Part III, Sections 2, 3, 5. In turn, these regulations most often simply cite the Statute and Rules of the Tribunal as the basis for the authority to create them.

69 For the ICTY, see Rules Governing the Detention of Persons Awaiting Trial or Appeal Before the Tribunal or Otherwise Detained on the Authority of the Tribunal, UN Doc. IT/38/Rev.9, 21 July 2005. Other ICTY regulations and orders relating to detention appear at www.icty.org/sections/LegalLibrary/Detention. For the ICTR, see Rules Covering the Detention of Persons Awaiting Trial or Appeal Before the Tribunal or Otherwise Detained on the Authority of the Tribunal, 5 June 1998, available at www.ictr.org/ENGLISH/basicdocs/detention/detention_07.pdf. For a detailed discussion of detention at the Tribunals, see Chapter 4, Section 4.3.

70 For the ICTY, see Directive on Assignment of Defence Counsel, UN Doc. IT/73/Rev.11, 11 July 2006; Code of Professional Conduct for Counsel Appearing Before the International Tribunal, UN Doc. IT/125/Rev.3, 22 July 2009. For the ICTR, see Directive on Assignment of Defence Counsel, Directive No. 1/96, 14 March 2008, available at www.ictr.org/ENGLISH/basicdocs/080314/05-Directive%20Assignment.pdf. For a detailed discussion on the assignment of defence counsel, see Chapter 5, Section 5.2.1.

71 See Practice Direction for the Determination of Applications for Pardon, Commutation of Sentence, and Early Release of Persons Convicted by the International Tribunal, UN Doc. IT/146/Rev.2, 1 September 2009. For a detailed discussion on procedures for determining eligibility for early release, see Chapter 10, Section 10.5.

utilised this class of apparently limited administrative powers to create an elaborate set of powerful regulations going into areas that impact the fair conduct of proceedings.

2.2 The International Criminal Court

2.2.1 Structure of the ICC procedural framework

The Rome Statute stands in sharp contrast to the Statutes of the *ad hoc* Tribunals in providing significantly greater detail in relation not only to its substantive law, but especially to its procedural law. Following the successful negotiation of the Rome Statute,[72] the ASP negotiated the ICC Rules of Procedure and Evidence as a supplement to the Statute; the Rules finally entered into force in September 2002. Like the *ad hoc* Tribunal model, the ICC Rules reflect the general ordering of provisions in the Rome Statute. Unlike the *ad hoc* Tribunals, however, most rules in the ICC Rules do not stand alone, but instead elaborate on procedures already set forth in some detail in the Statute itself. The Rules must therefore be read in conjunction with the Statute, both as mandated in Article 21 of the Statute, and indeed in order for them to make sense. Read together, the Statute and Rules cover the structure of the Court, its peculiar jurisdictional characteristics, and the progression of proceedings, from initiation of an investigation through to final appeal, revision, and enforcement, as well as a host of other procedural issues. In all, the ICC Rules themselves – like the Rome Statute – are far more detailed than their *ad hoc* Tribunal counterparts.

The Rome Statute and ICC Rules together embody approximately 350 separate provisions. They have since been supplemented by the ICC Court Regulations – a document envisaged by the Statute, and currently composed of 126 provisions[73] – and the ICC Registry Regulations, containing 223 provisions.[74] The resulting framework consists of over 700 separate provisions. Claus Kreß refers to the regime of international criminal procedure at the ICC as an 'architecture … of unprecedented complexity'.[75] The Court has also been referred to more candidly as having a 'Byzantine procedural structure', its codification process being 'voluminous, needlessly fragmented, and hierarchically ambiguous'.[76]

[72] For a concise history of the creation of the ICC, see Ratner, Abrams, and Bischoff, *supra* note 46, pp. 230–232.

[73] For more on the ICC Court Regulations, see *infra* Section 2.2.3.

[74] For more on the ICC Registry Regulations, see *infra* Section 2.2.3.

[75] Claus Kreß, 'The Procedural Texts of the International Criminal Court', (2007) 5 *Journal of International Criminal Justice* 537, 537.

[76] B. Don Taylor III, 'Demystifying the Procedural Framework of the International Criminal Court: A Modest Proposal for Radical Revision', in Carsten Stahn and Göran Sluiter (eds.), *The Emerging Practice of the International Criminal Court* (2009), pp. 755–756.

2.2.2 Creation and amendment of procedural rules in the Rome Statute and ICC Rules

As noted above, the Rome Statute itself contains numerous articles dealing with procedure and evidence. As with all provisions in the Statute, these articles are the product of often intense debates at the Rome Conference in 1998, and the negotiations and multiple drafts leading up to the Rome Conference.[77] Like the rest of the Statute, these provisions can only be amended by a two-thirds majority of states parties.[78] No procedural or evidentiary provisions have yet been amended, but a review conference is scheduled for 2010.

The ICC Rules were prepared and finalised by the Preparatory Commission[79] following the Rome Conference, and were based upon a draft prepared initially by the Australian delegation and a detailed response prepared by France (thereby representing the two predominant legal traditions – common and civil law).[80] The content of the Rules was heavily influenced by the Rules and jurisprudence of the *ad hoc* Tribunals, particularly in some areas, although there were areas of regulation under the Rome Statute (such as victim participation) for which no international criminal tribunal analogue existed.[81] Article 51 of the Rome Statute governs the formal adoption and amendment of the Rules, and under this provision, the first iteration of the Rules entered into force in September 2002, upon approval by a two-thirds majority of members of the ASP.[82] While new rules and amendments to existing rules may be proposed by any state party, the Prosecutor, or the judges acting by absolute majority, they become effective only upon adoption by a two-thirds majority of states parties voting.[83] In this way, the drafters of the ICC Statute made a clear break from the approach the Security Council took to the creation of the *ad hoc* Tribunals. As discussed above, the broad and flexible rule-making powers bestowed on the ICTY and ICTR judges gave rise to unprecedented adaptability, which facilitated the extraordinarily fast development of international criminal procedure, but also gave rise to some legitimacy concerns.

[77] See Silvia Fernández de Gurmendi and Håkan Friman, 'The Rules of Procedure and Evidence and the Regulations of the Court', in José Doria, Hans-Peter Gasser, and M. Cherif Bassiouni (eds.), *The Legal Regime of the International Criminal Court* (2009), pp. 797, 808; Bruce Broomhall, 'Article 51 Rules of Procedure and Evidence', in Otto Triffterer (ed.), *Commentary on the Rome Statute of the International Criminal Court* (2nd edn 2008), pp. 1037–1039.

[78] Rome Statute, Art. 121(3).

[79] The Preparatory Commission consisted of representatives of all states that signed the Rome Statute Final Act and other states invited to participate in the drafting process. See Fernández de Gurmendi and Friman, *supra* note 77, p. 798.

[80] See Broomhall, *supra* note 77, p. 1038.

[81] See Silvia A. Fernández de Gurmendi and Håkan Friman, 'The Rules of Procedure and Evidence of the International Criminal Court', (2000) 3 *Yearbook of International Humanitarian Law* 289, 290–291; Fernández de Gurmendi and Friman, *supra* note 77, pp. 81–82.

[82] Rome Statute, Art. 51(1). [83] *Ibid.*, Art. 51(2).

The ASP had the opportunity to follow the same procedural path. Indeed, in 1994 the International Law Commission (ILC) submitted a draft statute to the General Assembly which formed the basis for negotiations, in which the ILC expressed the view that the judges of the Court should draft the rules, like the judges of the ICTY, subject to the approval of states parties. Article 19(3) of the ILC Draft Statute provided that once the initial rules were passed by active agreement of the states parties, amendments to the Rules would be subject only to their passive approval – that is, amendments would be transmitted and confirmed by the Presidency[84] six months thereafter, unless a majority of states parties objected.[85]

Notwithstanding the ILC's recommendation, the ASP chose a methodology by which, in theory at least, states would maintain control over the further creation and amendment of the ICC Rules.[86] Article 51(3) of the Rome Statute contains an important provision to govern emergencies:

> After the adoption of the Rules of Procedure and Evidence, in urgent cases where the Rules do not provide for a specific situation before the Court, the judges may, by a two-thirds majority, draw up provisional Rules to be applied until adopted, amended or rejected at the next ordinary or special session of the Assembly of States Parties.[87]

Compared with Article 15 of the ICTY Statute and ICTY Rule 6, however, it was immediately apparent that the procedures in place for the adoption and amendment of the ICC Rules are far more cumbersome. Article 51(3) appeared to give the Court some means of amending and applying its rules where proceedings dictated that necessity. The primary difficulty with utilising such a provision, quite apart from the clear preference for the ASP to control the creation and amendment of Rules, was the uncertainty regarding the status of an order made under a rule implemented pursuant to Article 51(3). What is to happen in circumstances in which a provisional rule is created, and then a chamber issues an order pursuant to this rule, if the ASP

[84] The Presidency of the Court is made up of three judges (the President and the First and Second Vice-Presidents) and is an organ of the Court that presides over its administration. Pursuant to Articles 34 and 38 of the Statute, the members of the Presidency are elected by an absolute majority of the judges and serve terms of three years.

[85] Draft Statute for an International Criminal Court, in Report of the International Law Commission on Its Forty-Sixth Session, UN Doc. A/49/10 (Supp.) (1994), Art. 19. See also Timothy L.H. McCormack and Gerry Simpson, 'Achieving the Promise of Nuremberg: A New International Criminal Law Regime', in Timothy L.H. McCormack and Gerry Simpson (eds.), *The Law of War Crimes, National and International Approaches* (1997), pp. 248–249.

[86] Of course, it is possible – given the very detailed nature of the Rome Statute – that the judges would have been more constrained than their counterparts at the *ad hoc* Tribunals, even if the ILC's recommendation had been adopted.

[87] ICC Rule 3 sets out the procedure for amendment:

1. Amendments to the rules that are proposed in accordance with article 51, paragraph 2, shall be forwarded to the President of the Bureau of the Assembly of States Parties.
2. The President of the Bureau of the Assembly of States Parties shall ensure that all proposed amendments are translated into the official languages of the Court and are transmitted to the States parties.
3. The procedure described in sub-rules 1 and 2 shall also apply to the provisional rules referred to in article 51, paragraph 3.

subsequently rejects the rule? Neither the Statute nor the Rules as they are drafted answer this question, and the case law has likewise not yet addressed it.

Because the ICC Rules, like the Court's Statute, are designed to discourage amendment, it initially appeared as though the judges of the ICC would have considerable difficulty finding the flexibility to adjust to the procedural realities of conducting complex international criminal trials with a relatively static procedural framework. Indeed, all this detailed regulation of the Court's functions was undertaken before it was ever operational, and while the jurisprudence of the *ad hoc* Tribunals, with its important lessons for the ICC and future tribunals on how to address discrete procedural scenarios that arise in practice, was still in relative infancy. In considering the procedure for the adoption and amendment of rules under Article 51 of the ICC Statute, Antonio Cassese noted:

> It appears likely that this was a reaction against the ICTY and ICTR precedents, where the judges were, in a sense, both rule-makers and decision-makers. There were good reasons, however, for allocating this role to the judges of the *ad hoc* tribunals and for the extensive amendments they made in discharging this role. The ICTY's and ICTR's Rules of Procedure and Evidence constituted the first international criminal procedural and evidentiary codes ever adopted and they had to be amended gradually to deal with a panoply of contingencies which were not anticipated by the framers of their Statutes.[88]

Nonetheless, as already discussed, it seems inevitable that the ICC, notwithstanding its different Statute and some very significant procedural differences from the *ad hoc* Tribunals, would have similar need for regulatory amendment. Indeed, in light of the manner in which the Court has dealt with its less flexible procedural framework, it may be considered unfortunate that the ASP did not officially sanction a more flexible regime for amending procedural rules in the Statute and Rules.

2.2.3 Quasi-legislating via the back door: the Regulations of the Court and Registry

As it turned out, the ICC judges did identify a solution that would allow them – and especially the Presidency – considerable flexibility in crafting their procedural rules: the provision for the creation of Regulations of the Court under Article 52 of the ICC Statute. Article 52 provides for the judges to adopt, 'by an absolute majority, the Regulations of the Court necessary for its *routine functioning*'.[89] The judges are required to consult the Prosecutor and Registrar,[90] to circulate the Regulations

[88] Antonio Cassese, 'The Statute of the International Criminal Court: Some Preliminary Reflections', (1999) 10 *European Journal of International Law* 144, 163.

[89] Rome Statute, Art. 52(1) (emphasis added). No discussion of what was intended by this phrase appears in the Statute's *travaux préparatoires*.

[90] *Ibid.*, Art. 52(2).

and any amendments to states parties and, if they receive no objections within six months, the Regulations shall remain in force.[91] Together with the Regulations of the Registry, they constitute nearly 250 provisions.

It is clear that the Regulations of the Court promulgated thus far have gone well beyond governance of 'routine functioning'. This reality has prompted the concern that the judges are utilising this mechanism, which they control, as a 'backdoor' way to create and amend procedural rules of considerable import and substance.[92] The current Regulations set forth functions of the pre-trial chambers that make them even more powerful than they would be under the Statute and Rules alone;[93] delineate powers of the prosecution and pre-trial chamber;[94] and provide much of the framework for the Court's cooperation with states, among other important procedures.[95]

Furthermore, Regulation 55 empowers a trial chamber to 'change the legal characterization of facts to accord with crimes' under the Court's jurisdiction, 'or to accord with the form of participation of the accused'. In its decision confirming the charges against Thomas Lubanga, the Pre-Trial Chamber determined that an element of a group of charges that it confirmed concerned the existence of an international armed conflict.[96] Subsequently, the prosecution urged the Trial Chamber to amend the Pre-Trial Chamber's confirmation decision, arguing that Regulation 55 allowed the Trial Chamber to modify the legal character of the facts presented by the prosecution to render the international character of the armed conflict irrelevant to establishing responsibility under the charges.[97] Lubanga argued that Regulation 55 was *ultra vires*, exceeding the judges' power to create Regulations for the 'routine functioning' of the Court.[98]

[91] *Ibid.* See also Hans-Jörg Behrens, 'Article 52 Regulations of the Court', in Otto Triffterer (ed.), *Commentary on the Rome Statute of the International Criminal Court: Observers' Notes, Article by Article* (1999), p. 683.

[92] See, e.g., Kreß, *supra* note 75, pp. 540–541; Taylor, *supra* note 76, pp. 761–762, 764.

[93] ICC Court Regulation 46 (rendering the pre-trial chamber 'responsible for any matter, request or information arising out of the situation assigned to it').

[94] ICC Court Regulation 48 (broadly empowering the pre-trial chamber to order the production of documents from the prosecution).

[95] ICC Court Regulations 107–118. See also Kreß, *supra* note 75, pp. 540–541.

[96] *Prosecutor* v. *Lubanga*, Doc. No. ICC-01/04-01/06-678, Decision on the Schedule and Conduct of the Confirmation Hearing, 7 November 2006, p. 9. For further discussion on Regulation 55, see Chapter 6, Section 6.1.2.

[97] *Prosecutor* v. *Lubanga*, Doc. No. ICC-01/04-01/06-1084, Decision on the Status Before the Trial Chamber of the Evidence Heard by the Pre-Trial Chamber and the Decisions of the Pre-Trial Chamber in Trial Proceedings, and the Manner in Which Evidence Shall Be Submitted, 13 December 2007 ('*Lubanga* December 2007 Trial Decision'), para. 48. For a detailed discussion of this decision, see Taylor, *supra* note 76, p. 759. On ICC Court Regulation 55, see Kreß, *supra* note 75, p. 541; Carsten Stahn, 'Modification of the Legal Characterization of Facts in the ICC System: A Portrayal of Regulation 55', (2005) 16 *Criminal Law Forum* 3. See also *Prosecutor* v. *Lubanga*, Doc. No. ICC-01/04-01/06-2049, Decision Giving Notice to the Parties and Participants that the Legal Characterisation of the Facts May Be Subject to Change in Accordance with Regulation 55(2) of the Regulations of the Court, 14 July 2009 ('*Lubanga* July 2009 Trial Decision').

[98] *Lubanga* December 2007 Trial Decision, *supra* note 97, para. 35.

The Trial Chamber simply rejected Lubanga's challenge without answering the substantive question relating to the character of the Regulation. Perhaps it considered that Article 52(3) of the Statute provides an opportunity for states parties to reject a Regulation and, in this case, they had chosen not to do so, thus rendering Regulation 55 effectively adopted by the states parties.[99] Yet the absence of objection can, at best, show acquiescence on the part of the ASP.[100] Indeed, the lack of responsiveness by the ASP may indicate that those states parties initially unwilling to grant judges the sort of rule-making power available to their colleagues at the *ad hoc* Tribunals are now prepared to allow the ICC judges greater control over significant areas of the procedure of the Court.

The Trial Chamber issued a separate ruling in July 2009, in which the majority gave 'notice to the parties and participants that it appear[ed] to the majority of the Chamber that the legal characterisation of facts may be subject to change',[101] so as to allow the accused to be tried for sexual slavery and inhuman or cruel treatment – alleged crimes which had not been confirmed by the Pre-Trial Chamber. In dissent, Judge Fulford argued that 'a modification to the legal characterisation of the facts under Regulation 55 must not constitute an amendment to the charges, an additional charge, a substitute charge or a withdrawal of a charge'.[102] The Appeals Chamber ultimately agreed, and reversed the Trial Chamber's ruling, finding that 'Regulation 55 (2) and (3) of the Regulations of the Court may not be used to exceed the facts and circumstances described in the charges or any amendment thereto'.[103] However, in doing so, the Appeals Chamber disagreed – although somewhat unpersuasively – with the appellant's argument that Regulation 55 is *ultra vires* the Rome Statute (in particular, Article 52(1)).[104] The Appeals Chamber relied upon a handful of scholarly opinions that the term 'routine functioning' was meant to be a 'broad concept' and repeated the Trial Chamber's finding that because the ASP had a chance to reject the Regulation as drafted and had not done so, it had endorsed it.[105] The Appeals Chamber held that, far from violating any provisions of the Rome Statute, Regulation 55 'complements and completes' the Statute.[106] As noted above, the absence of objection by the ASP does not change the character

[99] *Ibid.*, para. 47. [100] See Taylor, *supra* note 76, p. 761.

[101] *Lubanga* July 2009 Trial Decision, *supra* note 97, para. 35.

[102] *Prosecutor* v. *Lubanga*, Doc. No. ICC-01/04-01/06-2069-Anx 1, Second Corrigendum to Minority Opinion on the 'Decision Giving Notice to the Parties and Participants that the Legal Characterisation of Facts May Be Subject to Change in Accordance with Regulation 55(2) of the Regulations of the Court', 31 July 2009, para. 17.

[103] *Prosecutor* v. *Lubanga*, Doc. No. ICC-01/04-01/06-2205, Judgement on the Appeals of Mr Lubanga Dyilo and the Prosecutor Against the Decision of Trial Chamber I of 14 July 2009 entitled 'Decision Giving Notice to the Parties and Participants that the Legal Characterisation of the Facts May Be Subject to Change in Accordance with Regulation 55(2) of the Regulations of the Court', 8 December 2009 ('*Lubanga* Characterisation of Facts Appeal Decision'), para. 1.

[104] *Lubanga* Characterisation of Facts Appeal Decision, *supra* note 103, paras. 69–72.

[105] *Ibid.* (quotation at para. 69). [106] *Ibid.*, para. 88.

of Regulation 55. Common sense would suggest that its potential impact upon an accused's fundamental rights takes it outside the definition of 'routine functioning', but given the position taken by the Appeals Chamber it would seem that argument has, for now, been resolved. It will be critical how chambers apply the Regulation in practice.

The ICC Registry Regulations also include provisions that may be of significant import to the running of the Court and its major facilities, including regulations relating to the file management system of the Court, the funding of international duty counsel, and provisional detention.[107] These Regulations, drafted by the Registry, are approved by the Presidency of the Court and are not subject to review by the ASP.[108]

The availability of the urgent amendment provision relating to the Rules of Procedure and Evidence,[109] and the use of the Court and Registry Regulations to regulate procedural areas of significant importance (as sanctioned by the ICC Appeals Chamber), suggest that the judges intend to wrest as much control as possible over the development of the Court's procedure from the ASP. Whether this phenomenon gives rise to concerns similar to those expressed in relation to the *ad hoc* Tribunals – especially that the powers have been used in potential violation of the separation of powers and legality doctrines – or poses a threat to the institution's legitimacy remains to be seen. It also remains to be seen whether the ASP – which, after all, retains ultimate control – will eventually act to amend the Statute or Rules to remove this power from the judges or, for example, to clarify what it meant by 'routine functioning'. This prospect is unlikely, as amendments require substantial consensus among states parties and are extremely difficult to effect.

2.3 Conclusion

The process by which rules of international criminal procedure are created and amended is in practice far from administrative in nature. As is clear from the use of sweeping rule-making powers by ICTY and ICTR judges, questions can arise as to whether the scope of this power accords with the separation-of-powers doctrine or other generally recognised principles of law. The power of judges to apply and interpret the rules they create is one thing; where they can subsequently vote to amend any aspect of the content of that same rule, the resulting legitimacy concerns may ultimately pose a challenge to the international criminal justice system itself. As discussed above, the judges of the *ad hoc* Tribunals have used their

[107] See ICC Registry Regulations 33–38, 48, 77, 81, 107–118. See also Kreß, *supra* note 75, p. 541.
[108] ICC Rule 14(1). On the definition of the Presidency, see *supra* note 84.
[109] Rome Statute, Art. 51(3).

quasi-legislative powers to overrule judicial determinations, even of the Appeals Chambers, on important procedural matters. This activity reasonably gives rise to inquiry into the independent and impartial exercise of judicial authority and stands in contrast to equally legitimate claims that these Tribunals must have a flexible approach to rule-making. The perception of misapplication of judicial authority is serious in any jurisdiction; in international criminal law, where there are few of the safeguards of a domestic jurisdiction in which the separation of powers is clearly established and applied, it becomes a matter of imperative significance.

While there might be an argument that the *ad hoc* Tribunals were the first such institutions – and that they therefore needed flexibility and may have made errors in good faith – the ICC, created with very different perceived needs and procedural architecture, is in less of a position to make the same argument. The ASP devised a regulatory structure under which judges were not intended to create and amend rules with the same freedom enjoyed in the *ad hoc* Tribunals. However, the ICC judges have made use of the Regulations, over which they have significant control, to formulate and enforce procedural rules far exceeding the 'routine' functions these Regulations were presumably meant to address.

These developments suggest a tendency on the part of judges serving in the international criminal tribunals to exercise significant control over making the rules they apply. No doubt, this is due to several factors: the lack of a clear parliamentary structure that could monitor judicial functioning and less cumbrously address codification needs; the requirement for speed and flexibility in responding to the already complex and variegated nature of trials dealing with war crimes, crimes against humanity, and genocide; a sense that international law, lacking a clear doctrine of separation of powers, leaves greater latitude to those applying its rules and principles, whether they be judges or policy-makers; a lack of genuine oversight; and an opacity to the functioning of these tribunals. The extent to which the rule-making activities of the judges of these institutions serve the rule of law is a difficult question to answer. Their efforts have no doubt been, in many respects, profoundly successful. This does not mean, however, that the process should be free from scrutiny, or that public transparency should not be required of those who have taken on the enormous duty of judging those most responsible for mass atrocity.

3

Procedures related to primacy and complementarity

CONTENTS

National courts bear the primary responsibility for trying international crimes, under one or more of five bases of jurisdiction recognised in international law: territoriality, nationality, the protective principle, passive personality, and universality.[1] Yet for a variety of reasons, states have usually failed to exercise any of these forms of jurisdiction to prosecute domestically. Most common among these reasons are a lack of domestic implementing legislation; a structural inability to prosecute, such as a dearth of judicial competence or catastrophic events damaging the legal system's integrity; or an unwillingness to prosecute, as could result from a judiciary that is corrupt, biased, or not independent from political leaders' whims. Seeking to prevent impunity for those who would otherwise escape prosecution in a national court, the international community has set up various international and hybrid criminal tribunals in the last two decades as supplements to or substitutes for national courts. In the principal tribunals examined in this series – the ICTY, ICTR, ICC, and SCSL – the tribunal's statute does not purport to strip national courts of jurisdiction, but instead establishes the tribunal's jurisdiction as concurrent with that of national courts.

Concurrent jurisdiction reinforces the obligation of states, in the first instance, to prosecute international crimes,[2] but also acknowledges the inability of international tribunals to handle the hundreds or thousands of potential cases themselves. The international tribunals were only designed – and have only been able – to dispose of a small fraction of such cases, and rely on national courts to try the remainder. In order to govern the exercise of concurrent jurisdiction, the international tribunals' governing instruments define the jurisdictional hierarchy between themselves and national courts and other national authorities.[3] As with many of the topics discussed in this volume and series, two major paradigms have emerged. The paradigm chosen for each tribunal depends on the unique circumstances and divergent goals surrounding its creation.[4] The first is that of the *ad hoc* Tribunals, which enjoy 'primacy', meaning that they are hierarchically superior to national courts and, with some exceptions, can demand that national authorities defer to their jurisdiction by not prosecuting a given case or ceasing an ongoing prosecution or investigation.[5] They can also issue a myriad of other orders for compliance and cooperation not only to national authorities, but also to international organizations and even private individuals.[6] The second paradigm is that of the ICC, which under the principle of

[1] For a brief overview of these jurisdictional bases, see Steven R. Ratner, Jason S. Abrams, and James L. Bischoff, *Accountability for Human Rights Atrocities in International Law: Beyond the Nuremberg Legacy* (3rd edn 2009), pp. 178–180.

[2] See, e.g., *Prosecutor* v. *Katanga and Ngudjolo*, Doc. No. ICC-01/04-01/07-1497, Judgment on the Appeal of Mr. Germain Katanga Against the Oral Decision of Trial Chamber II of 12 June 2009 on the Admissibility of the Case, 25 September 2009 ('*Katanga and Ngudjolo* Admissibility Appeal Judgement'), para. 85 ('States have a duty to exercise their criminal jurisdiction over international crimes.').

[3] See Rome Statute, Arts. 1, 17; ICTY Statute, Arts. 9, 29; ICTR Statute, Arts. 8, 28; SCSL Statute, Art. 8.

[4] For a thoughtful discussion of these and other possible jurisdictional relationships between domestic courts and international tribunals, see William W. Burke-White, 'The Domestic Influence of International Criminal Tribunals: The International Criminal Tribunal for the Former Yugoslavia and the Creation of the State Court of Bosnia & Herzegovina', (2008) 46 *Columbia Journal of Transnational Law* 279, 296–302.

[5] See *infra* Section 3.1.1. [6] See *infra* Section 3.1.4.

'complementarity' can only divest national authorities of jurisdiction over a given case if they are unwilling or genuinely unable to investigate or prosecute.[7] In many respects, complementarity puts the Court on equal or even subordinate hierarchical footing vis-à-vis national courts, as it faces considerable restrictions in its authority to compel deference and issue orders to states and other entities.[8]

This chapter looks at the procedures governing the international criminal tribunals' assertion of jurisdiction despite the concurrent jurisdiction of one or more national courts. It also introduces several related procedures – examined in later chapters – allowing the tribunals to issue orders for cooperation and compliance to national authorities, international organizations, and individuals. Section 3.1 explores the operation of primacy in the *ad hoc* Tribunals, with occasional reference to the SCSL, and how the principle affects procedures in those Tribunals. This section also touches upon some of the corollaries of primacy that have been developed in the case law, such as the *ad hoc* Tribunals' ability to refer a case to a national court and then monitor it. Section 3.2, in turn, explores the complementarity principle in the ICC, beginning with a review of the several mechanisms that may trigger ICC jurisdiction. The section describes, for those cases where jurisdiction is triggered, the criteria a chamber applies to determine whether the Court may exercise its jurisdiction notwithstanding the jurisdictional claims of national authorities. It also briefly lists other procedures, explained more fully in later chapters, that emanate from the Court's complementary relationship with national authorities.

3.1 Primacy

The existing international criminal tribunals lack law enforcement agencies of their own, and tribunal officials from their respective Registries and the Offices of the Prosecutor have only limited authority to operate directly on the territory of sovereign states.[9] For these and other reasons, cooperation from states, national courts, other national authorities, international organisations, and individuals is essential to the tribunals' operation. These entities provide the tribunals with critical assistance in locating witnesses and crime sites; procuring evidence; arresting alleged offenders and sending them to the tribunal for prosecution; imprisoning convicted persons and monitoring the conditions of their imprisonment; encouraging or compelling witnesses to testify and protecting them where cooperation puts them at risk; financing

[7] See *infra* Section 3.2.3.1.

[8] By virtue of its status as a hybrid tribunal created by treaty between the United Nations and the government of Sierra Leone, the SCSL lies somewhere in the middle of these two paradigms. It enjoys substantial authority over Sierra Leonean national authorities, but lacks broad power vis-à-vis third states. On the SCSL's powers, see *infra* notes 17, 24, 45.

[9] On the authority of ICTY and ICTR officials to operate directly on the territory of sovereign states, see *infra* note 94 and accompanying text.

the tribunals; and a myriad of other activities.[10] Without such cooperation, and the power to compel it in certain circumstances, international criminal tribunals could not function.

Each of the *ad hoc* Tribunals enjoys broad powers to compel the cooperation of national authorities, and this power has since been extended through judicial rule-making and case law to international organisations and individuals.[11] These powers, which establish a vertical relationship between the Tribunals on the one hand and states and international organisations on the other,[12] derive from the Tribunals' status as Security Council enforcement measures under Chapter VII of the UN Charter. As one ICTY chamber put it:

> As a judicial body created by the Security Council pursuant to Chapter VII of the UN Charter, the Tribunal occupies a unique position in the international legal hierarchy. The rules governing the horizontal relationship between sovereign and co-equal states, including those concerning interstate cooperation in criminal matters, do not apply to the distinctive vertical relationship between the Tribunal, on the one hand, and the member states of the United Nations, on the other.[13]

[10] See generally Jacob Katz Cogan, 'International Courts and Fair Trials: Difficulties and Prospects', (2002) 27 *Yale Journal of International Law* 111; Ratner, Abrams, and Bischoff, *supra* note 1, pp. 297–301. Many of these activities are discussed in other chapters. See, e.g., Chapter 4, Section 4.1 (investigations); Chapter 4, Section 4.3 (detention); Chapter 7, Section 7.4.2 (protective measures for witnesses); Chapter 10, Section 10.5 (enforcement of prison sentences).

[11] See, e.g., *Prosecutor* v. *Blaškić*, Case No. IT-95-14-AR108*bis*, Judgement on the Request of the Republic of Croatia for Review of the Decision of Trial Chamber II of 18 July 1997, 29 October 1997 ('*Blaškić* Subpoena Appeal Decision'), paras. 26–30, 55–56 (Tribunal may issue binding orders to states and subpoenas to individuals); *Prosecutor* v. *Milutinović, Šainović, Ojdanić, Pavković, Lazaraveić, and Lukić*, Case No. IT-05-87-AR108*bis*.1, Decision on Request of the North Atlantic Treaty Organisation for Review, 15 May 2006, paras. 8–10 (Tribunal may issue binding orders to international organisations); *Prosecutor* v. *Haradinaj, Balaj, and Brahimaj*, Case No. IT-04-84-PT, Order Requesting Assistance of UNMIK with Certain Investigations, 19 October 2006 (ordering United Nations civilian administration to assist defence in performing exhumations); *Prosecutor* v. *Bagosora, Kabiligi, Ntabakuze, and Nsengiyumva*, Case No. ICTR-98-41-T, Decision on Request for a Subpoena for Major Jacques Biot, 14 July 2006 (issuing subpoena *ad testificandum* to member of UN peacekeeping force); *Prosecutor* v. *Milutinović, Šainović, Ojdanić, Pavković, Lazaraveić, and Lukić*, Case No. IT-05-87-PT, Decision on Second Application of Dragoljub Ojdanić for Binding Orders Pursuant to Rule 54*bis*, 17 November 2005 ('*Milutinović et al.* NATO Trial Decision'), paras. 35–38 and p. 17 (ordering NATO and certain member states to produce certain documents and other materials in their possession); *Prosecutor* v. *Simić, Simić, Tadić, Todorović, and Zarić*, Case No. IT-95-9-T, Decision on Motion for Judicial Assistance by SFOR and Others, 18 October 2000, paras. 46–49, 58, 61–62 (ordering North Atlantic Council, its member states, and SFOR (a subunit of NATO) to produce certain documents and other materials, and individual NATO commander to testify); *Prosecutor* v. *Kordić and Čerkez*, Case No. IT-95-14/2-T, Order for the Production of Documents by the European Community Monitoring Mission and Its Member States, 4 August 2000 (ordering subunit of European Community and member states to hand over certain documents); *Prosecutor* v. *Krstić*, Case No. IT-98-33-PT, Binding Order to the Republika Srpska for the Production of Documents, 12 March 1999 (ordering sub-state political entity to hand over certain documents). Judicial rule-making is discussed in Chapter 2, Sections 2.1.1, 2.2.2.

[12] The seminal ICTY decision expounding the distinction between the 'horizontal' relationship between national courts of different states, and the 'vertical' relationship between the ICTY and national courts is the *Blaškić* Subpoena Appeal Decision, *supra* note 11. On these relationships, see especially *ibid.*, paras. 47, 54. For an overview on how the horizontal relationship functions between states, see Ratner, Abrams, and Bischoff, *supra* note 1, pp. 295–297.

[13] *Prosecutor* v. *Lukić and Lukić*, Case No. IT-98-32/1-PT, Decision on Referral of Case Pursuant to Rule 11 *bis*, 5 April 2007 ('*Lukić and Lukić* Referral Decision'), para. 108 (footnotes omitted) (citing *Blaškić* Subpoena Appeal Decision, *supra* note 11, para. 47).

Another chamber remarked in the same vein:

As national jurisdictions function concurrently on an equal level, it is of utmost importance that any exercise of such national jurisdiction be exercised in full respect of other national jurisdictions ... [S]overeignty and equality between States go hand in hand. The role of the Tribunal, as an enforcement measure under Chapter VII of the UN Charter, is from that perspective[] fundamentally different. Consequently, in this vertical relationship, sovereignty by definition cannot play the same role.[14]

Just as the Security Council can order states to comply with the measures it dictates when it is acting under Chapter VII in response to a threat to international peace and security, so it can delegate such authority to a judicial institution created as its subsidiary organ.[15] The Council has cemented this vertical relationship through resolutions obligating states to cooperate with the ICTY and ICTR,[16] and in Articles 29 and 28 of the *ad hoc* Tribunals' respective Statutes.[17]

[14] *Prosecutor* v. *Dragan Nikolić*, Case No. IT-94-2-PT, Decision on Defence Motion Challenging the Exercise of Jurisdiction by the Tribunal, 9 October 2002, para. 100.

[15] See *Prosecutor* v. *Tadić*, Case No. IT-94-1-A, Decision on the Defence Motion for Interlocutory Appeal on Jurisdiction, 2 October 1995 ('*Tadić* Jurisdiction Appeal Decision'), Separate Opinion of Judge Sidhwa, para. 86. See also, e.g., Report of the Secretary-General Pursuant to Paragraph 2 of Security Council Resolution 808, UN Doc. S/25704, 3 May 1993 ('Secretary-General's ICTY Report'), para. 28 (ICTY a subsidiary organ of the Security Council, created as an enforcement measure under Chapter VII); Charter of the United Nations, 26 June 1945, entered into force 24 October 1945, 3 Bevans 1153, Art. 48 ('[A]ction required to carry out the decisions of the Security Council for the maintenance of international peace and security shall be taken by all Members of the United Nations or by some of them, as the Security Council may determine.'); *ibid.*, Art. 103 ('In the event of a conflict between the obligations of the Members of the United Nations under the present Charter and their obligations under any other international agreement, their obligations under the present Charter shall prevail.').

[16] See Security Council Resolution 827, UN Doc. S/RES/827 (1993), para. 4; Security Council Resolution 955, UN Doc. S/RES/955 (1994), para. 2. The Dayton Peace Accords, concluded among the states of the former Yugoslavia and Republika Srpska, also provide for a duty to cooperate with the ICTY. See *Blaškić* Subpoena Appeal Decision, *supra* note 11, para. 53.

[17] See *Prosecutor* v. *Kordić and Čerkez*, Case No. IT-95-14/2-AR108*bis*, Decision on the Request of the Republic of Croatia for Review of a Binding Order, 9 September 1999, para. 16 (affirming ICTY Statute Article 29 power to issue binding orders to states); *Prosecutor* v. *Blaškić*, Case No. IT-95-14-T, Order to the Republic of Croatia for the Production of Documents, 21 July 1998, Separate Opinion of Judge Mohamed Shahabuddeen, p. 10 (ICTY Statute Article 29's '*requirement* to cooperate is an obligation, and that obligation has to be obeyed.') (emphasis in original). In contrast to the *ad hoc* Tribunals, the SCSL was not created by the Security Council acting under Chapter VII, but by bilateral treaty between the United Nations and the government of Sierra Leone. See generally Agreement Between the United Nations and the Government of Sierra Leone on the Establishment of a Special Court for Sierra Leone, UN Doc. S/2002/246, 16 January 2002, 2178 UNTS 138. Thus, while Sierra Leone has consented through a binding international agreement to concede primacy to the Special Court vis-à-vis its own national courts, neither it nor the United Nations – absent a Security Council Chapter VII resolution – had the authority to confer primacy on the SCSL in relation to third states. While the Secretary-General suggested that the Council endow the Special Court with the power to order the surrender of accused taking refuge outside Sierra Leone, see Report of the Secretary-General on the Establishment of a Special Court for Sierra Leone, UN Doc. S/2000/915, 4 October 2000 ('Secretary-General's SCSL Report'), para. 10, the Council never acted on the suggestion. Consequently, the SCSL lacks the power to order the surrender of accused persons from states other than Sierra Leone. See Nicole Fritz and Alison Smith, 'Current Apathy for Coming Anarchy: Building the Special Court for Sierra Leone', (2001) 25 *Fordham International Law Journal* 391, 416–417; Micaela Frulli, 'The Special Court for Sierra Leone: Some Preliminary Comments', (2000) 11 *European Journal of International Law* 857, 862 (lamenting this weakness as possibly allowing a large number of suspects to flee Sierra Leone and take refuge in neighbouring states). Another consequence is that the SCSL does not benefit from compulsory assessed contributions of UN member states, in contrast to the ICTY and ICTR. See Fritz and Smith, *supra*, pp. 416–418.

In this section of the chapter, we discuss the rules and procedures governing the exercise of concurrent jurisdiction between the *ad hoc* Tribunals and national courts – deferral, admissibility, and referral – and touch briefly upon the many other procedures which are manifestations of the vertical relationship between them, such as the power to issue binding orders and subpoenas. We elaborate on some of these latter procedures in other chapters.

3.1.1 Deferral of cases from national authorities to the ICTY or ICTR

Deferral is a procedural mechanism through which an international criminal tribunal orders a national court exercising concurrent jurisdiction over a given case to suspend its jurisdiction in favour of the tribunal's. Of the several rationales posited for the grant of this power to the *ad hoc* Tribunals by their architects,[18] two appear most frequently. Judge Sidhwa attempted to encapsulate the first in a separate opinion to the ICTY Appeals Chamber's seminal 1995 *Tadić* decision on jurisdiction:

> At the root of primacy is a demand for justice at the international level by all States … The rule [whereby the ICTY may order a national court to suspend proceedings in a given case and defer to the Tribunal's jurisdiction] … compels States to accept the fact that certain domestic crimes are really international in character and endanger international peace and that such international crimes should be tried by an international tribunal … The rule cuts national borders to bring to justice persons guilty of serious international crimes, as they concern all States and require to be dealt with [*sic*] for the benefit of all civilised nations … [T]he rule recognises the right of all nations to ensure the prevention of such violations by establishing international criminal tribunals appropriately empowered to deal with these matters, or else international crimes would be dealt with as ordinary crimes and the guilty would not be adequately punished.[19]

[18] For other rationales, see, e.g., Bartram S. Brown, 'Primacy or Complementarity: Reconciling the Jurisdiction of National Courts and International Criminal Tribunals', (1998) 23 *Yale Journal of International Law* 383, 398, 407–408.

[19] *Tadić* Jurisdiction Appeal Decision, *supra* note 15, Separate Opinion of Judge Sidhwa, para. 83. Judge Sidhwa's statement about 'inadequate' punishment of those convicted of ordinary crimes in national courts is ironic in light of the fact that sentences handed down by the ICTY for crimes against humanity and war crimes are often far lighter than those for ordinary crimes handed down by national courts. See Chapter 10, Section 10.2.4 and note 251 (discussing this troubling phenomenon); see also Gideon Boas, James L. Bischoff, and Natalie L. Reid, *Elements of Crimes Under International Law* (2008) ('Boas, Bischoff, and Reid, *Elements of Crimes*'), pp. 357–358, 362–363 (same). It is also perhaps somewhat exaggerated given that Tadić's international crimes were minor compared to those of accused later brought into the ICTY's custody. Indeed, the ICTY would almost certainly have left this case to be prosecuted in Germany, or asserted jurisdiction over the case but then referred it to Bosnia for national prosecution, had his whereabouts only become known several years later. See *infra* note 49 (later cases where the ICTY could have, but did not, request deferral); *infra* text accompanying notes 43–44 (discussing deferral of Tadić's case by Germany); *infra* Section 3.1.3 (discussing referral of the cases of lower-level accused to national courts).

Though early jurisprudence and literature sometimes invoked a version of this rationale,[20] it is not entirely convincing, especially in light of developments since 1995. The very fact that the *ad hoc* Tribunals were given concurrent jurisdiction with national courts demonstrates that, despite the Security Council's conclusion that such crimes constituted a threat to international peace and security,[21] they were never intended to try every international crime committed in the former Yugoslavia and Rwanda, and would have to share the burden in some way with national courts.[22] Judge Sidhwa's statement also seems to assume, incorrectly, that national courts are generally incapable of trying international crimes, and would instead routinely characterize the accused's acts as ordinary domestic crimes – for example, simple murder or assault instead of war crimes or crimes against humanity. As their workload has increased, the *ad hoc* Tribunals have shifted their focus to mid- and high-level political and military leaders, and have come to rely more heavily on national courts to try the bulk of persons thought responsible for crimes within their jurisdiction – including extremely grave crimes that surely threatened international peace and security.[23] A more accurate rendition of this rationale would thus centre on the accused rather than the crimes. The *ad hoc* Tribunals enjoy primacy, in part, so that those most responsible for the crimes within their jurisdiction, and thus most responsible for creating and perpetuating the threat to peace and security which concerns the international community as a whole, may be held to account by that community in a forum in which all states have the opportunity to participate.

The second rationale also stems from the situation on the ground at the time the *ad hoc* Tribunals were created. Conditions in Yugoslavia and Rwanda necessitated that the *ad hoc* Tribunals have primacy over national courts because the latter were very often biased, corrupt, unavailable, or otherwise incapable of administering justice of a quality sufficient to meet universally accepted standards. At the time of the ICTY's 1993 inception, a brutal ethnic war plagued much of the territory and had severely disrupted the judiciary and legal system. It was also widely feared that the national courts of the various Yugoslav successor states would refuse to initiate prosecutions against members of favoured ethnic groups, or would

[20] See, e.g., *Tadić* Jurisdiction Appeal Decision, *supra* note 15, para. 58 (majority warning that if the Tribunal did not enjoy primacy over national courts, 'human nature being what it is, there would be a perennial danger of international crimes being characterised as "ordinary crimes"'); Brown, *supra* note 18, pp. 407–408.

[21] See Security Council Resolution 827, *supra* note 16, preambular para. 4; Security Council Resolution 955, *supra* note 16, preambular para. 5. See also, e.g., Security Council Resolution 978, UN Doc. S/RES/978 (1995), para. 1 (urging states to detain suspects who allegedly committed crimes within the jurisdiction of the ICTR for prosecution by competent national courts *or* the ICTR).

[22] See, e.g., Secretary-General's ICTY Report, *supra* note 15, para. 64 (ICTY not intended to preclude exercise of jurisdiction by national courts).

[23] See generally *infra* Section 3.1.3 (discussing referral of cases from the ICTY and ICTR to national courts). The SCSL has, since its inception, been required to focus on those thought most responsible for crimes within its jurisdiction. See SCSL Statute, Art. 1(1).

judicially persecute members of a rival ethnicity. When the ICTR was created in 1994, Rwanda's legal system had been virtually destroyed during the genocidal frenzy and civil war between Hutu-dominated government forces and the Tutsi Rwandan Patriotic Front. The judiciary did not recover for several years thereafter, and still today has grave difficulty fairly trying the tens of thousands of cases arising out of the events of 1994.[24]

Article 9, the first article in the ICTY Statute defining the Tribunal's relationship with national authorities, provides that the ICTY and national courts 'shall have concurrent jurisdiction to prosecute persons' for international crimes in the former Yugoslavia, but that the Tribunal 'shall have primacy over national courts'. Further, '[a]t any stage of the procedure, the International Tribunal may formally request national courts to defer to the competence of the International Tribunal'. The ICTR Statute's analogous article is nearly identical, though it clarifies in paragraph 2 that '[t]he International Tribunal for Rwanda shall have the primacy over the national courts *of all States*'.[25] The ICTY's practice vis-à-vis states outside the former Yugoslavia evinces that Tribunal's view that Article 9 likewise gives it primacy over all national courts, or at least those of UN member states,[26] despite the absence of those words in the article.[27]

Each of the *ad hoc* Tribunals' Statutes also has a related article on the '*non bis in idem*' principle, listing the conditions under which a person already tried in one of the Tribunals may be tried before a national court, and vice versa, without violating the fundamental principle that no person may stand trial twice for the same

24 See John T. Holmes, 'Complementarity: National Courts Versus the ICC', in Antonio Cassese, Paola Gaeta, and John R.W.D. Jones (eds.), *The Rome Statute of the International Criminal Court: A Commentary*, Vol. 1 (2002), pp. 667, 668–669; Brown, *supra* note 18, p. 398. See also Ratner, Abrams, and Bischoff, *supra* note 1, pp. 195–197 (problems with Rwandan national trials). Indeed, it was Rwanda itself that proposed the creation of an international tribunal to prosecute the genocide's perpetrators. See Madeline H. Morris, 'The Trials of Concurrent Jurisdiction: The Case of Rwanda', (1997) 7 *Duke Journal of Comparative and International Law* 349, 353. See also *infra* text accompanying note 88 (discussing ICTR chambers' refusal to order referral of cases to Rwanda due to concerns that the accused would not receive a fair trial or, if convicted, would be subjected to prison conditions that violate his or her human rights). The decimation of Sierra Leone's legal system after that country's ghastly nine-year civil war similarly prompted the creation of the SCSL, a hybrid tribunal hierarchically superior to the national judiciary. See Secretary-General's SCSL Report, *supra* note 17, para. 9. As noted above, due to its creation by treaty between the United Nations and Sierra Leone, instead of by the Security Council under Chapter VII, the SCSL enjoys primacy only over the national courts of Sierra Leone. See *supra* note 17.

25 ICTR Statute, Art. 8(2) (emphasis added). But see *Prosecutor* v. *Bagosora, Kabiligi, Ntabakuze, and Nsengiyumva*, Case No. ICTR-98-41-T, Decision on Defence Motion to Obtain Cooperation from the Vatican Pursuant to Article 28, 13 May 2004 (only UN member states are bound to give effect to deferral requests).

26 See *supra* note 25. Cf. *Prosecutor* v. *Milošević, Milutinović, Šainović, Ojdanić, and Stojilković*, Case No. IT-99-37-I, Decision on Review of Indictment and Application for Consequential Orders, 24 May 1999, para. 23 (Switzerland, at the time a non-member of the UN, not bound by Tribunal orders).

27 See Robert Cryer, *Prosecuting International Crimes: Selectivity and the International Criminal Law Regime* (2005), pp. 129–130 (arguing that interpretive statements given by four members of the Security Council attempting to confine the ICTY's primacy to the states of the former Yugoslavia do not bind the Tribunal). See also *infra* notes 43–44 (deferral by Germany). Cf. note 83 (case concerning ICTY primacy vis-à-vis Argentina).

offence.[28] The application of this principle represents another manifestation of the Tribunals' hierarchical superiority over national courts: the latter are categorically barred from trying an individual for conduct constituting a serious violation of international criminal law where the Tribunal has already tried the individual for such conduct, whereas the converse is not always true. The Tribunals may try an individual even though a national court has already tried him or her if any of the following three factors are present: (1) the national court characterised the conduct in question as an 'ordinary crime'; (2) the proceedings were not impartial, independent, or were designed to shield the accused from international criminal responsibility; or (3) the national authorities did not prosecute the case diligently.[29] In the same vein, the *ad hoc* Tribunals are not bound by other determinations of national courts.[30]

Part Two of the Rules of each *ad hoc* Tribunal, entitled 'Primacy of the Tribunal', contains several rules elaborating these statutory provisions on concurrent jurisdiction and *non bis in idem*.[31] ICTY and ICTR Rule 8 give the Prosecutor authority to request information from state authorities regarding ongoing investigations or proceedings for a crime within the jurisdiction of the Tribunal. Rule 9 then sets forth the grounds on which the Prosecutor may request a trial chamber to order a national court to defer a case to the Tribunal. In the ICTY, these are: (1) the conduct in question is characterised in the national proceedings as an 'ordinary crime'; (2) the relevant national authorities are partial or not independent, the proceedings are designed to shield the accused from responsibility, or the case is not prosecuted diligently; or (3) 'what is in issue [in the domestic proceedings] is closely related to, or otherwise involves, significant factual or legal situations which may have implications for investigations or prosecutions before the Tribunal'.[32] The first two grounds simply reflect the circumstances in which the ICTY may try an accused despite the *non bis in idem* prohibition, and roughly correspond to the two rationales discussed above for why the *ad hoc* Tribunals' creators endowed them with primacy.[33] ICTR Rule 9 sets forth grounds that differ somewhat from those of ICTY Rule 9. The ICTR Rule gives the Prosecutor authority to petition a trial chamber

[28] See, e.g., International Covenant on Civil and Political Rights, 16 December 1966, entered into force 23 March 1976, UN Doc. A/6316 (1966), 999 UNTS 171, Art. 14(7).

[29] ICTY Statute, Art. 10; ICTR Statute, Art. 9; SCSL Statute, Art. 9 (referring specifically to Sierra Leonean national courts). Where the *ad hoc* Tribunals or the SCSL convict an accused who has already been convicted by a national court for the same act, their respective Statutes obligate them to take account of the extent to which the accused has already served the sentence imposed by the national court. ICTY Statute, Art. 10(3); ICTR Statute, Art. 9(2); SCSL Statute, Art. 9(2).

[30] ICTY Rule 12; ICTR Rule 12. See also SCSL Rule 12.

[31] By statutory mandate, the SCSL applies the Rules of the ICTR, modified by the SCSL judges to deal with unique situations arising in the Special Court. SCSL Statute, Art. 14. The SCSL Rules' analogue to Part Two of the ICTY and ICTR Rules is entitled 'Cooperation with States and Judicial Assistance'. See SCSL Rules, Part II (setting forth rules on cooperation by national courts of *any* state, not just Sierra Leonean courts).

[32] ICTY Rule 9(i), 9(ii), and 9(iii), respectively.

[33] See *supra* text accompanying notes 18–24 (discussing Article 10 of the ICTY Statute).

for a deferral order where the alleged crimes are the subject of ICTR investigations or charges.[34] Reflecting the first rationale discussed above, the Prosecutor can also request deferral where the crimes 'should be' the subject of investigations based on, among other things, the seriousness of the crimes, the status of the accused, and '[t]he general importance of the legal questions involved in the case'.[35] As Robert Cryer has observed, while these rules theoretically limit the *ad hoc* Tribunals' right to demand deferral to those contexts in which it is justified, the breadth of Rule 9 in each Tribunal effectively gives them the power to 'demand transfer of an individual case whenever [they] want[] to', and not only when there is some infirmity in the national proceedings, 'making the limits more illusory than real'.[36] As discussed below, this observation has been borne out in practice, especially at the ICTY.[37]

If the trial chamber agrees that one or more of the Rule 9 grounds has been triggered, it may issue a formal, binding request to the state concerned 'that its court defer to the competence of the Tribunal'.[38] The *ad hoc* Tribunals' power to compel deferral is discretionary[39] – though in practice trial chambers have tended to order deferral whenever the Prosecutors request it.[40] As noted above, the Tribunals were never intended – nor do they have the capacity – to try the vast majority of persons suspected of crimes within their jurisdiction, and in recent years the ICTY and ICTR have returned many of their indicted accused to national courts for prosecution.[41] When the Tribunals choose to order deferral, the state is obliged to transfer the accused to the Tribunal regardless of any intentions it may have had to try the accused or otherwise dispose of his or her case.[42]

[34] ICTR Rule 9(i) and 9(iii), respectively.

[35] *Ibid.*, Rule 9(ii). Alexander Zahar and Göran Sluiter suggest that the ICTR judges' formulation of such a sweeping rule 'may be explained by the Tribunal's wish to strengthen its position in relation to Rwanda's expanding investigation of crimes and prosecution of persons in which the ICTR prosecutor is also interested'. Alexander Zahar and Göran Sluiter, *International Criminal Law: A Critical Introduction* (2008), p. 450. Rule 9 of the SCSL Rules is essentially identical to the ICTR formulation.

[36] Cryer, *supra* note 27, p. 130. Accord Brown, *supra* note 18, p. 397; William A. Schabas, *The UN International Criminal Tribunals: The Former Yugoslavia, Rwanda and Sierra Leone* (2006), p. 124.

[37] See *infra* notes 45–47 and accompanying text.

[38] ICTY Rule 10; ICTR Rule 10 (at paragraph (C), making explicit the request's binding nature). See also SCSL Rule 10 (the SCSL can only issue such orders to Sierra Leonean courts). If the state fails to comply with such a request, the ICTY and ICTR may refer the matter to the Security Council; the SCSL may refer the matter to the SCSL President. ICTY Rule 11; ICTR Rule 11; SCSL Rule 11. On the ineffectiveness of this remedy generally, see *infra* text accompanying notes 103–104.

[39] The relevant rules all use the word 'may'. Accord *Tadić* Jurisdiction Appeal Decision, *supra* note 15, Separate Opinion of Judge Sidhwa, para. 81.

[40] See, e.g., *infra* note 45 and cases cited therein. For a rare partial denial of the Prosecutor's deferral request, see *In re Republic of Macedonia*, Case No. IT-02-55-Misc.6, Decision on the Prosecutor's Request for Deferral and Motion for Order to the Former Yugoslav Republic of Macedonia, 4 October 2002 ('Macedonia Deferral Decision'), paras. 45–52 (refusing to order deferral of 'all current and future investigations' of alleged crimes in 2001 involving Macedonian forces and the National Liberation Army in Macedonia, where the Macedonian prosecutor opposed deferral and the chamber was concerned about the 'intense frustrating effect' deferral would have on Macedonia's exercise of jurisdiction over future cases) (quotation at para. 50).

[41] See *infra* Section 3.1.3 (discussing referral).

[42] Cryer, *supra* note 27, p. 128 (discussing an episode in which Rwanda was obligated to transfer an accused to the ICTR notwithstanding its preference to try him in its own courts). For the *ad hoc* Tribunals, the binding nature of the order stems from the Tribunals' creation under Chapter VII of the UN Charter. See *infra* Section 3.1.4.

The most significant challenge to the *ad hoc* Tribunals' authority to order deferral arose in the *Tadić* case. German authorities captured Duško Tadić, a low-level Bosnian Serb suspected of participating in several atrocities, and instituted criminal proceedings against him. On the ICTY Prosecutor's urging, a trial chamber ordered the German court to defer the case to the ICTY, and the national court readily complied. In his subsequent challenge to the Tribunal's jurisdiction, Tadić argued, among other things, that the ICTY's primacy violated Germany's and Bosnia's sovereignty because it infringed on their domestic jurisdiction, as protected under Article 2(7) of the UN Charter.[43] Noting that Article 2(7) explicitly lists an exception for Security Council enforcement measures under Chapter VII of the Charter, the Appeals Chamber also cited teleological reasons for rejecting Tadić's objection, namely that without primacy, national authorities would be free to prosecute accused for 'ordinary' crimes, not prosecute such crimes diligently, or shield the accused from prosecution altogether.[44] Interestingly, no one had suggested that the German authorities, who had charged Tadić with murder, grievous bodily harm, and aiding and abetting genocide, would fail to prosecute him diligently or try him fairly, and the Appeals Chamber did not address this question.

This early experience reinforced the notion that the *ad hoc* Tribunals may order deferral in virtually any circumstance, and set a strong precedent for future cases. On the Prosecutor's request, the *ad hoc* Tribunals have ordered the deferral of many cases and investigations. Deferral requests seem to fall into two categories, and trial chambers have granted deferral for both categories of request in almost all cases. In the first category, the Prosecutor requests deferral of a particular case involving a specific individual or individuals.[45] In the second, the Prosecutor requests deferral of a more general group of incidents potentially involving several suspects.[46]

[43] *Tadić* Jurisdiction Appeal Decision, *supra* note 15, para. 50.

[44] *Ibid.*, paras. 56, 58, 60, 64.

[45] See, e.g., *Prosecutor* v. *Mrkšić, Sljivančanin, and Radić*, Case No. IT-95-13-R61, Decision on the Proposal of the Prosecutor for a Request to the Federal Republic of Yugoslavia (Serbia and Montenegro) to Defer the Pending Investigations and Criminal Proceedings to the Tribunal, 10 December 1998 ('*Mrkšić et al.* Deferral Decision') (under ICTY Rule 9(iii)); *In the Matter of Théoneste Bagosora*, Case No. ICTR-96-7-D, Decision of the Trial Chamber on the Application by the Prosecutor for a Formal Request for Deferral to the Competence of the International Criminal Tribunal for Rwanda in the Matter of Théoneste Bagosora (Pursuant to Rules 9 and 10 of the Rules of Procedure and Evidence), 17 May 1996 (deferral request to Belgium, under ICTR Rule 9(iii)); *In the Matter of Alfred Musema*, Case No. ICTR-96-5-D, Decision of the Trial Chamber in the Application by the Prosecutor for a Formal Request for Deferral by Switzerland in the Matter of Alfred Musema (Pursuant to Rules 9 and 10 of the Rules of Procedure and Evidence), 12 March 1996 (under ICTR Rule 9(iii)); *In the Matter of a Proposal for a Formal Request for Deferral to the Competence of the Tribunal Addressed to the Republic of Bosnia and Herzegovina in Respect of Radovan Karadžić, Ratko Mladić, and Mićo Stanišić*, Case No. IT-95-5-D, Decision, 16 May 1995 (under ICTY Rule 9(iii)); *Tadić* Jurisdiction Appeal Decision, *supra* note 15.

[46] See, e.g., Macedonia Deferral Decision, *supra* note 40 (under ICTY Rule 9(iii)); *In the Matter of Radio Télévision Libre des Mille Collines SARL*, Case No. ICTR 96-6-D, Decision of the Trial Chamber on the Application by the Prosecutor for a Formal Request for Deferral to the Competence of the International Criminal Tribunal for Rwanda in the Matter of Radio Télévision Libre des Mille Collines SARL (Pursuant to Rules 9 and 10 of the

For the ICTY, the most common vehicle for deferral has been Rule 9(iii) – the conduct under investigation in the national proceedings is closely related to, or involves questions that may affect, the Tribunal's work.[47] For the ICTR, the most common vehicle has been the ICTR's different Rule 9(iii) – the conduct is the subject of an ICTR indictment.[48] Especially beginning in the early 2000s when ICTY and ICTR dockets began filling up, the Prosecutors have refrained from requesting deferral in many cases over which the Tribunals could have asserted jurisdiction; these cases have usually involved lower-level suspects or incidents of lesser relative importance.[49] The *ad hoc* Tribunals have issued very few deferral decisions since the late 1990s, a phenomenon Alexander Zahar and Göran Sluiter attribute to the 'ever improving coordination between states and the ad hoc tribunals, given that states may consult with them before starting investigations', and the Prosecutors' 'more transparent prosecutorial policy'.[50] In conformity with the *ad hoc* Tribunals' completion strategies, the Prosecutors issued their final indictments in late 2004 and early 2005. Considering that the Tribunals are scheduled to finish their work in a few years, they are unlikely ever to order another deferral, though the important precedent they have established may prove useful for future international criminal tribunals.

3.1.2 Admissibility of cases in the ICTY

In contrast to the ICC,[51] 'admissibility' as a procedural concept was not often mentioned with respect to the *ad hoc* Tribunals prior to the adoption of their completion strategies. As long as they had subject-matter and temporal jurisdiction over the criminal conduct at issue, the *ad hoc* Tribunals could take a case with no

Rules of Procedure and Evidence), 12 March 1996 (deferral request to Belgium, under ICTR Rule 9(iii)); *In the Matter of a Proposal for a Formal Request for Deferral to the Competence of the Tribunal Addressed to the Republic of Bosnia and Herzegovina in Respect of Crimes Against the Population of the Lašva River Valley*, Case No. IT-95-6-D, Decision, 11 May 1995 (under ICTY Rule 9(iii)). Because there have been no prosecutions of crimes within the SCSL's jurisdiction in Sierra Leonean national courts, the SCSL has never had occasion to exercise its power of deferral vis-à-vis Sierra Leonean courts. Zahar and Sluiter, *supra* note 35, p. 452 n. 21. See also *supra* notes 17, 24 (discussing the SCSL's limited deferral power).

47 See, e.g., Macedonia Deferral Decision, *supra* note 40, para. 28 (ordering deferral of case involving leaders of National Liberation Army under Rules 9(iii) and 10(A) where the Macedonian prosecution was 'closely related, if not even identical, with the investigation and future prosecution … by the [ICTY] Prosecutor'); *ibid.*, para. 41 (ordering deferral of case involving twenty-three suspects under Rules 9(iii) and 10(A), and including in deferral order two suspects whom the ICTY Prosecutor declared she had no intention of prosecuting). See also *supra* note 45 and sources cited therein. See also Zahar and Sluiter, *supra* note 35, pp. 450–451 (discussing *Mrkšić et al.* Deferral Decision, *supra* note 45, in which the Trial Chamber avoided examining the ICTY Prosecutor's allegations that proceedings in the Federal Republic of Yugoslavia were not independent and impartial, and instead ordered deferral under the '"diplomatic" Rule 9(iii) ground').

48 See, e.g., *supra* note 45 and sources cited therein.

49 See, e.g., Sean D. Murphy, 'Progress and Jurisprudence of the International Criminal Tribunal for the Former Yugoslavia', (1999) 93 *American Journal of International Law* 57, 65 (discussing the *Djajić* and *Jorgić* cases before the German courts). See also *supra* note 19.

50 Zahar and Sluiter, *supra* note 35, p. 452.

51 See *infra* Section 3.2.3.

requirement that the national legal system that would ordinarily exercise jurisdiction was somehow inadequate.[52]

In 2004, the judges of the ICTY introduced a rule on admissibility. After the Prosecutor issued an indictment but before confirmation by a reviewing judge,[53] a panel composed of the ICTY President, Vice-President, and the presiding judges of the Trial Chambers was now required to examine the indictment to determine whether, 'prima facie, [it] concentrates on one or more of the most senior leaders suspected of being most responsible for crimes within the jurisdiction of the Tribunal'.[54] Believing such a rule would unduly infringe the Prosecutor's independence, the ICTR judges opted not to follow the ICTY's lead.[55]

3.1.3 Referral of cases from the ICTY or ICTR to national authorities

Just as the *ad hoc* Tribunals can order national courts to suspend their jurisdiction over a case and defer to the Tribunal's, they can also suspend their own jurisdiction and refer an indicted case to national authorities for prosecution. This aspect of concurrent jurisdiction was introduced into both Tribunals' Rules several years into their existence in the form of Rule 11 *bis*. Like many procedures discussed in this volume, the current version of Rule 11 *bis* is a product of the completion strategy.[56] By the early 2000s, it had become evident that it would take the *ad hoc* Tribunals too long to try all their remaining indictees. At the ICTY, these included not only political and military leaders, but also a large number of low-level foot-soldiers and detention camp guards.[57] At the same time, the Security Council began to pressure the Tribunals to speed up their work, focus on those thought most responsible for crimes,

[52] William A. Schabas, *An Introduction to the International Criminal Court* (2nd edn 2004), p. 85. In the ICTY, however, when a national legal system is actually seised of a case or investigations and the Tribunal must divest the national system of jurisdiction through a deferral order, one of the possible grounds on which it may do so is the inadequacy of the national system. See *supra* note 32 and accompanying text.

[53] Review of indictments is discussed in Chapter 6, Section 6.1.1.

[54] ICTY Rule 28(A).

[55] Vincent Sautenet, 'The International Criminal Tribunal for the Former Yugoslavia: Activities in 2004', (2005) 4 *Chinese Journal of International Law* 515, 562 n. 248. For an argument that ICTY Rule 28(A) infringes prosecutorial prerogatives, see Daryl A. Mundis, 'The Judicial Effects of the "Completion Strategies" on the Ad Hoc International Criminal Tribunals', (2005) 99 *American Journal of International Law* 142, 147–148. For a contrary view, see Sarah Williams, 'The Completion Strategy of the ICTY and the ICTR', in Michael Bohlander (ed.), *International Criminal Justice: A Critical Analysis of Institutions and Procedures* (2007), pp. 170–172.

[56] For an excellent and comprehensive review of Rule 11 *bis* case law in the ICTY (with some treatment of the ICTR), see Tilman Blumenstock and Wayde Pittman, 'The Transfer of Cases Before the International Criminal Tribunal for the Former Yugoslavia to Competent National Jurisdictions', (2008) 21(2) *Journal of International Law of Peace and Armed Conflict (Humanitäres Völkerrecht-Informationsschriften)* 106. For overviews focusing on the ICTR, see Cecile Aptel, 'Closing the U.N. International Criminal Tribunal for Rwanda: Completion Strategy and Residual Issues', (2008) 14 *New England Journal of International and Comparative Law* 169, 175–183; Erik Møse, 'The ICTR's Completion Strategy – Challenges and Possible Solutions', (2008) 6 *Journal of International Criminal Justice* 667, 672–674.

[57] See, e.g., Report on the Operation of the International Criminal Tribunal for the former Yugoslavia, UN Doc. A/55/382-S/2000/865, 12 May 2000, Annex I, para. 35 (predicting that the ICTY would not close before 2016 – an

and refer other cases to national jurisdictions.[58] As a result, the judges amended Rule 11 *bis* to make referral easier,[59] and began to employ it in both Tribunals.

The three-judge panel that determines whether to refer a case to national authorities is called the 'Referral Bench' at the ICTY, and has consisted of the same three judges – Orie, Kwon, and Parker – but has no special name or composition at the ICTR. For convenience, we will refer to the panel in both Tribunals generically as the 'referring chamber', and use 'Referral Bench' when speaking specifically of the ICTY's panel. Under Rule 11 *bis*, the referring chamber may, on its own initiative or at the request of the Prosecutor,[60] transfer an indicted case to national authorities provided certain conditions are met. First, the receiving state must be the locus of the crimes at issue, the place where the accused was arrested, or must otherwise have jurisdiction and be willing and adequately prepared to accept the case.[61] To better assess this third alternative option, referring chambers have customarily invited representatives of the receiving state to make written and oral submissions. The prosecution and accused, if in custody, must be heard.[62] Where more than one state fulfils these jurisdictional criteria, the chamber has discretion to choose the state of referral.[63] In practice, the ICTY Referral Bench has chosen the state with the strongest nexus to the alleged criminal conduct.[64]

Second, the referring chamber must be satisfied that the accused will receive a fair trial in the receiving state and will not be subject to a prospective death penalty.[65] For the ICTY, these conditions reflect in part the concerns over the adequacy of the judicial systems in the former Yugoslavia noted above.[66] In determining whether

alarming estimate at the time). See also, e.g., Antonio Cassese, 'The ICTY: A Living and Vital Reality', (2004) 2 *Journal of International Criminal Justice* 585, 595 ('early prosecution strategy of starting with … low-level defendants flooded the Tribunal with minor cases and created a backlog of (relatively) petty defendants').

58 See, e.g., Security Council Resolution 1534, UN Doc. S/RES/1534 (2004), paras. 4–5.

59 For a survey of the various amendments made to ICTY Rule 11 *bis* since its 1997 inception, see *Lukić and Lukić* Referral Decision, *supra* note 13, paras. 2–3 and nn. 2–8.

60 The accused cannot request referral. See, e.g., *Prosecutor* v. *Karemera, Ngirumpatse, and Nzirorera*, Case No. ICTR-98-44-AR11 *bis*, Decision on Joseph Nzirorera's Appeal from Denial of a Request for Designation of a Trial Chamber to Consider Referral to a National Jurisdiction, 3 July 2007, para. 11. Where the accused agrees with the Prosecutor's referral request, the chamber must still ensure that the rule's requirements for referral are met. See *Prosecutor* v. *Trbić*, IT-05-88/1-PT, Decision on Referral of Case Under Rule 11 *bis*, 27 April 2007 ('*Trbić* Referral Decision'), para. 9.

61 ICTY Rule 11 *bis*(A); ICTR Rule 11 *bis*(A). On the bases for a national court's exercise of jurisdiction, see Ratner, Abrams, and Bischoff, *supra* note 1, pp. 178–180. For decisions holding that the proposed receiving state lacked subject-matter jurisdiction, see *infra* notes 74, 79 and cases cited therein.

62 ICTY Rule 11 *bis*(B); ICTR Rule 11 *bis*(B).

63 See, e.g., *Prosecutor* v. *Mejakić, Gruban, Fuštar, and Knežević*, Case No. IT-02-65-PT, Decision on Prosecutor's Motion for Referral of Case Pursuant to Rule 11 *bis*, 20 July 2005, para. 39; *Lukić and Lukić* Referral Decision, *supra* note 13, para. 37.

64 Blumenstock and Pittman, *supra* note 56, pp. 111–112 (citing cases and criteria used by the ICTY Referral Bench to determine the most appropriate state for referral – e.g. the state that can best guarantee availability of evidence and witnesses).

65 ICTY Rule 11 *bis*(B); ICTR Rule 11 *bis*(C). See also, e.g., *Prosecutor* v. *Kanyarukiga*, Case No. ICTR-2002-78-R11 *bis*, Decision on Prosecutor's Request for Referral to the Republic of Rwanda, 6 June 2008 ('*Kanyarukiga* Referral Decision'), para. 25 (Rwanda's 2007 abolition of death penalty fulfils requirement).

66 See *supra* text accompanying note 24.

the fair-trial guarantees in the proposed receiving state are adequate, the referring chamber looks at the catalogue of rights set forth in the Tribunal's Statute, the International Covenant on Civil and Political Rights, and other international human rights instruments. These guarantees include, among others, the presumption of innocence, the right against self-incrimination, the right to counsel of one's choosing, the right to a free lawyer for indigents, the right to be tried in one's presence, the right to confront witnesses, and the right to be tried without undue delay.[67]

Third, for the ICTY but not the ICTR, the referring chamber must consider the gravity of the crimes charged and the accused's level of responsibility.[68] In all cases, the referring chamber determines these factors by looking at the indictment as it stands at the time it makes its decision, including any amendments since its first iteration.[69] Analysis of the gravity of the crimes and the accused's level of responsibility has formed a key part of the ICTY Referral Bench's decisions, and neither factor alone is determinative of the result. Nevertheless, the chamber has tended to place greater emphasis on level of responsibility. It has declined, for example, to refer the cases of two high-ranking generals,[70] but has referred a case charging a mid-level police commander with genocide for his involvement in the massacre of thousands of Bosnian Muslims at Srebrenica.[71] The ICTY Referral Bench seems more likely to order referral where the crimes alleged are temporally

[67] See Blumenstock and Pittman, *supra* note 56, pp. 113–114. See also, e.g., *Lukić and Lukić* Referral Decision, *supra* note 13, paras. 67–93 (analysing Bosnian fair-trial guarantees and determining that they were satisfactory); *Prosecutor* v. *Rašević and Todović*, Case No. IT-97-25/1-AR11*bis*, Decision on Savo Todović's Appeals Against Decisions on Referral Under Rule 11 *bis*, 4 September 2006 ('*Rašević and Todović* Appeal Decision'), paras. 55–59, 62–63, 68–69, 72–75 (affirming referring chambers' favourable conclusions on guarantees in Bosnia); *Prosecutor* v. *Bagaragaza*, Case No. ICTR-05-86-11*bis*, Decision on Prosecutor's Request for Referral of the Indictment to the Kingdom of the Netherlands, 13 April 2007 ('*Bagaragaza* Referral Decision'), paras. 32–35 (Dutch courts satisfy requirement); *Prosecutor* v. *Munyeshyaka*, ICTR-2005–87-I, Decision on the Prosecutor's Request for the Referral of Wenceslas Munyeshyaka's Indictment to France, 20 November 2007 ('*Munyeshyaka* Referral Decision'), paras. 20–24 (French courts satisfy requirement); *Kanyarukiga* Referral Decision, *supra* note 65, paras. 34–62 (considering and rejecting defence and NGO arguments that a number of fair-trial guarantees would be unavailable in Rwanda); *ibid.*, paras. 66–81 (expressing concerns over harassment of witnesses and inability of accused to secure availability of witnesses residing outside Rwanda); *ibid.*, para. 96 (expressing concerns that accused would face lifetime solitary confinement if convicted); *ibid.*, para. 104 (ultimately rejecting referral request based on these concerns).

[68] ICTY Rule 11 *bis*(C). The ICTR judges did not introduce these criteria into Rule 11 *bis*. The reason may be that most of the accused in the ICTR's custody have been relatively high in rank. See Stephen J. Rapp, 'Achieving Accountability for the Greatest Crimes: The Legacy of the International Tribunals', (2007) 55 *Drake Law Review* 259, 269–273.

[69] *Prosecutor* v. *Todović*, Case No. IT-97-25/1-AR11 *bis*.1, Decision on Rule 11*bis* Referral, 23 February 2006, para. 14; *Lukić and Lukić* Referral Decision, *supra* note 13, paras. 16–19.

[70] See *Prosecutor* v. *Delić*, Case No. IT-04-83-PT, Decision on Motion for Referral of Case Pursuant to Rule 11 *bis*, 9 July 2007, paras. 24–26 (accused was the most senior officer in the Army of Bosnia and Herzegovina); *Prosecutor* v. *Dragomir Milošević*, Case No. IT-98-29/1-PT, Decision on Referral of Case Pursuant to Rule 11 *bis*, 8 July 2005, paras. 21–24 (accused had high rank and commanded shelling campaign of Sarajevo over several months). See also *Prosecutor* v. *Lukić and Lukić*, Case No. IT-98-32/1-AR11*bis*.1, Decision on Milan Lukić's Appeal Regarding Referral, 11 July 2007 ('*Lukić and Lukić* Appeal Decision'), paras. 21–22 (Milan Lukić one of the most important paramilitary leaders in the Yugoslav conflict).

[71] See *Trbić* Referral Decision, *supra* note 60, paras. 16–19.

or geographically limited, the number of victims is limited, or the accused had a limited leadership role.[72]

Appeal from the referring chamber's decision is as of right, directly to the Appeals Chamber.[73] Once referred, the national prosecutor adapts the Tribunal indictment to charge crimes within the national court's jurisdiction. The national crimes available to be charged must be 'substantially analogous' to those charged at the Tribunal.[74]

Rule 11 *bis* and the jurisprudence construing it set forth several other principles that derive their force from the *ad hoc* Tribunals' primacy. First, the Tribunals' Prosecutors may send monitors to observe the referred national proceedings.[75] In the former Yugoslavia, monitoring is undertaken in practice by the Organisation for Security and Cooperation in Europe through agreement with the Prosecutor, and the ICTY Appeals Chamber has given its blessing to this arrangement.[76] Rule 11 *bis* explicitly allows the referring chamber, before the accused is convicted or acquitted, to revoke the referral and compel the case's deferral back to the Tribunal.[77] Presumably, the chamber would only exercise such authority if it were not satisfied that the accused was, in fact, receiving a fair trial, or if subsequent rulings in the national courts demonstrated that those courts lacked jurisdiction over the accused's crimes.[78] To date, the ICTY Referral Bench has not invoked

[72] Blumenstock and Pittman, *supra* note 56, p. 111 and nn. 68–71 (citing cases).

[73] Apart from decisions remanding to the referring chamber to remedy infirmities in its original decision, the ICTY Appeals Chamber has only reversed one referral decision on its merits, concluding that referral was inappropriate for notorious paramilitary leader Milan Lukić. See generally *Lukić and Lukić* Appeal Decision, *supra* note 70. Lukić and co-accused Sredoje Lukić, his cousin, were then tried at the ICTY and convicted of various crimes. See generally *Lukić and Lukić* Referral Decision, *supra* note 13. See also *Prosecutor* v. *Lukić and Lukić*, Case No. IT-98-32/1-T, Judgement, 20 July 2009.

[74] *Prosecutor* v. *Stanković*, Case No. IT-96-23/2-PT, Decision on Referral of Case Under Rule 11 *bis*, 17 May 2005 ('*Stanković* Referral Decision'), para. 39. For more on the substantive law to be applied by the state of referral, see Blumenstock and Pittman, *supra* note 56, pp. 109, 112–113. See also *Prosecutor* v. *Bagaragaza*, Case No. ICTR-05-86-R11*bis*, Decision on the Prosecution Motion for Referral to the Kingdom of Norway, 19 May 2006, paras. 16–17 (refusing referral of case charging genocide, conspiracy to commit genocide, and complicity in genocide to Norway because that country lacked these crimes in its national penal code, and a trial for ordinary homicide would not allow 'Bagaragaza's alleged criminal acts [to] be given their full legal qualification'), affirmed by *Prosecutor* v. *Bagaragaza*, Case No. ICTR-05-86-AR11*bis*, Decision on Rule 11 *bis* Appeal, 30 August 2006, paras. 17–18. See also *infra* note 79 and case cited therein (ICTR revoking earlier referral of Bagaragaza's case to the Netherlands for same reason).

[75] ICTY Rule 11 *bis*(D)(iv); ICTR Rule 11 *bis*(D)(iv).

[76] See, e.g., *Rašević and Todović* Appeal Decision, supra note 67, paras. 101–107. If an ICTR case is referred to Rwanda or another African state, the African Commission on Human and People's Rights will presumably monitor the proceedings, an approach the ICTR Appeals Chamber has sanctioned. See *Prosecutor* v. *Kanyarukiga*, Case No. ICTR-2002-78-R11*bis*, Decision on the Prosecution's Appeal Against Decision on Referral Under Rule 11 *bis*, 30 October 2008 ('*Kanyarukiga* Appeal Decision'), para. 38.

[77] ICTY Rule 11 *bis*(F)–(G) (obliging the receiving state to accede to the deferral order); ICTR Rule 11 *bis*(F)–(G) (same); *Kanyarukiga* Referral Decision, *supra* note 65, para. 102 (noting obligation on state to comply deriving from Article 28 of the ICTR Statute).

[78] See, e.g., *Trbić* Referral Decision, *supra* note 60, paras. 41, 46 (referring chamber noting that it 'keeps itself well informed of the progress of referred cases through the reports of the Office of the Prosecutor, as well as through other means', and that 'if a given case is not being satisfactorily prosecuted or tried, [it] maintains the power … to revoke the referral and compel the return of the accused to the seat of the Tribunal') (quotations at para. 46); *Lukić and Lukić* Referral Decision, *supra* note 13, para. 98 (similar).

this provision, though a referring chamber at the ICTR has.[79] Second, the referring chamber may order that protective measures for victims and witnesses remain in place in proceedings before the national court.[80] The national court, or a party appearing before the national court, must seek leave from the Tribunal to modify these measures.[81]

Third, ordinary rules of state-to-state extradition law do not apply to the *ad hoc* Tribunals' referral proceedings. A state, in surrendering an accused to the Tribunal, cannot invoke the rule of speciality to dictate the crimes for which the Tribunal must try the accused, or cite national laws or constitutional provisions on non-extradition of nationals to avoid surrendering one of its nationals.[82] By the same token, according to the ICTY referral chamber, a surrendering state cannot require a third state to which the Tribunal then refers the accused to obtain the surrendering state's prior approval to try the accused for crimes within the Tribunal's jurisdiction. The ICTY referral chamber expressly declined to opine on whether the receiving state can try the accused for crimes other than those for which the Tribunal referred him or her, and over which the Tribunal has no jurisdiction (such as organised crime, drug trafficking, or terrorism), though the Bench has cautioned that doing so without the surrendering state's prior approval may violate bilateral obligations the receiving state owes to the surrendering state.[83]

The United Nations has fostered a programme to strengthen the capacity of the courts in the former Yugoslavia to try referred cases fairly, and the ICTR and NGOs have worked with the Rwandan judicial system in an effort to achieve the

[79] See *Prosecutor* v. *Bagaragaza*, Case No. ICTR-2005-86-11*bis*, Decision on Prosecutor's Extremely Urgent Motion for Revocation of the Referral to the Kingdom of the Netherlands Pursuant to Rule 11 *bis* (F) & (G), 17 August 2007 ('*Bagaragaza* Revocation Decision'), para. 11 and p. 5 (upon Prosecutor's request, revoking referral to Netherlands in light of post-referral Dutch court decision concerning a different Rwandan accused, where the court held that it did not have jurisdiction over crimes committed by Rwandans in Rwanda, where none of the victims was Dutch).

[80] ICTY Rule 11 *bis*(D)(ii); ICTR Rule 11 *bis*(D)(ii). See also, e.g., *Trbić* Referral Decision, *supra* note 60, para. 43 (so ordering).

[81] See ICTY Rule 75(H) (national court or parties in that jurisdiction 'may seek to rescind, vary, or augment protective measures ordered in [ICTY] proceedings … by applying to the President of the Tribunal'); Chapter 7, Section 7.4.3 (discussing protective measures generally); Chapter 7, text accompanying notes 112–115 (discussing modification of protective measures cases). See also, e.g., *Prosecutor* v. *Blagojević and Jokić*, Case No. IT-02-60-A, Decision on the Request of the Court of Bosnia and Herzegovina for Variation of Protective Measures Pursuant to Rule 75(H), 13 December 2007, para. 14 (granting variation of measures to allow Bosnian court access to protected witness ICTY testimony); *Prosecutor* v. *Milošević*, Case No. IT-02-54-R75H.1, Decision on Application Pursuant to Rule 75(H), 30 January 2008 (denying request to vary measures). The victim or witness for whom the protective measures were ordered may also move the Tribunal to vary, augment, or rescind the measures. ICTY Rule 75(H).

[82] See *Prosecutor* v. *Mejakić, Gruban, Fuštar, and Knežević*, Case No. IT-02-65-AR11*bis*, Decision on Joint Defence Appeal Against Decision on Referral Under Rule 11 *bis*, 7 April 2006, para. 31 ('The referral procedure envisaged in Rule 11 *bis* is implemented pursuant to [Security Council Resolution 1503] which, under the United Nations Charter, overrides any state's extradition requirements under treaty or national law.'). See also ICTY Rule 58; ICTR Rule 58.

[83] See *Lukić and Lukić* Referral Decision, *supra* note 13, paras. 108, 111, 120, 122. See also generally Michael Bohlander, 'Referring an Indictment from the ICTY and ICTR to Another Court: Rule 11*bis* and the Consequences for the Law of Extradition', (2006) 55 *International and Comparative Law Quarterly* 219.

same goal. To date, the ICTY has referred ten cases to Bosnia, two to Croatia, and one to Serbia, in each case finding that the courts met the fair trial standards required by Rule 11 *bis*.[84] The ICTY Prosecutor will not likely seek further referrals, as all remaining indictees are relatively high in rank.[85] As for Rwanda, that country has made efforts to improve its judiciary and has abolished the death penalty. It has expressed willingness to accept cases from the ICTR, and even some resentment over cases that have been transferred to third countries.[86] The ICTR Prosecutor has filed several requests with trial chambers to refer cases to national authorities, both in Rwanda and in Western Europe.[87] Referring chambers of the ICTR, however, have rejected referral requests to Rwanda, based on concerns that the accused would not receive a fair trial or, if convicted, would be subjected to prison conditions that violate his or her human rights.[88] As a result, the handful of referred ICTR cases thus far have gone to courts in Western Europe.[89]

The Rule 11 *bis* referral process has reduced both *ad hoc* Tribunals' caseloads. The degree to which the process may be replicated in future international or hybrid tribunals remains to be seen, but the *ad hoc* Tribunals have provided a sound framework to serve as a model.

[84] Blumenstock and Pittman, *supra* note 56, pp. 109–110 (citing cases and affirmances on appeal). See also, e.g., *Stanković* Referral Decision, *supra* note 74, paras. 68, 77 (sufficient fair-trial safeguards in place in Bosnia). For analysis questioning the ICTY Referral Bench's conclusion that the courts of the former Yugoslavia are prepared to conduct fair trials, see Sarah Williams, 'ICTY Referrals to National Jurisdictions: A Fair Trial or a Fair Price?', (2006) 17 *Criminal Law Forum* 177, 216–221. For a completed Bosnian case, see *Prosecutor* v. *Janković*, X-KRZ-05/161, Verdict, 29 January 2008.

[85] See Blumenstock and Pittman, *supra* note 56, p. 110 and n. 38 (citing Prosecutor's statement).

[86] See Human Rights Watch, *World Report 2008*, January 2008, pp. 144, 146, available at www.hrw.org/en/reports/2008/01/30/world-report-2008; Aptel, *supra* note 56, p. 179 (discussing several efforts Rwanda has made to prepare itself to accept referred cases, including a new law setting forth fair-trial guarantees, another abolishing the death penalty, and promises to improve conditions of imprisonment and allow ICTR monitors to observe trials; and citing Organic Law Relating to the Abolition of the Death Penalty of Rwanda, No. 31/2007, 25 July 2007, and Organic Law Concerning the Transfer of Cases to the Republic of Rwanda from the International Criminal Tribunal for Rwanda, No. 11/2007, 16 March 2007).

[87] At least five of these requests have asked for referral of accused to Rwanda: Fulgence Kayishema (11 June 2007); Gaspard Kanyarukiga (7 September 2007); Yussuf Munyakazi (7 September 2007); Idelphonse Hategekimana (7 September 2007); and Jean-Baptiste Gatete (28 November 2007).

[88] See, e.g., *Kanyarukiga* Referral Decision, *supra* note 65, para. 104 (summarising findings that defence witnesses might be too afraid to testify, and that Kanyarukiga would thus be at a disadvantage relative to the prosecution; and that, if convicted, Kanyarukiga may face lifetime solitary confinement), affirmed by *Kanyarukiga* Appeal Decision, *supra* note 76, para. 16 (concerns about life imprisonment in solitary confinement); *ibid.*, para. 21 (concerns about impediments for defence in obtaining documents from Rwandan government and in meeting witnesses); *ibid.*, paras. 26–27 (concerns about harassment of witnesses); *ibid.*, para. 31 (concerns about ability of accused to call witnesses residing outside Rwanda); *Prosecutor* v. *Munyakazi*, Case No. ICTR-97-36-R11*bis*, Decision on the Prosecution's Appeal Against Decision on Referral Under Rule 11 *bis*, 8 October 2008 (also affirming refusal to refer case for these reasons, but overturning trial chamber's determination that the Rwandan judiciary is insufficiently independent).

[89] See, e.g., *Munyeshyaka* Referral Decision, *supra* note 67 (referral to France); *Prosecutor* v. *Bucyibaruta*, Case No. ICTR-05-85-I, Decision on Prosecutor's Request for Referral of Laurent Bucyibaruta's Indictment to France, 20 November 2007. See also *Bagaragaza* Referral Decision, *supra* note 67 (referral to Netherlands), revoked by *Bagaragaza* Revocation Decision, *supra* note 79; Aptel, *supra* note 56, pp. 177–178 (discussing reports that African states are not prepared to accept ICTR cases, and few states in Africa and elsewhere have expressed willingness to do so).

3.1.4 Other procedures on cooperation deriving from the primacy regime

Many rules in the ICTY's and ICTR's Rules of Procedure and Evidence find their origins in the *ad hoc* Tribunals' primacy and the obligation to cooperate with them, derived from Security Council mandate and reflected in Article 29 of the ICTY Statute and Article 28 of the ICTR Statute.[90] Beyond the transfer of national prosecutions to the Tribunals, discussed earlier in this chapter,[91] cooperation from states, international organisations, and individuals is especially important in four additional areas: locating, arresting, and transferring indictees to the Tribunals; assisting in investigations; producing evidence in the form of documents, testimony, and other information; and enforcing and monitoring sentences imposed by the Tribunals.[92] A number of ICTY and ICTR Rules derive from the obligation to cooperate.[93] We sketch a few of the more important ones here, and elaborate on some of them in later chapters.

First, states must allow the *ad hoc* Tribunals' Prosecutors and their teams of investigators to operate directly on their territory, collecting evidence and questioning witnesses and suspects, without the need for letters rogatory or other traditional state-to-state requests for assistance.[94] Second, states must arrest and surrender, upon request, any person indicted by the Tribunals present on their territory and, as discussed above, must defer any investigation or prosecution of the accused upon the Tribunals' request.[95] Moreover, they may not dictate, as a condition for surrender, the

[90] On the legal sources of this obligation to cooperate, see *supra* notes 11–17 and sources cited therein.

[91] See *supra* Section 3.1.1 (on deferral).

[92] See Zahar and Sluiter, *supra* note 35, p. 457. On the *ad hoc* Tribunals' coercive powers vis-à-vis states, international organisations, and individuals, see *supra* note 11 and accompanying text. Chapter 4, Section 4.1, discusses investigations and evidence-gathering; Chapter 10, Section 10.5, discusses enforcement of sentences in national prisons.

[93] Many of these rules are codifications of principles first established in the jurisprudence. See, e.g., ICTY Rules 54 *bis*, 70. Rule 54 allows a judge or chamber to 'issue such orders, summonses, subpoenas, warrants and transfer orders as may be necessary for the purposes of an investigation or for the preparations or conduct of the trial'. ICTY Rule 54; ICTR Rule 54. On judicial rule-making, see Chapter 2.

[94] See ICTY Statute, Art. 18(2); ICTR Statute, Art. 17(2); ICTY Rules 39–40; ICTR Rules 39–40; *Blaškić* Subpoena Appeal Decision, *supra* note 11, paras. 53–54. On the difficulties faced in such investigations, see generally Mark B. Harmon and Fergal Gaynor, 'Prosecuting Massive Crimes with Primitive Tools: Three Difficulties Encountered by Prosecutors in International Criminal Proceedings', (2004) 2 *Journal of International Criminal Justice* 403.

[95] See Chapter 4, Section 4.2.6 (on arrest and surrender); Section 3.1.1, *supra* (on deferral). See also ICTY Rules 55–58; ICTR Rules 55–58. Whether states are obliged to surrender persons accused by the *ad hoc* Tribunals of contempt, as opposed to crimes against humanity, war crimes, or genocide, is less clear. Article 29(1) of the ICTY Statute and Article 28(1) of the ICTR Statute require states to cooperate in the investigation and prosecution of persons accused of 'serious violations of international humanitarian law'; Article 29(2)(d) and Article 28(2)(d), respectively, require states to comply with the Tribunals' orders for 'arrest and detention of persons'. See also Boas, Bischoff, and Reid, *Elements of Crimes*, *supra* note 19, p. 4 (explaining that the phrase 'international humanitarian law' in the ICTY and ICTR Statutes is 'understood ... to cover not only war crimes, but also crimes against humanity and genocide'). One could argue that state cooperation in the Tribunals' investigation and prosecution of war crimes, crimes against humanity, and genocide encompasses surrendering accused contemnors, because holding contemnors responsible deters others from

crimes for which the Tribunals may try the accused.[96] Third, the Tribunals may issue orders to states and international organisations to hand over documents even where the information may implicate national security interests,[97] though certain procedures allow states and organisations to supply the information to one of the parties on condition that it not be disclosed or used in court without the provider's consent.[98] Fourth, the Tribunals may subpoena private individuals, state officials, and officials of international organisations; and they may compel those individuals to testify and to hand over documents, though exceptions exist for documents obtained in an official capacity, and certain classes of persons are immune from subpoena.[99] Fifth, a sentence handed down by the Tribunals is binding on the state of enforcement; the state may not modify the sentence or release the prisoner early without the tribunal's consent, and the tribunal maintains the authority and duty to supervise enforcement.[100]

Entities that fail to obey an order to cooperate face one of several possible consequences, depending on the circumstances. For states, and presumably international organisations as well, the *ad hoc* Tribunals' main remedy is to make a formal finding that the state has failed to cooperate, and to report the failure to the Security Council.[101] The Security Council, in turn, is expected to impose whatever sanctions

engaging in similar disruptive conduct and thereby aids the Tribunals in fulfilling their primary mandate of prosecuting the international crimes. Alexander Zahar asserts, on the other hand, that the absence of any explicit mention of contempt in these articles means that states are not obligated to surrender private individuals for the judge-made offence of contempt. See Alexander Zahar, 'International Court and Private Citizen', (2009) 12 *New Criminal Law Review* 569, 578–579; see also *ibid*., pp. 579–584 (arguing that the ICTY judges' asserted power to order accused contemnors arrested and surrendered to the Tribunal is *ultra vires*); *ibid*., pp. 571–573 (discussing contempt charges against a prosecution witness and U.S. resident who refused to testify in the ICTY's *Haradinaj* trial, and the United States's refusal to surrender him to The Hague because the surrender agreement between the ICTY and the United States does not list contempt as a ground for surrender).

96 See *supra* note 82 and sources cited therein (on the rule against conditional surrender). States may not invoke ordinary rules of extradition law to refuse the surrender of an accused or put conditions on the crimes for which the *ad hoc* Tribunals may try him or her. See ICTY Rule 58; ICTR Rule 58; *Lukić and Lukić* Referral Decision, *supra* note 13, paras. 109–113; *supra* note 82 and accompanying text.

97 See Chapter 6, Sections 6.3.2, 6.5.1.4. See also *Blaškić* Subpoena Appeal Decision, *supra* note 11, paras. 26–29, 61–69 (states); *Milutinović et al.* NATO Trial Decision, *supra* note 11, paras. 35–38 (international organisations); *supra* note 11 and sources cited therein (states, international organisations, and sub-state entities).

98 See Chapter 6, Sections 6.3.2, 6.5.1.4. See also ICTY Rule 70; ICTR Rule 70; ICTY Rule 54 *bis*; *Prosecutor* v. *Milutinović, Šainović, Ojdanić, Pavković, Lazarević, and Lukić*, Case No. IT-05-87-AR108*bis*.2, Decision on Request of the United States of America for Review, 12 May 2006, para. 37.

99 See Chapter 6, Section 6.3.2; Chapter 9, Section 9.3.2 (on testimonial privileges). See also *Prosecutor* v. *Krstić*, Case No. IT-98-33-A, Decision on Application for Subpoenas, 1 July 2003, paras. 24, 26–28; *Prosecutor* v. *Simić, Simić, Tadić, Todorović, and Zarić*, Case No. IT-95-9-T, Decision on the Prosecution Motion Under Rule 73 for a Ruling Concerning the Testimony of a Witness, 27 July 1999, paras. 72–74 (special rules for International Committee for the Red Cross employees); *Prosecutor* v. *Brđanin and Talić*, Case No. IT-99-36-AR73.9, Decision on Interlocutory Appeal, 11 December 2002, para. 50 (special rules for war correspondents).

100 See Chapter 10, Section 10.5. See also ICTY Statute, Arts. 27–28; ICTR Statute, Arts. 26–27; ICTY Rules 123–125; ICTR Rules 123–125.

101 See, e.g., ICTY Rule 7 *bis* (general authorisation of Tribunal and Prosecutor to report non-compliance); ICTY Rule 11 (authorisation to report non-compliance with deferral orders); ICTY Rule 13 (authorisation to report a state's violation of *non bis in idem* by trying an accused already tried by the Tribunal); ICTY Rules 59(B), 61(E) (authorisation to report a state's failure to act on an arrest warrant); ICTR Rules 7, 11, 13, 59(B), 61(E) (same); *Blaškić* Subpoena Appeal Decision, *supra* note 11, paras. 33–37 (clarifying at para. 36 that this finding 'must not include any recommendations or suggestions as to the course of action the Security Council

are necessary to compel the state to comply.[102] This remedy, however, has proven cumbersome to employ, and ineffective, as it transforms the legal question of whether a state has failed to cooperate with a judicial order into the subject of political debate among the members of the Security Council.[103] Indeed, the Security Council has seldom taken action in response to complaints by the Tribunals notwithstanding frequent recalcitrance by the Yugoslav successor states, especially in the early years of the ICTY,[104] and periodic obstructionism by the Rwandan government.[105] Much more effective in achieving cooperation from these states have been incentives from influential powers, such as U.S. or Western European financial aid or the prospect of European Union membership conditioned upon the surrender of suspects.

Individuals who fail to cooperate with an order from the *ad hoc* Tribunals may be charged with an offence against the administration of justice, such as contempt,[106] and put on trial under the procedures set forth in Rule 77 of both Tribunals. The Tribunals have held several contempt trials resulting in fines, and occasionally short jail terms.[107] Offences against the administration of justice are discussed in detail in Chapter 7.[108]

may wish to take as a consequence of that finding'); Daryl A. Mundis, 'Reporting Non-Compliance: Rule 7 *bis*', in Richard May, David Tolbert, and John Hocking (eds.), *Essays on ICTY Procedure and Evidence in Honour of Gabrielle Kirk McDonald* (2001). See also, e.g., Letter Dated 8 September 1998 from the President of the International Tribunal for the Prosecution of Persons Responsible for Serious Violations of International Humanitarian Law Committed in the Territory of the Former Yugoslavia to the President of the Security Council, UN Doc. S/1998/839, 8 September 1998 (reporting Federal Republic of Yugoslavia's failure to arrest and transfer three indictees involved in the Vukovar Hospital incident).

[102] See *Blaškić* Subpoena Appeal Decision, *supra* note 11, paras. 26–31.

[103] See Harmon and Gaynor, *supra* note 94, pp. 418–419; Jacob Katz Cogan, 'The Problem of Obtaining Evidence for International Criminal Courts', (2000) 22 *Human Rights Quarterly* 404, 423–427.

[104] See, e.g., Daphna Shraga, 'Politics and Justice: The Role of the Security Council', in Antonio Cassese (ed.), *The Oxford Companion to International Criminal Justice* (2009), p. 173 (despite more than twelve reports of non-compliance under Rule 59(B) by the Presidents of both Tribunals, the Security Council has never acted on the reports). See also Cryer, *supra* note 27, p. 137 (record of compliance with the Tribunals has been mixed).

[105] See, e.g., Theodor Meron, 'Reflections on the Prosecution of War Crimes by International Tribunals', (2006) 100 *American Journal of International Law* 551, 561; Letter Dated 8 August 2002 from the President of the International Criminal Tribunal for [Rwanda] Addressed to the President of the Security Council, UN Doc. S/2002/923, 13 August 2002 (enumerating specific instances of Rwandan obstructionism during a damaging period in 2002, including new restrictions on witness travel to the ICTR to testify, and withholding investigators' access to evidence and crime sites); *Prosecutor* v. *Niyitegeka*, Case No. ICTR-96-14-T, Decision to Adjourn Proceedings Due to the Unavailability of Witnesses, 19 June 2002 (postponing trial due to the lack of available witnesses, and reminding Rwanda of its obligation to cooperate).

[106] *Blaškić* Subpoena Appeal Decision, *supra* note 11, para. 59.

[107] See, e.g., *Prosecutor* v. *Jokić*, Case No. IT-05-88-R77.1, Judgement on Allegations of Contempt, 27 March 2009 (finding accused guilty of contempt for refusing to obey a subpoena to testify in the *Popović* trial, and sentencing him to four months); *Prosecutor* v. *Margetić*, Case No. IT 95-14 R77.6, Judgement on Allegations of Contempt, 7 February 2007 (finding accused guilty of contempt for, among other misconduct, publishing list of protected witnesses on website, and sentencing him to three months' imprisonment and a fine of €10,000).

[108] See Chapter 7, Section 7.8.

3.2 Complementarity

The ICC's jurisdiction over the crimes in its Statute is, like that of the ICTY and ICTR, concurrent with that of national authorities. Drawing inspiration from the model of the *ad hoc* Tribunals, the Court's architects did not design it to try all cases involving war crimes, crimes against humanity, and genocide committed in the territories or by the persons subject to its jurisdiction. Instead, they intended the ICC to share jurisdiction over these crimes with national authorities, and indeed for the latter to take the lead in investigating and prosecuting the vast majority of crimes. Departing sharply from the model of the *ad hoc* Tribunals, the ICC's architects designed the Court as a backstop measure that would intervene to investigate and try cases only where national authorities were unwilling or unable to genuinely perform this task themselves. This compromise, which states insisted upon as a safeguard against the perceived risk of unjustified intervention by an international body in their sovereign affairs, forms the core of the Court's relationship with national authorities.[109] As a consequence, the ICC's powers to assert jurisdiction over a case are much weaker than those enjoyed by the *ad hoc* Tribunals.[110] More broadly, the Court's powers to compel cooperation from states and other entities are also much less extensive, both as a corollary of the complementarity regime and as the result of the Rome Statute's creation by multilateral agreement rather than by Security Council resolution.[111]

Two principal reasons for the ICC's relative weakness are its prospective nature and its potentially global reach. The Court has jurisdiction over the crimes listed in its Statute committed on or after 1 July 2002 by one of the nationals of an ICC state party or in the territory of a state party.[112] As a consequence, a national of any state in the world, and not just of a state that has consented to the ICC's jurisdiction, is potentially subject to prosecution before the Court.[113] States, in crafting the

[109] For an overview of these negotiations by the coordinator of complementarity discussions in the Preparatory Commission leading up to the Rome Statute, see Holmes, *supra* note 24, pp. 672–674.

[110] See Rome Statute, preambular para. 10 and Art. 1 (ICC complementary to national criminal jurisdictions). See also *supra* text accompanying note 10 (giving some reasons why international criminal tribunals, including the ICC, must rely on national authorities, international organisations, and other entities to help carry out many activities essential to their functioning); William W. Burke-White, 'The International Criminal Court and the Future of Legal Accountability', (2003) *ILSA Journal of International and Comparative Law* 195, 197 ('Even if an individual is within the ICC's jurisdiction and the prosecutor wants to pursue the case, if a national court – any national court – investigates or prosecutes, the ICC is effectively stopped in its tracks ... despite the Court's best efforts to act[.]').

[111] See Göran Sluiter, 'Cooperation of States with International Criminal Tribunals', in Cassese, *supra* note 104, p. 188 (describing how negotiations on the Court's structure involving the entire international community necessarily resulted in compromises on the ICC's powers to compel action on the part of states). For a broader discussion of how states' fears of a powerful ICC resulted in 'compromises that effectively undercut the Court at every turn', see Burke-White, *supra* note 110, pp. 196–200 (quotation at p. 196).

[112] These two limitations do not apply where the Security Council has referred a case. Rome Statute, Arts. 11(1), 12(2). States can also accept the jurisdiction of the court on an *ad hoc* basis without ratifying the Rome Statute. *Ibid.*, Art. 12(3).

[113] This jurisdictional arrangement was one of the United States' major objections to the Rome Statute. For a summary of this and other U.S. objections that led to the United States' unwillingness to ratify the Statute,

Rome Statute, wanted to reserve for themselves the ability to dispose of such cases without ICC involvement. At the same time, complementarity acknowledges the reality that the ICC's limited size and resources give it the capacity to try only a small fraction of the international crimes that fall within its jurisdiction. Moreover, the complementarity relationship was thought potentially more efficient because national authorities may be in a better position than the Court to carry out the activities that form an essential part of criminal investigations, including collecting evidence, locating suspects and witnesses, and arresting suspects.[114]

In theory at least, complementarity also encourages national courts to prosecute in the first instance, and in the process to build the legal and institutional capacity necessary to undertake prosecutions the ICC will consider adequate to preclude its jurisdiction.[115] As discussed below, however, complementarity as the Court has thus far defined it may in reality have the reverse effect for some countries, such as the Democratic Republic of the Congo ('DRC'), which has effectively abdicated in favour of the ICC any responsibility for investigating and prosecuting certain serious crimes committed in the eastern DRC.[116]

3.2.1 Situations and cases

The Rome Statute employs two key terms of art throughout its complementarity provisions – 'situation' and 'case' – but does not define either term. An early pre-trial decision explained that a case concerns an identified person or persons suspected of conduct constituting a crime under the Statute, while a situation encompasses the broader geographical and temporal context – usually an international or internal armed conflict or other major episode of civil strife – within which such crimes were allegedly committed. One situation may ultimately generate many cases. A case emerges from a situation when the Court issues an arrest

see Ratner, Abrams, and Bischoff, *supra* note 1, pp. 245–246. For a partial list of the bewildering number of academic articles written in support of or against the U.S. position, see William A. Schabas, 'United States Hostility to the International Criminal Court: It's All About the Security Council', (2004) *European Journal of International Law* 701, 703, nn. 5–7.

[114] See ICC Office of the Prosecutor, *Informal Expert Paper: The Principle of Complementarity in Practice*, December 2003, www.icc-cpi.int/iccdocs/doc/doc654724.pdf, paras. 1–2. See also *supra* text accompanying note 10.

[115] Rome Statute, preambular paras. 4, 6 (affirming national authorities' obligation to prosecute serious international crimes). On national authorities' duty to prosecute, see *supra* note 1 and accompanying text. On the ICC's effect on prompting national authorities to establish a domestic framework for the effective prosecution of international crimes, see, e.g., Jann K. Kleffner, 'The Impact of Complementarity on National Implementation of Substantive International Criminal Law', (2003) 1 *Journal of International Criminal Justice* 86. On ICC states parties' promulgation of new laws giving them the ability to prosecute the crimes listed in the Rome Statute in their own courts, thereby potentially precluding the Court from asserting jurisdiction on the basis of national authorities' inability to prosecute, see Burke-White, *supra* note 110, pp. 201–203.

[116] See *infra* Section 3.2.3.1.1; *infra* notes 169–175, 261–264 and accompanying text.

warrant or a summons for a specific person suspected of criminal conduct within the situation.[117]

As of 1 December 2009, five situations appeared on the ICC's docket: in the DRC; Darfur, Sudan; Uganda; the Central African Republic ('CAR'); and Kenya. In turn, three cases have emerged from the situation in the DRC: trial continues in the case of Thomas Lubanga and in the joined case of Germain Katanga and Mathieu Ngudjolo, while Bosco Ntaganda remains at large. Several cases have also emerged from the *Situation in Darfur*, with the Court's issuance of arrest warrants for Omar al-Bashir, Bahr Abu Garda, Ahmad Harun, and Ali Kushayb, all of whom remain at large. Similarly, a number of cases have arisen out of the *Situation in Uganda*, with arrest warrants for at-large suspects Joseph Kony, Vincent Otti, Okot Odhiambo, and Dominic Ongwen. The *Situation in the Central African Republic* has generated one case, that of Jean-Pierre Bemba. The Court has confirmed some of the charges against Bemba and he will soon stand trial on those charges.[118] In the *Situation in Kenya*, the Prosecutor has, for the first time, sought the Court's permission to use his '*proprio motu*' power[119] to initiate an investigation into crimes committed in the post-election violence of 2007 and 2008.[120] No arrest warrants for particular individuals, and thus no cases, have yet emerged from the Kenya situation.

3.2.2 Trigger mechanisms placing a situation before the ICC

The Rome Statute provides for a complex procedure by which the ICC assesses the legality and prudence of asserting jurisdiction over a case and taking it away from national authorities. This procedure, which was designed to tilt decisively in favour of investigation and trial by national authorities, is triggered in one of three circumstances.[121]

First, a state party to the Rome Statute may refer a situation to the Prosecutor for possible investigation where it appears that crimes within the ICC's jurisdiction

117 See *Situation in the Democratic Republic of the Congo*, Doc. No. ICC-01/04-101-t, Decision on the Applications for Participation in the Proceedings of VPRS 1, VPRS 2, VPRS 3, VPRS 4, VPRS 5 and VPRS 6, 17 January 2006, para. 65 (situations 'generally defined in terms of temporal [and] territorial … parameters', while cases 'comprise specific incidents during which one or more crimes within the jurisdiction of the Court seem to have been committed by one or more identified suspects'). Accord, e.g., ICC Informal Expert Paper, *supra* note 114, p. 10 n. 10 ('a "case" would require a higher degree of specificity … and normally that the suspect has been identified and would occur later into the criminal investigation').As an alternative to an arrest warrant, the Rome Statute provides for the Prosecutor to apply for the issuance of a 'summons' for the appearance at the ICC of a person suspected of crimes, which the pre-trial chamber may issue with or without restrictions on the person's liberty. Rome Statute, Art. 58(7).

118 On procedures for the issuance of arrest warrants, see Chapter 6, Section 6.3.1; on confirmation of charges procedures, see Chapter 6, Section 6.1.1.

119 See *infra* text accompanying notes 128–134.

120 See *Situation in the Republic of Kenya*, Doc. No. ICC-01/09-3, Request for Authorisation of an Investigation Pursuant to Article 15, 29 November 2009 ('*Kenya* Request for Authorisation').

121 For an in-depth analysis of these trigger mechanisms and admissibility procedures generally, see Héctor Olásolo, *The Triggering Procedure of the International Criminal Court* (2005).

have been committed, whether on the referring state's own territory or elsewhere, as long as the alleged crimes were committed by a national of a state party or on the territory of a state party.[122] The referral is a formal written request to the ICC Prosecutor to investigate the matter, accompanied by supporting documentation.[123] Most of the cases currently before the ICC were placed there by state party referrals – specifically, by governments alleging crimes committed by rebels fighting against them on their own territory. This phenomenon is known as 'self-referral', and is discussed in greater detail below.[124] Three of the five situations currently before the Court were self-referred: the DRC, Uganda, and the CAR.

Second, the UN Security Council may refer a situation to the Prosecutor for possible investigation.[125] In so doing, the Council must be acting under Chapter VII of the UN Charter. By virtue of these Chapter VII powers, and in contrast to state-party referral, the Council may refer situations occurring anywhere in the world, and not only those where the crimes were allegedly committed by a national of a state party or on the territory of a state party to the Rome Statute.[126] To date, the Council has referred one situation, in Darfur, Sudan. Sudan is a non-party, and has vehemently protested what it sees as an infringement of its sovereignty.[127]

Third, the Prosecutor may investigate a situation *proprio motu* in the absence of state party or Security Council referral, upon seeking and receiving authorisation in advance from a pre-trial chamber. The Prosecutor decides whether to use this

[122] Rome Statute, Arts. 12(2), 13(a), 14(1). See also *ibid.*, Art. 42(1) (Prosecutor responsible for receiving referrals and examining them). For the definition of 'situation', see *supra* Section 3.2.1.

[123] *Ibid.*, Art. 14; ICC Rule 45. The Rome Statute's drafters did not contemplate that states parties might use the state-referral mechanism to request the Prosecutor to investigate crimes committed on their own soil. See William A. Schabas, *An Introduction to the International Criminal Court* (3rd edn 2007), pp. 145–147. Ironically, three of the five situations now before the Court were referred by the affected state itself. 'Self-referral' is discussed in Section 3.2.4. For examples of governments' self-referral letters, see *infra* note 257 and sources cited therein.

[124] See *infra* Section 3.2.4.

[125] Rome Statute, Art. 13(b). See also *ibid.*, Art. 42(1) (Prosecutor responsible for receiving referrals and examining them).

[126] *Ibid.*, Arts. 12(2), 13(b). The Security Council may also require the Prosecutor and Court to defer investigations and prosecutions for up to twelve months at a time. See *ibid.*, Art. 16. For more on deferral, see *infra* Section 3.2.5. The explicit inclusion of a power on the part of the Council, acting under Chapter VII, to invoke the ICC's jurisdiction, helped settle an earlier debate as to whether the Council's use of Chapter VII to create the *ad hoc* Tribunals was lawful. The legitimacy of these two tribunals, and the Council's power to create judicial organs to conduct international criminal trials or to refer cases to existing tribunals, is now generally accepted. For discussion of this issue, see, e.g., Nsongurua J. Udombana, 'Pay Back Time in Sudan? Darfur in the International Criminal Court', (2005) 13 *Tulsa Journal of Comparative and International Law* 1, 14–18.

[127] See Security Council Resolution 1593, UN Doc. S/RES/1593 (2005) (United States abstaining). See also generally Luigi Condorelli and Annalisa Ciampi, 'Comments on the Security Council Referral of the Situation in Darfur to the ICC', (2005) 3 *Journal of International Criminal Justice* 590. For a sharp critique of certain aspects of Resolution 1593, see Schabas, *supra* note 123, pp. 154–159.

discretionary power by examining information provided by NGOs, intergovernmental organisations, UN organs, and other sources, and determining whether a 'reasonable basis' exists for proceeding with an investigation.[128] As with state party referral, the alleged crimes must have been committed by a national of a state party or on the territory of a state party.[129] This 'reasonable basis' analysis requires the Prosecutor to examine, among other things, whether the case is admissible before the Court and whether the crimes are sufficiently grave.[130]

Many states at Rome objected to giving the Prosecutor a *proprio motu* power at all, fearing that he or she might use it to launch politically motivated prosecutions. The view that such a power was necessary to preserve the Prosecutor's independence eventually won the day.[131] Still, the Prosecutor's independence is much more circumscribed in the ICC than in the ICTY or ICTR, and he or she is subject to considerable oversight by the pre-trial chamber.[132] For his part, the first Prosecutor asserted that he 'will use this power with responsibility and firmness, ensuring strict compliance with the Statute'.[133] Despite a great number of communications from NGOs and other informants accompanied by requests that the Prosecutor initiate an investigation *proprio motu*, the Prosecutor has only sought the ICC's authorisation to use his *proprio motu* power on one occasion, in November 2009, in the situation in Kenya.[134] The remainder of the situations before the Court were referred to it by a state party or the Security Council.

[128] See, e.g., Schabas, *supra* note 123, p. 163 (discussing statistics). See also Luis Moreno-Ocampo, Prosecutor of the International Criminal Court, *Address to the Assembly of States Parties*, 14 November 2008, p. 2, available at www.icc-cpi.int/NR/rdonlyres/8FA4F619-D1E7-4F64-ADBB-3FC86AD2EA9C/280353/20081114_speech.pdf (Office of the Prosecutor received 4,248 communications from 1 January to 14 November 2008 alleging crimes and was, as of 14 November 2008, analysing situations in Colombia, Georgia, Kenya, Côte d'Ivoire, and Afghanistan with a view toward possibly opening an investigation); Fatou Bensouda, Deputy Prosecutor of the International Criminal Court, *Overview of Situations and Cases Before the ICC, Linked with a Discussion of the Recent Bashir Arrest Warrant*, 15 April 2009, pp. 9–10, available at www.icc-cpi.int/NR/rdonlyres/243B605F-5940-4ADD-8E3A-530B371D696E/280280/20090414Pretoria.pdf (discussing some of the communications received by the Office of the Prosecutor as of that date); *Kenya* Request for Authorisation, *supra* note 120, p. 3 (in request to Pre-Trial Chamber to permit *proprio motu* investigation, Prosecutor noting that he had received thirty communications from individuals, groups, and others regarding post-election crimes in Kenya).

[129] Rome Statute, Arts. 12(2), 13(c), 15(1)–(3); ICC Rules 46–48.

[130] See *infra* text accompanying notes 206–224 (discussing 'reasonable basis' analysis and related procedures).

[131] See Silvia A. Fernández de Gurmendi, 'The Role of the International Prosecutor', in Roy S. Lee (ed.), *The International Criminal Court: The Making of the Rome Statute* (1999), pp. 176–181.

[132] See, e.g., Giuliano Turone, 'Powers and Duties of the Prosecutor', in Cassese, Gaeta, and Jones, *supra* note 24, Vol. II, pp. 1141–1143.

[133] ICC Office of the Prosecutor, *Annex to the 'Paper on Some Policy Issues Before the Office of the Prosecutor': Referrals and Communications*, September 2003, p. 4, available at www.icc-cpi.int/NR/rdonlyres/278614ED-A8CA-4835-B91D-DB7FA7639E02/143706/policy_annex_final_210404.pdf.

[134] See *Kenya* Request for Authorisation, *supra* note 120, para. 114. See also *ibid.*, p. 3 (ICC Prosecutor explaining that his office gleaned the information in the request from a number of reliable reports, including those of the Office of the High Commissioner for Human Rights and the UN Special Rapporteur on Extrajudicial, Summary, or Arbitrary Executions). Procedures for seeking authorisation for *proprio motu* investigations are discussed in Section 3.2.3.2.1 below.

3.2.3 *Admissibility of cases in the ICC*

The ICC cannot assert jurisdiction over a case that is inadmissible before it.[135] The principle of complementarity, in turn, requires the Court or the Prosecutor to deem a given case inadmissible if they find one or more of the subparagraphs of Article 17(1) of the Rome Statute satisfied:

(a) The case is being investigated or prosecuted by a State which has jurisdiction over it, unless the State is unwilling or unable genuinely to carry out the investigation or prosecution;
(b) The case has been investigated by a State which has jurisdiction over it and the State has decided not to prosecute the person concerned, unless the decision resulted from the unwillingness or inability of the State genuinely to prosecute;
(c) The person concerned has already been tried for conduct which is the subject of the complaint, and a trial by the Court is not permitted under article 20, paragraph 3;
(d) The case is not of sufficient gravity to justify further action by the Court.

Article 20(3), in turn, provides:

No person who has been tried by another court for conduct also proscribed under article 6, 7 or 8 shall be tried by the Court with respect to the same conduct unless the proceedings in the other court:

(a) Were for the purpose of shielding the person concerned from criminal responsibility for crimes within the jurisdiction of the Court; or
(b) Otherwise were not conducted independently or impartially in accordance with the norms of due process recognized by international law and were conducted in a manner which, in the circumstances, was inconsistent with an intent to bring the person concerned to justice.

As interpreted in the jurisprudence, the inquiry into these various factors – which we will call the 'admissibility factors' – consists of a two-pronged inquiry that explores a series of questions related to state action (or lack thereof) with respect to the case; and whether the case is sufficiently grave to warrant ICC involvement. With respect to the state action prong, the Prosecutor or relevant chamber must ask a sequence of questions:

- Has a state with jurisdiction already prosecuted the person concerned for the same conduct? If so, then the case is inadmissible before the ICC, *unless* the national trial was intended to shield the person from criminal responsibility, was conducted in a manner inconsistent with internationally recognised due process standards, or was otherwise inconsistent with an intent to bring the person concerned to justice.
- If a state with jurisdiction has not already prosecuted the person concerned, did any such state investigate the person and consider prosecuting, but ultimately decide not

[135] Rome Statute, Art. 19(1).

to prosecute? If so, then the case is inadmissible, *unless* the decision not to prosecute resulted from the state's unwillingness or inability to genuinely prosecute.
- Is a state with jurisdiction currently investigating or prosecuting the person concerned? If so, the case is inadmissible, *unless* the state is unable or unwilling to genuinely carry out the investigation or prosecution.

The case is presumptively admissible where no state is investigating or prosecuting or where any of the 'unless' caveats are triggered. A finding of presumptive admissibility, in turn, engages the second prong of the two-pronged inquiry: even though presumptively admissible, is the case of sufficient gravity to justify further action by the ICC or its Prosecutor? If the case is sufficiently grave, then it is admissible. If not, then the case is not admissible and the ICC leaves it in the hands of the national authorities.

Section 3.2.3.1 explores the meaning and scope of the admissibility factors by focusing on five principal components of the two-pronged inquiry: state inaction; unwillingness of a state to investigate or prosecute; inability of a state to investigate or prosecute; *non bis in idem* – that is, the circumstances in which national court conviction or acquittal has the effect of precluding ICC admissibility; and gravity. Some of these components, including unwillingness, inability, and gravity, cut across the inquiry and arise in various different parts of it. Section 3.2.3.2 then reviews the practical application of the complementarity principle through separate stages of ICC proceedings in which the ICC Prosecutor or a chamber of the Court evaluates the admissibility factors to determine whether a given case is admissible. Throughout these sections, we use the term 'presumptively admissible' to describe a case for which all but one of the admissibility factors are satisfied – gravity – and which still must be assessed to determine if its gravity is sufficient to warrant ICC involvement.

3.2.3.1 Definition and scope of the admissibility factors

3.2.3.1.1 State inaction In its jurisprudence the ICC has recognised a key principle not explicitly listed in the Rome Statute, but which the Appeals Chamber has identified as inherent in the Statute's complementarity structure: a case is presumptively admissible if no state with jurisdiction is investigating or prosecuting it, and if no state has already done so.[136] Hence, provided the other personal, subject-matter,

[136] *Katanga and Ngudjolo* Admissibility Appeal Judgement, *supra* note 2, para. 78 (holding that 'inaction on the part of a State having jurisdiction (that is, the fact that a State is not investigating or prosecuting, or has not done so) renders a case admissible before the court' unless the gravity requirement is not satisfied). The Appeals Chamber applied textual and 'purposive' interpretations of the Rome Statute to arrive at this conclusion, and noted its support in a number of academic works. See *ibid.* Accord *Prosecutor* v. *Lubanga*, Doc. No. ICC-01-04-01/06-8-US-Corr, Decision Concerning Pre-Trial Chamber I's Decision of 10 February 2006 and the Incorporation of Documents into the Record of the Case Against Mr. Thomas Lubanga Dyilo, 10 February 2006 ('*Lubanga* Arrest Warrant Decision'), para. 30 ('[T]he first requirement for a case arising from the investigation of a situation to be declared inadmissible is that at least one State with jurisdiction over the case is investigating, prosecuting or trying that case, or has done so').

and temporal jurisdictional requirements are met, the ICC Prosecutor or chamber assessing admissibility may deem such a case presumptively admissible.[137] Where no state has even initiated an investigation, the Prosecutor or chamber need not examine unwillingness and inability.[138] Applying this principle, the Pre-Trial Chamber in *Bemba* found that the authorities in the CAR, the state where Bemba allegedly committed the crimes for which the ICC Prosecutor sought to try him, had abandoned all attempts to investigate or prosecute him due to his immunity as then Vice-President of the DRC. The case was therefore admissible before the ICC because no state was investigating or prosecuting his alleged crimes.[139]

The *Lubanga* Pre-Trial Chamber added an important gloss to the principle that inaction by any state equals presumptive admissibility before the ICC. In 2004, the President of the DRC referred the situation in his country to the ICC Prosecutor, declaring that the DRC's national authorities were unable to investigate or prosecute the alleged international crimes.[140] The Pre-Trial Chamber, ruling in 2006, declined to regard this statement as still accurate and instead found that a reopened DRC court had issued arrest warrants against Lubanga, and that the latter had been detained there pending trial for crimes under national law seemingly committed during certain military attacks by his rebel forces, the Forces Patriotiques pour la Libération du Congo ('FPLC').[141] The ICC Prosecutor sought to charge Lubanga for enlisting children into the FPLC, a war crime under the Rome Statute, and an activity that apparently overlapped temporally with the conduct alleged by the DRC authorities.[142] Citing no authority in the Rome Statute's *travaux préparatoires* or elsewhere, the Pre-Trial Chamber held that to trigger an ICC inquiry into

[137] Even if a state has decided after investigation not to prosecute, the case will still be presumptively admissible if the decision resulted from an unwillingness or inability to genuinely prosecute. See *infra* Section 3.2.3.1.2. Moreover, even if a state has already prosecuted, the case will still be presumptively admissible if certain conditions that obviate the need for ICC deferral on *non bis in idem* grounds, discussed in Section 3.2.3.1.4 *infra*, are satisfied.

[138] See *Katanga and Ngudjolo* Admissibility Appeal Judgement, *supra* note 2, paras. 78, 80. Accord, e.g., ICC Informal Expert Paper, *supra* note 114, paras. 18–19.

[139] See *Prosecutor* v. *Bemba*, Doc. No. ICC-01/05-01/08-14-tENG, Decision on the Prosecutor's Application for a Warrant of Arrest Against Jean-Pierre Bemba Gombo, 10 June 2008 ('*Bemba* Arrest Warrant Decision'), paras. 21–22. See also *Prosecutor* v. *Bashir*, Doc. No. ICC-02/05-01/09-3, Decision on the Prosecution's Application for a Warrant of Arrest Against Omar Hassan Ahmad Al Bashir, 4 March 2009, paras. 49–51 (in decision granting ICC Prosecutor's application for an arrest warrant, noting lack of investigations or prosecutions in Sudan, but declining to determine admissibility at this stage); *Katanga and Ngudjolo* Admissibility Appeal Judgement, *supra* note 2, para. 42 (pre-trial chamber need not find a case admissible as a prerequisite to issuing an arrest warrant).

[140] Letter from DRC President Joseph Kabila to ICC Prosecutor Luis Moreno Ocampo, 3 March 2004, available at http://wwwold.icc-cpi.int/library/cases/ICC-01-04-01-06-32-AnxA1_French.pdf.

[141] See *Lubanga* Arrest Warrant Decision, *supra* note 136, paras. 35–36. The Pre-Trial Chamber in the Uganda cases has apparently been more trusting of the continued validity of Uganda's declaration of its own ability to investigate and prosecute. See, e.g., *Situation in Uganda*, Doc. No. ICC-02/04-01/05-53, Warrant of Arrest for Joseph Kony Issued on 8 July 2005 as Amended on 27 September 2005, 27 September 2005 ('*Kony* Arrest Warrant Decision'), para. 38 (simply noting Uganda government's letter of referral declaring inability to prosecute, and finding that the case against Kony 'appears to be admissible').

[142] See Rome Statute, Art. 8(2)(e)(vii). For more on this case, see Boas, Bischoff, and Reid, *Elements of Crimes*, *supra* note 19, pp. 302–303.

unwillingness and inability, the domestic proceedings 'must encompass both the person and the conduct which is the subject of the case before the Court'.[143] The Chamber held that since the DRC arrest warrants for Lubanga 'contain[ed] no reference to his alleged responsibility for the alleged ... FPLC's policy/practice of enlisting [children] into the FPLC', 'the DRC cannot be considered to be acting in relation to the specific case before the [ICC]'.[144] The Chamber accordingly found this 'same person/same conduct' test not satisfied, and deemed the case admissible without examining willingness or ability.[145]

Subsequently, at least one Pre-Trial Chamber – in the *Katanga* and *Ngudjolo* cases, which were later joined into a single case – has applied *Lubanga*'s same person/same conduct test.[146] Finding reasonable grounds to believe that the rebel forces under the command of Katanga and Ngudjolo committed war crimes and crimes against humanity during an attack on the eastern DRC village of Bogoro, and relying on information on Congolese investigations presented by the Prosecutor, the Chamber held cursorily that 'the proceedings against [Katanga and Ngudjolo] in the DRC do not encompass the same conduct which is the subject of the Prosecution Application'.[147] Like the Chamber in *Lubanga*, it declared the cases admissible without looking at unwillingness or inability.[148]

Under the same person/same conduct test, it is not necessary for national investigations or prosecutions to be completely nonexistent. Instead, where investigations or prosecutions exist but concern other suspects, even for the same criminal episode, or the same suspect but for conduct other than that referred to the ICC, the case is presumptively admissible.[149] Yet the reasoning in the decisions in *Lubanga*, *Katanga*, and *Ngudjolo* is too sparse to ascertain whether the Pre-Trial Chambers actually looked at the alleged conduct that gave rise to the DRC criminal charges against the

[143] *Lubanga* Arrest Warrant Decision, *supra* note 136, para. 31. Accord, e.g., *Prosecutor* v. *Katanga*, Doc. No. ICC-01/04-01/07-55, Decision on the Evidence and Information Provided by the Prosecution for the Issuance of a Warrant of Arrest for Germain Katanga, 6 July 2007 ('*Katanga* Arrest Warrant Decision'), para. 20; *Prosecutor* v. *Ngudjolo*, Doc. No. ICC-01/04-02/07-3, Decision on the Evidence and Information Provided by the Prosecution for the Issuance of a Warrant of Arrest for Mathieu Ngudjolo Chui, 6 July 2007 ('*Ngudjolo* Arrest Warrant Decision'), para. 21.

[144] *Lubanga* Arrest Warrant Decision, *supra* note 136, paras. 38–39.

[145] *Ibid.*, para. 40.

[146] *Katanga* Arrest Warrant Decision, *supra* note 143, paras. 20–21; *Ngudjolo* Arrest Warrant Decision, *supra* note 143, paras. 21–22 (same three judges, same cursory finding as *Katanga*). By finding admissibility based on inaction under the same person/same conduct test, the *Lubanga*, *Katanga*, and *Ngudjolo* Pre-Trial Chambers avoided the difficult questions that could surround an evaluation of a state's willingness and ability to genuinely investigate and prosecute the conduct at issue in those cases, even in instances of self-referral.

[147] *Katanga* Arrest Warrant Decision, *supra* note 143, para. 20; *Ngudjolo* Arrest Warrant Decision, *supra* note 143, para. 21 (same).

[148] *Katanga* Arrest Warrant Decision, *supra* note 143, para. 21; *Ngudjolo* Arrest Warrant Decision, *supra* note 143, para. 22. The Pre-Trial Chamber in the Uganda cases took a different approach, simply finding that the cases 'appear[ed]' to be admissible on the basis of the Uganda government's declaration of inability. See, e.g., *Kony* Arrest Warrant Decision, *supra* note 141, para. 38.

[149] On the gravity threshold, see *infra* Section 3.2.3.1.5.

three suspects, or merely determined from the face of the DRC arrest warrants that their alleged ICC crimes were not listed there. In other words, it is unclear whether these Chambers compared the *crimes* alleged in the DRC against the crimes alleged in the ICC, or the underlying *conduct* giving rise to those crimes, whatever its characterisation in arrest warrants or charging documents. The former approach – requiring complete parity between the list of alleged crimes in the national proceedings and the list in the ICC – would likely make it easier to find a given case admissible than the Rome Statute's drafters intended. Some states have not yet implemented the international crimes in the Rome Statute in their domestic penal codes. Even in states that have implemented the international crimes, in a given case the national prosecutor may make a strategic decision, based on the available evidence and the input of the victims, not to charge an international crime, and instead to charge only domestic crimes such as murder or assault. A national prosecution for grave domestic crimes should be considered sufficient to preclude the ICC from taking a case. A conviction on such charges avoids the impunity of the individual and satisfies the victims' need for justice, and leaving prosecutions to the national authorities saves the international prosecutor the need to prove the burdensome additional elements that must be shown for a crimes against humanity or genocide conviction.[150] Katanga himself proposed an alternative approach that would instead compare the gravity of the national charges against the gravity of the proposed ICC charges.[151]

After ICC charges were confirmed against Katanga and he became aware of the Pre-Trial Chamber's previously *ex parte* decision on admissibility, he lodged an admissibility challenge with the Trial Chamber, assailing the same person/same conduct test on several grounds.[152] The Trial Chamber chose not to address the merits of the same person/same conduct test and, as described below, instead opted to characterise the DRC's lack of investigations into crimes committed in Bogoro as 'unwillingness' – a separate basis for admissibility.[153]

[150] See Schabas, *supra* note 123, p. 183.

[151] *Prosecutor* v. *Katanga and Ngudjolo*, Doc. No. ICC-01/04-01/07-949, Motion Challenging the Admissibility of a Case by the Defence of Germain Katanga, Pursuant to Article 19(2)(a) of the Statute, 11 March 2009 ('*Katanga* Admissibility Challenge'), para. 46.

[152] Among other criticisms, Katanga accused the Pre-Trial Chamber of apparently ignoring documentation showing that the DRC authorities were investigating and prosecuting him for a number of serious crimes, including genocide and crimes against humanity, committed during the same conflict out of which the ICC charges arose. *Ibid.*, paras. 11–12, 15, 61. Recalling complementarity's goal of fostering prosecutions at the national level, he argued that when the ICC Prosecutor is dissatisfied with charges brought at the national level, he should approach the national authorities to convince them to charge different or graver crimes, rather than remove the case to the ICC. See *ibid.*, paras. 40, 49. Katanga asserted in addition that the test as applied allowed the Court to declare a case admissible in all but a small number of cases, and that the resulting loose application of the complementarity principle amounted to *de facto* primacy, contrary to the intentions of the states who negotiated the Rome Statute. See *ibid.*, paras. 18–19.

[153] *Prosecutor* v. *Katanga and Ngudjolo*, Doc. No. ICC-01/04-01/07-1213-tENG, Reasons for the Oral Decision on the Motion Challenging the Admissibility of the Case (Article 19 of the Statute), 16 June 2009 ('*Katanga and Ngudjolo* Admissibility Trial Decision'), paras. 93–95 and p. 138. See also *infra* text accompanying notes 169–175.

In one of its key decisions on complementarity to date, the Appeals Chamber affirmed the admissibility of Katanga's case.[154] Yet it did so on different grounds than either the Pre-Trial Chamber or the Trial Chamber, and declined to give its views on the merits of either the same person/same conduct test or the Trial Chamber's 'unwillingness' analysis.[155] The DRC assured the Appeals Chamber that it had not investigated or prosecuted crimes committed during the Bogoro incident, that it did not intend to do so in the future, and that it preferred that such crimes be investigated by the ICC.[156] The Appeals Chamber dismissed as irrelevant Katanga's assertion that the DRC had been investigating him for Bogoro crimes in the past but stopped in order to leave such investigations to the ICC Prosecutor.[157] The Chamber construed Article 17 in the following manner:

> [I]n considering whether a case is inadmissible ... the initial questions to ask are (1) whether there are ongoing investigations or prosecutions, or (2) whether there have been investigations in the past, and the State having jurisdiction has decided not to prosecute the person concerned. It is only when the answer[] to [either question is] in the affirmative that one has to ... examine the question of unwillingness and inability. To do otherwise would be to put the cart before the horse. It follows that in case of inaction, the question of unwillingness or inability does not arise; inaction on the part of a State having jurisdiction (that is, the fact that a State is not investigating or prosecuting, or has not done so) renders a case admissible before the Court, subject to article 17(1)(d) of the Statute [setting forth the gravity requirement].[158]

The Appeals Chamber remarked that the alternative construction urged by Katanga would contravene the Rome Statute's goal of ending impunity, as '[t]he Court would be unable to exercise its jurisdiction over a case as long as the State is theoretically willing and able to investigate and to prosecute the case, even though that State has no intention of doing so', and thus 'a potentially large number of cases would not be prosecuted by domestic jurisdictions or by the International Criminal Court'.[159] The Appeals Chamber then determined that the DRC authorities' voluntary cessation of investigations into possible crimes by Katanga, even though such

[154] *Katanga and Ngudjolo* Admissibility Appeal Judgement, *supra* note 2, para. 116.

[155] See *ibid.*, para. 81 ('In light of the above, the Appeals Chamber does not have to address in the present appeal the correctness of the "same-conduct test" used by the Pre-Trial Chambers to determine whether the same "case" is the object of domestic proceedings.'); *ibid.*, para. 97 (declining to address Katanga's argument that the Trial Chamber's construction of 'unwillingness' was erroneous).

[156] *Ibid.*, para. 68.

[157] Katanga argued that the Trial Chamber erred in looking at the facts as they currently stood, instead of looking at them as they stood at the time the Pre-Trial Chamber issued its admissibility decision and warrant of arrest – that is, February 2006. He argued that in February 2006, the DRC was indeed investigating possible Bogoro crimes. The Appeals Chamber dismissed this argument, and held that a chamber deciding whether a case *is* admissible must look at the facts as they currently exist, not as they may have existed at an earlier stage of the ICC proceedings. See *ibid.*, paras. 56, 80.

[158] *Ibid.*, para. 78. The gravity requirement is discussed in Section 3.2.3.1.5 below.

[159] *Ibid.*, para. 79. Accord *ibid.*, para. 83.

forbearance was prompted by the DRC's desire to see Katanga prosecuted before the ICC, constituted inaction rendering the case admissible before the ICC.[160]

3.2.3.1.2 Unwillingness Even where a state has jurisdiction over a case, and is investigating or prosecuting it or has decided not to prosecute the person concerned, the case will still be presumptively admissible before the ICC if the state is unwilling or unable to carry out the investigation or prosecution genuinely, or the decision not to prosecute resulted from an unwillingness or inability to prosecute genuinely.[161] This subsection discusses unwillingness; the following subsection examines inability.[162]

The Rome Statute seems to contemplate that, when assessing a state's willingness to investigate or prosecute, the ICC Prosecutor or chamber must look into state officials' motives, intentions, and good faith or lack thereof – the type of inquiry that could prove politically sensitive. The Statute lists three grounds that would prompt a finding of unwillingness: (1) the national proceedings were designed to shield the person concerned from responsibility for war crimes, crimes against humanity, or genocide; (2) the proceedings suffer from an unjustified delay inconsistent with an intent to bring the person to justice; or (3) the national authorities did not conduct or are not conducting the proceedings independently or impartially, and in a manner consistent with an intent to bring the person to justice.[163] As an informal group of experts noted in 2003, these factors touch upon procedural and institutional factors affecting the national proceedings, and not on whether the accused was ultimately convicted or acquitted.[164] Essentially, they aim at precluding an obligation for the Court to defer to sham proceedings in a national jurisdiction.

The group of experts proffered a list of indicia from which an unwillingness to bring the person to justice may be inferred, depending on the circumstances. These include direct political interference in the judicial proceedings; institutional deficiencies that allow for indirect political influence, such as the subordination of the prosecutorial or judicial authorities to the political branches; friendship, political alliance, or some other close linkage between the suspect or accused and the political authorities, police, investigators, prosecutors, or judges; a focus on lower-level perpetrators of the crimes at issue and a failure to investigate or indict leaders; the adequacy of the charges against the accused in light of the gravity of the alleged

[160] See *ibid.*, paras. 80, 82, 116.

[161] Rome Statute, Art. 17(1)(a)–(b). Information on a state's willingness and ability can come from a number of sources, including a statement filed with the Court by the state itself. See ICC Rule 51. The delegates at Rome chose the word 'genuinely' as preferable to terms such as 'diligently', 'efficiently' and 'sufficiently', as they thought the former a more objective term. Holmes, *supra* note 24, p. 674 (explaining the negotiations and noting that 'genuinely' was an unprecedented term, but not proffering a clear definition for it).

[162] See *infra* Section 3.2.3.1.3.

[163] Rome Statute, Art. 17(2).

[164] ICC Informal Expert Paper, *supra* note 114, para. 46.

crimes; insufficient resources allocated to the case compared to cases of similar complexity and gravity; long delays compared to cases of similar complexity and gravity; procedures and rulings that deviate from previous or ordinary practice and inure to the benefit of the suspect or accused; and inadequate steps taken by the authorities to protect at-risk victims and witnesses from intimidation.[165] A noteworthy characteristic of many of these proposed indicia is that they are to be evaluated, in the first instance, by comparison to the state's usual handling of similar cases, and not in comparison to other states.[166] The group also underscored that unwillingness on the part of one government institution may create an inability to prosecute in another – for example, a blanket amnesty granted by the legislature can preclude the judicial authorities from proceeding with trial.[167]

After charges were confirmed against him and the case passed to the Trial Chamber, the accused Germain Katanga challenged the Pre-Trial Chamber's determination from two years prior that his case was admissible.[168] In rejecting that challenge, the Trial Chamber added a fourth basis for a finding of unwillingness in addition to the three explicitly listed in the Statute (the national proceedings were designed to shield the person; they suffer from unjustified delay; or the national authorities did not conduct them with an intent to bring the person to justice): that the state simply expresses its unwillingness to investigate or prosecute, and its preference for prosecution in the ICC. The Chamber thus expanded the scope of 'unwillingness' beyond the notion that the national authorities are conducting sham proceedings or are otherwise behaving in a manner inconsistent with an intent to bring the person to justice:

> [T]he Statute makes explicit provision for … unwillingness motivated by the desire to obstruct the course of justice. There is also the case of a State which may not want to protect an individual, but, for a variety of reasons, may not wish to exercise its jurisdiction over him or her. This second form of 'unwillingness', which is not expressly provided for in article 17 of the Statute, aims to see the person brought to justice, but not before national courts. The Chamber considers that a State which chooses not to investigate or prosecute a person before its own courts, but has nevertheless every intention of seeing that justice is done, must be considered as lacking the will referred to in article 17.[169]

The *Katanga and Ngudjolo* Trial Chamber reasoned that this expansion was consistent with the Rome Statute's object and purpose because it furthers the drafters'

165 *Ibid.*, *supra* note 114, para. 47 and Annex 4 (at pp. 28–31, listing several additional indicia). See also Holmes, *supra* note 24, pp. 675–676 (listing some of these and adding that '[t]he transfer of the case(s) to secret tribunals would also be relevant') (quotation at p. 675).

166 See Holmes, *supra* note 24, pp. 673–674 (describing states' concerns that their performance would be judged in comparison to that of the Court or other, presumably wealthier, states with more robust judicial systems).

167 ICC Informal Expert Paper, *supra* note 114, paras. 45–46.

168 See *supra* note 152 and accompanying text (outlining Katanga's arguments before the Trial Chamber).

169 *Katanga and Ngudjolo* Admissibility Trial Decision, *supra* note 153, para. 77.

desire to end impunity: while states have the right and duty to exercise their criminal jurisdiction, they may freely choose to waive this right where they 'consider[] that it is more opportune for the Court to carry out an investigation or prosecution', and 'still be complying with [their] duties under the complementarity principle'.[170]

In the case before the Trial Chamber, the DRC itself had referred to the ICC the broader situation in which Katanga's alleged crimes were committed, and had informed the ICC Prosecutor and the Trial Chamber that it had no intention of prosecuting Katanga for any of the crimes or conduct at issue in the ICC proceedings.[171] The Trial Chamber found this expression of unwillingness sufficient to render the case admissible, and did not delve into the motives the DRC may have had for deciding not to investigate or prosecute.[172] While this interpretation of 'unwillingness' is consistent with the ordinary meaning of the term, it goes beyond the text of the Rome Statute and probably the intent of the drafters, as the factors explicitly listed in the Statute – which appear to be exhaustive – clearly contemplate that the state's unwillingness will be shown in a more subtle and devious fashion.[173] As explained above,[174] the Appeals Chamber affirmed the admissibility of Katanga's case, but chose to characterise the DRC's forbearance not as unwillingness, but as complete inaction – an independent ground of admissibility.[175] While the Appeals Chamber did not expressly reject the Trial Chamber's expanded definition of 'unwillingness', future chambers will likely choose to follow the Appeals Chamber in characterising a state's voluntary relinquishment of jurisdiction to the ICC as inaction, instead of unwillingness.

3.2.3.1.3 Inability The assessment of a state's ability to prosecute is likely a more objective and straightforward exercise than assessing unwillingness.[176] The Rome Statute requires the ICC Prosecutor or chamber to examine 'whether, due to a total

[170] *Ibid.*, paras. 78–79 (citing Rome Statute, preambular para. 5).

[171] *Ibid.*, paras. 93–94. See also *ibid.*, para. 95 ('[T]he Chamber cannot but note the clear and explicit expression of unwillingness of the DRC to prosecute this case.'). The Trial Chamber dismissed as vague the documentation proffered by Katanga allegedly showing that DRC authorities had investigated crimes in the village of Bogoro. See *ibid.*, paras. 68–72. For more on the DRC's self-referral, see *supra* text accompanying notes 140–145; *infra* text accompanying note 262.

[172] *Ibid.*, p. 38. In addressing Katanga's arguments on the invalidity of the Pre-Trial Chamber's 'same person/ same conduct' test, see *supra* note 152, the Trial Chamber also suggested that it would have found the case admissible even had the DRC been investigating and those investigations involved the same person and same conduct as the ICC investigations: 'Even assuming that investigations had been underway in a State against an accused person for crimes wholly identical to those which are the subject of a warrant issued for his or her arrest by the Court, the expression of the unwillingness of the State to bring the accused to justice before its own courts can be such that it can only result in a Chamber declaring the case admissible.' *Ibid.*, para. 88.

[173] See Olásolo, supra note 121, pp. 150–153; John T. Holmes, 'The Principle of Complementarity', in Roy S. Lee (ed.), *The International Criminal Court: The Making of the Rome Statute* (1999), p. 50.

[174] See *supra* text accompanying notes 154–160.

[175] *Katanga and Ngudjolo* Admissibility Appeal Decision, *supra* note 2, para. 97.

[176] Holmes, *supra* note 24, p. 677.

or substantial collapse or unavailability of its national judicial system, the State is unable to obtain the accused or the necessary evidence and testimony or otherwise unable to carry out its proceedings'.[177] State authorities may be willing and even eager to investigate or prosecute, and yet unable to do so because of a collapsed or otherwise unavailable judicial system, and in such cases the ICC's architects envisioned prosecution at the Court. Judicial systems suffering from total or substantial collapse may include those of failed or conflict-ridden states, where the national courts are no longer functioning. They may also include states whose courts are not functioning in the region affected by a conflict and where a court in another part of the country cannot effectively try the case, or where the authorities cannot effectively gather evidence or gain custody of the accused.[178]

An 'unavailable' judicial system may be one that lacks the legal infrastructure necessary to charge and try the accused criminally, such as one where the legislature has granted the accused an amnesty; or one where the accused's conduct, at least as the ICC Prosecutor seeks to charge it, has not been criminalised under national law.[179] A judicial system may also be 'unavailable' if the judges, investigators, prosecutors, or other staff necessary to carry out an investigation and trial of the type and complexity required in light of the accused's alleged criminal conduct are lacking.[180]

3.2.3.1.4 Non bis in idem Consistent with the *non bis in idem* principle discussed earlier in this chapter,[181] the ICC Prosecutor or chamber may not deem a case admissible where the person concerned has already been tried in a national court for the same conduct. Notwithstanding conviction or acquittal in a national court, however, the case will be presumptively admissible if the national proceedings were intended to shield the accused, or otherwise were not conducted independently and impartially or in a manner consistent with an intent to bring the person to justice.[182] An examination of these exceptions likely considers the same factors as those discussed above for assessing unwillingness.[183] The actual crime charged by the national authorities is irrelevant; if the underlying conduct is the same, and neither of the exceptions applies, the ICC cannot assume jurisdiction over the case,

177 Rome Statute, Art. 17(3).

178 An earlier draft of the Rome Statute provided for a finding of inability due to mere 'partial' collapse of the judicial system; this was later changed to 'substantial' collapse. Thus, a partial collapse will be insufficient for a finding of inability where the state can still genuinely investigate and prosecute the case using the non-collapsed portion of its judicial infrastructure. See Holmes, *supra* note 24, pp. 677–678.

179 See *supra* text accompanying notes 149–150 (discussing uncertainty in the definition of the same person/same conduct test).

180 ICC Informal Expert Paper, *supra* note 114, para. 50 and Annex 4 (at p. 31, also listing other indicia); Holmes, *supra* note 24, p. 678.

181 See *supra* text accompanying notes 28–30.

182 Rome Statute, Arts. 17(2)(c), 20(3).

183 See *supra* Section 3.2.3.1.2 and especially text accompanying notes 164–167.

even if the national conviction or acquittal was for an 'ordinary' domestic crime such as assault, and the ICC Prosecutor intends to seek to charge a far graver crime, such as torture as a crime against humanity.[184]

3.2.3.1.5 Gravity Even if the ICC Prosecutor or chamber finds a case presumptively admissible due, for example, to the state's inaction or unwillingness to prosecute, they must ultimately determine the case to be inadmissible if it lacks sufficient gravity to justify trial before the ICC. This factor may evince the intent of the ICC's architects that the Court remain a forum for trying major offenders, like the SCSL and the ICTY subsequent to the adoption of its completion strategy,[185] and that it not become burdened with trials of low-level perpetrators or perpetrators of isolated crimes.[186]

In a joint decision on the ICC Prosecutor's application for arrest warrants for Lubanga and Ntaganda, the Pre-Trial Chamber gave prominent weight to the gravity factor as indispensable for a finding of admissibility.[187] The Chamber held that it is not enough merely that the person in question is suspected of committing one of the crimes listed in the Rome Statute.[188] Instead, 'the relevant

[184] The Rome Statute's drafters purposely chose a 'conduct-based' test in defining the operation of *ne bis in idem* where the national court has tried the person first, and the ICC subsequently intends to try him or her. See Immi Tallgren, 'Article 20: *Ne Bis in Idem*', in in Otto Triffterer (ed.), *Commentary on the Rome Statute of the International Criminal Court: Observers' Notes, Article by Article* (1999), pp. 430–431. Curiously, the drafters chose a different formula for the converse scenario. While an ICC conviction or acquittal categorically bars national courts from re-trying the accused, they are only barred from re-trying for the precise *crimes* for which the ICC tried him or her, and not for any other domestic or international crime, even if based on the same underlying conduct. See Rome Statute, Art. 20(2). Thus, for example, where the ICC has tried a person for torture as a crime against humanity and convicted or acquitted the person, a national court can later try him or her for torture or assault under the national penal code, or even for torture as a war crime, without running afoul of Article 20(2). Some delegates protested this formulation as weakening the protection that *ne bis in idem* should afford the person. See Tallgren, *supra*, p. 428. Delegates on the prevailing side pointed out the widely recognized practice of many national systems of allowing a person to be tried for a crime even if he or she has already been tried for the same crime abroad. They also expressed the view that 'since the ICC does not have jurisdiction over crimes under *national* law, there is a need to ensure that a person who commits such a crime does not escape responsibility simply because in the ICC trial it is not proved beyond reasonable doubt that the acts amounted to a crime in the jurisdiction of the ICC'. *Ibid.*, p. 428 (emphasis in original). See also Lorraine Finlay, 'Does the International Criminal Court Protect Against Double Jeopardy: An Analysis of Article 20 of the Rome Statute', (2009) 15 *U.C. Davis Journal of International Law and Policy* 221, 229–232 (elaborating on the arguments of the two camps).

[185] See *supra* notes 23, 53–55, 58, 68–72 and accompanying text. On gravity in the ICC generally, see Margaret M. De Guzman, 'Gravity and the Legitimacy of the International Criminal Court', (2009) 32 *Fordham International Law Journal* 1400; American University Washington College of Law War Crimes Research Office, *The Gravity Threshold of the International Criminal Court*, March 2008, www.wcl.american.edu/warcrimes/icc/ documents/WCROReportonGravityMarch2008.pdf?rd=1.

[186] See generally Ray Murphy, 'Gravity Issues and the International Criminal Court', (2006) 17 *Criminal Law Forum* 281.

[187] See *Lubanga* Arrest Warrant Decision, *supra* note 136, paras. 43, 62. The *Lubanga* Arrest Warrant Decision was apparently a corrected version and largely a copy of the joint decision, which does not appear on the ICC's website and may still be under seal, but was cited and quoted extensively in the now-public Appeals Chamber ruling. The partial citation of the joint decision is *Situation in the Democratic Republic of the Congo*, Doc. No. ICC-01/04-118-US-Exp-Corr, Decision on the Prosecutor's Application for Warrants of Arrest, Article 58, [date unknown] ('*Lubanga and Ntaganda* Arrest Warrant Decision').

[188] *Lubanga* Arrest Warrant Decision, *supra* note 136, para. 41.

conduct must present particular features which render it especially grave'.[189] In particular, the conduct must be either systematic or large-scale, and must cause 'social alarm' in the international community.[190] According to the Chamber, the gravity factor also requires the ICC to focus on senior leaders suspected of being most responsible for crimes, a standard that mandates analysis of the position of the person in the hierarchy; the role he or she played in the government, rebel faction, or other group in committing crimes; and the criminal role played by the government or organisational entity to which the person belonged.[191] The Pre-Trial Chamber found that the case against Lubanga fulfilled these requirements. Lubanga's rebel army, the FPLC, was suspected of enlisting hundreds of children, a grave war crime causing social alarm in the international community; and Lubanga was sufficiently senior, as he had ultimate control over the FPLC's activities, including the enlistment of children.[192] Ntaganda, by contrast, was not sufficiently senior, as he was not a key decision-maker in the FPLC or its political wing, and did not have authority to change those entities' policies, or to change or prevent their practices.[193] The Pre-Trial Chamber accordingly issued an arrest warrant for Lubanga but denied one for Ntaganda, finding the case against the latter inadmissible.[194]

[189] *Ibid.*, para. 45. Accord *Situation in the Democratic Republic of the Congo*, Doc. No. ICC-01/04-169, Judgment on the Prosecutor's Appeal Against the Decision of Pre-Trial Chamber I Entitled 'Decision on the Prosecutor's Application for Warrants of Arrest, Article 58', 13 July 2006 ('*Ntaganda* Arrest Warrant Appeal Judgement'), para. 59 (quoting *Lubanga and Ntaganda* Arrest Warrant Decision, *supra* note 187, para. 46).

[190] *Lubanga* Arrest Warrant Decision, *supra* note 136, para. 46. Accord *Ntaganda* Arrest Warrant Appeal Judgement, *supra* note 189, para. 56 (quoting *Lubanga and Ntaganda* Arrest Warrant Decision, *supra* note 187, para. 64). Kevin Jon Heller has endorsed the *Lubanga* Pre-Trial Chamber's consideration of what he terms 'situational gravity'. Heller argues that, in choosing which situations to investigate, the ICC Prosecutor has placed too much emphasis on the number of victims and given little weight to other factors that, in Heller's view, are better indicators of a crime's gravity. These factors largely overlap with those identified by the *Lubanga* Pre-Trial Chamber: (1) systematicity, on the theory that crimes committed as part of an organised plan or policy are inherently more grave than those that are not, even though they may involve fewer victims; (2) social alarm in the international community, on the theory that certain crimes – e.g., torture, attacks on peacekeepers, and forced disappearance – cause significant damage to the global rule of law and universal values, even though they often involve far fewer victims than mass atrocities; and (3) state criminality, on the theory that states are generally able to carry out what Heller deems 'system crimes' (among which Heller includes genocide and torture) more effectively than rebel groups. See generally Kevin Jon Heller, 'Situational Gravity Under the Rome Statute', in Carsten Stahn and Larissa van den Herik (eds.), *Future Perspectives on International Criminal Justice* (2010).

[191] See *Lubanga* Arrest Warrant Decision, *supra* note 136, paras. 51–52, 63. Accord *Ntaganda* Arrest Warrant Appeal Judgement, *supra* note 189, para. 60 (citing *Lubanga and Ntaganda* Arrest Warrant Decision, *supra* note 187, paras. 52–53). As support, the Pre-Trial Chamber cited Security Council Resolution 1534, ICTY Rule 28(A), and ICTY Rule 11 *bis*(C), all of which were intended to focus the ICTY's work on senior leaders suspected of being most responsible for crimes. See *Lubanga* Arrest Warrant Decision, *supra* note 136, paras. 55–57. For a discussion of Resolution 1534, ICTY Rule 28(A), and ICTY Rule 11 *bis*(C), see *supra* text accompanying notes 51–55, 58, 68–72.

[192] See *Lubanga* Arrest Warrant Decision, *supra* note 136, paras. 64–75.

[193] *Ntaganda* Arrest Warrant Appeal Judgement, *supra* note 189, para. 63 (citing *Lubanga and Ntaganda* Arrest Warrant Decision, *supra* note 187, para. 87).

[194] *Ibid.*, *supra* note 189, para. 55 (citing generally *Lubanga and Ntaganda* Arrest Warrant Decision, *supra* note 187).

The Appeals Chamber vacated the Pre-Trial Chamber's decision with respect to Ntaganda. It rejected the Pre-Trial Chamber's holding that any crime must be systematic or large-scale to be admissible in the ICC as 'blur[ring] the distinction' between the Rome Statute's jurisdictional requirements for war crimes and crimes against humanity. The Appeals Chamber also noted that the drafters explicitly rejected an absolute requirement that a war crime be systematic or large-scale.[195] The Pre-Trial Chamber's purported 'social alarm' requirement, moreover, is nowhere mentioned in the Statute and would depend, inappropriately, on 'subjective and contingent reactions to crimes rather than on their objective gravity'.[196] The Appeals Chamber also rejected the Pre-Trial Chamber's restriction of admissible cases to the most senior leaders, as such a rule would send a signal to all mid- and low-level offenders that they may engage in criminal conduct free from the spectre of ICC prosecution. Indeed, the Appeals Chamber refused to adopt a categorical test for determining whether a person's role is significant enough to render the case admissible, as governments and other organisations may have 'highly variable constitutions and operations', and 'individuals who are not at the very top ... may still carry considerable influence and commit ... very serious crimes'.[197] The Appeals Chamber remanded the case to the Pre-Trial Chamber for a proper determination of whether to issue an arrest warrant against Ntaganda,[198] and the Pre-Trial Chamber ultimately issued such a warrant.[199] Subsequent chambers that have followed *Lubanga*'s pronouncements on other aspects of the admissibility test have not given prominence to the gravity factor.[200]

Notwithstanding *Ntaganda*, the ICC Prosecutor maintains a policy of focusing on high-level offenders.[201] He has outlined several other factors relevant to his gravity assessment: 'the scale of the crimes; the nature of the crimes; the manner

[195] *Ibid.*, paras. 70–71 (quotation at para. 70). See also Boas, Bischoff, and Reid, *Elements of Crimes*, *supra* note 19, pp. 293–294 (discussing Rome conference debate over whether to exclude isolated war crimes from ICC's jurisdiction).

[196] *Ntaganda* Arrest Warrant Appeal Judgement, *supra* note 189, para. 72. But see Heller, *supra* note 190, p. 233 (arguing that the Appeals Chamber did not foreclose the ICC Prosecutor from considering social alarm when determining whether a given situation is grave enough to warrant an investigation).

[197] *Ntaganda* Arrest Warrant Appeal Judgement, *supra* note 189, paras. 73–77 (quotation at para. 77). See also *ibid.*, paras. 78–80 (finding that the drafters did not intend to limit the ICC's reach to senior leaders, and that the Pre-Trial Chamber's reliance on completion-strategy-induced seniority restrictions in the *ad hoc* Tribunals was misplaced).

[198] *Ibid.*, para. 91.

[199] See *Prosecutor* v. *Ntaganda*, Doc. No. ICC-01/04-02/06-1-US, Décision relative à la requête de l'Accusation aux fins de délivrance d'un mandat d'arrêt, 22 August 2006; *Prosecutor* v. *Ntaganda*, Doc. No. ICC-01/04-02/06-2-Anx-tENG, Warrant of Arrest, 22 August 2006.

[200] See, e.g., *Ngudjolo* Arrest Warrant Decision, *supra* note 143, paras. 21–22; *Katanga* Arrest Warrant Decision, *supra* note 143, paras. 19–21; *Bemba* Arrest Warrant Decision, *supra* note 139, paras. 21–22. See also *supra* text accompanying notes 140–160 (discussing *Lubanga*'s 'same person/same conduct' test, followed in at least two subsequent pre-trial decisions on admissibility).

[201] ICC Office of the Prosecutor, *Report on Prosecutorial Strategy*, September 2006, p. 5, available at www.icc-cpi.int/NR/rdonlyres/699AA4B3-E8C2-4E41-9EFA-EBA503BDBF7F/143694/OTP_ProsecutorialStrategy20060914_English.pdf.

of commission of the crimes; and the impact of the crimes'.[202] The Prosecutor has accordingly declined human rights groups' requests that he proceed against British troops who may have committed war crimes against a handful of victims in Iraq, explaining that the scale of the crimes was too small compared to those involved in the ICC's other cases in the DRC, Uganda, Sudan, and elsewhere.[203] This early practice suggests that the scale of atrocities must be quite extensive before the ICC Prosecutor will agree to devote resources to a case, at least under current budget and staffing restraints.[204] Cases deemed to be of insufficient gravity are left to national authorities, regardless of whether those authorities intend to investigate or prosecute and, if so, are willing or able to do so genuinely.

3.2.3.2 Proceedings on admissibility

The admissibility factors come into play at various stages of the ICC's proceedings on admissibility, when one of the three trigger mechanisms discussed above places a situation on the Court's agenda and the Prosecutor or relevant chamber must then determine whether the case is admissible.[205] The subsections that follow discuss these procedures.

3.2.3.2.1 Preliminary examination by the Prosecutor and pre-trial chamber authorisation for proprio motu *investigation* When a state or the Security Council refers a situation to the Prosecutor, the Prosecutor is not then obliged to open an investigation, but instead must first determine that a 'reasonable basis' exists to do so. The Prosecutor must also perform this 'reasonable basis' inquiry when contemplating whether to open an investigation *proprio motu*.[206]

[202] *Ibid.* ('The policy also means that the Office selects a limited number of incidents and as few witnesses as possible are called to testify. This allows the Office to carry out short investigations and propose expeditious trials while aiming to represent the entire range of criminality'). See also Moreno-Ocampo, *supra* note 128, p. 3 (reiterating in November 2008 the prosecutorial policy of 'focussing on those most responsible'); see ICC Office of the Prosecutor, *Paper on Some Policy Issues before the Office of the Prosecutor*, September 2003, www.icc-cpi.int/library/ organs/otp/030905_Policy_Paper.pdf, p. 3.

[203] See Luis Moreno Ocampo, Letter Dated February 9, 2006, www.icc-cpi.int/library/organs/otp/OTP_ letter_ to_senders _re_Iraq_9_February_2006.pdf. It is quite possible that in this circumstance, the Prosecutor made a pragmatic determination that investigating British soldiers for conduct in the Iraq War would have provided ammunition for opponents of the fledgling Court to brand it as a political tool under the control of opponents of the United States or other Western powers. See generally Heller, *supra* note 190. For more on the Prosecutor's strategy of focusing on the most serious crimes and high-level offenders, which has contributed to his decision to turn down invitations to investigate alleged situations in several countries, see *infra* note 208; William A. Schabas, 'Prosecutorial Discretion v. Judicial Activism at the International Criminal Court', (2008) 6 *Journal of International Criminal Justice* 731, 736–741; De Guzman, *supra* note 185, pp. 1429–1435.

[204] Heller sharply criticises this policy, arguing that the ICC Prosecutor places far too much focus on the number of victims in assessing the gravity of a situation, and not enough on other factors, such as the social alarm caused by the suspected crimes. See *supra* note 190.

[205] See *supra* Section 3.2.2.

[206] Rome Statute, Art. 53(1); ICC Rule 48. See also Turone, *supra* note 132, pp. 1147–1148 (explaining why the 'reasonable basis' test in Article 53 applies to all three trigger mechanisms, despite the confusing wording of the relevant statutory provisions).

The 'reasonable basis' standard is set forth in Article 53 of the Rome Statute, and requires the Prosecutor to forbear from initiating an investigation if one or more of the following four factors is satisfied: (1) the information available provides no reasonable grounds to believe that a crime has been or is being committed; (2) even though such grounds may exist, the crime falls outside the Court's jurisdiction;[207] (3) even though such grounds may exist and the crime appears to fall within the Court's jurisdiction, the case is inadmissible according to one or more of the admissibility factors;[208] and (4) even though reasonable grounds exist to believe a crime within the Court's jurisdiction is being or has been committed and the case would be admissible, '[t]aking into account the gravity of the crime and the interests of victims, there are nonetheless substantial reasons to believe that an investigation would not serve the interests of justice'.[209]

For the third factor, where the Prosecutor finds that a state is genuinely investigating or prosecuting; has prosecuted and convicted or acquitted the person concerned; or has decided not to prosecute, he or she must defer his or her own investigation. The Prosecutor must also decline to investigate where he or she finds that the crimes alleged are not sufficiently grave to warrant prosecution before the ICC, as he has done with alleged crimes in several countries.[210] For the fourth factor, the Office of the Prosecutor has declared that it 'is not required to establish that an investigation or prosecution is in the interests of justice. Rather, [it] shall proceed with investigation unless there are specific circumstances which provide substantial reasons to believe it is not in the interests of justice to do so at that time'.[211] The criteria the Prosecutor considers in making the 'interests of justice' assessment are the gravity of the crimes, including their scale, nature, manner of commission, and impact; and the interests of victims, including their desire to see justice done and the need to protect them.[212] To aid in examining all four factors, the Prosecutor may seek information from states, UN organs, NGOs, and other reliable sources.[213]

If, after examining the four factors, the Prosecutor concludes that no reasonable basis exists to open an investigation into a situation referred by a state party

[207] Rome Statute, Art. 53(1)(a).

[208] *Ibid.*, Art. 53(1)(b).

[209] *Ibid.*, Art. 53(1)(c).

[210] See *supra* text accompanying notes 202–203 (also outlining criteria Prosecutor uses to assess gravity). See also ICC Informal Expert Paper, *supra* note 114, para. 25 (noting that, at this point, 'admissibility is not an issue for litigation and judicial determination, but rather a matter for the OTP to consider and assess in reaching decisions').

[211] ICC Office of the Prosecutor, *Policy Paper on the Interests of Justice*, September 2007, p. 3, available at www.icc-cpi.int/NR/rdonlyres/772C95C9-F54D-4321-BF09-73422BB23528/143640/ ICCOTPInterestsOfJustice.pdf. Accord *Kenya* Request for Authorisation, *supra* note 120, para. 60.

[212] *Ibid.*, pp. 4–6. The highly discretionary nature of this exercise accounts for the pre-trial chamber's ability to compel the Prosecutor to open an investigation where the decision not to investigate is based solely on this factor. See *infra* text accompanying note 219.

[213] Rome Statute, Art. 15(2); ICC Rule 104(2) (providing that such information may be received in the form of written or oral testimony, under the procedure set forth in ICC Rule 47).

or the Security Council, he or she must notify the state or Council and provide the reasons behind the decision.[214] If the Prosecutor decides not to open an investigation *proprio motu*, he or she must similarly notify the NGO, UN organ, or other entity that provided information on the alleged crimes.[215] These latter entities have no recourse to challenge the Prosecutor's decision not to proceed.[216] By contrast, where a state or the Council has referred a situation, it may request the pre-trial chamber assigned to follow the situation to review the Prosecutor's decision. After review, the chamber may request the Prosecutor to reconsider, but with the exception of the circumstance described in immediately below, the Prosecutor retains the discretion, upon reconsideration, to reaffirm the decision not to investigate.[217]

Where the Prosecutor based the decision not to investigate solely on the fourth factor of Article 53 – that is, it is not in the interests of justice to proceed with an investigation – the Prosecutor must additionally notify the pre-trial chamber of the decision and explain the reasons.[218] In this narrow circumstance, and regardless of the trigger mechanism that brought the case before the Prosecutor, the pre-trial chamber may review the decision on its own initiative, and may compel the Prosecutor to investigate notwithstanding the latter's reluctance.[219] The Office of the Prosecutor has adopted a policy whereby it considers a refusal to investigate solely on this ground to be 'exceptional in its nature', and that a 'presumption in favour of investigation' exists 'wherever the [other] criteria [in Article 53] have been met'.[220] If the Prosecutor determines that a reasonable basis to investigate does exist, or the pre-trial chamber orders an investigation, a number of other procedures come into play. These are set forth in Articles 18 and 19 of the Rome Statute, discussed below.[221]

Article 15 provides for several unique additional steps in those situations where the Prosecutor has decided to begin an investigation *proprio motu*. Under Article 15, the Prosecutor must submit a written request for authorisation to the pre-trial chamber, appending supporting material.[222] The pre-trial chamber may then hold

214 ICC Rule 105(1), (3). 215 Rome Statute, Art. 15(6); ICC Rules 49, 105(2).

216 These entities may, however, provide the Prosecutor with new facts or evidence regarding the same situation, and he may reconsider his decision based on this new information. Rome Statute, Art. 15(6).

217 Rome Statute, Art. 53(3)(a); ICC Rule 107 (providing, *inter alia*, that the chamber may request additional documentation from the Prosecutor and further observations from the referring state or Council); ICC Rule 108 (providing, *inter alia*, that the Prosecutor shall inform the pre-trial chamber of his final decision in writing and give his reasons). See also Turone, *supra* note 132, pp. 1156–1157 (the purpose of such judicial review is to avoid 'arbitrary and non-transparent' decisions not to investigate).

218 Rome Statute, Art. 53; ICC Rule 105(4)–(5).

219 Rome Statute, Art. 53(3)(b); ICC Rule 110(2).

220 ICC Office of the Prosecutor, *supra* note 209, p. 1; accord *ibid.*, pp. 2–3.

221 See *infra* Sections 3.2.3.2.2, 3.2.3.2.3.

222 Rome Statute, Art. 15(3); ICC Rule 50(2); see also ICC Court Regulation 49 (setting forth the items the request for authorisation must contain). Victims may make representations to the pre-trial chamber at this stage, and the Prosecutor must notify them of his intent to seek authorisation unless doing so would jeopardise the investigation or the safety of victims and witnesses. Rome Statute, Art. 15(3); ICC Rule 50(1), (3). See also, e.g., *Situation in the Republic of Kenya*, Doc. No. ICC-01/09-11, Victim's Response to the Application

a hearing on the request. If the chamber agrees that a reasonable basis exists for opening an investigation, and that the case appears to fall within the ICC's jurisdiction, it may approve all or part of the request; if not, it may deny it in its entirety. In this assessment, the chamber considers the same four factors considered by the Prosecutor under Article 53, including whether a case arising out of the situation would be admissible.[223] If the chamber denies the request, the Prosecutor may make a subsequent request based on new facts.[224]

In November 2009, the Prosecutor filed his first request for authorisation to begin an investigation *proprio motu*. In seeking permission to investigate crimes committed during the violent episode following Kenya's disputed December 2007 presidential elections, the Prosecutor assessed each of the four Article 53 factors in turn. He argued first that a large quantum of supporting material from UN bodies, NGOs, and other sources provided reasonable grounds to believe crimes against humanity had been committed in Kenya,[225] and urged the Trial Chamber to apply a permissive standard:

> The expression 'reasonable basis' … indicates that a decision to authorize the commencement of an investigation shall be made pursuant to a lower standard than the one required for the issuance of a warrant of arrest or summons to appear. The test of reasonable basis is the lowest found in the Rome Statute.[226]

'To this end', the Prosecutor continued, 'the procedure should be expeditious and summary in nature, without prejudice to subsequent determinations on questions of fact and law'.[227] Second, he asserted that the ICC has jurisdiction over the alleged crimes, as they were committed on the territory of a state party, Kenya, subsequent to the date the Rome Statute entered into force for it, and they constitute crimes against humanity listed in Article 7 of the Statute.[228] Third, he urged the Chamber

of Professors Max Hilaire and William A. Cohn to Appear as Amici Curiae, 20 January 2010. Chapter 8 explores the role and status of victims in international criminal proceedings. See also Turone, *supra* note 132, pp. 1159–1160 (describing this additional step required for *proprio motu* investigations as a compromise motivated by states' wariness of a fully independent Prosecutor, and questioning the wisdom of allowing a single referring state to bypass similar judicial scrutiny).

[223] See ICC Informal Expert Paper, *supra* note 114, para. 26. See also *supra* text accompanying notes 207–209. The chamber's conclusions at this stage do not bind it to reach the same result in subsequent determinations of admissibility and jurisdiction of cases arising out of the situation. Rome Statute, Art. 15(4); ICC Rule 50(5).

[224] Rome Statute, Art. 15(5).

[225] See *Kenya* Request for Authorisation, *supra* note 120, para. 114, pp. 3–4; para. 48. Appended to the request are thirty-four annexes of supporting material. See also *ibid.*, paras. 23–44 (summarising the supporting material).

[226] *Ibid.*, para. 103 (citing, among other academic works, Olásolo, supra note 121, p. 61).

[227] *Ibid.*, para. 106. See also *ibid.*, para. 112 (Prosecutor noting that, in a widely publicised 23 November 2009 notification on Kenya, he provided notice to victims and their legal representatives of his intention to seek authorisation to investigate).

[228] See *ibid.*, paras. 48–50; see also *ibid.*, paras. 62–101 (explaining how the alleged crimes constitute various crimes against humanity listed in the Rome Statute).

to conclude, as he had done, that the cases he would investigate within the situation would be admissible before the ICC because Kenya had instituted no investigations into crimes committed by 'those bearing the greatest responsibility for the crimes against humanity allegedly committed';[229] and the alleged crimes satisfied the Rome Statute's gravity threshold on account of their widespread, systematic, and brutal nature, as well as their devastating impact on the victims.[230] Fourth, the Prosecutor stated that he 'has no reason to believe that the opening of an investigation into the situation would not be in the interests of justice'.[231] The Pre-Trial Chamber will likely rule on the request sometime in 2010.

3.2.3.2.2 Preliminary rulings on admissibility Article 18 of the Rome Statute contains a set of procedures designed to give a state that purports to be dealing with a situation the opportunity to request or require the ICC Prosecutor to defer any investigations to the state's national authorities.[232] These procedures come into play when the Prosecutor is poised to open an investigation, whether *proprio motu* with pre-trial authorisation; on the basis of a state party referral for which the Prosecutor has found a reasonable basis to proceed; or where the pre-trial chamber has ordered the Prosecutor to investigate. They do not apply to investigations opened as a result of Security Council referral.[233] Commentators have explained that this carve-out for Council-referred situations derives from the Council's primacy over states: once the Council has decided under Article VII of the UN Charter that ICC investigations and prosecutions are an appropriate means of maintaining or restoring international peace and security with respect to a given situation, states have no opportunity to request or compel deferral (though they can later challenge jurisdiction or admissibility under Article 19, as described below).[234] Another reason for the carve-out may be because the Council resolution referring the situation is presumed to put all UN member states on notice that investigations may be forthcoming.

Before opening an investigation, Article 18 requires the Prosecutor to provide notification to all states parties to the Rome Statute as well as 'those States

[229] *Ibid.*, paras. 52–55 (quotation at para. 55) (relying on *Katanga and Ngudjolo* Admissibility Appeal Judgment, *supra* note 2, para. 78). See also *supra* text accompanying notes 154–160 (discussing the *Katanga and Ngudjolo* Appeals Chamber's holding that a state's inaction in investigating or prosecuting renders a case admissible, provided the gravity threshold is met).

[230] See *ibid.*, paras. 56–59.

[231] *Ibid.*, para. 61.

[232] Giuliano Turone characterises Article 18 as 'providing a frankly exaggerated protection to the primacy of national jurisdiction'. Turone, *supra* note 132, p. 1164.

[233] Rome Statute, Art. 18(1). By contrast, the procedures under Article 19 discussed below apply to all situations regardless of the trigger mechanism. See *infra* text accompanying notes 242–255.

[234] See, e.g., Daniel D. Ntanda Nsereko, 'Article 18: Preliminary Rulings Regarding Admissibility', in Triffterer, *supra* note 184, pp. 397–398; see also Leila Nadya Sadat, *The International Criminal Court and the Transformation of International Law: Justice for the New Millennium* (2002), pp. 122–123 (Council referral places the situation on the 'fast track' with respect to challenging admissibility because Article 18 will not apply). On Article 19 challenges to admissibility, see *infra* Section 3.2.3.2.3.

which, taking into account the information available, would normally exercise jurisdiction over the crimes concerned'.[235] Within a month of this notification, a state may notify the Prosecutor that it is investigating or has investigated a person for criminal conduct possibly qualifying as crimes against humanity, war crimes, or genocide, where such conduct relates to the information in the Prosecutor's notification. If the state so requests, the Prosecutor must defer any investigation unless the pre-trial chamber rules, upon the Prosecutor's motion, that the investigation may proceed.[236] In deciding whether to allow the investigation to proceed or to order deferral, the pre-trial chamber examines the Prosecutor's motion along with any submissions the state may file before the chamber, and may hold a hearing. The chamber analyses the state's investigation or prosecution through the lens of the admissibility factors to consider, among other factors, the genuineness of the national proceedings, including the state's willingness and ability to prosecute.[237]

Whether the Prosecutor chooses to defer to the state's investigation,[238] or is ordered to do so by the pre-trial chamber, the deferral is open to review after six months, or whenever 'there has been a significant change of circumstances based on the State's unwillingness or inability genuinely to carry out the investigation'.[239] In such a circumstance, the Prosecutor may reapply to the pre-trial chamber for authorisation to investigate.[240] Pending a ruling by the pre-trial chamber or at any time after the Prosecutor has deferred an investigation, the Prosecutor may seek pre-trial authorisation 'to pursue necessary investigative steps for the purpose of preserving evidence where there is a unique opportunity to obtain important

[235] Rome Statute, Art. 18(1); ICC Rule 52 (Prosecutor shall provide information about the alleged crimes, and state may ask for more information within one month). See also, e.g., *Kenya* Request for Authorisation, *supra* note 120, para. 114, para. 114 (prosecution submitting that, should the Pre-Trial Chamber grant the request to begin an investigation into possible Kenya crimes *proprio motu*, 'it will provide the notice foreseen in Article 18(1) of the Statute'). See also Turone, *supra* note 132, p. 1163 (criticising as 'unacceptable' the need to notify non-party states as such states 'might have no other interest than simply preventing justice from being done'). The Prosecutor may notify states confidentially, and may limit the scope of the information provided to prevent the destruction of evidence or the absconding of persons. Rome Statute, Art. 18(1). See also Prosecutor Opens Investigation in the Central African Republic, Doc. No. ICC-OTP-20070522-220, www.icc-cpi.int/menus/icc/press%20and%20media/press%20releases/ 2007/prosecutor%20opens%20 investigation%20in%20the%20central%20african%20republic?lan=en-GB (publicly announcing decision to open investigation).

[236] Rome Statute, Art. 18(2); ICC Rule 53 (state must provide Prosecutor with information concerning its investigation); ICC Rule 54 (procedure for Prosecutor's application to pre-trial chamber to authorise investigation notwithstanding state's concurrent investigation, and for notification to state that this application was made). The Prosecutor may revisit his deferral where circumstances have changed, and may request the state to report periodically on the progress of its investigations and prosecutions. Rome Statute, Arts. 18(3), 18(5).

[237] ICC Rule 55(1)–(2). See also *supra* Section 3.2.3.1 (Article 17 factors). The Prosecutor or state may appeal the pre-trial chamber's decision to the Appeals Chamber. Rome Statute, Art. 18(4).

[238] Where he defers, the Prosecutor may request periodic updates from the state on the progress of its investigations and prosecutions. *Ibid.*, Art. 18(5).

[239] *Ibid.*, Art. 18(3).

[240] *Ibid.*; ICC Rule 56 (providing, among other things, that the same procedures apply to a challenge made prior to deferral, as set forth in Rules 54 and 55).

evidence or there is a significant risk that such evidence may not be subsequently available'.[241]

3.2.3.2.3 Challenges to admissibility In an additional manifestation of the Rome Statute's significant deference to states' prerogative to exercise their own criminal jurisdiction over international crimes, Article 19 of the Rome Statute provides a further layer of protection to states that purport to be dealing with a case, as well as suspects or accused who object to jurisdiction or admissibility before the ICC. Regardless of the trigger mechanism that brought a case before the Court, the pre-trial chamber, or another chamber in a later phase of proceedings, may on its own motion determine the case's admissibility under the admissibility factors discussed above, and must satisfy itself that the Court has jurisdiction.[242]

Furthermore, several other entities can raise challenges to admissibility or jurisdiction. These include (1) a suspect for whom the Court has issued an arrest warrant; (2) the accused; (3) a state party with jurisdiction that purports to be investigating or prosecuting the case or to have done so; or (4) a non-party state that has accepted the Court's jurisdiction on an *ad hoc* basis.[243] The Prosecutor may then request a ruling from the relevant chamber on whether the investigation or ICC proceedings can move forward notwithstanding the challenge.[244] In evaluating a challenge under Article 19, the chamber accepts submissions from the Prosecutor and the challenging entity, and may hold a hearing.[245]

Each challenging entity has just one opportunity to raise a jurisdiction or admissibility challenge and must do so prior to or at 'the commencement of the trial'.[246] The relevant chamber will consider the merits of additional challenges filed by the same entity, or any challenge filed after 'the commencement of the trial', only where the chamber has granted leave for the entity to make the challenge.[247] Where the entity is challenging admissibility and waits until after 'the commencement of

241 Rome Statute, Art. 18(6); see also ICC Rule 57. Investigations are discussed in greater detail in Chapter 4, Section 4.1.

242 Rome Statute, Art. 19(1). The Appeals Chamber has expressed disapproval of *sua sponte* admissibility reviews in *ex parte* proceedings in which only the prosecution participates, particularly where '(a) admissibility was not raised in the Prosecutor's ex parte application, (b) the review was ex parte without the participation of the suspect, victims or entities and (c) no ostensible cause or self evident factor was manifest impelling the exercise of proprio motu review'. *Ntaganda* Arrest Warrant Appeal Judgement, *supra* note 189, para. 53 (disapproving of Pre-Trial Chamber's decision to examine admissibility *sua sponte* before granting *ex parte* application for arrest warrant).

243 Rome Statute, Art. 19(2), (4). Where the challenging entity is a state, it 'shall make the challenge at the earliest opportunity', *ibid.*, Art. 19(5), and the Prosecutor must cease his investigation until the relevant chamber decides on the challenge, *ibid.*, Art. 19(7).

244 *Ibid.*, Art. 19(3).

245 ICC Rule 58. Victims who have already communicated with the Court in relation to the case, or the entity that referred the related situation, may also make representations to the chamber. ICC Rule 59(3). The participation of entities other than the prosecution may be restricted, however, where *ex parte* proceedings are necessary, for example, to maintain confidentiality to prevent a suspect from going into hiding. See *Ntaganda* Arrest Warrant Appeal Judgement, *supra* note 189, paras. 30–31.

246 Rome Statute, Art. 19(4). 247 *Ibid.*

the trial', and even if the chamber has granted leave to file the challenge, the entity may only base the challenge on a *non bis in idem* argument that the accused has already been tried and convicted or acquitted in a national court.[248]

Katanga filed an admissibility challenge before the Trial Chamber after the Pre-Trial Chamber had confirmed the charges against him (the point at which the case passed from the Pre-Trial Chamber to the Trial Chamber), but prior to opening statements or the presentation of evidence in his trial, arguing that the DRC was willing and able to try him.[249] He had not first sought the Trial Chamber's leave to file the challenge. After a lengthy examination of the Rome Statute, its *travaux*, and other sources, the Trial Chamber determined that 'the commencement of the trial' has several potential meanings in the different places where it appears in the Statute, but that in Article 19 it means prior to the confirmation of charges decision, not prior to opening statements – an event that typically takes place several months after the confirmation of charges.[250] Nevertheless, because the meaning of 'the commencement of the trial' for purposes of Article 19 had been murky up to that point, the Trial Chamber found that Katanga had been reasonably unaware that he should have filed the challenge prior to the confirmation of charges decision.[251] The Trial Chamber thus opted to consider the challenge on its merits and, as discussed above, ultimately denied it, and the denial was affirmed on appeal.[252]

As the *Katanga and Ngudjolo* case demonstrates, it is the pre-trial chamber that rules on Article 19 challenges to admissibility prior to the confirmation of charges; after the confirmation of charges, the trial chamber handles such challenges.[253] Where the chamber has ruled in favour of the challenging entity and adjudged the case inadmissible, the Prosecutor may ask the chamber to revisit its decision if new facts arise which the Prosecutor believes render the case admissible.[254] In any event, where the Prosecutor defers an investigation voluntarily or on the chamber's order, the Prosecutor may request updates from the state that claims to be dealing with the case.[255]

[248] *Ibid.*, Art. 19(4) (challenge may only be based on Article 17(1)(c)); see also *supra* Section 3.2.3.1.4. At his initial appearance before the Pre-Trial Chamber in February 2008, Ngudjolo, represented by duty counsel, raised a challenge his case's admissibility on the ground that a DRC court had already tried and acquitted him. His permanent counsel chose not to pursue this challenge subsequently, however, probably because Ngudjolo had not, in fact, been tried in the DRC. See Finlay, *supra* note 184, pp. 245–247.

[249] See *Katanga* Admissibility Challenge, *supra* note 151, para. 61; *Katanga and Ngudjolo* Admissibility Trial Decision, *supra* note 153, para. 8 (Katanga explaining that he filed the motion so late, among other reasons, because it was only after the hearing on the confirmation of charges that he had enough information to determine whether he had grounds to challenge admissibility).

[250] See *ibid.*, paras. 29–50.

[251] See *ibid.*, paras. 56–58.

[252] See *supra* text accompanying notes 153–160, 175.

[253] Rome Statute, Art. 19(6); ICC Rule 133. Decisions on jurisdiction or admissibility may be appealed to the Appeals Chamber. On procedures related to the confirmation of charges in the ICC, see Chapter 6.

[254] Rome Statute, Art. 19(10); ICC Rule 62.

[255] Rome Statute, Art. 19(11).

3.2.4 Self-referral

As mentioned above,[256] most situations currently before the ICC were referred by the states parties on whose soil the alleged crimes were committed, and which would ordinarily be expected to exercise territorial jurisdiction over them. As early as 2003, the Prosecutor began to encourage this practice for a number of reasons, including that the self-referring state is more likely to cooperate with the investigation, which gives the Prosecutor's staff more freedom of movement and security on the territory.[257] Moreover, while the Security Council has referred one situation to the Court, Council referrals and referrals by third states will probably be rare in practice.[258] And despite the recent request for pre-trial chamber authorisation to use the *proprio motu* power to begin investigations in Kenya,[259] the Prosecutor may be generally expected to make sparing use of this power, given the additional procedural steps required to secure approval of a *proprio motu* investigation and states' concerns with respect to the power.[260]

As predicted by the Prosecutor, the states that have referred situations from their own territories have tended to be cooperative. Self-referral has also allowed states to avoid the diplomatic complications that would ensue from denouncing other states. In cases arising out of self-referred situations, chambers have tended to apply the ICC's admissibility procedures rather laxly. In the *Uganda* situation, the Pre-Trial Chambers did not even analyse the facts through the lens of the admissibility factors discussed above, but instead gave significant weight to Uganda's own pronouncement as to its inability to investigate or prosecute, and found cursorily that the cases 'appear[] to be admissible'.[261] The Pre-Trial Chambers in *Lubanga* and the subsequently joined *Katanga* and *Ngudjolo* cases have been less willing to regard the DRC's declaration of inability from its 2004 self-referral letter as still true, yet they have easily found the cases admissible based on the 'same person/same conduct' test described above, without delving into the sensitive question of the DRC's inability or unwillingness to investigate or prosecute.[262] While not following the same person/same conduct test, the Trial and Appeals Chambers in

[256] See *supra* text accompanying note 124.

[257] ICC Office of the Prosecutor, *supra* note 129, p. 5. For an example of a government's letter referring a situation to the Prosecutor on the ground that it is unable to investigate and prosecute, see Letter from DRC President Joseph Kabila to ICC Prosecutor Luis Moreno Ocampo, *supra* note 140. See also *Kony* Arrest Warrant Decision, *supra* note 141, para. 37 (quoting relevant portion of Uganda government's referral letter).

[258] Paola Gaeta, 'Is the Practice of "Self-Referrals" a Sound Start for the ICC?', (2004) 2 *Journal of International Criminal Justice* 949, 950–951.

[259] See *supra* text accompanying notes 119–120, 134, 225–231.

[260] On the additional steps required, see *supra* text accompanying notes 222–224; on states' anxiousness over the *proprio motu* power and the Prosecutor's response to this anxiousness, see *supra* text accompanying notes 131–134.

[261] See, e.g., *Kony* Arrest Warrant Decision, *supra* note 141, para. 38. See also *supra* notes 141, 148. The Article 17 factors are discussed in Section 3.2.3.1, *supra*.

[262] See *supra* text accompanying notes 140–148.

Katanga and Ngudjolo readily found the case admissible as well. At a later stage of the case, the DRC reaffirmed to the Trial Chamber that it still had no intention of trying Katanga, and the Trial Chamber, like the Pre-Trial Chambers in the *Uganda* situation, took the DRC at its word and construed the lack of intention as 'unwillingness' under the Rome Statute.[263] And as the Pre-Trial Chamber had done before it, the Appeals Chamber skirted the question of unwillingness and inability entirely, finding that the DRC authorities' voluntary cessation of investigations into possible crimes by Katanga, even though prompted by the DRC's desire to see Katanga prosecuted before the ICC, constituted inaction rendering the case admissible before the ICC.[264] The *Katanga and Ngudjolo* case thus presents the scenario in which a Chamber in each of the three Divisions of the ICC reached the same conclusion – that Katanga's case is admissible – through its own unique interpretation of the various admissibility factors in the Rome Statute.[265] None of the Chambers expressly disavowed the others' construction of the Rome Statute's complementarity provisions, and a future chamber could theoretically employ any of them. All of these constructions make finding admissibility a straightforward task whenever a state such as the DRC wishes to abdicate its responsibilities to investigate or prosecute in favour of the ICC.

Even though self-referral has helped get the ICC off the ground, and the ICC Prosecutor and judges at all levels seem to have embraced it wholeheartedly, some commentators have been sharply critical of the practice, for two main reasons. First, a key purpose behind the Rome Statute is to encourage states to prosecute crimes themselves, with the ICC stepping in only as a last resort. Yet self-referral allows even states with relatively robust judicial systems, such as Uganda, to hand off to the resource-limited Court cases they may have been able to genuinely investigate and prosecute themselves. Second, and more alarmingly, self-referral has allowed states like Uganda to seek the Court's intervention as a means of driving rebel enemies into hiding and weakening their war effort.[266] In such situations, states might withdraw their cooperation if the Prosecutor were to begin actively investigating the government's own alleged war crimes, which may serve as a deterrent to investigations. By comparison, the ICTR Office of the Prosecutor, dependent on cooperation from the Rwandan government in conducting investigations and securing the attendance of witnesses, has been accused of one-sidedness for its failure

[263] See *supra* text accompanying notes 169–172.

[264] See *supra* text accompanying notes 154–160, 174–175.

[265] See *supra* Section 3.2.3.1 (discussing the admissibility factors).

[266] For more on these and other reasons, see Gaeta, *supra* note 258, p. 952; Claus Kreß, '"Self-Referrals" and "Waivers of Complementarity": Some Considerations in Law and Policy', (2004) 2 *Journal of International Criminal Justice* 944, 946–948; Schabas, *supra* note 123, pp. 147–151; Mahnoush H. Arsanjani and W. Michael Reisman, 'The Law-in-Action of the International Criminal Court', (2005) 99 *American Journal International Law* 385, 392–397; William W. Burke-White, 'Complementarity in Practice: The International Criminal Court as Part of a System of Multi-Level Global Governance in the Democratic Republic of Congo', (2005) 18 *Leiden Journal of International Law* 557, 567–568.

to investigate alleged crimes committed by the Rwandan Patriotic Front, in power in Rwanda since mid-1994.[267] The ICC Prosecutor has attempted to deflect similar accusations. [268]

3.2.5 Security Council deferral

Article 16 of the Rome Statute gives the Security Council the unique power to preclude the Prosecutor or Court from commencing or continuing an investigation or prosecution for a twelve–month renewable period, provided the Council acts under Chapter VII of the UN Charter. The Council can impose this suspension regardless of the trigger mechanism that put the case before the Court.[269] Article 16 was a compromise intended to assuage the concerns of some states that the ICC might interfere with the Council's prerogative to deal with threats to peace and security by inserting itself into the matter improvidently. The provision has been used twice – in 2002 and in 2003 – both times at the prompting of the United States. The United States threatened to veto Council resolutions renewing the mandate of peacekeeping missions unless the Council passed a resolution prohibiting the ICC from investigating or prosecuting peacekeepers from non-parties to the ICC, a large number of whom are U.S. nationals.[270] In the operative text of the 2003 resolution, the Council:

Requests, consistent with the provisions of Article 16 of the Rome Statute, that the ICC, if a case arises involving current or former officials or personnel from a contributing State not a Party to the Rome Statute over acts or omissions relating to a United Nations established

[267] See especially Luc Reydams, 'The ICTR Ten Years On: Back to the Nuremberg Paradigm?', (2005) 3 *Journal of International Criminal Justice* 977.

[268] Moreno-Ocampo, *supra* note 128, p. 6 ('[M]y Office evaluates the crimes committed, their gravity and national proceedings. I have to apply the law. Nothing more, nothing less. The decision that ending impunity will ensure lasting peace and security was taken in Rome. I should not, and I will not take into consideration political considerations.'). Some quarters have criticised the Prosecutor's decision to push ahead with investigations in Sudan because to do so not only hinders humanitarian aid efforts in Darfur, but also jeopardises the fragile peace in South Sudan, which is scheduled to hold a referendum on self-determination in 2011, and weakens the prospects of a negotiated end to the Darfur conflict. See, e.g., CNN News, 'African Union Urges United Nations to Halt al-Bashir Case', 5 February 2010, www.cnn.com/2010/WORLD/africa/02/05/sudan.bashir.genocide/index.html#cnn STCText (discussing African Union request to UN Security Council to order deferral of case of Sudanese President Bashir on these grounds); 'Compounding the Crime', *The Economist*, 12 March 2009 (describing disruptions in foreign humanitarian activities after the ICC issued an arrest warrant for Bashir), available at www.economist.com/opinion/displaystory.cfm?story_id=E1_TPNSRNDJ. The Prosecutor's insistence on pressing for the apprehension of the Sudan suspects – and especially Bashir – lends some credibility to his assurances that politics do not play a role in his decision-making. See, e.g., Luis Moreno-Ocampo, Statement to the United Nations Security Council on the Situation in Darfur, Sudan, 5 June 2009, para. 37 ('There will be no impunity in Darfur. Justice proceedings are in motion.'), available at www.icc-cpi.int/NR/rdonlyres/8A4EAC94-694F-4365-90E4-862438D1731D/280453/OTPSpeech05062009_Engl.pdf; Luis Moreno-Ocampo, Address at Yale Law School, 6 February 2009, www.icc-cpi.int/NR/rdonlyres/F04CB063-1C1E-463E-B8FB-5ECE076FB1E0/ 279792/090206_ProsecutorskeynoteaddressinYale.pdf, p. 9. His refusal to investigate possible British war crimes in Iraq, however, may produce the opposite impression. See *supra* note 203.

[269] Turone, *supra* note 132, pp. 1144–1145.

[270] See Security Council Resolution 1422, UN Doc. S/RES/1422 (2002); Security Council Resolution 1487, UN Doc. S/RES/1487 (2003) (France, Germany, and Syria abstaining). For criticism of this use of Article 16,

or authorized operation, shall for a 12-month period starting 1 July 2003 not commence or proceed with investigation or prosecution of any such case, unless the Security Council decides otherwise.[271]

The 2002 resolution was unanimous. When the Security Council voted on the 2003 resolution, however, France, Germany, and Syria abstained. Following the revelation in early 2004 that detainees at Abu Ghraib prison in Iraq had been abused by U.S. servicemembers, support among the Council's members for another exemption waned significantly, and the United States withdrew its request to renew the exemption for another year. No country has since sought to invoke Article 16.

3.2.6 Other procedures on cooperation deriving from the complementarity regime

As it is for the *ad hoc* Tribunals, the assistance of states, along with international organisations and individuals, is critically important to the functioning of the ICC, for reasons given earlier in this chapter.[272] Like Article 28 of the ICTY and ICTR Statutes, the Rome Statute has a general provision – Article 86 – obliging states to 'cooperate fully' with the Court. Yet the lengthy and complex articles that follow Article 86 reveal that, in contrast to the *ad hoc* Tribunals, the ICC's powers to compel cooperation are severely circumscribed, with many grounds on which a state may permissibly refuse to cooperate.[273] This weakness derives from the negotiating process that led to the Rome Statute and the latter's status as a creature of multilateral consent binding only on those states that choose to ratify it, as opposed to an instrument created by the Security Council through a Chapter VII resolution binding on all UN member states, regardless of consent.[274] The resulting cooperation regime is partly vertical and partly horizontal, with many provisions resembling rules of state-to-state cooperation in legal matters.[275] We sketch here some of the ICC's more important cooperation rules.

see, e.g., Carsten Stahn, 'The Ambiguities of Security Council Resolution 1422 (2002)', (2003) 14 *European Journal of International Law* 85.

271 Security Council Resolution 1487, *supra* note 270, para. 1.

272 See *supra* text accompanying note 92 (providing four main reasons).

273 For an analysis of the many limitations imposed on the Court by these grounds of refusal, see Cryer, *supra* note 27, pp. 149–160.

274 The lack of obligation on non-party states has at least two exceptions, however. First, when the Security Council invokes Article 13(b) of the Rome Statute to refer a case under Chapter VII of the UN Charter, and specifically requires the cooperation of a non-party, as it did with Sudan. See Security Council Resolution 1593, *supra* note 127, para. 2 (deciding that Sudan 'shall cooperate fully with and provide any necessary assistance to the Court and the Prosecutor' and recognising that other 'States not party to the Rome Statute have no obligation under the Statute', but urging 'all States and concerned regional and other international organizations to cooperate fully'). Second, when a non-party state accepts the ICC's jurisdiction on an *ad hoc* basis under Article 12(3), and enters into an agreement with the Court under Article 87(5) to provide assistance. See Rome Statute, Arts. 12(3), 87(5).

275 See Bert Swart, 'General Problems', in Cassese, Gaeta, and Jones, *supra* note 24, p. 1594. See also generally Phakiso Mochochoko, 'International Cooperation and Judicial Assistance', in Lee, *supra* note 129, p. 305.

First, states have a duty to comply with requests to arrest suspects and surrender them to the ICC. Where another state has also made a request for the suspect's extradition, however, a complex procedure derived from state-to-state extradition law applies; in some circumstances, the procedure may allow the requested state to refuse the Court's request in favour of the requesting state's. Moreover, in another provision inspired by extradition law, where a state surrenders to the Court a suspect on the condition that he or she only be tried for certain crimes, the Court may not try him or her for other crimes without the surrendering state's consent.[276] This contrasts sharply with the ICTY, which has held unequivocally that it is not bound by extradition-law restrictions.[277]

Second, states have a duty to comply with a number of other requests for cooperation including, for example, to gather and preserve evidence, question suspects, execute searches and seizures, and protect victims and witnesses. Several exceptions apply to this broad duty, however. For example, the carrying out of such requests is subject to 'procedures of national law'; the state may postpone action if it would interfere with its own ongoing investigations or prosecutions; and the Court must modify the request where the state insists that the request conflicts with an 'existing fundamental legal principle of general application'.[278] This latter term is left undefined in the Statute, has benefited from little elucidation in academic literature, and seems to provide states with a vague and shifting basis on which to refuse cooperation.[279] Third, as a corollary of these rules and exceptions, the Prosecutor faces significant limitations on his power to investigate. The Rome Statute envisions that investigative and law enforcement functions will be carried out by the authorities of the state, and not, as in the ICTY and ICTR, by teams from the Office of the Prosecutor. Two narrow exceptions allow the Prosecutor to operate directly on the state's territory: if the activity is essential and can be carried out in a public place without compulsory measures, provided the state is the territory of the alleged crime and the case has been deemed admissible, or the state consents;

276 On the duty to arrest and surrender, including in urgent situations, see Rome Statute, Arts. 89, 91, 92; ICC Rules 181–184, 187–189; on competing requests, see Rome Statute, Art. 90; ICC Rule 186; on conditional surrender, see Rome Statute, Art. 101; ICC Rule 196.

277 See *supra* text accompanying note 82.

278 Rome Statute, Arts. 93(1) (first quotation), 93(3) (second quotation), 94, 96, 99(1). Moreover, states do not have to comply with requests for assistance not enumerated in Article 93(1) if such compliance would be prohibited under national law, but any such state must first determine whether the assistance can be provided subject to conditions or in an alternative manner. Rome Statute, Art. 93(1)(l), (5). States may also refuse assistance where providing it would prejudice national security. A complex procedure governs the determination of whether the state has properly invoked national security concerns. Rome Statute, Arts. 72, 93(4).

279 See, e.g., David Hunt, 'The International Criminal Court: High Hopes, "Creative Ambiguity" and an Unfortunate Mistrust of International Judges', (2004) 2 *Journal of International Criminal Justice* 56, 69; Claus Kreß, 'The Procedural Law of the International Criminal Court in Outline: Anatomy of a Unique Compromise', (2003) 1 *Journal of International Criminal Justice* 603, 615–616.

or if a pre-trial chamber authorises a limited investigation after finding that the state is clearly unable to execute a request for cooperation.[280]

Fourth, the ICC lacks the power to subpoena individuals, whether in a private or official capacity.[281] Judging from the great frequency with which chambers have used the subpoena power in the *ad hoc* Tribunals to summon recalcitrant witnesses and compel them to testify, this restriction could have especially grave consequences for the ability of the ICC to effectively conduct trials. Fifth, states that have agreed to imprison persons convicted in the ICC are generally bound to accept the sentence handed down by the Court. Like the *ad hoc* Tribunals, the Court retains the authority to supervise the enforcement of the sentence, and has sole authority to decide on requests for revision or reduction of the sentence.[282]

The Rome Statute contains similar remedies for the failure of states and individuals to cooperate with the Court to those contained in the *ad hoc* Tribunals' Statutes and Rules. With regard to states, a chamber of the Court may make a judicial finding that the state has failed to cooperate. Once such a finding is made, the Court may then report the matter to the Assembly of States Parties or, if the Security Council referred the situation in question, to the Council.[283] While either remedy can be expected to be cumbersome and ineffectual, referral to the Assembly will be especially so, as that body's sanctioning powers appear to be very limited.[284] For individuals, the Rome Statute lists a number of offences against the administration of justice, including giving false testimony and intimidating witnesses, for which the Court may put the individual on trial.[285] Persons convicted of an offence against the administration of justice may be sentenced to a term of imprisonment or fined, or both.[286]

3.3 Conclusion

Primacy and complementarity have emerged as the two main alternatives for structuring the legal relationship between an international criminal tribunal and national

[280] See Chapter 4, Section 4.1.3.2. See also Rome Statute, Arts. 57(3)(d), 99(4); ICC Rule 115.

[281] See also Rome Statute, Art. 93(1)(e), (7).

[282] See Chapter 10, Section 10.5. See also Rome Statute, Arts. 103(2), 105, 106, 110; ICC Rules 211, 223–224.

[283] Rome Statute, Art. 87(7). See also *ibid.*, Art. 87(5)(b) (Court may submit to Assembly report on non-party state's violation of duty to cooperate under *ad hoc* agreement with Court). On *ad hoc* agreements, see *supra* note 274; on Security Council referral of a case to the ICC, see *supra* text accompanying notes 125–127.

[284] See, e.g., Rome Statute, Art. 112(2)(f) (giving the Assembly the power to '[c]onsider … any question relating to non–co-operation', but failing to go into further detail). See also Antonio Cassese, *International Criminal Law* (2nd edn 2008), p. 351 (lamenting the Rome Statute's silence on whether Assembly can agree on countermeasures or to authorise a state to adopt countermeasures, and the lack of a provision allowing the Security Council to adopt sanctions even in cases not referred to the Court by the Council).

[285] See Chapter 7, Section 7.8.

[286] Rome Statute, Art. 70(1) (listing offences), 70(3); ICC Rules 162–169 (setting forth procedures for investigation and trial). Importantly, the Statute envisions that persons suspected of these offences may be tried in national courts in lieu of the ICC. See Rome Statute, Art. 70(4); ICC Rule 162.

courts, and by extension national prosecutors, international organisations, and individuals.[287] Primacy affords the *ad hoc* Tribunals extraordinary powers vis-à-vis these entities. As an institution created by states seeking to preserve their prerogative to try crimes committed on their territory and keep their nationals out of the ICC's dock, states withheld such broad powers from the ICC, or so they believed.

In recent years, however, the two models have undergone some convergence. As for the *ad hoc* Tribunals, their completion strategies have prompted procedural rules and jurisprudence designed to focus their work on those thought most responsible for particularly heinous crimes. The ICTY, for example, has introduced an admissibility test giving a panel of judges the authority to veto an indictment if it finds that the accused is insufficiently senior.[288] Similarly, ICTY chambers have recognised national courts' interest in trying offenders at home and their competence to do so fairly,[289] and the Tribunal has made some attempts at helping to strengthen judicial, investigative, and prosecutorial capacity in the former Yugoslav states.[290] Departing from the Tribunal's early practice of granting deferral whenever the Prosecutor requested, moreover, at least one ICTY chamber has refused to order a blanket cessation of national investigations into a series of criminal incidents, despite the Prosecutor's assertions that such investigations might interfere with her own.[291] Notwithstanding some early missteps, the ICTR has also referred the cases of some of its indictees to national courts in Europe – though a tense relationship with Rwanda persists.[292]

As for the ICC, prior to the development of jurisprudence on the question, several commentators expressed concerns that the Rome Statute's complex complementarity provisions may give states too many avenues through which to block the Court's ability to assert its jurisdiction over a case.[293] Yet the manner in which chambers at all levels have applied the admissibility test has allowed them to readily find

[287] Academic commentators have posited alternative models. See, e.g., Burke-White, *supra* note 4, pp. 296–302; Frédéric Megret, 'In Defense of Hybridity: Towards a Representational Theory of International Criminal Justice', (2005) 38 *Cornell International Law Journal* 725, 743–748.

[288] ICTY Rule 28(A). See also, e.g., ICTY Rule 11 *bis*. These mechanisms are discussed in Sections 3.1.2 and 3.1.3, *supra*.

[289] See Section 3.1.3, *supra*.

[290] See Burke-White, *supra* note 4, pp. 335–342. For critical views on the ICTY's accomplishments in this regard, see Jane E. Stromseth, 'Pursuing Accountability for Atrocities After Conflict: What Impact on Building the Rule of Law?', (2007) 38 *Georgetown Journal of International Law* 251, 269–276; David Tolbert, 'The International Criminal Tribunal for the Former Yugoslavia: Unforeseen Successes and Foreseeable Shortcomings', (2002) 26 *Fletcher Forum of World Affairs* 7, 13–15.

[291] See Macedonia Deferral Decision, *supra* note 40, paras. 45–52. See also Burke-White, *supra* note 4, pp. 319–328 (giving several reasons why the ICTY's completion strategy has 'shifted the governance structure from one of absolute international primacy toward a new relationship with incentives similar to those of complementarity').

[292] See *supra* note 89 and accompanying text. On the Rwandan judicial system's capacity and ICTR tensions with Rwanda, see, e.g., Ratner, Abrams, and Bischoff, *supra* note 1, pp. 195–198, 228–229.

[293] See, e.g., Burke-White, *supra* note 110, pp. 197–198; Mohamed M. El Zeidy, 'The Principle of Complementarity: A New Machinery to Implement International Criminal Law', (2002) 23 *Michigan Journal of International Law* 869, 909–910, 918, 969–970; Turone, *supra* note 132, p. 1163.

admissibility, particularly in cases where the state that would ordinarily exercise jurisdiction disclaims any intention of investigating or prosecuting, or prefers for some other reason that the ICC assume these responsibilities.[294] These decisions open the Court up to a new criticism: that it has so watered down complementarity that the relationship with national authorities is beginning to resemble a form of primacy, and that this lack of judicial restraint will deter wary non-party states from ratifying the Statute.[295] Indeed, much like the development of the sweeping judge-made Regulations discussed in Chapter 2,[296] the ICC's judges appear to have appropriated for themselves significant new powers not contemplated by the delegates who drafted the Rome Statute.[297]

The extent to which either model will be replicated in future international criminal tribunals is difficult to predict. For a number of reasons, including states' fatigue with funding the expensive ICTY and ICTR bureaucracies for many years beyond their anticipated lifespan,[298] and anxiety on the part of some permanent members of the Security Council at the astonishing degree of activism exhibited by ICTY and ICTR judges since their earliest cases, the Council is unlikely to create another *ad hoc* tribunal vested with extraordinary powers derived from Chapter VII of the UN Charter. The ICC, a permanent court with potentially global reach, is also one of a kind. In contrast to its substantive provisions, it is doubtful that future tribunals will copy the Court's cumbersome complementarity provisions – although some simpler version could be conceivable.[299]

Nevertheless, the *ad hoc* Tribunals and the ICC do provide some lessons for the amount of power a future international or hybrid criminal tribunal may be expected to wield in its relationship of concurrent jurisdiction with national courts. A key factor will be whether the national courts in the relevant country have, or are perceived to have, the wherewithal and willingness to try persons fairly. Where they clearly cannot, the tribunal will be given broad authority to compel the deferral of cases; where they can – or may someday be able to – an admissibility test with elements of complementarity may be the right solution. If recent experience is any guide, one relevant factor will be the suspect's rank or alleged degree of responsibility over physical perpetrators, and another will be the gravity of the

[294] See *supra* Sections 3.2.3.1.1, 3.2.3.1.2; *supra* notes 261–265 and accompanying text.

[295] See, e.g., *Katanga* Admissibility Challenge, *supra* note 151, para. 19.

[296] See Chapter 2, Section 2.2.3.

[297] For more on judicial appropriation of power, see Chapter 12, Section 12.4.

[298] On the phenomenon known as 'tribunal fatigue', see, e.g., Ralph Zacklin, 'The Failings of Ad Hoc International Tribunals', (2004) 2 *Journal of International Criminal Justice* 541.

[299] East Timor's Special Panels for Serious Crimes and the Supreme Iraqi Criminal Tribunal largely copied the Rome Statute's crimes and forms of responsibility, but their procedural rules vary significantly from those of the ICC. See Gideon Boas, James L. Bischoff, and Natalie L. Reid, *Forms of Responsibility in International Criminal Law* (2007), pp. 133, 137, 268, 272, 336, 339, 376, 378; Boas, Bischoff, and Reid, *Elements of Crimes*, *supra* note 19, pp. 120, 132, 207, 210, 311, 314.

accused's and the physical perpetrators' crimes, as gauged by the nature and scale of the crimes, their impact on victims, and perhaps the degree to which the crimes shock the conscience of the international community, or are perceived to do damage to global respect for the rule of law.[300] A future international or hybrid tribunal will probably have greater latitude to divest national courts of graver cases involving higher-level individuals, leaving isolated incidents and lower-level perpetrators to be tried at home, or not at all.[301] Finally, if the Security Council gets involved in the tribunal's creation, or in referring cases to the tribunal, the tribunal is likely to have greater freedom of action in addressing those cases.[302]

[300] See *supra* notes 190, 202 and accompanying text.

[301] But see *Ntaganda* Arrest Warrant Appeal Judgement, *supra* note 189, paras. 73–79 (declining to restrict admissible cases before the ICC to those involving senior leaders).

[302] Any future international or hybrid criminal tribunal will also need the capacity to maintain close links with national prosecutors and courts, to monitor how they carry out investigations, how they search for and arrest suspects, how they try cases, and how they apply the law. The tribunal will also rely on national authorities' assistance in carrying out its own investigations, arrests, and the procurement of witnesses, and in providing a prison for persons it convicts. To perform these duties, the tribunal will need lawyers with expertise in a vast array of domestic laws and judicial, prosecutorial, police, and political infrastructures, so that it may ascertain whether and why the authorities of a given state cannot adequately do the tasks themselves, or when they might be able to resume them following a period of disruption.

4

Investigations, rights of suspects, and detention

CONTENTS

In the predominantly adversarial framework of international criminal law, the investigative phase of international criminal proceedings is largely driven by the prosecution. Although the regulatory structure of each of the international criminal tribunals accords the chambers varying measures of control during the investigative phase, investigative decisions and activities remain largely within the purview and discretion of the prosecution. That discretion, however, is also bounded by rules which explicitly recognise and protect the rights of suspects and other relevant actors during the investigative phase.

At the ICTY, ICTR, and SCSL, the chamber plays only a minor and relatively reactive role in the investigative phase. With no input into the initiation of investigations or regulatory control over the conduct of the investigation, the chamber's role is largely a facilitative one, issuing such orders in aid of the prosecution's work as may be necessary to secure state cooperation.[1] The ICC pre-trial chamber, conversely, plays an authoritative role in certain aspects of the prosecution's investigative activities. Investigations initiated by the ICC Prosecutor *proprio motu* must be authorised by the pre-trial chamber before they can proceed. Additionally, the ICC Prosecutor's decisions not to initiate an investigation or not to prosecute following an investigation are both subject to confirmation by the pre-trial chamber in certain instances. Apart from this enlarged gatekeeping function, however, the ICC pre-trial chamber's role in the conduct of the investigation is largely similar to the other tribunals – facilitating without controlling.

Consistent with the human rights law protections the tribunals are bound to recognise and protect, the rights of suspects during investigations are enshrined in the tribunals' governing instruments. These include the right against self-incrimination; the right to counsel during investigative interviews; the right to the free services of an interpreter and pre-interview rights advisements in a language the suspect understands; the right to be free from arbitrary arrest and detention; the right not to be coerced, threatened, or subjected to torture or cruel and inhuman or degrading treatment; and the right to judicial review of the legality of arrest or detention. The right to judicial review of the legality of detention, however, has been of limited value to accused individuals. When faced with situations in which accused have been transferred to the custody of the tribunals following legally questionable arrests – or even patently unlawful arrests – the tribunals have not found that such arrests deprive them of jurisdiction.

The adjudication of cases before the *ad hoc* Tribunals can be a very lengthy process and it is not uncommon for accused to spend years in detention awaiting trial. The early experience of the ICC suggests that pre-trial detention may similarly be quite lengthy, much of that detention spent awaiting the pre-trial chamber's confirmation hearing. This directly implicates international human rights law in three important respects: the conditions of detention, the right to be tried without undue delay, and the right to apply for release from detention pending trial. While the detention conditions of accused before the international criminal tribunals have generally met – or exceeded – human rights norms, detention pending trial for lengthy periods without release has been more problematic. Lengthy pre-trial

[1] For more on these orders, see Chapter 3, Sections 3.1.4, 3.2.6; Chapter 6, Section 6.3.2.

detentions, shockingly long in comparison to national criminal prosecutions, are quite common. Moreover, despite amendments to the provisional release rules of the *ad hoc* Tribunals and the SCSL designed to bring detention and release practices into compliance with human rights norms, detention appears to be the rule, release the exception. Thus, the provisional release decisions of these Tribunals reveal a gap between the normative aspirations of the rules and the actual treatment accorded the accused.

This chapter begins with a description of the prosecution's discretionary authority to initiate and conduct investigations, detailing the oversight role – if any – that the chamber plays in that process. Section 4.2 discusses the rights of suspects during the investigative phase of proceedings, rights which attach even before arrest and remain applicable throughout the course of the proceedings. The section also details those instances in which accused have challenged the legality of the manner in which they were detained and transferred to the *ad hoc* Tribunals, and the decisions in which those Tribunals have continued to exercise jurisdiction over the cases. Finally, Section 4.3 discusses detention issues, focusing on those which directly implicate international human rights law concerns: the conditions of detention, the length of pre-trial detention, and the tribunals' rules regarding release from detention pending trial.

4.1 Investigations

4.1.1 Initiating investigations

In all the international criminal tribunals, the prosecution is the organ that initiates the investigations.[2] In the ICTY, ICTR, and SCSL, the prosecution's power to initiate and conduct an investigation of crimes within each tribunal's jurisdiction is absolute.[3] Although information may come to the prosecution from virtually any source, there is no formal 'referral' mechanism. Nor is the standard particularly rigorous. The ICTY and ICTR Statutes note that the prosecution 'shall assess the information received or obtained and decide whether there is sufficient basis to proceed'.[4] Moreover, at the *ad hoc* Tribunals, the decision to initiate an investigation is not subject to review, as the prosecution requires no authorisation from the Tribunals' judges to launch or conduct an investigation.

[2] Rome Statute, Art. 15(1) (Prosecutor may initiate investigations *proprio motu* on the basis of information on crimes within the jurisdiction of the Court); ICTY Statute, Art. 18(1) (Prosecutor initiates investigations *ex officio* or on the basis of information obtained from any source); ICTR Statute, Art. 17(1) (same); SCSL Statute, Art. 15 ('The Prosecutor shall be responsible for the investigation and prosecution of persons who bear the greatest responsibility for serious violations of international humanitarian law and crimes under Sierra Leonean law committed in the territory of Sierra Leone since 30 November 1996').

[3] See Robert Cryer, Håkan Friman, Darryl Robinson, and Elizabeth Wilmshurst, *An Introduction to International Criminal Law and Procedure* (2007), p. 366.

[4] ICTY Statute, Art. 18(a); ICTR Statute, Art. 17(1).

With certain well-defined exceptions, the ICC Prosecutor also enjoys a fair degree of autonomy.[5] The ICC Prosecutor must obtain the permission of the pre-trial chamber to conduct an investigation initiated *proprio motu*.[6] The procedures regulating the prosecution's preliminary examinations and the pre-trial chamber's role in authorising *proprio motu* investigations are discussed fully in Chapter 3.[7]

Once the pre-trial chamber has authorised the prosecution to conduct a *proprio motu* investigation, or where the prosecution initiates an investigation following referral, the pre-trial chamber exercises little control over the manner in which the investigation proceeds. Nor does the pre-trial chamber have the authority to order an investigation to end. It would appear that only the Security Council has the authority to stop an investigation, pursuant to its power under Article 16 of the Rome Statute to request the deferral of an investigation or prosecution.[8] Moreover, this power accorded the Security Council is not limited to those situations that were initially referred to the ICC Prosecutor by the Council.

4.1.2 The prosecution's investigative powers and duties

The prosecution's investigatory powers at all the international criminal tribunals are largely similar. It has the power to conduct onsite investigations,[9] collect and examine evidence,[10] and summon and question witnesses, victims, and suspects.[11] In carrying out any of these particular tasks, the prosecution may seek the assistance of the state authorities concerned or, where appropriate, relevant international organisations.[12]

[5] See Carsten Stahn, 'Judicial Review of Prosecutorial Discretion: Five Years On', in Carsten Stahn and Göran Sluiter (eds.), *The Emerging Practice of the International Criminal Court* (2009), p. 249 (noting that, like his counterparts at the *ad hoc* Tribunals, the ICC Prosecutor 'enjoys wide autonomy regarding the selection of cases and the framing of the charges').

[6] As discussed in Chapter 3, Section 3.2.2, there are three 'trigger mechanisms' by which an ICC investigation may begin: (1) a state party may refer a 'situation' to the Prosecutor; (2) the Security Council may refer a situation to the Prosecutor; and (3) the Prosecutor may initiate an investigation *proprio motu* on the basis of information received from any source. Rome Statute, Arts. 13, 15.

[7] See Chapter 3, Section 3.2.3.2.1.

[8] Rome Statute, Art. 16. See also Chapter 3, Section 3.2.5 (discussing Security Council deferral). The request must be made by the Security Council in a resolution adopted under Chapter VII of the Charter. Although the deferral is for a period of twelve months, such requests may be renewed indefinitely. Rome Statute, Art. 16.

[9] Rome Statute, Art. 54(2); ICTY Statute, Art. 18(2); ICTR Statute, Art. 17(2); SCSL Statute, Art. 15(2) (noting also that the SCSL Prosecutor shall be assisted, as appropriate, by the Sierra Leonean authorities concerned); ICTY Rule 39; ICTR Rule 39; SCSL Rule 39. On the manner by which the prosecution conducts onsite investigations, see Chapter 3, Section 3.1.4 (for the *ad hoc* Tribunals); *ibid.*, Section 3.2.6 (for the ICC).

[10] Rome Statute, Art. 54(3)(a); ICTY Statute, Art. 18(2); ICTR Statute, Art. 17(2); SCSL Statute, Art. 15(2); ICTY Rule 39; ICTR Rule 39; SCSL Rule 39.

[11] Rome Statute, Art. 54(3)(b); ICTY Statute, Art. 18(2); ICTR Statute, Art. 17(2); SCSL Statute, Art. 15(2); ICTY Rule 39; ICTR Rule 39; SCSL Rule 39.

[12] Rome Statute, Art. 54(3)(c); ICTY Statute, Art. 18(2); ICTR Statute, Art. 17(2); SCSL Statute, Art. 15(2); ICTY Rule 39; ICTR Rule 39; SCSL Rule 39. On the obligations of states to cooperate with the tribunals, see Chapter 3, Sections 3.1.4, 3.2.6.

The prosecution may also request such orders from the tribunals' judges as may be necessary to conduct the investigation.[13]

Unlike the ICTY, ICTR, and SCSL Prosecutors, the ICC Prosecutor is statutorily required to investigate incriminating and exonerating circumstances equally 'in order to establish the truth'.[14] It remains unclear whether this prosecutorial duty to investigate exculpatory evidence has any practical substantive effect.[15] Whether the duty to investigate exculpatory evidence represents a meaningful departure from the manner in which the Prosecutors at the ICTY, ICTR, and SCSL conduct their investigations is debatable. To the extent that considering conflicting evidence is simply sound investigative practice, it is arguably something which all the international prosecutors engage in, legally duty-bound or not. Moreover, because the duty to investigate exculpatory evidence is broadly defined, its extent is unclear.[16] As yet, the ICC has had no occasion to consider the extent of the duty to investigate exculpatory evidence.

In addition, the ICC Prosecutor is also required to 'respect the interests and personal circumstances of victims and witnesses, including age, gender ... and health, and take into account the nature of the crime, in particular where it involves sexual violence, gender violence or violence against children'.[17] Finally, the ICC Prosecutor has a duty to fully respect the rights of 'persons arising under [the Rome] Statute'.[18] As with the duty to investigate exculpatory evidence, it is unclear whether the addition of these statutory duties represents a substantive departure from previous practice at the other international criminal tribunals.

4.1.3 Prosecutorial requests for state assistance

4.1.3.1 The ad hoc *Tribunals*

During the course of an investigation and 'in case of urgency', the ICTY, ICTR, and SCSL Prosecutors may request any state to provisionally arrest and detain a

[13] Rome Statute, Art. 54(3)(b); ICTY Statute, Art. 18(2); ICTR Statute, Art. 17(2); SCSL Statute, Art. 15(2); ICTY Rule 39; ICTR Rule 39; SCSL Rule 39.

[14] Rome Statute, Art. 54(1)(a). For an argument that the *ad hoc* Tribunals' prosecutors may have a similar duty, see Salvatore Zappalà, 'The Prosecutor's Duty to Disclose Exculpatory Materials and the Recent Amendment to Rule 68 ICTY RPE', (2004) 2 *Journal of International Criminal Justice* 620, 622 (arguing that the duty to search for the truth necessarily implies the obligation to search for any exculpatory evidence, and that such reasoning finds support in the jurisprudence of the ICTY and the ICTR).

[15] See, e.g., Cryer, Friman, Robinson, and Wilmshurst, *supra* note 3, p. 367 (noting the argument that the ICC Prosecutor's obligation to investigate exculpatory evidence, if properly carried out, has the potential to narrow the scope of the case, reducing the number of charges, and possibly the length of the subsequent proceedings).

[16] See, e.g., Alexander Zahar and Göran Sluiter, *International Criminal Law: A Critical Introduction* (2008), p. 374 (noting a need for realism in respect of the prosecution's perceived impartial role in this regard and asking whether it is to be realistically expected that a truly impartial approach is possible in an adversarial model). On the prosecution's obligation to disclose materials of an exculpatory character in the prosecution's possession, see Chapter 6, Section 6.5.1.2.

[17] Rome Statute, Art. 54(1)(b). [18] *Ibid.*, Art. 54(1)(c).

suspect or accused, seize physical evidence, or take any necessary measures to prevent the escape of a suspect or accused, the destruction of evidence, or injury to or intimidation of a victim or witness.[19] Although denoted in the Rules as 'requests', such communications from either the ICTY or ICTR Prosecutors are binding on states because those two tribunals' statutes are an exercise of the Security Council's authority under Chapter VII of the UN Charter.[20] The SCSL Prosecutor enjoys no such enforcement authority. Accordingly, the SCSL Prosecutor's requests for state cooperation are just that – merely requests.

4.1.3.2 The ICC

Unlike the ICTY or ICTR Prosecutors, the ICC Prosecutor has no authority to issue binding orders – or even requests – directly to states. He or she cannot ask states directly to seize evidence, protect witnesses, or arrest suspects or accused. Each of these aspects of the investigation is, instead, dependent upon the pre-trial chamber either requesting the cooperation of the state concerned (a request with which states parties are obligated to comply and non-party states may comply) or authorising investigative activities on the territory of a state party that is unable to execute a request for cooperation.[21]

Part Nine of the Rome Statute details the cooperation that states parties have agreed to provide the Court and, by extension, the ICC Prosecutor. The detailed cooperation regime includes virtually any investigative activity that the prosecution may need to undertake. In addition to agreeing to surrender persons to the custody of the Court,[22] states parties have agreed to comply with the Court's requests to provide the following assistance in relation to investigations or prosecutions: (1) the identification and whereabouts of persons or the location of items; (2) the taking of evidence, including testimony under oath, and the production of evidence, including expert opinions and reports necessary to the Court; (3) the questioning of any person being investigated or prosecuted; (4) the service of documents, including judicial documents; (5) the facilitation of the voluntary appearance of persons as witnesses or experts before the Court; (6) the temporary transfer of persons in custody for purposes of identification or for obtaining testimony or other assistance; (7) the examination of places or sites, including the exhumation and examination of grave sites; (8) the execution of searches and seizures; (9) the provision of records and documents, including official records and documents; (10) the protection of victims and witnesses and the preservation of evidence; (11) the identification, tracing, and freezing or seizure of proceeds, property, and assets and instrumentalities

[19] ICTY Rule 40; ICTR Rule 40; SCSL Rule 40.

[20] See ICTY Statute, Art. 29; ICTR Statute, Art. 28; ICTY Rule 40(A); ICTR Rule 40(A). On the obligations of states to cooperate with the *ad hoc* Tribunals, see Chapter 3, Section 3.1.4.

[21] Rome Statute, Art. 57(3)(d).

[22] See Chapter 3, Section 3.2.6.

of crimes for the purpose of eventual forfeiture, without prejudice to the rights of bona fide third parties; and (12) any other assistance not prohibited by the law of the requested state, with a view to facilitating the investigation and prosecution of crimes within the jurisdiction of the Court.[23]

Additionally, the Court may 'invite' non-party states to provide such investigative assistance, and although not obligated, such states are certainly free to provide that assistance, consistent with any other applicable international or domestic legal constraints.[24] The Court may also seek the assistance of intergovernmental organisations.[25]

Finally, where the prosecution considers an investigation to present a 'unique opportunity to take testimony or a statement from a witness or to examine, collect or test evidence, which may not be available subsequently for the purposes of a trial', the prosecution must notify the pre-trial chamber.[26] Following such notification, the pre-trial chamber may authorise the prosecution to undertake investigative activities within the territory of a state party

> without having secured the cooperation of that State under Part 9 if, whenever possible having regard to the views of the State concerned, the Pre-Trial Chamber has determined in that case that the State is clearly unable to execute a request for cooperation due to the unavailability of any authority or any component of its judicial system competent to execute the request for cooperation.[27]

Given the extensive list of investigative activities that states parties have pledged to facilitate, the opportunity for non-party states to voluntarily cooperate, and the pre-trial chamber's authority to authorise investigative activities on the territory of states parties that are unable to comply, the ICC's regulatory framework does not appear to diminish the ICC Prosecutor's investigative capabilities vis-à-vis those of the prosecution at the *ad hoc* Tribunals. It does, however, subject those investigative activities to the enforcement authority and, in some cases, discretionary oversight of the pre-trial chamber.

4.2 Rights of suspects during investigations

Consistent with the human rights law obligations that the international criminal tribunals are bound to recognise and protect,[28] suspects before the tribunals enjoy

[23] Rome Statute, Art. 93.
[24] *Ibid.*, Art. 87(5) (assistance to be provided 'on the basis of an *ad hoc* arrangement, an agreement with such State or any other appropriate basis').
[25] *Ibid.*, Art. 87(6). [26] *Ibid.*, Art. 56(1)(a). [27] *Ibid.*, Art. 57(3)(d).
[28] For a discussion of the extent to which the international criminal tribunals are bound by international human rights law, see Zahar and Sluiter, *supra* note 16, pp. 276–281 (noting the ways in which human rights 'enter' the legal framework of the various tribunals, and arguing that human rights must be respected

certain rights during the investigative phase of the proceedings just as they do during trial proceedings. These rights are consistently enshrined in the constitutive legal instruments creating the tribunals.

'Suspects' are defined for the *ad hoc* Tribunals and the SCSL as persons 'concerning whom the Prosecutor possesses reliable information which tends to show that the person may have committed a crime over which the Tribunal has jurisdiction'.[29] While the Rome Statute does not use the term suspect, it regulates the prosecution's behaviour – and the behaviour of state authorities acting at the Court's behest – '[w]here there are grounds to believe that a person has committed a crime within the jurisdiction of the Court and that person is about to be questioned either by the Prosecutor, or by national authorities'.[30] The rights enjoyed by such persons are virtually identical to those accorded suspects before the *ad hoc* Tribunals. We refer to such persons generically as 'suspects' throughout this volume.

4.2.1 The right against self-incrimination

Before each of the tribunals, suspects have the right not to be compelled to incriminate themselves or confess guilt. In the *ad hoc* Tribunals, this right is characterised as the right to remain silent 'and to be cautioned that any statement the suspect makes shall be recorded and may be used in evidence'.[31] The right to remain silent – along with the rights to the presence of counsel and the free assistance of an interpreter (discussed below) – are found in Rule 42, common to the ICTY, ICTR, and the SCSL. According to one trial chamber of the ICTY, Rule 42 is 'an adaptation *mutatis mutandi*' of Article 6(3) of the ECHR and Article 14(3) of the ICCPR and is 'based on the most elementary and fundamental provisions for the protection of individual human rights'.[32]

The required advisement by the ICC Prosecutor goes a bit further, informing the suspect that he or she not only has the right to remain silent, but that such silence may not serve as 'a consideration in the determination of guilt or

and applied by the *ad hoc* Tribunals as organs of the UN, and to achieve international cooperation in promoting and encouraging respect for human rights and fundamental freedoms). See also Chapter 1, Section 1.1.5.

29 ICTY Rule 2(A); ICTR Rule 2(A); SCSL Rule 2(A).

30 Rome Statute, Art. 55(2).

31 ICTY Rule 42(A)(iii); ICTR Rule 42(A)(iii); SCSL Rule 42(A)(iii). The right against compelled self-incrimination by a witness during testimony is discussed in Chapter 9, Section 9.3.2.1.

32 *Prosecutor* v. *Delalić, Mucić, Delić, and Landžo*, Case No. IT-96-21-T, Decision on Zdravko Mucić's Motion for the Exclusion of Evidence, 2 September 1997 ('*Čelebići* Trial Decision on Evidence Exclusion'), para. 60. See also *ibid*., para. 43 (characterising Art. 6(3) of the ECHR and Art. 14(3) of the ICCPR as 'the internationally accepted basic and fundamental rights accorded to the individual to enable the enjoyment of a right to a fair hearing during trial').

innocence'.[33] Thus, suspects cannot be compelled to be interviewed by the prosecution, and that refusal cannot be held against them in any subsequent proceedings. Nor can the refusal to answer any specific questions during an interview to which the suspect has voluntarily submitted be held against him or her.

4.2.2 The right to the assistance of counsel during interviews

During any interviews with the prosecution, the suspect has the right to have legal assistance of his or her choosing present, or to appointed counsel if he or she does not have sufficient means to secure counsel.[34] This right to the assistance of counsel has been described as an 'unfettered' right.[35] Although at the *ad hoc* Tribunals the right to the assistance of counsel during questioning nominally applies only to questioning 'by the Prosecutor', the importance of this protection has led to its extension to questioning by other law enforcement authorities.[36] At the ICC, the right to the assistance of counsel applies during questioning either by the prosecution, or by national authorities acting pursuant to a request by the Court.[37] At the ICTY, ICTR, and SCSL, if the suspect waives his or her right to counsel during an interview, but subsequently expresses a desire to have counsel present, questioning must cease, and may resume only once the suspect is represented by counsel.[38]

4.2.3 The right to prior advisement in a language the suspect understands

Prior to any interview with a suspect, the prosecution is required to inform the suspect of the above rights. For each of the tribunals, it must make this advisement in a language the suspect understands. Accordingly, the suspect enjoys the right to an interpreter, free of charge, during the advisement of any of these rights, as well as during the interview itself.[39] However, the suspect is entitled merely to be advised of the applicable rights; there is no requirement that the prosecution explain the rights or their meaning.[40]

[33] Rome Statute, Art. 55(2)(b).

[34] *Ibid.*, Art. 55(2)(c)–(d); ICTY Statute, Art. 18(3); ICTR Statute, Art. 17(3); ICTY Rule 42(A)(i); ICTR Rule 42(A)(i); SCSL Rule 42(A)(i).

[35] *Čelebići* Trial Decision on Evidence Exclusion, *supra* note 32, para. 51 (finding that provisions of Austrian law which restricted the right to the presence of counsel during questioning were 'inconsistent with the unfettered right to counsel in [ICTY Statute] Article 18(3) and [ICTY] Sub-rule 42(A)(i)').

[36] *Čelebići* Trial Decision on Evidence Exclusion, *supra* note 32, para. 55 (holding that questioning by Austrian police which did not comply with the requirements of Rule 42(A)(i) and Rule 42(B) must be excluded). For more on the exclusion of evidence as a remedy for violation of this right, see Chapter 9, Section 9.1.1.2.

[37] Rome Statute, Art. 55(2).

[38] ICTY Rule 42(B); ICTR Rule 42(B); SCSL Rule 42(B).

[39] Rome Statute, Art. 55(1)(c); ICTY Rule 42(A); ICTR Rule 42(A); SCSL Rule 42(A).

[40] See *Čelebići* Trial Decision on Evidence Exclusion, *supra* note 32, para. 58 (rejecting the defence argument that the prosecution's investigators had a duty to explain the provisions of Rule 42, being satisfied that 'the duty is only to interpret to the suspect the rules in a language he or she understands').

4.2.4 *The right to have any interview recorded*

Although not delineated as a 'right' held by the suspect, the Rules of each of the international criminal tribunals require the prosecution to record interviews with suspects. The particular rules regulating the recording of suspect interviews are quite detailed as to the procedures to be followed. At the ICTY, whenever the prosecution questions a suspect, the questioning must be audio- or video-recorded using the following procedure: the suspect must be informed that the questioning is being recorded; breaks in the course of the questioning are to be identified on the recording; at the conclusion, the suspect must be offered the opportunity to clarify anything he or she has said and to add anything he or she wishes to say; a copy of the recording is to be supplied to the suspect; and if the suspect later becomes an accused, the recording must be transcribed.[41]

The ICTR, SCSL, and ICC Rules require the same procedures as the ICTY,[42] and also provide that the suspect is entitled to receive a transcription of the recording whether or not he or she later becomes an accused.[43] Additionally, the original recording is to be sealed in the presence of the suspect and the suspect's counsel under the signatures of the prosecution attorney, the suspect, and the suspect's counsel.

While the *ad hoc* Tribunals' rules do not provide any exceptions to the recording requirement, the ICC envisions two possible exceptions. First, if the suspect refuses to be audio- or video-recorded, the interview may proceed with only a written record being made.[44] Second, a suspect may be questioned without such a recording 'where the circumstances prevent such recording taking place'.[45] Such an interview must proceed with a written record being made, and the reasons preventing audio- or video-recording must be noted in the written record.

4.2.5 *The right not to be coerced, threatened, or tortured*

The Rome Statute provides certain explicit rights to suspects during investigations that have no direct counterpart in the governing instruments of the *ad hoc* Tribunals or the SCSL. At the ICC, suspects shall not be subjected to 'any form of coercion, duress or threat, to torture or to any other form of cruel, inhuman or degrading treatment or punishment'.[46]

While the *ad hoc* Tribunals' and SCSL's governing instruments contain no similar provisions, each of their Rules provides the chambers with ample authority

[41] ICTY Rule 43. [42] ICC Rule 112; ICTR Rule 43; SCSL Rule 43.
[43] ICC Rule 112(1)(e); ICTR Rule 43(iv); SCSL Rule 43(iv).
[44] ICC Rule 112(1)(a). [45] ICC Rule 112(2).
[46] Rome Statute, Art. 55(1)(b) (applicable not only to suspects but to any person 'in respect of an investigation' under the Rome Statute).

to recognise and appropriately sanction any such violations by the prosecution. No evidence obtained from a suspect under circumstances amounting to coercion, torture, or cruel, inhuman or degrading treatment is admissible at trial against the person.[47] Indeed, even treatment of a suspect falling arguably short of coercion, torture, or cruel, inhuman or degrading treatment may give rise to the exclusion of evidence obtained under circumstances of 'oppressive conduct'.[48] Moreover, one ICTY Trial Chamber has said that 'in a situation where an accused is very seriously mistreated, maybe even subjected to inhuman, cruel or degrading treatment, or torture, before being handed over to the Tribunal, this may constitute a legal impediment to the exercise of jurisdiction over such an accused'; and further noted that '[t]his would certainly be the case where persons acting for [the arresting authorities] or the Prosecution were involved in such very serious mistreatment'.[49]

4.2.6 The right to be free from arbitrary arrest

The Rome Statute provides suspects an explicit right to be free from arbitrary arrest. In respect of an investigation, a person '[s]hall not be subjected to arbitrary arrest or detention, and shall not be deprived of his or her liberty except on such grounds and in accordance with such procedures as are established in [the Rome] Statute'.[50] Moreover, any person who has been the victim of unlawful arrest or detention by the ICC – or by national authorities acting on the Court's behalf – 'shall have an enforceable right to compensation'.[51]

While the *ad hoc* Tribunals' and the SCSL's governing instruments provide no explicit prohibition against arbitrary arrest or detention, each of their Rules – like the ICC's – provides a detailed arrest and surrender regime.[52] As discussed above, the *ad hoc* Tribunals' Prosecutors may, in cases of urgency, directly request any state to provisionally arrest a suspect. Where the prosecution has made such a request and the state has provisionally arrested a suspect, a judge of the tribunal may order the suspect transferred to the tribunal if the judge considers that there is

[47] See ICTY Rule 95 ('No evidence shall be admissible if obtained by methods which cast substantial doubt on its reliability or if its admission is antithetical to, and would seriously damage, the integrity of the proceedings'); ICTR Rule 95 (same); SCSL Rule 95 ('No evidence shall be admitted if its admission would bring the administration of justice into serious disrepute'). See Chapter 9, Section 9.1.1.2 (discussing exclusion of evidence in more detail).

[48] See, e.g., *Čelebići* Trial Decision on Evidence Exclusion, *supra* note 32, paras. 63–70 (noting that statements obtained from suspects by oppressive conduct may also be inadmissible under ICTY Rule 95, and defining oppressive conduct as that which 'saps the concentration and has sapped the free will of the suspect through various acts and weakens resistance rendering it impossible for the suspect to think', and listing the factors to be considered in such an analysis as the characteristics of the person making the statement, the duration of the questioning, and the manner of the exercise of the questioning).

[49] *Prosecutor* v. *Dragan Nikolić*, Case No. IT-94-2-PT, Decision on Defence Motion Challenging the Exercise of Jurisdiction by the Tribunal, 9 October 2002 ('*Dragan Nikolić* Trial Decision on Jurisdiction'), para. 114.

[50] Rome Statute, Art. 55(1)(d). [51] *Ibid.*, Art. 85(1).

[52] See Chapter 3, Section 3.1.4 (for the *ad hoc* Tribunals and SCSL); *ibid.*, Section 3.2.6 (for the ICC).

a reliable and consistent body of material which tends to show that the suspect may have committed a crime over which the tribunal has jurisdiction, and provisional detention is considered necessary to prevent the escape of the suspect, injury to or intimidation of a victim or witness, destruction of evidence, or any other reason necessary for the conduct of the investigation.[53] Such provisional detention is capped at ninety days following the transfer of the suspect to the tribunal's detention facility. In the event that an indictment has not been confirmed and an arrest warrant signed at the end of the ninety-day period, the suspect must be released from detention by the tribunal.[54]

At the ICC, conversely, a suspect may only be arrested following the issuance of an arrest warrant by the pre-trial chamber.[55] The Court will then submit a detailed request for arrest and surrender of the person to any state on the territory of which that person may be found.[56] In urgent cases, the Court may request a state to provisionally arrest a person pending formal presentation of the request for surrender.[57] Such detention is potentially capped at sixty days from the date of the provisional arrest. In the event that the Court's formal request for surrender has not been received within that time, the detaining state may release the person, although such release is without prejudice to the subsequent arrest and surrender of the person if the formal request is later received.[58]

4.2.7 The right to judicial review of the legality of arrest or detention

A problematic aspect of arrest and detention at the *ad hoc* Tribunals is the way in which chambers have dealt with challenges to the legality of an accused's detention

[53] ICTY Rule 40 *bis*(A)–(B); ICTR Rule 40 *bis*(A)–(B); SCSL Rule 40 *bis*(A)–(B).

[54] ICTY Rule 40 *bis*(D); ICTR Rule 40 *bis*(C), (F)–(H); SCSL Rule 40 *bis*(C), (F)–(H). The initial period of provisional detention is capped at thirty days. However, each of the tribunals provides that the prosecution may request, and the tribunal may order, two successive extensions of thirty days each. The maximum permissible provisional detention period is thus ninety days.

[55] See Rome Statute, Art. 58 (providing that the pre-trial chamber shall issue a warrant of arrest on the application of the prosecution if it is satisfied (1) that there are reasonable grounds to believe that the person has committed a crime within the jurisdiction of the Court; and (2) that the arrest of the person appears necessary to ensure the person's appearance at trial, or to ensure that the person does not obstruct or endanger the investigation or the court proceedings, or, where applicable, to prevent the person from continuing with the commission of that crime or a related crime). See also *ibid.*, Art. 91(2) (providing that a request for arrest and surrender shall include a copy of the warrant of arrest).

[56] For more on states' obligations to cooperate with the ICC in arresting and surrendering suspects, see Chapter 3, Section 3.2.6.

[57] Rome Statute, Art. 92(1).

[58] See *ibid.*, Art. 92(3) (providing that a person who is provisionally arrested may be released from custody if the requested state has not received the request for surrender within the time limits prescribed in the ICC Rules); ICC Rule 188 (providing that for the purposes of Art. 92(3), the time limit for receipt by the requested state of the request for surrender shall be sixty days from the date of the provisional arrest). See also Rome Statute, Art. 92(4) (providing that the release of the person from custody is without prejudice to the subsequent arrest and surrender of the person if the request for surrender and the documents supporting the request are delivered at a later date).

arising from the manner in which some accused have been detained by national authorities, under dubious circumstances, prior to their surrender. The ICTY and ICTR Statutes contain no provision permitting a person directly to challenge the legality of his or her detention. Thus, there is no explicit counterpart of the common law right to *habeas corpus* review.[59] Despite its absence in the constitutive texts of the *ad hoc* Tribunals, however, the jurisprudence has recognised such a right. Early in the *Barayagwiza* case at the ICTR, the accused filed a petition for writ of *habeas corpus* challenging the length of time he was detained by both the Government of Cameroon, where he had been arrested pursuant to an ICTR warrant, and the ICTR. The Trial Chamber failed to rule on the accused's motion, a failure later criticised by the ICTR Appeals Chamber, which found that

> [a]lthough neither the Statute nor the Rules specifically address *writs of habeas corpus* as such, the notion that a detained individual shall have recourse to an independent judicial officer for review of the detaining authority's acts is well-established by the Statute and Rules. Moreover, this is a fundamental right and is enshrined in international human rights norms, including Article 8 of the Universal Declaration of Human Rights, Article 9(4) of the ICCPR, Article 5(4) of the ECHR and Article 7(6) of the [American Convention on Human Rights]. The Inter-American Court of Human Rights has defined the *writ of habeas corpus* as: '[A] judicial remedy designed to protect personal freedom or physical integrity against arbitrary decisions by means of a judicial decree ordering the appropriate authorities to bring the detained person before a judge so that the lawfulness of the detention may be determined and, if appropriate, the release of the detainee be ordered.' Thus, this right allows the detainee to have the legality of the detention reviewed by the judiciary.[60]

In addition to finding that the Trial Chamber had the inherent power to undertake review of the legality of Barayagwiza's detention, the Appeals Chamber held that the Trial Chamber could, as a matter of discretion, decline to exercise jurisdiction over a case 'where to exercise that jurisdiction in light of serious and egregious violations of the accused's right would prove detrimental to the court's integrity'.[61]

Barayagwiza's challenge concerned primarily the length of time he was detained by national authorities and the ICTR before being informed of the charges against him and being given any opportunity to challenge the legality of his detention.[62] Other accused, however, have sought similar review of the legality of their detention based on the manner in which they were taken into custody, arguing that the

[59] See Cryer, Friman, Robinson, and Wilmshurst, *supra* note 3, p. 371 (describing the writ of *habeas corpus* as a 'fundamental feature of the common law jurisdiction' which has long been used domestically as a means of testing the validity of detentions, and noting that it is not applicable, as such, in international criminal proceedings).

[60] *Barayagwiza* v. *Prosecutor*, Case No. ICTR-97-19-AR72, Decision, 3 November 1999, para. 88.

[61] *Ibid.*, para. 74.

[62] For a detailed description of the Appeals Chambers' decisions in Barayagwiza's case, see William A. Schabas, 'Barayagwiza v. Prosecutor', (2000) 94 *American Journal of International Law* 563.

tribunal should decline to exercise jurisdiction over their cases. None of these has successfully convinced a chamber to dismiss the indictment.

Slavko Dokmanović was indicted by the ICTY in 1996 and arrested in 1997, after being enticed by investigators from the ICTY Office of the Prosecutor to travel from Serbia to Croatian territory controlled by the United Nations Transitional Administration for Eastern Slavonia, Baranja, and Eastern Sirmium ('UNTAES'). Dokmanović challenged his arrest, claiming, among other things, that the way he was lured out of Serbia to be arrested constituted kidnapping in violation of the sovereignty of the Federal Republic of Yugoslavia ('FRY'). Acknowledging that the prosecution had deceived Dokmanović, the Trial Chamber nevertheless refused to dismiss the indictment, finding that Dokmanović had not been forcibly abducted or kidnapped, and that 'luring [was] consistent with principles of international law and the sovereignty of the FRY'.[63] For a time following this case, the ICTY Prosecutor appears to have adopted the position of *male captus, bene detentus*,[64] arguing that the legality of arrest was irrelevant because irregularities prior to or during arrest did not affect the jurisdiction of the tribunals.[65]

In the *Dragan Nikolić* case, however, the ICTY rejected the proposition that irregularities in the manner of arrest could never rise to a serious enough level so as to require the Tribunal to refuse to exercise jurisdiction over a case. In April 2000, Dragan Nikolić was kidnapped in Serbia by a number of individuals unconnected to the ICTY, transported across the border to Bosnia and Herzegovina, and delivered into the hands of the NATO Stabilisation Force ('SFOR'), which arrested him and transferred him to the Tribunal's custody. Nikolić challenged the legality of his continued detention, arguing among other things that his forcible abduction violated the sovereignty of the FRY and the due process rights guaranteed to him

[63] *Prosecutor* v. *Mrkšić, Radić, Šljivančanin, and Dokmanović*, Case No. IT-95-13a-PT, Decision on the Motion for Release by the Accused Slavko Dokmanović, 22 October 1997, para. 57. The Trial Chamber acknowledged that there was some authority for the proposition that it may be difficult to distinguish forcible abduction from coercion or fraudulent luring, and that the elements of kidnapping in some national jurisdictions acknowledged that kidnapping could be committed through fraud. However, the Trial Chamber noted that 'on the continuum between force and fraud', it did not believe that the accused was coerced in a way that would justify comparing his luring to a forcible abduction or kidnapping case. *Ibid.*, para. 57 n. 73.

[64] The maxim *male captus, bene detentus* 'expresses the principle that a court may exercise jurisdiction over an accused person regardless of how that person has come into the jurisdiction of the court'. *Dragan Nikolić* Trial Decision on Jurisdiction, *supra* note 49, para. 70. See also *ibid.*, para. 78 (noting that the principle has long caused intensive and sometimes heated debates in judicial, executive, and academic circles); *ibid.*, paras. 79–93 (discussing at length the application of principles similar to *male captus, bene detentus* in national jurisdictions as diverse as the United States, Israel, the United Kingdom, New Zealand, Australia, South Africa, France, Germany, and Zimbabwe).

[65] See Zahar and Sluiter, *supra* note 16, p. 291 (noting that certain NATO states appear to have taken the same position as the ICTY Prosecutor, and describing the case of accused Stevan Todorović, who alleged that he was abducted in Serbia by unknown persons who transported him out of the country to be arrested by NATO forces, and the manner in which 'an escalating cooperation dispute, which would seriously damage the prosecutor's arrest strategy' led to the settlement of the case by plea agreement). See also *ibid.*, p. 290 (arguing that in subsequent cases 'the *ad hoc* Tribunals "as human rights courts" have distanced themselves from *male captus bene detentus* as a matter of principle').

by the ICTY Statute to such an extent that dismissal of the indictment against him was the only appropriate remedy. Relying on the Appeals Chamber's decision in *Barayagwiza*, the Trial Chamber found that it had the inherent power to decide whether or not to exercise jurisdiction over Dragan Nikolić.[66] Although deeply concerned about the illegal arrest and abduction of Nikolić, the Trial Chamber found that his treatment did not rise to the required level, and rejected his request that it decline to exercise jurisdiction over his case.

In denying Nikolić's appeal of the Trial Chamber's decision declining to dismiss the indictment, the Appeals Chamber recognised that in the case of what it termed 'Universally Condemned Offences', the international community as a whole has a legitimate expectation that persons accused of such offences will be brought to justice swiftly.[67] The Appeals Chamber went on to note that the international community's legitimate expectation must be balanced against both the principle of state sovereignty and the fundamental human rights of the accused. At least where an illegal abduction is carried out by private individuals who are apprehending a fugitive from international justice, such balancing would normally fall against the accused. Further, agreeing with the ICTR Appeals Chamber's approach in *Barayagwiza*, the *Dragan Nikolić* Appeals Chamber held that assessing human rights violations cannot be made *in abstracto*, and instead depends upon the circumstances of the case. Certain human rights violations are of such a serious nature that they require that the tribunal decline to exercise jurisdiction.[68] Although the Appeals Chamber declined to list which human rights violations would qualify, it approvingly noted the Trial Chamber's holding that jurisdiction should not be exercised 'in circumstances where an accused is very seriously mistreated, maybe even subject to inhuman, cruel or degrading treatment, or torture', and that this would certainly be the case where persons acting on behalf of SFOR or the prosecution were involved in such serious mistreatment.[69] Apart from such exceptional cases, however, 'the remedy of setting aside jurisdiction will, in the Appeals Chamber's view, usually be disproportionate'.[70] Thus, the test for whether a chamber will refuse to exercise jurisdiction appears to be heavily dependent both upon the level of mistreatment and the identity of the individuals delivering that mistreatment.

[66] *Dragan Nikolić* Trial Decision on Jurisdiction, *supra* note 49, para. 74.

[67] *Prosecutor* v. *Dragan Nikolić*, Case No. IT-94-2-AR73, Decision on Interlocutory Appeal Concerning Legality of Arrest, 5 June 2003, para. 25 (noting that accountability for these crimes is a necessary condition for the achievement of international justice, which plays a critical role in the reconciliation and rebuilding, based on the rule of law, of countries and societies torn apart by international and internecine conflicts). See also *ibid.*, para. 24 (defining genocide, crimes against humanity, and war crimes as 'Universally Condemned Offences').

[68] *Ibid.*, para. 30.

[69] *Ibid.*, para. 28 (quoting *Dragan Nikolić* Trial Decision on Jurisdiction, *supra* note 49, para. 114).

[70] *Ibid.*

Zdravko Tolimir's case at the ICTY illustrates well how exceptional the remedy of setting aside jurisdiction has proven to be. Tolimir alleged that at 3 a.m. on May 2007, he was abducted from his apartment in Belgrade by a well-organised group of twenty men who claimed to be police officers. The reputed police officers set off explosives at the door of the apartment, put a sack over Tolimir's head, and transported him in a van escorted by other vehicles to a detention facility in Belgrade, denying him any opportunity to contact counsel. Tolimir was then driven to a border crossing between Serbia and the Republika Srpska ('RS') in Bosnia and Herzegovina, and was handed over to NATO forces, which subsequently transferred him to The Hague.[71] Tolimir challenged the legality of his arrest, arguing that the prosecution acted in collusion with the men who abducted him in Belgrade, which the prosecution denied. Although the prosecution requested information from Serbia regarding the events in Belgrade, no information was provided.[72] Because the judges had no evidence regarding the events in Belgrade other than Tolimir's allegations, it accepted his factual allegations as true for the limited purpose of its decision whether or not to decline jurisdiction in the case. The Trial Chamber said:

> What is before the Trial Chamber – with reference to each phase of the arrest individually and cumulatively – does not amount to a human rights violation of such a serious nature so as to require that the exercise of jurisdiction be declined. In fact, the only irregular aspect of the arrest is the alleged circumstances surrounding the Accused's removal from his apartment in Belgrade. Assuming those allegations to be true, even that scenario however is not so egregious as to merit declining jurisdiction over this Accused in relation to the grave crimes charged against him.[73]

The *Tolimir* Trial Chamber appears to have gone further than the *Nikolić* Chambers. Taking Tolimir's version of events as true certainly raised the possibility that his abductors were not private individuals but were, in fact, acting with the implicit acquiescence of Serbian authorities and the explicit cooperation of Bosnian authorities. Indeed, in a subsequent decision denying what it construed as a motion from Tolimir for reconsideration of its decision, the Trial Chamber acknowledged that for the purposes of the original decision, it had accepted as true that Serbian

[71] *Prosecutor* v. *Tolimir*, Case No. IT-05-88/2-PT, Decision on Preliminary Motions on the Indictment Pursuant to Rule 72 of the Rules, 14 December 2007 ('*Tolimir* First Trial Decision on Legality of Arrest'), para. 9. Tolimir also alleged many details about what happened at the border crossing. He claimed that the RS authorities wanted him to speak with the RS Minister of Police about a deal in which the RS authorities would surrender him to the ICTY with certain, unspecified privileges. Tolimir refused any deal and demanded to be returned to Serbia. Following a two-hour telephone conversation 'with Belgrade and Banja Luka which were in contact with The Hague', Tolimir's demand to be returned to Serbia was denied, and Tolimir was driven to Bratunac, RS, where he was detained in a vehicle and continuously filmed 'in order to deceive the public that he had been arrested in the Bratunac area'. *Ibid.*

[72] *Ibid.*, para. 24. Serbia later provided an official report. According to the Trial Chamber, it provided nothing beyond the information the Chamber already possessed. See *Prosecutor* v. *Tolimir*, Case No. IT-05-88/2-PT, Decision on Submissions of the Accused Concerning Legality of Arrest, 18 December 2008 ('*Tolimir* Second Trial Decision on Legality of Arrest'), para. 16.

[73] *Tolimir* First Trial Decision on Legality of Arrest, *supra* note 71, para. 25.

authorities were involved in Tolimir's abduction from his apartment in Belgrade.[74] The Trial Chamber's decisions were not reviewed by the Appeals Chamber as interlocutory appeals and thus will not be subject to appellate review unless Tolimir is convicted following his trial and raises them at that time. As of 1 December 2009, Tolimir's trial had not yet begun.

4.3 Detention and release pending trial and appeal

The adjudication of cases before international criminal tribunals can be a lengthy process and it is not uncommon for accused to spend years in detention awaiting trial. Nor is it uncommon for trials and appeals involving complex international crimes to last for years.[75] This directly implicates international human rights law in three important respects: the conditions of detention, the length of detention, and release from detention pending trial. While the detention conditions of accused before the international criminal tribunals have generally met – or exceeded – human rights norms, the tribunals have routinely dismissed challenges to the lengthy detentions of their accused awaiting trial and during trial and appeal proceedings. Additionally, pre-trial detention for lengthy periods without temporary release has been problematic.

4.3.1 Conditions of detention

The detention conditions of accused before the *ad hoc* Tribunals and the SCSL are not addressed directly in either their Statutes or their Rules. Nevertheless, the ICTY, ICTR, and SCSL have all adopted detailed rules and regulations governing detention conditions and the rights accorded detained persons.[76] Each has put in

[74] See *Tolimir* Second Trial Decision on Legality of Arrest, *supra* note 72, para. 17. Tolimir had submitted what he characterised as new facts to the Trial Chamber. These included Tolimir's claim that former ICTY Prosecutor Carla del Ponte published a book in which she elaborated on the circumstances of his arrest and said that a Serbian 'special unit' was involved, and a televised statement of the Serbian Interior Minister in which the Minister claimed that the former Serbian government arrested Tolimir and turned him over to the ICTY. *Ibid.*, paras. 6–7.

[75] See Chapter 7, notes 3–5 and accompanying text (discussing some of the reasons trials are so lengthy).

[76] See Rules Governing the Detention of Persons Awaiting Trial or Appeal Before the Tribunal or Otherwise Detained on the Authority of the Tribunal, UN Doc. IT/38/Rev. 9, as amended 21 July 2005; United Nations Detention Unit Regulations for the Establishment of a Disciplinary Procedure for Detainees, UN Doc. IT/97, April 1995 (issued by the ICTY Registrar); United Nations Detention Unit Regulations to Govern the Supervision of Visits to and Communications with Detainees, UN Doc. IT/98/Rev. 4, amended as of August 2009 (issued by the ICTY Registrar); United Nations Detention Unit House Rules for Detainees, UN Doc. IT/99, April 1995 (issued by the ICTY Registrar); Rules Covering the Detention of Persons Awaiting Trial or Appeal Before the Tribunal or Otherwise Detained on the Authority of the Tribunal, 5 June 1998 ('ICTR Rules of Detention'), www.ictr.org/ ENGLISH/basicdocs/rulesdet.htm; Rules Governing the Detention of Persons Awaiting Trial or Appeal before the Special Court for Sierra Leone or Otherwise Detained on the Authority of the Special Court for Sierra Leone, as amended on 14 May 2005 ('SCSL Rules of Detention'), www.sc-sl.org/LinkClick.aspx?fileticket= sSNS1UL5T3w%3d&tabid=176.

place formal complaint mechanisms to assist detainees in challenging the conditions of their detention.[77] Detention conditions at the tribunals are also monitored by the International Committee of the Red Cross (ICRC).[78] Individuals detained by the ICC are housed in a separate section of the same detention facility used by the ICTY. Additionally, the ICC's Regulations of the Court contain extensive provisions regulating detention conditions that are largely reflective of those in place at the *ad hoc* Tribunals.[79]

The tribunals' commitment to safeguarding the human rights of the accused must always be balanced against the need to ensure appropriate security, especially as the accused are often former – in some cases current – high-profile political or military figures with considerable influence. In general, detention conditions at the international criminal tribunals have complied with international human rights norms and some of the tribunals have been proactive in taking steps to improve conditions even where minimum standards are already met.[80]

4.3.2 The length of pre-trial detention

Recognising the human rights implications of lengthy detentions awaiting trial – accused persons shall be entitled to trial 'within a reasonable time or to release'[81] – each of the international criminal tribunals' Statutes secures to the

[77] See United Nations Detention Unit Regulations for the Establishment of a Complaints Procedure for Detainees, UN Doc. IT/96, April 1995 (issued by the ICTY Registrar); ICTR Rules of Detention, *supra* note 76, Rules 82–86; SCSL Rules of Detention, *supra* note 76, Rules 59–60.

[78] See, e.g., Appointment of Inspecting Authority for the Detention Unit, 28 April 1995, www.icty.org/x/file/Legal%20Library/Detention/UNDUappointment_of_inspect1995_en.pdf.

[79] See ICC Court Regulations 89–106 (providing, in relevant part, that all detained persons be treated with humanity and with respect for the 'inherent dignity of the human person' (ICC Court Regulation 91(1)); that there shall be no discrimination of detained persons on grounds of gender, age, race, colour, language, religion or belief, political or other opinion, national, ethnic or social origin, wealth, birth, or other status (ICC Court Regulation 91(2)); that detention records are to remain confidential (ICC Court Regulation 92); that the detention centre shall undergo regular and unannounced inspections by an independent inspecting authority (ICC Court Regulation 94); that detained persons shall have access to confidential communications with counsel (ICC Court Regulation 97); that detained persons shall have access to diplomatic and consular assistance (ICC Court Regulation 98); that detained persons shall be generally entitled to participate in a work programme, keep personal possessions, procure reading and writing materials, have daily exercise in the open air, receive correspondence and communicate with family (ICC Court Regulation 99); and that detained persons shall be entitled to receive visits (ICC Court Regulation 100)).

[80] See Zahar and Sluiter, *supra* note 16, p. 319 (noting that the tribunals' detention units offer 'more than satisfactory conditions for treatment'). As an example of proactive measures, an independent audit of the ICTY's detention unit in 2006 revealed that several detainees felt the social conditions at the detention facility could be improved if detainees who had already been convicted could be separated from those involved in intensive preparations before or during trial. President Pocar ordered the Registrar to implement the audit's recommendation to separate convicted and non-convicted detainees. Case No. IT-06-89-Misc.1, Order to the Registrar to Separate Convicted and Non-Convicted Detainees Held in the Detention Unit, 15 June 2006.

[81] See ICCPR, Art. 9(3) ('Anyone arrested or detained on a criminal charge … shall be entitled to trial within a reasonable time or to release'); ECHR, Art. 5(3) ('Everyone arrested or detained … shall be entitled to trial within a reasonable time or to release pending trial'); ACHR, Art. 7 ('Any person detained … shall be entitled to trial within a reasonable time or to be released without prejudice to the continuation of the proceedings').

accused the right to be tried 'without undue delay'.[82] Given the complexity of the cases before the tribunals and the seriousness of the crimes charged, the length of pre-trial detention can be considerable when compared to the length of pre-trial detention in national criminal proceedings. Indeed, the tribunals have yet to find a pre-trial detention period so unreasonably lengthy as to dismiss an indictment on this basis.

While the *ad hoc* Tribunals have no specific mechanism for addressing the length of pre-trial detention, the Rome Statute provides the ICC's judges with specific regulatory authority in this regard. The pre-trial chamber has an express obligation to 'ensure that a person is not detained for an unreasonable period prior to trial due to inexcusable delay by the Prosecutor'.[83] The Appeals Chamber has held that the unreasonableness of any period of detention prior to trial cannot be determined in the abstract, but has to be determined in the circumstances in each case.[84] Moreover, where the pre-trial chamber finds that the detention period is not unreasonable, there is no requirement for it to address whether the prosecution has caused inexcusable delay.[85] It remains unclear, however, whether finding the length of the detention to be unreasonable based upon prosecutorial delay obligates the pre-trial chamber to release the person detained. No pre-trial chamber has yet found any period of detention unreasonable, and the Rome Statute provides only that in such a case, the pre-trial chamber 'shall consider' releasing the person.[86]

Nothing in the ICC's procedural framework requires a trial chamber to review an accused's detention in the manner required of the pre-trial chamber. Nevertheless, when the *Lubanga* case was transferred to the Trial Chamber following the confirmation of charges, that Chamber issued a decision noting that '[w]hile the Statute and Rules require only the Pre-Trial Chamber to undertake this periodic review of any decision on interim release, Article 61(11) vests the relevant powers of the Pre-Trial Chamber in the Trial Chamber ... Accordingly, the Chamber has undertaken a review of the Decision'.[87] The Trial Chamber then undertook to review the overall period of detention. Without elaboration, the Trial Chamber found that the period of detention

[82] Rome Statute, Art. 67(1)(c); ICTY Statute, Art. 21(4)(c); ICTR Statute, Art. 20(4)(c); SCSL Statute, Art. 17(4)(c).

[83] Rome Statute, Art. 60(4).

[84] *Prosecutor* v. *Lubanga*, Doc. No. ICC-01/04-01/06-824, Judgment on the Appeal of Mr. Thomas Lubanga Dyilo Against the Decision of Pre-Trial Chamber I Entitled '*Décision sur la demande de mise en liberté provisoire de Thomas Lubanga Dyilo*', 13 February 2007 ('*Lubanga* Appeal Decision on Interim Release'), para. 122 (finding that the Pre-Trial Chamber had not erred by refusing to consider the period of time Lubanga had spent in detention and house arrest in the DRC prior to the issuance of the ICC's arrest warrant, and that the seven months and three days he had spent in detention since his arrest by the ICC was not *per se* unreasonably long).

[85] *Ibid.*, para. 124 (noting that the Pre-Trial Chamber's approach of not addressing the prosecution's conduct was acceptable because after having determined that the period of detention was reasonable, the question of inexcusable delay had become moot).

[86] Rome Statute, Art. 60(4).

[87] *Prosecutor* v. *Lubanga*, Doc. No. ICC-01/04-01/06-976, Decision Reviewing the 'Decision on the Application for the Interim Release of Thomas Lubanga Dyilo', 9 October 2007 ('*Lubanga* Trial Decision on Interim Release'), para. 8.

was reasonable, that no inexcusable delay had been caused by the prosecution, and that preparations for trial were proceeding expeditiously.[88] The Trial Chamber continued to periodically review the overall length of Lubanga's pre-trial detention in the same manner, something which other trial chambers have emulated.[89]

Chambers of the *ad hoc* Tribunals and the SCSL conduct no such periodic review of the overall length of detention. Moreover, where accused have raised a specific challenge to the length of pre-trial detention – most often at the ICTR – those challenges have been rejected. In rejecting one such claim, the *Kanyabashi* Trial Chamber noted that

> the issue of reasonable length of proceeding has been addressed by the U.N. Human Rights Committee, the European Court of Human Rights and the Inter-American Commission on Human Rights. 'The reasonableness of the period cannot be translated into a fixed number of days, months or years, since it is dependent on other elements which the judge must consider'. In the opinion of the European Court of Human Rights, 'the reasonableness of the length of proceedings coming within the scope of Article 6(1) [of the ECHR] must be assessed in each case according to the particular circumstances. The Court has to have regard, *inter alia*, to the complexity of the factual or legal issues raised by the case, to the conduct of the applicants and the competent authorities and to what was at stake for the former, in addition to complying with the "reasonable time" requirement'.[90]

Under the *Kanyabashi* Trial Chamber's standard, the applicable analysis thus requires review of a host of factors, which appears to leave ample discretion for trial chambers to find the length of pre-trial detention not unreasonable.

The *Mugiraneza* case illustrates the difficulties facing an accused hoping to prevail on such a claim. Mugiraneza had been detained for four years awaiting trial when he filed a motion alleging a breach of his right to be tried without undue delay. Citing *Kanyabashi*, the Trial Chamber reasoned that any inquiry into an alleged breach of the right to be tried without undue delay would necessarily involve the consideration of a number of factors, including the fundamental purpose of the ICTR, which was 'prosecuting persons responsible for genocide and other serious violations of international humanitarian law committed in the territory of Rwanda'.[91] With reference only to these general factors, and no analysis specific

[88] *Ibid*., paras. 10–12.

[89] *Prosecutor* v. *Lubanga*, Doc. No. ICC-01/04-01/06-1151, Decision Reviewing the Trial Chamber's Ruling on the Detention of Thomas Lubanga Dyilo in Accordance with Rule 118(2), 1 February 2008; *Prosecutor* v. *Lubanga*, Doc. No. ICC-01/04-01/06-1359, Decision Reviewing the Trial Chamber's Ruling on the Detention of Thomas Lubanga Dyilo in Accordance with Rule 118(2), 29 May 2008.

[90] *Prosecutor* v. *Kanyabashi*, Case No. ICTR-96-15-I, Decision on the Defence Extremely Urgent Motion on Habeas Corpus and for Stoppage of Proceedings, 23 May 2000, para. 68.2 (citing *Firmenich* v. *Argentina*, Inter-American Commission on Human Rights Resolution No. 17/89, 13 April 1989, and *Zimmerman and Steiner* v. *Switzerland*, ECHR (1983), Series A, No. 66, para. 24).

[91] *Prosecutor* v. *Mugiraneza*, Case No. ICTR-99-50-I, Decision on Prosper Mugiraneza's Motion to Dismiss the Indictment for Violation of Article 20(4)(c) of the Statute, Demand for Speedy Trial and for Appropriate Relief, 2 October 2003, para. 11.

to the accused's situation, the Trial Chamber found that the four and a half years between Mugiraneza's arrest and the 'imminent commencement of his trial [was] not be to assessed as being undue'.[92] Additionally, the Trial Chamber found no need to consider whether the delay was attributable to the conduct of the prosecution.[93] Almost five months later, the Appeals Chamber reversed the Trial Chamber's decision, holding that five factors must be determined when considering whether there has been a violation of the right to be tried without undue delay: (1) the length of the delay; (2) the complexity of the proceedings, such as the number of charges, the number of accused, the number of witnesses, the volume of evidence, and the complexity of facts and law; (3) the conduct of the parties; (4) the conduct of the relevant authorities; and (5) the prejudice to the accused, if any.[94] Thus, the Trial Chamber erred in considering the purpose of the Tribunal in its analysis, as well as in failing to consider the prosecution's conduct. On remand over a year after its first decision denying Mugiraneza's claim, the Trial Chamber again denied the challenge, this time determining that no delay was attributable to the prosecution.[95]

Short of outrageous delaying behaviour by the prosecution, the balancing analysis used at the *ad hoc* Tribunals appears to ensure that with the types of cases before them, undue delay will not be found. This approach, which appears to highlight a gap between actual practice and the accused's statutory right to be tried within a 'reasonable time', has subjected the Tribunals to criticism.[96] In perhaps the most egregious case, Théoneste Bagosora was arrested in March 1996 and finally convicted by the Trial Chamber in a judgement rendered on 18 December 2008.[97] Bagosora thus spent twelve years in detention awaiting a disposition on his case, without the benefit of provisional release. As of 1 December 2009, he remained in detention with his appeal pending.

4.3.3 Release pending and during trial

Each of the international criminal tribunals' Rules provide for the possibility of the accused's release from detention pending and during trial. Although called different things – provisional release at the *ad hoc* Tribunals, bail at the SCSL, and interim

[92] *Ibid.*, para. 13. [93] *Ibid.*, para. 14.

[94] *Prosecutor* v. *Mugiraneza*, Case No. ICTR-99-50-AR73, Decision on Prosper Mugiraneza's Interlocutory Appeal from Trial Chamber II Decision of 2 October 2003 Denying the Motion to Dismiss the Indictment, Demand for Speedy Trial and for Appropriate Relief, 27 February 2004.

[95] *Prosecutor* v. *Mugiraneza*, Case No. ICTR-99-50-T, Decision on Prosper Mugiraneza's Application for a Hearing or Other Relief on his Motion for Dismissal for Violation of his Right to a Trial Without Undue Delay, 3 November 2004.

[96] See, e.g., Zahar and Sluiter, *supra* note 16, p. 300 (citing the case of ICTR accused Théoneste Bagosora, who was arrested in March 1996 with his trial beginning in April 2002, and noting that 'this shocks the sense of justice of every reasonable observer').

[97] *Prosecutor* v. *Bagosora, Kabiligi, Ntabakuze, and Nsengiyumva*, Case No. ICTR-98-41-T, Judgement and Sentence, 18 December 2008.

release at the ICC – the legal considerations attending such a release are broadly similar. One crucial difference, explained below, involves the discretionary authority of the *ad hoc* Tribunals' judges to deny applications for release even where the accused makes the required showing. For judges at the ICC, no such discretion exists.

4.3.3.1 The ad hoc *Tribunals and the SCSL*

Once detained at the ICTY, ICTR, or SCSL, an accused may not be released except upon an order of the chamber seised of the case, prior to or during trial.[98] As initially promulgated in all three tribunals, the relevant rule provided that release could be ordered by a chamber '*only in exceptional circumstances*, after hearing the host country and only if [the chamber] is satisfied that the accused will appear for trial and, if released, will not pose a danger to any victim, witness or other person'.[99] This formulation, clearly establishing release as the exception and detention as the rule, was heavily criticised, both by commentators and judges.[100] The ICTY deleted the exceptional circumstances element from its rule in 1999, as did the ICTR and SCSL in 2003.[101] While extant, the parameters of the exceptional circumstances limitation were typically defined negatively in the jurisprudence. The judges were often clear on what did not constitute exceptional circumstances; less so in defining what they were.[102] Additionally, even after the exceptional circumstances limitation

[98] ICTY Rule 65(A) ('an accused may not be released except upon an order of a Chamber'); ICTR Rule 65(A) ('an accused may not be provisionally released except upon an order of a Trial Chamber'); SCSL Rule 65(A) ('an accused shall not be granted bail except upon an order of a Judge or Trial Chamber').

[99] See Rules of Procedure and Evidence of the International Criminal Tribunal for the former Yugoslavia, UN Doc. IT/32/Rev.14, as amended 17 December 1998, available at www.icty.org/x/file/Legal%20Library/Rules_procedure_evidence/IT032_rev14_en.pdf, Rule 65(B) (emphasis supplied); Rules of Procedure and Evidence of the International Criminal Tribunal for Rwanda, as amended 6 July 2002, available at http://ictr.org/ENGLISH/ rules/060702/060702.pdf, Rule 65(B). See also *Prosecutor* v. *Norman, Fofana, and Kondewa* ('*CDF* Case'), Case No. SCSL-04-14-T, Fofana – Decision on Application for Bail Pursuant to Rule 65, 5 August 2004, para. 87 (noting that Rule 65(B) formerly provided that bail could only be granted 'in exceptional circumstances' and that the phrase was deleted by an amendment to the Rule).

[100] On this, and for a critical analysis of Rule 65(B) and its application in cases before the *ad hoc* Tribunals, see Zahar and Sluiter, *supra* note 16, pp. 286–289 (characterising the exceptional circumstances formulation of Rule 65(B) as a 'flagrant violation of international human rights law' and calling the inadequate enforcement of the right not to be subject to arbitrary arrest or detention one of the 'weakest spots of the law of international criminal procedure'). See also Cryer, Friman, Robinson, and Wilmshurst, *supra* note 3, p. 370 (noting that the exceptional circumstances limitation was the major obstacle to provisional release and that it was abandoned after extensive internal debates and external criticism); *Prosecutor* v. *Krajišnik and Plavšić*, Case Nos. IT-00-39-PT and IT-00–40-PT, Decision on Momčilo Krajišnik's Notice of Motion for Provisional Release, 8 October 2001 ('*Krajišnik and Plavšić* Provisional Release Decision'), Dissenting Opinion of Judge Patrick Robinson, paras. 2, 8 (noting that the exceptional circumstances limitation was removed from Rule 65(B) because the ICTY judges concluded that it conflicted with customary international law as reflected in the main international human rights instruments, and arguing that any system of mandatory detention is *per se* incompatible with Article 9(3) of the ICCPR).

[101] See SCSL Rule 65(B) ('Bail may be ordered by a Judge or a Trial Chamber after hearing the State to which the accused seeks to be released and only if it is satisfied that the accused will appear for trial and, if released, will not pose a danger to any victim, witness or other person').

[102] See, e.g., *Prosecutor* v. *Ndayambaje*, Case No. ICTR-98-42-T, Decision on the Defence Motion for the Provisional Release of the Accused, 21 October 2002 ('*Ndayambaje* Provisional Release Decision'), para. 25 (finding that the accused being a long distance from his family and lacking the opportunity for family visits did

was removed from the ICTY's rule, its chambers took pains to note that despite the removal of the limitation, provisional release continued 'to be the exception and not the rule, a position justified by the absence of any power in the [ICTY] to execute its own arrest warrants'.[103] Despite an increasing willingness on the part of ICTY chambers to grant provisional release, owing largely to the stabilisation of security in the states of the former Yugoslavia, applications for provisional release are more often denied than granted. By sharp contrast, the ICTR has yet to provisionally release any of its accused. Nor has the SCSL ever found it appropriate to grant bail.[104] At the ICTY and ICTR, appeals from decisions on applications for provisional release are as of right.[105] At the SCSL, leave to appeal must be obtained from a judge of the Appeals Chamber, and is only available upon good cause being shown.[106]

For a chamber at the ICTY or ICTR to release an accused from detention during the pendency of the accused's case, it must: (1) hear the views of the host state and the state to which the accused seeks to be released; (2) be satisfied that, if released, the accused will appear for trial; and (3) be satisfied that, if released, the accused will not pose a danger to any victim, witness, or other person.[107] The only difference for the SCSL is that the rule does not require the chamber to hear the views of the host state.[108] The burden rests on the accused to satisfy the trial chamber that the accused will appear for trial and will not pose a danger to any victim, witness, or other person.[109] Additionally, satisfaction of the two showings

not constitute exceptional circumstances); *Prosecutor* v. *Nahimana*, Case No. ICTR-99-52-T, Decision on the Defence's Motion for the Release or Alternatively Provisional Release of Ferdinand Nahimana, 5 September 2002, para. 10 (finding that 'a decision to provisionally release an accused charged with serious violations of international law, including genocide, must weigh the request of the accused against community interests and the need to complete trial proceedings in an orderly manner', and rejecting the application for release). See also *Prosecutor* v. *Rutaganda*, Case No. ICTR-96-3-T, Decision on the Request Filed by the Defence for Provisional Release of Georges Rutaganda, 7 February 1997 (finding that if the Trial Chamber was not satisfied of the existence of exceptional circumstances, with the accused bearing the burden of proof, no provisional release could be ordered, and it was not necessary to consider the other criteria of Rule 65(B)).

103 *Prosecutor* v. *Brđanin and Talić*, Case No. IT-99-36-T, Decision on Motion by Momir Talić for Provisional Release, 28 March 2001, paras. 17–18 (noting that it cannot be said that provisional release became the rule rather than the exception following the amendment of Rule 65(B)). Accord *Krajišnik and Plavšić* Provisional Release Decision, *supra* note 100, para. 12. See also *Prosecutor* v. *Sesay, Kallon, and Gbao* ('*RUF* Case'), Case No. SCSL-04-15-AR65, Sesay – Decision on Appeal Against Refusal of Bail, 14 December 2004 ('*RUF* Appeal Decision on Bail'), para. 28 (affirming the Trial Chamber's assertion that the need to rely upon local authorities to effect arrests placed a substantial burden upon any applicant but did not constitute a re-introduction of the previous 'exceptional circumstances' limitation).

104 Unlike the ICTY and the ICTR, at which there is no limit on the number of times an accused may apply for provisional release, the SCSL Rules permit only one bail application per accused 'unless there has been a material change in circumstances'. SCSL Rule 65(C). See, e.g., *RUF* Appeal Decision on Bail, *supra* note 103 (Sesay's only application for bail denied by the Trial Chamber, with the denial upheld by the Appeals Chamber).

105 ICTY Rule 65(D); ICTR Rule 65(D). On interlocutory appeals, see Chapter 11, Section 11.4.

106 SCSL Rule 65(E).

107 ICTY Rule 65(B); ICTR Rule 65(B).

108 SCSL Rule 65(A) (requiring the trial chamber to hear only the state to which the accused seeks to be released).

109 *Prosecutor* v. *Popović, Beara, Nikolić, Miletić, Borovčanin, Gvero, and Pandurević*, Case No. IT-05-88-AR65.7, Decision on Vujadin Popović's Interlocutory Appeal Against the Decision on Popović's Motion for Provisional Release, 1 July 2008 ('*Popović et al.* July 2008 Appeal Decision on Provisional Release'),

is a necessary but not a sufficient condition for the granting of provisional release. The ICTY, ICTR, and SCSL Rules all provide that granting such release is wholly within the chamber's discretion.[110]

For the ICTY and the ICTR, both situated outside of the states involved in the conflicts that spawned their existence, the host state notice requirement is largely a formality, aimed at recognising the political niceties and practical considerations involved. The Netherlands, for example, has never asserted any interest in the merits of such an application beyond noting its understanding that the accused, if released, will leave Dutch territory.[111] The requirement to hear the state to which the accused seeks to be released rests upon similar practical concerns, coupled with the opportunity for such states to assure the trial chamber of their genuine willingness to admit the accused within their territory and their ability to guarantee the accused's return.[112]

Of the two elements that the accused must prove to gain provisional release – that is, that the accused will return for trial; and that he or she will not pose a danger to any victim, witness, or other person – the jurisprudence has primarily focused upon the former. Decisions on applications for provisional release have tended to analyse the validity of governmental guarantees of return, the flight risk posed by the accused with respect to the stage of the proceedings, and whether the accused self-surrendered to the tribunal or was captured while a fugitive.[113] If an accused has once been granted provisional release and fully complied with the trial

para. 17 (noting that in requesting provisional release once an order on detention has been issued, the onus is on the accused to demonstrate entitlement to provisional release under Rule 65(B)); *Krajišnik and Plavšić* Provisional Release Decision, *supra* note 100, para. 11; *CDF* Case, Case No. SCSL-04-14-AR65, Fofana – Appeal Against Decision Refusing Bail, 11 March 2005 ('*CDF* Appeal Decision on Bail'), para. 33 (noting that it is a precondition to any grant of bail that the applicant must satisfy the court that he will appear for trial and will not endanger witnesses or any other potential victim, including himself).

110 ICTY Rule 65(B) ('Release may be ordered by a Trial Chamber …'); ICTR Rule 65(B) ('Provisional release may be ordered by a Trial Chamber …'); SCSL Rule 65(B) ('Bail may be ordered by a Judge or a Trial Chamber …').

111 See, e.g., *Prosecutor* v. *Milutinović, Šainović, Ojdanić, Pavković, Lazarević, and Lukić*, Case No. IT-05-87-T, Correspondence from Host Country Re: Request for Provisional Release, 16 December 2008 (noting that the Netherlands 'as host country and limiting itself to the practical consequences relating to … provisional release, does not have any objections', and that it is the understanding of the Netherlands that 'upon his provisional release, Mr. Milan Milutinović will leave Dutch territory').

112 See, e.g., *CDF* Appeal Decision on Bail, *supra* note 109, para. 5 (recognising the submissions by the government of Sierra Leone with regard to Fofana's bail application that police resources were inadequate to maintain surveillance of the accused should he be released).

113 See, e.g., *Prosecutor* v. *Popović, Beara, Nikolić, Miletić, Borovčanin, Gvero, and Pandurević*, Case No. IT-05-88-T, Decision on Gvero's Motion for Provisional Release, 10 December 2008 ('*Popović et al.* 10 December 2008 Trial Decision on Gvero's Provisional Release'), paras. 18, 25 (granting provisional release, noting that Gvero voluntarily surrendered to the Tribunal upon notification of the charges against him, and noting Trial Chamber's satisfaction with the security guarantees provided by the Serbian Government that Gvero would return to the Tribunal); *Prosecutor* v. *Popović, Beara, Nikolić, Miletić, Borovčanin, Gvero, and Pandurević*, Case No. IT-05-88-T, Decision on Miletić's Motion for Provisional Release, 10 December 2008 ('*Popović et al.* 10 December 2008 Trial Decision on Miletić's Provisional Release'), paras. 18, 25 (same). See also *Prosecutor* v. *Popović, Beara, Nikolić, Miletić, Borovčanin, Gvero, and Pandurević*, Case No. IT-05-88-T, Decision on Borovčanin's Motion for Custodial Visit, 17 December 2008 ('*Popović et al.* 17 December 2008 Trial Decision on Borovčanin's Custodial Release'), para. 28 (denying provisional release,

chamber's orders, subsequent decisions on provisional release will typically count this as a factor in the accused's favour.[114]

Decisions on motions for provisional release are fact-intensive, and each case must be considered on an individual basis in light of the particular circumstances of the accused making the application.[115] In deciding whether the accused has made the requisite showing, the chamber must consider all the relevant factors and provide a reasoned opinion indicating its views on each of those factors.[116] Additionally, the chamber is required to assess the accused's individual circumstances not only as they exist at the time it reaches its decision on provisional release but also, as much as can be foreseen, at the time the accused is expected to return to detention.[117] Largely because a chamber's decision on provisional release is focused on the individual circumstances of the accused, an applicant's reference to the treatment of other accused, even co-accused in the same case, is of no relevance.[118]

If the chamber decides to grant provisional release, it has the authority to impose such conditions 'as are necessary to ensure the presence of the accused at trial and the protection of others'.[119] Such conditions have often taken the form of restricting the accused's movement while on release and requiring the accused to reside at a specific address, with monitoring by national authorities.[120] Custodial

even under full custodial conditions, noting that the accused was arrested and surrendered to the Tribunal after two-and-a-half years as a fugitive).

114 See, e.g., *Popović et al.* 10 December 2008 Trial Decision on Gvero's Provisional Release, *supra* note 113, para. 18 (granting provisional release and noting that Gvero had previously been granted provisional release on several occasions and had always been compliant with the conditions imposed upon him during those periods of release); *Popović et al.* 10 December 2008 Trial Decision on Miletić's Provisional Release, *supra* note 113, para. 18 (same). Even previous compliance with release conditions, however, may not be enough where the chamber considers the accused a serious flight risk. See, e.g., *Popović et al.* 17 December 2008 Trial Decision on Borovčanin's Custodial Release, *supra* note 113, para. 28 (denying release and noting that although the accused had been compliant with previous conditions of release, the Chamber continued to have serious concerns about his risk of flight).

115 *Prosecutor* v. *Popović, Beara, Nikolić, Miletić, Borovčanin, Gvero, and Pandurević*, Case Nos. IT-05-88-AR65.4, AR65.5 and AR65.6, Decision on Consolidated Appeal Against Decision on Borovčanin's Motion for a Custodial Visit and Decisions on Gvero's and Miletić's Motions for Provisional Release During the Break in the Proceedings, 15 May 2008 ('*Popović et al.* May 2008 Appeal Decision on Provisional Release'), para. 13.

116 *Prosecutor* v. *Prlić, Stojić, Praljak, Petković, Ćorić and Pušić*, Case No. IT-04-74-AR65.7, Decision on 'Prosecution's Appeal from *Décision relative à la Demande de mise en liberté provisoire de l'Accusé Petković* Dated 31 March 2008', 21 April 2008, para. 7; *Popović et al.* May 2008 Appeal Decision on Provisional Release, *supra* note 115, para. 13.

117 *Prosecutor* v. *Mićo Stanišić*, Case No. IT-04-79-AR65.1, Decision on Prosecution's Interlocutory Appeal of Mićo Stanišić's Provisional Release, 17 October 2005, para. 8.

118 See, e.g., *Popović et al.* July 2008 Appeal Decision on Provisional Release, *supra* note 109, paras. 14–15 (rejecting the accused's argument alleging inconsistency of treatment with respect to his co-accused, noting that the trial chamber properly considered only the individual circumstances of the accused).

119 ICTY Rule 65(C); ICTR Rule 65(C); SCSL Rule 65(D).

120 See, e.g., *Popović et al.* 10 December 2008 Trial Decision on Miletić's Provisional Release, *supra* note 113, para. 26(iv) (granting provisional release and ordering the accused and the authorities of the Serbian Government, including the local police, to comply with, in relevant part, the following conditions: that the accused provide the Serbian authorities and the ICTY Registrar with the address in Belgrade where he would be staying during his release; that the accused remain within the confines of Belgrade; that the accused surrender his passport to the Serbian authorities; that the accused report each day to the Belgrade police; that

release, in which the accused is delivered to national authorities under the condition that he or she remains in custody during the release, is the most extreme such measure used by chambers.[121] As the security situation has gradually stabilised in the former Yugoslavia, ICTY trial chambers have granted provisional release with increasing frequency. Accused have been released pending trial, as well as temporarily during trial to seek medical treatment,[122] to visit ailing family members,[123] and to attend memorial services for family members.[124]

Although the ICTY has never had an accused fail to return from provisional release, in 2008 the Appeals Chamber significantly curtailed trial chambers' discretionary authority to grant provisional release following any decision by the trial chamber denying an accused's motion for a judgement of acquittal. In the *Prlić* case, the Trial Chamber granted provisional release to five of the six accused following the close of the prosecution's case and one day before it declined to enter judgements of acquittal. The prosecution appealed, and the Appeals Chamber found that the Trial Chamber's decision not to enter a judgement of acquittal at that stage of the proceedings – generally referred to as a Rule 98 *bis* decision[125] – was 'a significant enough change in circumstance to warrant the renewed and explicit consideration by the Trial Chamber of the risk of flight by the Accused'.[126] Substituting its judgement that the various justifications offered for provisional release by the five accused were 'not sufficiently compelling', the Appeals Chamber reversed the Trial

the accused have no contact with the co-accused in his case; and that the accused not discuss his case with anyone other than counsel).

121 See, e.g., *Prosecutor* v. *Popović, Beara, Nikolić, Miletić, Borovčanin, Gvero, and Pandurević*, Case No. IT-05-88-T, Decision on Nikolić's Motion for Provisional Release, 21 July 2008 ('*Popović et al.* 21 July 2008 Decision on Nikolić's Provisional Release'), para. 22 (granting provisional release under the condition that the accused be in the custody at all times of the armed members of the Republika Srpska (RS) police, and that he spend every night in the Bratunac, RS, detention facility).

122 See, e.g., *Prosecutor* v. *Milutinović, Šainović, Ojdanić, Pavković, Lazarević, and Lukić*, Case No. IT-05-87-A, Public Redacted Version of the 'Decision on Vladimir Lazarević's Second Motion for Temporary Provisional Release on the Grounds of Compassion' Issued on 21 May 2009, 22 May 2009 ('*Milutinović et al.* 22 May 2009 Appeal Decision on Provisional Release'), para. 11 (noting that although medical treatment for the accused's condition was available in the Netherlands, there was a sufficient basis to conclude that the required treatment and subsequent therapy had a greater chance to succeed if performed in Serbia, so special circumstances existed warranting provisional release).

123 See, e.g., *Popović et al.* 10 December 2008 Trial Decision on Miletić's Provisional Release, *supra* note 113, para. 24 (granting provisional release to the accused to visit his seriously ill wife and to attend a memorial service for his sister).

124 See, e.g., *Popović et al.* 21 July 2008 Decision on Nikolić's Provisional Release, *supra* note 121, para. 18 (granting provisional release under full custodial conditions in order for the accused to attend a memorial service for his father).

125 On mid-trial proceedings involving judgements of acquittal, see Chapter 7, Section 7.6.5.

126 *Prosecutor* v. *Prlić, Stojić, Praljak, Petković, Ćorić, and Pušić*, Case No. IT-04-74-AR65.5, Decision on Prosecution's Consolidated Appeal Against Decisions to Provisionally Release the Accused Prlić, Stojić, Praljak, Petković, and Ćorić, 11 March 2008, para. 19; see also *ibid.*, para. 19 (finding that the Trial Chamber committed a discernable error in failing to explicitly discuss the impact of its Rule 98 *bis* decision when granting provisional release, and that this caused the Trial Chamber to err by not assessing the requirements of Rule 65(B) in the 'present context of the proceedings').

Chamber's decision.[127] Thus, the Appeals Chamber has decreed that when considering an application for provisional release at the post-Rule 98 *bis* stage of the proceedings a trial chamber should not exercise its discretion to grant provisional release unless 'serious and sufficiently compelling humanitarian reasons exist'.[128] In several partly dissenting opinions, Judge Güney criticised the Appeals Chamber's holding, characterising it as imposing an additional element to the two criteria listed in Rule 65(B), 'contrary to both the Rules and the continuing presumption of innocence, and effectively suspending the grant of discretion to the Trial Chamber by the Rules'.[129] This, he argued, amounted to reinstating for post-Rule 98 *bis* proceedings the exceptional circumstances limitation of Rule 65(B) which the judges had specifically abrogated in 1999.[130] Judge Güney was later joined in this criticism by Judge Liu,[131] further dividing the Appeals Chamber on this issue, and at least one trial chamber judge has refused to acknowledge the Appeals Chamber's holding as legitimate.[132]

There is some merit to the dissenters' views. It is difficult to argue that the Appeals Chamber has not jurisprudentially reinstated a narrow 'exceptional circumstances' limitation on provisional release – albeit one that generally applies for a relatively short period of time and occurs at a point in the proceedings during which provisional release applications would always have come under heavy

[127] *Ibid.*, para. 21 (finding that, because none of the bases upon which the five accused applied for release were sufficiently compelling to warrant provisional release, a trial chamber properly exercising its discretion would have denied the applications). On the Appeals Chamber's interference in trial chamber discretionary decisions generally, see Chapter 11, Section 11.4.3.

[128] *Prosecutor* v. *Popović, Beara, Nikolić, Miletić, Borovčanin, Gvero, and Pandurević*, Case No. IT-05-88-AR65.10, Decision on Radivoje Miletić's Appeal Against Decision on Miletić's Motion for Provisional Release, 19 November 2009 ('*Popović et al.* 19 November 2009 Appeal Decision on Provisional Release'), para. 7.

[129] *Prosecutor* v. *Prlić, Stojić, Praljak, Petković, Ćorić and Pušić*, Case No. IT-04-74-AR65.8, Decision on 'Prosecution's Appeal from *Décision relative à la Demande de mise en liberté provisoire de l'Accusé Prlić* Dated 7 April 2008', 25 April 2008 ('*Prlić et al.* 25 April 2008 Appeal Decision on Provisional Release'), Partly Dissenting Opinion of Judge Güney, para. 1. Accord *Popović et al.* May 2008 Appeal Decision on Provisional Release, *supra* note 115, Partly Dissenting Opinion of Judge Güney. See also *Prosecutor* v. *Prlić, Stojić, Praljak, Petković, Ćorić and Pušić*, Case No. IT-04-74-AR65.11, Partly Dissenting Opinion of Judge Güney to Decision on Praljak's Appeal of the Trial Chamber's 2 December 2008 Decision on Provisional Release, 4 February 2009, para. 3 (dissenting from the majority's holding because it endorsed the Trial Chamber's denial of provisional release on the sole basis that the humanitarian grounds raised by the defence were not sufficiently compelling, and concluding: 'Should I decide to remain silent on this matter in future cases, my silence should not in any way be construed as an approval of the additional requirement adopted by the majority of the Judges of the Appeals Chamber').

[130] *Prlić et al.* 25 April 2008 Appeal Decision on Provisional Release, *supra* note 129, Partly Dissenting Opinion of Judge Güney, para. 5.

[131] See *Popović et al.* 19 November 2009 Appeal Decision on Provisional Release, *supra* note 128, Joint Dissenting Opinion of Judges Güney and Liu, para. 1.

[132] *Prosecutor* v. *Popović, Beara, Nikolić, Miletić, Borovčanin, Gvero, and Pandurević*, Case No. IT-05-88-T, Decision on Gvero's Motion for Provisional Release with Judge Agius'[s] Dissenting Opinion and Judge Prost's Separate Declaration, 17 December 2009, Judge Prost's Separate Declaration, para. 3 (arguing that the mandatory application of the Appeals Chamber's 'sufficient humanitarian grounds' requirement following Rule 98 *bis* proceedings is *ultra vires* and 'constitutes an improper fettering of the discretion accorded to a Trial Chamber in matters of provisional release').

scrutiny. The legal merits of the dissenters' views aside, there is no doubt that the Appeals Chamber's decisions have made it more difficult for accused to be granted provisional release following a trial chamber's decision under Rule 98 *bis*.

4.3.3.2 The ICC

Release from detention at the ICC is broadly governed by the same legal standards applicable at the *ad hoc* Tribunals. There are some important differences, however, most notably with regard to the discretionary authority of the chamber to grant or deny an application once the accused has made the requisite showing.

Once an individual has been detained at the Court, and prior to the confirmation hearing, he or she may apply to the pre-trial chamber for 'interim release' pending trial.[133] The pre-trial chamber's decision on the application is guided by the same standards applicable to the issuance of the initial arrest warrant, which require that the arrest of a person (for whom reasonable grounds exist to believe that he or she has committed a crime within the jurisdiction of the Court) appears necessary (1) to ensure the person's appearance at trial; (2) to ensure that the person does not obstruct or endanger the investigation or the court proceedings; or (3) where applicable, to prevent the person from continuing with the commission of the alleged crime or a related crime which is within the jurisdiction of the Court and which arises out of the same circumstances.[134] If the pre-trial chamber is satisfied that the conditions attending the issuance of the initial arrest continue to be met, no release is possible. If the pre-trial chamber is not satisfied that the conditions continue to be met, the person must be released, with or without conditions. The pre-trial chamber is required to review its ruling on an application for interim release *proprio motu* at least every 120 days, and may do so at any time on the request of the prosecution or the detained person.[135] Appeals against decisions on interim release are as of right for both parties.[136]

[133] See Rome Statute, Art. 60(2) ('A person subject to a warrant of arrest may apply for interim release pending trial. If the Pre-Trial Chamber is satisfied that the conditions set forth in Article 58, paragraph 1, are met, the person shall continue to be detained. If it is not so satisfied, the Pre-Trial Chamber shall release the person, with or without conditions'). In addition to the possibility of interim release after being surrendered to the Court, the Rome Statute also provides a mechanism whereby a person who has been provisionally arrested by national authorities upon the request of the Court may apply to the competent authority in the custodial state for interim release pending surrender to the Court. *Ibid.*, Art. 59(3). While the custodial state may release the person, it must consider whether there are 'urgent and exceptional circumstances to justify interim release, and whether necessary safeguards exist to ensure that the custodial State can fulfill its duty to surrender the person to the Court'. *Ibid.*, Art. 59(4). Additionally, the relevant pre-trial chamber must be notified of any such request for interim release and is required to make 'recommendations to the competent authority in the custodial state', recommendations to which the custodial state must give full consideration. *Ibid.*, Art. 59(5).

[134] *Ibid.*, Art. 58(1).

[135] *Ibid.*, Art. 60(3); ICC Rule 118(2); see *Lubanga* Appeal Decision on Interim Release, *supra* note 84, paras. 93–102 (rejecting Lubanga's argument that the required periodic review was triggered by the issuance of the arrest warrant and, therefore, that the Pre-Trial Chamber had neglected its obligations of review).

[136] Rome Statute, Art. 82(1)(b). On interlocutory appeals, see Chapter 11, Section 11.4.

In the *Lubanga* case, the Appeals Chamber strictly construed the language of the Rome Statute and rejected the prosecution's argument that the pre-trial chamber's decisions on interim release are discretionary. The Appeals Chamber noted that '[d]epending upon whether or not the conditions of Article 58(1) of the [Rome] Statute continue to be met, the detained person *shall* be continued to be detained or *shall* be released'.[137] Thus, unlike decisions on provisional release at the *ad hoc* Tribunals, such decisions at the ICC are not of a discretionary character.

As at the *ad hoc* Tribunals and the SCSL, the questions on which the pre-trial chamber must be satisfied before ordering release focus on the necessity of ensuring that the detained person will appear for trial, and that he or she will not obstruct the proceedings of the court; the latter of these factors is most often characterised as whether the person is likely to endanger witnesses, or exert pressure upon them while released.[138] Also as at the *ad hoc* Tribunals and the SCSL, these factors operate in the alternative; either one alone is enough to require continued detention.[139] Unlike at the *ad hoc* Tribunals and the SCSL, however, because these factors are necessarily taken into account in the issuance of the initial arrest warrant by the pre-trial chamber – with at least one of them being found against the accused as a necessary predicate for arrest – every application for interim release begins from the baseline assumption that continued detention is necessary absent a change of circumstances. According to the Appeals Chamber, the requirement of changed circumstances 'imports either a change in some or all of the facts underlying a previous decision on detention, or a new fact satisfying a Chamber that a modification of its prior ruling is necessary'.[140]

The *Bemba* Pre-Trial Chamber was the first to grant interim release to a person detained by the ICC, and the case is illustrative of the changed circumstances requirement. On Bemba's fourth application for release, and following the confirmation of his charges, the Pre-Trial Chamber found a 'substantial change in

[137] *Lubanga* Appeal Decision on Interim Release, *supra* note 84, para. 134; see also *Prosecutor* v. *Bemba*, Doc. No. ICC-01/05-01/08-631-Red, Judgment on the Appeal of the Prosecutor Against Pre-Trial Chamber II's 'Decision on the Interim Release of Jean-Pierre Bemba Gombo and Convening Hearings with the Kingdom of Belgium, the Republic of Portugal, the Republic of France, the Federal Republic of Germany, the Italian Republic, and the Republic of South Africa', 2 December 2009 ('*Bemba* Appeal Decision on Interim Release'), para. 59.

[138] See, e.g., *Lubanga* Appeal Decision on Interim Release, *supra* note 84, para. 139 (noting the Pre-Trial Chamber's observation that Lubanga knew the identities of some of the witnesses in his case and that there would be a risk that he would exert pressure on them if released, and recalling its earlier finding in its decision to issue the warrant of arrest of the potential endangerment of certain witnesses).

[139] *Bemba* Appeal Decision on Interim Release, *supra* note 137, para. 89 (noting that if one of the conditions set forth in Article 58(1)(b) of the Rome Statute is fulfilled, the other conditions do not have to be addressed, and detention must be maintained; and declining to address the Pre-Trial Chamber's analysis of additional factors after finding the Pre-Trial Chamber had erred in its analysis of the first factor); accord *Lubanga* Appeal Decision on Interim Release, *supra* note 84, para. 139.

[140] *Bemba* Appeal Decision on Interim Release, *supra* note 137, para. 60.

circumstances' since its decision denying Bemba's third application for release.[141] In granting the prosecution's appeal of the Pre-Trial Chamber's decision to release Bemba, the Appeals Chamber analysed in detail the various changed circumstances described by the Pre-Trial Chamber, rejecting each one as representing either no change at all, or something which the Pre-Trial Chamber did not adequately explain.[142] Ultimately, the Appeals Chamber found that the only relevant changed circumstance was the confirmation of the charges, something which made Bemba more likely to abscond.[143] As a result, Bemba remained in detention.

As at the *ad hoc* Tribunals and the SCSL, should the pre-trial chamber decide to grant an application for interim release, it may impose conditions on that release. Such conditions may include that the released person (1) must not travel beyond certain territorial limits without the explicit agreement of the chamber; (2) must not go to certain places or associate with certain persons; (3) must not contact victims or witnesses directly or indirectly; (4) must not engage in certain (unspecified) professional activities; (5) must reside at a particular address; (6) must respond when summoned; (7) must post bond or provide real or personal security or surety; or (8) must supply the Registrar with all identity documents, including his or her passport.[144] Should the pre-trial chamber decide to grant interim release and impose conditions, it must specify the appropriate conditions and identify a state willing to accept the person and enforce the conditions in the same decision in which the release is granted. When the *Bemba* Pre-Trial Chamber granted interim release, its decision deferred implementation of that release 'pending a decision in which State [he] will be released and which set of conditions shall be imposed on him'.[145] In addition to reversing the Pre-Trial Chamber's decision for the reasons specified above, the Appeals Chamber also held that the Pre-Trial Chamber had erred by failing to specify the appropriate conditions of release once it had decided that some conditions would be appropriate.[146]

[141] *Prosecutor* v. *Bemba*, Doc. No. ICC-01/05-01/08-475, Decision on the Interim Release of Jean-Pierre Bemba Gombo and Convening Hearings with the Kingdom of Belgium, the Republic of Portugal, the Republic of France, the Federal Republic of Germany, the Italian Republic, and the Republic of South Africa, 14 August 2009 ('*Bemba* Fourth Pre-Trial Decision on Interim Release'), para. 69.

[142] *Bemba* Appeal Decision on Interim Release, *supra* note 137, paras. 66–88 (noting that the Pre-Trial Chamber had incorrectly failed to acknowledge that the confirmation of charges increased the likelihood the accused would abscond; that the Pre-Trial Chamber had incorrectly assessed the accused's political and professional position and international ties, in that nothing about them had changed since the previous decision on interim release; that the Pre-Trial Chamber had inadequately assessed the accused's financial situation and resources; that the Pre-Trial Chamber had inappropriately given weight to the accused's previous offer to surrender and his professed willingness to cooperate; and that the Pre-Trial Chamber had weighed the accused's good behaviour while in detention too heavily).

[143] *Ibid.*, para. 70 (noting that the finding by the Pre-Trial Chamber that there were substantial grounds to believe that the accused committed the crimes charged increased the likelihood that he might abscond).

[144] ICC Rule 119(1).

[145] *Bemba* Fourth Pre-Trial Decision on Interim Release, *supra* note 141, para. 79.

[146] *Bemba* Appeal Decision on Interim Release, *supra* note 137, paras. 104–109.

As with the overall length of pre-trial detention – discussed above – nothing in the ICC's procedural framework requires a trial chamber to review *proprio motu* whether an accused should be granted interim release. Nevertheless, when the *Lubanga* case was transferred to the Trial Chamber following the confirmation of charges, the Trial Chamber undertook *proprio motu* to review whether circumstances had changed such that Lubanga should be granted interim release. In an exceedingly brief analysis, the Chamber then noted that Lubanga faced grave charges and, if released, was likely to return to the Democratic Republic of the Congo, with the probable consequence that the Court would no longer be able to secure his attendance at trial voluntarily. Thus, detention remained necessary.[147] The Trial Chamber continued to periodically review Lubanga's detention in the same manner, something which other trial chambers have emulated.[148]

4.3.4 Detention and release pending appeal on the merits

The Rules of the *ad hoc* Tribunals and the SCSL all provide that an acquitted person may continue to be held in custody pending the prosecution's appeal.[149] Convicted persons are automatically detained, even where one or both parties file an appeal,[150] and the Appeals Chamber may grant provisional release to a convicted person pending an appeal if it is satisfied (1) that the appellant, if released, will either appear at the hearing of the appeal or will surrender into detention at the appointed time; (2) that the appellant will not pose a danger to any victim, witness, or other person; and (3) that 'special circumstances exist warranting such release'.[151] These conditions must be considered cumulatively, and must be demonstrated by the appellant 'on a balance of probabilities, and the fact that an individual has already been sentenced is a matter to be taken into account by the Appeals Chamber when balancing the probabilities'.[152] Should the Appeals Chamber decide

[147] *Lubanga* Trial Decision on Interim Release, *supra* note 87, para. 8.

[148] *Prosecutor* v. *Lubanga*, Doc. No. ICC-01/04-01/06-1151, Decision Reviewing the Trial Chamber's Ruling on the Detention of Thomas Lubanga Dyilo in Accordance with Rule 118(2), 1 February 2008; *Prosecutor* v. *Lubanga*, Doc. No. ICC-01/04-01/06-1359, Decision Reviewing the Trial Chamber's Ruling on the Detention of Thomas Lubanga Dyilo in Accordance with Rule 118(2), 29 May 2008.

[149] ICTY Rule 99(B) ('If, at the time the judgement is pronounced, the Prosecutor advises the Trial Chamber in open court of the Prosecutor's intention to file notice of appeal ... the Trial Chamber may, on application in that behalf by the Prosecutor and upon hearing the parties, in its discretion, issue an order for the continued detention of the accused, pending the determination of the appeal'). Accord ICTR Rule 99(B); SCSL Rule 99(B). Trial chambers at the *ad hoc* Tribunals have both granted and denied such prosecution motions for continued detention of the acquitted person pending appeal. See Chapter 10, Section 10.4.2.

[150] See Chapter 10, Section 10.4 (noting that, where a trial chamber convicts the accused and one or both of the parties files an appeal, the tribunal continues to hold the convicted person until resolution of the appeal).

[151] ICTY Rule 65(I); ICTR Rule 65(I).

[152] *Prosecutor* v. *Delić*, Case No. IT-04-83-A, Decision on Motion of Rasim Delić for Provisional Release, 11 May 2009, para. 5; *Prosecutor* v. *Strugar*, Case No. IT-01-42-A, Decision on the Renewed Defence Request Seeking Provisional Release on Compassionate Grounds, 15 April 2008 ('*Strugar* Appeal Decision on Provisional Release'), para. 5.

that provisional release is appropriate, it may impose such conditions as are appropriate to ensure the return of the convicted person.[153]

The requirement to demonstrate 'special circumstances' for post-conviction release pending appeal is difficult to satisfy, as the Appeals Chamber has held that special circumstances related to humane and compassionate considerations exist only 'where there is an *acute justification*, such as the appellant's medical need or a memorial service for a close family member'.[154] Post-conviction release pending appeal remains rare, although the Appeals Chamber has exceptionally granted provisional release for an accused to visit a close family member in extremely poor health whose death was believed to be imminent.[155]

Whether similarly difficult standards will be applied to post-conviction applications for release at the ICC remains to be seen. The Rome Statute mandates that a convicted person shall remain in custody pending an appeal '[u]nless the Trial Chamber orders otherwise'.[156] No specific standards govern the issuance of such an order, but presumably a trial chamber would be governed at a minimum by the standards applicable to interim release pending trial. The Rome Statute also provides that, upon the request of the prosecution, an acquitted person may continue to be held in detention pending the prosecution's appeal. Here, however, the presumption is against detention, as the acquitted person must be released except where the trial chamber finds 'exceptional circumstances ... having regard, *inter alia*, to the concrete risk of flight, the seriousness of the offence charged and the probability of [the prosecution's] success on appeal'.[157]

4.4 Conclusion

During the investigation phase of international criminal cases, prosecutorial independence is at its zenith. With few substantive restrictions, the prosecution's discretion in deciding which cases to investigate, how to conduct those investigations, and which individuals to ultimately indict, is near absolute. While the ICC pre-trial chamber certainly encroaches somewhat on the exercise of the prosecution's discretion in specific instances, the ICC Prosecutor largely enjoys the same independence as the Prosecutors at the *ad hoc* Tribunals.

[153] ICTY Rule 65(I); ICTR Rule 65(I).

[154] See, e.g., *Milutinović et al.* 22 May 2009 Appeal Decision on Provisional Release, *supra* note 122, paras. 9–10 (emphasis added) (granting provisional release after finding that the accused's necessary medical treatment was more likely to be successful if conducted in Serbia, and that this constituted 'acute justification'). See also *Prosecutor* v. *Brđanin*, Case No. IT-99-36-A, Decision on Radoslav Brđanin's Motion for Provisional Release, 23 February 2007, para. 6; *Prosecutor* v. *Simić*, Case No. IT-95-9-A, Decision on Motion of Blagoje Simić Pursuant to Rule 65(I) for Provisional Release for a Fixed Period to Attend Memorial Services for his Father, 21 October 2004, para. 20.

[155] *Strugar* Appeal Decision on Provisional Release, *supra* note 152, para. 10.

[156] Rome Statute, Art. 81(3)(a). See also Chapter 10, Section 10.4.

[157] *Ibid.*, Art. 81(3)(c)(1). See also Chapter 10, Section 10.4.2.

The investigative phase at the tribunals is the first phase during which international human rights norms relative to the rights of suspects come into play. It is during investigations that the prosecution first comes into contact with a suspect *as* a suspect, and the point at which the prosecution's obligation to respect certain rights is engaged. Those rights are enshrined in the governing instruments of the tribunals and traceable directly to international human rights instruments. The tribunals have taken great pains to acknowledge the importance of human rights norms and the seriousness of their obligations to respect them. For the most part, they have fulfilled those obligations. Suspects before any of the tribunals enjoy rights similar to suspects in national criminal proceedings. The right against self-incrimination, the right to the presence of counsel when questioned by the prosecution, the right to be informed of rights and to the services of an interpreter, and the right not to be subjected to cruel treatment during investigations all appear to be reasonably well respected by the prosecution and well guarded by the judges. Additionally, the tribunals have generally ensured that the conditions of detention meet or exceed international human rights standards.

At least with regard to the *ad hoc* Tribunals, the same cannot be categorically said for the right to be free from arbitrary arrest or detention, the right to be tried without undue delay, and the right to apply for release from detention pending and during trial. The Tribunals' approaches to all three of these rights seem to weigh heavily against the accused. Although accused are able to obtain judicial review of the legality of their detentions, chambers have yet to find it appropriate to decline to exercise jurisdiction in those instances in which the accused was haled before the court under questionable – or admittedly unlawful – circumstances. *Male captus, bene detentus*, although formally eschewed by the Tribunals, is alive and well. The complexity of the cases, the number of witnesses, the limited resources available to the Tribunals, and the voluminous amounts of evidence – particularly in multi-accused trials – virtually guarantee pre-trial detention at the Tribunals will be shockingly lengthy by comparison to national criminal cases. Moreover, the practice of the Tribunals demonstrates that the statutory right of each accused to be brought to trial without undue delay is expansively construed in favour of the prosecution.

Release from detention pending or during trial remains exceedingly difficult to obtain. In practice, even though such a presumption no longer appears in the tribunals' constitutive texts,[158] detention remains the rule, release the exception. Even as the stabilisation of security conditions in the former Yugoslavia has made provisional release more palatable to the ICTY's trial chamber judges, the Appeals Chamber has narrowed the discretion available to them to grant provisional release in the later stages of proceedings.

[158] See *supra* Section 4.3.3.1 (discussing the deletion of the 'exceptional circumstances' requirement).

It is too early to tell whether the ICC will improve on these aspects of the treatment of accused in international criminal trials. The Rome Statute certainly provides a framework better suited to the protection of these rights. Whether the ICC's judges will mould that framework in favour of the accused, or whether they will invoke the serious nature and complexity of the crimes within the Court's jurisdiction to mimic the *ad hoc* Tribunals, remains to be seen.

5

Defence counsel, *amici curiae*, and the different forms of representation of accused

CONTENTS

In any criminal justice system, including those set up to try persons thought responsible for international crimes, fundamental human rights principles demand that accused persons have the ability to defend themselves against criminal allegations. Among these fundamental rights are the right to be represented by qualified defence counsel, at no cost if the accused cannot afford counsel; and, with certain limitations developed in the jurisprudence, the right to conduct their own defence. Defence representation before international criminal tribunals can take many forms, including privately funded defence counsel; tribunal-funded defence counsel; self-representation, which implicates a range of procedural and resource issues; and even the use of *amici curiae* to perform many of the tasks traditionally performed by defence counsel. There are two basic categories of legal representation in international criminal law: representation by counsel and self-representation. As will be discussed in some depth, these two different models of representation give rise to variants that impact significantly on the capacity of international criminal tribunals to deliver a fair trial.

This chapter considers the regulatory structure and jurisprudence relating to these different procedural models. Like most chapters in this volume, the chapter focuses mainly on the ICC, ICTY, and ICTR, with occasional reference to the SCSL, Special Tribunal for Lebanon ('STL'), or another internationalised tribunal if their relevant procedures illustrate an innovative approach or otherwise aid the analysis of the key issues surrounding representation of accused persons. Where procedures across the tribunals vary significantly, we discuss each tribunal in a separate subsection.

Section 5.1 begins by exploring the human rights foundation for legal representation in international criminal law, noting its modern roots in the ICCPR and its status as part of the *jus cogens* norm guaranteeing the right to a fair trial. Section 5.2 considers the myriad procedural rules and issues related to representation by defence counsel at the different international criminal tribunals. Sections 5.3 to 5.7 look at self-representation, its growing significance in relation to the efficiency and legitimacy of international criminal proceedings, the various ways of providing resources to self-represented accused, and the many fair trial issues implicated by this form of representation. This chapter concludes with some reflections on the different models of representation, how these impact on the procedural framework of international criminal law, and where these issues might be heading as international criminal law continues to develop.

5.1 Legal representation as a human right

While the international criminal tribunals have defence models and procedures that differ from one another in certain respects, they are all premised on the same human rights provisions contained in Article 14(3)(b) and (d) of the ICCPR. These clauses provide that, in the determination of a criminal charge against them, everyone is entitled

> [t]o have adequate time and facilities for the preparation of his defence and to communicate with counsel of his own choosing[;] ... to defend himself ... through legal assistance of his own choosing; to be informed, if he does not have legal assistance, of this right; and to have legal assistance assigned to him, in any case where the interests of justice so require, and without payment by him in any such case if he does not have sufficient means to pay for it.[1]

Chapter 1 of this volume considers in detail the relevance of the human rights regime to the creation and interpretation of international criminal procedure. The regulatory framework giving effect to rights and obligations in respect of defence, defence counsel and other forms of representation, and resources for the defence of accused persons in international criminal tribunals reflects significant adherence to the articulation of the right to counsel in human rights law, as well as to the interpretation and application of that right in the human rights regime.

The right to counsel forms part of the *jus cogens* norm[2] guaranteeing a fair trial to persons accused of crimes.[3] The constellation of rights that makes up the fair trial norm, often referred to as 'due process rights' or 'minimum guarantees', is articulated in the subparagraphs of Article 14 of the ICCPR.[4] These individual rights, including the right to counsel, do not themselves amount to *jus cogens* norms because they may be interpreted contextually or even derogated from in order to achieve the higher purpose of a fair trial.[5] Furthermore, international criminal law is a *sui generis* system of law in which human rights must be interpreted in a manner consistent with the particularities of that

[1] ICCPR, Art. 14(3)(b), (d). This formulation is reflected in other regional human rights instruments. See, e.g., ECHR, Art. 6(3)(c); ACHR, Art. 8(2)(d).

[2] A *jus cogens* norm, or peremptory norm of international law, is defined as 'a norm accepted and recognized by the international community of States as a whole as a norm from which no derogation is permitted and which can be modified only by a subsequent norm of general international law having the same character'. Vienna Convention on the Law of Treaties, 23 May 1969, entered into force 27 January 1980, 1155 UNTS 331, Art. 53. See also Robert Y. Jennings and Arthur Watts (eds.), *Oppenheim's International Law* (9th edn 1992), pp. 7–8; Christos L. Rozakis, *The Concept of Jus Cogens in the Law of Treaties* (1976), p. 11.

[3] The right to a fair trial is sometimes described as a 'derivative *jus cogens* norm', because, while it does not appear in nonderogable provisions of multilateral treaties or other sources, it is essential to the protection of other *jus cogens* norms. See Francisco F. Martin, Stephen J. Schnably, Richard Wilson, Jonathan S. Simon, and Mark V. Tushnet, *International Human Rights and Humanitarian Law: Treaties, Cases, and Analysis* (2006), p. 36.

[4] These rights are reflected in an array of human rights instruments and in the constitutional frameworks of the international criminal tribunals, as discussed in Section 5.2, *infra*.

[5] See Gideon Boas, *The Milošević Trial: Lessons for the Conduct of Complex International Criminal Proceedings* (2007), pp. 15–21, 69–78.

system.[6] Nevertheless, it does not appear that any decision of the international criminal tribunals in relation to the right to counsel as set out in Article 14(3)(d) of the ICCPR has significantly altered the understanding of this right in human rights law.

5.2 Defence counsel representation

As with many areas of international criminal procedure, the regulatory framework for defence counsel representation before many of the international tribunals is not enshrined in the respective Statutes.[7] Unlike the other 'party' to international criminal proceedings – the prosecution – the defence is largely not an integrated part of the institutional structure. Instead, defence counsel and representation issues are handled by the Registry of each tribunal, with an internal unit or office dedicated to developing rules and practices relating to the appointment of counsel, their remuneration, professional conduct, conflicts of interest, termination, and withdrawal. This lack of procedural parity with the prosecution might suggest that the defence exists more as the 'second-class' party to the proceedings. Indeed, the unequal place of the defence in the tribunal structure,[8] particularly at the ICC, which has had the opportunity to benefit from the experience of the *ad hoc* Tribunals in its evolution, has led some commentators to express regret.[9]

It is certainly difficult to rebut the argument that the prosecution is given considerable time and resources to prepare cases for trial, while accused persons are accorded far less time. As with Slobodan Milošević, who (over considerable objection) found himself at trial within eight months of arrest,[10] Radovan Karadžić was

[6] See *ibid.*, pp. 69–78; Patrick L. Robinson, 'Ensuring Fair and Expeditious Trials at the International Criminal Tribunal for the Former Yugoslavia', (2000) 11 *European Journal of International Law* 569, 572–573. See also Martin, Schnably, Wilson, Simon, and Tushnet, *supra* note 3, p. 36 n. 43; cf. Salvatore Zappalà, *Human Rights in International Criminal Proceedings* (2003), p. 5; Christoph Safferling, *Towards an International Criminal Procedure* (2001), p. 36. But see Gabrielle McIntyre, 'Defining Human Rights in the Arena of International Humanitarian Law: Human Rights in the Jurisprudence of the ICTY', in Gideon Boas and William A. Schabas (eds.), *International Criminal Law Developments in the Case Law of the ICTY* (2002), p. 193.

[7] As noted below, the SCSL is an exception to this general observation. See *infra* Section 5.2.1.3.

[8] Save for the recently created Special Tribunal for Lebanon. See *infra* Section 5.2.1.4.

[9] See, e.g., Alexander Zahar and Göran Sluiter, *International Criminal Law: A Critical Introduction* (2008), pp. 19, 60; M. Cherif Bassiouni and Peter Manikas, *The Law of the International Criminal Tribunal for the Former Yugoslavia* (1996), p. 298.

[10] The prosecution acknowledged early in the proceedings the enormity of its case. In relation to the search for exculpatory material alone, the prosecution stated that it had expended 'the equivalent of twenty-six "person years" of labour and cost nearly 1.5 million U.S. dollars' in identifying potentially relevant material to serve on the accused. *Prosecutor* v. *Slobodan Milošević*, Case No. IT-02-54-T, Transcript, 29 November 2005, p. 46687. Despite complaints to the Trial Chamber that this volume of material made it impossible to prepare and proceed to trial in the time stipulated by the Chamber, the trial proceeded, *Prosecutor* v. *Slobodan Milošević*, Case No. IT-02-54-T, Transcript, 25 July 2002, p. 8639, stalling only when the accused became too sick to attend trial. See Boas, *supra* note 5, pp. 211–213.

also rushed to trial shortly after his arrest and transfer to The Hague; he was ostensibly given a matter of months to assemble his defence, while the prosecution had many years to prepare for trial.[11] This different position for the defence vis-à-vis the prosecution offices at the international criminal tribunals does give the impression that the former is at a disadvantage in the adversarial proceedings.[12]

Compensating for a lack of procedural depth in the Statutes of the international criminal tribunals, the judges and Registry officials have developed Rules of Procedure and Evidence, along with relevant directives, regulations, and codes of conduct, that dictate the manner in which an accused is availed of legal assistance, and the extent of that assistance.[13] These rules, regulations, and directives have lent a degree of coherence and structure to defence representation before international criminal tribunals.

In general, defence representation in the international criminal tribunals provides for three representation scenarios: (1) the accused chooses and engages qualified counsel, remunerated directly by the accused or a third party; (2) if indigent, the accused is assigned counsel by the tribunal under its legal aid scheme; or (3) the accused defends himself or herself directly, without counsel. The subsections that follow discuss the first two scenarios, which encapsulate the classic defence counsel representation model, and the rules of professional conduct applicable to defence counsel. Section 5.3 explores the third – and far more complex – scenario.

5.2.1 The appointment and assignment of defence counsel

5.2.1.1 Defence counsel at the ad hoc *Tribunals*

For appointment to defend accused in the *ad hoc* Tribunals, counsel must fulfil the requirements set out in Rule 44(A) in the ICTY Rules and ICTR Rules, derived from the ICCPR, which provide for certain minimum qualifications, such as the requirements that counsel be admitted to practice law in a domestic jurisdiction or be a university professor of law; be proficient in one of the Tribunal's working languages; and be a member in good standing of an association of defence counsel recognised by the Registrar. If accused do not have

[11] See *Prosecutor* v. *Karadžić*, Case No. IT-95-5/18-T, Decision on Appointment of Counsel and Order on Further Trial Proceedings, 5 November 2009.

[12] But see *infra* Section 5.2.1.3 (discussing the significantly different position of the defence at the SCSL).

[13] See Rome Statute, Arts. 55(2)(c)–(d), 56(2)(d), 61(1), 67(1)(b), 67(1)(d); ICTY Statute, Arts. 18, 21; ICTR Statute, Arts. 17, 20; ICC Rules 20–22, 27(3), 121(2); ICTY Rules 44–46; ICTR Rules 44–46; Code of Professional Conduct for Counsel, 2 December 2005 ('ICC Code'); Directive on Assignment of Defence Counsel, 11 July 2006 ('ICTY Directive'); Code of Professional Conduct for Counsel Appearing Before the International Tribunal, 22 July 2006 ('ICTY Code'); Directive on Assignment of Defence Counsel, 14 March 2008 ('ICTR Directive'); Code of Professional Conduct for Defence Counsel, 8 June 1998 ('ICTR Code'). The ICTY and ICTR Directives and Codes are approved by the judges in plenary and promulgated thereafter by a decision of the Registrar. The ICC Code was adopted by the Assembly of States Parties. Full citations for these Codes and Directives appear in the Table of Short Forms.

sufficient means to pay for legal assistance, they are entitled – 'where the interests of justice so require' – to have legal assistance assigned at the expense of the Tribunal.

The UN Human Rights Committee has found that the interests of justice will mandate the provision of counsel where the charges confronted by the accused are of sufficient gravity.[14] As Michael Bohlander has pointed out, the 'interests of justice' condition is effectively superfluous in international criminal law, as the interests of justice require that all persons accused of war crimes who request counsel, and who are without sufficient means to pay for it, be provided with counsel free of charge.[15] Assignment of counsel to an accused or a suspect is governed by Rule 45 in the ICTY Rules and ICTR Rules, as well as the procedure set out in their respective Directives on Assignment of Defence Counsel, which are promulgated by the Registrar of each Tribunal. In most cases, the accused makes a request to the Registrar, who is the responsible authority in such matters, to have counsel assigned.[16] The Registrar maintains a list of persons eligible to be assigned as counsel. As articulated in the Rules[17] and the Directives[18] of the two Tribunals, persons on the list must fulfil the requirements of Rule 44(A), as well as possess established competence in 'criminal law and/or international criminal law/international humanitarian law/international human rights law';[19] have at least seven years' experience in criminal proceedings;[20] be fluent in one of the working languages, English or French, or in exceptional circumstances, in the language of the accused;[21] and must have indicated their willingness and availability to act as assigned counsel to any indigent person detained at the Tribunal.[22]

[14] See General Comment No. 32, 'Article 14: Right to equality before courts and tribunals and to a fair trial', UN Doc. CCPR/C/GC/32, 23 August 2007 ('General Comment No. 32'), para. 38. See also *Lindon* v. *Australia*, Human Rights Committee, Communication No. 646/1995, UN Doc. CCPR/C/64/D/646/1995, 25 November 1998, para. 6.5; *Z.P.* v. *Canada*, Human Rights Committee, Communication No. 341/1988, UN Doc. CCPR/C/41/D/341/1988, para. 5.4.

[15] See Michael Bohlander, 'The Defence', in Gideon Boas and William A. Schabas, *International Criminal Law Developments in the Case Law of the ICTY* (2003), p. 39.

[16] See ICTY Directive, Art. 7; ICTR Directive, Art. 7. The Office of Legal Affairs and Detention Matters ('OLAD') at the ICTY estimates that eighty per cent of all accused in the past two years have declared themselves indigent. Author interview with Martin Petrov, ICTY OLAD representative, 20 April 2006.

[17] ICTY Rule 45(A)–(B).

[18] ICTY Directive, Art. 14; ICTR Directive, Art. 14. [19] ICTY Rule 45(B)(ii).

[20] This amendment was introduced at the ICTY in July 2004. See Rules of Procedure and Evidence of the International Criminal Tribunal for the former Yugoslavia, UN Doc. IT/32/Rev.33, as amended 17 December 2004, available at www.icty.org/x/file/Legal%20Library/Rules_procedure_evidence/IT032_rev33_ en.pdf, Rule 45(B)(iii). Existing counsel who lacked these qualifications were permitted to remain. The ICTR similarly requires seven years' minimum experience. ICTR Rule 45(A).

[21] ICTY Rule 44(A)(ii); ICTR Rule 45(A). Despite the 'exceptional circumstances' terminology, it was common practice at the ICTY, at least for some time, for counsel to be assigned even though they did not speak either of the working languages of the Tribunal. See, e.g., *Prosecutor* v. *Stanišić*, Case No. IT-04-79-PT, Decision of Deputy Registrar, 7 July 2008.

[22] ICTY Rule 45(B); ICTR Rule 45(A).

The suspect or accused can review the list and request particular counsel.[23] In practice, a suspect or accused can also request a particular counsel to be added to the list.[24] The right to choose counsel, however, is not absolute. The Registrar may disregard a request in the interests of justice,[25] such as to avoid possible conflicts of interest.[26] When assigning counsel, the Registrar may also take into account 'the resources of the Tribunal, competence and recognised experience of counsel, geographical distribution, and a balance of the principal legal systems of the world, irrespective of the age, gender, race or nationality of the candidates'.[27]

Detainees held under the authority of the Tribunal, suspects to be questioned by the Office of the Prosecutor, and accused persons in pre-trial, trial, and appeal proceedings are entitled to appointment of counsel.[28] In the event of a review proceeding,[29] appointment of counsel is possible only after review has been granted by the Appeals Chamber, or, if deemed necessary, at the stage at which a request for review is being considered by the Chamber.[30]

The burden of establishing indigence rests on persons seeking the appointment of counsel,[31] who must show that they are unable to remunerate counsel and therefore entitled to assigned counsel at the expense of the tribunal. The suspect or accused must complete a declaration of means[32] and the Registrar is authorised to

[23] ICTY Directive, Art. 11(D)(i).

[24] See, e.g., *Prosecutor* v. *Delalić, Mucić, Delić and Landžo*, Case No. IT-96-21-T, Decision on Request by Accused Mucić for Assignment of New Counsel, 24 June 1996, para. 2.

[25] See, e.g., *Prosecutor* v. *Akayesu*, Case No. ICTR-96-4-A, Judgement, 1 June 2001, paras. 60–64 (noting that 'the issue of the right of an indigent accused to counsel of his own choosing' requires balancing 'affording the accused as effective a defence as possible to ensure a fair trial' with 'proper use of the Tribunal's resources'; and concluding that 'the Registrar is not necessarily bound by the wishes of an indigent accused', but 'has wide discretion, which he exercises in the interests of justice', and that 'the Trial Chamber had a duty to ensure that the rights of the Accused were respected and that the trial proceeded fairly and expeditiously' in accordance with the ICTR Statute).

[26] See, e.g., *Prosecutor* v. *Knežević*, Case Nos. IT-95-4-PT, IT-95-8/1-PT, Decision on Accused's Request for Review of Registrar's Decision as to Assignment of Counsel, 6 September 2002 ('*Knežević* September 2002 Decision'). Knežević initially requested an attorney, Miodrag Deretić, who was already assigned as co-counsel to another accused formerly charged in the same indictment. That initial request was denied. Knežević then requested a different attorney, Draško Zeć, who worked in the same law office as Deretić. Upon request for clarification from the Registry, the attorneys did not sufficiently clarify their professional relationship, and in a non-privileged conversation Zeć told Knežević he should request Zeć's appointment as it would allow Deretić to act alongside him. The Trial Chamber found that the Registrar was justified in refusing to appoint Zeć as counsel, and that Zeć's intention to allow Deretić to act alongside him constituted improper conduct. *Ibid.*, p. 5.

[27] *Prosecutor* v. *Nyiramasuhuko and Ntahobali*, Case No. ICTR-97-21-T, Decision on a Preliminary Motion by the Defence for the Assignment of a Co-counsel to Pauline Nyiramasuhuko, 13 March 1998, para. 17.

[28] ICTY Directive, Art. 5(iii) (detainees); ICTY Directive, Art. 5(ii) (suspects); ICTY Directive, Art. 5(iii) (accused); ICTR Directive, Art. 2(B) (detainees); ICTR Directive, Art. 2(A) (suspects and accused).

[29] An exceptional remedy which can be granted following an appellate judgement on the merits. See Chapter 11, Section 11.7.

[30] See *Barayagwiza* v. *Prosecutor*, Case No. ICTR-99-52A-R, Decision on Jean-Bosco Barayagwiza's Motion of 6 March 2008, 11 April 2008.

[31] ICTY Directive, Art. 8(A); ICTR Directive, Art. 3.

[32] ICTY Directive, Art. 9; ICTR Directive, Art. 7.

gather information to assist in making a determination.[33] If the suspect or accused is found not to be truly indigent, the Registrar can refuse to assign counsel,[34] or, at the ICTY, can order only partial coverage of costs of counsel.[35] During the Registrar's consideration of the request, he or she can assign counsel temporarily to prevent prejudice to the suspect or accused.[36]

Appointment of co-counsel, legal assistants, consultants, investigators, and interpreters is also within the administrative powers of the Registrar; however, it is lead counsel who requests those appointments and selects and supervises defence team members.[37] The Registrar has primary responsibility for the assignment of counsel, and an accused may appeal the Registrar's decision to the President of the tribunal.[38] In exceptional circumstances, the trial chamber may review the decision insofar as the fairness or integrity of the particular proceedings has been engaged.[39]

Both *ad hoc* Tribunal Registries operate a department that provides assistance to defence counsel: the Office of Legal Aid and Detention Matters at the ICTY, and Defence Counsel Support Services Management at the ICTR. While both Tribunals also have affiliated defence lawyers' associations, only the ICTY officially recognises its defence organisation.[40]

5.2.1.2 Defence counsel at the ICC

The Rome Statute contains a representation provision in Article 67(1)(d) that is similar to that of the *ad hoc* Tribunals, but which expressly limits the right of the accused concerning representation and presence during the trial. The system of representation before the ICC is established by its Statute, but as with the *ad hoc* Tribunal Statutes, there is little elaboration on the procedural framework for defence counsel representation within the ICC jurisdiction. The ICC Rules, drafted by states parties and adopted by the ASP, provide some detail, although instruments created by the Judges of the ICC – the Regulations of both the Court and the

[33] ICTY Directive, Art. 7; ICTR Directive, Art. 9.

[34] ICTY Directive, Art. 11(A); ICTR Directive, Art. 10(A).

[35] ICTY Directive, Art. 11(A).

[36] ICTY Directive, Art. 11(B); ICTR Directive, Art. 10(B). The temporary period lasts not more than 120 days at the ICTY; not more than thirty days at the ICTR.

[37] ICTY Directive, Art. 16(C)–(E); ICTR Directive, Art. 15(C).

[38] ICTY Directive, Art. 13(A); ICTR Directive, Art. 12(A).

[39] See ICTY Rule 54; ICTR Rule 54; ICTY Directive, Art. 13(B); ICTR Directive, Art. 12(B). See also, e.g., *Knežević* September 2002 Decision, *supra* note 26, p. 4 (Trial Chamber holding that while it was within its powers to intervene in determinations relating to the assignment of counsel where the fairness of the proceedings is implicated, the Registrar had not erred in his determination of the matter under review). See also *Prosecutor* v. *Blagojević and Jokić*, Case No. IT-02-60-AR73.4, Public and Redacted Reasons for Decision on Appeal by Vidoje Blagojević to Replace His Defense Team, 7 November 2003 ('*Blagojević and Jokić* Defense Appeal Decision') (ICTY Appeals Chamber holding that trial chambers may intervene in the Registrar's domain where fair trial issues are raised).

[40] This group is called the 'Association of Defence Lawyers appearing before the ICTY'. For an example of this official recognition, see ICTY Directive, Articles 2, 4, 33.

Registry, and the Code of Professional Conduct for Counsel – create the detailed procedural structure relating to defence counsel representation.

Through the Court Regulations, the ICC judges have established the Office of Public Counsel for the Defence (OPCD)[41] as a form of in-house defence counsel to provide advice and *ad hoc* representation. The OPCD has two specific functions: (1) representing and protecting the rights of the accused during the initial stages of the investigation;[42] and (2) providing support and assistance to defence counsel and to the suspect or accused, including, where appropriate, legal research and advice, and appearing before the relevant chamber 'in respect of specific issues'.[43]

Similar to the *ad hoc* Tribunals, an indigent suspect or accused is entitled to assigned counsel paid for by the ICC.[44] The Registrar investigates and confirms claims of indigence,[45] and maintains a list of qualifying counsel from which accused persons or suspects may choose, or to which they may request that particular counsel be added.[46] Counsel acting for, and paid by, non-indigent accused must still be placed on the list of counsel authorised to appear before the Court. Interim counsel may be assigned where urgently required or until permanent counsel is assigned.[47] A chamber may also, in consultation with the Registrar, appoint counsel 'where the interests of justice so require'.[48]

The President of the Court reviews decisions of the Registrar concerning assignment of defence counsel prior to the confirmation of charges;[49] the pre-trial or trial chamber plays this role once charges against the accused have been confirmed.[50] Furthermore, like the *ad hoc* Tribunals, ICC chambers will most likely have power to review assignment decisions that affect the trial's fairness or expeditiousness, though no jurisprudence on this question yet exists.[51]

Qualification for eligibility as counsel is based on experience in international law or criminal law and procedure, either as a judge, prosecutor, advocate, or in a similar role, for at least ten years.[52] Counsel must also have no record of conviction of a serious criminal or disciplinary offence,[53] and be fluent in either English or

41 ICC Court Regulation 77. See also ICC Court Regulation 81 (noting that the Registrar shall also develop an Office of Public Counsel for victims).

42 ICC Court Regulation 77(4). 43 ICC Court Regulation 77(5).

44 Rome Statute, Art. 67(1)(d). 45 ICC Court Regulation 132.

46 ICC Rule 21(2); ICC Court Regulation 75; ICC Registry Regulation 122.

47 ICC Court Regulation 73; ICC Registry Regulation 129.

48 ICC Court Regulation 76(1). See also Rome Statute, Art. 56(2)(d).

49 ICC Rule 21(3); ICC Court Regulation 72.

50 Rome Statute, Arts. 61(11), 64(6)(a). Confirmation of charges in the ICC is discussed in Chapter 6, Section 6.1.1.

51 See Rome Statute, Art. 64(2) ('The Trial Chamber shall ensure that a trial is fair and expeditious and is conducted with full respect for the rights of the accused and due regard for the protection of victims and witnesses.'). While not expressly providing for such judicial review, it can be expected that the ICC will follow the *ad hoc* Tribunal practice in respect of this issue.

52 ICC Rule 22(1); ICC Court Regulation 67(1).

53 ICC Court Regulation 67(2).

French, the two working languages of the Court.[54] An interpreter will be provided at no cost to the defence if necessary to meet the requirements of fairness; which will be the case if a suspect is questioned in a language they do not fully understand or speak,[55] or if any of the proceedings or documents presented to the Court are in a language the accused does not fully understand or speak.[56]

Lead counsel for an accused assigned by the Court can choose assistants from a list maintained by the Registrar.[57] Inclusion on the list requires either five years of relevant experience in criminal proceedings or specific competence in international law or criminal law and procedure.[58] The ICC Rules anticipate that the ASP will facilitate the formation of an affiliated defence association at the ICC.[59] The International Criminal Defence Attorneys Association (ICDAA) launched the International Criminal Bar (ICB) to ensure a unified voice and independence for counsel practising before the ICC, although the ICB has not been recognised by the ASP as a legitimate body for the Registrar or Court to consult on issues related to the legal profession.[60] Both the ICB and the International Bar Association (IBA) submitted to the ICC Registry draft codes of conduct for counsel practising before the ICC, but it would appear that the Court has not yet adopted any such code. The IBA currently submits regular monitoring reports to the ICC with a focus on the rights of accused.[61] The lack of an official defence counsel association may create problems for the ICC in obtaining consensus on issues such as training and discipline; by comparison, resolution of these issues at the ICTY was assisted by that Tribunal's Association of Defence Counsel.[62]

5.2.1.3 Defence counsel at the SCSL

For the most part, the internationalised criminal tribunals follow the approaches of the *ad hoc* Tribunals and ICC in their provisions on defence counsel. However, the SCSL Rules formally establish a Defence Office, dedicated to 'ensuring the rights of suspects and accused'.[63] The Defence Office can assist in all three representation scenarios – that is, privately funded defence counsel, tribunal-funded defence counsel, and self-representation. The law governing the system of representation at the SCSL is set forth in the Statute, Rules, Directive on the Assignment of Counsel,[64]

[54] ICC Rule 22(1). [55] Rome Statute, Art. 55(1)(c).
[56] Rome Statute, Art. 67(1)(f).
[57] ICC Court Regulation 68; ICC Registry Regulations 125(1), 127.
[58] ICC Registry Regulation 124. [59] ICC Rule 20(3).
[60] Karen Corrie, Coalition for the International Criminal Court, 'Questions & Answers on Defense Counsel at the International Criminal Court', 30 June 2008, www.amicc.org/docs/Corrie%20Defense %20Q&A.pdf.
[61] These reports are available at www.ibanet.org/Human_Rights_Institute/ICC_Outreach_Monitoring/ ICC_ Monitoring.aspx.
[62] See Sylvia de Bertodano, 'What Price Defence? Resourcing the Defence at the ICTY', (2004) 2 *Journal of International Criminal Justice* 503, 503–508.
[63] SCSL Rule 45.
[64] Adopted on 1 October 2003. See www.sc-sl.org/LinkClick.aspx?fileticket=1FClI7mri4k%3d&tabid=176.

and Code of Professional Conduct for Counsel with the Right of Audience before the Special Court for Sierra Leone.[65] The Registrar is responsible for establishing, maintaining, and developing the Defence Office, which indicates that it is not an entirely independent organ of the Court. The Defence Office is headed by the Special Court Principal Defender, who is supported by a team of lawyers, duty counsel, and defence advisors.

Although it was originally conceived that the Defence Office would represent all accused at all stages of the proceedings, it soon became apparent that conflicts of interest between accused in interrelated cases or a multi-accused case would prevent such broad representation.[66] As such, the mandate of the Defence Office is to provide initial advice and assistance.[67] However, in providing such assistance, duty counsel must ensure they are not privy to any attorney–client confidences or arguments that will later be raised by the accused.

The Defence Office coordinates the legal aid programme[68] and 'renders a variety of assistance to appointed and assigned counsel, including administrative assistance, vetting of investigators, substantive legal research and aid in drafting motions and applications'; it also 'identifies legal issues that need to be raised before the judges of the Special Court, researches those issues, prepares briefs and then shares the fruits of that research with Defence Counsel'.[69] Furthermore, the Defence Office coordinates an outreach programme separate from the general Registry outreach programme.[70]

As noted, although an advance on the models used in the *ad hoc* Tribunals and the ICC, the Defence Office is still subject to the overall supervision of the Registrar, with the implicit limitations on independence. Funding and equality of arms with the Office of the Prosecutor have remained an issue.[71]

[65] Adopted on 14 May 2005. See www.sc-sl.org/LinkClick.aspx?fileticket=IbTonPmXLHk%3d&tabid=176.

[66] Unlike a domestic public defender model, where counsel may represent several accused with completely unrelated cases, in international criminal proceedings many of the defendants have related cases on similar facts. As such, no single public defender is able to represent all of the indigent defendants coming before the Court without grave conflicts of interest arising, as one accused may implicate another in the course of their defence. See John R.W.D. Jones, Claire Carlton-Hanciles, Haddijatou Kah-Jallow, Sam Scratch, and Ibrahim Yillah, 'The Special Court for Sierra Leone, A Defence Perspective', (2004) 2 *Journal of International Criminal Justice* 211, 213.

[67] See SCSL Rule 45(B)(i).

[68] See SCSL Rule 45(C). Assignment of counsel, however, is subject to the approval of the Registrar. SCSL Rule 44.

[69] Jones, Carlton-Hanciles, Kah-Jallow, Scratch, and Yillah, *supra* note 66, p. 215.

[70] *Ibid.*

[71] On the difference in resources available to the prosecution and defence, respectively, see, e.g., *ibid.*, pp. 229–230. The right to equality of arms is derived from Article 14 of the ICCPR. The UN Human Rights Committee has stated that the right is engaged in a number of provisions, including the requirement in Article 14(3)(b) to ensure an accused has adequate time and facilities to prepare a defence, and to be represented by and consult with counsel. See General Comment No. 32, *supra* note 14, para. 32. Accord *Smith* v. *Jamaica*, Communication No. 282/1988, UN Doc. CCPR/C/47/D/282/1988, para. 10.4; *Sawyers, McLean and McLean* v. *Jamaica*, Communication Nos. 226/1987 and 256/1987, UN Doc. CCPR/C/41/D/256/1987, para. 13.6.

5.2.1.4 Defence counsel at the Special Tribunal for Lebanon

The Special Tribunal for Lebanon (STL), established in 2007, builds on the innovation of the SCSL and goes further in an endeavour to improve the equality of arms between the defence and the prosecution. The STL is the first international criminal tribunal to institutionalise a Defence Office in its founding text.[72] The STL Statute also establishes the Defence Office as an independent organ of the Court, not a subsidiary of the Registry, as at the SCSL.[73] The Government of Lebanon has bound itself to cooperate with all organs of the Court, especially the prosecution and defence counsel.[74]

Although the Statute provides that the Defence Office may include one or more public defenders, similar to the system intended at the SCSL, this is not reflected in the STL Rules of Procedure and Evidence. Under these Rules, the staff of the Defence Office cannot take any instructions from suspects or accused persons or be involved in factual allegations or matters relating to a specific case.[75]

The Defence Office has a mandate to protect the rights of the defence, and provide support and assistance to defence counsel, including legal research, collection of evidence, and appearing before the chamber on specific issues.[76] Similar to the SCSL, the list of available defence counsel is maintained by the Defence Office, not the Registry.[77] In practice, although the Registry controls the overall budget for the Tribunal, the Defence Office maintains a significant level of independence, as its decisions are not subject to supervision by the Registrar.[78] The Office provides an array of support services to counsel, including providing facilities, advice, and training to defence counsel; maintaining a list of experts, investigators, legal assistants, and case managers who may be assigned to assist counsel; appearing before the chambers with regard to general defence issues; and seeking any cooperation

[72] Statute of the Special Tribunal for Lebanon, UN Doc. S/RES/1757 (2007), Annex ('STL Statute'), Art. 7. By contrast, the SCSL Defence Office was not established in that Court's Statute, but only its Rules of Procedure and Evidence. See SCSL Rule 45.

[73] STL Statute, *supra* note 72, Art. 7. See also *ibid.*, Art. 13(1) (providing that the Head of the Defence Office is to be independent).

[74] STL Statute, *supra* note 72, Art. 15(1) ('The Government shall cooperate with all organs of the Special Tribunal, in particular with the Prosecutor and defence counsel, at all stages of the proceedings. It shall facilitate access of the Prosecutor and defence counsel to sites, persons and relevant documents required for the investigation.').

[75] Rules of Procedure and Evidence, Doc. No. STL/BD/2009/01/Rev. 2, as amended 30 October 2009, Rule 57(I).

[76] STL Statute, *supra* note 72, Art. 13(2) ('The Defence Office, which may also include one or more public defenders, shall protect the rights of the defence, provide support and assistance to defence counsel and to the persons entitled to legal assistance, including, where appropriate, legal research, collection of evidence and advice, and appearing before the Pre-Trial Judge or a Chamber in respect of specific issues.').

[77] STL Statute, *supra* note 72, Art. 13(1).

[78] Gideon Boas and Gabriel Oosthuizen, International Criminal Law Services, 'Suggestions for Future Lessons-Learned Studies: The Experience of Other International and Hybrid Criminal Courts of Relevance to the International Criminal Court', January 2010, www.iclsfoundation.org/wp-content/uploads/2009/11/icls-report-lessonslearnedgapsstudy-final.pdf, p. 7.

that the defence may require from any third parties, including states.[79] The Defence Office has promulgated a Code of Professional Conduct for Counsel and is developing a resource pack for new defence counsel, including information on legal and practical issues. Also, to mitigate against a possible lack of communication, the Office is designed so that each defence counsel has a designated representative within the Office, thereby facilitating closer working relationships between counsel and the Office.[80]

The establishment of the Defence Office as an independent organ has been commended as a 'highly remarkable and welcome innovation'[81] in international criminal law, granting the defence 'a higher formal status'[82] with the aim of equality of arms,[83] and representing an 'advancement in the further development of effective but fair instruments for international adjudication [that] demonstrates many lessons learned from other existing international criminal tribunals'.[84] The STL model has, with good reason, been lauded as 'a precedential model for any future international courts in relation to defence',[85] and it will be interesting to see whether the experience of the STL fulfils its promise and influences further developments in the defence regime before the ICC.

5.2.2 Professional conduct of counsel

In every international criminal tribunal, defence counsel are bound by the governing instruments of the tribunal. While no comprehensive regime of ethics exists in international criminal law,[86] each tribunal has set forth certain ethical guidelines. Counsel owe obligations to the client and to the tribunal itself. The ICC, ICTY, and ICTR have all adopted a Code of Conduct which details the rights and duties outlined in their Statutes and Rules.[87] These Codes have many features in common and each provides basic principles focusing on the appropriate role of an advocate in the administration of justice. They suggest – and in the case of the ICTR state expressly – that the Code is not a comprehensive rendition of the

[79] See 'About the Defence Office', www.stl-tsl.org/sid/28.
[80] Boas and Oosthuizen, *supra* note 78, p. 43.
[81] Bert Swart, 'Cooperation Challenges for the Special Tribunal for Lebanon', (2007) 5 *Journal of International Criminal Justice* 1153, 1155.
[82] Jan Erik Wetzel and Yvonne Mitri, 'The Special Tribunal for Lebanon: A Court "Off the Shelf" for a Divided Country', (2008) 7 *Law and Practice of International Courts and Tribunals* 81, 97–98.
[83] See Cécile Aptel, 'Some Innovations in the Statute of the Special Tribunal for Lebanon', (2005) 5 *Journal of International Criminal Justice* 1107, nn. 29, 36 (citing Report of the Secretary-General on the Establishment of a Special Tribunal for Lebanon, UN Doc. S/2006/893, 15 November 2006, para. 30 and noting that institutionalisation of the Defence Office serves to ensure equality of arms); accord Swart, *supra* note 81, note 12.
[84] Wetzel and Mitri, *supra* note 82, p. 112.
[85] Boas and Oosthuizen, *supra* note 78, p. 45.
[86] See Laurel Baig, 'International Criminal Law and Legal Ethics: The Need for Shared Expectations', in (2009) *Proceedings of the 103rd Annual Meeting of the American Society of International Law.*
[87] See *supra* note 13 and accompanying text.

rights and obligations of counsel and that the inherent jurisdiction of the tribunal and any applicable national code of conduct will also be relevant to the conduct of counsel.[88]

5.2.2.1 Hierarchy and primacy of sources

The Code of Conduct of each institution applies to all defence counsel before the court or tribunal.[89] Counsel must follow the Statute and Rules governing the tribunal[90] and, to the extent there exists any inconsistency, the Codes must be read subject to these documents.[91] Moreover, each institution's Code states that, in case of inconsistency, the Code prevails in respect of counsel's conduct before the tribunal over any other codes of practice to which counsel may be subject, such as those regulating counsel's practice before the courts of his or her home country.[92] Nevertheless, the institution's Code of Conduct should not be considered exhaustive; counsel may still be held responsible for breaches of the other codes of practice to which they remain subject while practising before the tribunal, or through the institution's inherent jurisdiction to impose other standards or requirements on counsel appearing before it.[93]

As an example of these principles, in one case before the ICTY, defence counsel Deyan Ranko Brashich delayed informing the Tribunal of earlier disciplinary findings against him by the New York City Bar Association, which had determined that Brashich had breached its code of conduct on several occasions.[94] Such findings made him ineligible to practise at the ICTY.[95] The ICTY's disciplinary board imposed a fine of US$10,000.[96]

5.2.2.2 Obligations to the client

Generally, obligations to the client include acting professionally with competence, skill, and integrity;[97] and acting diligently and promptly to protect all client interests within the scope of the legal representation.[98] These obligations apply from

[88] ICTY Code, Art. 3; ICTR Code, Art. 1(4) (expressly stating that the Code should not be read as a full or complete listing of duties).
[89] ICC Code, Art. 1; ICTY Code, Art. 1(A); ICTR Code, Art. 3(2).
[90] See ICC Code, Art. 31(a); ICTY Code, Art. 35(i); ICTR Code, Art. 12(1).
[91] See ICTR Code, Article 1(2) (conflict between ICTR Code and ICTR Directive).
[92] ICC Code, Art. 4; ICTY Code, Art. 4; ICTR Code, Art. 19.
[93] See ICC Code, Arts. 30, 31(a), 38; ICTY Code, Art. 35(i); ICTR Code, Art. 1(4).
[94] See *In the Matter of Mr Deyan Ranko Brashich, Attorney at Law from the United States*, Case No. IT-00-39-A, Decision in the Appeal by the Registrar to the Disciplinary Board, 22 March 2007 ('March 2007 Disciplinary Board Decision'), Annex III (noting decisions regarding disciplinary complaints against Brashich from 25 January 2002, 1 April 2003, and other dates).
[95] See ICTY Directive, Art. 14(A)(ii) (disqualifying counsel if found guilty of local disciplinary actions); ICTY Code, Art. 35(v) (requiring counsel to disclose relevant information to the Registry).
[96] March 2007 Disciplinary Board Decision, *supra* note 94, paras. 44, 54–55.
[97] ICC Code, Arts. 7(2), 13(2)(c), 14(1); ICTY Code, Art. 10(i), (iv); ICTR Code, Art. 5(a), (d).
[98] ICC Code, Art. 13(2)(b); ICTY Code, Art. 11; ICTR Code, Art. 6.

initial dealings with a prospective client, through to conclusion of the matter, termination by the client, or the Registrar's withdrawal of the lawyer's authorisation to practise before the tribunal.[99]

Counsel must follow the objectives of the representation as outlined by the client.[100] Counsel must exercise his or her own judgement as to the best course of action in pursuing those objectives; but must also consult the client,[101] and keep the client informed as the proceedings progress.[102] Counsel's communication with the client may be restricted by the Chamber if the client chooses to testify. For example, in the *Popović* case, the Chamber ordered that the accused Pandurević could not communicate with his counsel about the substance of his testimony during cross-examination without leave of the Chamber.[103] Counsel must exercise independent professional judgement,[104] and must not be swayed by external pressures.[105] At the ICTY, this latter obligation includes the situation where counsel suspects that inducement from any person, organisation or state has influenced the client's instructions.[106] For the ICC, a mere 'reasonable inference' that the independence of counsel has been compromised is enough to constitute a breach of the Code of Conduct.[107]

Counsel must take into account the client's personal circumstances, such as any disability.[108] They cannot exert undue influence over the client or engage in improper conduct with the client.[109] Counsel cannot advise or assist a client to engage in criminal or fraudulent conduct, including acting contrary to the Statute or Rules of the tribunal.[110]

Unlike other ethical obligations, the requirements of confidentiality in a counsel's dealings with his or her client continue after the representation has ended,[111] unless the client consents to disclosure or discloses the information himself or herself.[112] Suspects or accused persons in detention have the right to privileged communication with their counsel.[113] Defence team members can generally pass

[99] ICC Code, Arts. 17(1), 18; ICTY Code, Art. 8(A); ICTR Code, Art. 4(1).
[100] ICC Code, Art. 14(2)(a); ICTY Code, Art. 8(B)(i); ICTR Code, Art. 4(2)(a).
[101] See ICC Code, Art. 14(2)(b); ICTY Code, Art. 8(B)(ii); ICTR Code, Art. 4(2)(b).
[102] ICC Code, Art. 15(1); ICTY Code, Art. 12; ICTR Code, Art. 7.
[103] *Prosecutor* v. *Popović, Beara, Nikolić, Miletić, Borovčanin, Gvero, and Pandurević*, Case No. IT-05-88-T, Transcript, 26 January 2009, pp. 30637–30638.
[104] ICC Code, Art. 6(1); ICTY Code, Art. 10(ii); ICTR Code, Art. 5(b)–(c).
[105] ICC Code, Art. 6(2)(a); ICTY Code, Art. 10(iii), (v); ICTR Code, Art. 5(e).
[106] See ICTY Code, Art. 8(B)(iii).
[107] ICC Code, Art. 6(2)(b).
[108] *Ibid.* Art. 9(2)–(3); ICTY Code, Art. 16; ICTR Code, Art. 10.
[109] ICC Code, Art. 9(1), (4); ICTY Code, Art. 15.
[110] ICC Code, Art. 31(b); ICTY Code, Arts. 8(C), 35(i); ICTR Code, Arts. 4(3), 20(a).
[111] ICC Code, Arts. 8(1), 15(3), 17(2), 18(2); ICTY Code, Art. 13(A); ICTR Code, Art. 8(1).
[112] ICC Rule 73; ICTY Code, Art. 13(B)(i)–(ii); ICTR Code, Art. 8(2)(a)–(b).
[113] For the ICC, see Rome Statute, Art. 67(1)(b); ICC Rule 73. For the ICTY, see Rules Governing the Detention of Persons Awaiting Trial or Appeal Before the Tribunal or Otherwise Detained on the Authority of the Tribunal, Doc. No. IT/38/Rev. 9, as amended 21 July 2005, Rule 67(A). For the ICTR, see Rules Covering the

confidential information among themselves for the purpose of performing their duties,[114] although the ICC Code contains stricter limits, especially in relation to protected victims and witnesses.[115] The *ad hoc* Tribunals have express exceptions to the rule of confidentiality when disclosure is necessary for counsel to defend himself or herself against a criminal or disciplinary charge in relation to the conduct of the defence;[116] to prevent an act which may be criminal or result in a person's death or any other substantial bodily harm;[117] or, in the case of the ICTY, to substantiate a remuneration claim to the Registrar.[118] The ICC Rules relating to confidential information are much more detailed than those of the *ad hoc* Tribunals, and certain rules apply to determine information that is precluded from disclosure.[119]

5.2.2.3 Obligations to the tribunal

Counsel are personally responsible to the tribunal for the conduct and presentation of their client's case.[120] They may not knowingly make an incorrect statement of fact or law to the tribunal,[121] and therefore have an obligation to take all reasonable steps to correct, as soon as practicable, statements they later discover were incorrect.[122] The ICC Code expressly extends this obligation to include statements to the Court made by any member of a counsel's defence team.[123] Counsel must maintain the integrity of evidence,[124] and cannot offer evidence known to be 'incorrect'.[125] Other than in exceptional circumstances and where specifically authorised, counsel cannot contact a judge in relation to the merits of a case outside of the proceedings,[126] and can only make such submissions by filing them formally through the Registry.[127]

The *ad hoc* Tribunals may withhold payment to counsel who bring meritless or frivolous claims,[128] while the ICC Code attempts to regulate the same behaviour by obliging counsel to represent their client expeditiously with the purpose of avoiding

Detention of Persons Awaiting Trial or Appeal Before the Tribunal or Otherwise Detained on the Authority of the Tribunal, 5 June 1998, www.ictr.org/ENGLISH/basicdocs/rulesdet.htm, Rule 65.

114 ICC Code, Art. 8(3); ICTY Code, Art. 13(A); ICTR Code, Art. 8(1).

115 ICC Code, Art. 8(4) ('In particular, Counsel shall not reveal the identity of protected victims and witnesses, or any confidential information that may reveal their identity and whereabouts, unless he or she has been authorized to do so by an order of the Court').

116 ICTY Code, Art. 13(B)(iii); ICTR Code, Art. 8(2)(c).

117 ICTY Code, Art. 13(C); ICTR Code, Art. 8(2)(d).

118 ICTY Code, Art. 13(B)(iv) (pursuant to ICTY Directive, Art. 17).

119 For example, information regarding national security or related to protected victims and witnesses. See generally ICC Code, Art. 8; ICC Rule 73. For disclosure of work to the Registry, see ICC Registry Regulation 130.

120 ICC Code, Art. 24(2); ICTY Code, Art. 23(A); ICTR Code, Art. 13(1).

121 See ICC Code, Art. 24(3); ICTY Code, Art. 23(B)(i); ICTR Code, Art. 13(2)(a).

122 ICC Code, Art. 24(3); ICTY Code, Art. 23(D); ICTR Code, Art. 13(4).

123 ICC Code, Art. 24(3).

124 *Ibid.*, Art. 25(1); ICTY Code, Art. 24; ICTR Code, Art. 14.

125 ICC Code, Art. 25(1); ICTY Code, Art. 23(B)(ii); ICTR Code, Art. 13(2)(b).

126 ICC Code, Art. 23(a); ICTY Code, Art. 22(i).

127 ICC Code, Art. 23(b) ; ICTY Code, Art. 22(ii).

128 See ICTY Code, Art. 25; ICTY Rule 73(D); ICTR Rule 73(F). See also *Prosecutor* v. *Dragomir Milošević*, Case No. IT-98-29/1-A, Decision on Dragomir Milošević's Third Motion to Present Additional Evidence, 8

unnecessary expense or delay.[129] Counsel also have a general obligation not to bring the tribunal, or its proceedings, into disrepute.[130]

5.2.2.4 Obligations to others in the proceedings

Counsel are required to be courteous towards all others involved in the proceedings.[131] The ICC Code also prohibits discrimination by counsel towards anyone taking part in the case.[132] Unless otherwise provided, counsel are restricted from communicating with other represented persons in the proceeding without their client's authorisation.[133] For communication with unrepresented persons in relation to the case, the Codes impose various limits[134] as well as obligations, such as advising the unrepresented person of the counsel's role in the matter[135] and of his or her right to representation.[136] The ICC Code further regulates counsel's communication with other counsel involved in the proceedings.[137]

Rules of communication for counsel with victims and witnesses have been developed over time. The ICTR Code does not address the issue, despite the existence of witness-protection provisions within the Statute and Rules of that Tribunal.[138] The ICTY has protective provisions in its Statute and Rules,[139] and its Code also specifies that counsel cannot needlessly embarrass, delay, or burden witnesses,[140] nor can they seek to unduly influence witnesses through payments.[141] By comparison, the ICC has wide-ranging protections for victims and witnesses enshrined within its Statute, and the Court has broad discretionary powers to enforce those protections.[142] The ICC Code exerts those powers by requiring counsel to refrain from any 'intimidating, harassing or humiliating behaviour' and not to subject witnesses to 'disproportionate or unnecessary pressure within or outside the Courtroom'.[143] The ICC Code also imposes an express obligation on counsel to supervise their defence team members,[144] and holds counsel responsible when a team member engages in misconduct[145] or where they ordered or knew of a breach by a subordinate member

September 2009, para. 21 (ICTY Appeals Chamber deeming motion frivolous; and ordering sanctions for defence counsel and non-payment of fees relating to the motion, under ICTY Rule 73(D)).

[129] ICC Code, Art. 24(5).

[130] *Ibid.*, Art. 24(1); ICTY Code, Art. 3(v); ICTR Code, Art. 15(1).

[131] ICC Code, Art. 7(1); ICTY Code, Art. 27(A); ICTR Code, Art. 17(1). Reference is made to 'respect' in the ICTR and ICC Codes, 'integrity' in the ICTY Code, and 'fairness and honesty' in the ICTR Code.

[132] ICC Code, Art. 9(1).

[133] ICC Code, Art. 28; ICTY Code, Art. 27(D); ICTR Code, Art. 17(2).

[134] ICC Code, Art. 26; ICTY Code, Art. 29; ICTR Code, Art. 18.

[135] ICC Code, Art. 26(2)(b); ICTY Code, Art. 29(B)(i); ICTR Code, Art. 18(2).

[136] ICC Code, Art. 26(2)(a); ICTY Code, Art. 29(B)(ii); see also ICTR Code, Art. 18(1)(b).

[137] ICC Code, Art. 27.

[138] ICTR Statute, Art. 14; ICTR Rule 69.

[139] ICTY Statute, Art. 22; ICTY Rule 75.

[140] ICTY Code, Art. 28(A). [141] ICTY Code, Art. 28(B). [142] Rome Statute, Art. 68.

[143] ICC Code, Art. 29. Counsel must also have 'particular consideration for victims of torture or of physical, psychological or sexual violence, or children, the elderly or the disabled'.

[144] ICC Code, Art. 7(4). [145] *Ibid.*, Art. 31.

of their defence team.[146] Sanctions for misconduct range from admonishment to fines, suspension, or a permanent ban on practising before the Court.[147]

5.2.3 *Conflicts of interest*

Counsel must ensure that no conflict arises between their client's interests and their own and, within the confines of the governing instruments of the tribunal, the client's interests must come before any other person, organisation, or state.[148]

Counsel must not become involved in a proceeding where they will likely be required as a witness, unless the testimony relates to an uncontested issue[149] or to the nature or value of the legal services rendered.[150] The *ad hoc* Tribunals' Codes allow an exception to this rule if it would otherwise cause substantial hardship to the client.[151] Counsel are also prevented from becoming involved in cases which may harm the interests of other clients, are substantially related to another client they have represented, or about which they have been privy to confidential information.[152] Where a conflict of interest arises, counsel must notify all potentially affected parties and either withdraw from representation of one or more clients with the consent of the tribunal, or seek the full and informed consent of all potentially affected clients to continue to act.[153]

5.2.4 *Misconduct*

The tribunals can refuse audience to a counsel who has been found to be offensive, abusive, or otherwise obstructive.[154] Counsel can be banned from further engagements with the tribunal either temporarily or permanently,[155] and a fine can also be imposed.[156] Both the ICTY and the ICC Codes outline a procedure for appeal of misconduct findings.[157] The *ad hoc* Tribunals may inform the professional body of counsel's national jurisdiction,[158] while the ICC Code sets up a communication procedure with the governing professional body of counsel's national jurisdiction

146 *Ibid.*, Art. 32.
147 *Ibid.*, Art. 42.
148 See *ibid.*, Art. 16(1); ICTY Code, Art. 14(A)–(B); ICTR Code, Art. 9(1).
149 ICC Code, Art. 12(3)(a); ICTY Code, Art. 26(i); ICTR Code, Art. 16.
150 ICC Code, Art. 12(3)(b); ICTY Code, Art. 26(ii). See also ICTR Code, Art. 16 (formulated differently, allowing counsel to testify only where 'the testimony relates to an uncontested issue or where substantial hardship would be caused to the client if that Counsel does not so act').
151 ICTY Code, Art. 26(iii); ICTR Code, Art. 16.
152 ICC Code, Art. 12(1); ICTY Code, Art. 14(D); ICTR Code, Art. 9(3).
153 ICC Code, Art. 16(3); ICTY Code, Art. 14(E); ICTR Code, Art. 9(5).
154 ICTY Rule 46(A)(i); ICTR Rule 46(A), (C).
155 ICC Code, Art. 42(1)(d)–(e); ICTY Rule 46(A)(ii); ICTY Code, Art. 47(C)(v)–(vi); ICTR Rule 46(B).
156 ICC Code, Art. 42(1)(c); ICTY Code, Art. 47(C)(iv).
157 ICC Code, Art. 43; ICTY Code, Art. 48.
158 ICTY Rule 46(B); ICTY Code, Art. 47(F); ICTR Rule 46(B); ICTR Code, Art. 21(2).

to prevent double disciplinary measures.[159] Ignorance of the tribunal's rules and procedures may amount to misconduct,[160] as may absences and tardiness.[161] At the *ad hoc* Tribunals, counsel have the additional responsibility of reporting any known misconduct of other counsel.[162] Counsel are also subject to criminal or administrative sanctions for conduct qualifying as offences against the administration of justice.[163]

5.2.5 Termination, suspension, and withdrawal

A defence counsel's representation agreement may be terminated by the client,[164] or withdrawn or suspended by the tribunal as a result of disciplinary procedures.[165] In certain circumstances, counsel may request termination of the agreement so long as it has no material adverse effect on the client.[166] Any party requesting termination of the agreement must show it is in the interests of justice.[167]

The process of withdrawal or removal of counsel can be complicated, as it affects not only the interests of the accused, but also any co-accused, the prosecution, and the broader interests of justice in achieving an expeditious trial. Indeed, this has been an area of considerable difficulty in the management of defence issues before the *ad hoc* Tribunals. In the *Butare* case, for example, the Trial Chamber granted defendant Ntahobali's request for withdrawal of his current counsel and co-counsel, granted his request for self-representation until new counsel and co-counsel were appointed, and ordered a new 'duty counsel' to assist Ntahobali during the interim period of self-representation.[168] The Chamber noted, however, that for such an order

159 ICC Code, Art. 38.

160 See *Prosecutor* v. *Galić*, Case No. IT-98-29-T, Order on the Defence Motion for Discovery, 11 May 2000.

161 See *Nahimana, Barayagwiza, and Ngeze* v. *Prosecutor*, Case No. ICTR-99-52-A, Judgement, 28 November 2007, para. 139 (holding that where counsel and co-counsel absent themselves from proceedings, this amounts to gross misconduct warranting sanctioning by the Tribunal).

162 ICTY Code, Art. 36; ICTR Code, Art. 21(1).

163 See Chapter 7, Section 7.8.

164 ICC Code, Art. 18(3); ICTY Code, Art. 9(A)(iii); ICTR Code, Art. 4(1).

165 See ICC Code, Arts. 38(4), 42; ICTY Code, Arts. 45, 47; ICTY Directive, Art. 20; ICTR Directive, Arts. 18–20.

166 ICC Code, Art. 18; ICTY Code, Art. 9(B).

167 See *Prosecutor* v. *Blagojević and Jokić*, Case No. IT-02-60-A, Judgement, 9 May 2007, para. 17.

168 *Prosecutor* v. *Nyiramasuhuko and Ntahobali*, Case No. ICTR-97-21-T, Decision on Ntahobali's Motion for Withdrawal of Counsel, 22 June 2001 ('*Ntahobali* June 2001 Decision'), p. 7. For the full procedural history, see *Prosecutor* v. *Nyiramasuhuko and Ntahobali*, Case No. ICTR-97-21-T, Registrar's Decision to Reject Shalom Ntahobali's Request for Withdrawal of His Lead Counsel, Me René Saint-Léger, 4 April 2001; *Prosecutor* v. *Nyiramasuhuko and Ntahobali*, Case No. ICTR-97-21-T, President's Decision on Review, in Accordance with Article 19(E) of the Directive on Assignment of Defence Counsel, 4 June 2001; *Prosecutor* v. *Nyiramasuhuko and Ntahobali*, Case No. ICTR-97-21-T, Requête en extrême urgence aux fins de retrait de la commission d'office des conseils Me St-Léger et de Me Michael Bailey, 11 June 2001; *Prosecutor* v. *Nyiramasuhuko and Ntahobali*, Case No. ICTR-97-21-T, Prosecutor's Reply to Ntahobali's Motion to Remove Counsel, 14 June 2001; *Prosecutor* v. *Nyiramasuhuko and Ntahobali*, Case No. ICTR-97-21-T, Response to Arsène Shalom Ntahobali's Urgent Motion for Withdrawal of Counsel Me St-Leger and Me James Michael Bailey Counsel for Ntahobali, 14 June 2001.

to be granted, the chamber must ultimately be satisfied that exceptional circumstances exist, that good cause exists warranting withdrawal of counsel, and that the request is not designed to delay proceedings.[169]

A contrasting example arose in the *Blagojević and Jokić* case, in which counsel for Vidoje Blagojević, Michael Karnavas, resisted attempts by Blagojević to capriciously seek his removal. Although counsel had a history of cooperation with and instruction from Blagojević before they fell out, issues related to the appointment of co-counsel in the case displeased the accused, who purported to sack his entire defence team.[170] The Trial Chamber refused to grant the withdrawal of counsel by the accused, relying upon its inherent powers to ensure the fairness of the trial.[171] The ruling, supported by the Appeals Chamber,[172] is an example of how counsel might remain and represent an unwilling and uncooperative accused.[173] In another ICTY case, Sefer Halilović changed counsel on numerous occasions during the pre-trial phase, which made the preparation and commencement of his trial very difficult.[174]

Whatever the position of counsel vis-à-vis their client, there remains an obligation to return all material and evidence to the Registry,[175] and more generally, to protect the client's interests until replacement counsel has been appointed.[176]

5.2.6 Fees and costs

Except as authorised by the governing instruments, counsel must not accept remuneration from any source other than the client[177] or the Registry, depending on whether they have been appointed by the client or the Registry.[178] If client-funded, counsel's fees must be agreed upon between the client and counsel before

[169] *Ntahobali* June 2001 Decision, *supra* note 168, para. 12.

[170] See *Blagojević and Jokić* Defense Appeal Decision, *supra* note 39, para. 3.

[171] *Ibid.*, para. 6.

[172] *Prosecutor* v. *Blagojević and Jokić*, Case No. IT-02-60-AR73.4, Public and Redacted Reasons for Decision on Appeal by Vidoje Blagojević, 7 November 2003, para. 7.

[173] In contrast, assigned counsel in the *Milošević* case sought to escape their role as imposed counsel after it became apparent that Milošević was not only uncooperative, but that he would call their professional integrity into question. See *Prosecutor* v. *Slobodan Milošević*, Case No. IT-02-54-T, Assigned Counsel's Motion for Withdrawal with Annex A, 8 November 2004. The Trial Chamber refused counsel's application. *Prosecutor* v. *Milošević*, Case No. IT-02-54-T, Decision on Assigned Counsel's Motion for Withdrawal, 7 December 2004 ('*Milošević* Decision on Assigned Counsel Withdrawal'). See also *infra* Section 5.3.1.1 (discussing this case).

[174] See *Prosecutor* v. *Halilović*, Case No. IT-01-48-T, Judgement, 16 November 2005, Annex 2, paras. 3–10.

[175] See ICC Code, Arts. 15(2), 18(5); ICTY Code, Art. 9(D); ICTR Code, Art. 14(2); ICTR Directive, Art. 20(B).

[176] ICTY Code, Art. 9(C); ICTY Directive, Art. 21; ICTR Directive, Art. 20.

[177] For example, Article 19(B) of the ICTY Code stipulates that fully informed written consent must be obtained from the client and there must be no conflict of interest in the lawyer-client relationship. Accord ICC Code, Art. 21; ICTR Code, Art. 9(4).

[178] ICC Code, Art. 22; ICTY Code, Art. 19(C); ICTY Directive, Art. 24(D); ICTR Code, Art. 9(4); ICTR Directive, Art. 22(B).

commencement of representation.[179] If appointed by the Registry, counsel's remuneration is guided by the adopted policies of the court or tribunal.[180]

If appointed, counsel must not give any portion of the fees obtained from the Registry to the client; this practice is known as fee-splitting and is strictly prohibited.[181] Under certain circumstances, the Registry also has the power to invoke so-called 'clawback' provisions and demand the restitution of fees paid.[182]

5.3 Self-representation

The right to self-representation is reflected in international and regional human rights conventions, in particular Article 14(3)(d) of the ICCPR.[183] This provision has generally been interpreted as recognising a right to self-representation which reposes in an accused, but which can be limited for various reasons.[184]

5.3.1 Self-representation at the ad hoc *Tribunals*[185]

The position before the ICTY is unequivocally one of a robust right to self-representation. Article 21(4)(d) of the ICTY Statute, which has been repeated in the statutes of other international criminal tribunals, mirrors Article 14(3)(d) of the ICCPR. The provision has been interpreted by the ICTY Appeals Chamber as

179 ICC Code, Art. 20; ICTY Code, Art. 19(A).

180 See, e.g., ICC Registry Regulation 133; ICTY Directive, Arts. 23–31.

181 ICC Code, Art. 22(2)–(5); ICTY Code, Art. 18; ICTR Code, Art. 5 *bis*.

182 ICC Court Regulation 85(4); ICTY Rule 45(E); ICTR Rule 45(I).

183 See also *supra* note 1 (citing other treaties).

184 See *Croissant* v. *Germany*, Case No. 13611/88, Judgment, 25 September 1992 (European Court of Human Rights interpreting an analogous provision); accord *Correia de Mateos* v. *Portugal*, Case No. 48188/99, Decision on Admissibility, 15 November 2001; *X* v. *Norway*, Case No. 5923/72, Decision on Admissibility, 30 May 1975; *Weber* v. *Switzerland*, Case No. 11034/84, Judgment, 22 May 1990; *X* v. *Austria*, Case No. 7138/75, Decision on Admissibility, 5 July 1977. But see *Michael and Brian Hill* v. *Spain*, Communication No. 526/1993, UN Doc. CCPR/C/59/D/526/1993, 2 April 1997 (Human Rights Committee concluding that Spain was in breach of the relevant provision by not allowing the accused to to represent themselves, even though Spain's Criminal Code required persons accused of such crimes to be represented). The relevance of the latter decision was challenged by trial chambers in the *Milošević* and *Šešelj* cases. See *Prosecutor* v. *Slobodan Milošević*, Case No. IT-02-54-T, Reasons for Decision on Assignment of Defence Counsel, 22 September 2004 ('*Milošević* Trial Decision on Representation'), para. 44; *Prosecutor* v. *Šešelj*, Case No. IT-03-67-PT, Decision on Prosecution's Motion for Order Appointing Counsel to Assist Vojislav Šešelj with His Defence, 9 May 2003 ('*Šešelj* Standby Counsel Decision'), para. 18. For a challenge to the view that Article 14(3)(d) of the ICCPR, on which the relevant provisions are based, supports a right to self-representation, see Michael P. Scharf and Christopher M. Rassi, 'Do Former Rogue Leaders Have an International Right to Act as Their Own Lawyers in War Crimes Trials?', (2004) 20 *Ohio State Journal on Dispute Resolution* 1, 11. For further analysis, see Boas, *supra* note 5, ch. 4; David Weissbrodt, *The Right to a Fair Trial under the Universal Declaration of Human Rights and the International Covenant on Civil and Political Rights* (2001), p. 45; Manfred Nowak, *U.N. Covenant on Civil and Political Rights: CCPR Commentary* (1993), p. 258.

185 Most of the relevant jurisprudence on these questions emerged from the ICTY. While these issues have been considered at the ICTR, see, e.g., *Prosecutor* v. *Barayagwiza*, Case No. ICTR-97-19-T, Decision on Defence Counsel Motion to Withdraw, 2 November 2000; *Ntahobali* June 2001 Decision, *supra* note 168, the leading decisions in this area are those of the ICTY Appeals Chamber, which will be the focus of this section.

granting the right to self-representation, which it characterised in turn as an 'indispensable cornerstone of justice'.[186] This proposition, first set out in the *Milošević* case, has been reaffirmed in both the *Šešelj* and *Krajišnik* cases.[187] In particular, the Appeals Chamber, in a series of decisions in the *Šešelj* case, has shown that even where an accused appearing *pro se* significantly obstructs the proceedings, his or her right to self-representation will still be preserved. The Appeals Chamber has further ruled that while an accused's right to self-representation may be limited in rare circumstances, any such limitation must be to the minimum extent necessary to protect the Tribunal's interest in assuring a reasonably expeditious trial.[188] In applying this precedent, and in response to the refusal of the accused to attend the commencement of his trial, the *Karadžić* Trial Chamber simply ordered an adjournment of some four months – effectively giving in to the accused's wishes, and despite threatening to proceed in his absence and to appoint counsel to conduct his case. The Chamber instructed the Registrar to appoint counsel to prepare to step in if in the future it should determine that Karadžić had lost his right to self-representation.[189]

Despite this jurisprudence, the Appeals Chamber has also acknowledged that, at least in principle, the right to self-representation is not absolute,[190] and can be limited if exercise of the right is 'substantially and persistently obstructing the proper and expeditious conduct of the trial',[191] whether or not such obstruction is the accused's intent.[192]

Unfortunately, the ICTY Appeals Chamber has established a confusing and unsatisfactory set of precedents, which leave the status of this increasingly important area of international criminal procedure unclear. This line of authority commenced with the Appeals Chamber's ostensible reversal of the Trial Chamber's imposition of defence counsel on Slobodan Milošević.

5.3.1.1 Milošević *case*

For some time during the course of the trial, the *Milošević* Trial Chamber had refused to prevent the accused from representing himself, or impose any but the

186 *Prosecution* v. *Slobodan Milošević*, Case No. IT-02-54-AR73.7, Decision on Interlocutory Appeal of the Trial Chamber's Decision on the Assignment of Defence Counsel, 1 November 2004 ('*Milošević* Appeal Decision on Representation'), para. 11.

187 See *Šešelj* Standby Counsel Decision, *supra* note 184; *Prosecutor* v. *Šešelj*, Case No. IT-03-67-PT, Decision on Assignment of Counsel, 21 August 2006 ('Second *Šešelj* Decision'); *Prosecutor* v. *Šešelj*, Case No. IT-03-67-AR73.3, Decision on Appeal Against the Trial Chamber's Decision on Assignment of Counsel, 20 October 2006 ('*Šešelj* Appeal Decision'); *Prosecutor* v. *Krajišnik*, Case No. IT-00-39-T, Reasons for Oral Decision Denying Mr Krajišnik's Request to Proceed Unrepresented by Counsel, 18 August 2005.

188 *Milošević* Appeal Decision on Representation, *supra* note 186, para. 17.

189 *Prosecutor* v. *Karadžić*, Case No. IT-95-5/18-T, Decision on Appointment of Counsel and Order on Further Trial Proceedings, 11 November 2009.

190 *Milošević* Appeal Decision on Representation, *supra* note 186, paras. 12–13.

191 *Ibid.*, para. 13. 192 *Ibid.*, para. 14.

most minimal restrictions on his exercise of that right, apparently on the basis of a mistaken belief that the accused had a right under customary international law to represent himself.[193] In 2004, some two and a half years into the trial, the Trial Chamber finally assigned defence counsel over Milošević's objections, citing his parlous state of health, manipulation of his medication regime, and the obstructive impact of these factors on the capacity of the Chamber to ensure that the accused receive a fair and appropriately expeditious trial.[194] Far from removing the accused from the courtroom or terminating his involvement in presenting his defence, the Trial Chamber issued an order detailing the manner in which his defence would proceed, including allowing him the opportunity to both cooperate with assigned counsel and, where appropriate, to examine witnesses and make submissions directly to the Chamber.[195]

The Appeals Chamber, however, overruled the Trial Chamber, characterising the decision as having imposed 'sharp restrictions' on Milošević that 'were grounded on a fundamental error of law' because 'the Trial Chamber failed to recognize that any restrictions on Milošević's right to represent himself must be limited to the minimum extent necessary to protect the Tribunal's interest in assuring a reasonably expeditious trial'.[196] Although reluctantly upholding the Trial Chamber's conclusion that an accused's right to represent himself could be limited,[197] the Appeals Chamber found that the Trial Chamber's restriction on Milošević's right of self-representation was not proportionate to the Tribunal's interest in an expeditious resolution of the case.[198] The Appeals Chamber purported to show the existence of the principle of 'proportionality' on which it relied through an odd assortment of authorities on topics unrelated to assignment of counsel. Indeed, with one exception, the decisions cited by the Appeals Chamber were based on domestic administrative or constitutional law issues having no bearing upon an international criminal trial, the determination of the issue of a fair trial for an accused, or even the status of the principle in question in international law.[199]

5.3.1.2 Šešelj *case*

The interlocutory appeal decision in *Milošević* appears to have established a jurisprudential attitude in the Appeals Chamber that has resonated in later

193 See *Milošević* Trial Decision on Representation, *supra* note 184, paras. 7, 8. This position was criticised by Scharf and Rassi, who noted that neither a proper reading of the *travaux préparatoires* of the ICCPR, nor a survey of practice by states, supports this conclusion. See Scharf and Rassi, *supra* note 184, p. 14.

194 *Milošević* Trial Decision on Representation, *supra* note 184, paras. 64–68.

195 See *Prosecutor* v. *Slobodan Milošević*, Case No. IT-02-54-T, Order on the Modalities to be Followed by Court Assigned Counsel, 3 September 2004.

196 *Milošević* Appeal Decision on Representation, *supra* note 186, para. 17.

197 *Ibid.*, para. 15.

198 *Ibid.*

199 The ICTY Appeals Chamber cited *Elloy de Freitas* v. *Permanent Secretary of Ministry of Agriculture, Fisheries, Lands, and Housing*, [1998] 1 AC 69 (Privy Council considering whether the appellant acted

decisions. In August 2006, almost two years after the Appeals Chamber Decision in *Milošević*, the Trial Chamber preparing for trial in the *Šešelj* case determined that the time had come to impose defence counsel, abandoning a more tentative 'standby counsel' mechanism employed earlier in the proceedings.[200] After recounting Šešelj's extraordinary obstructionist behaviour,[201] the Chamber revoked his right to self-representation and imposed counsel. On 20 October 2006, the Appeals Chamber promptly overturned the Trial Chamber's decision, ruling that the Trial Chamber had not previously explicitly warned Šešelj that his conduct might have the effect of the court removing his right to act in his own defence; the Trial Chamber had therefore, according to the Appeals Chamber, acted precipitously.[202]

Following the Appeals Chamber's ruling, the Trial Chamber reinstated the terms of its initial ruling imposing standby counsel on Šešelj on 25 October 2006, and was forced to delay the scheduled start of trial.[203] Šešelj objected to re-imposition of standby counsel and went on a hunger strike in protest.[204] In the meantime, in accordance with the Appeals Chamber's ruling, the Trial Chamber issued regular warnings during the hunger strike, articulating in detail Šešelj's obstructive behaviour and stating that if he persisted, the Chamber would again impose counsel. Ultimately, on 27 November 2006, the Trial Chamber again decided to revoke Šešelj's right to represent himself, and ordered standby counsel to take over the conduct of his defence.[205]

in violation of statutory restrictions prohibiting civil servants from publishing their political views on any matter to anyone in a public place); *McConnell* v. *Federal Election Commission*, 540 U.S. 93 (2003) (US Supreme Court considering whether the Bipartisan Campaign Reform Act of 2002 violated the US constitutional guarantee of freedom of speech and association); *Chassagnou* v. *France*, Case No. 25088/94, Judgment, 29 April 1999 (European Court of Human Rights considering a challenge based on proportionality by a French landowner required under French law to automatically transfer hunting rights over his land because it did not meet a certain size); *Edmonton Journal* v. *Alberta*, [1989] CarswellAlta 198 (Supreme Court of Canada concluding that a restrictive ban imposed on publication by certain legislation did not, as required, impair the right to freedom of expression as little as possible and went much further than necessary to protect privacy); and *Prosecutor* v. *Limaj, Bala, and Musliu*, Case No. IT-03-66-AR65, Decision on Fatmir Limaj's Request for Provisional Release, 31 October 2003 (Appeals Chamber itself holding that, when interpreting provisions of the ICTY Rules governing interim release of accused pending or during trial or appeal, the general principle of proportionality must be taken into account). For a detailed discussion of the *Milošević* ruling and its implications, see Boas, *supra* note 5, pp. 218–222.

200 See *Šešelj* Standby Counsel decision, *supra* note 184 (the original standby counsel ruling). See also *infra* Section 5.4 (discussing the standby counsel model).

201 Second *Šešelj* Decision, *supra* note 187, Part III. Among other things, Šešelj has published books entitled *Genocidal Israeli Diplomat Theodor Meron*, *In the Jaws of the Whore Del Ponte*, and *The Lying Hague Homosexual, Geoffrey Nice*. See *ibid*., para. 30. He has written to the Tribunal in one submission stating 'you, all you members of the Hague Tribunal Registry, can only accept to suck my cock', *ibid*., para. 48, among many other obscene and improper statements.

202 *Šešelj* Appeal Decision, *supra* note 187, paras. 23–26.

203 *Prosecutor* v. *Šešelj*, Case No. IT-03-67-PT, Order Concerning Appointment of Standby Counsel and Delayed Commencement of Trial, 25 October 2006 ('*Šešelj* Decision Reinstating Standby Counsel').

204 *Ibid*., para. 8.

205 *Prosecutor* v. *Šešelj*, Case No. IT-03-67-PT, Reasons for Decision (No. 2) on Assignment of Counsel, 27 November 2006.

In a convoluted ruling on 8 December 2006, the Appeals Chamber once again overruled the Trial Chamber. Yet the Appeals Chamber did not impugn the reasoning in the Trial Chamber's 27 November 2006 decision – the decision that the Appeals Chamber admitted it was actually seised of; in fact, it declared the decision a lawful application of the principles it set forth in its 20 October 2006 ruling.[206] The Appeals Chamber instead faulted the Trial Chamber's 25 October 2006 decision reinstating standby counsel, revealing its preoccupation with the 'collision course' on which the 25 October decision had placed Šešelj and the Trial Chamber, most obviously articulated in Šešelj's hunger strike.[207] The Appeals Chamber acknowledged that Šešelj had not satisfied the formal requirements entitling his appeal against the 25 October decision to be heard on the merits, but intimated that the hunger strike justified the exceptional measure of the Chamber allowing the appeal to proceed.[208] Šešelj thus effectively blackmailed the Appeals Chamber into hearing his appeal and, it would seem, granting him relief.[209]

Commentators have questioned whether the 8 December 2006 decision was a sound development in the case law. They have argued, for example, that the Appeals Chamber was 'capitulating to pressure'[210] and in so doing, 'twisting process and law'[211] to move against the emerging case law that entitled a Trial Chamber to curtail self-representation if obstructionist conduct could be established.[212]

5.3.1.3 Krajišnik *case*

In May 2007, the question of self-representation again returned to the Appeals Chamber for consideration. The issue was whether to allow the convicted Bosnian Serb leader, Momčilo Krajišnik, to represent himself on appeal. The majority concluded, on the basis of its reasoning in the *Milošević* and *Šešelj* rulings, that the right extended to appeal and that Krajišnik could represent himself.[213]

206 *Prosecutor* v. *Šešelj*, Case No. IT-03-67-AR73.4, Decision on Appeal Against the Trial Chamber's Decision (No. 2) on Assignment of Counsel, 8 December 2006 ('Second *Šešelj* Appeal Decision'), para. 20.

207 *Ibid.*

208 *Ibid.*, paras. 13–14.

209 See *ibid.*, para. 15. Following the Appeals Chamber ruling, preparations for trial in the *Šešelj* case were placed on hold. His trial, which commenced later before a different Trial Chamber, has been plagued by continuing obstructions and delays, including, most recently, a contempt trial and finding of guilt against Šešelj, resulting in a fifteen-month jail term. *Prosecutor* v. *Šešelj*, Case No. IT-03-67-R77.2, Decision on Allegation of Contempt, 21 January 2009.

210 Göran Sluiter, 'Compromising the Authority of International Criminal Justice: How Vojislav Šešelj Runs His Trial', (2007) 5 *Journal of International Criminal Justice* 529, 534.

211 Alexander Zahar, 'Legal Aid, Self-Representation, and the Crisis at the Hague Tribunal', (2008) 19 *Criminal Law Forum* 241, 244.

212 Sluiter, *supra* note 210, p. 535 (comparing the decision to the ICTR's decision in *Barayagwiza* where, under threat from the Rwandan government to cease all cooperation, the Appeals Chamber reversed termination of the case in a final decision with dubious legal reasoning). See *Prosecutor* v. *Barayagwiza*, Case No. ICTR-97-19-AR72, Decision, 3 November 1999; *Prosecutor* v. *Barayagwiza*, Case No. ICTR-97-19-A, Decision (Prosecutor's Request for Review or Reconsideration), 31 March 2000.

213 *Prosecutor* v. *Krajišnik*, Case No. IT-00-39-A, Decision on Momčilo Krajišnik's Request to Self-Represent, on Counsel's Motion in Relation to Appointment of Amicus Curiae, and on the Prosecutor's Motion of 16 February 2007, 11 May 2007 ('*Krajišnik* Appeal Decision'), paras. 13, 24.

In an extraordinary statement of dissent that reveals the discord in the Appeals Chamber in this area, Judge Schomburg registered his 'fundamentally dissenting opinion', which he opened by stating: 'If I were tasked to show that international criminal jurisdiction cannot work I would draft the decision in the same way as was done by the majority of the Appeals Chamber. Therefore, with all due respect, I have to fundamentally disagree with the decision.'[214] Referring to the standing authority on self-representation, Judge Schomburg continued:

> Due to time constraints and considering the particular question before this bench of the Appeals Chamber, I have to restrict my analysis to whether there is a right to self-representation in proceedings at the appellate level. This does not mean, however, that I hold the Appeals Chamber's past jurisprudence on self-representation during trial to be correct, having never been assigned to a bench of the Appeals Chamber ruling on this issue. My necessary self-restraint is based on the fact that this is the first Appeals Chamber decision dealing with self-representation on appeal.[215]

Judge Schomburg argued at length that the extension of this right to appeal proceedings, as understood by the Appeals Chamber, added to a line of authority that already renders it unlikely that a self-represented accused charged with such complex crimes will receive a fair trial.

5.3.2 Self-representation at the SCSL

Following the lead of Slobodan Milošević, an increasing number of senior-level accused – especially civilian leaders – have opted to represent themselves in international criminal trials. While the ICTY has been the venue of the most spectacular examples, the phenomenon has spread to other international tribunals. Of particular note are two cases before the SCSL.

5.3.2.1 Norman *case*

In a decision rendered in June 2004, a Trial Chamber of the SCSL considered an application filed by Samuel Hinga Norman on the day his trial began, requesting the Chamber to remove his counsel and allow him to represent himself. The Chamber held that while 'as a matter of statutory construction, Article 17(4)(d) of the SCSL Statute guarantees to an accused person … the right to self-representation',[216] that right is not absolute.[217] The Chamber reasoned:

[214] *Ibid.* Fundamentally Dissenting Opinion of Judge Schomburg on the Right to Self-Representation. Judge Pocar also dissented from this decision.

[215] *Ibid.*, para. 5.

[216] *Prosecutor* v. *Norman, Fofana, and Kondewa* ('*CDF* Case'), Case No. SCSL-04-14-T, Decision on the Application of Samuel Hinga Norman for Self Representation Under Article 17(4)(d) of the Statute of the Special Court, 8 June 2004 ('*Norman* Decision on Self-Representation'), para. 8. Article 17(4) of the SCSL Statute reproduces the language of Article 21(4) of the ICTY Statute and Article 20(4) of the ICTR Statute.

[217] *Norman* Decision on Self-Representation, *supra* note 216, para. 8.

The question to put here is whether the attendant consequences that would flow from our granting the request … would, in the overall interests of justice, be consistent with the statutory guarantees to a fair and expeditious trial to be reserved by the Court to the accused particularly where, as in this case, his detention has been as long as over one year.[218]

The Chamber considered that, as a co-accused, Norman should not be permitted to exercise 'his qualified right to self-representation' to the detriment of the right of his two co-accused to a fair and expeditious trial,[219] and that to allow him to represent himself would tarnish the integrity of the proceedings and threaten the interests of justice.[220] The Chamber identified six considerations for determining whether the right to self-representation should be limited: (1) the right to counsel is predicated upon the notion that representation by counsel is an essential and necessary part of a fair trial; (2) counsel relieves the burden on the trial judges of explaining and enforcing basic rules of courtroom protocol and assisting the accused; (3) given the complexity of such trials, permitting an inexperienced (and likely untrained) accused to present his or her own defence risks unfairness to the accused; (4) there is a public interest, national and international, in the expeditious completion of the trial; (5) there is the high potential that self-representation would further disrupt the Court's timetable and calendar; and (6) there is a tension between giving effect to the right of an accused to self-representation and the right of his co-accused to a fair and expeditious trial as required by law.[221]

These six considerations contain elements that appear more broadly conceived than those referred to by the ICTY Appeals Chamber. The *Norman* decision appears to address the specific trial-related concerns relating to an accused and, where relevant, co-accused, as well as engaging the fundamental issue of the fairness of the trial and apprehending the broader public interest at stake.

5.3.2.2 Gbao *case*

In the *RUF* case, the Trial Chamber refused an application by the accused Gbao to withdraw the counsel that had been appointed for him, and rejected the accused's argument that such a step was necessary because he no longer recognised the legitimacy of the SCSL.[222] On appeal, the Appeals Chamber agreed with the Trial Chamber:

218 *Ibid.*, para. 12. 219 *Ibid.*, para. 14. 220 *Ibid.*, para. 22.

221 *Ibid.*, para. 26. Following the decision, standby counsel were imposed. When Norman subsequently refused to appear in Court, however, his right to self-representation was revoked and standby counsel were transformed into court-appointed counsel. *CDF* Case, Case No. SCSL-04-14-PT, Ruling on the Issue of Non-Appearance of the First Accused Samuel Hinga Norman, the Second Accused Moinina Fofana, and the Third Accused, Allieu Kondewa at the Trial Proceedings, 1 October 2004; *CDF* Case, Case No. SCSL-04-14-PT, Consequential Order on the Role of Court Appointed Counsel, 1 October 2004. See also Nina H.B. Jørgensen, 'The Problem Of Self-Representation at International Criminal Tribunals: Striking a Balance between Fairness and Effectiveness', (2006) 4 *Journal of International Criminal Justice* 64, 67–68 (discussing this case).

222 *Prosecutor* v. *Sesay, Kallon, and Gbao* ('*RUF* Case'), Case No. SCSL-04-15-T, Decision on Application for Leave to Appeal: Gbao – Decision on Application to Withdraw Counsel, 4 August 2004, para. 29 (quoting a written declaration by Gbao).

> It is clear from examining all of the circumstances of this case that the interests of justice would not be served by allowing Mr. Gbao to be unrepresented before the Court. The Trial Chamber accordingly takes the position that it must safeguard the rights of the accused and the integrity of the proceedings before the Court by insisting that Mr. Gbao should continue to be represented by the Counsel that have represented him throughout these proceedings. We hold in this regard that an accused person cannot waive his right to a fair and expeditious trial whatever the circumstances.[223]

The Appeals Chamber of the SCSL has thus established that the Special Court could assign counsel or insist on assigned counsel continuing to represent the accused, even *in absentia*, in 'the interests of justice and a fair hearing'.[224] This conclusion reflects the basic principle that an accused cannot be allowed to frustrate the proceedings by an act of obstruction, whatever form that obstruction takes. Once again, this solution is preferable to that of the ICTY; indeed, the failure to adopt an approach that strikes a similar balance between pragmatism and principle may well be one reason why issues relating to self-representation have continued to plague the ICTY so deeply.

5.4 Standby counsel

'Standby counsel' is a term used to denote an attorney the court appoints to assist a self-represented accused, and is a model of assisted representation developed and applied in some U.S. jurisdictions. In discussing the appointment of such counsel in the context of rights granted by the U.S. Constitution, one commentator notes:

> [T]he judge may find it advisable to appoint standby counsel, especially if the case is expected to be long or complicated, or if there are multiple defendants ... [T]he role of counsel in such a situation is a sensitive and sometimes difficult one. Thus, although counsel may expect to take part in such tasks as investigating the facts and law of the case, preparing and presenting pretrial motions, helping the defendant present the case in court, and assembling and presenting information relevant to sentencing, counsel may find it prudent to keep in mind that it is the defendant who still has the right to control all strategic decisions and speak for the defence unless the court specifically directs otherwise.[225]

In the leading case on this form of representation, the U.S. Supreme Court in *McKaskle* v. *Wiggins* reversed the intermediate appellate court's ruling that the accused's right to self-representation had been violated by the unsolicited participation of standby counsel, and held that the accused had been accorded all the rights encompassed within the right to self-representation, including the right to make motions, argue points of law,

[223] *RUF* Case, Case No. SCSL-04-15-AR73, Gbao – Decision on Appeal Against Decision on Withdrawal of Counsel, 23 November 2004, para. 46.
[224] *Ibid.*
[225] Daniel A. Klein, 'Annotation: Right, Under Federal Constitution, of Accused to Represent Himself or Herself in Criminal Proceeding – Supreme Court Cases', (2004) 145 *United Supreme Court Reports, Lawyers' Edition (Second)* 1177, § 2[b].

and question witnesses.[226] Participation by standby counsel had not interfered with the accused's right to present his own defence, and the accused was given ample opportunity to present his own positions to the trial court on every matter discussed.[227]

Standby counsel have been used in the ICTY, ICTR, and SCSL.[228] In the most extended discussion of the employment of standby counsel in these tribunals, the ICTY Trial Chamber in *Šešelj* considered the role standby counsel would play and concluded that the model might be preferable to the more radical approach of imposing counsel on an unwilling accused. According to that Chamber, among the tasks that could be undertaken by standby counsel are: (1) assisting in the preparation of the defence case during the pre-trial or trial phases when requested by the accused; (2) receiving copies of all court documents, filings, and disclosed materials that are received by or sent to the accused; (3) being present in the courtroom during the proceedings; (4) being engaged actively in the substantive preparation of the case and participating in the proceedings, in order to be prepared to take over from the accused at trial; (5) addressing the chamber whenever the accused or chamber so requests; (6) offering advice or making suggestions to the accused, in particular on evidentiary and procedural issues; (7) in the event of abusive conduct by the accused towards witnesses (in particular sensitive or protected witnesses), stepping in to conduct examination or cross-examination if so ordered by the trial chamber, without depriving the accused of his right to control the content of the examination; and (8) in exceptional circumstances, taking over the defence from the accused at trial should the trial chamber conclude that the accused is engaging in disruptive conduct or conduct requiring his removal from the courtroom.[229]

The model maintains certain fundamental characteristics of self-representation, but at the same time provides the court with some comfort that counsel – acting in the interests of an accused, even if uninstructed – is able to step into the proceedings in some capacity, possibly even taking over the functional role of defence counsel. As a result, even though international criminal tribunals (with the possible exception of the SCSL) appear to retain a profound predisposition for allowing accused persons to represent themselves, the standby counsel model provides a compromise between self-representation and full representation by counsel. This compromise may, however, be illusory; if the chamber determines that standby counsel should take over the presentation of the defence case from the accused, the result is a radically different role for the accused, who is no longer at the forefront of the presentation of his or her own defence.

[226] *McKaskle* v. *Wiggins*, 465 U.S. 168, 174 (1984).

[227] *Ibid.*, p. 181.

[228] See, e.g., *supra* Section 5.3.2.1 (discussing the *Norman* case); notes 185, 212 and accompanying text (referring to the *Baryagwiza* case); and Section 5.3.1.2 (discussing the *Šešelj* case).

[229] *Šešelj* Standby Counsel Decision, *supra* note 184, para. 30. In the ICTY, such removal would occur pursuant to ICTY Rule 80(B).

5.5 Imposing defence counsel

The increasing trend of self-representation in international criminal trials has given rise to circumstances in which chambers have decided to impose defence counsel – in all cases to date, over the vociferous objections of an accused. Most notoriously, imposition of counsel occurred at the ICTY, at least temporarily, in the *Milošević*[230] and *Šešelj*[231] cases. In both cases, the Trial Chamber reasoned that defence counsel could be imposed because the accused had, in differing ways, obstructed the conduct of the proceedings to such an extent that the Trial Chamber was not persuaded that a fair and expeditious trial could be delivered.

Where defence counsel is forced upon an accused, the crucial ingredient of an instructed defence may be missing. The imposition of counsel on an unconsenting accused can radically alter the nature of the defence, affecting not only the rights of the accused vis-à-vis his or her defence, but also the conduct of the entire proceedings. In adversarial criminal proceedings, one of the crucial elements to the conduct of a defence is that counsel be instructed by the client as to the defence strategy and all manner of crucial details that arise day after day in a trial. Acting without instructions critically limits counsel's ability to truly defend an accused, particularly in complex international criminal proceedings.

Other issues may arise for an unwanted defence counsel, including ethical issues relating to the position in which imposed counsel find themselves. Such ethical issues were raised in the *Milošević* case by imposed counsel, Stephen Kay and Gillian Higgins, who sought to withdraw from appointment as court-assigned counsel on the grounds that representing an unwilling accused compromised their professional integrity and was not in the interests of justice.[232] The Trial Chamber considered these arguments at length and ultimately held that the interests of justice would best be served by the continued service of counsel, despite their desire to be withdrawn, and refused their request for withdrawal.[233] The decision of the Appeals Chamber reversing the Trial Chamber's imposition of counsel on the ground that it violated Milošević's right to represent himself renders the imposition of counsel in such circumstances increasingly unlikely in the ICTY in the future. Other international criminal tribunals, particularly the ICC, may in time provide a more sound jurisprudential lead in this area. These tribunals should look closely at the approach to self-representation taken by the SCSL and STL in light of the considerable harm done to both individual proceedings and the broader reputation of the ICTY caused by that Tribunal's approach.

[230] See *supra* Section 5.3.1.1. [231] See *supra* Section 5.3.1.2.
[232] See *Milošević* Decision on Assigned Counsel Withdrawal, *supra* note 173, para. 5.
[233] *Ibid.*, paras. 31–35.

5.6 *Amici curiae*

The *amicus curiae*, or 'friend of the court', is an institution in many legal systems and is increasingly recognised in international proceedings. While not, strictly speaking, a form of defence representation, international criminal tribunals have often used *amici curiae* to assist them in augmenting legal argumentation on an issue of considerable import to an accused or to the chamber. *Amici* have generally assisted in the 'proper determination of a case', either through appearing before the chamber or making submissions on an issue specified by the chamber.[234] In the words of another international tribunal, *amici curiae* can provide a court with 'special perspectives, arguments, or expertise on the dispute, usually in the form of a written … brief or submission'.[235] In one case in particular – *Milošević* – the *amicus* model has even been used as a form of *de facto* defence counsel.[236]

5.6.1 Amici curiae *at the* ad hoc *Tribunals*

Rule 74 of the ICTY Rules and ICTR Rules authorises a chamber, 'if it considers it desirable for the proper determination of the case, [to] invite or grant leave to a State, organization or person to appear before it and make submissions on any issue specified by the Chamber'. This rule therefore confers on chambers an explicit power to appoint *amici curiae*. Both Tribunals have used this power in a broad array of circumstances relating to substantive and procedural issues, including deferral proceedings;[237] failure to execute a warrant;[238] jurisdictional proceedings

[234] *Prosecutor* v. *Slobodan Milošević*, Case No. IT-99-37-PT, Order Inviting Designation of *Amicus Curiae*, 30 August 2001, pp. 2–3 (quoting ICTY Rule 74). See also *infra* Section 5.6.4.

[235] *Aguas Argentinas S.A. and Others* v. *Argentine Republic*, International Centre for Settlement of Investment Disputes, Case No. ARB/03/19, Order in Response to a Petition for Transparency and Participation as *Amicus Curiae*, 19 May 2005. See also Lance Bartholomeusz, 'The *Amicus Curiae* Before the International Courts and Tribunals', (2005) 5 *Non-State Actors and International Law* 211.

[236] See *infra* Section 5.6.4.

[237] See *Prosecutor* v. *Tadić*, Case No. IT-94-1-D, In the Matter of a Proposal for a Formal Request for Deferral to the Competence of the International Tribunal, Decision of the Trial Chamber on the Application by the Prosecutor for a Formal Request for Deferral to the Competence of the International Criminal Tribunal for the Former Yugoslavia in the Matter of Duško Tadić (Pursuant to Rules 9 and 10 of the Rules of Procedure and Evidence), 8 November 1994; *Prosecutor* v. *Erdemović*, Case No. IT-96-22-D, In the Matter of a Proposal for a Formal Request for Deferral to the Competence of the International Tribunal Addressed to the Federal Republic of Yugoslavia in the Matter of Drazen Erdemović, 29 May 1996; *Prosecutor* v. *Mladić and Stanišić*, Case No. IT-95-5-D, In the Matter of a Proposal for a Formal Request for Deferral to the Competence of the Tribunal Addressed to the Republic of Bosnia and Herzegovina in Respect of Radovan Karadžić, 16 May 1995. See also Rodney Dixon, Aga Khan, and Richard May (eds.), *Archbold International Criminal Courts: Practice, Procedure and Evidence* (2003), pp. 379–384; Ascensio Hervé, 'L'*amicus curiae* devant les juridictions internationales', (2001) 105 *Revue générale de droit international public* 4. For more on deferral and the *Tadić* case in particular, see Chapter 3, Section 3.1.1.

[238] The ICTY has permitted some *amicus* participation in Rule 61 proceedings, convened early in the Tribunal's history when it proved impossible to execute certain warrants. See *Prosecutor* v. *Karadžić and Mladić*, Case Nos. IT-95-5-R61 and IT-95–18-R61, Review of the Indictments Pursuant to Rule 61 of the Rules of Procedure and Evidence, 16 July 1996, para. 2 (inviting a Special Rapporteur of the UN Commission on Human Rights and a member of the Commission of Experts established by Security Council Resolution 780 (1992) to hearing in Rule 61 proceedings concerning Karadžić and Mladić). But see Report of the

concerning whether the ICTY was 'established by law';[239] questions relating to the protection of victims and witnesses;[240] the ICTY's power to address subpoenas to sovereign states and their high government officials, and the appropriate remedies for non-compliance;[241] evidentiary issues arising in trials involving crimes of sexual violence;[242] testimony by war correspondents;[243] the scope of Common Article 3 of the Geneva Conventions and Additional Protocol II;[244] the exercise of prosecutorial discretion in respect of sexual offences charges not pleaded in the *Akayesu* case;[245] and a wide variety of other issues.[246] Section 5.6.4 discusses the role of *amici curiae* as developed in the *Milošević* trial, including their role as *de facto* defence counsel.

International Tribunal for the Prosecution of Persons Responsible for Serious Violations of International Humanitarian Law Committed in the Territory of the former Yugoslavia Since 1991, UN Doc. A/51/292-S/1996/665, 16 August 1996, para. 65 (noting that in same proceedings, permission to appear as *amicus* was refused to the Republic of Croatia and Human Rights Watch).

239 See Dixon, Khan, and May, *supra* note 237, p. 698 (noting that, on the basis of 'its special interest and knowledge as a Permanent Member of the UN Security Council and its substantial involvement in the adoption of the Statute of the Tribunal', the U.S. Government successfully intervened in *Tadić* on this important question of general international law).

240 See *Prosecutor* v. *Tadić*, Case No. IT-94-1, Decision on the Prosecutor's Motion Requesting Protective Measures for Victims and Witnesses, 10 August 1995, para. 10 (permitting Professor Christine Chinkin to file an *amicus* brief relating to the appropriate principles in international criminal proceedings concerning witness confidentiality and witness anonymity).

241 The Trial Chamber invited requests to participate as *amicus curiae* and specified the questions to be addressed. It received a number of requests from individuals, mainly distinguished international law professors, and some NGOs such as Juristes sans Frontières and Lawyers Committee for Human Rights. The Trial Chamber granted leave to thirteen applicants to make written submissions, of whom seven were allowed to participate in the hearing. See *Prosecutor* v. *Blaskić*, Case No. IT-95-14-T, Decision on the Objection of the Republic of Croatia to the Issuance of Subpoenae Duces Tecum, 18 July 1997, paras. 7, 8, 10, 12. On appeal, the Appeals Chamber extended a similar invitation for *amici* to participate, to which five states responded with *amicus curiae* briefs. See *Prosecutor* v. *Blaskić*, Case No. IT-95-14, Judgement on the Request of the Republic of Croatia for Review of the Decision of Trial Chamber II of 18 July 1997, 29 October 1997, para. 17.

242 In the *Furundžija* case, the Trial Chamber accepted an *amicus* brief from a coalition of women's groups about the credibility of a rape victim's evidence as a witness and about appropriate protective measures for such a witness. Proceedings had been re-opened because of the Prosecutor's late disclosure of evidence that, after being raped, the witness had received medical, psychological, or psychiatric treatment or counselling. See *Prosecutor* v. *Furundžija*, Case No. IT-95-17/1-T, Judgement, 10 December 1998, paras. 35, 107. See also Chapter 9, Section 9.1.4 (discussing evidentiary rules in such cases).

243 *Prosecutor* v. *Brđanin and Talić*, Case No. 99-36-PT, Second Decision on Motions by Radoslav Brđanin and Momir Talić for Access to Confidential Documents, 15 November 2000 (permitting written and oral *amicus* participation on behalf of thirty-four media companies and journalists' associations). See also Chapter 9, Section 9.3.2.2 (discussing the qualified privilege accorded war correspondents).

244 *Prosecutor* v. *Semanza*, Case No. ICTR-97-20-T, Decision on the Kingdom of Belgium's Application to File an *Amicus Curiae* Brief and on the Defence Application to Strike the Observations of the Kingdom of Belgium Concerning the Preliminary Response by the Defence, 9 February 2001, para. 10. Belgium complained that the ICTR had interpreted these provisions too restrictively.

245 *Prosecutor* v. *Akayesu*, Case No. ICTR-96-4-T, Order Granting Leave for *Amicus Curiae* to Appear, 6 March 1997. Indeed, this intervention had the unusual effect of causing the prosecution to seek amendment of its indictment *during the trial* to reflect the concerns set out in the brief.

246 See, e.g., *Prosecutor* v. *Krajišnik*, Case No. IT-00-39-A, Public and Redacted *Amicus Curiae*'s Appellate Brief, 31 August 2007 (discussing the failure of the Chamber to accord the accused a fair trial, specific aspects of the right allegedly violated, and the implications of misconduct and ineffective assistance of counsel early in proceedings).

5.6.2 *Amici curiae at the SCSL*

Rule 74 of the SCSL Rules replicates the analogous rule on *amici curiae* used in the ICTY and ICTR. It has been used in proceedings against Charles Taylor, the former President of Liberia, on whether he had immunity from exercise of the Special Court's jurisdiction.[247] The Trial Chamber invited international law professors Diane Orentlicher and Philippe Sands to make written and oral submissions as *amici*. Sands made submissions about a head of state's immunity from indictments of international or national courts; on whether the SCSL was an international court or merely a Sierra Leonean domestic court; on whether it was lawful for the SCSL to issue the indictment and circulate the arrest warrant while Taylor was a serving head of state; and on the effect of Taylor's subsequent status as a former head of state. Orentlicher addressed two questions: whether the indictment was invalid because it violated the immunities accorded serving heads of state under international law; and whether Taylor had substantive immunity as a former head of state from prosecution for the specific crimes charged. The Chamber referred in detail to the *amicus* briefs and explicitly adopted Sands' conclusions that the Special Court was an international court and therefore unconstrained by the jurisdictional constraints relating to 'the question of immunity of a serving head of State' that apply to national courts.[248]

5.6.3 *Amici curiae at the ICC*

The ICC Rules explicitly provide for the use of *amici curiae* at all stages of the proceedings. Rule 103, entitled '*Amicus curiae* and other forms of submission', provides:

1. At any stage of the proceedings, a Chamber may, if it considers it desirable for the proper determination of the case, invite or grant leave to a State, organization or person to submit, in writing or orally, any observation on any issue that the Chamber deems appropriate.
2. The Prosecutor and the defence shall have the opportunity to respond to the observations submitted under sub-rule 1.
3. A written observation submitted under sub-rule 1 shall be filed with the Registrar, who shall provide copies to the Prosecutor and the defence. The Chamber shall determine what time limits shall apply to the filing of such observations.

Rule 103 is substantially similar to Rule 74 in each of the ICTY, ICTR, and SCSL Rules, although it emphasises that *amicus* participation may be appropriate at any stage of the proceedings. The Rule grants chambers a broad discretionary power

[247] *Prosecutor* v. *Taylor*, Case No. SCSL-2003-01-I, Decision on Immunity from Jurisdiction, 31 May 2004.
[248] See Bartholomeusz, *supra* note 235, pp. 253–254.

either to invite *amici curiae* to submit their observations or, in the case of entities who file briefs on an issue without invitation, to grant leave to such entities to have the status of *amici*. Competence to submit such observations is not limited; 'States, organizations and persons' may be invited or may apply for leave to submit observations. The term 'organizations' is not qualified, leaving the door open for the involvement of non-governmental organisations, mixed-membership organisations, and public intergovernmental organisations. The term 'persons' is also not qualified by either the adjectives 'natural' or 'legal', leaving it to the Court to invite or accept submissions from individuals and corporations or other legal persons. The only criterion for inviting or granting leave to submit observations is whether the Court considers it 'desirable for the proper determination of the case'. The range of issues upon which observations may be invited or accepted can be legal or factual and appears to be entirely within a Chamber's discretion. The prosecution and defence have a right to respond to the observations.[249]

Several applications for leave to file *amicus* observations have been made, and chambers have granted a few. A pre-trial judge in *Bemba*, for example, allowed Amnesty International to file an *amicus* brief on three issues: 'i) The requisite mental element for military commanders; ii) Liability for the failure to punish as applied to non-state actors; and iii) Whether causation is an element of superior responsibility'.[250]

The broadly legal nature of these matters, relating as they do to fundamental questions of the legal status of a form of responsibility charged against an accused in proceedings, revealed a very significant potential for the involvement of *amici curiae* before the ICC. Indeed, the Court ultimately endorsed Amnesty International's argument concerning negligence, the separateness of the duties imposed on superiors, and its alternative argument for causation.[251]

5.6.4 **Amicus curiae** ***as*** **de facto** ***defence counsel***

Early in the *Milošević* proceedings, before the trial had even begun but after it was clear that the accused would be allowed to represent himself, the Trial Chamber issued an order to the ICTY Registrar to appoint *amici curiae* to assist the Chamber in the proper determination of the case.[252] The Trial Chamber stressed that the role of the *amici* would not be to represent the accused, but to assist the court by: (1)

[249] ICC Rule 103(2); see also Bartholomeusz, *supra* note 235, p. 242.

[250] *Prosecutor* v. *Bemba*, Doc. No. ICC-01/05-01/08-401, Decision on Application for Leave to Submit Amicus Curiae Observations Pursuant to Rule 103 of the Rules of Procedure and Evidence, 9 April 2009. Natalie L. Reid co-authored the brief for Amnesty International in this matter.

[251] *Prosecutor* v. *Bemba*, Doc. No. ICC-01/05-01/08-424, Decision Pursuant to Article 61(7)(a) and (b) on the Charges of the Prosecutor Against Jean-Pierre Bemba Gombo, 15 June 2009.

[252] *Prosecutor* v. *Slobodan Milošević*, Case No. IT-99-37-PT, Transcript, 30 August 2001, pp. 15–18.

making submissions properly open to Milošević by way of preliminary or other pre-trial motion; (2) making any submissions or objections to evidence properly open to him during the trial proceedings and cross-examining witnesses as appropriate; (3) drawing to the attention of the Trial Chamber any exculpatory or mitigating evidence on Milošević's behalf; and (4) acting 'in any other way which designated counsel considers appropriate in order to secure a fair trial'.[253] The Registrar complied with the Chamber's order by appointing three *amici curiae* in the case.[254]

While these counsel were appointed as friends of the court, their role was designed to augment the accused's resources and bolster legal argumentation and the cross-examination of witnesses – tasks quintessentially associated with defence counsel. In November 2001, the Trial Chamber further ordered the three *amici* to make submissions or objections on evidence presented that would be open to Milošević to make, and again stated that they were to act 'in any other way they consider appropriate in order to secure a fair trial'.[255]

Later in the trial, the Chamber issued another order to the *amici curiae*, authorising them to receive such information as the accused may provide to them and to act in any way to protect and further the accused's interests.[256] This order extended their role well beyond any traditional role normally played by *amicus curiae* and encouraged the development of their role into a form of *de facto* defence counsel. In practice, the *amici curiae* carried on a parallel quasi-defence function. They had no direct instructions from Milošević, but they provided him with considerable case management assistance out of court, and made submissions they perceived as being in his interests and consistent with his stated position in court. In this way, the *amici curiae* model employed in the *Milošević* trial had some utility. Yet it is far from an efficient model, and is unlikely to be easily transposed to other international criminal trials of self-represented accused, mainly because the marginal success of the approach was so specific to the personalities and relationships built up over a long period of cohabitation in the courtroom in that case.

Nevertheless, while an extreme and unorthodox use of the *amicus curiae* model, the *Milošević* precedent shows the potential innovation and transformation of the role of the friend of the court towards providing a high degree of assistance to accused in the conduct of their self-represented defence. If the ICTY Appeals Chamber precedent on the right to self-representation discussed above is to become

[253] *Ibid.*

[254] *Prosecutor* v. *Slobodan Milošević*, Case No. IT-99-37-PT, Decision by the Registrar, 6 September 2001.

[255] *Prosecutor* v. *Slobodan Milošević*, Case No. IT-01-51-PT, Order Inviting Designation of *Amicus Curiae*, 23 November 2001. The Registrar responded by formally appointing the three *amici* already identified in his decision of 6 September. *Prosecutor* v. *Slobodan Milošević*, Case No. IT-01-51-PT, Decision by the Registrar, 27 November 2001.

[256] *Prosecutor* v. *Slobodan Milošević*, Case No. IT-02-54-T, Order of Further Instruction to the *Amici Curiae*, 6 October 2003.

entrenched in international criminal proceedings – rendering the right next to absolute – then it may be necessary to consider unusual approaches such as that employed in the *Milošević* trial, along with standby counsel, so as to assist in the delivery of fair and expeditious trials.

5.7 Legal associates and unrepresented accused

Another way in which international criminal tribunals, in particular the ICTY, have sought to ensure adequate resources for self-represented accused is the employment of what the *Milošević* Trial Chamber termed 'legal associates' to assist the accused in the preparation and conduct of their defence. The use of this form of assistance is premised on a trial chamber's obligation to ensure that a trial is fair. An accused's *pro se* appearance in a highly complex international criminal trial clearly implicates the right to equality of arms.[257]

As with some other defence models discussed in this chapter, the use of legal associates to aid *pro se* accused was first developed early in the *Milošević* proceedings. The Trial Chamber realised that the accused, if he were to represent himself, needed at least to have access to lawyers whom he could trust and with whom he could communicate in a privileged manner. The Chamber reasoned that fair trial guarantees demanded that Milošević be able to communicate freely with persons who could give him legal advice, and supply them with copies of documents, subject to protective measures ordered by the Trial Chamber in relation to the protection of witnesses. In April 2002, it granted Milošević privileged communication with two Serbian lawyers, Zdenko Tomanović and Dragoslav Ognjanović, as legal associates.[258] The Trial Chamber stated that the accused 'shall be entitled to communicate fully and without restraint' with Tomanović and Ognjanović and that 'all correspondence and communications between them and the accused shall be privileged'. In October 2003, the Trial Chamber issued an order appointing Branko Rakić as a third legal associate to Milošević.[259]

[257] For more on the right to equality of arms, see *supra* note 71. The principle has been adopted and referred to in this context before the ICTY. See generally *Milošević* Trial Decision on Representation, *supra* note 184; *Prosecutor* v. *Karadžić*, Case No. IT-95-5/18-PT, Decision on Accused Motion for Adequate Facilities and Equality of Arms, 28 January 2009 ('*Karadžić* Adequate Facilities Decision').

[258] *Prosecutor* v. *Slobodan Milošević*, Case No. IT-02-54-T, Order, 16 April 2002. By this Order, the two legal associates became bound by all existing orders of the Trial Chamber, including the order for protective measures. Tomanović's power of attorney was filed with the Registry on 16 April 2002 and Ognjanović's power of attorney was filed on 22 April 2002.

[259] *Prosecutor* v. *Slobodan Milošević*, Case No. IT-02-54-T, Order Appointing Branko Rakić as Legal Associate to the Accused, 23 October 2003. The conditions imposed with respect to the other two legal associates also applied to Branko Rakić. It also appears that Milošević had at least one additional associate in Belgrade, Momo Raičević, who appeared to be involved in sourcing of information and briefing witnesses. See *Prosecutor* v. *Slobodan Milošević*, Case No. IT-02-54-T, Transcript, 22 September 2005, p. 44547; *ibid.*, 30 September 2005, p. 44973; *ibid.*, 3 October 2005, p. 45045.

The Trial Chamber never gave any clear definition of the role of legal associates. There is also little concrete evidence of what these legal associates actually did in relation to the trial. In December 2004, the Trial Chamber issued an order refusing Milošević's application to add four witnesses to his list of witnesses.[260] According to the Trial Chamber, the application to add the names had been filed by the '*pro se* liaison officer' – another post created specifically for the *Milošević* case, in which a Registry employee assisted the accused in obtaining and filing documents and with logistical questions surrounding the preparation of his defence, and served as an intermediary between the accused and the Registry.[261] The liaison officer, in turn, based the petition on a letter written by one of the associates, Ognjanović, stating the need for the witnesses.

The legal associates relayed information not only from the accused to the other participants in the case and to the Trial Chamber, but also from the prosecution to the accused. For example, the legal associates informed Milošević of the order in which the prosecution intended to call its witnesses and provided him with documents related to those witnesses.[262] At one stage, they also informed the Chamber of Milošević's poor health,[263] and provided information relating to other defence witnesses the accused intended to call.[264] Moreover, the associates appeared to collect information on Milošević's behalf from both the ICTY[265] and institutions in Serbia.[266] At times, the legal associates appeared to also act as translators.[267] In addition, it was clear that they reviewed exhibits provided to the defence by the prosecution.[268] In these ways – and surely in many others that never became public – the legal associates acted in some respects and at different times as both investigators and defence lawyers, although they never appeared in court or directly authored legal submissions on behalf of the accused that were filed with the Chamber.

In this respect, the model used in the *Milošević* case again appears to have set something of a precedent before the ICTY. Another senior accused appearing subsequently at the ICTY, Radovan Karadžić, also elected to represent himself. He sought the services of an experienced defence counsel who had represented other accused at the *ad hoc* Tribunals, Peter Robinson, who was appointed as Karadžić's 'legal associate'.[269] The interesting difference in Karadžić's case is the engagement of a large international team of *pro bono* lawyers working with Robinson and

[260] *Prosecutor* v. *Slobodan Milošević*, Case No. IT-02-54-T, Order on Application by the Accused to Add Four Witnesses to His Witness List, 3 December 2004.

[261] There is no provision for such an officer in the ICTY Rules. It seems to have been an *ad hoc* institution created for the *Milošević* trial, and it does not appear to have been used in any other proceedings before the ICTY or any other international tribunal.

[262] *Prosecutor* v. *Slobodan Milošević*, Case No. IT-02-54-T, Transcript, 11 June 2002, p. 6673.

[263] *Ibid.*, 7 October 2003, p. 27109. [264] *Ibid.*, 9 November 2004, p. 33197.

[265] *Ibid.*, 18 October 2005, p. 45316.

[266] *Ibid.*, 19 October 2005, p. 45472. See also *ibid.*, 26 October 2005, p. 45744; *ibid.*, 26 April 2005, p. 38812.

[267] *Ibid.*, 27 April 2005, p. 38858. [268] *Ibid.*, 9 May 2005, p. 39186.

[269] See *Karadžić* Adequate Facilities Decision, *supra* note 257, para. 2.

formal recognition by the Registry and Trial Chamber of these lawyers as rendering legal assistance to the accused.[270]

Up until close to the scheduled commencement of Karadžić's case, he was highly cooperative and appeared intent upon conducting a focused forensic defence – quite contrary to the clear position of Milošević from the start of his case. However, Karadžić had become frustrated by the refusal of the Tribunal to provide resources for the proper remuneration of his legal associate[271] and this, coupled with the sheer size of the case and limited time and resources for preparation, led him to inform the Chamber that he would refuse to attend court on the nominated date for commencement of trial. The Trial Chamber responded, in a rather unorthodox way, by writing to Karadžić to ask him to reconsider, and to advise that it had the power to proceed *in absentia* of the accused and to impose defence counsel if it determined that his conduct amounted to significant obstruction to the trial and the provision of a fair trial.[272] Karadžić responded that he would not move from his position.[273] In the end, as occurred in different ways in the *Milošević* and *Šešelj* cases, the Trial Chamber granted a four-month adjournment of proceedings, explaining that it would order the assignment of counsel to prepare and follow the case and (much like standby counsel) be prepared to step in should the need arise at some point in the future.[274]

5.8 Conclusion

The representation of accused persons before international criminal tribunals is a matter of some complexity. The same basic models of representation exist in international criminal law as in domestic criminal justice systems: the accused are either represented by counsel (self-funded or court-appointed) or they are self-represented. What renders these otherwise common factors distinctive in international criminal law is the complicated nature of the cases and tribunal structures. The international criminal tribunals have responded to these complexities with a number of provisions and approaches designed to ensure that effectuation of the

[270] See *Prosecutor* v. *Karadžić*, Case No. IT-95-5/18-PT, Transcript, 17 August 2009, pp. 145–148; Mike Corder, 'Karadzic Wages Paperwork Blitz in War Crimes Trial', Associated Press, 29 August 2009, available at http://abcnews.go.com/International/wireStory?id=7593069. Gideon Boas was one of the lawyers providing *pro bono* legal assistance in the preparation of preliminary motions and motions relating to points of law.

[271] See *Karadžić* Adequate Facilities Decision, *supra* note 257, para. 6.

[272] *Prosecutor* v. *Karadžić*, Case No. IT-95-5/18-PT, Transcript 26 October 2009, pp. 502–503 (Trial Chamber reading out relevant portion of the letter at a hearing which was not attended by the accused).

[273] See *Prosecutor* v. *Karadžić*, Case No. IT-95-5/18-PT, Response to Letter from the Chamber, 24 October 2009.

[274] *Prosecutor* v. *Karadžić*, Case No. IT-95-5/18, Decision on Appointment of Counsel and Order on Further Trial Proceedings, 11 November 2009, para. 28.

right to representation meets the obligation of these tribunals to comply with the *jus cogens* norm of a right to a fair trial.

Aspects of the treatment of representation have been innovative, including the extended use of *amici curiae* to perform many of the functions traditionally performed by defence counsel; and other forms of legal assistance and defence resources to self-represented accused, such as legal associates and *pro se* liaison officers to aid the accused in receiving and making filings before the court, performing research, and undertaking other logistical tasks. The ICTY Registrar, at least, appears prepared to provide a series of non-traditional forms of defence assistance without requiring means testing. Where counsel is retained or appointed, the international criminal tribunals and defence counsel associations have developed a strong network of rules and regulations to reinforce and support the crucial role of counsel in these institutions.

Where the accused elects self-representation, as has been the case with numerous senior-level accused, the appellate jurisprudence of the *ad hoc* Tribunals has significantly complicated the task of trial chambers seeking to maintain order by imposing defence counsel – even where the accused is intentionally being obstructionist, unruly, or otherwise contumacious. We hope the Appeals Chambers will depart from this unfortunate precedent in the short time left in their mandates, and that the ICC and internationalised tribunals will take a radically different path to regulating self-representation to ensure that the integrity of the tribunals is protected and that the obligation to provide a fair and expeditious trial is fully respected.

Significant progress can be seen through the evolution of the status of the defence before the internationalised criminal tribunals. The advancement of the defence as an independent organ of the court, as seen in the STL Statute,[275] is evidence of incremental progress, both in its independence and its assured place in the founding instrument.[276] The unique complexity of international criminal trials, including the different forms of defence representation, will continue to present unusual obstacles to the principle of equality of arms and the delivery of a fair and expeditious trial, especially in the case of obstructionist accused.[277] It is also clear that *de jure* protection of defence rights does not equate to *de facto* protection.[278] Provision for the defence as an independent organ in founding texts and rules must

[275] See *supra* Section 5.2.1.4.

[276] See *supra* Section 5.2.1.3 (discussing the SCSL).

[277] See *supra* Sections 5.3.1.1, 5.3.1.2, 5.5.

[278] See Gillian Higgins, 'Fair and Expeditious Pre-Trial Proceedings: The Future of International Criminal Trials', (2007) 5 *Journal of International Criminal Justice* 394, 400 (discussing Iraqi High Tribunal, where rules provided for the creation of a defence office, but poor implementation and funding prevented any real assistance).

be supported in practice by funding, resources, and judicial case management. The perceptible trend of the strengthening of the defence vis-à-vis the prosecution, along with evolving case management techniques to ensure fair and expeditious trials, give some indication of the future direction of international criminal defence and its representation.

6

Pre-trial proceedings

CONTENTS

The pre-trial phase at the international criminal tribunals begins with the prosecution's submission of proposed charges and ends with the commencement of trial. During this period, which can last up to several years,[1] the participants prepare for trial in those cases where the proposed charges have passed judicial scrutiny, and the accused has not pleaded guilty to some or all of those charges. At the ICC, this stage takes place under the supervision and control of both the pre-trial and trial chambers, as a case is transferred from one to the other after the charges have been confirmed, and typically well before opening statements.[2] At the SCSL, the same judges hear and manage the case through the pre-trial and trial phases.[3] While the same arrangement may occur at the *ad hoc* Tribunals in some cases,[4] in others, control of each phase is tasked to a different chamber.[5]

This chapter examines six sets of rules and practices that comprise and define the pre-trial phase of the proceedings. Section 6.1 discusses the law governing the submission, review, confirmation, amendment, and withdrawal of charges. Section 6.2 reviews the joinder and severance of charges, accused, and indictments or trials – tools which facilitate the large trials that have come to characterise proceedings at the ICTY, ICTR, and SCSL, and which may yet become an important feature of ICC procedure. Section 6.3 summarises the broad powers of chambers to issue warrants and other pre-trial orders in aid of investigations or the preparation and future conduct of the trial.

[1] See Chapter 4, Section 4.3.2 (discussing the length of pre-trial detention). The duration of the pre-trial phase is also determined in part by how long the accused manages to evade the custody of the tribunals. See *infra* Sections 6.1.3, 6.2.4.

[2] See *infra* Section 6.6.3.

[3] See, e.g., *Prosecutor* v. *Fofana and Kondewa* ('*CDF* Case'), Case No. SCSL-04-14-T, Judgement, 2 August 2007 ('*CDF* Trial Judgement'), para. 20 (noting the decisions made in the pre-trial phase by the same chamber, albeit with a rotating presidency).

[4] See, e.g., *Prosecutor* v. *Milutinović, Šainović, Ojdanić, Pavković, Lazarević, and Lukić*, Case No. IT-05-87-PT, Judgement, 26 February 2009 ('*Milutinović et al.* Trial Judgement'), Vol. I, paras. 15–16 (discussing the pre-trial phase in that case).

[5] See, e.g., *Prosecutor* v. *Halilović*, Case No. IT-01-48-T, Judgement, 16 November 2005, pp. 295–296 (referring to the pre-trial phase conducted before another trial chamber). See also Chapter 7, Sections 7.3.1, 7.6.1.

Section 6.4 examines guilty plea dispositions and discusses the *ad hoc* Tribunals' experiences with plea bargaining, a procedural transplant from the common law with the potential to expedite the conclusion of cases, but which has played a comparatively minor role in international criminal trials. Section 6.5 discusses the disclosure obligations of the parties to international criminal proceedings. Both the prosecution and the defence bear such obligations, although the prosecution's obligation is far heavier and tied directly to the tribunals' mandate to provide a fair trial to the accused. Section 6.6 explores the judges' case-management authority at each of the tribunals, outlining the various tools at their disposal to affect the scope of the trial. Faced with the inherent tension of ensuring that complex international criminal trials are both fair and expeditious, the *ad hoc* Tribunals' judges have given themselves significant – if underutilised – authority to shape the proceedings. Finally, Section 6.7 provides some concluding thoughts on the pre-trial process at the international criminal tribunals.

6.1 Charging instruments

The commencement of formal accusatory proceedings at the international criminal tribunals is guided by two complementary legal principles, both firmly rooted in international human rights law. First, an individual should not face the prospect of criminal liability unless there is an objectively reasonable basis to believe that his or her conduct warrants such liability.[6] Second, any person against whom criminal proceedings are instituted should be informed, in a timely fashion, of the legal and factual bases of the prosecution's allegations.[7] The institutions surveyed in this volume are all tribunals of limited jurisdiction – whether personal, temporal, or subject matter. Their governing instruments thus add another consideration, this time directed at the authority of the court or tribunal concerned to hear the case and pass judgement on the accused: are the allegations presented by the prosecution within the jurisdiction of the court or tribunal?

At the *ad hoc* Tribunals and the SCSL, these issues are dealt with in connection with a single document, the indictment containing the charges against the accused, which must be reviewed and confirmed by a judge before the accused may be arrested or detained. The alternative outcomes are the same at the ICC – either a determination that there are insufficient grounds to proceed against the individual,

[6] See ICCPR, Art. 9(1); ECHR, Art. 5(1)(c); ACHR, Art. 7.

[7] See ICCPR, Arts. 9(2), 14(3)(a); ECHR, Arts. 5(2), 6(3)(a); ACHR, Arts. 7, 8(2)(b); United Nations Human Rights Committee, General Comment No. 13 (1984), reprinted in UN Doc. HRI/GEN/1/Rev.1 p. 14 (1994), para. 8 (noting that the accused's right to be informed of the charges against him 'must arise when in the course of an investigation a court or an authority of the prosecution decides to take procedural steps against a person suspected of a crime or publicly names him as such'; and that the requirements of the ICCPR 'may be met by stating the charge either orally or in writing, provided that the information indicates both the law and the alleged facts on which it is based').

or preparation for trial on the basis of a formal charging document listing the allegations against the accused. The procedural path is quite different, however, requiring two rounds of judicial review and affording the accused an opportunity to challenge the prosecution's allegations before the charging instrument (termed the 'Document Containing the Charges', or DCC) may be confirmed.

Notwithstanding these differences, there are fundamental similarities between the procedural approaches to accusation in the international criminal tribunals. All combine prosecutorial discretion with judicial oversight in an effort to balance the independent investigation of international crimes with the impartial determination of compliance with the human rights principles discussed above. The subsections below examine how the instruments and practice of these tribunals strike this balance at three different points in the proceedings: judicial review of the proposed charges; amendment of the charges, including in response to challenges from the accused to the form of the indictment or charging instrument; and withdrawal of charges by the prosecution.

6.1.1 Review of proposed charges

Under the basic instruments governing the *ad hoc* Tribunals, the Prosecutor is tasked with drafting a proposed indictment, which is then presented to a single judge for review, along with supporting materials setting forth the factual basis for the proposed charges.[8] If that judge determines that the Prosecutor has established a *prima facie* case against the accused, the indictment is confirmed and is typically used as grounds for the issuance of an arrest warrant for the accused.[9] While it may be amended or withdrawn after confirmation,[10] or replaced with another indictment if additional accused are joined,[11] the indictment that is confirmed by the reviewing judge (in its original or amended form) is generally the basis for the ensuing trial of the accused. The Rules of each of these tribunals permit communications between

[8] See ICTY Statute, Art. 18(4) and ICTR Statute, Art. 17(4), which provide, in identical terms: 'Upon a determination that a *prima facie* case exists, the Prosecutor shall prepare an indictment containing a concise statement of the facts and the crime or crimes with which the accused is charged under the Statute. The indictment shall be transmitted to a judge of the Trial Chamber.' See also ICTY Rule 47 (implementing this article of the Statute); ICTR Rule 47 (same). Pursuant to the completion strategies at the *ad hoc* Tribunals, the prosecution's investigations were completed and the final indictments confirmed in 2004 at the ICTY, and 2005 at the ICTR. See www.icty.org/sections/AbouttheICTY/OfficeoftheProsecutor; Letter Dated 5 December 2005 from the President of the International Criminal Tribunal for the Prosecution of Persons Responsible for Genocide and Other Serious Violations of International Humanitarian Law Committed in the Territory of Rwanda and Rwandan Citizens Responsible for Genocide and Other Such Violations Committed in the Territory of Neighbouring States Between 1 January and 31 December 1994 Addressed to the President of the Security Council, UN Doc. S/2005/782, 14 December 2005, p. 2 and para. 35.

[9] ICTY Statute, Art. 19(1); ICTR Statute, Art. 18(1). See *infra* Section 6.3 for a discussion of judicial authority to issue warrants and orders.

[10] See *infra* Sections 6.1.2, 6.1.3.

[11] See *infra* Section 6.2.

the reviewing judge and the prosecution during the review process,[12] but it is only after confirmation of the indictment – or upon the actual arrest, if the indictment is sealed after confirmation[13] – that the accused is informed of the pending charges.

A similar approach is applied at the SCSL, where the procedural rules are explicitly modelled on those of the ICTR.[14] The governing instruments of the SCSL, however, mandate a structure for charging instruments that is quite different from the indictments at the *ad hoc* Tribunals, which are frequently quite long and include all the factual allegations the prosecution intends to prove at trial. As the SCSL Appeals Chamber explained, in the course of scolding the prosecution for adopting the model used at the ICTY and ICTR, an indictment at the SCSL should contain only the counts 'encapsulating the offence[s] with which the subject is charged' and a brief description of 'the particulars of the offence[s]' such as time, place, and co-offenders; attached to this indictment as a separate document is the case summary 'briefly setting out the allegations [the Prosecutor] proposes to prove – a *précis*, as it were, of his opening speech'.[15]

At the ICC, unlike the process at the *ad hoc* Tribunals and the SCSL, the confirmation of charges against the accused is the culmination of two successive interactions between the parties and the pre-trial chamber.[16] The first, an *ex parte* exchange between the prosecution and the chamber that may occur '[a]t any time after the initiation of an investigation', is triggered by the prosecution's request for the issuance of an arrest warrant or summons for a potential accused (the 'suspect'). The request

[12] See ICTY Rule 47(F) (providing that the reviewing judge may, *inter alia*, 'request the Prosecutor to present additional material in support of any or all counts' or 'adjourn the review so as to give the Prosecutor the opportunity to modify the indictment'); ICTR Rule 47(F) (same, except the judge may also request the Prosecutor 'to take any further measures which appear appropriate').

[13] See ICTY Rule 53(B)–(C) (permitting a judge or chamber, on consultation with the prosecution, to prohibit public disclosure of all or part of an indictment until served on all accused, or if required to give effect to a rule, to protect confidential information, or by the interests of justice); ICTR Rule 53(B)–(C) (same); SCSL Rule 53(B)–(C) (same).

[14] SCSL Rule 47; see also SCSL Statute, Art. 14 ('The Rules of Procedure and Evidence of the International Criminal Tribunal for Rwanda obtaining at the time of the establishment of the Special Court shall be applicable *mutatis mutandis* to the conduct of the legal proceedings before the Special Court'). In contrast to the *ad hoc* Tribunals, however, Rule 47 of the SCSL Rules does not explicitly provide for communication between the judge and the prosecution between submission and confirmation of the indictment. The SCSL Statute does not contain provisions concerning the review, amendment, or withdrawal of indictments. Eleven accused were indicted by the SCSL in 2003: two died soon after they were indicted, see *infra* Section 6.1.3; one is still at large, see www.sc-sl.org/CASES/JohnnyPaulKoroma/tabid/188/Default.aspx (discussing Johnny Paul Koroma); and as of 31 May 2009, the Special Court's administration expected that all judicial proceedings would be concluded by the end of 2010. See Sixth Annual Report of the President of the Special Court for Sierra Leone, p. 33, available at www.sc-sl.org/LinkClick.aspx?fileticket=%2fuI3lqaO5D0%3d&tabid=53.

[15] *CDF* Case, Case No. SCSL-04-14-AR73, Decision on Amendment of the Consolidated Indictment, 16 May 2005 ('*CDF* Indictment Appeal Decision'), para. 51.

[16] Under the Rome Statute, 'unless otherwise provided for in the Rules of Procedure and Evidence or by a majority of the Pre-Trial Chamber', the functions and powers of the pre-trial chamber may be exercised by a single judge of that chamber, except for orders or rulings issued under Articles 15, 18, 19, 54(2), 61(7), or 72, which require approval by a majority of the three-judge panel. Rome Statute, Art. 57(2). The exceptions relate generally to authorisation of a *proprio motu* investigation by the Prosecutor, rulings regarding admissibility or the Court's jurisdiction, or protection of information relevant to national security. In addition, formal confirmation of charges may only be ordered by a majority of the pre-trial chamber.

is granted only if the judge or chamber to which the application is made determines that there are '*reasonable* grounds to believe that the person has committed a crime within the jurisdiction of the Court',[17] and that the requested warrant or summons is necessary or sufficient to achieve the purpose for which it is sought.[18] The second interaction is a formal *inter partes* hearing 'to confirm the charges on which the Prosecutor intends to seek trial',[19] at which the prosecution must 'support each charge with sufficient evidence to establish *substantial* grounds to believe that the person committed the crime charged',[20] and the suspect has the right to object to the charges, challenge the prosecution's evidence, or offer evidence of his or her own.[21] During the period between these two interactions, the prosecution may continue its investigation, and is permitted to amend or withdraw the proposed charges.[22]

6.1.1.1 The applicable standards

6.1.1.1.1 A prima facie *case* The ICTY and ICTR Statutes and the ICTY Rules all require that the prosecution establish a *prima facie* case before an indictment may be confirmed,[23] but none of those instruments actually defines that standard. While there has been some frustration expressed in the jurisprudence over the lack

[17] Rome Statute, Art. 58 (emphasis added). Notwithstanding the plain text of this provision, it is clear that arrest warrants may be issued for persons alleged to be responsible for international crimes through forms of participation other than commission. See, e.g., *Prosecutor* v. *Lubanga*, Case No. ICC-01/04-01/06, Decision on the Prosecutor's Application for a Warrant of Arrest, Article 58, 10 February 2006, Annex A to Doc. No. ICC-01/04-01/06-8-Corr, reclassified as public by Doc. No. ICC-01/04-01/06-37 ('*Lubanga* Arrest Warrant Decision'), paras. 77–78. See also Gideon Boas, James L. Bischoff, and Natalie L. Reid, *Forms of Responsibility in International Criminal Law* (2007) ('Boas, Bischoff, and Reid, *Forms of Responsibility*'), for an in-depth overview of this area of substantive international criminal law and pp. 2–5 for the distinction between physical commission and other forms of responsibility.

[18] If an arrest warrant is requested, Article 58(1)(b) of the Rome Statute requires the pre-trial judge or chamber to determine whether a warrant 'appears necessary' to ensure the appearance of the potential accused; to remove the risk of obstruction or endangerment of the investigation; or to prevent the commission (or continued commission) of the alleged crime, or a related crime within the Court's jurisdiction and arising from the same circumstances. If, on the other hand, the prosecution requests a summons, the task of the judge or chamber under Article 58(7) is to determine (in addition to the existence of reasonable grounds to believe that the person committed the alleged crime(s)) whether a summons 'is sufficient to ensure the person's appearance'.

[19] Rome Statute, Art. 61(1).

[20] *Ibid.*, Art. 61(5) (emphasis added). This formulation is consistent with the rare international criminal case in which commission is the only form of responsibility charged, and where the allegations in the charging instruments thus do not extend much beyond the bare facts necessary to establish the commission of the crime. As noted elsewhere, however, most suspects in international criminal proceedings are charged with forms of responsibility other than physical commission. Boas, Bischoff, and Reid, *Forms of Responsibility*, *supra* note 17, pp. 2, 19, 384, 420. The actual application of this standard by ICC pre-trial chambers is more promising, in that it demonstrates an appreciation of the distinction between the elements of crimes and the elements of forms of responsibility, and includes consideration of whether the prosecution has met its burden with regard to its allegations for each element of the form or forms of responsibility charged. See *infra* text accompanying notes 34–35.

[21] Rome Statute, Art. 61(6). See also William A. Schabas, 'International Criminal Tribunals: A Review of 2007', (2008) 6 *Northwestern University Journal of International Human Rights* 382, 410 (describing ICC confirmation of charges hearings as 'ensur[ing] that a prosecution is not frivolous and that there is sufficient evidence for a finding of guilt, thereby protecting the accused from prosecutorial abuse').

[22] Rome Statute, Art. 61(4).

[23] ICTY Statute, Arts. 18, 19; ICTR Statute, Arts. 17, 18; ICTY Rule 47.

of clear guidance on this question,[24] over the years, reviewing judges at the ICTY have settled on a definition that focuses on the sufficiency of the prosecution's evidence in support of the proposed charges. In perhaps the clearest articulation of the standard, Judge May defined a '*prima facie* case' as 'a credible case which, if accepted and uncontradicted, would be a sufficient basis on which to convict the accused'.[25]

At the ICTR, the corresponding rule itself provides a definition similar to that developed in ICTY case law: Rule 47(B) provides that, in performing its duties under Article 18 of the ICTR Statute, the prosecution shall prepare and forward an indictment for confirmation 'if satisfied in the course of an investigation that there is sufficient evidence to provide reasonable grounds for believing that a suspect has committed a crime within the jurisdiction of the Tribunal'. Though the Rule does not state explicitly that this standard is a clarification of the term '*prima facie*' as used in Article 18 to describe the duties of both the prosecution and the reviewing judge, it has been applied and interpreted as such by ICTR judges.[26]

The SCSL has no analogous provision in its Statute regarding review of the indictment, but has nevertheless applied a standard similar to that developed by reviewing judges of the *ad hoc* Tribunals.[27] The key distinction between the standard applied in the *ad hoc* Tribunals and the SCSL appears to be that the reviewing judge in the latter court is not required to review the supporting materials to test the prosecution's assertion that it will be able to prove its case. As the Appeals Chamber explained, the practice of reviewing an indictment at the SCSL 'does not, as in certain other courts, require a judicial finding of a *prima facie* case: the judge is concerned only to ensure that the particulars which the Prosecution claims it can

[24] See, e.g., *Prosecutor* v. *Mladić*, Case No. IT-95-5/18–1, Order Granting Leave to File an Amended Indictment and Confirming the Amended Indictment, 8 November 2002, paras. 12–18 (discussing the lack of unanimity in past decisions determining the test to be applied, and noting the 'absence of a definition in … customary or conventional [international] law') (quotation at para. 18).

[25] *Prosecutor* v. *Milošević*, Case No. IT-01-51-I, Decision on Review of Indictment, 22 November 2001, para. 14 (slightly modifying the test first set forth by Judge McDonald in *Prosecutor* v. *Kordić, Blaškić, Čerkez, Šantić, Skopljak, and Aleksovski*, Case No. IT-95-14-I, Decision on Review of the Indictment, 10 November 1995, pp. 2–3); accord *Prosecutor* v. *Karadžić*, Case No. IT-95-5/18-PT, Decision on Prosecution Motion to Amend the First Amended Indictment, 16 February 2009 ('*Karadžić* Pre-Trial Indictment Decision'), para. 35; *Prosecutor* v. *Haradinaj, Balaj, and Brahimaj*, Case No. IT-04-84-PT, Decision on Motion to Amend the Indictment and on Challenges to the Form of the Amended Indictment, 25 October 2006 ('*Haradinaj et al.* Pre-Trial Indictment Decision'), para. 19.

[26] See, e.g., *Prosecutor* v. *Gacumbitsi*, Case No. ICTR-2001-64-I, Decision on the Prosecutor's Application for Confirmation of an Indictment and Related Orders, 20 June 2001 (interpreting Article 18(1) of the ICTR Statute 'consistent with Rule 47', as requiring that the reviewing judge 'determine whether the Prosecutor has presented within the Indictment and the supporting materials allegations as would provide "reasonable grounds for believing" that the identified suspect has committed crimes falling within the jurisdiction of the Tribunal').

[27] See, e.g., *Prosecutor* v. *Taylor*, Case No. SCSL-2003-01-I, Decision Approving the Indictment and Order for Non-Disclosure, 7 March 2003 (approving the indictment because the reviewing judge was 'satisfied from the material tendered by the Prosecutor that there is sufficient evidence to provide reasonable grounds for believing that the suspect has committed crimes within the jurisdiction of the Court and that the allegations would, if proven, amount to the crimes specified and particularised in the said Indictment').

prove would amount to a triable offence' within the jurisdiction of the Court.[28] If this was in fact the standard applied by SCSL judges,[29] it would appear inconsistent with the practice of the other international tribunals surveyed here, which all require judges to assess the sufficiency of the evidence on which the prosecution relies before a suspect is detained, and therefore seem more protective of the rights of the suspect.

6.1.1.1.2 'Reasonable grounds' and 'substantial grounds' In considering the prosecution's applications for arrest warrants, pre-trial chambers at the ICC have concluded that the determination of whether there are 'reasonable grounds' to believe that the suspect is responsible for crimes within the jurisdiction of the Court should be guided by international human rights law, especially decisions interpreting the ECHR and the case law of the Inter-American Court of Human Rights ('IACHR').[30] Cases applying the ECHR have interpreted the 'reasonable suspicion' standard of Article 5(1)(c) to mean 'the existence of facts or information which would satisfy an objective observer that the person concerned may have committed the offence';[31] while the IACHR cases cited by the ICC have emphasised the importance of judicial supervision of the deprivation of personal liberty on suspicion of criminal liability.[32]

The hearing to determine whether the charges against the suspect will be confirmed is the second point at which the prosecution's allegations are subject to judicial review. The *Katanga and Ngudjolo* Pre-Trial Chamber emphasised that this stage of the proceedings is intended solely to protect 'the rights of the Defence against wrongful and wholly unfounded charges', and that as such, the confirmation hearing 'should not be seen as a mini-trial or a trial before the trial'.[33] As a practical matter, to meet its burden of establishing 'substantial grounds' to conclude

28 *CDF* Indictment Appeal Decision, *supra* note 15, para. 49.

29 See, e.g., *supra* note 27 (describing the standard applied in the 2003 *Taylor* decision, which preceded the Appeals Chamber's edict in the *CDF* Indictment Appeal Decision, *supra* note 15). By the time of the latter decision in 2005, however, all SCSL indictments had already been confirmed, so the holding would apply only to judicial review of any future amendment to the indictments.

30 See, e.g., *Prosecutor* v. *Harun and Kushayb*, Doc. No. ICC-02/05-01/07-1-Corr, Decision on the Prosecution Application Under Article 58(7) of the Statute, 27 April 2007 (corrected 15 May 2007) ('*Harun and Kushayb* Arrest Warrant Decision'), para. 28 (concluding that 'the expression "reasonable grounds to believe" must be interpreted and applied in accordance with internationally recognized human rights', and determining accordingly that 'the Chamber will be guided by the "reasonable suspicion" standard of Article 5(1)(c) of the [ECHR] and the jurisprudence of the [IACHR]').

31 *Fox, Campbell, and Hartley* v. *United Kingdom*, Judgement, 13 Eur. H.R. Rep. 157, 30 August 1990, para. 32 (noting also that '[w]hat may be regarded as "reasonable" will however depend upon all the circumstances'); accord *Labita* v. *Italy*, Judgment, 2000-IV Eur. Ct. H.R., 6 April 2000, para. 155.

32 See, e.g., *Bámaca Velásquez* v. *Guatemala*, Judgement, 25 November 2000, Series C, No. 70, paras. 138–144; *Loayza-Tamayo* v. *Peru*, Judgement, 17 September 1997, Series C, No 33, paras. 49–55; *Gangaram Pandray* v. *Suriname*, Judgement, 21 January 1994, Series C, No. 16, paras. 46–51 (cited in *Harun and Kushayb* Arrest Warrant Decision, *supra* note 30, para. 28 n. 22; *Lubanga* Arrest Warrant Decision, *supra* note 17, para. 12 n. 6).

Prosecutor v. *Katanga and Ngudjolo*, Doc. No. ICC-01/04-01/07-717, Public Redacted Version of Decision on the Confirmation of Charges, 30 September 2008 ('*Katanga and Ngudjolo* Confirmation Decision'), paras. 3, 64 (internal quotation marks and footnote omitted).

the suspect bears liability for the crimes alleged in the charging instrument, the prosecution 'must present concrete and tangible evidence which "demonstrates a clear line of reasoning underpinning its specific allegations"' as to each element of the crimes and forms of responsibility alleged.[34] For example, in *Katanga and Ngudjolo*, where the suspects faced charges that they jointly committed war crimes through other persons, the Pre-Trial Chamber considered whether the prosecution had provided sufficient evidence to permit the conclusions that the armed groups that physically committed the crimes were subject to the control of the suspects, and were organised and comprised in such a manner as to ensure compliance with the suspects' orders.[35]

6.1.1.2 The prosecution's burden and the court's considerations

With the possible exception of the SCSL,[36] the governing instruments of all the international tribunals surveyed here place particular emphasis on judicial review of the evidence underlying the prosecution's charges. Accordingly, their statutes, rules, or jurisprudence expressly require that the prosecution provide the judge or chamber reviewing the indictment, or considering whether to issue an arrest warrant or confirm the charges against the suspect, with the documents and other materials that would justify the arrest, detention, and trial of the suspect.[37] In addition, judges at the *ad hoc* Tribunals and the ICC may insist that the prosecution provide additional supporting materials if the documents included in the initial submission are insufficient to meet either the *prima facie* standard or the 'reasonable grounds' standard, respectively.[38]

[34] *Ibid.*, para. 65 (quoting *Prosecutor* v. *Lubanga*, Doc. No. ICC-01/04-01/06-803-tEN, Decision on the Confirmation of Charges, 29 January 2007 ('*Lubanga* Confirmation Decision'), paras. 38–39) (alterations omitted); see also *ibid.*, paras. 540–581; *Lubanga* Confirmation Decision, *supra*, paras. 321, 396–399.

[35] See, e.g., *Katanga and Ngudjolo* Confirmation Decision, *supra* note 33, paras. 540–545.

[36] See *supra* text accompanying note 28.

[37] See ICTY Rule 47(B), (D), (E) (referring to the supporting or accompanying material that the prosecution must provide to the reviewing judge along with the proposed indictment); ICTR Rule 47(B), (D), (E) (same); Rome Statute, Arts. 58(2)(d), 58(7)(d) (providing that a prosecution application for an arrest warrant must include '[a] summary of the evidence and any other information which establish reasonable grounds to believe that the person committed' the crimes alleged, and that an application for a summons must include '[a] concise statement of the facts which are alleged to constitute the crime' the prosecution intends to charge).

[38] See ICTY Rule 47(F)(i) (providing that the reviewing judge 'may … request the Prosecutor to present additional material in support of any or all counts'); ICTR Rule 47(F) (same); *Situation in Darfur, Sudan*, Doc. No. ICC-02/05-160, Decision Requesting Additional Supporting Materials in Relation to the Prosecution's Request for a Warrant of Arrest Against Omar Hassan Al Bashir, 15 October 2008 (directing the prosecution to provide the information identified in an *ex parte* annex by mid-November 2008); *Situation in Darfur, Sudan*, Doc No. ICC-02/05-166, Decision Requesting Additional Information and Supporting Materials, 9 December 2008 (directing the prosecution to provide the information identified in an *ex parte* annex by the end of January 2009). See also *Lubanga* Arrest Warrant Decision, *supra* note 17, para. 9 (noting that in the event of an invitation to submit additional material, the prosecution retains the discretion 'to decide what t present to the Chamber in order to convince it (i) that there are reasonable grounds to believe that the pers has committed a crime within the jurisdiction of the Court and (ii) that the arrest of the person appears nec sary', but that 'unless … the two above-mentioned conditions have been met, [the Chamber] will declin issue any warrant of arrest').

At the ICC, and initially over the objections of the Prosecutor, pre-trial chambers have interpreted their task as requiring review of both the factual and legal sufficiency of the prosecution's allegations before an arrest warrant may be issued.[39] In this expansive view of their role at this stage of the proceedings, these chambers have considered not only whether there is sufficient evidence to establish 'reasonable grounds' to believe that the suspect is responsible for the crimes alleged, but have also undertaken detailed analyses of whether the prosecution's submission establishes both the forms of responsibility and all the elements of the crimes charged, including the underlying offences, the general requirements, and any applicable specific requirements.[40]

Few judges at the *ad hoc* Tribunals have expressly included such analyses in their written decisions on review of the indictment, so most of their jurisprudence evaluating the legal sufficiency of charges arises in the context of preliminary motions from the defence.[41] In fact, many of the decisions at the ICTY and ICTR reviewing indictments before arrest and detention of accused contain remarkably little analysis of the prosecution's allegations, and some even refer to the process as one of 'confirmation', not 'review' of an indictment, so it is often unclear whether the judge has fully exercised the powers of review available under each tribunal's statute and rules.[42] In many cases in these tribunals, therefore, there is insufficient detail provided in such decisions for the conclusion that the prosecution has provided adequate factual support for the charges in the indictment, and the legal sufficiency of those allegations will often go untested until trial unless the accused challenges the form of the indictment.[43] There is thus considerable merit to the ICC approach, which requires considering, at this early stage of the proceedings, whether the proposed indictment adequately alleges legal bases on which these tribunals of limited jurisdiction could convict the suspect. It provides greater protection for the rights

[39] See, e.g., *Lubanga* Arrest Warrant Decision, *supra* note 17, paras. 79–96; *Harun and Kushayb* Arrest Warrant Decision, *supra* note 30, pp. 10–27; see also *ibid.*, pp. 27–36 (considering separately whether there are reasonable grounds to believe that the suspects are criminally responsible for the alleged crimes).

[40] See Gideon Boas, James L. Bischoff, and Natalie L. Reid, *Elements of Crimes Under International Law* (2008) ('Boas, Bischoff, and Reid, *Elements of Crimes*'), p. 9, for definitions of these building blocks of an international crime, and distinctions between the elements that constitute an underlying offence (such as murder); the elements, termed 'general requirements', which would render that offence an international crime (such as wilful killing as a grave breach of the Geneva Conventions or murder as a crime against humanity); and other elements, termed 'specific requirements', which would mark the offence as one of a unique subset of international crimes (such as murder as a form of persecution as a crime against humanity).

[41] See *infra* Section 6.1.2.1 (discussing amendment of the indictment in response to challenges from the accused).

[42] See, e.g., *Prosecutor* v. *Limaj, Bala, Musliu, and Murtezi*, Case No. IT-03-66-I, Confirmation of Indictment, 27 January 2003; *Prosecutor* v. *Orić*, Case No. IT-03-68-I, Confirmation of Indictment and Order for Non-Disclosure, 28 March 2003.

[43] See *Prosecutor* v. *Krnojelac*, Case No. IT-97-25-PT, Decision on Prosecutor's Response to Decision of 24 February 1999, 20 May 1999, para. 18 (stating that 'it is never the function of a Trial Chamber to approve of the form of an indictment unless and until there is some complaint by the accused that the form of that indictment (original or amended) is defective'); see also *infra* Section 6.1.2.1 (discussing amendment of the indictment in response to challenges from the accused).

of the suspect, enhances the credibility of the court or tribunal, and could reduce inefficiency in later stages of the proceedings.[44]

6.1.2 Amendment of charges

All the international tribunals surveyed in this volume permit amendment of the charging instrument both before and after judicial review. Under the applicable rules at the ICTY, ICTR, and SCSL, the prosecution may amend an indictment without prior judicial authorization at any time before it is confirmed or approved.[45] Though the Rome Statute and ICC Rules are silent on whether the prosecution may amend an application for a summons or arrest warrant for a suspect, such an approach would seem both logical and consistent with the nature of the two-stage process at the Court: at that early point in the proceedings, the prosecution's allegations are presented in the form of an *ex parte* motion, not a proposed charging instrument, so there should be no requirement for prior judicial approval of amendments to the application. Between the issuance of the arrest warrant and the confirmation hearing, both the Statute and the Rules explicitly authorize the ICC prosecution to continue its investigation and amend the proposed charges, provided that it notifies the pre-trial chamber and the suspect of the proposed amendments and provides a list of the supporting evidence no later than fifteen days before the confirmation hearing.[46]

Once a judge or pre-trial chamber confirms the charges against the accused, any amendments to the charging instrument may be made only with leave of the pre-trial chamber or the trial chamber hearing the case.[47] While the tribunals apply slightly different tests to determine whether the proposed amendments will be allowed, all incorporate factors that reflect the fundamental task of the judiciary in criminal proceedings – to ensure a fair and expeditious trial that respects the rights of the accused.

[44] But see Salvatore Zappalà, 'Foreword, Symposium: Lubanga Before the ICC', (2008) 6 *Journal of International Criminal Justice* 467, 469 (2008) (noting that the lengthy confirmation of charges decision in Lubanga 'will fail to represent a sustainable precedent' because, among other things, 'there is reason for concern … in relation to the sustainability of such an approach given the other cases the court has to try'); Michela Miraglia, 'Admissibility of Evidence, Standard of Proof, and Nature of the Decision in the ICC Confirmation of Charges in Lubanga', (2008) 6 *Journal of International Criminal Justice* 489, 501, 503 (2008) (concluding that 'the choice to render such a lengthy and detailed decision (contrary to all other confirmation decisions at the *ad hoc* Tribunals) creates concerns with regard to the preservation of the trial judges' impartiality and efficient case management' and that 'shortening the drafting process of the confirmation decision will help judges to manage cases in an efficient way when the ICC caseload increases').

[45] ICTY Rule 50; ICTR Rule 50; SCSL Rule 50.

[46] See Rome Statute, Art. 61(4); ICC Rule 121(4).

[47] ICTY Rule 50; ICTR Rule 50; SCSL Rule 50; Rome Statute, Art. 61(9); ICC Rule 128. See also *infra* Section 6.1.2.1 (discussing amendment during trial). As discussed below, under recent amendments to the ICTY Rules, pre-trial chambers also have the authority to 'invite the Prosecutor to reduce the number of counts charged in the indictment' and to 'fix a number of crime sites or incidents … in respect of which evidence may be presented by the Prosecutor which' in the view of the chamber, 'are reasonably representative of the crimes

In practice, charging instruments at the international tribunals are amended for one or more of a handful of reasons – some of them unique to the context and demands of international trials, but others found in any domestic jurisdiction – including: to reflect new trial strategies or additional evidence uncovered since the indictment was initially confirmed;[48] to bring the legal allegations in the instrument into compliance with developments in the case law on the elements of crimes and forms of responsibility, and in particular, the law on cumulative charging;[49] to add or remove accused to reflect joinder, recent rendition to the Tribunal, severance, or withdrawal of charges;[50] and, as discussed below, when ordered by a trial chamber in response to defence challenges to the form of the accusatory instrument.

At the ICTY, chambers will generally exercise their discretion to permit amendment of an indictment if the modifications 'ensure that the real issues in the case will be determined'.[51] Leave to amend will not be granted, however, unless two

charged'. ICTY Rule 73 *bis*(D); see *infra* Section 6.6.2. A judicial determination that the prosecution may only present evidence on 'representative' crime sites or incidents is not, strictly speaking, an amendment to the indictment. See, e.g., *Milutinović et al.* Trial Judgement, *supra* note 4, Vol. I, para. 16 ('The legal result' of the pre-trial chamber's decision to bar presentation of evidence with respect to three crime sites or incidents in the indictment 'is that the [related] charges in the Indictment … still exist and the Accused are still charged in relation thereto'). Nevertheless, it has the practical effect of reducing the allegations that are tested at trial and eventually the subject of a final judgement on the merits. See *ibid.* (noting that 'the Chamber refused to allow evidence to be led in relation to each of the crime sites … on the ground that what allegedly occurred there was not, unlike other killing sites, associated with locations from which persons were allegedly forcibly displaced, and thus did not fall within "the nature or theme" of the Prosecution case').

48 See, e.g., *Prosecutor* v. *Haradinaj, Balaj, and Brahimaj*, Case No. IT-04-84-PT, Decision on Motion to Amend the Amended Indictment, 12 January 2007, paras. 4–5, 9; *Prosecutor* v. *Taylor*, Case No. SCSL-03-01-I, Decision on Prosecution's Application to Amend Indictment and on Approval of Amended Indictment, 16 March 2006, paras. 9–11.

49 See, e.g., *Prosecutor* v. *Kanyarukiga*, Case No. ICTR-02-78-I, Decision on Prosecution Request to Amend the Indictment, 14 November 2007 ('*Kanyarukiga* Pre-Trial Indictment Decision'), para. 2 (noting prosecution submission that proposed amendments serve, among other things, to 'clarif[y] … the alleged modes of participation … through which the Accused is alleged to have participated in the charged crimes'); *Prosecutor* v. *Karadžić*, Case No. IT-95-5/18-PT, Motion to Amend the First Amended Indictment, 22 September 2008 (prosecution seeking to amend, *inter alia*, allegations in respect of JCE and co-perpetration to reflect recent jurisprudence); *Prosecutor* v. *Gotovina, Čermak, and Markač*, Case No. IT-06-90-PT, Decision on Ante Gotovina's Motion Pursuant to Rule 73 Requesting Pre-Trial Chamber to Strike Parts of Prosecution Pre-Trial Brief Constituting Effective Amendment of the Joinder Indictment, and on Prosecution's Motion to Amend the Indictment, 14 September 2008 (same). The *ad hoc* Appeals Chambers permit cumulative charging where 'prior to the presentation of all the evidence, it is not possible to determine to a certainty which of the charges brought against an accused will be proved'. *Prosecutor* v. *Delalić, Mucić, Delić and Landžo*, Case No. IT-96-21-A, Judgement, 20 February 2001, para. 400; accord *Prosecutor* v. *Musema*, Case No. ICTR-96-13-A, Judgement, 16 November 2001, para. 363 (deciding to adopt ICTY test for multiple convictions under ICTR Statute). See also Boas, Bischoff, and Reid, *Elements of Crimes*, *supra* note 40, pp. 319–323 (discussing law on cumulative charging).

50 See, e.g., *Prosecutor* v. *Čermak and Markač*, Case No. IT-03-73-PT and *Prosecutor* v. *Gotovina*, Case No. IT-01-45-PT, Decision on Prosecution's Consolidated Motion to Amend the Indictment and for Joinder, 14 July 2006 ('*Gotovina et al.* Indictment and Joinder Decision') (permitting prosecution to file amended joinder indictment). But see *Prosecutor* v. *Sesay, Kallon, and Gbao* ('*RUF Case*'), Case No. SCSL-04-15-T, Decision on Prosecution Application for Leave to Amend the Indictment, 31 July 2006, para. 33 (rejecting prosecution's request to extend time period in indictment by eighteen months because doing so would 'not only change the goal posts that were fixed by the indictment … but will also be prejudicial to the rights of the Accused'). See also *infra* Section 6.1.3 (discussing withdrawal of charges); Section 6.2 (discussing joinder).

51 *Karadžić* Pre-Trial Indictment Decision, *supra* note 25, para. 29 (quoting *Prosecutor* v. *Brđanin and Talić*, Case No. IT-99-36-PT, Decision on Form of Further Amended Indictment and Prosecution Application to

conditions are satisfied: first, granting the proposed amendment must not cause unfair prejudice to the accused in the circumstances of the case;[52] and second, any material amendment[53] must be supported by evidence that satisfies the *prima facie* standard applied to the review of indictments.[54] In order to determine whether permitting the amendment would cause unfair prejudice to the accused, pre-trial and trial chambers focus on two considerations,[55] both informed by the timing of the prosecution's motion to amend:[56] (1) has the accused been provided with sufficient notice of the scope and nature of the prosecution's allegations to provide an adequate opportunity to prepare an effective defence;[57] and (2) would granting the amendment adversely affect the accused's right to trial without undue delay?[58] The question of undue delay, in turn, will depend in part on whether the amendment introduces a new charge to the indictment, because under the ICTY Rules, new charges trigger automatic procedural consequences that may postpone the start of trial – a further appearance must be scheduled for entry of a plea to the new charges, and the accused has an additional period of thirty days to file preliminary

Amend, 26 June 2001, para. 50); accord *Prosecutor* v. *Popović, Beara, Nikolić, Borovčanin, Tolimir, Miletić, Gvero, and Pandurević* and *Prosecutor* v. *Trbić*, Case Nos. IT-05-88-PT and IT-05–88/1-PT, Decision on Further Amendments and Challenges to the Indictment, 13 July 2006 ('*Popović et al.* Pre-Trial Indictment Decision'), para. 8.

52 *Karadžić* Pre-Trial Indictment Decision, *supra* note 25, para. 29; *Popović et al.* Pre-Trial Indictment Decision, *supra* note 51, para. 8; *Prosecutor* v. *Halilović*, Decision on Prosecutor's Motion Seeking Leave to Amend the Indictment, 17 December 2004 ('*Halilović* Pre-Trial Indictment Decision'), para. 22.

53 See *Popović et al.* Pre-Trial Indictment Decision, *supra* note 51, para. 8 (collecting cases holding that supporting material need only be provided for material amendments); *ibid.*, para. 20 (requiring supporting material for any amendment other than those which 'seek[] merely to rectify minor, non-substantive errors'). See also *infra* Section 6.1.2.1 (discussing materiality in the context of the law on the form of the indictment).

54 *Karadžić* Pre-Trial Indictment Decision, *supra* note 25, para. 29; *Popović et al.* Pre-Trial Indictment Decision, *supra* note 51, para. 8; *Prosecutor* v. *Rasim Delić*, Case No. IT-04-84-PT, Decision on the Prosecutor's Submission of Proposed Amended Indictment and Defence Motion Alleging Defects in Amended Indictment, 30 June 2006, para. 31; ICTY Statute, Art. 19(1); ICTY Rule 50(A)(ii). See *supra* Section 6.1.1.1.1 on the *prima facie* standard.

55 *Karadžić* Pre-Trial Indictment Decision, *supra* note 25, para. 30 & n. 59 (collecting cases identifying these as the two principal factors in the undue prejudice inquiry); *Halilović* Pre-Trial Indictment Decision, *supra* note 52, paras. 22, 23.

56 See *Karadžić* Pre-Trial Indictment Decision, *supra* note 25, para. 31 ('[A]s a general rule, the closer to trial the Prosecution moves to amend the indictment, the more likely it is that the Trial Chamber will deny the motion' because it would deprive the accused an adequate opportunity to prepare an effective defence); *ibid.*, para. 32 (holding that the prosecution's diligence and the timeliness of the motion are also relevant to the consideration of undue delay) (citing *Prosecutor* v. *Karemera, Ngirumpatse, Nzirorera, and Rwamakuba*, Case No. ICTR-98-44-AR73, Decision on Prosecutor's Interlocutory Appeal Against Trial Chamber III Decision of 8 October 2003 Denying Leave to File an Amended Indictment, 19 December 2003, para. 15).

57 *Popović et al.* Pre-Trial Indictment Decision, *supra* note 51, para. 21 (holding that the sufficiency of notice will determine whether accused has adequate opportunity to prepare defence); *Karadžić* Pre-Trial Indictment Decision, *supra* note 25, para. 31 ('Where an amendment clarifies the Prosecution's case and provides further notice to the Accused … the Trial Chamber will be more likely to hold that the accused has not been deprived of an adequate opportunity to prepare his defence.').

58 See *Popović et al.* Pre-Trial Indictment Decision, *supra* note 51, para. 21 (holding that the possibility of delay must be weighed against the potential benefits to the accused and trial chamber of an improved indictment, such as 'simplification of the proceedings, a more complete understanding of the Prosecution's case, and the avoidance of possible challenges to the indictment or evidence presented at trial'); *Karadžić* Pre-Trial Indictment Decision, *supra* note 25, para. 32 (same).

motions in respect of those charges.[59] Under settled ICTY jurisprudence, a proposed amendment to an indictment will result in a new charge if it 'introduces a basis for conviction that is factually and/or legally distinct from any already alleged in the indictment'.[60]

While ICTR decisions on motions to amend tend to be less structured in their analysis, the considerations remain the same, and trial chambers generally consider four factors in determining whether to grant leave to amend: (1) whether the proposed changes will improve 'the clarity and precision of the case to be met'; (2) whether the prosecution's request to amend is submitted 'in a timely manner that avoids creating an unfair tactical advantage'; (3) whether the amendment will cause 'delay or other possible prejudice' to the accused; and (4) if the proposed amendment entails new charges, whether a *prima facie* case exists with respect to such new charges.[61]

The judges at the SCSL have been even plainer in identifying the considerations that inform the decision on whether to grant leave to amend an indictment. In one of the few decisions to discuss the issue, the Appeals Chamber explained that amendments generally fall into three categories: (1) 'formal or semantic changes, which should not be opposed'; (2) '[c]hanges which give greater precision to the charge or its particulars, either by narrowing the allegation or identifying times, dates or places with greater particularity or detail', which 'will normally be allowed, even during the trial'; and (3) '[s]ubstantive changes, which seek to add fresh allegations amounting either to separate charges or a new allegation in respect of an existing charge'.[62] The latter substantive amendments should be allowed when sought at the pre-trial stage 'so long as the Defence can adequately prepare', though the Chamber noted that 'obviously more justification is required the closer to the date fixed for trial'.[63] When sought late in the proceedings – that is, once trial is underway[64] – amendments are subject to a 'much more rigorous' test: in addition to

[59] ICTY Rule 50(B), (C) (providing also that 'where necessary, the date for trial may be postponed to ensure adequate time for the preparation of the defence') (quotation in ICTY Rule 50(C)).

[60] *Halilović* Pre-Trial Indictment Decision, *supra* note 52, para. 30; see also *ibid.*, para. 34 ('[W]here the new allegation could be the sole action or omission of the Accused that justifies his conviction, that amendment is a "new charge" for the purposes of Rule 50.'); *Popović et al.* Pre-Trial Indictment Decision, *supra* note 51, para. 11 and n. 26 (collecting cases endorsing the *Halilović* definition of 'new charge' and explaining that '[i]t is each charge … that holds the potential of exposing the accused to individual criminal liability' while '[t]he counts in an indictment, by contrast, merely reflect the way in which the Prosecution chose to organise the charges in relation to the crimes allegedly committed'); *Haradinaj et al.* Pre-Trial Indictment Decision, *supra* note 25, para. 13 (same); *Karadžić* Pre-Trial Indictment Decision, *supra* note 25, para. 34. For more on what constitutes a 'charge', see *infra* note 106.

[61] *Kanyarukiga* Pre-Trial Indictment Decision, *supra* note 49, para. 4. See also *ibid.* n. 6 (collecting ICTR decisions on the standards applied).

[62] *CDF* Indictment Appeal Decision, *supra* note 15, para. 79.

[63] *Ibid.*, para. 81. See also *ibid.*, para. 88 ('Amendments that do not amount to new counts should generally be admitted, even at a late stage, if they will not prejudice the defence or delay the trial process.').

[64] At each of the *ad hoc* Tribunals and the SCSL, indictments may be amended at any stage of the proceedings. See, e.g., *Popović et al.* Pre-Trial Indictment Decision, *supra* note 51, para. 8 (noting that an indictment

demonstrating that the amendments will not prejudice the accused, and are warranted in the interests of justice, the prosecution must satisfy the chamber that the proposed substantive changes will neither delay nor interrupt the trial.[65]

The law governing amendment of indictments at the *ad hoc* Tribunals and SCSL reflects the fundamentally adversarial nature of the process before those tribunals, because it assumes that the impetus for amendment will come from the prosecution. The distinctions between this approach and that employed at the ICC are perhaps nowhere more evident than in Regulation 55, the provision in the ICC's Court Regulations that authorises a Trial Chamber, after hearing evidence in the case, to 'change the legal characterisation of facts to accord with the crimes … or to accord with the form of participation of the accused' provided for in the Rome Statute, albeit 'without exceeding the facts and circumstances described in the charges and any amendments to the charges'.[66] This power of a trial chamber is in addition to the authority of the pre-trial chamber in the case to determine whether the prosecution may be allowed to amend the charges between the confirmation hearing and the start of trial.[67]

The bounds of Regulation 55 have been tested in the very first case to go to trial at the ICC. In response to a submission from the legal representatives of the victims in the *Lubanga* case, the Trial Chamber determined that the latter limitation on its authority to amend the charges did not apply, and that it wished to consider changing the legal characterisation of the facts alleged in the charging instrument to take account of additional facts adduced at trial – effectively expanding the charges against the accused.[68] Application of the authority

may be amended at any time, even in the late stages of pre-trial proceedings or after trial has begun); *CDF* Indictment Appeal Decision, *supra* note 15, para. 78 (holding that amendment may be granted 'up to the conclusion of the trial'); *Prosecutor* v. *Akayesu*, Case No. ICTR-96-4-T, Leave to Amend the Indictment, 17 June 1997 (granting leave to amend the indictment to add new charges arising in connection with testimony heard in the course of the trial).

65 *CDF* Indictment Appeal Decision, *supra* note 15, paras. 77–78 (quotation at para. 77); see also *ibid.*, para. 80 (explaining that this stricter standard arises out of the concern, 'fundamental to the adversarial system of criminal justice[,] that once a trial is underway with live witnesses it should proceed straight-forwardly without change of goal-posts').

66 ICC Court Regulation 55(1). See also generally Carsten Stahn, 'Modification of the Legal Characterization of Facts in the ICC System: A Portrayal of Regulation 55', (2005) 1 *Criminal Law Forum* 31. For more on the unusual and controversial nature of the ICC Court Regulations in the context of the governing instruments of that Court, see Chapter 2, Section 2.2.3.

67 See Rome Statute, Art. 61(9).

68 See *Prosecutor* v. *Lubanga*, Doc. No. ICC-01/04-01/06-2049, Decision Giving Notice to the Parties and Participants that the Legal Characterisation of the Facts May Be Subject to Change in Accordance with Regulation 55(2) of the Regulations of the Court, 14 July 2009, paras. 5, 33 (decision by a two-judge majority); *Prosecutor* v. *Lubanga*, Doc. No. ICC-01/04-01/06-2093, Clarification and Further Guidance to Parties and Participants in Relation to the 'Decision Giving Notice to the Parties and Participants that the Legal Characterisation of the Facts May Be Subject to Change in Accordance with Regulation 55(2) of the Regulations of the Court', 27 August 2009, para. 7 (explaining that 'the specific new legal characterisations that the Chamber may consider' are sexual slavery as a crime against humanity and a war crime, inhuman treatment as a war crime, and cruel treatment as a war crime).

conferred by this Regulation in this manner was extremely controversial,[69] and within six months the ICC Appeals Chamber overturned the decision, holding that 'Regulation 55 (2) and (3) of the Regulations of the Court may not be used to exceed the facts and circumstances described in the charges or any amendment thereto'.[70]

6.1.2.1 Challenges to the form of the charging instrument

At the *ad hoc* Tribunals and the SCSL, the initial *ex parte* review of an indictment is generally focused on its factual sufficiency – that is, whether the prosecution has enough evidence to support its allegations and justify the provisional detention and trial of the accused.[71] It is therefore only on the initiative of the accused – after transfer to the tribunal and following disclosure by the prosecution – that trial chambers are required to assess the legal sufficiency of the indictment, in response to defence motions challenging the jurisdiction of the tribunal and asserting defects in the form of the indictment.[72] Challenges to jurisdiction may be broad, such as the motion in the *Tadić* case asserting that the ICTY could not try the accused for the alleged crimes because the Tribunal's establishment and primacy over domestic courts 'constitute[d] an infringement upon the sovereignty of the states directly

[69] See, e.g., *Prosecutor* v. *Lubanga*, Doc. No. ICC-01/04-01/06-2069-Anx1, Minority Opinion on the 'Decision Giving Notice to the Parties and Participants that the Legal Characterisation of Facts May Be Subject to Change in Accordance with Regulation 55(2) of the Regulations of the Court', 17 July 2009 (as corrected on 31 July 2009) (Presiding Judge Fulford dissenting and arguing *inter alia* that the majority opinion is inconsistent with Article 61(9) of the Statute, which confers 'the power to frame and alter the charges ... exclusively [on] ... the Pre-Trial Chamber'; Article 74(2) of the Statute, which limits a final conviction to charges set out in the charging instrument; and the plain text of Regulation 55 itself); *Prosecutor* v. *Lubanga*, Doc. No. ICC-01/04-01/06-1975, Defence Response to the 'Joint Application of the Legal Representatives of the Victims for the Implementation of the Procedure Under Regulation 55 of the Regulations of the Court' of 22 May 2009 and to the 'Prosecution's Response to the Legal Representatives' "Demande conjointe des représentants légaux des victimes aux fins de mise en oeuvre de la procédure en vertu de la norme 55 du Règlement de la Cour"' of 12 June 2009, 19 June 2009, para. 23 ('Any amendment to the charges that involves adding new legal characterisations or replacing initial characterisations with more serious characterisations, can only be made in accordance with the combined provisions of articles 61(4) and 61(9) and rules 121(4) and 128, which give the Pre-Trial Chamber sole jurisdiction and require that the accused be informed of the new charges before the start of the trial'); Kevin Jon Heller, '"Recharacterizing" Facts in Lubanga', 10 August 2009, http://opiniojuris.org/2009/08/10/recharacterizing-facts-in-lubanga/ (arguing that 'the majority's decision represents a very significant intrusion into prosecutorial discretion').

[70] *Prosecutor* v. *Lubanga*, Doc. No. ICC-01/04-01/06-2205, Judgment on the Appeals of Mr Lubanga Dyilo and the Prosecutor Against the Decision of Trial Chamber I of 14 July 2009, 8 December 2009, para. 1 (labelling this holding the 'key finding' of the decision); see also *ibid*., para. 72 (nevertheless upholding the validity of Regulation 55); Chapter 2, Section 2.2.3 (discussing the latter holding).

[71] See *supra* Section 6.1.1.2.

[72] See ICTY Rule 72(A); ICTR Rule 72(A); SCSL Rule 72(B). As one Trial Chamber noted, alleged defects in an indictment may not be perceptible at the pre-trial stage, but 'may arise at a later stage of the proceedings if the evidence at trial does not conform to the indictment's allegations'. *Prosecutor* v. *Stanišić and Župljanin*, Case No. IT-08-91-PT, Decision on Mićo Stanišić's and Stojan Župljanin's Motions on Form of the Indictment, 19 March 2009 ('*Stanišić and Župljanin* Form of Indictment Decision'), para. 17. In those circumstances, the trial chamber will exercise its discretion to determine the appropriate course to ensure a fair trial. *Ibid.* (listing amendment of the indictment, adjournment of the trial, or exclusion of evidence as possible solutions).

affected';[73] or quite narrow, such as the motion in the *Karadžić* case asserting that the Tribunal lacked jurisdiction over the charges of hostage-taking as alleged in the indictment.[74] Challenges to the form of an indictment, on the other hand, are directed at a single overarching question: does the indictment set forth the prosecution's allegations in sufficient detail to inform the accused of the case against him or her and allow the preparation of an adequate defence?

The right to be informed of the legal and factual bases of the prosecution's allegations is reflected in the provisions of the governing instruments of the international criminal tribunals, which require that the charging instrument identify the crimes with which the accused is charged, and include a concise rendition of the underlying facts.[75] Read together with the accused's right to have 'adequate facilities for the preparation of his defence',[76] these provisions have been interpreted in the case law of the *ad hoc* Tribunals and the SCSL as obliging the prosecution 'to plead the material facts underpinning the charges with enough detail to inform the accused clearly of the charges against him or her so that he or she may prepare an

[73] *Prosecutor* v. *Tadić*, Case No. IT-94-1-T, Motion on the Jurisdiction of the Tribunal, 23 June 1995, p. 2. The decisions by the Trial Chamber and Appeals Chamber in this case, affirming the jurisdiction and legitimacy of the ICTY and presenting the first systematic analysis of the elements of the crimes set forth in the Statute, were a significant milestone in the development of contemporary international law. See *Prosecutor* v. *Tadić*, Case No. IT-94-1-T, Decision on Defence Motion on Jurisdiction, 10 August 1995; *Prosecutor* v. *Tadić*, Case No. IT-94-1-AR72, Decision on the Defence Motion for Interlocutory Appeal on Jurisdiction, 2 October 1995. Tadić was not the last ICTY accused to level such broad accusations at the Tribunal. More recently, the accused Zdravko Tolimir asserted that the ICTY lacked jurisdiction because, among other things, its creation was an unlawful exercise of power by the Security Council. See *Prosecutor* v. *Tolimir*, Case No. IT-05-88/2-PT, Preliminary Motions on the Indictment in Accordance with Rule 72 of the Rules, 7 November 2007, pp. 6–7; see also *Prosecutor* v. *Tolimir*, Case No. IT-05-88/2-PT, Decision on Preliminary Motions on the Indictment Pursuant to Rule 72 of the Rules, 14 December 2007 (rejecting this argument).

[74] *Prosecutor* v. *Karadžić*, Case No. IT-95-5/18-PT, Preliminary Motion to Dismiss Count 11 for Lack of Jurisdiction, 18 March 2009 (arguing that the crime as defined under customary international law concerned only civilian victims, not the non-civilian persons involved in the incident alleged in the indictment); see also *Prosecutor* v. *Karadžić*, Case No. IT-95-5/18-PT, Decision on Six Preliminary Motions Challenging Jurisdiction, 17 December 2009 (rejecting this and other arguments).

[75] See Rome Statute, Art. 61(3) (requiring that, '[w]ithin a reasonable time before the [confirmation of charges] hearing', the suspect must '[b]e provided with a copy of the document containing the charges on which the Prosecutor intends to bring the person to trial; and … [b]e informed of the evidence on which the Prosecutor intends to rely at the hearing'); ICTY Statute, Art. 18(4) (the indictment presented for review and possible confirmation must contain 'a concise statement of the facts and the crime or crimes with which the accused is charged'); ICTR Statute, Art. 17(4) (same); SCSL Rule 47 (indictment must contain 'a statement of each specific offence of which the named suspect is charged and a short description of the particulars of the offence', and must 'be accompanied by a Prosecutor's case summary briefly setting out the allegations he proposes to prove in making his case'). See also Rome Statute, Art. 67(1)(b) (same, using simply 'the accused'); ICTY Statute, Art. 21(4)(a) (enshrining the accused's right 'to be informed promptly and in detail in a language which he understands of the nature and cause of the charge against him'); ICTR Statute, Art. 20(4)(a) (same, with addition of feminine pronouns); SCSL Statute, Art. 17(4)(a) (same); ICC Rule 121(3) (requiring the prosecution to provide the pre-trial chamber and the suspect with 'a detailed description of the charges together with a list of the evidence which he or she intends to present at the [confirmation] hearing'); ICC Court Regulation 52 (providing that charging instrument must include 'a statement of the facts, including the time and place of the alleged crimes, which provides a sufficient legal and factual basis to bring the person or persons to trial, including relevant facts for the exercise of jurisdiction by the Court').

[76] ICTY Statute, Art. 21(4)(b). Accord ICTR Statute, Art. 20(4)(b) (same, with addition of feminine pronouns); SCSL Statute, Art. 17(4)(b) (same); Rome Statute, Art. 67(1)(b) (same, using simply 'the accused').

adequate defence'.[77] In this context, 'charges' are understood broadly to include not only the crimes alleged, but also the form or forms of responsibility that link the accused to those crimes.[78]

Determinations of materiality are inherently case-specific and depend on the elements of the crimes and forms of responsibility alleged in the indictment.[79] In particular, the form of responsibility – that is, the actual conduct of the accused with regard to the crime and thus the proximity to the events alleged – is the chief determinant of the degree of specificity required for the charges in the indictment.[80] For example, decisions at the ICTY and ICTR direct the prosecution, when contending that the accused committed the crimes charged through participation in a joint criminal enterprise ('JCE'), to specify the form of JCE alleged,[81] the purpose of the enterprise, the identity or affiliation of the other members of the JCE, and the nature of the accused's participation in the JCE.[82] Similarly, allegations that the accused failed to prevent or punish the criminal conduct of subordinates, and is therefore liable for their crimes under the doctrine of superior responsibility, should specify the names or affiliations of those subordinates.[83]

Nevertheless, decisions of the *ad hoc* Tribunals and the SCSL acknowledge the sheer scale of the criminal transactions that give rise to proceedings before those tribunals, and do not, for example, require the prosecution to identify the names

[77] *Haradinaj et al.* Pre-Trial Indictment Decision, *supra* note 25, para. 22 & n. 57 (collecting cases). See also *Prosecutor* v. *Nchamihigo*, Case No. ICTR-01-63-T, Judgement and Sentence, 12 November 2008, paras. 32–33 (describing the amount of detail required); *CDF* Trial Judgement, *supra* note 3, paras. 17–25 (citing relevant rules and regulations and summarising case law on indictments).

[78] See, e.g., *Halilović* Pre-Trial Indictment Decision, *supra* note 52, para. 34 (concluding that an allegation regarding superior responsibility qualified as a new charge against the accused); see also *supra* notes 59–60 and accompanying text, *infra* note 106.

[79] See, e.g., *Prosecutor* v. *Bagaragaza*, Case No. ICTR-2005-86-I, Decision on the Prosecutor's Application for Leave to Amend the Indictment, 30 November 2006 ('*Bagaragaza* Indictment Decision'), para. 11 ('The Prosecution's characterisation of the alleged criminal conduct and the proximity of the accused to the underlying crime are decisive factors in determining the degree of specificity with which the Prosecution must plead the material facts of its case in the indictment in order to provide the accused with adequate notice'); *Prosecutor* v. *Sesay*, Case No. SCSL-03-05-PT, Decision and Order on Defence Preliminary Motion for Defects in the Form of the Indictment, 13 October 2003 ('*RUF* Pre-Trial Indictment Decision'), para. 8: '[T]he degree of specificity required must necessarily depend upon such variables as (i) the nature of the allegations, (ii) the nature of the specific crimes charged, (iii) the scale or magnitude on which the acts or events allegedly took place, (iv) the circumstances under which the crimes were committed, (v) the duration of ... the acts or events [that] occurred, (vi) the time span between the ... events and the filing of the indictment, and (vii) the totality of the circumstances surrounding the commission of the alleged crime.'

[80] See *Haradinaj et al.* Pre-Trial Indictment Decision, *supra* note 25, para. 23; *Prosecutor* v. *Popović, Beara, Nikolić, Borovčanin, Tolimir, Miletić, Gvero, Pandurević, and Trbić*, Case No. IT-05-88-PT, Decision on Motions Challenging the Indictment Pursuant to Rule 72 of the Rules, 31 May 2006, para. 4.

[81] See Boas, Bischoff, and Reid, *Forms of Responsibility*, *supra* note 17, pp. 33–83, 426 (discussing the categories of JCE and the elements that define and distinguish each category).

[82] See, e.g., *Prosecutor* v. *Karadžić*, Case No. IT-95-5/18-PT, Decision on Two Motions Alleging Defects in the Form of the Indictment, 12 May 2009, para. 16; *Bagaragaza* Indictment Decision, *supra* note 79, para. 12.

[83] See, e.g., *Prosecutor* v. *Deronjić*, Case No. IT-02-61-PT, Decision on Form of the Indictment, 25 October 2002, paras. 19–20 (holding indictment to be defective because subordinates were not 'sufficiently identified'); *Bagaragaza* Indictment Decision, *supra* note 79, para. 17. See also Boas, Bischoff, and Reid, *Forms of Responsibility*, *supra* note 17, pp. 174–252, 427 (discussing the forms of superior responsibility and the elements that define and distinguish each form).

of individual victims or describe each offence committed by the subordinates of a high-level accused.[84] If the indictment alleges that the accused physically committed crimes, however, it must include 'the identity of the victim, the time and place of the events, and the means by which the offence was committed'.[85] The indispensable requirement in all cases, regardless of the form of responsibility that is alleged, is that the indictment must state the particular acts or course of conduct by the accused that form the basis for the charges in question.[86]

At the ICC, there has been relatively little discussion of how the legal provisions governing the form and contents of the charging instrument are to be interpreted. While each accused that has gone through the confirmation of charges stage of the procedure has challenged the form of the DCC,[87] the discussions of the principles informing the chambers' consideration of those challenges have been somewhat sparse. Nevertheless, the holdings in these first few decisions do provide some guidance about judicial expectations with regard to specificity of pleading. First, while the crimes and forms of responsibility must be 'clearly articulated', the prosecution is not obliged to provide a statement or explanation of its understanding

[84] See, e.g., *Haradinaj et al.* Pre-Trial Indictment Decision, *supra* note 25, para. 23 (excusing the prosecution from identifying victims 'where the scale of the crimes renders it impractical to require a high degree of specificity'); *Prosecutor* v. *Bagosora, Kabiligi, Ntabakuze, and Nsengiyumva*, Case No. ICTR-98-41-T, Judgement and Sentence, 18 December 2008, para. 114 (noting that 'in certain circumstances, the sheer scale of the alleged crimes makes it impracticable to require a high degree of specificity in such matters as the identity of the victims and the dates of the commission of the crimes'); *Prosecutor* v. *Kondewa*, Case No. SCSL-03-12-PT, Decision and Order on Defence Preliminary Motion for Defects in the Form of the Indictment, 27 November 2003, para. 7 (endorsing the approach of another Trial Chamber and holding that 'the degree of specificity required in indictments' alleging the core international crimes within the jurisdiction of these tribunals 'is different from and perhaps not as high as, the particularity required in domestic criminal law jurisdictions'). But see *RUF* Case, Case No. SCSL-04-15-A, Judgment, 26 October 2009 ('*RUF* Appeal Judgment'), Partially Dissenting and Concurring Opinion of Justice Shireen Avis Fisher, para. 71 (arguing that 'it is not enough simply to find the cataclysmic dimensions of the alleged criminality' because 'the "sheer scale" exception is grounded in the impracticability of pleading in greater detail *as a consequence* of the scale of the alleged crimes', so a chamber must thus 'assess not only the general dimensions of the criminality, but … whether the scale of the crimes charged made it "impracticable" for the Prosecution to plead locations with greater specificity').

[85] *Stanišić and Župljanin* Form of Indictment Decision, *supra* note 72, para. 10.

[86] See, e.g., *Prosecutor* v. *Prlić, Stojić, Praljak, Petković, Ćorić, and Pušić*, Case No. IT-04-74-PT, Decision on Defence Preliminary Motions Alleging Defect[s] in the Form of the Indictment, 22 July 2005, para. 11; *Prosecutor* v. *Krnojelac*, Case No. IT-97-25-PT, Decision on Preliminary Motion on Form of Amended Indictment, 11 February 2000, paras. 18–19. See also *Prosecutor* v. *Ndindabahizi*, Case No. ICTR-01-71-A, Judgment, 16 January 2007, paras. 20–22 (noting that '[t]he precision with which dates have to be charged varies from case to case' and concluding that a date range of thirteen days 'sufficiently specified the date range for the crimes alleged' in the particular case); *Prosecutor* v. *Kamuhanda*, Case No. ICTR-99-54A-A, Judgement, 19 September 2005, paras. 18–20 (finding indictment defective because it simply alleged that the accused distributed arms 'on several occasions', without specifying the dates or locations of these distributions); *RUF* Pre-Trial Indictment Decision, *supra* note 79, para. 6 (explaining that indictment must 'state the material facts underpinning the charges, but need not elaborate on the evidence by which such material facts are the be proved').

[87] See *Lubanga* Confirmation Decision, *supra* note 34, paras. 146–153 (discussing the suspect's challenge to the form of the DCC); see also *Prosecutor* v. *Bemba*, Doc. No. ICC-01/05-01/08-424, Decision on Confirmation of the Charges, 15 June 2009, paras. 63–70; *Prosecutor* v. *Katanga and Ngudjolo*, Doc. No. ICC-01/04-01/07-648, Decision on the Three Defences' Requests Regarding the Prosecution's Amended Charging Document, 25 June 2008 ('*Katanga and Ngudjolo* Form of DCC Decision').

of the law underlying those charges.[88] Second, although the prosecution is not strictly required to do so under the governing instruments, it may (and is encouraged to) provide additional details on the context in which the crimes occurred, such 'event[s] occurring before or during the commission of the acts or omission with which the suspect is charged'.[89] Finally, as in the SCSL,[90] the two instruments that collectively comprise the prosecution's statement of its case against the suspect are to be read together when determining whether the prosecution has adequately informed the suspect of the charges.[91]

6.1.3 Withdrawal of charges

At the *ad hoc* Tribunals and the SCSL, the Prosecutors may, on their own authority, withdraw an indictment at any time before the judicial review is complete; if they wish to do so after the indictment has been confirmed, they must first notify or seek permission from the assigned judge or chamber.[92] At the ICC, the prosecution may withdraw any charges before the confirmation hearing as long as the suspect is given reasonable notice and the pre-trial chamber is provided with an explanation of the reasons for the withdrawal;[93] after trial has begun, permission of the trial chamber is required to withdraw any charges.[94]

While the circumstances of particular cases may vary widely, in practice there are three principal reasons for which the Prosecutors at the *ad hoc* Tribunals, the SCSL, and the ICC have withdrawn indictments or otherwise dropped all charges against a particular suspect:[95]

Death of the accused. Two of the eleven individuals indicted by the SCSL died soon after they were indicted: Foday Sankoh, the leader of the Revolutionary United

88 *Lubanga* Confirmation Decision, *supra* note 34, para. 151; accord *Katanga and Ngudjolo* Form of DCC Decision, *supra* note 87, para. 21.

89 *Lubanga* Confirmation Decision, *supra* note 34, paras. 152–153 (quotation at para. 152).

90 See *supra* note 15 and accompanying text.

91 See *Katanga and Ngudjolo* Form of DCC Decision, *supra* note 87, paras. 21(c), 24–26 (holding that the DCC is to be read together with the prosecution list of evidence).

92 See ICTY Rule 51 (providing that the prosecution may withdraw an indictment (1) before it is confirmed, without leave; (2) between confirmation and the assignment of the case to a trial chamber, with leave of the reviewing judge or another judge assigned by the President of the Tribunal; or (3) after the case has been assigned to a trial chamber, with leave of that chamber; and that in any event, the suspect or accused and defence counsel must be notified of the withdrawal); ICTR Rule 51 (same, except providing that the prosecution must seek trial chamber authorisation for withdrawal at any point after the initial appearance of the accused); SCSL Rule 51 (providing that the prosecution may withdraw an indictment (1) before it is confirmed, ostensibly without leave; (2) between confirmation and the commencement of trial, upon providing reasons for the withdrawal in open court; or (3) after trial has begun, only with leave of that chamber; and that in any event, the accused and defence counsel must be notified of the withdrawal).

93 Rome Statute, Art. 61(4).

94 *Ibid.*, Art. 61(9).

95 In addition to the reasons discussed here, see also Chapter 3, Section 3.1.3 (discussing suspension of ICTY or ICTR indictments while cases are transferred to national jurisdictions for trial).

Front ('RUF'), was indicted on 3 March 2003 and died of natural causes in custody on 29 July 2003; and Sam Bockarie, a former RUF battlefield commander, was indicted on 7 March 2003 and was killed in Liberia in May 2003. The prosecution formally withdrew the indictments against Sankoh and Bockarie on 8 December 2003 with the endorsement of the Trial Chamber.[96] At the *ad hoc* Tribunals, in contrast, if an accused dies at any point between the confirmation of the indictment and the issuance of the trial judgement, all proceedings in respect of that accused are terminated, and there is no need for the prosecution to move to withdraw the indictment or the charges pertaining to that accused.[97]

Prosecutorial strategy. Of the 161 individuals indicted by the ICTY, twenty have had their indictments withdrawn.[98] For at least four of those twenty, the prosecution explicitly invoked the large number of suspects involved in the crimes at issue, its comparatively limited resources, and the improvement in states' compliance and cooperation with the Tribunal as grounds for withdrawing the indictment against certain accused.[99] Similarly, in at least one ICTR case during the same period, the prosecution sought to withdraw the indictment against an accused charged with a single count of murder as a crime against humanity arising from the murder of the Prime Minister of Rwanda and ten Belgian soldiers serving under UN auspices in July 1994, citing a trial strategy 'aimed at shedding light on the events that occurred in Rwanda in 1994 and highlighting the complete landscape of the criminal acts perpetrated at the time', and asserting that this goal 'would not be achieved through the prosecution of a single count indictment' arising from a

[96] *Prosecutor* v. *Sankoh*, Case No. SCSL-2003-02-PT, Withdrawal of Indictment, 8 December 2003; *Prosecutor* v. *Bockarie*, Case No. SCSL-2003-04-PT, Withdrawal of Indictment, 8 December 2003.

[97] See, e.g., *Prosecutor* v. *Slobodan Milošević*, Case No. IT-02-54-T, Order Terminating the Proceedings, 14 March 2006 (noting that 'in the case of the death of an accused, the proceedings have to be terminated'); *Prosecutor* v. *Musabyimana*, Case No. ICTR-01-62-I, Order Terminating the Proceedings Against Samuel Musabyimana, 20 February 2003 (observing that 'in the case of the death of an accused, the proceedings are terminated *as regards that accused*') (emphasis added). See also *CDF* Case, Case No. SCSL-04-14-T, Decision on Registrar's Submission of Evidence of Death of Accused Samuel Hinga Norman and Consequential Issues, 21 May 2007, paras. 18, 21 (holding, in a case where one of the accused died between trial's end and issuance of the judgement, that 'there can be no further proceedings in respect of the Accused Norman, such proceedings or process having been frustrated by the doctrine of extinguishment or abatement', and ruling the proceedings against him 'terminated effective the date of death'). But see *ibid.*, para. 22 (concluding that 'it is neither possible nor desirable to separate the evidence presented at the trial against the Accused Norman from the entire evidentiary record', and since the parties did not object, 'the Chamber ... must render its verdict against the two remaining Accused on the basis of the entire evidentiary record before it').

[98] See 'Key Figures of ICTY Cases', www.icty.org/sections/TheCases/KeyFigures (as of 1 December 2009).

[99] See *Prosecutor* v. *Sikirica, Došen, Fuštar, Kolundžija, Banović, Banović, Janjić, Knežević, Kondić, Lajić, Saponja, and Timarac*, Case No. IT-95-8-I, Order Granting Leave for Withdrawal of Charges Against Janjić, Kondić, Lajić, Saponja, Timarac, 5 May 1998 (granting the prosecution motion to withdraw the indictment in respect of four accused considering 'the resources available to the Office of the Prosecutor', and that the 'increase in the number of arrests and surrenders of accused to the custody of the International Tribunal has compelled [the Prosecutor] to re-evaluate all outstanding indictments vis-à-vis the overall investigative and prosecutorial strategies of the Office of the Prosecutor', and of the other accused – Janjić – because of his death).

single incident.[100] Though the Trial Chamber rejected this and the other arguments it attributed to the prosecution, it nevertheless concluded that the motion was 'well founded', apparently on the grounds of prosecutorial discretion, and granted the request to withdraw the indictment.[101]

Insufficient evidence. In at least one case at the ICTR, the prosecution sought leave to withdraw an indictment after its confirmation because '[t]he evidence obtained in the course of further investigation of the Accused [was] found to be insufficient at [that] time to proceed to trial'.[102] Although the prosecution reserved the right to seek another indictment against the suspect 'on the same counts or other counts in the future, based on evidence gathered in ongoing investigations',[103] none was forthcoming. At the ICTY, the prosecution withdrew indictments against at least five different accused for lack of evidence, including the indictment jointly charging Marinko Katava, Ivan Šantić, and Pero Skopljak.[104]

In most cases, withdrawal of charges at the *ad hoc* Tribunals is considered in the context of amendment of the indictment in preparation for a trial, which is discussed in the previous subsection of this chapter. However, if the accused agrees to plead guilty in exchange for lenience, the prosecution will often seek trial chamber permission to withdraw many or most of the charges in the indictment, with the caveat that it will seek reinstatement if the accused does not fulfil the terms of the plea arrangement.[105]

6.2 Joinder and severance

As a result of the complex crimes within the jurisdiction of international tribunals and the circumstances in which they are likely to arise, it is extremely rare that a trial will proceed against a single accused based on a single indictment comprised of a single count. Moreover, as discussed above in the context of amendments, a single count in an indictment at one of these tribunals may in fact encompass

[100] *Prosecutor* v. *Ntuyuhaga*, Case No. ICTR-98-40-T, Decision on the Prosecutor's Motion to Withdraw the Indictment, 18 March 1999 (summarising the prosecution's arguments).
[101] *Ibid.*
[102] *Prosecutor* v. *Rusatira*, Case No. ICTR-2002-80-I, Decisions on the Prosecutor's *Ex Parte* Application for Leave to Withdraw the Indictment, 14 August 2002 (summarising the prosecution's contentions).
[103] *Ibid.*
[104] See ICTY Press Release No. CC/PIO/279-E, 19 December 1997, available at www.icty.org/sid/7425 (noting that 'since their voluntary surrender on 6 October 1997 … further investigations have been made by the Office of the Prosecutor who became satisfied that "there is insufficient basis to justify proceeding to trial" against them', and thus that 'their indictment should be withdrawn'; and that '[c]onsidering the "urgency of the matter", the [Chamber] held hearings on Friday afternoon [19 December 1997] and ordered the release of the three men "in the interests of justice"').
[105] See, e.g., *Prosecutor* v. *Todorović*, Case No. IT-95-9/1-I, Decision on Prosecution Motion to Withdraw Counts of the Indictment and Defence Motion to Withdraw Pending Motions, 26 February 2001, p. 2 (withdrawing counts 2 to 27 of the indictment without prejudice, and confirming the prosecution's 'right … to apply to reinstate the counts should the accused fail to comply fully with the Plea Agreement').

myriad charges: if a charge is understood as the minimum combination of factual and legal allegations sufficient to justify the imposition of criminal liability, then even the eight-page *Halilović* indictment with its sole count of murder as a violation of the laws or customs of war included no fewer than ninety-six distinct charges.[106]

The practice of joining charges, accused, and trials, which is explicitly authorised by the governing instruments of the international criminal tribunals, reflects a formal recognition of the context in which international crimes are committed and the resource constraints under which all these tribunals operate. Simply put, it is frequently more efficient, and provides a better understanding of the events in question, to consider the alleged responsibility of different accused for different crimes arising from the same incident or incidents in a single trial. On the other hand, international criminal trials can be staggeringly complicated, but must still comply with the international human rights requirements of fairness and expedition, so there is a point when a trial is frankly too large for efficient management or effective control of the proceedings.[107] The tension between these two sets of considerations, while present to varying degrees at all the tribunals surveyed here, is especially heightened at the *ad hoc* Tribunals because of the larger numbers of accused and their completion strategies.

6.2.1 *Joinder of charges*

The Rules of the ICTY, the ICTR, and the SCSL authorise the joinder of 'two or more crimes' in a single indictment 'if the series of acts committed together form the same transaction' and the same accused is alleged to bear responsibility for the crimes alleged.[108] These Rules also define a criminal 'transaction' as '[a] number of acts or

[106] See *supra* notes 59–60 and accompanying text; see also *Prosecutor* v. *Halilović*, Case No. IT-01-48-I, Indictment, 10 September 2001 (charging the accused with superior responsibility for murder as a violation of the laws or customs of war arising from his alleged failures to (1) prevent thirty-three alleged murders in one Bosnian village, (2) punish the alleged perpetrators of those deaths, and (3) prevent thirty alleged murders in another Bosnian village). The total of ninety-six charges reflects the number of distinct combinations of factual and legal allegations that would be sufficient to ground the conviction of the accused for the crime and form of responsibility charged: failure to prevent thirty-three murders + failure to punish thirty-three murders + failure to prevent thirty murders. That is, because a trial chamber's finding that the accused was responsible for either failure to prevent or failure to punish a single murder would be grounds for conviction of superior responsibility for murder as a violation of the laws or customs of war, each such combination of underlying offence and basis of responsibility qualifies as a charge. For more on the two distinct obligations that underlie superior responsibility in international criminal law (prevention and punishment of the criminal conduct of subordinates), see Boas, Bischoff, and Reid, *Forms of Responsibility*, *supra* note 17, pp. 222–224, 227–237.

[107] See generally Gideon Boas, *The Milošević Trial: Lessons for the Conduct of Complex International Criminal Proceedings* (2007).

[108] ICTY Rule 49; ICTR Rule 49; SCSL Rule 49. Although the text of the rule, which is identical in all these instruments, refers to commission of the crimes by the same accused, it has not been interpreted as restricting joinder to only the few cases where the accused is charged with physical commission of the alleged crimes. For a discussion of the (likely unintentionally) narrow terms in which other early judicial pronouncements

omissions whether occurring as one event or a number of events, at the same or different locations and being part of a common scheme, strategy or plan'.[109] There are no provisions in the Rome Statute or the ICC Rules expressly authorising the joinder of charges alleging responsibility for the core categories of crimes within the Court's jurisdiction,[110] though the Rules do contemplate the possibility of joining contempt charges with charges alleging violations of substantive international criminal law.[111] Nevertheless, the lack of explicit authorisation has not prevented the ICC Prosecutor from seeking and securing confirmation of multiple charges against suspects.[112]

The prosecutors at the *ad hoc* Tribunals have taken full advantage of the provisions in their governing instruments. For example, the indictment against Milorad Krnojelac, the Bosnian Serb commander of the Kazneno-Popravni Dom detention camp in Foča between April 1992 and August 1993, charged him with the following crimes, all arising from his alleged acts or omissions in his role at the camp: various forms of persecution as crimes against humanity, torture as a crime against humanity, torture as a violation of the laws or customs of war, inhumane acts as a crime against humanity, cruel treatment as a violation of the laws or customs of war, murder as a crime against humanity, murder as a violation of the laws or customs of war, imprisonment as a crime against humanity, enslavement as a crime against humanity, and slavery as a violation of the laws or customs of war.[113]

at the *ad hoc* Tribunals were couched, see Boas, Bischoff, and Reid, *Elements of Crimes*, *supra* note 40, pp. 35–41, 157–159, 238–239 (discussing early definitions of particular elements that reflect a similar focus on commission to the apparent exclusion of other forms of responsibility).

109 ICTY Rule 2; ICTY Rule 2; SCSL Rule 2.

110 These core categories are genocide, crimes against humanity, war crimes, and aggression. Rome Statute, Art. 5(1). The term 'core categories of crimes' reflects the structure of international crimes: as explained in Volume II of this Series, genocide, crimes against humanity, and war crimes are properly understood as categories characterised by distinct sets of general requirements that may be fulfilled with regard to a particular underlying offence. For example, the underlying offence of murder becomes the international crime of murder as a crime against humanity if the victim is a civilian, the murder is committed in the context of a widespread or systematic attack directed against a civilian population, and either the physical perpetrator or another relevant actor knows that the murder is part of that attack. The same underlying offence qualifies as genocide by killing if the physical perpetrator or other relevant actor intends by that murder (and presumably, others) to contribute to the partial or complete destruction of a group protected under the Genocide Convention; and as the war crime of wilful killing as a grave breach of the Geneva Conventions if it is committed in territory controlled by one of the parties to an international conflict, is closely related to that conflict, and the victim is a person protected by the Geneva Conventions. See Boas, Bischoff, and Reid, *Elements of Crimes*, *supra* note 40, pp. 9–13 (discussing the structure of international crimes).

111 See ICC Rules 162(2)(c), 165(4) (referring to joinder of charges of offences against the administration of justice under Article 70 of the Rome Statute with charges under Articles 5 to 8, which set forth the international crimes within the jurisdiction of the Court).

112 See, e.g., *Lubanga* Confirmation Decision, *supra* note 34 (confirming charges against Thomas Lubanga for co-perpetration of the war crimes of enlisting, conscripting, and using children as active participants in hostilities, arising from his role as a commander of the Forces Patriotiques du Libération du Congo, the military wing of the Union des Patriotes Congolais in the Democratic Republic of the Congo between September 2002 and August 2003).

113 *Prosecutor* v. *Krnojelac*, Case No. IT-97-25-I, Third Amended Indictment, 25 June 2001. Note the pairings of different international crimes with the same underlying offence, such as enslavement as a crime against humanity and slavery as a violation of the laws or customs of war. For an explanation of the different general requirements that must be satisfied before the underlying offence of slavery qualifies as either a crime

Similarly, the indictment against Charles Taylor, the former Liberian president, charges him with the following crimes, arising chiefly from the conduct of armed forces under his control in Sierra Leone between 1996 and 2002: acts of terrorism in violation of Article 3 common to the Geneva Conventions ('Common Article 3') and Additional Protocol II to the Geneva Conventions ('Additional Protocol II'); murder as a crime against humanity; violence to life, health, and physical or mental well-being of persons in violation of Common Article 3 and Additional Protocol II; rape as a crime against humanity; sexual slavery and other sexual violence as a crime against humanity; outrages upon personal dignity in violation of Common Article 3 and Additional Protocol II; other inhumane acts as a crime against humanity; conscription or enlistment of child soldiers in violation of international humanitarian law; enslavement as a crime against humanity; and pillage in violation of Common Article 3 and Additional Protocol II.[114]

Although accused at the tribunals frequently challenge this practice of cumulative or alternative charging, it has been repeatedly upheld by trial and appeals chambers as both permissible and advisable, in light of the express authorisation in the rules, the complex structure of the crimes at issue, and the continual development of the law on the elements of the crimes.[115]

6.2.2 *Joinder of accused*

Most of the crimes tried by the international criminal tribunals are committed in the context of armed conflicts with large numbers of combatants and multiple levels of formal command or informal control in the groups that are parties to the

against humanity or a violation of the laws or customs of war, see Boas, Bischoff, and Reid, *Elements of Crimes*, *supra* note 40, at 35–56, 65–68, 232–263, 281. For similar examples of multiple-charge indictments at the ICTR, see, e.g., *Prosecutor* v. *Muhimana*, Case No. ICTR-95-1B-I, Revised Amended Indictment, 29 July 2004 (charging Mikaeli Muhimana, a former counsellor of a sector in the Rwandan prefecture of Kibuye, with genocide, or alternatively complicity in genocide; murder as a crime against humanity; and rape as a crime against humanity); *Prosecutor* v. *Musema*, Case No. ICTR-96-13-I, Amended Indictment, 14 December 1998 (charging Alfred Musema, former director of a tea factory in Kibuye, with genocide, or alternatively complicity in genocide; conspiracy to commit genocide; murder, extermination, and inhumane acts as crimes against humanity; and serious violations of Common Article 3 and Additional Protocol II arising out of the conduct underlying the other crimes).

114 *Prosecutor* v. *Taylor*, Case No. SCSL-2003-01-I, Amended Indictment, 16 March 2006.

115 See, e.g., *Prosecutor* v. *Brđanin and Talić*, Case No. IT-99-36-PT, Decision on Objections by Momir Talić to the Form of the Amended Indictment, 20 February 2001, para. 40 ('There is no readily identifiable prejudice to an accused in permitting cumulative charging, when the issues arising from an accumulation of offences are determined after all of the evidence has been presented, whereas the very real possibilities of prejudice to the prosecution in restricting such charging are manifest'). Accord *Prosecutor* v. *Galić*, Case No. IT-98-29-A, Judgment, 30 November 2006, para. 161; *Prosecutor* v. *Musema*, Case No. ICTR-96-13-A, Judgment, 16 November 2001, para. 369; *Prosecutor* v. *Bagosora, Kabiligi, Ntabakuze, and Nsengiyumva*, Case No. ICTR-98-41-T, Decision on Kabiligi Request for Particulars of the Amended Indictment, 27 September 2005, para. 7 ('The Prosecution is not barred from cumulative charging on the basis of the same factual allegations. Cumulative charging has been standard practice at both the ICTR and ICTY.'). For more on ICTY jurisprudence regarding cumulative and alternative charging, see Boas, Bischoff, and Reid, *Elements of Crimes*, *supra* note 40, pp. 319–323.

hostilities. Moreover, the offences that are not charged as war crimes (but rather genocide or crimes against humanity) generally arise from conflicts or criminal transactions of long duration and wide geographic scope. Accordingly, in an effort to capture the range of alleged criminal conduct and the roles played by different individuals with regard to the alleged crimes, many of the indictments brought by the Prosecutors of the *ad hoc* Tribunals and the SCSL charge one or more accused with responsibility for crimes committed by multiple physical perpetrators. This charging practice is explicitly authorised in the Rules of the ICTY, ICTR, and SCSL.[116] At the latter court, however, it was never invoked at the very outset of the proceedings to ground an initial indictment against two or more accused. Rather, as discussed below, the SCSL Prosecutor indicted each accused separately, and then later sought to join subsets of those indictments into trials of multiple accused from the armed factions in the conflict.[117] At the ICC, the Statute and Rules contemplate instruments bringing charges against multiple accused,[118] and in at least one case to date, a pre-trial chamber has granted joinder and confirmed a charging instrument jointly accusing two or more individuals.[119]

6.2.3 Joinder of indictments or trials

As a result of the long periods of investigation and pre-trial preparation at the international criminal tribunals – and the sporadic nature of the transfers of accused to the tribunals – the prosecution will often request joint trials of multiple accused charged under different indictments; or seek to merge two or more existing indictments into a single joint indictment that will underpin a single trial against the accused who had surrendered or been apprehended to date. This practice is particularly prevalent at the *ad hoc* Tribunals, and can be traced to several factors,

116 See ICTY Rule 48 ('Persons accused of the same or different crimes committed in the course of the same transaction may be jointly charged and tried'); ICTR Rule 48 (same); SCSL Rule 48(a) (same, except substituting the term 'indicted' for 'charged'). For examples of initial indictments against two or more accused in the *ad hoc* Tribunals, see *Prosecutor* v. *Naletilić and Martinović*, Case No. IT-98-34-I, Indictment, 18 December 1998 (as permitted by Rules 48 and 49 of the ICTY Rules, charging both accused with multiple crimes in a single indictment); *Prosecutor* v. *Nyiramasuhuko and Ntahobali*, Case No. ICTR-97-21-I, Indictment, 26 May 1997 (similarly charging both accused with multiple crimes).

117 See *infra* text accompanying notes 132–135. A similar practice is reflected in ICTR proceedings, where almost all accused were initially indicted separately before some indictments were joined for trial. The exceptions to this practice were the parent-child pairings of Nyiramasuhuko and Ntahobali, see *supra* note 116, and the Ntakirutimanas, see *infra* text accompanying notes 129–131.

118 Rome Statute, Art. 64(5); ICC Rule 136(1) (expressing a presumption in favour of joint trials for '[p]ersons accused jointly').

119 See *Prosecutor* v. *Katanga and Ngudjolo*, Doc. No. ICC-01/04-01/07-257, Decision on Joinder of the Cases Against Germain Katanga and Mathieu Ngudjolo Chui, 10 March 2008 ('*Katanga and Ngudjolo* Joinder Decision'), pp. 6–11; *Katanga and Ngudjolo* Confirmation Decision, *supra* note 33, pp. 207–212 (confirming charges of murder, sexual slavery, and rape as crimes against humanity; and wilful killing, use of child soldiers, intentionally directing attacks on a civilian population, pillaging, destruction of property, sexual slavery, and rape as war crimes against Germain Katanga and Mathieu Ngudjolo for their role in the perpetration of these crimes in the Democratic Republic of the Congo between 2001 and 2004).

including the tendency of the ICTR prosecution to indict accused separately, even if they were alleged to have participated in the same criminal transaction; the practice of the ICTY prosecution of charging many accused with criminal liability through the form of responsibility known as JCE;[120] the marked increase in accused rendered to the ICTY in the last few years, an improvement over previously sporadic and uncertain rendition practices; and the completion strategies at both the ICTY and ICTR. In these circumstances, the prosecution will frequently use the opportunity to submit a proposed amended joinder indictment that reflects an ostensibly 'streamlined' account of the factual and legal bases of the charges against the accused, but also incorporates additional amendments, some of which may have a substantive effect on the charges faced by the accused.[121]

At the ICTY, a chamber reviewing a motion to join indictments applies a two-step test that is guided by the Rules and considerations of efficiency and fairness: (1) are the criteria in the rule permitting joinder of accused satisfied under the circumstances and, if so, (2) should the chamber nevertheless exercise its discretion to deny joinder?[122] The first prong of the test is satisfied by a *prima facie* showing that the crimes in question were committed in the course of the same criminal transaction.[123] The second prong requires a case-specific consideration of several factors, including (1) whether joinder would avoid duplication of the presentation of evidence on the crimes and forms of responsibility alleged against the multiple accused, would minimise hardship to witnesses, or would otherwise promote judicial economy; (2) whether joinder would create a conflict of interest or otherwise prejudice the right of any of the accused to a fair and expeditious trial; and (3) whether there is any other factor that persuades the trial chamber it will not be able to manage the proposed joint trial.[124]

[120] By an allegation of JCE, the prosecution contends that the accused intentionally participated in a common plan, design or purpose with one or more other persons involving the perpetration of one or more of the crimes within the jurisdiction of the Tribunal. For more on this form of responsibility unique to international criminal law, see Boas, Bischoff, and Reid, *Forms of Responsibility*, *supra* note 17, pp. 7–141, 426. Note that the definition of a criminal 'transaction' for joinder purposes also requires that the conduct in question be 'part of a common scheme, strategy or plan'. See *supra* text accompanying note 109.

[121] See, e.g., *Gotovina et al.* Indictment and Joinder Decision, *supra* note 50 (granting in part prosecution's request to amend the indictment in each of the two cases (*Čermak and Markač*, and *Gotovina*), granting the request for joinder, and granting leave to amend and file the proposed joint amended indictment). See also *Haradinaj et al.* Pre-Trial Indictment Decision, *supra* note 25, para. 6 (regarding a proposed second consolidated amended indictment).

[122] See *Prosecutor* v. *Me[j]akić, Gruban, and Knežević*, Case No. IT-95-4-PT, and *Prosecutor* v. *Fuštar, Banović, and Knežević*, Case No. IT-95-8/1-PT, Decision on Prosecution's Motion for Joinder of Accused, 17 September 2002 ('*Mejakić et al.* Joinder Decision') (citing ICTY Rules 48 and 82(B), the latter of which provides that a 'Trial Chamber may order that persons accused jointly under Rule 48 be tried separately if it considers it necessary in order to avoid a conflict of interests that might cause serious prejudice to an accused, or to protect the interests of justice').

[123] See *supra* notes 109, 116 and accompanying text; see also *Prosecutor* v. *Milutinović, Šainović, and Ojdanić*, Case No. IT-99-37-PT, and *Prosecutor* v. *Pavković, Lazarević, Đorđević, and Lukić*, Case No. IT-03-70-PT, Decision on Prosecution Motion for Joinder, 8 July 2005 ('*Milutinović et al.* Joinder Decision').

[124] *Milutinović et al.* Joinder Decision, *supra* note 123. See also *Prosecutor* v. *Norman*, Case No. SCSL-2003-08-PT, *Prosecutor* v. *Fofana*, Case No. SCSL-2003-11-PT, and *Prosecutor* v. *Kondewa*, Case No.

Unlike joinder of charges, the joinder of indictments or trials is less a consequence of the nature of international crimes, and more a result of a combination of limited resources, prosecutorial strategy, and external pressures such as the completion strategies at the *ad hoc* Tribunals. It is thus not surprising that, at the ICTY, the practice has both increased in frequency and come under criticism in recent years. For example, in response to one accused's assertion that 'the Completion Strategy should not influence the Trial Chamber in its determination of the joinder motion or be allowed to influence the right of an accused to a speedy trial', Judge Robinson took pains to note, in a separate opinion to the unanimous decision granting joinder, that 'the Security Council resolution [urging the ICTY to complete its work by 2010] does not impose an obligation on the Tribunal to do anything other than adopt all reasonable measures to meet the deadlines set' and should not 'be interpreted as requiring the Chambers to exercise their judicial function in a manner that enables the Tribunal to meet the deadline, but breaches the fundamental principle of fairness in the trial process'.[125] Judge Robinson concluded:

> While it would be quite proper for the Prosecutor to be influenced by the Completion Strategy in determining her prosecutorial strategy, including the joinder of accused, the Completion Strategy would, as the Appeals Chamber has held, be an 'improper consideration' in the decision of a Trial Chamber. This is true even though the implementation of the Strategy may have implications for factors (such as judicial economy) of which a Trial Chamber may properly and quite independently take account.[126]

At the ICTR, in addition to the rule providing that two or more individuals 'may be jointly charged and tried', the judges adopted a separate rule providing that '[p]ersons who are separately indicted, accused of the same or different crimes committed in the course of the same transaction, may be tried together, with leave granted by a Trial Chamber'.[127] Although ICTR chambers generally apply the same

SCSL-203-12-PT, Decision and Order on Prosecution Motions for Joinder, 27 February 2004 ('*CDF* Joinder Decision'), para. 18 (compiling an extensive list of considerations applied by chambers of the *ad hoc* Tribunals when ruling on joinder motions).

125 *Prosecutor* v. *Popović*, Case No. IT-02-57-PT, *Prosecutor* v. *Beara*, Case No. IT-02-58-PT, *Prosecutor* v. *Nikolić*, Case No. IT-02-63-PT, *Prosecutor* v. *Borovčanin*, Case No. IT-02-64-PT, *Prosecutor* v. *Tolimir, Miletić, and Gvero*, Case No. IT-04-80-PT, and *Prosecutor* v. *Pandurević and Trbić*, Case No. IT-05-86-PT, Decision on Motion for Joinder, 21 September 2005, Separate Opinion of Judge Patrick Robinson, para. 2.

126 *Ibid.*, para. 4 (quoting *Prosecutor* v. *Milošević*, Case No. IT-02-54-AR73.6, Decision on the Interlocutory Appeal by the *Amici Curiae* Against the Trial Chamber Order Concerning the Presentation and Preparation of the Defence Case, 20 January 2004, para. 18). But see Boas, *supra* note 107, pp. 115–121 (discussing joinder); *ibid.*, pp. 68–69 (discussing Judge Hunt's criticism of his colleagues on the Appeals Chamber for reversing or ignoring carefully considered precedent on the basis of an improper contemplation of the completion strategy).

127 ICTR Rule 48 *bis* (entitled 'Joinder of Trials'). But see *Prosecutor* v. *Ntagerura* and *Prosecutor* v. *Bagambiki, Imanishimwe, and Munyakazi*, Case Nos. ICTR-96-10-I and ICTR-97-36-I, Decision on Prosecutor's Motion for Joinder, 11 October 1999, para. 27 (explaining that '[a]t the 1999 Plenary Session, the Tribunal added Rule 48 *bis* to the Rules' and that '[t]his was merely a clarification of Rule 48'). There is no separate rule in this regard at the ICTY, where the parties and chambers have been content to apply Rule 48 as permitting

test employed by ICTY chambers,[128] the issue of whether the acts alleged formed part of the same transaction for purposes of a joinder motion proved particularly contentious at the ICTR. In response, trial chambers placed a judicial gloss on the plain language of the Rules, and developed a three-pronged guideline:

[T]he acts of the accused need not be criminal [or] illegal in themselves. However … :

1. [The acts of the accused should be] connected to material elements of a criminal act. For example the acts of the accused may be non-criminal [or] legal acts in furtherance of future criminal acts;
2. The criminal acts [to] which the acts of the accused are connected … must be capable of specific determination in time and space; and
3. The criminal acts [to] which the acts of the accused are connected … must illustrate the existence of a common scheme, strategy or plan.[129]

In one such case, the prosecution moved to join two indictments, each of which charged two accused with several crimes in a different village in the Rwandan prefecture of Kibuye. Applying these guidelines to the submissions of the parties, the Trial Chamber ruled that 'the acts of the accused may form part of the same transaction notwithstanding that they were carried out in different areas and over different periods, providing that there is a sufficient nexus between the acts committed in the two areas'.[130] The Chamber granted the joinder motion because it found that 'a joinder of the … indictments would enable the parties to make a more consistent and detailed presentation of evidence', would permit 'better protection for the witnesses by limiting their travel to the Tribunal', and would cause no prejudice to the rights of the accused.[131]

When the much smaller number of accused at the SCSL is taken into consideration, the comparative incidence of joinder is even higher: three of the four trials heard by this court have proceeded on the basis of amended joint indictments, each charging multiple accused from the same armed group.[132] These proceedings are known by the names of the respective factions that were parties to the conflict in Sierra Leone. The *Armed Forces Revolutionary Council* or *AFRC* case against

both joint accusation in the initial indictment and motions to join separate indictments. See, e.g., *Mejakić et al.* Joinder Decision, *supra* note 122; *Milutinović et al.* Joinder Decision, *supra* note 123.

128 See *supra* text accompanying notes 122–124.

129 *Prosecutor* v. *Ntakirutimana, Ntakirutimana, and Sikubwabo*, Case Nos. ICTR-96-10-I and ICTR 96-17-T, Decision on the Prosecutor's Motion to Join the Indictments ICTR 96–10-I and ICTR 96–17-T, 22 February 2001, para. 18 (quoting *Prosecutor* v. *Ntabakuze and Kabiligi*, Case ICTR-97–34-I, Decision on the Defence Motion Requesting an Order for Separate Trials, 30 September 1998, p. 2, and noting that '[these] guidelines have been followed by the Tribunal in several decisions on joinder').

130 *Ibid.*, para. 21 (concluding that 'under each separate indictment, the Prosecution has alleged in relation to the accused that the acts committed at the Mugonero Complex were closely linked to the acts that followed in the area of Bisesero').

131 *Ibid.*, para. 27.

132 Charles Taylor is the sole accused in the fourth trial.

Alex Tamba Brima, Ibrahim Bazzy Kamara, and Santigie Borbor Kanu concluded in February 2008 with the confirmed sentences of fifty, forty-five, and fifty years respectively for acts of terrorism, collective punishments, violence to life, health, and physical or mental well-being of persons (in particular murder and mutilation), outrages upon personal dignity, and pillage as violations of Common Article 3 and Additional Protocol II; conscripting children or using them to participate actively in hostilities, as another war crime; and extermination, murder, rape, and enslavement as crimes against humanity.[133] The *Civil Defence Forces* or *CDF* case against Sam Norman, Moinina Fofana, and Allieu Kondewa concluded in May 2008 with sentences of fifteen years and twenty years for Fofana and Kondewa, respectively, for murder and inhumane acts as crimes against humanity; and violence to life, health, and physical or mental well-being of persons (in particular murder and cruel treatment), and pillage as violations of Common Article 3 and Additional Protocol II.[134] Finally, the *Revolutionary United Front* or *RUF* case against Issa Hassan Sesay, Morris Kallon, and Augustine Gbao concluded in October 2009 with sentences of fifty-two years, forty years, and twenty-five years respectively, for (1) extermination, murder, rape, enslavement, sexual slavery and other sexual violence, and other inhumane acts as crimes against humanity; (2) acts of terrorism; collective punishments; violence to life, health, and physical or mental well-being of persons (in particular murder and mutilation); outrages upon personal dignity; and pillage as violations of Common Article 3 and Additional Protocol II; and (3) conscripting, enlisting, and using children as active participants in the hostilities; and intentionally directing attacks against humanitarian or peacekeeping personnel as other serious violations of international humanitarian law.[135]

In the first SCSL decision on a prosecution request to join indictments, the Trial Chamber went through a detailed analysis of the applicable law, and relied on the jurisprudence of the *ad hoc* Tribunals interpreting the similar provisions of their own Rules. 'Convinced that the legislative intent' behind the applicable rule in the SCSL Rules was 'to render joinder permissible only in cases where the acts and omissions of [separately indicted] accused persons … amount to … crimes committed in the course of the same transaction simpliciter', the Trial Chamber concluded that to win joinder, the prosecution must establish that (1) the accused

[133] See *Prosecutor* v. *Brima, Kamara, and Kanu*, Case No. SCSL-04-16-A, Appeal Judgement, 22 February 2008, pp. 11–12, 105–106.

[134] See *CDF* Case, Case No. 04-14-A, Appeal Judgement, 28 May 2008, pp. 187–192. Only Fofana was convicted of pillage as a war crime. Norman died in custody in February 2007, and proceedings against him were terminated as of the date of his death. See *supra* note 97 and accompanying text.

[135] See *RUF* Appeal Judgment, *supra* note 84, pp. 477–480 (referring to counts in *RUF* Case, Case No. SCSL-04-15-PT, Corrected Amended Consolidated Indictment, 2 August 2006). The *RUF* case also comprised charges against Foday Saybana Sankoh and Sam Bockarie, but the indictments against those two accused were withdrawn in December 2003 following their deaths. See *supra* text accompanying note 96. For a discussion and criticism of these various terms of years, see Chapter 10, Section 10.2.4.

are charged with crimes committed in the course of the same transaction; (2) 'the factual allegations in the Indictments will, if proven, show a consistency between the said crimes ... and the Prosecution's theory that they were committed in furtherance, or were the product of a common criminal design'; and (3) with due regard to the rights of the accused, 'it will be in the interests of justice to try the Accused jointly'.[136] Applying this test to the prosecution's request for a joint trial of six accused, the Trial Chamber concluded that 'it would be more conducive to the interests of justice' and that the accused's 'chances of a fair and expeditious trial could be greatly enhanced' if the three accused allegedly belonging to the RUF were tried separately from the three accused allegedly belonging to the AFRC.[137] The Trial Chamber therefore ordered separate joint trials of these respective groups of accused.[138]

In the sole decision on joinder by an ICC chamber as of 1 December 2009, the *Katanga and Ngudjolo* Pre-Trial Chamber granted the prosecution's request for a joint trial of the two accused, and applied the same factors as those considered by *ad hoc* and SCSL chambers, albeit in a different procedural framework. Concluding that the applicable statutory and regulatory provisions established a presumption in favour of joint proceedings for persons accused jointly,[139] the Chamber placed the burden on the accused to demonstrate that joinder was not appropriate under the circumstances, rather than on the prosecution to show that joinder should be granted, as is the case in the other tribunals.[140] After noting several benefits of joint trials – including judicial economy, minimised impact on potential witnesses, and equal treatment for the accused[141] – the Chamber held that 'neither Defence has shown that joining the cases would prejudice the suspects or would be contrary to the interests of justice' and granted joinder, although it noted that the ruling would not preclude either accused from later seeking severance.[142]

[136] *Prosecutor* v. *Sesay*, Case No. SCSL-2003-05-PT, *Prosecutor* v. *Brima*, Case No. SCSL-2003-06-PT, *Prosecutor* v. *Kallon*, Case No. SCSL-2003-07-PT, *Prosecutor* v. *Gbao*, Case No. SCSL-2003-09-PT, *Prosecutor* v. *Kamara*, Case No. SCSL-2003-10-PT, and *Prosecutor* v. *Kanu*, Case No. SCSL-2003-13-PT, Decision and Order on Prosecution Motions for Joinder, 27 January 2004 ('*AFRC* and *RUF* Joinder Decision'), para. 31; see also *ibid.*, para. 22 (terming this 'the consistency or product test'). The decision granting joinder in the *CDF* case was issued on the same day by the same bench, and includes an identical discussion of the applicable law. See *CDF* Joinder Decision, *supra* note 124, para. 21.

[137] *AFRC* and *RUF* Joinder Decision, *supra* note 136, para. 46.

[138] *Ibid.*, para. 48. The Chamber later denied the prosecution leave to file an interlocutory appeal of the decision, see *RUF* Case, Case No. SCSL-2004-15-PT, Decision on Prosecution's Application for Leave to File an Interlocutory Appeal Against the Decision on the Prosecution Motions for Joinder, 13 February 2004, so the trials proceeded as ordered. See *supra* text accompanying notes 132–135.

[139] *Katanga and Ngudjolo* Joinder Decision, *supra* note 119, p. 7.

[140] *Ibid.*, pp. 9–10 ('[A]bsent any declaration of guilt by Germain Katanga or Mathieu Ngudjolo Chui, the above-mentioned circumstances require the application of the general rule for joint proceedings for persons prosecuted jointly unless it is shown that separate proceedings are necessary in order to avoid serious prejudice to Germain Katanga or Mathieu Ngudjolo Chui or to protect the interests of justice').

[141] *Ibid.*, p. 8. [142] *Ibid.*, p. 10.

6.2.4 Severance

The governing instruments of all these tribunals also grant chambers the power to order separate trials of jointly accused persons if necessary to avoid prejudice to the rights of any of the accused or to protect the interests of justice.[143] As with joinder, trial chambers thus have broad discretion to order severance in appropriate circumstances,[144] and have done so in cases where delays caused by the ill health of one accused would prejudice the rights of his co-accused to trial without undue delay,[145] or similarly, where one or more of the accused on a joint indictment had not yet been rendered to the custody of the tribunal.[146] As one ICTY trial chamber noted, '[m]ost requests for severance' at that tribunal 'have been denied on the basis that continuing with joined proceedings would best protect the interests of justice'.[147] ICTR chambers have also regularly declined to sever accused, particularly where the party seeking severance did not demonstrate that the absence of one or more co-accused would cause a delay in the trial against the accused in custody,[148] and have held that 'severance will only be granted if serious prejudice to a specific right of an accused can be shown'.[149]

6.3 Orders and warrants

The ICTY, ICTR, and SCSL Rules each include what is termed a 'general provision' on the power of a pre-trial or trial chamber to issue binding orders in aid of a trial: 'At the request of either party or *proprio motu*, a Judge or a Trial Chamber may issue such orders, summonses, subpoenas, warrants and transfer orders as

[143] See ICC Rule 136; ICTY Rule 82; ICTR Rule 82; SCSL Rule 82.

[144] See, e.g., *Prosecutor* v. *Brđanin and Talić*, Case No. IT-99-36-AR72.2, Decision on Request to Appeal, 16 May 2000, p. 4; *Prosecutor* v. *Karemera, Ngirumpatse, and Nziorera*, Case No. ICTR-98-44-AR73.16, Decision on Appeal Concerning the Severance of Matthieu Ngirumpatse, 19 June 2009, para. 16 (reaffirming, at the outset of its analysis of an appeal of an order for severance, that '[d]ecisions related to the general conduct of trial are matters within the discretion of the Trial Chamber').

[145] See, e.g., *Prosecutor* v. *Brđanin and Talić*, Case No. IT-99-36-T, Decision on Prosecution's Oral Request for the Separation of Trials, 20 September 2002, paras. 26–29 and p. 9; *Prosecutor* v. *Strugar and Kovačević*, Case No. IT-01-42-PT, Decision on the Prosecutor's Motion for Separate Trial and Order to Schedule a Pre-Trial Conference and the Start of the Trial against Pavle Strugar, 26 November 2003, pp. 2–3.

[146] See, e.g., *Prosecutor* v. *Bizimana and Nzabonimana*, Case No. ICTR-98-44-I, Decision on Prosecution Motion for Severance and Amendment of Indictment, 7 November 2008, para. 5; *Prosecutor* v. *Muvunyi, Nizeyimana, and Hategekimana*, Case No. ICTR-2000-55-I, Decision Regarding the Prosecutor's Motion for Leave to Sever an Indictment and for Directions on the Trial of Tharcisse Muvunyi, 11 December 2003, para. 7.

[147] *Prosecutor* v. *Popović, Beara, Nikolić, Borovčanin, Tolimir, Miletić, Gvero, Pandurević, and Trbić*, Case No. IT-05-88-PT, Decision on Severance of Case Against Milorad Trbić, 26 June 2006, p. 3 n. 13 (collecting cases).

[148] See, e.g., *Prosecutor* v. *Muhimana and Seven Others*, Case No. ICTR-95-1-I, Decision on the Prosecutor's Motion for Leave to Sever an Indictment, 6 July 2000; *Prosecutor* v. *Nsabimana*, Case No. ICTR-97-29-I, Decision on the Defence Motion for Orders to Sever Proceedings, Set a Date for a Status Conference and for the Return of Personal Effects, 8 July 1998.

[149] *Prosecutor* v. *Karemera, Ngirumpatse, and Nzirorera*, Case No. ICTR-98-44-T, Decision on Remand Regarding Continuation of Trial, 10 September 2009, para. 6.

may be necessary for the purposes of an investigation or for the preparation or conduct of the trial.'[150] ICC judges and chambers enjoy a similarly broad grant of power, which is expressed in a number of different provisions throughout the Rome Statute, ICC Rules, and Regulations of the Court.[151] In the political and diplomatic context in which all these international tribunals operate, the assertion of judicial authority pursuant to these provisions and the somewhat chequered history of compliance with the ensuing orders[152] reflect both a commitment to the development of an international rule of law, and the unique challenges posed in running complex international criminal trials.

6.3.1 Warrants

The arrest warrant issued at the outset of criminal proceedings at the international tribunals is essentially a specialised type of court order. Issued pursuant to a grant of authority in the Statute and Rules of each institution,[153] the warrant typically sets forth (in varying degrees of detail) the conclusion of the judge or chamber that the allegations against the suspect or accused have satified the relevant legal standards, and directs the competent authorities to arrest, detain, and transfer the individual to the custody of the court.[154] At the ICC, as befits the more nuanced relationship of complementarity between that court and national authorities,[155] the decision issuing an arrest warrant typically includes a direction to the administrative arm of the Court to prepare a 'request' to the custodial state for arrest and surrender of the suspect.[156]

At the *ad hoc* Tribunals and the SCSL, issuance of an arrest warrant is an automatic procedural step once an indictment is confirmed, and there are no separate

[150] ICTY Rule 54; see also ICTR Rule 54 (same); SCSL Rule 54 (replacing the Latin phrase '*proprio motu*' with the English translation 'of its own motion').

[151] See, e.g., Rome Statute, Arts. 19(8), 56, 57; ICC Court Regulations 29(1), 54–55; *infra* notes 165–169.

[152] See, e.g., Jelena Pejić, 'The Tribunal and the ICC: Do Precedents Matter?', (1997) 60 *Albany Law Review* 841, 848 (noting challenges in early years of ICTY in obtaining surrender of indicted persons); Mary Margaret Penrose, 'Lest We Fail: The Importance of Enforcement in International Criminal Law', (1999–2000) 15 *American University International Law Review* 321, 358–359 (noting disparity in early years of ICTY between number of indictments and accused in custody); Statement by the President of the Security Council, UN Doc. S/PRST/1996/34, 8 August 1996 (condemning failure of states to cooperate with ICTY).

[153] See ICTY Statute, Art. 19(2); ICTR Statute, Art. 18(2); ICTY Rule 55; ICTR Rule 55; SCSL Rule 55.

[154] See, e.g., *Prosecutor* v. *Župljanin*, Case No. IT-99-36-I, Warrant of Arrest, 23 March 2005, p. 6 (directing the European Union stabilization force in Bosnia-Herzegovina, a legal successor to the NATO mission there, to 'search for, arrest and surrender to the International Tribunal … Stojan Župljanin').

[155] See generally Chapter 3, Sections 3.2, 3.2.6.

[156] See, e.g., *Prosecutor* v. *Bashir*, Doc. No. ICC-02/05-01/09-21, Public Redacted Version of Decision on the Prosecution's Application for a Warrant of Arrest Against Omar Hassan Ahmad Al Bashir, 4 March 2009, p. 93 (deciding that the Registry 'shall prepare a request for cooperation seeking the arrest and surrender of Omar Al Bashir … and shall transmit such request to the competent Sudanese authorities', and directing the Registry 'as appropriate, to prepare and transmit to any other State any additional request for arrest and surrender which may be necessary').

legal requirements that must be fulfilled;[157] at the ICC, as discussed above, the arrest warrant is the crucial first step in the pre-trial process, because it is the stage at which the prosecution's allegations are first subject to judicial testing.[158] Even when simultaneously issued with indictments, however, international tribunals' arrest warrants have outsize procedural significance. After all, refusals by the competent authorities to comply with arrest warrants have a direct effect on the perceived success of the tribunals' efforts to try the grave violations of international law that are subject to their respective jurisdictions.

In the early years of the ICTY, arrest warrants were routinely ignored by the parties to the ongoing conflicts, and were inconsistently enforced by the international forces tasked with locating and detaining the accused.[159] Recent years have seen much better results: there have been some high-profile arrests of accused pursuant to longstanding warrants, such as Ante Gotovina and Radovan Karadžić,[160] and many more ostensibly voluntary surrenders by accused and renditions by states seeking better relations with the European Union.[161] The ICTR has faced similar challenges in securing the transfer of accused to its custody for trial, with the added complication of an even greater dispersion of accused around the world,[162] while

[157] See ICTY Statute, Art. 19(2); ICTR Statute, Art. 18(2); SCSL Rule 47(H).

[158] See *supra* Section 6.1.1.1 for a discussion of the standards applied to a request for issuance of an arrest warrant at the ICC. While the Rome Statute and ICC Rules contemplate the issuance of a summons instead of a warrant to ensure the presence of the accused, it is the latter form of compulsion that has been used in almost all the cases currently pending before the Court. The sole exception is in a case arising out of the Situation in Darfur, Sudan. See *Prosecutor* v. *Abu Garda*, Doc. No. ICC-02/05-02/09-2, Summons to Appear, 7 May 2009 (unsealed 12 May 2009).

[159] See *supra* note 152.

[160] See Fifteenth Annual Report of the International Tribunal for the Prosecution of Persons Responsible for Serious Violations of International Humanitarian Law Committed in the Territory of the Former Yugoslavia Since 1991, UN Doc. A/63/210-S/2008/515, 4 August 2008, para. 65 (reporting arrest of Karadžić and Župljanin in 2008).

[161] Between 1 September 2004 and 31 December 2006, close to thirty accused were transferred to the ICTY by state authorities in the region of the former Yugoslavia. See Eleventh Annual Report of the International Tribunal for the Prosecution of Persons Responsible for Serious Violations of International Humanitarian Law Committed in the Territory of the Former Yugoslavia Since 1991, UN Doc. A/59/215-S/2004/627, 16 August 2004 (noting that 'overall there has been no major progress' in the Prosecutor's cooperation with governments except for Croatia, which handled two indictments 'in an efficient manner'); Twelfth Annual Report of the International Tribunal for the Prosecution of Persons Responsible for Serious Violations of International Humanitarian Law Committed in the Territory of the Former Yugoslavia Since 1991, UN Doc. A/60/267-S/2005/532, 17 August 2005 (noting that a combination of the Prosecutor's efforts and international pressure brought about 'the significant results' of transfer of twenty-four accused to The Hague); Thirteenth Annual Report of the International Tribunal for the Prosecution of Persons Responsible for Serious Violations of International Humanitarian Law Committed in the Territory of the Former Yugoslavia Since 1991, UN Doc. A/61/271-S/2006/666, 21 August 2006 (noting that three accused were transferred in 2006).

[162] See, e.g., BBC World News, 'US Deports Rwandan Pastor', 24 March 2000, http://news.bbc.co.uk/2/hi/africa/690082.stm (reporting on decision by American immigration authorities to deport alleged participant in Rwandan genocide in order to stand trial in Arusha); BBC World News, 'Genocide Suspect Sent to Rwanda', 25 April 2000, http://news.bbc.co.uk/2/hi/africa/726094.stm (reporting on extradition by Belgian government of prominent participant in Rwandan genocide); Linda Keller, 'Belgian Jury to Decide Case Concerning Rwandan Genocide', *ASIL Insights*, May 2001, www.asil.org/insigh72.cfm (summarizing case against four Rwandans on trial in Belgium for alleged human rights violations during 1994 genocide).

the difficulties of the ICC in obtaining compliance with its arrest warrants are well known.[163]

6.3.2 Pre-trial orders

For pre-trial proceedings, the general authority conferred on chambers and judges to issue orders is supplemented by specific provisions directed at the investigation, arrest, detention, and transfer of suspects or accused.[164] These provisions include authorisation for orders on provisional release,[165] protective measures,[166] victim participation,[167] disclosure of evidence,[168] and general trial preparation.[169]

As with other aspects of the tribunals' respective legal regimes, the content and application of many of these rules reflect the differing contexts in which the tribunals operate and the distinct challenges that are anticipated or experienced in their daily functioning. For example, although prosecutors at the ICTY and ICTR may ask a chamber to issue orders to a custodial state, or one in which relevant evidence may be found, directing it to provide assistance to the prosecution in the apprehension of the accused, the preservation of evidence, and the protection of witnesses,[170] the ICTY Rules go further, and contain detailed provisions on judicial orders compelling the production of evidence from recalcitrant states or those with national security concerns. This specific regime arose in large part because a significant portion of the non-testimonial evidence that is potentially available to the parties is either kept in the archives of the successor states of the former Yugoslavia, or was

[163] As of 1 December 2009, of the thirteen individuals for whom arrest warrants have been issued, one has died, and five have been transferred to the custody of the ICC. See generally www.icc-cpi.int/Menus/ICC/Situations+and+Cases/Cases/; see also *Prosecutor* v. *Kony, Otti, Odhiambo, Lukwiya, and Ongwen*, Doc. No. ICC-02/04-01/05-248, Decision to Terminate the Proceedings Against Raska Lukwiya, 11 July 2007 (terminating proceedings and voiding arrest warrant after suspect's death).

[164] See, e.g., Rome Statute, Art. 57 (setting forth the extensive powers and functions of pre-trial chambers); ICTY Statute, Art. 19(2) ('Upon confirmation of an indictment, the judge may, at the request of the Prosecutor, issue such orders and warrants for the arrest, detention, surrender or transfer of persons, and any other orders as may be required for the conduct of the trial'); ICTR Statute, Art. 18(2) (same); SCSL Rule 47(H)(i) (replacing the phrase 'as may be required for the conduct of the trial' in the last phrase with 'as may be required for the proceedings in accordance with these Rules').

[165] See ICC Rule 119 (entitled 'Conditional Release'); ICTY Rule 65; ICTR Rule 65; SCSL Rule 65 (entitled 'Bail'); Chapter 4, Sections 4.3.3, 4.3.4.

[166] See ICC Rule 87; ICTY Rule 69; ICTR Rule 69; SCSL Rule 69; Chapter 7, Section 7.4.2.

[167] See ICC Rules 89–93; see also generally Chapter 8.

[168] See ICC Rules 79–84; ICTY Rules 66, 68–68 *bis*; ICTR Rules 66, 68; SCSL Rules 66, 68; *infra* Section 6.5.

[169] See, e.g., Rome Statute, Art. 57; ICC Rules 132–134; ICTY Rules 65 *bis*, 65 *ter*, 73 *bis*; ICTR Rules 65 *bis*, 73 *bis*; SCSL Rules 65 *bis*, 73 *bis*; ICC Court Regulation 54; *infra* Section 6.6.2.

[170] See ICTY Statute, Art. 18(2); ICTR Statute, Art. 17(2); ICTY Rules 39–40; ICTR Rules 39–40. See also *Prosecutor* v. *Blaškić*, Case No. IT-95-14-AR108*bis*, Judgement on the Request of the Republic of Croatia for Review of the Decision of Trial Chamber II of 18 July 1997, 29 October 1997 ('*Blaškić* Subpoena Appeal Decision'), paras. 53–54. On the difficulties faced in such investigations, see generally Mark B. Harmon and Fergal Gaynor, 'Prosecuting Massive Crimes with Primitive Tools: Three Difficulties Encountered by Prosecutors in International Criminal Proceedings', (2004) 2 *Journal of International Criminal Justice* 403.

gathered by the military or intelligence arms of other states that were involved in the armed conflicts in question.[171] At the ICC, on the other hand, public knowledge of a particular investigation generally comes much earlier than is the case at the other international tribunals,[172] and its Statute includes specific authorisation for chambers to issue orders for the preservation of evidence during an investigation, well before a trial begins.[173]

The rules governing the obligation of states, international organisations, and individuals to testify in a trial before the *ad hoc* Tribunals, or to hand over documents or other materials, have developed over time as the Tribunals have had to address parties' requests for assistance by such entities in concrete cases. These rules reflect the judges' pragmatism regarding the extent to which states can be expected to cooperate where a party seeks sensitive information, especially national security information. With respect to states and international organisations, the Tribunals have affirmed their prerogative to issue orders to these entities compelling them to hand over documents, even where the information may implicate national security interests.[174] In the ICTY, however, the party seeking such information must first go through an elaborate procedure, including approaching the state or organisation to try to obtain the information voluntarily, before a chamber will order that the information be handed over,[175] and the Tribunal will not issue such an order if the state or organisation is not the owner or originator of the information.[176] Moreover, under Rule 70 of both Tribunals, the state or organisation may supply information to the prosecution or defence on the condition that the party not disclose it to others. The state or organisation must consent before the party may use the information in court,[177] and it cannot be compelled to hand over information it has already offered

[171] See *infra* notes 174–179 and accompanying text (discussing Rules 54 *bis* and 70 in the ICTY Rules). While the ICTR has its own difficult relationship with the Rwandan government, there was no perceived need for explicit rules governing the production of documentary evidence, and there is no analogue to the ICTY's provisions in this respect.

[172] See Chapter 3, Section 3.2.3.2.2 (discussing rules for providing notice to states that may be investigating or prosecuting, or intending to do so).

[173] Rome Statute, Art. 18(6) (if an investigation is deferred, or pending a decision on the prosecution's request for authorisation to continue an investigation notwithstanding a state's request that it be deferred, 'the Prosecutor may, on an exceptional basis, seek authority from the Pre-Trial Chamber to pursue necessary investigative steps for the purpose of preserving evidence where there is a unique opportunity to obtain important evidence or there is a significant risk that such evidence may not be subsequently available').

[174] See *Blaškić* Subpoena Appeal Decision, *supra* note 170, paras. 26–29, 61–69 (states); see also Chapter 3, note 11 and sources cited therein (states, international organisations, and sub-state entities).

[175] See ICTY Rule 54 *bis*. Although the text of Rule 54 *bis* refers only to 'States', the Appeals Chamber has since held that it also applies to information sought from an international organization. See *Prosecutor* v. *Milutinović, Šainović, Ojdanić, Pavković, Lazaraveić, and Lukić*, Case No. IT-05-87-AR108*bis*.1, Decision on Request of the North Atlantic Treaty Organisation for Review, 15 May 2006 ('*Milutinović et al.* NATO Appeal Decision'), para. 8. There is no corresponding provision in the ICTR Rules.

[176] *Milutinović et al.* NATO Appeal Decision, *supra* note 175, paras. 19–20.

[177] See ICTY Rule 70; ICTR Rule 70; see also generally *Prosecutor* v. *Slobodan Milošević*, Case No. IT-02-54-AR108*bis* and AR73.3, Public Version of the Confidential Decision on the Interpretation and Application of Rule 70, 23 October 2002.

on a restricted basis under Rule 70.[178] The limited remedies available for a state's failure to comply with an order of one of these international tribunals are discussed in Chapter 3.[179]

The ICTY and ICTR may also subpoena individuals.[180] They may order private individuals to appear in court to testify or to hand over documents, and may also order state officials or officials of international organisations – including NATO and UN peacekeeping forces – to testify or appear for a pre-testimonial interview, including with respect to matters witnessed in the course of official duties.[181] The Tribunals may not, however, issue an order to a state official for the production of documents in his or her custody in an official capacity, and must instead direct such an order to the state.[182] Moreover, the case law has established that certain classes of individuals are immune from being subpoenaed to testify or hand over documents generated in the course of performing official duties, including members of the International Committee for the Red Cross and, unless certain conditions are met, war correspondents.[183] When the Tribunal issues a subpoena to an individual, the state in which he or she is located is expected to secure the witness's agreement

[178] Hence, a party dissatisfied with the restrictions a state imposes on certain information may not circumvent the state's prerogative under Rule 70 by seeking a court order for unrestricted access to it under Rule 54 *bis*. See *Prosecutor* v. *Milutinović, Šainović, Ojdanić, Pavković, Lazarević, and Lukić*, Case No. IT-05-87-AR108*bis*.2, Decision on Request of the United States of America for Review, 12 May 2006, para. 37. See also generally Laura Moranchek, 'Protecting National Security Evidence While Prosecuting War Crimes: Problems and Lessons for International Justice from the ICTY', (2006) 31 *Yale Journal of International Law* 477, 486–90.

[179] See Chapter 3, Section 3.1.4.

[180] While the subpoena power lacks explicit support in the ICTY and ICTR Statutes, the ICTY Appeals Chamber has held that it derives from the Tribunal's 'inherent powers'. *Blaškić* Subpoena Appeal Decision, *supra* note 170, para. 55.

[181] See *Prosecutor* v. *Krstić*, Case No. IT-98-33-A, Decision on Application for Subpoenas, 1 July 2003 ('*Krstić* Subpoena Appeal Decision'), paras. 24, 26–28; *Prosecutor* v. *Slobodan Milošević*, Case No. IT-02-54-T, Decision on Assigned Counsel Application for Interview and Testimony of Tony Blair and Gerhard Schröder, 9 December 2005, paras. 30, 33. See also, e.g., *Prosecutor* v. *Bagosora, Kabiligi, Ntabakuze, and Nsengiyumva*, Case No. ICTR-98-41-T, Decision on Request for a Subpoena, 11 September 2006 (subpoena *ad testificandum* to Rwandan Minister of Defence); *Prosecutor* v. *Bagosora, Kabiligi, Ntabakuze, and Nsengiyumva*, Case No. ICTR-98-41-T, Decision on Request for a Subpoena for Major Jacques Biot, 14 July 2006 (subpoena *ad testificandum* to commander in UN peacekeeping force); *Prosecutor* v. *Simić, Simić, Tadić, Todorović, and Zarić*, Case No. IT-95-9-T, Decision on Motion for Judicial Assistance by SFOR and Others, 18 October 2000, paras. 46–49, 58, 61–62 (order to North Atlantic Council to disclose certain documents and other information to defence, and subpoena *ad testificandum* to General Eric Shinseki, then-commander of NATO-led multinational force in Bosnia).

[182] *Blaškić* Subpoena Appeal Decision, *supra* note 170, paras. 39–44; *Krstić* Subpoena Appeal Decision, *supra* note 181, paras. 24, 26–28.

[183] *Prosecutor* v. *Simić, Simić, Tadić, Todorović, and Zarić*, Case No. IT-95-9-T, Decision on the Prosecution Motion Under Rule 73 for a Ruling Concerning the Testimony of a Witness, 27 July 1999, paras. 72–74 (ICRC has right to confidentiality with respect to information gathered by former employee in the course of official duties); *Prosecutor* v. *Brđanin and Talić*, Case No. IT-99-36-AR73.9, Decision on Interlocutory Appeal, 11 December 2002, para. 50 (Appeals Chamber setting forth two-pronged test that must be met before chamber may subpoena a war correspondent: (1) 'the petitioning party must demonstrate that the evidence sought is of direct and important value in determining a core issue in the case'; and (2) 'it must demonstrate that the evidence sought cannot reasonably be obtained elsewhere'). See also Chapter 9, Section 9.3.2 (discussing testimonial privileges).

to testify or hand over the documents to the Tribunal, under threat of civil or criminal penalty.[184] Unlike a state, which may be subject only to remedial action by the Security Council for flouting a tribunal order, an individual who fails to comply with a subpoena or other judicial order may be subject to prosecution for contempt before that tribunal.[185]

At the ICC, a pre-trial chamber has specific statutory and regulatory authorisation to issue orders or decisions that are necessary for, among other things, assistance of the prosecution's investigation, preparation of the defence, protection and privacy of victims and witnesses, and preservation of evidence.[186] In the execution of those powers, the Pre-Trial Chamber in the *Situation in the Democratic Republic of the Congo* issued several decisions over the four years between the initiation of the investigation and the confirmation of charges against the accused Katanga and Ngudjolo, including authorisation for the prosecution to request assistance from the Netherlands Forensic Institute, an independent specialist laboratory, with regard to a 'unique investigative opportunity';[187] formally requesting the cooperation of the Congolese government in providing documents required by the defence;[188] and ordering that redacted copies of applications for official status as victims be provided to defence counsel.[189] For the ICC, the international body to which complaints of non-compliance by states are generally made is the Assembly of States Parties, though non-compliance may also be addressed to the Security Council where that body originally referred the situation to the Court.[190]

6.4 Guilty pleas and plea bargaining

Long a staple in domestic adversarial criminal justice systems,[191] guilty pleas and plea bargaining did not take place at the Nuremberg or Tokyo Tribunals,

184 *Blaškić* Subpoena Appeal Decision, *supra* note 170, para. 27.

185 See Chapter 7, Section 7.8 (discussing contempt and other offences against the administration of justice).

186 Rome Statute, Arts. 56, 57(3); ICC Rules 114–116. The ICC has no power to subpoena individuals. See Chapter 3, Section 3.2.6.

187 *Situation in the Democratic Republic of the Congo*, Doc. No. ICC-01/04-21, Decision on the Prosecutor's Request for Measures under Article 56, 26 April 2005. The quoted language reflects the title of Article 56, the text of which refers to 'a unique opportunity … to examine, collect or test evidence, which may not be available subsequently for the purposes of a trial'. See also Chapter 4, Section 4.1 (discussing investigations in detail).

188 *Situation in the Democratic Republic of the Congo*, Doc. No. ICC-01/04-444, Decision on the 'Defence Application Pursuant to Article 57(3)(b) of the Statute to Seek the Cooperation of the Democratic Republic of Congo (DRC)', 25 April 2008.

189 See, e.g., *Prosecutor* v. *Katanga and Ngudjolo*, Doc. No. ICC-01/04-01/07-509, Decision Authorising the Filing of Observations on the Applications for Participation in the Proceedings, 26 May 2008, pp. 4, 6.

190 Rome Statute, Art. 87(7). See also Chapter 3, Section 3.2.6.

191 See, e.g., Nancy Amoury Combs, 'Procuring Guilty Pleas for International Crimes: The Limited Influence of Sentence Discounts', (2006) 59 *Vanderbilt Law Review* 69, 70–71 (noting that approximately ninety per cent of all criminal cases in the United States involve guilty pleas and that a large percentage of cases in England, Australia, and other common law jurisdictions are similarly disposed). Despite some movement towards what Mirjan Damaška terms consensual justice following the Second World War, Anglo-American-style

and the very concept of negotiated dispositions was initially rejected by the judges of the ICTY.[192] Nevertheless, guilty pleas have become an accepted – although not universally acclaimed – form of case disposition at the *ad hoc* Tribunals.[193] Guilty pleas are almost always the product of negotiations between the accused and the prosecutor, and much has been written about plea bargaining at the *ad hoc* Tribunals, a practice lauded by some for its beneficial effects, but viewed with deep suspicion by others for its perceived capacity to thwart the goals of international criminal justice.[194] From the practitioner's perspective, normative debates about whether plea bargaining is appropriate to the adjudication of international crimes have been largely mooted by practice at the ICTY and ICTR. Although the SCSL Rules also provide for guilty pleas, no accused has ever pleaded guilty before that Tribunal.[195] Nevertheless, plea bargaining is entrenched in the procedural practice of the *ad hoc* Tribunals and is likely to play some role at the ICC. The subsections that follow outline the procedures relevant to plea dispositions at the various tribunals, which can take place during the pre-trial or trial phase at the *ad hoc* Tribunals, and occur at the commencement of trial at the ICC.

plea bargaining does not fit easily within continental European criminal justice systems. See Mirjan Damaška, 'Negotiated Justice in International Criminal Courts', (2004) 2 *Journal of International Criminal Justice* 1018, 1021–1024. But see also Henri D. Bosly, 'Admission of Guilt Before the ICC and in Continental Systems' (2004) 2 *Journal of International Criminal Justice* 1040, 1042, 1044–1045 (noting that although at first glance the institution of guilty pleas seems quite extraneous to Romano-Germanic criminal justice systems, several continental European states, including Spain, Italy, and France have adopted forms of guilty pleas).

192 In their first annual report following the adoption of the Rules, the ICTY judges said that the granting of immunity and the practice of plea bargaining 'find no place in the rules'. Annual Report of the [ICTY], UN Doc. A/49/342-S/1994/1007, 29 August 1994, para. 74.

193 See, e.g., Christoph Safferling, *Towards an International Criminal Procedure* (2001), p. 276 (arguing that the process of pleading 'should be removed from the system altogether').

194 See, e.g., Nancy Amoury Combs, *Guilty Pleas in International Criminal Law: Constructing a Restorative Justice Approach* (2007) (describing plea bargaining at international criminal tribunals and arguing for the enhanced use of pleas in the construction of a restorative justice approach to the adjudication of international crimes); John R.W.D. Jones and Steven Powles, *International Criminal Practice* (3rd edn 2003), p. 641 (questioning the appropriateness of guilty plea dispositions for tribunals adjudicating international crimes); Bosly, *supra* note 191, pp. 1047, 1049 (noting that continental jurists are sceptical of guilty pleas and plea bargaining discussions and arguing that guilty pleas should not be allowed for serious offences); Julian A. Cook, III, 'Plea Bargaining at The Hague', (2005) 30 *Yale Journal of International Law* 473, 477 (contending that defects in the plea bargaining procedures at the ICTY produce guilty pleas 'of dubious validity' that threaten to undermine the integrity of the Tribunal); Alexander Zahar and Göran Sluiter, *International Criminal Law: A Critical Introduction* (2008), p. 42 (noting that plea bargaining has found an important place at the ICTY due to the significant increase in its caseload over time and the presence of a compelling completion strategy); Michael Bohlander, 'Plea-Bargaining Before the ICTY', in Richard May, David Tolbert, John Hocking, Ken Roberts, Bing Bing Jia, Daryl Mundis, and Gabriel Oosthuizen (eds.), *Essays on ICTY Procedure and Evidence in Honour of Gabrielle Kirk McDonald* (2001), pp. 151–163. For the view that plea bargaining at international criminal tribunals produces benefits that go beyond the resource and investigative advantages that prompted their use at the ICTY, see Alan Tieger and Milbert Shin, 'Plea Agreements at the ICTY' (2005) 3 *Journal of International Criminal Justice* 666.

195 See *infra* note 204.

6.4.1 Guilty pleas at the ad hoc *Tribunals*

As initially adopted, both the ICTY and ICTR Rules provided that during an accused's initial appearance before the Tribunal, the chamber was required to call upon the accused to enter a plea of guilty or not guilty and set the case either for trial or a pre-sentencing hearing. Implicit in these rules was that the accused could – at a very early stage of the proceedings – forgo the right to a trial.[196] However, neither the Statutes nor the initial Rules of either Tribunal defined the character of a guilty plea nor provided guidance as to the attendant legal or procedural considerations.[197]

The *Erdemović* Trial Chamber of the ICTY was the first to grapple with defining the legal requirements for a valid guilty plea.[198] Referring to what it characterised as the 'formal' validity of a plea, the Trial Chamber noted that it was concerned with ensuring the plea was voluntary and made with a full understanding of the nature of the charge and its consequences.[199] Turning to what it termed the 'substantive' validity of the plea, the Trial Chamber pointed out

> that the choice of pleading guilty relates not only to the fact that the accused was conscious of having committed a crime and admitted it, but also to his right, as formally acknowledged in the procedures of the International Tribunal and as established *in common law* legal systems, to adopt his own defence strategy. The plea is one of the elements which constitute such a defence strategy.[200]

Finally, the Trial Chamber addressed whether Erdemović's plea was ambiguous or equivocal, an issue the Chamber felt compelled to address in light of the accused's assertion that he had committed the acts to which he was pleading guilty while under duress. Rejecting duress as an affirmative defence to a crime against humanity, the Trial Chamber found Erdemović's guilty plea valid.[201]

[196] With the minor exception that the ICTY rule was subsequently amended to permit the accused to enter his or her plea within thirty days of the initial appearance, the chronological structure has not changed. See ICTY Rule 62(A)(iii). As noted in Chapter 2, Section 2.1.3, the process by which the Tribunal's judges amend the Rules is not public and it is impossible to determine whether their reason for this amendment to Rule 62 was specifically related to guilty pleas. Jones and Powles note that the purpose of the amendment appears to have been to ensure that the accused would have time to consider the plea and consult with counsel on the matter. Jones and Powles, *supra* note 194, p. 633.

[197] Indeed, the only acknowledgement of pleas in the Statute, the reference in Article 20 to the trial chamber instructing the accused 'to enter a plea', was characterised as procedurally ambiguous and employing 'vague and imprecise language' by Judges McDonald and Vohrah of the ICTY Appeals Chamber. ICTY Statute, Art. 20(3); *Prosecutor* v. *Dražen Erdemović*, Case No. IT-96-22-A, Judgement, 7 October 1997 ('*Erdemović* Appeal Judgement'), Joint Separate Opinion of Judge McDonald and Judge Vohrah, para. 6.

[198] Erdemović's case was widely commented upon and noteworthy not only because he was the first accused to plead guilty at the ICTY, but also because he pleaded guilty without the benefit of an agreement with the Prosecutor. For a detailed explanation of the facts and circumstances surrounding his guilty plea, see Nancy Amoury Combs, 'Copping a Plea to Genocide: The Plea Bargaining of International Crimes', (2002) 151 *University of Pennsylvania Law Review* 1, 109–115.

[199] *Prosecutor* v. *Dražen Erdemović*, Case No. IT-96-22-T, Sentencing Judgement, 29 November 1996 ('*Erdemović* November 1996 Sentencing Judgement'), para. 11.

[200] *Ibid.*, para. 13 (emphasis in original).

[201] *Ibid.*, paras. 14–20.

Although the Appeals Chamber found that Erdemović's plea was not 'informed', it approved the Trial Chamber's exposition of the requirements for a valid guilty plea. Looking explicitly to the common law roots of the guilty plea disposition,[202] the Appeals Chamber concluded that to be valid, a guilty plea must be voluntary, informed, and unequivocal.[203] Following the *Erdemović* Appeal Judgement, the judges of each *ad hoc* Tribunal amended the Rules to incorporate these three elements, along with the requirement that the trial chamber be satisfied as to the existence of a sufficient factual basis for the crime charged and the accused's participation.[204] Except for subsequent amendment of both the ICTY and ICTR Rules to ensure that guilty pleas are entered before a full trial chamber rather than a single judge,[205] the fundamental procedure and the attendant legal requirements have not changed since Erdemović's case.

6.4.1.1 Legal requirements for a valid guilty plea

Given the relatively small number of accused who have opted to waive their right to a full trial,[206] the guilty plea disposition appears to play a comparatively minor

[202] *Erdemović* Appeal Judgement, *supra* note 197, Joint Separate Opinion of Judge McDonald and Judge Vohrah, para. 6 (noting that Rule 62 substantially reflected Rule 15 of the suggested rules of procedure and evidence offered by the United States).

[203] *Erdemović* Appeal Judgement, *supra* note 197, paras. 18–20 (noting each of the requirements and making reference to the reasoning set forth in the Joint Separate Opinion of Judge McDonald and Judge Vohrah); *ibid.*, Joint Separate Opinion of Judge McDonald and Judge Vohrah, paras. 8–9. The Appeals Chamber remanded the case to the Trial Chamber, which accepted the plea and considered duress to be a mitigating factor at sentencing. See Chapter 10, note 165.

[204] ICTY Rule 62 *bis*; ICTR Rule 62(B). Although the texts of the ICTY and ICTR rules are slightly different, there appears to be no substantive difference. Like the ICTY and the ICTR, the SCSL provides for the possibility of a guilty plea at the initial appearance, and its Rules, first adopted in 2002, included these requirements from their inception. SCSL Rules 61, 62. None of the accused before the SCSL ever opted to plead guilty.

[205] See ICTY Rule 62(A)(iii). This amendment followed an amendment to Rule 62 which permitted initial appearances to be held before single judges rather than full trial chambers.

[206] Of 161 accused indicted by the ICTY, twenty have pleaded guilty: Dražen Erdemović, Case No. IT-96-22 (plea on 14 January 1998; sentenced to five years); Goran Jelisić, Case No. IT-95-10 (plea on 29 October 1998; sentenced to forty years); Stevan Todorović, Case No. IT-95-9/1 (plea on 13 December 2000; sentenced to ten years); Dragan Kolundžija, Case No. IT-95-8 (plea on 4 September 2001; sentenced to three years); Damir Došen, Case No. IT-95-8 (plea on 19 September 2001; sentenced to five years); Duško Sikirica, Case No. IT-95-8 (plea on 19 September 2001; sentenced to fifteen years); Milan Simić, Case No. IT-95-9/2 (plea on 15 May 2002; sentenced to two concurrent terms of five years); Biljana Plavšić, Case No. IT-00-39 and 40/1 (plea on 2 October 2002; sentenced to eleven years); Momir Nikolić, Case No. IT-02-60/1 (plea on 7 May 2003; sentenced to twenty-seven years, reduced to twenty years by Appeals Chamber); Dragan Obrenović, Case No. IT-02-60/2 (plea on 21 May 2003; sentenced to seventeen years); Predrag Banović, Case No. IT-02-65/1 (plea on 26 June 2003; sentenced to eight years); Darko Mrđa, Case No. IT-02-59 (plea on 24 July 2003; sentenced to seventeen years); Miodrag Jokić, Case No. IT-01-42 (plea on 27 August 2003; sentenced to seven years); Dragan Nikolić, Case No. IT-94-2 (plea on 4 September 2003; sentenced to twenty-three years, reduced to twenty years by Appeals Chamber); Miroslav Deronjić, Case No. IT-02-61 (plea on 30 September 2003; sentenced to ten years); Ranko Češić, Case No. IT-95-10/1 (plea on 8 October 2003; sentenced to eighteen years); Milan Babić, Case No. IT-03-72 (plea on 27 January 2004; sentenced to thirteen years); Miroslav Bralo, Case No. IT-95-17 (plea on 19 July 2005; sentenced to twenty years); Ivica Rajić, Case No. IT-95-12 (plea on 26 October 2005; sentenced to twelve years); Dragan Zelenović, Case No. IT-96-23/2 (plea on 17 January 2007; sentenced to fifteen years). Eight accused indicted by the ICTR have pleaded guilty: Jean Kambanda, Case No. ICTR-97-23 (plea on 1 May 1998; sentenced to life imprisonment); Omar Serushago,

role in cases before international criminal tribunals.[207] One result is that the *ad hoc* Tribunals have little explored the legal requirements for a valid guilty plea since their establishment in *Erdemović*.[208] Indeed, most of the legal disputes attending guilty pleas since *Erdemović* have focused on the extent to which a guilty plea should be considered as a mitigating factor in the trial chamber's sentencing decision.[209]

6.4.1.1.1 Is the plea voluntary? The ICTY Appeals Chamber noted that it is a requirement in all common law jurisdictions that a guilty plea be made voluntarily, and that voluntariness includes two elements. First, the accused must be mentally competent to understand the consequences of pleading guilty. Second, the plea must not result from threats or inducements other than the expectation of a reduction in sentence. As described by one judge who participated in the *Erdemović* case, 'guilty pleas from those who are mentally incompetent to offer them, or which are the result of torture, threats or improper inducements, offend the international community's sense of fairness and justice and must not be accepted'.[210]

In principle, the competence prong of the inquiry would appear to be co-extensive with the requirement that the accused be competent to stand trial, a determination that the trial chamber has the authority to make with the consultation of experts.[211] After Erdemović's initial appearance and attempt to plead guilty, he was found to have been incompetent by a panel of experts. However, because Erdemović was adjudged competent to stand trial in a second analysis prior to the time when his guilty plea was again

Case No. ICTR-98-39 (plea on 14 December 1998; sentenced to fifteen years); Georges Ruggiu, Case No. ICTR-97-32 (plea on 15 May 2000; sentenced to two terms of twelve years to run concurrently); Vincent Rutaganira, Case No. ICTR-95-1 (plea on 8 December 2004; sentenced to six years); Joseph Serugendo, Case No. ICTR-05-84 (plea on 15 March 2005; sentenced to six years); Paul Bisengimana, Case No. ICTR-00-60 (plea on 7 December 2005; sentenced to fifteen years); Joseph Nzabirinda, Case No. ICTR-01-77 (plea on 14 December 2006; sentenced to seven years); Juvénal Rugambarara, Case No. ICTR-00-59 (plea on 13 July 2007; sentenced to eleven years).

[207] For some explanations why guilty plea dispositions have been used so sparingly at the ICTY and the ICTR, see *infra* Section 6.4.2.

[208] See, e.g., *Prosecutor* v. *Momir Nikolić*, Case No. IT-02-60/1-S, Sentencing Judgement, 2 December 2003 ('*Momir Nikolić* Sentencing Judgement'), para. 52 (merely noting the requirements that the guilty plea be voluntary, informed, and unequivocal, and citing the *Erdemović* Appeal Judgement, *supra* note 197, as authority).

[209] See Chapter 10, Section 10.2.2.5.

[210] Gabrielle Kirk McDonald, 'Trial Procedures and Practices', in Gabrielle Kirk McDonald and Olivia Swaak-Goldman (eds.), *Substantive and Procedural Aspects of International Criminal Law: The Experience of International and National Courts* (2000), pp. 575–576.

[211] See, e.g., ICTY Rule 74 *bis* (authorising the Trial Chamber, *proprio motu* or at the request of a party, to order a medical, psychiatric, or psychological examination of the accused). Competence to stand trial requires that the accused have at least the capacity to understand the nature of the charges, the course of the proceedings, the details of the evidence, and the consequences of the proceedings. Additionally, the accused must have the capacity to instruct counsel and to testify. This minimum standard is met 'when an accused has those capacities, viewed overall and in a reasonable and commonsense manner, at such a level that it is possible for the accused to participate in the proceedings … and sufficiently exercise the identified rights'. *Prosecutor* v. *Strugar*, Case No. IT-01-42-T, Decision Re the Defence Motion to Terminate the Proceedings, 26 May 2004, paras. 36–37. Additionally, the burden of proving incompetence rests upon the accused, using 'the balance of probabilities' as the standard of proof. *Ibid.*, para. 38. Accord *Prosecutor* v. *Strugar*, Case No. IT-01-42-A, Judgement, 17 July 2008, paras. 55–56.

made and formally accepted by the Trial Chamber, the Appeals Chamber stated that it had no doubt that he was competent to enter the plea.[212] Underscoring that competence to plead guilty is largely co-extensive with competence to stand trial, the ICTR Appeals Chamber in the *Kambanda* case found that an accused being depressed due to his isolation in detention did not rise to the level of incompetence to plead guilty.[213]

As for the second prong of the voluntariness inquiry, examples of inducements that will serve to invalidate a guilty plea include promises to discontinue improper harassment; misrepresentation, including unfulfilled or impossible promises; and promises, such as bribes, that by their nature have no proper relationship to the Prosecutor's authority.[214] The ICTR Appeals Chamber put it succinctly in the *Kambanda* case: '[N]o pressure must have been brought to bear upon [the accused] to sign the plea agreement'.[215] Thus, the inquiry appears to focus on threats or promises that are external to the appropriate scope of the Prosecutor's powers or to any agreement which underlies the plea. Accordingly, the ICTR Appeals Chamber has held that an accused's subsequently unfulfilled hope for a lighter sentence does not qualify as improper inducement which would negate the voluntary nature of the guilty plea, and it refused to invalidate a plea agreement on this ground.[216]

6.4.1.1.2 Is the plea informed? For a guilty plea to be informed, the accused must understand the charge or charges and the nature and consequences of the guilty plea. The *Erdemović* Appeals Chamber clarified that an informed plea requires that the accused understand (1) the nature of the charges and the consequences of pleading guilty generally; and (2) where applicable, the nature and distinction between alternative charges and the consequences of pleading guilty to one rather than the other.[217]

Erdemović's case remains emblematic of the informed plea requirement. The Appeals Chamber noted that Erdemović was not clearly told by the Trial Chamber that by pleading guilty he would lose his right to a trial. Moreover, the Appeals Chamber was not convinced that Erdemović's counsel fully appreciated that a guilty

[212] *Erdemović* Appeal Judgement, *supra* note 197, Joint Separate Opinion of Judge McDonald and Judge Vohrah, paras. 11–12. It is also worth noting that the Appeals Chamber implied that being incompetent to stand trial might not necessarily equate to incompetence to plead. Although it did not have to reach the issue because the second psychiatric report found Erdemović competent, the Appeals Chamber noted that it found persuasive the prosecution's argument that because the first report had focused on Erdemović's fitness to withstand the rigours of trial, it should not form the sole basis of any conclusion that Erdemović was also unfit to plead guilty. *Ibid.*, Joint Separate Opinion of Judge McDonald and Judge Vohrah, para. 12.

[213] *Prosecutor* v. *Kambanda*, Case No. ICTR-97-23-A, Judgement, 19 October 2000 ('*Kambanda* Judgement on Sentencing Appeal'), para. 62.

[214] *Erdemović* Appeal Judgement, *supra* note 197, Joint Separate Opinion of Judge McDonald and Judge Vohrah, para. 10 (quoting approvingly from the U.S. Supreme Court's opinion in *Brady* v. *United States*, 397 U.S. 742 (1970)).

[215] *Kambanda* Judgement on Sentencing Appeal, *supra* note 213, para. 61.

[216] *Ibid.*, para. 63 (noting that the accused could not subsequently claim his guilty plea was involuntary simply because he received a life sentence after pleading guilty in the hope of receiving a lesser sentence).

[217] *Erdemović* Appeal Judgement, *supra* note 197, Joint Separate Opinion of Judge McDonald and Judge Vohrah, para. 14; *Kambanda* Judgement on Sentencing Appeal, *supra* note 213, para. 75.

plea would finally decide the issue of conviction or acquittal. Finally, the Appeals Chamber was deeply concerned that neither Erdemović nor his counsel had a full understanding of the nature of – or fundamental differences between – war crimes and crimes against humanity. Nor had the Trial Chamber adequately informed Erdemović of those differences, and the Appeals Chamber was convinced that Erdemović unknowingly pleaded guilty to a more serious charge – murder as a crime against humanity rather than as a war crime – than he otherwise would have.[218]

6.4.1.1.3 Is the plea unequivocal? At first blush, the requirement that a guilty plea be unequivocal might appear linguistically similar to the voluntariness requirement. However, it is conceptually separate and depends on a consideration of whether the plea is accompanied or qualified by words describing facts which establish a recognised defence in law.[219] Here again, *Erdemović* represents the high-water mark in the jurisprudence. While pleading guilty, Erdemović appeared to be maintaining that his (otherwise) criminal acts were legally justified. Only after the Appeals Chamber concluded that duress was not available as a legal justification precluding criminal responsibility could it find that Erdemović's plea was unequivocal. According to the *Erdemović* Appeals Chamber, this requirement upholds the presumption of innocence and protects the accused against an unwitting forfeiture of the right to a trial where the accused appears to have a defence he or she may not realise.[220] *Kambanda* is illustrative of the discrete and narrow character of the inquiry into whether the accused's plea is unequivocal. In rejecting Kambanda's claim that his guilty plea had been equivocal, the ICTR Appeals Chamber noted that, unlike Erdemović, Kambanda had never raised – much less persisted in – any explanation of his actions that would have amounted to a legal defence to the charges.[221]

6.4.1.2 The plea proceeding

Guilty pleas at the *ad hoc* Tribunals follow extensive consultation between the accused and defence counsel, who bears initial responsibility for ensuring that the accused fully understands the nature and consequences of the decision to plead

[218] *Erdemović* Appeal Judgement, *supra* note 197, Joint Separate Opinion of Judge McDonald and Judge Vohrah, paras. 15–19. Despite this holding, the *ad hoc* Tribunals' Appeals Chambers subsequently ruled that there is no hierarchy in the crimes within their jurisdiction. For criticism of this holding, see Boas, Bischoff, and Reid, *Elements of Crimes*, *supra* note 40, pp. 141–142, 363–367; see also Chapter 10, Section 10.2.2.1.1.

[219] *Erdemović* Appeal Judgement, *supra* note 197, Joint Separate Opinion of Judge McDonald and Judge Vohrah, para. 31. See also *Kambanda* Judgement on Sentencing Appeal, *supra* note 213, para. 85 (noting that Kambanda had not persisted in explaining his actions either at the time he pleaded guilty or later at the sentencing hearing).

[220] *Erdemović* Appeal Judgement, *supra* note 197, Joint Separate Opinion of Judge McDonald and Judge Vohrah, para. 29.

[221] *Kambanda* Judgement on Sentencing Appeal, *supra* note 213, paras. 79, 85.

guilty.[222] Final responsibility for ensuring the validity of the plea, however, rests squarely with the trial chamber. Considering the grave consequences of a guilty plea – a disposition characterised by one domestic court as 'a solemn act not to be disregarded because of belated misgivings about [its] wisdom'[223] – the ICTY and ICTR Rules are decidedly minimalist in approach, requiring only that the trial chamber satisfy itself that the requirements are met, without further reference to any specific advisements to be made or questions to be asked.[224]

Lacking further guidance in the Rules themselves, trial chambers at the *ad hoc* Tribunals have taken widely varying approaches to the manner in which they satisfy themselves as to the legal validity of guilty pleas. During the formal acceptance of the plea, some have been content to accept one- or two-word responses to broad inquiries tracking the text of the pertinent rules.[225] Others have asked detailed questions and examined the accused regarding his or her knowledge of the charges and the rights being waived.[226] This diversity of approach has prompted at least one commentator to criticise the 'bare-bones' nature of the rules, arguing that each of the trial rights the accused is forfeiting by pleading guilty should appear in the text of the rules and that the accused should be examined closely by the trial chamber with regard to each of them.[227] In at least a partial answer to this concern, written plea agreements at the *ad hoc* Tribunals often list the individual trial rights the accused is giving up.[228] Attached to the written agreement are signed

[222] For a good discussion of the issues facing defence counsel in this regard, see Rodney Dixon and Alexis Demirdjian, 'Advising Defendants About Guilty Pleas Before International Courts' (2005) 3 *Journal of International Criminal Justice* 680. See also Cook, *supra* note 194, p. 502.

[223] *United States* v. *Morrison*, 967 F.2d 264, 268 (8th Cir. 1992).

[224] ICTY Rule 62 *bis*; ICTR Rule 62(B).

[225] For example, the trial chamber's inquiry into the validity of Biljana Plavšić's plea agreement was exceedingly short. Judge May asked, 'Mrs. Plavšić, in the plea agreement which we have read, you signed a declaration that you entered into the agreement freely and voluntarily, understanding its terms, and have been advised by your lawyers. You have also signed a statement to the same effect in which is added that the plea is informed and unequivocal. Do you confirm that these declarations are correct?' Plavšić answered, 'I do', which was enough for the Trial Chamber. *Prosecutor* v. *Plavsić*, Case No. IT-00-39 and 40-I, Transcript, 2 October 2002, p. 338. See also *Prosecutor* v. *Češić*, Case No. IT-95-10/1-PT, Transcript, 8 October 2003, pp. 71–72 (with the accused being asked by the Trial Chamber whether he came to the agreement of his own free will, not being forced or threatened in any way, and answering, 'Yes, Your Honour').

[226] Indeed, such questioning has at times revealed that the accused was not fully aware of the consequences of the plea, or was not in agreement with the characterisation of his or her conduct. See, e.g., *Prosecutor* v. *Kunarac*, Case No. IT-96-23-I, Transcript, 13 March 1998, pp. 22–46 (with Judge Cassese noting during Kunarac's attempt to plead guilty that it was clear that the Chamber could only enter a not guilty plea, and further noting that the accused appeared not to have been well advised by counsel, thereby putting the Chamber in an awkward position).

[227] See Cook, *supra* note 194, pp. 481, 502 (arguing that the trial chamber should examine the accused regarding the right to be presumed innocent and to have guilt proven beyond a reasonable doubt; the right to call witnesses on the accused's behalf; the right to examine the witnesses against the accused; the right to be tried without undue delay; the right not to be compelled to be a witness against oneself; the fact that the trial chamber is not bound to follow any sentencing recommendations and has the authority to impose a life sentence; the elements of the crime(s) to which the accused is pleading guilty; the facts in support of the plea; and whether the plea is the product of undue threats or inducements).

[228] See, e.g., *Prosecutor* v. *Blagojević, Obrenović, Jokić, and Nikolić*, Case No. IT-02-60-PT, Joint Motion for Consideration of Amended Plea Agreement Between Momir Nikolić and the Office of the Prosecutor,

declarations by the accused and defence counsel that the accused has carefully read and reviewed every part of the written agreement, and that the accused has been fully advised of his or her rights and of the consequences of the plea, including the maximum possible sentence.[229]

6.4.2 Plea bargaining at the **ad hoc** *Tribunals*

Plea bargaining generally occurs in two forms: sentence bargaining, in the form of prosecutorial concessions to recommend a lesser sentence in exchange for a guilty plea to the charged counts, and charge bargaining, with the prosecution agreeing to ask the trial chamber to dismiss a count or counts in exchange for the guilty plea. Both forms of bargaining have been used at the *ad hoc* Tribunals, the latter garnering more controversial attention for what some observers consider its potential to distort the truth-telling aim of international criminal justice by failing to capture the full scope of the accused's criminal acts.[230]

As with the contours of the guilty plea proceeding itself, the parties' plea negotiation powers at the *ad hoc* Tribunals are not addressed in the Statutes, nor did the Rules as originally adopted address the practice.[231] This changed in 2001, however, when the ICTY adopted Rule 62 *ter* – largely a codification of existing practice – which described the negotiation powers of the Prosecutor and the attendant authority of the trial chamber.[232] The ICTR's judges followed suit shortly thereafter in ICTR Rule 62 *ter.* The Rule provides that the Prosecutor and the accused may agree that, in exchange for a plea of guilty on one or more counts in the indictment, the Prosecutor shall do one or more of the following: (1) apply to amend the indictment; (2) submit that a specific sentence or sentencing range is appropriate;

7 May 2003 ('Momir Nikolić Plea Agreement'), para. 17; *Prosecutor* v. *Blagojević, Obrenović, and Jokić*, Case No. IT-02-60-T, Joint Motion for Consideration of Plea Agreement Between Dragan Obrenović and the Office of the Prosecutor, 20 May 2003 ('Obrenović Plea Agreement'), para. 17; *Prosecutor* v. *Sikirica*, Case No. IT-95-8-T, Joint Submission of the Prosecution and the Accused Duško Sikirica Concerning a Plea Agreement and Admitted Facts, 6 September 2001 ('Sikirica Plea Agreement'), para. 4. Plea agreements at the ICTR seem to be somewhat less extensive in listing the rights being waived. See, e.g., *Prosecutor* v. *Bisengimana*, Case No. ICTR-2000-60-I, Joint Motion for Consideration of a Guilty Plea Agreement Between Paul Bisengimana and the Office of the Prosecutor, 30 November 2005 ('Bisengimana Plea Agreement'), para. 51.

229 See, e.g., Momir Nikolić Plea Agreement, *supra* note 228, pp. 6–7; Obrenović Plea Agreement, *supra* note 228, pp. 8–9; Sikirica Plea Agreement, *supra* note 228, pp. 11–12; Bisengimana Plea Agreement, *supra* note 228, paras. 52–53.

230 See, e.g., Ralph Henham and Mark Dumbl, 'Plea Bargaining at the International Criminal Tribunal for the Former Yugoslavia', (2005) 16 *Criminal Law Forum* 49, 81–82 (noting that when charges are dismissed the plea bargain 'may bury allegations and consequently erase those victims and bar the determination of the truths of their claims').

231 For a detailed exposition and analysis of plea agreements at the *ad hoc* Tribunals through 2005, see Combs, *supra* note 194, chs. 4–5. For a similar analysis specific to plea agreements at the ICTY, see generally Cook, *supra* note 194.

232 The ICTR adopted an identical rule in 2003. See ICTR Rule 62 *bis*.

or (3) not oppose a request by the accused for a particular sentence or sentencing range.[233] Any negotiated agreement must be disclosed in open session, unless good cause can be shown for this occurring in closed session.[234] Additionally, both the accused and the Prosecutor may submit to the trial chamber any relevant information that might assist in determining the appropriate sentence.[235]

With regard to the sentence, Rule 62 *ter* provides that the trial chamber is not bound by the agreement.[236] Although the judges have often stressed that they are in no way bound by the parties' agreements or expectations, most sentences following a guilty plea disposition are within the range contemplated by the parties.[237] As discussed below, however, some trial chambers have imposed sentences significantly in excess of the prosecution's recommendation.[238] While reiterating the independence of the judges, the Appeals Chamber has said that any deviation from the agreed-upon terms must be explained.[239]

The plea agreements reached in cases before the *ad hoc* Tribunals are quite detailed and, although generally outlined initially to the trial chamber in confidential pleadings, are made public during the plea proceedings and memorialised in the subsequent sentencing judgements.[240] Standard terms include an agreement between the parties as to the factual basis underlying the plea;[241] if applicable, a request by the prosecution to withdraw a charge or charges;[242] an acknowledgement

[233] ICTY Rule 62 *ter*(A). Accord ICTR Rule 62 *bis*(A). The SCSL has no equivalent rule, despite the fact that the SCSL Rules provide for the possibility of guilty pleas. See *supra* note 204.

[234] ICTY Rule 62 *ter*(C); ICTR Rule 62 *bis*(B). 'Closed session' proceedings are discussed in Chapter 7, Section 7.4.1.

[235] ICTY Rule 100(A); ICTR Rule 100(A).

[236] ICTY Rule 62 *ter*(B); ICTR Rule 62 *bis*(C).

[237] The most recent guilty plea dispositions at the *ad hoc* Tribunals are illustrative. At the ICTY, Dragan Zelenović agreed to plead guilty to three counts of torture and four counts of rape as crimes against humanity. The prosecution agreed to withdraw all remaining counts and to recommend a sentence of ten to fifteen years (as against Zelenović's recommended sentence of seven to ten years). The Trial Chamber sentenced Zelenović to fifteen years, which was confirmed by the Appeals Chamber. *Prosecutor* v. *Zelenović*, Case No. IT-96-23/2-S, Sentencing Judgement, 4 April 2007 ('*Zelenović* Sentencing Judgement'), paras. 10–13, affirmed by *Prosecutor* v. *Zelenović*, Case No. IT-96-23/2-A, Judgement on Sentencing Appeal, 31 October 2007, p. 13. At the ICTR, Juvénal Rugambarara agreed to plead guilty to one count of extermination as a crime against humanity and the prosecution agreed to recommend a sentence between nine and twelve years. Rugambarara made no specific sentencing suggestion and the Trial Chamber sentenced him to eleven years' imprisonment. *Prosecutor* v. *Rugambarara*, Case No. ICTR-00-59-T, Sentencing Judgement, 16 November 2007 ('*Rugambarara* Sentencing Judgement'), paras. 4–9, 48–49, 61.

[238] See *infra* text accompanying notes 252–255.

[239] *Prosecutor* v. *Babić*, Case No. IT-03-72-A, Judgement on Sentencing Appeal, 18 July 2005, para. 30; *Prosecutor* v. *Dragan Nikolić*, Case No. IT-94-2-A, Judgement on Sentencing Appeal, 4 February 2005 ('*Dragan Nikolić* Judgement on Sentencing Appeal'), para. 89.

[240] Sentencing judgements are discussed in Chapter 10, Section 10.1.6.

[241] See, e.g., Momir Nikolić Plea Agreement, *supra* note 228, para. 7 (making reference to the facts and allegations outlined in specific paragraphs of the indictment); Obrenović Plea Agreement, *supra* note 228, para. 7 (same); Sikirica Plea Agreement, *supra* note 228, paras. 6–16 (listing detailed facts regarding the role of the accused in the crimes to which he plead guilty); Bisengimana Plea Agreement, *supra* note 228, paras. 23–42.

[242] See, e.g., Momir Nikolić Plea Agreement, *supra* note 228, para. 4; Obrenović Plea Agreement, *supra* note 228, para. 4; Sikirica Plea Agreement, *supra* note 228, paras. 6–16 (with the Prosecutor agreeing not

that the accused understands the rights being waived;[243] and an acknowledgement by the prosecution that it will recommend either a specific sentence or sentencing range, or that it will not oppose the specified sentence or range that the accused intends to suggest.[244] A common term present in ICTY plea agreements is an undertaking by the accused to provide full cooperation to the Prosecutor, including testifying in other cases before the Tribunal,[245] and many accused convicted pursuant to guilty pleas have provided valuable testimony against other accused.[246] At times, however, such convicted persons have behaved contumaciously when called upon to fulfil their end of the bargain.[247] A common term of more recent plea agreements at the ICTR is an agreement that the Prosecutor will support the accused's request to serve his imprisonment in a European country.[248]

to appeal the Trial Chamber's Rule 98 *bis* mid-trial acquittal of the accused on the remaining charges); Bisengimana Plea Agreement, *supra* note 228, paras. 46–47 (with the prosecutor also agreeing not to refer any case against the accused to any other jurisdiction).

243 See, e.g., Momir Nikolić Plea Agreement, *supra* note 228, para. 17; Obrenović Plea Agreement, *supra* note 228, para. 17; Sikirica Plea Agreement, *supra* note 228, paras. 3–4; Bisengimana Plea Agreement, *supra* note 228, paras. 51–52.

244 See, e.g., Momir Nikolić Plea Agreement, *supra* note 228, para. 4; Obrenović Plea Agreement, *supra* note 228, para. 4; Sikirica Plea Agreement, *supra* note 228, para. 17; Bisengimana Plea Agreement, *supra* note 228, para. 48.

245 See, e.g., *Zelenović* Sentencing Judgement, *supra* note 237, paras. 10–13; Momir Nikolić Plea Agreement, *supra* note 228, paras. 9–11 (outlining Nikolić's cooperation obligations, including: meeting as often as necessary with the prosecutor to provide full and complete information and evidence regarding the attack and fall of the Srebrenica enclave in July 1995; truthfully, candidly, and freely answering all questions put to him by the prosecution; and testifying truthfully in any trials, hearings, or other proceedings as requested by the prosecution, without minimising his own involvement or fabricating the involvement of others); Obrenović Plea Agreement, *supra* note 228, paras. 9–11 (outlining the same obligations). Although apparently not an explicit term of the agreement, at least one accused at the ICTR 'offered' his full cooperation to the Prosecutor, although the Trial Chamber declined to consider such cooperation as a mitigating factor at sentencing. *See Prosecutor* v. *Nzabirinda*, Case No. ICTR-01-77-T, Sentencing Judgement, 23 February 2007 ('*Nzabirinda* Sentencing Judgement'), para. 97. Trial chambers consider cooperation with the prosecution, including testifying in subsequent trials, as a mitigating factor in sentencing. See Chapter 10, Section 10.2.2.3.

246 See, e.g., *Prosecutor* v. *Babić*, Case No. IT-03-72-S, Sentencing Judgement, 29 June 2004 ('*Babić* Sentencing Judgement'), para. 73 (noting that Babić testified in the proceedings against Slobodan Milošević, providing far-reaching insight into the decision-making, operation, and plans of the joint criminal enterprise around Milošević which no other insider witness had been able to provide).

247 Momir Nikolić, for example, pleaded guilty and agreed to provide substantial cooperation to the prosecution, although the trial chamber in accepting his guilty plea was less than impressed with his testimony in the *Blagojević and Jokić* case. Although the Appeals Chamber overturned the Trial Chamber's finding on this point, *Prosecutor* v. *Momir Nikolić*, Case No. IT-02-60/1-A, Judgement on Sentencing Appeal, 8 March 2006 ('*Momir Nikolić* Judgement on Sentencing Appeal'), paras. 98–103 (Appeals Chamber finding that the Trial Chamber committed a discernible error in finding Nikolić's testimony evasive at trial), the Trial Chamber might have had a better insight into the sincerity with which Nikolić expected to fulfil his agreement to provide substantial cooperation. See also Chapter 10, Section 10.2.2.3 (discussing Appeals Chamber's reduction of Nikolić's sentence upon finding that the Trial Chamber had underestimated Nikolić's degree of cooperation with the prosecution). Two years later, the prosecution in the *Popović* case dropped Nikolić from its witness list, explaining that Nikolić had become 'adverse to the Prosecution's case'. *Prosecutor* v. *Popović, Beara, Nikolić, Miletić, Borovčanin, Gvero, and Pandurević*, Case No. IT-05-88-T, Transcript, 2 November 2007, p. 17398. The *Popović* Trial Chamber itself later summoned Nikolić to testify as a chamber witness. *Prosecutor* v. *Popović, Beara, Nikolić, Miletić, Borovčanin, Gvero, and Pandurević*, Case No. IT-05-88-T, Order to Summon Momir Nikolić, 10 March 2009, pp. 2–3.

248 See, e.g., Bisengimana Plea Agreement, *supra* note 228, para. 49. When such requests are made, the trial chamber acknowledges the parties' submissions and notes that decisions regarding the location of the

Nancy Combs has analysed the ebb and flow of the evolution of plea bargaining at the *ad hoc* Tribunals, and argues that the attractiveness of negotiated dispositions at the ICTY depends greatly on the certainty of sentence discounts, something which itself is tied directly to the acceptance of the practice by the judges.[249] The primary incentive for most accused to enter any bargain with the prosecution is the expectation of more certainty with regard to the sentence. The greater the likelihood of substantial upward divergence from the agreed-upon terms, the less attractive any such bargain becomes. Yet judges at both the ICTY and the ICTR have demonstrated a willingness to impose sentences that exceed the accused's expectations. Indeed, the practice got off to a particularly bad start in the ICTR in 1998 with the guilty plea of Jean Kambanda, who received a life sentence from the judges despite his substantial cooperation with the prosecution.[250] Although other factors also played a role in the infrequency with which ICTR accused have chosen to plead guilty – especially in the Tribunal's early years – no ICTR accused following Kambanda could have found much comfort in the prospect of pleading guilty.[251]

Judges at the ICTY have also demonstrated a willingness to impose higher sentences than expected, most dramatically in the cases of Dragan Nikolić and Momir Nikolić. In Momir Nikolić's case, the prosecution recommended a sentence of fifteen to twenty years, while the accused argued for a ten-year term. Rejecting both recommendations, the Trial Chamber sentenced him to twenty-seven years.[252] In Dragan Nikolić's case, the prosecution recommended fifteen years and the Trial Chamber imposed twenty-three years.[253] Although the Appeals Chamber later reduced both men's sentence to twenty years,[254] the attractiveness of negotiated dispositions at the ICTY was greatly diminished. Few accused at the ICTY have since pleaded guilty.[255]

accused's incarceration are to be made by the Tribunal's President, in consultation with the trial chamber. See *Rugambarara* Sentencing Judgement, *supra* note 237, paras. 4–9, 48–49, 61; *Nzabirinda* Sentencing Judgement, *supra* note 245, paras. 97, 119; *Prosecutor* v. *Bisengimana*, Case No. ICTR-00-60-T, Judgement and Sentence, 13 April 2006, paras. 187, 203.

249 See Combs, *supra* note 191, pp. 92–100; Combs, *supra* note 194, pp. 89–90. See also Combs, *supra* note 191, p. 75 (noting that to induce an accused to plead guilty, a prosecutor must be able to offer the accused a fairly certain sentence reduction in exchange for the plea).

250 See Steven R. Ratner, Jason S. Abrams, and James L. Bischoff, *Accountability for Atrocities in International Law: Beyond the Nuremberg Legacy* (3rd edn 2009), pp. 227–228.

251 See *ibid.* See also Combs, *supra* note 191, pp. 118–124 (explaining that guilty pleas at the ICTR were rare prior to 2004 as most accused refused to accept that genocide occurred at all).

252 *Momir Nikolić* Sentencing Judgement, *supra* note 208, paras. 180, 183. Compared to many of the sentences imposed on persons convicted before the ICTY, Nikolić's sentence to twenty-seven years of imprisonment was high. For a thorough discussion of sentencing, see Chapter 10.

253 *Prosecutor* v. *Dragan Nikolić*, Case No. IT-94-2-S, Sentencing Judgement, 18 December 2003, paras. 275–284.

254 *Momir Nikolić* Judgement on Sentencing Appeal, *supra* note 247, para. 135; *Dragan Nikolić* Judgement on Sentencing Appeal, *supra* note 239, p. 44.

255 See Combs, *supra* note 191, p. 99 (noting that the primary reason the ICTY obtained fewer guilty pleas after 2003 was because the sentences imposed on Momir Nikolić, Dragan Nikolić, and Milan Babić resulted in ICTY accused no longer having the requisite certainty of receiving the sentence discounts they had bargained

6.4.3 Admissions of guilt and plea bargaining at the ICC

As a result of the two-step process leading to confirmation or rejection of proposed charges,[256] the ICC has no procedural equivalent of the initial appearances held at the *ad hoc* Tribunals. Moreover, it does not recognise a 'guilty plea' as such. Rather, Article 64 of the Rome Statute – in the context of addressing the functions and powers of the trial chamber – refers to affording the accused 'the opportunity to make an admission of guilt … or to plead not guilty'.[257] Terms such as 'guilty plea' were deliberately rejected at the Rome Conference, and while the applicable procedural provisions attending an admission of guilt impose similar responsibilities on the Court and provide similar protections to the accused as those attending a guilty plea proceeding at the *ad hoc* Tribunals, the process itself is quite different.[258] Where an accused before the *ad hoc* Tribunals might plead guilty as early as the initial appearance, an accused before the ICC is only afforded the opportunity to make an admission of guilt at the commencement of the trial.[259]

In principle – no accused before the ICC having yet exercised the option – the legal requirements for a valid admission of guilt are virtually identical to those for a valid guilty plea at the *ad hoc* Tribunals. The trial chamber must be satisfied that: (1) the accused understands the nature and consequences of his or her admission; (2) the admission is voluntarily made after sufficient consultation with defence counsel; and (3) the admission is supported by a sufficient factual basis.[260] There are, however, two differences between the ICC's admission of guilt and the *ad hoc* Tribunals' guilty pleas. The first – that the voluntariness inquiry requires the accused to have been afforded 'sufficient' consultation with counsel – seems minor. In cases where the accused is represented by counsel, this addition to the voluntariness inquiry may be a distinction without a difference, albeit one with potential implications for any subsequent ineffective assistance of counsel

for with the prosecution). Although less dramatic than either Dragan Nikolić's or Momir Nikolić's case, the Trial Chamber that accepted Milan Babić's guilty plea also imposed a thirteen-year sentence, two years longer than the sentence recommended by the prosecution. See generally *Babić* Sentencing Judgement, *supra* note 246.

256 See *supra* Section 6.1.1.

257 Rome Statute, Art. 64(8)(a). See also Fabricio Guariglia, 'Article 65', in Otto Triffterer (ed.), *Commentary on the Rome Statute of the International Criminal Court: Observers' Notes, Article by Article* (1999), pp. 825–826 (describing Article 65 as following a 'third avenue' between the classic common law and civil law approaches, with parallels in both, and noting that the clear-cut distinctions between the common law guilty plea and the civil law concept of summary or abbreviated procedures have been substantially eroded at the domestic level); Safferling, *supra* note 193, pp. 275–276 (noting that, in general, Article 65 of the Rome Statute treats the admission of guilt in the same way in which confessions by the accused are treated in continental Europe).

258 See Silvia A. Fernández de Gurmendi, 'International Criminal Law Procedures', in Roy S. Lee (ed.), *The International Criminal Court: The Making of the Rome Statute* (1999), pp. 241–242 (describing the negotiations leading to the construction of Article 65); Guariglia, *supra* note 257, pp. 824, 831.

259 Rome Statute, Art. 64(8)(a). See Chapter 3, Section 3.2.3.2.3 (discussing case law on the various different meanings of 'commencement of trial' in the Rome Statute).

260 Rome Statute, Art. 65(1).

allegation.[261] The second difference is the omission of any requirement that the admission of guilt be unequivocal. Whether this constitutes a substantive difference seems doubtful, however. It is difficult to imagine that an admission could be appropriately characterised as one made with a genuine understanding of the admission's nature and consequences if it is 'accompanied or qualified by words describing facts which establish a defence in law'.[262] Moreover, any such equivocation should also signal that the accused has certainly not had sufficient consultation with competent counsel, and the trial chamber would be remiss in accepting such an admission as valid.

As at the *ad hoc* Tribunals, where the trial chamber is satisfied as to the three requirements for a valid admission of guilt, it is required to consider the admission as establishing all the essential facts that are required to prove the crime to which the admission relates.[263] The trial chamber nevertheless retains discretion as to whether to enter a conviction despite the fact that the crime has been established. This discretion is directly related to Article 65(4), which permits the trial chamber to set the case for trial, or request the Prosecutor to present additional evidence, where it is of the opinion that this would be in the interests of justice, particularly with regard to the interests of victims.[264] The extent of any abbreviated procedures short of setting the case for a full trial – something which seems unnecessarily burdensome and costly where the accused truly does not wish to contest guilt – is wholly within the discretion of the trial chamber.

Despite the formal procedural differences, an accused before the ICC does not seem to be in an appreciably different position vis-à-vis admitting guilt and negotiating with the Prosecutor than an accused before the *ad hoc* Tribunals. It has been noted that, in principle, nothing in the Rome Statute prevents plea bargaining at the ICC.[265] In practice, however, whether the Prosecutor can bargain effectively may depend entirely on the ICC's judges. That the ICC's judges are not bound by any negotiations between the parties puts them in no different position than the

[261] Additionally, whether the text of the rule forecloses an admission of guilt by a self-represented accused will undoubtedly be tested at some point, and largely may depend on the evolving jurisprudence regarding the nature of the right to self-representation. See Chapter 5, Section 5.3.

[262] *Erdemović* Appeal Judgement, *supra* note 197, Joint Separate Opinion of Judge McDonald and Judge Vohrah, para. 31.

[263] Rome Statute, Art. 65(2).

[264] *Ibid.*, Arts. 65(2), 65(4). But see Guariglia, *supra* note 257, p. 829 (noting that one potential interpretation of this language could give leeway to the trial chamber to acquit an accused if it considers that the admission of guilt is not supported by a factual basis and that a full trial would not modify that situation).

[265] Robert Cryer, Håkan Friman, Darryl Robinson, and Elizabeth Wilmshurst, *An Introduction to International Criminal Law and Procedure* (2007), pp. 384–386. Virtually mirroring the Rome Statute, the Regulations of East Timor's Special Panels for Serious Crimes provided for the accused to make an admission of guilt, and similarly empowered the court to require a more complete presentation of evidence. See United Nations Transitional Administration in East Timor, Regulation No. 2000/30 on Transitional Rules of Criminal Procedure, UN Doc. UNTAET/REG/2000/30, 25 September 2000, as amended by Regulation No. 2001/25 of 14 September 2001, Section 29A. Combs has noted, however, that by the time the Special Panels closed in 2005, approximately half of its cases had been disposed of by guilty pleas. Combs, *supra* note 194, p. 117.

judges at the *ad hoc* Tribunals. That the ICC's judges may require additional evidence does not mean that they will require unnecessary trial-like proceedings.[266] Additionally, the extent to which the accused has a 'right' to plead guilty – as implied by the *Erdemović* Trial Chamber's assertion that the guilty plea is part of the right to adopt a defence strategy[267] – is yet to be explored.

6.5 Disclosure and its limits

Mirroring fundamental human rights protections, the international criminal tribunals secure to each accused the right to adequate time and facilities to prepare a defence.[268] Thus, the accused is entitled to discover the evidence which the prosecution will lead in its case against him or her in a timely and complete fashion. Additionally, the accused is entitled to the disclosure of materials of an exculpatory character, without regard to whether the materials are admissible at trial. The duty of appropriate disclosure to the accused rests squarely upon the prosecution, with the judges playing a largely passive oversight role.

While the accused's rights to discover evidence are extensive, they are not limitless. Certain materials may be withheld from the accused, temporarily or indefinitely, to the extent necessary to protect the security interests of victims, witnesses, or states. In all instances, the protection of such materials is subject to strict regulation by the judges. Nor is the accused free from disclosure obligations, as the prosecution is also – to varying degrees across the international criminal tribunals – entitled to discover the evidence upon which the accused will rely at trial. Because of the importance of timely disclosure to the parties' capacities to prepare for trial, the violation of disclosure obligations by either party is subject to sanctions by the judges.

6.5.1 Disclosure by the prosecution

Materials subject to the prosecution's duties of disclosure fall broadly into two categories: (1) non-exculpatory evidence or supporting materials which the prosecution has used to secure charges against the accused, or which it will lead against the accused at trial, or which are otherwise material to the preparation of the defence; and (2) material of an exculpatory character, whether or not the prosecution will lead it as evidence against the accused. As discussed below, for the broad range of

[266] See ICC Rule 139 (permitting the trial chamber to seek the views of the accused and the prosecution as to whether additional evidence should be required, and requiring the trial chamber to put its reasons for its decisions on the record).

[267] *Erdemović* November 1996 Sentencing Judgement, *supra* note 199, para. 13.

[268] ICCPR, Art. 14(3)(b); Rome Statute, Art. 67(1)(b); ICTY Statute, Art. 21(4)(b); ICTR Statute, Art. 20(4)(b); SCSL Statute, Art. 17(4)(b).

materials falling in the first category, different time-limits for disclosure are applicable, depending upon the nature of the materials and the particular rules of the tribunal in question. Additionally, the prosecution's duty to disclose some materials within this category is triggered only by a specific defence request. Disclosure of materials of an exculpatory character, by contrast, never requires a specific defence request. Moreover, the prosecution's duty is to disclose exculpatory materials 'as soon as practicable'.[269]

6.5.1.1 Non-exculpatory materials

In general, disclosure to the accused of non-exculpatory materials at the ICTY, ICTR, and SCSL takes place in defined stages. While certain disclosure is automatic, some require a specific defence request. The prosecution's first disclosure duties are automatically triggered by the accused's initial appearance. Within thirty days of the initial appearance of an accused at the ICTY and ICTR, the prosecution must make available to the accused the supporting materials accompanying the indictment, as well as all prior statements of the accused obtained by the prosecution.[270]

Next, within a time limit established by the trial chamber or pre-trial judge at the ICTY, and no later than sixty days before trial at the ICTR, the prosecution must disclose the statements of all witnesses it intends to call to testify at trial, as well as all transcripts and statements it intends to introduce in written form.[271] The SCSL accelerates this aspect of prosecution disclosure, requiring the statements of witnesses and written evidence in lieu of testimony to be disclosed within thirty days of the accused's initial appearance.[272] At all three tribunals, for any witnesses the prosecution subsequently decides to call at trial, or any written evidence the prosecution subsequently decides to lead, similar disclosure is to be made at the time of the prosecution's decision.[273] Additionally, the prosecution's disclosure obligation

[269] Rome Statute, Art. 67(2); ICTY Rule 68(i); ICTR Rule 68(A). While the 'as soon as practicable' language does not appear in the SCSL Rules, the SCSL Prosecutor's obligation to disclose exculpatory materials arises 'within 30 days of the initial appearance of the accused'. SCSL Rule 68(B). Subsequently, however, the SCSL Prosecutor is under a continuing duty to disclose such material, presumably as soon as practicable. *Ibid.*

[270] ICTY Rule 66(A)(i); ICTR Rule 66(A)(i). 'Supporting material' means the material submitted to the confirming judge and does not include other material such as a brief of arguments or statement of facts. See, e.g., *Prosecutor* v. *Kordić and Čerkez*, Case No. IT-95-14/2-PT, Order on Motion to Compel Compliance by the Prosecutor with Rules 66(A) and 68, 26 February 1999, p. 3. 'Prior statements' include not only statements made by the accused to the prosecution but statements made by the accused in any type of judicial proceeding which the prosecution has in its possession. *Ibid.* Prior statements also include the transcriptions required to be made from any audio- or video-recorded interviews of the accused with the prosecution. See, e.g., *Prosecutor* v. *Čermak and Markač*, Case No. IT-03-73-PT, Decision Relating to Prosecutor's Disclosure Obligation, 26 May 2004, para. 4.

[271] ICTY Rule 66(A)(ii); ICTR Rule 66(A)(ii). Regarding written evidence in lieu of testimony, see Chapter 9, Section 9.2.1.1.

[272] SCSL Rule 66(A)(i).

[273] ICTY Rule 66(A)(ii); ICTR Rule 66(A); SCSL Rule 66(A)(ii) (with the additional caveat that such disclosure should be not later than sixty days prior to the trial, except upon good cause being shown).

is a continuous one, such that new witness statements which come into the prosecution's possession after initial disclosure has been made must be disclosed on an ongoing basis.[274]

Upon a specific defence request, the prosecution shall permit the defence to inspect any books, documents, photographs, and tangible objects in the prosecution's custody or control, which are material to the preparation of the defence or which the prosecution intends to lead as evidence at trial, or which were obtained from or belonged to the accused.[275] With regard to inspecting items which are 'material to the preparation of the defence', the ICTR Appeals Chamber has used an expansive construction of preparation, characterising it as 'a broad concept … [that] does not necessarily require that the material itself counter the Prosecution evidence'.[276] Thus, the obligation to permit inspection includes statements of potential witnesses whom the prosecution has never intended to call at trial, and even the statements of defence witnesses that are in the prosecution's possession.[277] Broadly, the obligation to permit inspection 'requires that the Prosecution must make available all materials which will assist the Defence in countering the evidence to be presented by the Prosecution'.[278] As a practical matter, it is the prosecution that must decide which evidence in its possession is material to the defence as it is the only party fully aware of that evidence. If the defence believes that certain evidence or information in the prosecution's possession is material to the preparation of its case, it may request the chamber to decide the issue. To do so, however, it must 'specifically identify evidence material to the preparation of the Defence that is being withheld by the Prosecutor'.[279] For the chamber to order the prosecution to disclose the materials at issue, the defence must make a *prima facie* showing of

[274] See *RUF* Case, Case No. SCSL-04-15-T, Decision on Sesay Application for Disclosure Pursuant to Rules 89(B) and/or 66(A)(ii), 10 January 2008 ('*RUF* Disclosure Decision'), para. 12.

[275] ICTY Rule 66(B); ICTR Rule 66(B); SCSL Rule 66(A)(iii).

[276] *Prosecutor* v. *Bagosora, Kabiligi, Ntabakuze, and Nsengiyumva*, Case No. ICTR-98-41-AR73, Decision on Interlocutory Appeal Relating to Disclosure Under Rule 66(B) of the Tribunal's Rules of Evidence and Procedure, 25 September 2006, para. 9 (citing *United States* v. *Marshall*, 132 F.3d 63, 68 (D.C. Cir. 1998) and noting that 'even under United States Federal Rule of Criminal Procedure 16, which is limited to disclosure on matters material to the preparation of the defence against the prosecutor's case-in-chief, evidence is material as long as there is a strong indication that it will play an important role in uncovering admissible evidence, aiding witness preparation, corroborating testimony, or assisting impeachment or rebuttal', and further noting that it also extends to some extent to information which might dissuade a defendant from pursuing an unmeritorious defence).

[277] *RUF* Disclosure Decision, *supra* note 274, para. 32.

[278] *Ibid.*, para. 27. Accord *Prosecutor* v. *Bagosora, Kabiligi, Ntabakuze, and Nsengiyumva*, Case No. ICTR-98-41-T, Decision on Disclosure of Materials Relating to Immigration Statements of Defence Witnesses, 27 September 2005, para. 5.

[279] *RUF* Case, Case No. SCSL-04-15-T, Sesay – Decision on Defence Motion for Disclosure Pursuant to Rules 66 and 68 of the Rules, 9 July 2004, paras. 28–30 (quoting *Prosecutor* v. *Delalić, Mucić, Delić, and Landžo*, Case No. IT-96-21-T, Decision on the Motion by the Accused Zejnil Delalić for the Disclosure of Evidence, 26 September 1996, para. 11) (adopting a construction of SCSL Rule 66 consistent with the jurisprudence of both the ICTY and the ICTR, and rejecting the defence request for a disclosure order after finding that certain materials in the possession of the prosecution while 'in general, germane to the conflict that unravelled in Sierra Leone', were not specific to the alleged criminal responsibility of the accused).

materiality.[280] Thus, conclusory allegations or a general description of the information are not sufficient.[281]

The disclosure regime for non-exculpatory materials at the ICC is largely similar in character to that of the *ad hoc* Tribunals and the SCSL. Time limits are more fluid, however. The prosecution must provide the accused with the names of all witnesses it intends to call to testify, as well as any prior statements of those witnesses 'sufficiently in advance [of the proceeding] to enable the adequate preparation of the defence'.[282] If the proceeding in question is the confirmation hearing, the prosecution is required to provide a list of evidence upon which it will rely no later than thirty days before the hearing.[283] As at the ICTY, ICTR, and SCSL, where the prosecution subsequently decides to call a witness to testify, disclosure of the witness's name and a copy of the witness's prior statements must be made at the time of the prosecution's decision.[284] Accused before the ICC are also entitled to inspect books, documents, photographs, and other tangible objects in the possession or control of the prosecution which are material to the preparation of the defence, or which the prosecution intends to use as evidence at the confirmation hearing or the trial, or which were obtained from or belonged to the accused.[285] Although the ICC provisions for such inspection do not formally require a defence 'request', this is a distinction without a difference. The prosecution's obligation of access is the same and, as the objects are in the control of the prosecution, defence inspection will necessarily involve coordination between the parties.

6.5.1.2 Exculpatory materials

Each of the international criminal tribunals separates out materials of an exculpatory character for the purposes of defining the prosecution's disclosure obligation. So important is the prosecution's obligation to disclose materials of an exculpatory nature that the ICTY Appeals Chamber described such disclosure as 'essential for the fair conduct of proceedings before the Tribunal'.[286] It has also been

[280] *Ibid.*, para. 28 (citing *Prosecutor* v. *Ndayambaje*, Case No. ICTR-96-8-T, Decision on the Defence Motion for Disclosure, 25 September 2001, para. 11).

[281] See, e.g., *Prosecutor* v. *Naletilić and Martinović*, Case No. IT-98-34-T, Decision on Joint Motions for Order Allowing Defence Counsel to Inspect Documents in the Possession of the Prosecution, 16 September 2002 (rejecting a defence request to inspect materials in the prosecution's possession 'the source of which is the Government of Croatia and the archive of the ABiHC, to determine if they are relevant to the defence of the Accused', and noting that the defence might wish to state with more precision what documents it wishes to inspect and which it knows to be in the possession of the prosecution).

[282] ICC Rule 76(1). [283] ICC Rule 121(3).

[284] ICC Rule 76(2).

[285] ICC Rule 77. See also, e.g., *Prosecutor* v. *Lubanga*, Doc. No. ICC-01/04-01/06-649, Decision on the Defence Request for Order to Disclose Exculpatory Materials, 2 November 2006 ('*Lubanga* Exculpatory Materials Decision'), p. 4 (finding that the defence request for a list of all items seized during a search and seizure operation that was subsequently declared unlawful by the Court of Appeal of Kisingani, DRC, fell within the scope of Rule 77, and ordering the prosecution to provide the list).

[286] *Prosecutor* v. *Krstić*, Case No. IT-98-33-A, Judgement, 19 April 2004 ('*Krstić* Appeal Judgement'), para. 210. See also *Prosecutor* v. *Kordić and Čerkez*, Case No. IT-95-14/2-A, Judgement, 17 December 2004,

characterised as one of the most onerous responsibilities of the prosecution, forming part of the prosecutor's duty to act as a minister of justice.[287]

For the ICTY and ICTR, materials of an exculpatory character are those 'which in the actual knowledge of the Prosecutor may suggest the innocence or mitigate the guilt of the accused or affect the credibility of Prosecution evidence'.[288] The SCSL's definition differs only slightly, substituting 'known to the Prosecutor' for 'actual knowledge', and adding the slight modifier 'which in any way tends to suggest',[289] neither of which puts a significant legal gloss on the definition. The ICC's definition – which finds expression in the Rome Statute rather than the Rules – is substantively identical with regard to the character of the materials. Materials of an exculpatory character subject to disclosure by the ICC Prosecutor are those materials 'in the Prosecutor's possession or control which he or she believes shows or tends to show the innocence of the accused, or to mitigate the guilt of the accused, or which affect the credibility of prosecution evidence'.[290]

Material will be deemed to affect the credibility of prosecution evidence 'if it undermines the case presented by the Prosecution at trial'.[291] Moreover, any material which undermines the case presented by the prosecution at trial must be disclosed even if not in a form which itself could be presented as evidence at trial. Thus, materials subject to disclosure include those materials which may put the defence on notice that other exculpatory materials exist.[292]

Consistent with the largely adversarial framework of the trial process at the international criminal tribunals, it is the prosecution that is charged with determining whether material in its possession is of an exculpatory character and therefore subject to mandatory disclosure. Neither the accused nor the judges are privy to the voluminous amounts of information collected by the prosecution. Given its unique

paras. 183, 242; *Prosecutor* v. *Karemera, Ngirumpatse, and Nzirorera*, Case No. ICTR 98-44-AR73.6, Decision on Joseph Nzirorera's Interlocutory Appeal, 28 April 2006 ('*Nzirorera* Appeal Decision'), para. 27.

287 *Prosecutor* v. *Brđanin*, Case No. IT-99-36-A, Decision on Appellant's Motion for Disclosure Pursuant to Rule 68 and Motion for an Order to the Registrar to Disclose Certain Materials, 7 December 2004, p. 2.

288 ICTY Rule 68(i); ICTR Rule 68(A).

289 SCSL Rule 68(B).

290 Rome Statute, Art. 67(2). This includes, as at the *ad hoc* Tribunals, evidence which may affect the credibility of witnesses the prosecution intends to call, whether at the confirmation hearing or the trial. See, e.g., *Lubanga* Exculpatory Materials Decision, *supra* note 285, p. 3 (holding that information regarding the criminal record and the suspect status of any witness whose statements or summaries would be relied upon by the prosecution at the confirmation hearing fell within the disclosure obligations of Rule 67(2)). Accord *Prosecutor* v. *Lubanga*, Doc. No. ICC-01/04-01/06-1401, Decision on the Consequences of Non-Disclosure of Exculpatory Materials Covered by Article 54(3)(e) Agreements and the Application to Stay the Prosecution of the Accused, Together with Certain Other Issues Raised at the Status Conference on 10 June 2008, 13 June 2008 ('*Lubanga* Trial Decision on the Consequences of Non-Disclosure'), para. 59 (exculpatory material includes: (1) material that shows or tends to show the innocence of the accused; (2) material that mitigates the guilt of the accused; and (3) material that may affect the credibility of prosecution evidence).

291 *Krstić* Appeal Judgement, *supra* note 286, para. 178.

292 *Ibid.*

position with regard to the materials that it alone possesses, such that the defence and the judges are not aware of what they cannot see, the prosecution is the *de facto* arbiter of its disclosure obligations to the defence.[293] The Rome Statute, however, provides that 'in case of doubt … the Court shall decide'.[294]

Although in principle the jurisprudential framework governing the prosecution's obligation to disclose exculpatory material is relatively straightforward, in practice few issues have generated as much continuous litigation.[295] That litigation, however, is overwhelmingly very fact-specific, with the parties arguing the materiality of discrete pieces of information within the specific context of the case at hand. Nevertheless, some applicable guidelines are discernible from the jurisprudence. The prosecution must actively and continually review its files to determine the existence of exculpatory material subject to disclosure.[296] Where exculpatory material is identified, the prosecution's obligation is to disclose the material in its original form and not in the form of a summary.[297] The obligation to disclose exculpatory material does not entail the obligation to identify the material as exculpatory. Thus, the prosecution has no affirmative obligation to characterise it as such for the benefit of the defence, which is expected to be able to analyse the relevance of the material to its case.[298]

[293] *Nzirorera* Appeal Decision, *supra* note 286, paras. 16, 22.

[294] Rome Statute, Art. 67(2). Accord *Lubanga* Trial Decision on the Consequences of Non-Disclosure, *supra* note 290, para. 87 (noting that once the prosecution believes that evidence in its possession shows or tends to show the innocence of the accused, it is to be disclosed to the defence or, in case of doubt, put before the Court).

[295] See, e.g., David Scheffer, 'A Review of the Experiences of the Pre-Trial and Appeals Chambers of the International Criminal Court Regarding the Disclosure of Evidence', in Carsten Stahn and Göran Sluiter (eds.), *The Emerging Practice of the International Criminal Court* (2009), p. 585 (noting that one of the more reliable constants of criminal procedure, both domestic and international, is the discord among the prosecution, defence counsel, and judges over the timing and manner of disclosure of evidence). For a defence perspective on the practice of prosecutorial disclosure at international criminal tribunals, see Michael G. Karnavas, 'Gathering Evidence in International Criminal Trials – The View of the Defence Lawyer', in Michael Bohlander (ed.), *International Criminal Justice: A Critical Analysis of Institutions and Procedures* (2007), pp. 75–152.

[296] *Prosecutor* v. *Kajelijeli*, Case No. ICTR-98-44A-A, Judgement, 23 May 2005, para. 262. The Appeals Chamber has recognised that the voluminous nature of materials in the possession of the prosecution may give rise to delays in disclosure. See, e.g., *Prosecutor* v. *Blaškić*, Case No. IT-95-14-A, Judgement, 20 July 2004, para. 300. This volume does not, however, excuse the prosecution from reviewing the materials and assessing them for exculpatory value. See, e.g., *Krstić* Appeal Judgement, *supra* note 286, para. 197 ('The Appeals Chamber is sympathetic to the argument of the Prosecution that in most instances material requires processing, translation, analysis and identification as exculpatory material. The Prosecution cannot be expected to disclose material which – despite its best efforts – it has not been able to review and assess. Nevertheless, the Prosecution did take an inordinate amount of time before disclosing material in this case, and has failed to provide a satisfactory explanation for the delay.').

[297] *Prosecutor* v. *Brđanin*, Case No. IT-99-36-T, Decision on 'Motion for Relief from Rule 68 Violations by the Prosecutor and for Sanctions to Be Imposed Pursuant to Rule 68 bis and Motion for Adjournment While Matters Affecting Justice and a Fair Trial Can Be Resolved', 30 October 2002, para. 26 (noting further that if redaction is required of protected information, the redacted version of the statement must be sufficiently cohesive, understandable, and usable).

[298] See, e.g., *Krstić* Appeal Judgement, *supra* note 286, para. 190. But see *ibid.*, para. 191 (noting that the fact that the prosecution bears no *prima facie* responsibility to identify exculpatory materials as such for the defence does not prevent the accused from arguing, as a ground of appeal, that the accused suffered

Moreover, for the accused to be entitled to a remedy for the prosecution's violation of its obligation to disclose exculpatory material, it is not enough merely to demonstrate the breach. The accused must also show that his or her case suffered material prejudice as a result.[299]

6.5.1.3 Electronic disclosure

The amount of material collected by the prosecution at the international criminal tribunals is staggering, reaching into millions of documents. In recent years, the tribunals have had to contend with comprehensive data management of the vast amounts of material collected, in the form of electronic storage and searching.

As a result, the ICTY and the ICTR both have rules that permit the prosecution to comply with certain of its disclosure obligations 'in electronic form'.[300] Giving the defence access to an electronic database – known at the ICTY and the ICTR as the Electronic Disclosure Suite ('EDS') – which permits the defence to access all the prosecution's non-protected materials without restriction seems an eminently practical solution.[301] Managing defence access to the database in a manner fully consistent with the prosecution's disclosure obligations, however, is something that has proven difficult. Citing numerous practical difficulties with its use, one defence counsel has noted that the EDS, 'while it sounds idyllic[,] … is far from the silver bullet acclaimed by the prosecution'.[302]

Of greater concern than the practical difficulties associated with electronic disclosure, however, has been the prosecution's undifferentiated use of the EDS with regard to both non-exculpatory and exculpatory materials. In the *Karemera* case, the prosecution argued that by making its entire document collection available to the accused via EDS, which would permit the accused to search all the prosecution's materials for any exculpatory value, the prosecution had complied with its obligation to disclose exculpatory materials. In rejecting the prosecution's argument, the Appeals Chamber noted that 'the Prosecution's Rule 68 obligation to disclose extends beyond simply making available its entire evidence collection in a

prejudice from the prosecution's failure to identify the materials as exculpatory); *infra* text accompanying notes 303–304 (explaining that the prosecution cannot satisfy its obligation to disclose exculpatory materials simply by making its entire evidence database searchable by the defence, without at least notifying the defence of the existence of exculpatory materials).

299 See, e.g., *ibid.*, para. 153. See also *ibid.*, paras. 212–215 (finding the prosecution in breach of its obligations to disclose certain materials 'as soon as practicable', but imposing no sanction because the accused demonstrated no material prejudice from the breach).

300 ICTY Rule 68(ii); ICTR Rule 68(B).

301 Although it has received less attention, the ICC also has an electronic disclosure system, which the parties in at least one case have referred to as 'the most convenient' format for disclosure. See, e.g., *Prosecutor* v. *Lubanga*, Doc. No. ICC-01/04-01/06-102, Decision on the Final System of Disclosure and the Establishment of a Timetable, 15 May 2006, para. 68 (noting the parties' agreement that the electronic format would be the most convenient 'if security and practical arrangements do not prevent [the accused] from having unrestricted access to the electronic versions of the evidence and materials subject to exchange by the parties before the confirmation hearing').

302 Karnavas, *supra* note 295, p. 100.

searchable format. A search engine cannot serve as a surrogate for the Prosecution's individualized consideration of the material in its possession'.[303] Thus, the prosecution must still search the materials in its possession, analyse them for exculpatory value, and at the very least notify the defence of their existence.[304] It cannot fail to investigate the materials in its possession for their exculpatory value simply on the theory that the defence has unlimited access to the same materials.

6.5.1.4 Materials not subject to disclosure

Certain types of materials which would otherwise fall within the prosecution's disclosure obligations are specifically exempted from disclosure. These include work product of the prosecution, as well as materials provided to the prosecution on a confidential basis.

Reports, memoranda, or other internal documents prepared by a party, its assistants, or representatives in connection with the investigation or preparation of the case are generally not subject to disclosure.[305] Commonly referred to as 'work product', such materials are protected, except to the extent that any such materials within the possession or control of the prosecution are considered to be of an exculpatory character.[306] The ICTY has held that it is in the public interest that information related to the internal preparation of a case, including legal theories, strategies, and investigations should be privileged and not subject to disclosure to the opposing party.[307]

The prosecution is also not required to disclose information provided to it on a confidential basis that has been used solely for the purpose of generating new evidence.[308] Confidential information is most often provided to the prosecution by states or organisations with a security interest in the information. Thus, the Rules dictate that the provider of the information is in control of whether the information can be disclosed to the accused.[309] Without such consent and disclosure, the

[303] *Prosecutor* v. *Karemera, Ngirumpatse, and Nzirorera*, Case No. ICTR 98-44-AR73.7, Decision on Interlocutory Appeal Regarding the Role of the Prosecutor's Electronic Disclosure Suite in Discharging Disclosure Obligations, 30 June 2006, para. 10.

[304] *Ibid.*

[305] ICC Rule 81; ICTY Rule 70(A); ICTR Rule 70(A); SCSL Rule 70(A).

[306] ICTY Rule 70(A) (the materials are protected '[n]otwithstanding the provisions of Rules 66 [prosecution disclosure of materials of a non-exculpatory character] and 67 [defence disclosure]'); ICTR Rule 70(A) (same); SCSL Rule 70(A) (same). Strangely, the ICC Rule has no correlative provision removing materials of an exculpatory character from the general 'work product' exemption. Despite this, it seems inconceivable that an ICC chamber would countenance the non-disclosure of work product that contained exculpatory information. See *infra* text accompanying notes 316–323.

[307] *Prosecutor* v. *Blagojević and Jokić*, Case No. IT-02-60-T, Decision on Vidoje Blagojević's Expedited Motion to Compel the Prosecution to Disclose Its Notes from Plea Discussions with the Accused Nikolić & Request for an Expedited Open Session Hearing, 13 June 2003, p. 6. See also *Prosecutor* v. *Nahimana, Barayagwiza, and Ngeze*, Case No. ICTR-99-52-T, Decision on the Prosecutor's Ex Parte Application to Exclude Certain Documents from Defence Inspection of Microfiche Material, 25 October 2002, p. 4.

[308] Rome Statute, Art. 54(3)(e); ICTY Rule 70(B); ICTR Rule 70(B); SCSL Rule 70(B).

[309] See *supra* text accompanying notes 174–179 for an elaboration of the procedures involved.

material may not be led as evidence at trial.[310] Additionally, should the provider consent to the disclosure of the information followed by the evidence being led at trial, the trial chamber may not order the parties to produce further information from the provider, nor may the trial chamber summon the provider as a witness.[311] Should the prosecution call the provider of the confidential information as a witness at trial, the trial chamber may not compel the witness to answer any question which the witness declines to answer on grounds of confidentiality.[312]

The ICTY Appeals Chamber has reiterated that the purpose behind the exemption from disclosure for materials provided on a confidential basis is 'to encourage States, organizations, and individuals to share sensitive information with the Tribunal ... by permitting the sharing of information on a confidential basis and by guaranteeing information providers that the confidentiality of the information they offer and of the information's sources will be protected'.[313] There is an inherent tension, however, between the need to shield sensitive information from disclosure and the accused's fair trial right to the disclosure of exculpatory materials. The ICTY Appeals Chamber has held that sufficient safeguards exist to ensure the accused receives a fair trial.[314] As noted above, information provided confidentially to the prosecution may not be led at trial without prior disclosure to the accused. Additionally, trial chambers are empowered to exclude evidence from trial if its probative value is substantially outweighed by the need to ensure a fair trial.[315]

The tension between the need to protect information provided on a confidential basis and the accused's right to a fair trial was well illustrated by a dispute in the *Lubanga* case at the ICC which almost derailed the Court's first trial. There, the prosecution was in possession of over 200 documents which it conceded contained exculpatory or material information, but which it had agreed with the providers of the information not to disclose.[316] Moreover, under the terms of the confidentiality agreement between the prosecution and the information providers, the evidence could not be shown to the Court. The Trial Chamber found that the prosecution

310 ICC Rule 82(1).

311 ICTY Rule 70(C); ICTR Rule 70(C); SCSL Rule 70(C).

312 ICTY Rule 70(D); ICTR Rule 70(D); SCSL Rule 70(D).

313 *Prosecutor* v. *Blaškić*, Case No. IT-95-14-R, Decision on 'Defence Motion on Behalf of Rasim Delić Seeking Access to All Confidential Material in the *Blaškić* Case', 1 June 2006, p. 12. See also *Prosecutor* v. *Slobodan Milošević*, Case No. IT-02-54-AR108*bis* and AR73.3, Public Version of the Confidential Decision on the Interpretation and Application of Rule 70, 23 October 2002 ('*Milošević* Rule 70 Appeal Decision'), para. 19.

314 *Milošević* Rule 70 Appeal Decision, *supra* note 313, para. 26.

315 ICTY Rule 70(G) (providing that nothing in Rule 70 affects the trial chamber's authority to make such a determination under Rule 89(D)); ICTR Rule 70(F) (same); SCSL Rule 70(F) (providing that nothing in Rule 70 shall affect the trial chamber's power to exclude evidence pursuant to Rule 95, which stipulates that no evidence shall be admitted if its admission would bring the administration of justice into serious disrepute); *Milošević* Rule 70 Appeal Decision, *supra* note 313, para. 26.

316 *Lubanga* Trial Decision on the Consequences of Non-Disclosure, *supra* note 290, para. 64 (noting the prosecution's concession that approximately ninety-five items of evidence were 'potentially exculpatory', and that 112 items were 'material to defence preparation').

had invoked the confidentiality agreement regime of the Rome Statute incorrectly, as it had utilised the regime 'routinely, in inappropriate circumstances, instead of resorting to it exceptionally'.[317] Citing jurisprudence of the ICTY, the Trial Chamber stated that the fundamental right to a fair trial included an entitlement to disclosure of exculpatory material.[318] Because the accused could not be given access to potentially exculpatory materials, the Trial Chamber found that the trial process had been 'ruptured to such a degree that it is now impossible to piece together the constituent elements of a fair trial'.[319] Accordingly, the prosecution was given a choice; either it could disclose all the exculpatory information to the accused, or the trial could not go forward. As the prosecution could not disclose the information without violating the confidentiality agreements, the trial was stayed.[320] Although the crisis had passed before the prosecution's appeal of the decision was heard – the providers agreed to permit the evidence to be disclosed to the Trial Chamber – the Appeals Chamber ruled on the merits of the appeal and agreed with the Trial Chamber that the prosecution had inappropriately used the confidentiality agreements too broadly.[321] The Appeals Chamber noted that the case before it demonstrated that reliance on confidentiality agreements 'may lead to tensions with [the prosecution's] disclosure obligations'.[322] Accordingly, it is incumbent on the prosecution to make use of such agreements in a manner that permits the Court to resolve the tension between confidentiality and the accused's right to a fair trial.[323] Where such tensions cannot be resolved, they must be decided in favour of the accused's right to the disclosure of exculpatory evidence.

6.5.1.5 *Delayed disclosure*[324]

In 'exceptional circumstances', the prosecution may request the chamber to order the non-disclosure of the identity of a victim or witness who may be in danger or at risk, until such time as the person is brought under the protection of the tribunal.[325]

[317] *Ibid.*, para. 72.
[318] *Ibid.*, para. 77 (quoting *Krstić* Appeal Judgement, *supra* note 286, para. 180, and *Prosecutor* v. *Orić*, Case No. IT-03-68-T, Decision on Ongoing Complaints About Prosecutorial Non-Compliance with Rule 68 of the Rules, 13 December 2005, para. 20).
[319] *Ibid.*, para. 93. [320] *Ibid.*, para. 94.
[321] Accord *Prosecutor* v. *Lubanga*, Doc. No. ICC-01/04-01/06-1486, Judgment on the Appeal of the Prosecutor Against the Decision of Trial Chamber I Entitled 'Decision on the Consequences of Non-disclosure of Exculpatory Materials Covered by Article 54(3)(e) Agreements and the Application to Stay the Prosecution of the Accused, Together with Certain Other Issues Raised at the Status Conference on 10 June 2008', 21 October 2008, paras. 37–38 (finding no appealable error in the Trial Chamber's interpretation of the scope of the Rome Statute providing for confidentiality agreements).
[322] *Ibid.*, para. 43. [323] *Ibid.*, para. 44.
[324] Delayed disclosure is also discussed in Chapter 7, Section 7.4.2.
[325] ICTY Rule 69(A); ICTR Rule 69(A); SCSL Rule 69(A). At the ICTR and SCSL, the rule provides that either party may seek such delayed disclosure.

At the *ad hoc* Tribunals, this is generally referred to as the prosecution seeking protective measures[326] in the form of delayed disclosure.

Delayed disclosure of a witness's identity has been described as an 'extraordinary measure', justified only when the witness or his or her family would be placed in extreme danger should it become known that the witness will testify at trial.[327] In balancing the need to protect the safety of victims and witnesses against the accused's fair trial right to have adequate preparation time, the trial chambers consider the following criteria: (1) the likelihood that the witness will be interfered with or intimidated once the witness's identity is made known to the accused and his or her counsel (but not the public); (2) the extent to which the power to make protective orders can be used to protect the witness in the particular trial, as opposed to measures which simply make it easier for the prosecution to bring cases against other persons in the future; and (3) the length of time before the trial at which the identity of the witness must be disclosed to the accused.[328] In analysing these factors, trial chambers have recognised that the greater the length of time between the disclosure of the identity of the witness and the time of the witness's testimony, the greater the potential for interference will be.[329]

In striking this balance between the safety of witnesses and the accused's right to adequate time to prepare, trial chambers have recognised that 'the balance dictates clearly in favour of an accused's right to the identity of witnesses which the Prosecution intends to rely upon'.[330] Accordingly, the risk to the witness must not be illusory. The subjective fears of the potential witness are not in themselves sufficient to establish a real likelihood of risk from disclosure of the witness's identity to the accused. Nor will an indeterminate risk to witnesses in general due, for example, to the poor security situation in the former Yugoslavia and Rwanda be sufficient.[331] There must be an objective foundation to the witness's fears.[332] When such an objective foundation is present, and the risk is extreme, trial chambers have not shrunk

326 On protective measures generally, see Chapter 7, Section 7.4.2.

327 *Prosecutor* v. *Slobodan Milošević*, Case No. IT-02-54-T, First Decision on Prosecution Motion for Protective Measures for Sensitive Source Witnesses, 3 May 2002 ('*Milošević* Delayed Disclosure Decision'), para. 8 (noting the prosecution's argument that the witnesses it sought to protect with delayed disclosure were in extreme danger as they would testify in relation to matters bearing directly on the criminal responsibility of the accused, or matters that related to high-level operations of government agencies or to perpetrator groups identified in the indictments).

328 *Ibid.*, para. 3. See also Chapter 7, Section 7.4.2.

329 *Prosecutor* v. *Brđanin and Talić*, Case No. IT-99-36-PT, Decision on Third Motion by Prosecution for Protective Measures, 8 November 2000 ('*Brđanin* Protective Measures Decision'), para. 13.

330 *Prosecutor* v. *Milutinović, Ojdanić, and Šainović*, Case No. IT-99-37-PT, Decision on Prosecution's Motion for Protective Measures, 17 July 2003, p. 3 (noting further that while it is extremely important to provide adequately for the protection of witnesses, the accused's fair trial right dictates that protective measures should be granted only where it is properly shown in the circumstances of the witness that the protective measures sought meet the standards of the Statute and the Rules, as expanded by the jurisprudence of the ICTY).

331 See Chapter 7, Section 7.4.2.

332 See, e.g., *Brđanin* Protective Measures Decision, *supra* note 329, para. 13.

from withholding the identity of the witness from the accused and defence counsel, even to the extent of permitting delayed disclosure such that the accused may only learn the identity of the witness ten days prior to the witness's testimony.[333]

6.5.2 Disclosure by the accused

Like the prosecution, the defence bears disclosure obligations, although the defence's disclosure obligations are less extensive and vary widely across the international criminal tribunals. Just as described above for the prosecution, the defence is never required to disclose work product.[334] Additionally, at least at the ICTY, the defence may request the chamber to exempt information provided to the defence on a confidential basis from disclosure in the same manner as the prosecution.[335] With regard to the general disclosure obligations of the defence, the ICTY Rules provide for the most extensive obligations; the SCSL Rules provide the least.

6.5.2.1 Tangible objects and witness statements

At the ICTY, the defence must permit the prosecution to inspect and copy any books, documents, photographs, and tangible objects in the defence's custody or control which the defence intends to use as evidence at trial, and must provide the prosecution with copies of any existing statements of the witnesses it intends to call at trial.[336] Written evidence in lieu of testimony that the defence intends to introduce at trial must also be disclosed.[337] Although these materials largely mirror the disclosure obligation of the ICTY Prosecutor with respect to non-exculpatory materials, the defence is not required to disclose them during the prosecution's case-in-chief, but merely prior to the start of the defence case.[338]

At the ICC, ICTR, and SCSL, by contrast, there is no requirement in the Rules for the defence to disclose the statements of witnesses it will call at trial. The ICC does require the defence to permit the prosecution to inspect tangible objects in its possession or control.[339] Before the ICTR, however, the defence is not required to permit the prosecution to inspect tangible evidence in its possession, unless the defence has made such a reciprocal request to inspect tangible evidence in the possession of the prosecution.[340] Thus, accused before the ICTR may shield evidence in their possession from the prosecution, but only by forgoing their own right to inspect prosecution evidence. Moreover, the defence's reciprocal disclosure obligation with respect to the inspection of tangible objects is not as broad as the

[333] See, e.g., *Milošević* Delayed Disclosure Decision, *supra* note 327, para. 13.
[334] ICC Rule 81; ICTY Rule 70(A); ICTR Rule 70(A); SCSL Rule 70(A).
[335] ICTY Rule 70(F). [336] ICTY Rule 67(A). [337] ICTY Rule 67(A)(ii).
[338] ICTY Rule 67(A) (defence disclosure due at a time not prior to a ruling under Rule 98 *bis* for judgement of acquittal but not less than one week prior to the commencement of the defence case).
[339] ICC Rule 78. [340] ICTR Rule 67(C).

prosecution's. The prosecution's obligation to permit inspection extends not just to evidence the prosecution expects to use at trial, but also to evidence which is 'material to the preparation of the defence'.[341] Should the defence trigger for itself an obligation to permit the prosecution to inspect its materials, however, the disclosure obligation covers only materials that the defence will use at trial.[342] No provision in the SCSL Rules requires accused before that tribunal to permit the prosecution any inspection of tangible objects.

6.5.2.2 Certain defences

Each of the tribunals obliges the defence to provide disclosure regarding its intention to interpose certain defences. Thus, the defence must notify the prosecution of its intent to offer an alibi, or any special defence, including that of diminished or lack of mental responsibility.[343] For the ICC, 'special defences' are defined as grounds for excluding criminal responsibility, and are specified in the Rome Statute.[344] For accused before all the tribunals, such disclosure to the prosecution must be made as early as practicable and prior to the commencement of trial.[345]

Where the accused will offer an alibi, the defence disclosure is required to be specific regarding the place or places at which the accused claims to have been present at the time of the alleged crime.[346] Additionally, the accused must disclose the names and addresses of witnesses to the alibi, as well as any other evidence upon which he or she intends to rely to establish the alibi. Likewise, where the accused will offer any special defence, the evidence upon which the accused will rely must be disclosed.[347]

Defence disclosure related to alibi or other special defences triggers a further disclosure duty for the prosecution, which must notify the accused of the names of any witnesses the prosecution intends to call in rebuttal.[348] The failure of the accused to provide notice of alibi or any other ground for excluding criminal

[341] ICTR Rule 66(B).

[342] See, e.g., *Prosecutor* v. *Karemera, Ngirumpatse, and Nzirorera*, Case No. ICTR-98-44-T, Decision on Prosecution Cross-Motion for Enforcement of Reciprocal Disclosure Rule 67 of the Rules of Evidence and Procedure, 21 September 2007 ('*Karemera et al.* Rule 67 Decision'), paras. 7–8.

[343] ICC Rule 79(1); ICTY Rule 67(B); ICTR Rule 67(A)(ii); SCSL Rule 67(A)(ii).

[344] Rome Statute, Art. 31(1); ICC Rule 79(1)(b). The grounds for excluding criminal responsibility include: mental disease or defect which destroys the person's capacity to appreciate the unlawfulness or nature of his or her conduct, or capacity to control his or her conduct to conform to the requirements of law (Art. 31(1)(a)); that the person was in a state of involuntary intoxication that destroyed his or her capacity to appreciate the unlawfulness or nature of his or her conduct, or capacity to control his or her conduct to conform to the requirements of law (Art. 31(1)(b)); reasonable self-defence or defence of another (Art. 31(1)(c)); and duress and necessity (Art. 31(1)(d)). For a discussion of these defences, see Ratner, Abrams, and Bischoff, *supra* note 250, pp. 150–158.

[345] ICC Rule 80 (sufficiently in advance of the commencement of trial to enable the prosecution to prepare adequately); ICTY Rule 67(B) (within the time prescribed by the chamber or pre-trial judge); ICTR Rule 67(A)(ii)(a); SCSL Rule 67(A)(ii)(a).

[346] ICC Rule 79(1)(a); ICTY Rule 67(B)(i)(a); ICTR Rule 67(A)(ii)(a); SCSL Rule 67(A)(ii)(a).

[347] ICC Rule 79(1)(a), (b); ICTY Rule 67(B)(i)(a), (b); ICTR Rule 67(A)(ii)(a), (b); SCSL Rule 67(A)(ii)(a), (b).

[348] ICTY Rule 67(B)(ii); ICTR Rule 67(A)(i); SCSL Rule 67(A)(i).

responsibility does not limit the right of the accused to raise the alibi or defence at trial.[349] There is, however, a 'professional obligation' on defence counsel to file the required notice as soon as he or she knows that the accused intends to enter such a defence.[350]

The jurisprudence has added nuance to the defence disclosure obligation regarding an alibi. In the *Karemera* case, the Trial Chamber noted that the accused is only obliged to notify the prosecution of an alibi when the accused intends to show that he or she was at a particular place at the time the crime was alleged to have been committed. Accordingly, the accused's intention to show merely that the accused was not at the scene of the alleged crime, without more, does not require the defence to notify the prosecution.[351]

6.5.3 Sanctions for non-disclosure

Of all the international criminal tribunals, only the ICTY has a Rule authorising its judges to impose sanctions on a party which fails to fulfil its disclosure obligations.[352] The Rule leaves the character of such sanctions wholly undefined, and the jurisprudence establishes that sanctions are within the discretion of the relevant chamber.[353] The ICTR and SCSL exercise identical authority, however, basing this power on a rule granting the chamber general remedial power over the conduct of counsel.[354]

In principle, the sanctions available for a party's failure in its disclosure obligations include the trial chamber prohibiting the non-disclosing party from leading the untimely disclosed evidence at trial.[355] In practice, untimely disclosure is

[349] ICC Rule 79(3); ICTY Rule 67(C); ICTR Rule 67(B); SCSL Rule 67(B); see also, e.g., *Prosecutor* v. *Rutaganda*, Case No. ICTR-93-A, Judgement, 26 May 2003, para. 241.

[350] *Karemera et al.* Rule 67 Decision, *supra* note 342, para. 17.

[351] *Ibid.*, para. 16. [352] ICTY Rule 68 *bis*.

[353] See, e.g., *Krstić* Appeal Judgement, *supra* note 286, para. 212.

[354] ICTR Rule 46(A) ('A Chamber may, after a warning, impose sanctions against a counsel if, in its opinion, his conduct remains offensive or abusive, obstructs the proceedings, or is otherwise contrary to the interests of justice.'). The SCSL has an identical rule. SCSL Rule 46(A). See also, e.g., *Prosecutor* v. *Bizimungu, Mugenzi, Bicamumpaka, and Mugiraneza*, Case No. ICTR-99-50-T, Decision on Jérộme-Clément Bicamumpaka's Submissions for Stay of Proceedings and Motion for Disclosure Concerning Witness GKB, 19 May 2009, para. 8 (noting the authority of the Trial Chamber under Rule 46(A) to impose sanctions upon the prosecution for breach of its disclosure obligations); *Prosecutor* v. *Karemera, Ngirumpatse, and Nzirorera*, Case No. ICTR-98-44-T, Decision on Defence Oral Motions for Exclusion of Witness XBM's Testimony, for Sanctions Against the Prosecution and for Exclusion of Evidence Outside the Scope of the Indictment: Articles 17(4) and 20 of the Statute, Rule 47(C) of the Rules of Procedure and Evidence, 19 October 2006, para. 8 (acknowledging the Trial Chamber's authority to enter sanctions for disclosure violations under Rule 46 but finding it unwarranted under the facts at issue).

[355] See *Prosecutor* v. *Ndindiliyimana, Bizimungu, Nzuwonemeye, and Sagahutu*, Case No. ICTR-00-56-T, Decision on Defence Motions Alleging Violations of the Prosecutor's Disclosure Obligations Pursuant to Rule 68, 22 September 2008, para. 61 (noting that the determination of a suitable remedy for disclosure violations falls within the chamber's inherent power and responsibility to secure justice and ensure a fair trial for the accused, and noting a large number of remedial options available to the chamber, including: (1) recalling relevant prosecution witnesses for further cross-examination; (2) permitting the defence to call additional witnesses; (3) excluding relevant parts of the prosecution evidence; (4) drawing necessary inferences from

generally remedied by the trial chamber giving the opposing party additional time to prepare to meet the evidence, or permitting the opposing party to recall witnesses.[356] The *Orić* Trial Chamber noted that in the practice of the ICTY, the prosecution's violation of its obligation to disclose exculpatory materials 'is governed less by a system of "sanctions" than by the Judges' definitive evaluation of the evidence presented by either of the parties, and the possibility which the opposing party will have had to contest it'.[357] Although generally unwilling to prohibit parties from leading untimely disclosed evidence, trial chambers have not been shy in condemning parties that violate their disclosure obligations, particularly where the violator is the prosecution. In the *Furundžija* case, for example, the Trial Chamber was so dismayed at what it characterised as the prosecution's 'consistent pattern of non-compliance with the orders of the Trial Chamber' – much of that non-compliance in relation to disclosure obligations – that it took the rare step of issuing a formal complaint to the Prosecutor herself.[358]

6.5.4 Confidential material from other cases

Although not specifically provided for in the Rules of the tribunals, it has become quite common for the defence to request access to confidential information appearing in the record of other cases before the tribunal.[359] Indeed, it has become well established in the jurisprudence of the ICTY that an accused is always entitled to seek material from any source, including other cases before the tribunal, to assist it in the preparation of its case.

In order to be permitted access to confidential *inter partes* materials in another case, the moving party must identify or describe the information sought by its

exculpatory material; (5) dismissing charges touched upon by exculpatory material; and (6) ordering a stay of proceedings).

[356] See, e.g., *Prosecutor* v. *Orić*, Case No. IT-03-68-T, Judgement, 30 June 2006, para. 813 (detailing ongoing disclosure disputes during trial, and the Trial Chamber's decision to permit the defence to recall witnesses based on the prosecution's failure to meet its Rule 68 disclosure obligations). Zappalà argues that the determination of sanctions should not be left to the discretion of the judges, but should be specified in a set of rules specifying sanctions to be imposed. In Zappalà's view, when sanctions remain wholly in the discretion of the judges, the accused is substantially unprotected from the prosecution's violation of its disclosure obligations. Salvatore Zappalà, *Human Rights in International Criminal Proceedings* (2003), p. 146.

[357] *Prosecutor* v. *Orić*, Case No. IT-03-68-T, Decision on Urgent Defence Motion Regarding Prosecutorial Non-Compliance with Rule 68, 27 October 2005, p. 3; see also *ibid.*, pp. 4–5 (noting that the prosecution's failure of its disclosure obligation in the instance at bar represented the fifth occasion on which it was necessary for the Trial Chamber to address a the prosecution's failure to comply with its disclosure obligations, finding that no further remedy was warranted, and ordering the prosecution to conduct a thorough and complete search for exculpatory material and provide the Trial Chamber with a declaration of the result of the search).

[358] *Prosecutor* v. *Furundžija*, Case No. IT-95-17/1-PT, The Trial Chamber's Formal Complaint to the Prosecutor Concerning the Conduct of the Prosecution, 5 June 1998, para. 2 (noting that the prosecution's misconduct fell short of constituting knowing and wilful interference with the administration of justice and, therefore, fell outside the scope of the Trial Chamber's inherent contempt powers).

[359] Obtaining confidential material from other cases is also discussed in Chapter 7, text accompanying notes 114–118.

general nature, and must demonstrate a legitimate forensic purpose for access to the information.[360] The moving party can demonstrate such a legitimate forensic purpose by showing the existence of a nexus between the party's case and the case from which the material is sought. Such a nexus must consist of a geographic, temporal, or otherwise material overlap between the two cases.[361] If the chamber is satisfied that the requested material is likely to assist the moving party's case materially, or that there is at least a good chance that it would, access may be granted.[362]

6.6 Pre-trial case management

In keeping with the largely adversarial model of trial proceedings at the international criminal tribunals, the scope of the trial is governed largely by the decisions of the parties. It is the prosecution that decides which charges to bring, and which witnesses and evidence it will lead in support of the charges. Likewise, it is the defence which decides which witnesses and evidence – if any – it will lead. Subject to limitations in the Rules relative to relevance and admissibility, these decisions are largely within the sole discretion of the parties.[363] This is certainly one of the factors contributing to the extraordinary length of some international criminal trials.[364]

The judges, however, are not wholly powerless to intervene in the parties' decisions. Although great care must be taken to balance timeframes with the legitimate needs of the parties to prepare for trial, it is the judges who will determine when trial begins. Concomitantly, during the pre-trial process the judges play an important managerial role in shepherding the parties through their preparations, and the judges possess a number of case-management tools. Most of the judges' powers during the pre-trial phase are uncontroversial. Some are more problematic, particularly at the *ad hoc* Tribunals, where the judges have the authority to limit the number of witnesses a party may call, or to determine the overall time available to

[360] *Prosecutor* v. *Dragomir Milošević*, Case No. IT-98-29/1-A, Decision on Radovan Karadžić's Motion for Access to Confidential Material in the *Dragomir Milošević* Case, 19 May 2009 ('*Dragomir Milošević* Confidential Access Decision'), para. 7; *Prosecutor* v. *Martić*, Case No. IT-95-11-A, Decision on Motion by Jovica Stanišić for Access to Confidential Testimony and Exhibits in the Martić Case Pursuant to Rule 75(G)(i), 22 February 2008 ('*Martić* Confidential Access Decision'), para. 9; *Prosecutor* v. *Krajišnik*, Case No. IT-00-39-A, Decision on 'Motion by Mićo Stanišić for Access to All Confidential Materials in the Krajišnik Case', 21 February 2007, p. 4.

[361] *Dragomir Milošević* Confidential Access Decision, *supra* note 360, para. 8; *Martić* Confidential Access Decision, *supra* note 360, para. 9.

[362] *Martić* Confidential Access Decision, *supra* note 360, para. 9.

[363] See Chapter 7, text accompanying notes 295–298.

[364] See Boas, *supra* note 107, p. 280 (explaining that Offices of the Prosecutor, particularly at the *ad hoc* Tribunals, have shown that they are not yet prepared to take responsibility for reducing and focusing their cases in a way that impacts substantially and favourably on their length and manageability).

a party for presenting its case. As discussed below, judicial authority to limit the scope of the parties' case has been used sparingly, as the judges have been reluctant to wield a heavy hand.

6.6.1 Pre-trial case management at the ad hoc *Tribunals and the SCSL*

The ICTY Rules provide for the designation of 'a Judge responsible for the pre-trial proceedings'.[365] As a general matter, this pre-trial judge is charged with coordinating communications between the parties during the pre-trial phase, ensuring that the proceedings are not unduly delayed, and taking any appropriate measures necessary to prepare the case for a fair and expeditious trial.[366]

To fulfil the pre-trial judge's charge to expedite a smooth transition to the trial, the judge is required to establish a work plan for the parties, complete with specific deadlines the parties are expected to meet.[367] The pre-trial judge will order the parties to meet and discuss issues related to the preparation of the case.[368] Once any preliminary motions are disposed of, the pre-trial judge will establish a date for a pre-trial conference and set a timeframe within which the prosecution must file the final version of its pre-trial brief,[369] a list of witnesses the prosecution intends to call,[370] and a list of exhibits the prosecution intends to offer at trial.[371] Included in the prosecution's pre-trial brief is the total time estimated for the presentation of the prosecution's case.[372]

Following the submission of the prosecution's pre-trial brief, the pre-trial judge will submit a complete file to the trial chamber, and will set a deadline for the filing of the defence's pre-trial brief.[373] At this stage of the proceedings, the defence's pre-trial brief is much less comprehensive than the prosecution's, and includes 'in general terms' the nature of the accused's defence, the matters with which the accused takes issue in the prosecution's pre-trial brief, and the reasons why the

365 ICTY Rule 65 *ter*(A). 366 ICTY Rule 65 *ter*(B).

367 ICTY Rule 65 *ter*(D)(ii). 368 ICTY Rule 65 *ter*(D)(iv).

369 ICTY Rule 65 *ter*(E)(i). The brief is required to include, for each count charged, a summary of the evidence the prosecution intends to bring regarding the commission of the alleged crime and the form of responsibility incurred by the accused. Additionally, the brief must include any admissions by the parties and a statement of matters which are not in dispute between them, as well as a statement of contested matters of fact and law. *Ibid.*

370 ICTY Rule 65 *ter*(E)(ii). This list is extensive and includes the name or pseudonym of each proposed witness; a summary of the facts on which each witness will testify; the points in the indictment as to which each witness will testify, including specific references to counts and relevant paragraphs in the indictment; the total number of witnesses and the number of witnesses that will testify against each accused and on each count; an indication of whether the witness will testify *viva voce* or whether the witness's evidence will be led in the form of written evidence; the estimated length of time required for each witness to testify; and the total time estimated for presentation of the prosecution's case. *Ibid.*

371 ICTY Rule 65 *ter*(E)(iii). Where possible, the prosecution is required to indicate whether the defence has any objection to an exhibit based on authenticity. Additionally, the prosecution is required to serve the defence with copies of the exhibits on the list. *Ibid.*

372 ICTY Rule 65 *ter*(E)(ii)(f). 373 ICTY Rule 65 *ter*(L).

accused takes issue.[374] The pre-trial judge then submits a second file to the trial chamber.[375]

Although the ICTR and SCSL Rules do not provide for the designation of a pre-trial judge with a case management charge, each tribunal requires the prosecution to file a pre-trial brief largely similar in content to that filed by the ICTY prosecution.[376] In each of the *ad hoc* Tribunals, with the filing of the prosecution's pre-trial brief the trial chamber has a concrete picture of the scope of the prosecution's case and the time required for trial. It is at this point that the *ad hoc* Tribunal judges' authority to limit the scope of the trial is engaged.

6.6.2 Limiting the scope of the trial at the ad hoc *Tribunals and the SCSL*

Having been informed how many witnesses the prosecution intends to call at trial, as well as the general substance of each witness's expected testimony, trial chambers at the *ad hoc* Tribunals are empowered to limit the number of witnesses the prosecution may call.[377] Additionally, ICTY trial chambers have the authority to determine the maximum time available to the prosecution to present its case.[378] The ICTY Appeals Chamber has observed that in exercising its discretion to determine the time available to a party to present its case, a trial chamber has the responsibility to ensure that 'the proceedings do not suffer undue delays and that the trial is completed within a reasonable time, which is recognized as a fundamental right of due process under international human rights law'.[379] There is a balance to be struck here, however, as the Appeals Chamber has also recognised that considerations of judicial economy should never impinge on the rights of the parties to a fair trial.[380]

374 ICTY Rule 65 *ter*(F). Following the close of the prosecution's case-in-chief, the defence is required to file a new pre-trial brief similar in content to the prosecution's pre-trial brief. Included in the defence's pre-trial brief is the total time estimated for the presentation of the defence case. ICTY Rule 65 *ter*(G). During trial, following the close of the prosecution's case-in-chief, the defence is required to file a more comprehensive brief. See ICTY Rule 65 *ter*(G); ICTR Rule 73 *ter*(B); SCSL Rule 73 *ter*(B). See also Chapter 7, Sections 7.6.1, 7.6.2.

375 ICTY Rule 65 *ter*(G).

376 ICTR Rule 73 *bis*(B); SCSL Rule 73 *bis*(B).

377 ICTY Rule 73 *bis*(C) (trial chamber 'shall determine the number of witnesses the Prosecutor may call'); *Prosecutor* v. *Prlić, Stojić, Praljak, Petković, Ćorić, and Pušić*, Case No. IT-04-74-AR73.7, Decision on Defendant's Appeal Against '*Décision portant attribution du temps à la Défense pour la présentation des moyens à décharge*', 1 July 2008 ('*Prlić et al.* Appeal Decision on Defence Time'), para. 16; ICTR Rule 73 *bis*(D) (trial chamber may order the prosecution to reduce the number of witnesses it intends to call if the trial chamber considers that an excessive number of witnesses are being called to prove the same facts); SCSL Rule 73 *bis*(D) (same).

378 ICTY Rule 73 *bis*(C)(ii); see also, e.g., *Prlić et al.* Appeal Decision on Defence Time, *supra* note 377, para. 16.

379 *Prosecutor* v. *Prlić, Stojić, Praljak, Petković, Ćorić, and Pušić*, Case No. IT-04-74-AR73.2, Decision on Prosecution Appeal Concerning the Trial Chamber's Ruling Reducing Time for the Prosecution Case, 6 February 2007 ('*Prlić et al.* Appeal Decision on Prosecution Time'), para. 23.

380 *Prosecutor* v. *Orić*, Case No. IT-03-68-AR73.2, Interlocutory Decision on Length of Defence Case, 20 July 2005, para 8.

The potential difficulties in striking such a balance are illustrated by the Trial Chamber's decisions in the *Prlić* case involving six accused, one of the largest – and longest – trials heard before the ICTY. The Trial Chamber initially granted to the prosecution a total of 400 hours to present its case-in-chief. The Trial Chamber then reduced that total time to 293 hours. The prosecution appealed the decision, arguing that the Trial Chamber had unreasonably limited the prosecution's ability to fairly and effectively present its case. Looking at the specific method employed by the Trial Chamber in arriving at the imposed reduction in available time to the prosecution – a methodology which focused on a comparison of the time actually taken in trial to the overall time the Trial Chamber initially determined the trial should last – the Appeals Chamber found that the Trial Chamber had failed to adequately consider whether its ordered reduction would still allow the prosecution the opportunity to fairly present its case. In essence, the Trial Chamber appeared to have rendered its calculations based upon the amount of time it wished the trial to take, rather than the amount of time the prosecution fairly needed. The Appeals Chamber remanded the case to the Trial Chamber for a 'renewed assessment and consideration of whether the reduction of time would allow the Prosecution a fair opportunity to present its case in light of the complexity and number of issues that remain'.[381] On remand, the Trial Chamber reassessed its decision in light of the Appeals Chamber's guidance and granted the prosecution an additional twenty-three hours (for a total allocation of 316 hours).[382]

The Appeals Chamber was not finished with the consideration of time limits in the *Prlić* case, however. In determining the length of the various defence cases, the Trial Chamber allocated a total of 336.5 hours, divided unequally among the six accused. Four of the six appealed this time allotment arguing, among other things, that the Trial Chamber had simply made an arithmetic calculation in which it divided the amount of time used by the prosecution among the accused. The Appeals Chamber noted that such an approach would, indeed, constitute a discernible error, but did not accept that the Trial Chamber had actually made such an error. In affirming the Trial Chamber's decision, the Appeals Chamber held that the time allocated to an accused 'must be reasonably proportional to the time allocated to the Prosecution, and objectively adequate to permit the Accused to set forth his case in a manner consistent with his rights under Article 21 of the [ICTY] Statute'.[383] Accordingly, strict proportionality alone, divorced from a consideration of the actual time needed by the accused to fairly present a defence case, constitutes a potentially reversible error.

[381] *Prlić et al.* Appeal Decision on Prosecution Time, *supra* note 379, para. 24.

[382] *Prlić et al.* Appeal Decision on Defence Time, *supra* note 377, para. 2. In the event, the prosecution later closed its case-in-chief having used only 297 hours. *Ibid.*

[383] *Prlić et al.* Appeal Decision on Defence Time, *supra* note 379, para. 39.

The most controversial use of the judges' authority to limit the scope of the trial has come with trial chambers limiting the number of crime sites or incidents upon which the prosecution may present evidence.[384] At the ICTY, the judges may 'invite the Prosecutor to reduce the number of counts charged in the indictment' and may 'fix a number of crime sites or incidents … in respect of which evidence may be presented by the Prosecutor which', in the view of the chamber, 'are reasonably representative of the crimes charged'.[385] In the *Milutinović* case, another large trial involving six accused, the Trial Chamber specified certain crime sites in relation to which the prosecution would not be permitted to present evidence 'on the ground that what allegedly occurred there was not, unlike other killing sites, associated with locations from which persons were allegedly forcibly displaced, and thus did not fall within "the nature or theme" of the Prosecution case'.[386]

The judges' authority to limit the number of crime sites upon which the prosecution may present evidence has been used only sparingly over the objections of the prosecution. The power of the judges to do so, however, has provided the prosecution an incentive to identify ways in which it can streamline and shorten cases. In the *Karadžić* case, for example, the Trial Chamber threatened to use its authority to reduce the number of crime sites available to the prosecution '[s]hould the Prosecution not provide assistance in identifying specific counts and/or crime sites or incidents, the removal of which would be in the interests of a fair and expeditious trial'.[387] In response, the prosecution identified ten municipalities, and twenty specific crime sites, upon which it would not lead evidence, should the Trial Chamber 'consider it necessary'.[388] The Trial Chamber accepted the prosecution's proposal, and ordered the prosecution not to lead evidence in relation to the identified sites and incidents.[389]

Of all the international criminal tribunals, the ICTY's judges have gone the furthest in developing and applying pre-trial case management techniques designed to fairly and expeditiously try complex and often massive cases. In the early years of

[384] See Institute For War and Peace Reporting, 'Prosecution, Judges in Karadzic Case Stand-Off', 25 September 2009, www.iwpr.net/EN-tri-f-356134 (stating that a 'proposal that the prosecution cut the [*Karadžić*] indictment further after it had already agreed to make certain cuts in response to [an earlier] request' met opposition from the prosecution and 'sparked angry protest in the Bosnian capital, Sarajevo').

[385] ICTY Rule 73 *bis*(D) (providing that this determination is to be made 'having regard to all the relevant circumstances, including the crimes charged in the indictment, their classification and nature, the places where they are alleged to have been committed, their scale and the victims of the crimes').

[386] *Milutinović et al.* Trial Judgement, *supra* note 4, Vol. I, para. 16; accord *Prosecutor* v. *Milutinović, Šainović, Ojdanić, Pavković, Lazarević, and Lukić*, Case No. IT-05-87-T, Decision on Application of Rule 73 *bis*, 22 July 2006, para. 13.

[387] *Prosecutor* v. *Karadžić*, Case No. IT-95-5/18-PT, Order to the Prosecution Under Rule 73 *bis*(D), 22 July 2009, para. 5.

[388] *Prosecutor* v. *Karadžić*, Case No. IT-95-5/18-PT, Prosecution Submission Pursuant to Rule 73 *bis*(D), 31 August 2009, paras. 10–11.

[389] *Prosecutor* v. *Karadžić*, Case No. IT-95-5/18-PT, Decision on the Application of Rule 73 *bis*(D), 8 October 2009, paras. 6, 11.

the Tribunal, fairness concerns seemingly overrode the need to expedite proceedings. Under increasing pressure from the international community to complete its mandate and shut the Tribunal's doors, however, its judges have become increasingly concerned about the length of the trials.[390] To some observers, both inside and outside the Tribunal, the 'completion strategy' has driven this shift in focus. One respected Appeals Chamber judge, in forcefully dissenting from a decision which he viewed as driven by 'a desire to assist the prosecution to bring the Completion Strategy to a speedy conclusion',[391] opined that

> [t]he international community has entrusted the Tribunal with the task of trying persons charged with serious violations of international humanitarian law. It expects the Tribunal to do so in accordance with those rights of the accused to which reference is made in the previous paragraph. If the Tribunal is not given sufficient time and money to do so by the international community, then it should not attempt to try those persons in a way which does not accord with those rights. In my opinion, it is improper to take the Completion Strategy into account in departing from interpretations which had earlier been accepted by the Appeals Chamber where this is at the expense of those rights. This Tribunal will not be judged by the number of convictions which it enters, or by the speed with which it concludes the Completion Strategy which the Security Council has endorsed, but by the fairness of its trials. The Majority Appeals Chamber Decision and others in which the Completion Strategy has been given priority over the rights of the accused will leave a spreading stain on this Tribunal's reputation.[392]

Yet for all the concern about expeditious trial conclusion overshadowing the fairness of proceedings, the ICTY's judges have seemingly been reluctant to employ all the case management means at their disposal. As one of the authors has argued extensively elsewhere, the appropriate development and use of case management tools will be essential if international criminal tribunals are to establish best practices and successfully fulfil their mandates, both to the accused and to the international community.[393]

6.6.3 Pre-trial case management at the ICC

At the ICC, once a case arises from a situation,[394] the pre-trial chamber manages that case through the confirmation hearing. Although the confirmation hearings presided over by the pre-trial chambers are not as extensive or lengthy as trials,

[390] See Boas, *supra* note 107, p. 64 (noting that the expeditious conclusion of trials has become something of an obsession at the ICTY).

[391] *Prosecutor* v. *Slobodan Milošević*, Case No. IT-02-54-AR73.4, Dissenting Opinion of Judge David Hunt on Admissibility of Evidence in Chief in the Form of Written Statement (Majority Opinion Given 30 September 2003), 21 October 2003, para. 20.

[392] *Ibid.*, paras. 21–22.

[393] See Boas, *supra* note 107, p. 280 ('Achieving a tough but balanced approach to [case management] issues will go a long way to achieving best practice in the conduct of complex international criminal trials.').

[394] On this step, see Chapter 3, Section 3.2.1.

they are large and complex proceedings, arguably involving nearly as much managerial oversight as is required during preparation for trial. Yet the pre-trial chambers have no specific case management duties in facilitating the preparation of the case for trial. Their focus is solely on preparation of the case for the confirmation hearing.[395] Once charges are confirmed, it is the trial chamber that manages the case in preparation for trial.

During the entire pre-trial phase, pre-trial and trial chambers at the ICC exercise the same managerial functions over the parties as their counterparts at the *ad hoc* Tribunals. They set confirmation hearing and trial dates, establish deadlines for disclosure, facilitate meetings with and between the parties to discuss scheduling and identify legal issues to be decided, rule on motions, and are ultimately in control of the timing and the format of the proceedings. In addition, ICC judges also have to manage victim participation at all stages of the proceedings, something which has added considerably to the managerial workload.[396]

Unlike their counterparts at the *ad hoc* Tribunals, the ICC's judges have no direct procedural authority to limit the number of witnesses the parties may call or fix the number of crime sites or incidents upon which the prosecution may lead evidence. As discussed in the previous section, these case management tools – appropriately applied – could prove extremely valuable to the Court in its work.

6.7 Conclusion

More than just preparation for the ensuing trial, the pre-trial phase at the international criminal tribunals can be viewed as an effort to increase fairness and efficiency through a process of winnowing. First, the judges and parties decide which allegations warrant trial, through the review and confirmation of charges, and the negotiations that typically precede and produce guilty pleas. Second, there is further reduction in the number of trials – though certainly not their complexity – through consolidation, effected by joinder of charges, accused, and indictments. Third, and perhaps most controversially, there is constriction in the scope of trials through judicial intervention to limit the charges on which evidence may be adduced at trial, and even the type and extent of the evidence that can be presented on the charges that survive.

Viewed through this lens, it is not clear that the tribunals are successful in their efforts, or at least that (perceived) gains in efficiency have not come at the expense of procedural guarantees or institutional reputation. As the *Milošević* trial amply

[395] See Scheffer, *supra* note 295, p. 596 (characterising the confirmation hearing as 'the apex of the [pre-trial chamber's] engagement in a case'). On the confirmation hearing, see *supra* Sections 6.1.1.1.2, 6.1.1.2.
[396] On victim participation in proceedings before the ICC, see generally Chapter 8.

demonstrated, joinder of charges and indictments may in fact be counterproductive if the resulting trial is simply too unwieldy for a chamber to manage efficiently. At the same time, while the *ad hoc* Tribunals' judges have granted themselves the authority to intervene in the parties' decisions regarding the scope of the trial, the number of witnesses to be called, and the time to be taken in leading evidence, they do not appear to have significantly expedited the proceedings.[397] For all the concerns voiced over judicial meddling in the domain of the parties, the judges' touch has been rather light.

The ICC's judges may yet learn from the experience of their counterparts at the *ad hoc* Tribunals. The development and application of appropriate pre-trial and case management techniques will be crucial to fulfilling the promise of the Rome Statute. Indeed, given the permanence of the Court, what it does in its early years may be particularly important for generations to come. Yet its pre-trial and trial chambers currently lack certain procedural tools that may be of supreme importance to its functioning. As explained earlier in this volume, the ICC's judges have taken upon themselves a significant amount of legislative authority.[398] One beneficial use to which that power could be put would be the creation of regulatory tools that will enable them to efficiently manage and conclude the complex trials that are to come.

[397] On the judges' expanding power and efforts to expedite proceedings, see Chapter 12, Sections 12.2, 12.3.

[398] On the ICC's judges use of the Regulations of the Court to create rules with significant procedural impact, see Chapter 2, Section 2.2.2.

7

Trial proceedings

CONTENTS

Trial is the central and most visible phase of an international criminal prosecution.[1] In all the international criminal tribunals examined in this series, it is the public forum in which the prosecution and defence question witnesses, present documentary and other evidence, and make legal arguments before a panel of judges who serve as finders of both fact and law. Since the majority of accused before international criminal tribunals choose to contest the charges against them rather than plead guilty,[2] most cases to date have featured a trial, and the trial has usually been lengthy. Rarely has a trial chamber completed a trial in under a year, and trials lasting two or more years are common.[3] While the extended length of these trials has been criticised for potentially violating the rights of accused,[4] the reasons for delays are complex. Delay often occurs as a result of the unavoidable confluence of a challenging political context, complex substantive law, a heavy caseload, and persistent scarcity of resources.[5]

This chapter explores the trial phase of international criminal prosecutions, focusing on the *ad hoc* Tribunals, the ICC, and the SCSL. While differences exist in the trial procedures of these tribunals, trial before all of them is largely

1 See, e.g., 'Man of Peace, Man of War', *The Economist*, 29 August 2009, p. 52 (noting Liberian and Sierra Leonean public's close following of testimony in former Liberian president Charles Taylor's trial at the SCSL).

2 On guilty plea procedures and plea bargaining, see Chapter 6, Section 6.4; see also Steven R. Ratner, Jason S. Abrams, and James L. Bischoff, *Accountability for Human Rights Atrocities in International Law: Beyond the Nuremberg Legacy* (3rd edn 2009), pp. 221–222, 227–228 (explaining why so few accused plead guilty at the *ad hoc* Tribunals).

3 See, e.g., International Criminal Tribunal for the former Yugoslavia, Weekly Press Briefing, 15 January 2003, www.icty.org/sid/3446 (noting that '[t]he average length of trials at the [ICTY] is around 16 months'); Mark B. Harmon, 'The Pre-Trial Process at the ICTY as a Means of Ensuring Expeditious Trials: A Potential Unrealized', (2007) 5 *Journal of International Criminal Justice* 377, 383–384 (trials at ICTY 'breathtakingly long' when measured in calendar days). In the ICTR, final judgements are typically issued at least three or four years after the accused's initial appearance but in some cases the process has taken an entire decade. See Report on the Completion Strategy of the International Criminal Tribunal for Rwanda, UN Doc. S/2009/247, 14 May 2009 (providing information as of 4 May 2009).

4 See, e.g., Daniel J. Rearick, 'Innocent Until Alleged Guilty: Provisional Release at the ICTR,' (2003) 44 *Harvard International Law Journal* 577, 578.

5 See, e.g., O-Gon Kwon, 'The Challenge of an International Criminal Trial as Seen from the Bench', (2007) 5 *Journal of International Criminal Justice* 360, 364 (attributing delay to exceedingly complex crime base, elements of crimes and forms of responsibility that are far more complex than those in domestic criminal law, rambling testimony by witnesses unfamiliar with adversarial process, and similarly unfamiliar defence counsel who attempt to expose every inconsistency and error, 'even on irrelevant and trivial points'); David Wippman, 'The Costs of International Justice', (2006) 100 *American Journal of International Law* 861, 875 (noting greater complexity of issues before ICTY as compared to domestic criminal tribunals); Christina M. Carroll, 'An Assessment of the Role and Effectiveness of the International Criminal Tribunal for Rwanda and the Rwandan National Justice System in Dealing with Mass Atrocities of 1994', (2000) 18 *Boston University International Law Journal* 163, 181–184 (attributing delay at ICTR to its status as 'a nascent criminal court'; and noting lack of resources, dependence on state cooperation, and sheer volume of motions made by both prosecution and defence); Gabrielle Kirk McDonald, Address to the United Nations General Assembly, 8 November 1999, available at www.icty.org/sid/7725 (identifying length of ICTY proceedings as a 'primary concern' but noting that '[t]his process cannot be short-circuited'; that '[t]o do justice properly takes both time and resources'; and that delay is not surprising considering that ICTY 'is the first international criminal tribunal in 50 years and the law it applies must, in many instances, be interpreted and applied for the first time'); see also *infra* note 143.

adversarial and the corresponding rules are similar in nature, and they will thus be discussed in tandem.[6] Section 7.1 begins by looking at the process for appointing judges to a trial bench. It also examines procedures that apply when a judge falls ill, dies, or otherwise becomes unavailable after the start of trial, and what happens if a judge's impartiality is called into question. Section 7.2 reviews the rules governing the location of trial hearings. Section 7.3 surveys many of the means by which the trial chamber controls the conduct of proceedings, including by limiting the manner in which the parties may present evidence and their available time, and by removing disruptive persons from the courtroom or public gallery. Several additional procedures related to the trial chamber's control over the proceedings appear in other chapters of this volume.[7]

Chapter 7 continues in Section 7.4 by describing the requirement of a public trial and its exceptions, including closed trial sessions and protective measures, such as pseudonyms, for at-risk witnesses. Section 7.5 explores the requirement that the accused be present at trial and the exceptional circumstances in which trial may be held absent the accused. The subsections of Section 7.6 describe the procedures governing the various stages of the trial, including the transfer of the case from the pre-trial chamber to the trial chamber; opening statements; the presentation of each party's case; rebuttal, rejoinder, and reopening; and closing arguments. This section also discusses the practice known as witness 'proofing', as well as mid-trial proceedings for judgement of acquittal, during which the trial chamber may acquit the accused on some or all charges upon finding the prosecution's evidence insufficient. Section 7.7 examines the criteria under which a chamber may alter a previous ruling upon a motion for reconsideration. Section 7.8 describes the procedures relating to prosecution of persons for offences against the administration of justice, such as perjury, witness intimida-

[6] See Chapter 1, Section 1.3 (noting that some chapters discuss the tribunals in tandem, while others discuss them in separate subsections, mainly depending on whether their respective procedures differ significantly from one another).

[7] See, e.g., Chapter 4, Sections 4.3.3, 4.3.4 (trial chamber's power to order interim release of an accused from custody pending or during trial or appeal); Chapter 5, Sections 5.5, 5.6 (trial chamber's assignment or imposition of counsel, and use of *amici curiae* to make arguments on behalf of self-represented accused); Chapter 6, Section 6.2 (procedures for ordering two or more accused joined together into the same trial, or an accused severed from a joint trial); *ibid.*, Section 6.5.3 (trial chamber's supervision of parties' fulfilment of disclosure obligations); *ibid.*, Section 6.3.2 (trial chamber's orders to states, international organisations, and other entities for the production of documents or for testimony at trial); *ibid.* (trial chamber's power to subpoena witnesses and documents); *ibid.*, Section 6.4 (trial chamber's power to preside over guilty-plea proceedings when an accused pleads guilty at beginning of trial or after trial has begun); *ibid.*, Section 6.1.2 (ICC chamber's power to change the 'legal characterisation' of the facts charged against the accused); Chapter 11, Section 11.4 (trial chamber's prerogative to grant leave to file interlocutory appeal from certain types of decision).

tion, and the disclosure of protected witnesses' identities, and Section 7.9 offers some concluding remarks on the trial process.

7.1 Composition of the trial bench

7.1.1 Qualifications of judges and election to the tribunal

Judges at the international criminal tribunals must possess high moral character, impartiality, and integrity, and be qualified to serve in the highest judicial office of their home countries.[8] They must be independent and not engage in activities that may interfere with their judicial duties.[9] In the ICC, each judge must have experience in criminal law or the relevant areas of international law. In the *ad hoc* Tribunals and SCSL, the 'overall composition' of a trial chamber should reflect such experience.[10]

The manner in which judges are elected to serve on the various tribunals is patterned on the procedure at the International Court of Justice, but the details vary from tribunal to tribunal and, at the *ad hoc* Tribunals, depending on whether the judicial vacancy is for a permanent or an *ad litem* judge. For the ICTY and ICTR, UN member states and other entities with permanent observer status nominate candidates, and the UN Secretary-General forwards these nominations to the Security Council. The Council narrows the list, taking into account the need for representation from the world's principal legal systems and equitable geographical distribution. The General Assembly then elects the judges from the persons on the Council's list.[11] At the ICC, candidates are nominated by states parties to the Rome Statute and must be nationals of a state party. The candidates are organised into a list of candidates with expertise in criminal law and procedure, and another list of candidates with expertise in international law. The Assembly of States Parties elects the judges from the candidates on the two lists, having regard to the need for gender and geographical balance and representation of the principal legal systems.[12] Judges at the *ad hoc* Tribunals serve for four years and are eligible for re-election (except *ad litem* judges at the ICTR); judges at the ICC serve for nine years and may not be re-elected.[13] At the SCSL, judges

[8] Rome Statute, Art. 36(3)(a); ICTY Statute, Art. 13; ICTR Statute, Art. 12; SCSL Statute, Art. 13(1).

[9] See, e.g., Rome Statute, Art. 40.

[10] Rome Statute, Art. 36(3)(b); ICTY Statute, Art. 13; ICTR Statute, Art. 12; SCSL Statute, Art. 13(1).

[11] See generally ICTY Statute, Arts. 13 *bis*–13 *ter*; ICTR Statute, Arts. 12 *bis*–12 *ter*.

[12] See generally Rome Statute, Arts. 36–37. See also William A. Schabas, *An Introduction to the International Criminal Court* (3rd edn 2007), pp. 347–350 (detailing this process and the elections that occurred between 2003 and 2006).

[13] See Rome Statute, Art. 36(9) (also setting forth procedure by which one-third of ICC's judges is elected every three years); ICTY Statute, Arts. 13 *bis*(3) (permanent judges), 13 *ter*(1)(e) (*ad litem* judges); ICTR Statute, Arts. 12 *bis*(3) (permanent judges), 12 *ter*(1)(e) (*ad litem* judges).

are appointed – a majority by the UN Secretary-General, and a minority by the Sierra Leone government, upon nominations forwarded by states – and may be re-appointed.[14]

This nomination and election process has likely had adverse effects on the quality of justice dispensed by the international criminal tribunals. Many states nominate and elect judges based on politics rather than on their merit as judges.[15] Former ICTY Judge David Hunt opined as follows:

> The members of the General Assembly of the United Nations who elect the judges are mainly either diplomats or politicians, whose method of doing business is to make political compromises or to base their decisions upon diplomatic expediency. Such conduct is regarded as quite normal for diplomats and politicians. But it does not produce the most efficient form of judiciary, and it certainly does not produce the best judges who are available.[16]

Indeed, as a result of this process, a considerable percentage of the international judiciary, including at international criminal tribunals, is composed of former diplomats, government bureaucrats, parliamentarians and other domestic politicians, and academics, thereby diluting the number of judges with experience in judging actual cases.[17] In many countries, moreover, nominations are motivated by patronage, as service on an international tribunal is a lucrative, prestigious, and highly coveted position.[18] Furthermore, once elected, judges may be influenced by a need to show loyalty to the state that nominated them for election or, where re-election is a possibility, by a desire to curry favour with this state in order to guarantee re-nomination.[19]

[14] See SCSL Statute, Arts. 12–13 (three-year terms); Agreement Between the United Nations and the Government of Sierra Leone on the Establishment of a Special Court for Sierra Leone, 16 January 2002, 2178 UNTS 138, Art. 2(2)(a).

[15] See, e.g., Stephanos Bibas and William W. Burke-White, 'International Idealism Meets Domestic-Criminal-Procedure Realism', (2010) 59 *Duke Law Journal* 637, 667–671; *ibid.*, p. 668 ('In this context, bloc politics, bargaining, and horse-trading matter more than merit.'); *ibid.*, pp. 669–671 (proposals to improve the process); William A. Schabas, *The UN International Criminal Tribunals: The Former Yugoslavia, Rwanda and Sierra Leone* (2006), p. 595 (ICTY and ICTR elections 'do not show the most glorious side of international justice' and 'involve complex negotiations, often insincere pledges to vote for certain candidates, and commitments by States based on considerations that are far from judicial excellence and the need for the most qualified judges at the international tribunals').

[16] David Hunt, Address at the Conference of the Australian and New Zealand Society of International Law, Canberra, 19 June 2004 (on file with authors).

[17] See Erik Voeten, 'The Politics of International Judicial Appointments', (2009) 9 *Chicago Journal of International Law* 387, 390. See also, e.g., Kai Ambos, '"Witness Proofing" Before the International Criminal Court: A Reply to Karemaker, Taylor, and Pittman', (2008) 21 *Leiden Journal of International Law* 911, 915 (expressing serious doubts about the professional qualifications of many judges at international criminal tribunals, and pointing to the specific example of the late Fumiko Saiga, a Japanese woman with long diplomatic experience elected to the ICC judiciary despite her lack of a law degree).

[18] See, e.g., Bibas and Burke-White, *supra* note 15, p. 668; Voeten, *supra* note 17, pp. 397–398.

[19] See, e.g., Bibas and Burke-White, *supra* note 15, p. 669; Voeten, *supra* note 17, pp. 388–389. See also Gideon Boas, 'The Case for a New Appellate Jurisdiction for International Criminal Law', in Goran Sluiter and Sergey Vasiliev (eds.), *International Criminal Procedure: Towards a Coherent Body of Law* (2009), p. 445 (arguing for strict criteria for appointment of judges for election, including experience in judging criminal cases a proven record of excellence).

7.1.2 Appointment, composition, and general duties of trial judges

The trial bench is composed of three judges, with a fourth, non-voting judge in some ICC, ICTY, and SCSL cases. In the ICTY and ICTR, the bench may have two *ad litem* judges but must, with one narrow exception, have at least one permanent judge.[20] In those Tribunals, the judge who is senior in precedence among the three usually presides over trial hearings, by for instance administering the oath to witnesses, calling on counsel to speak, calling recesses, and ordering the hearing into private or closed session.[21] At the ICC and SCSL, the presiding judge is elected by his or her colleagues in the Trial Chamber.[22] The trial judges not only rule on matters of law, but also serve as the finders of fact and determine the accused's guilt or innocence, and decisions only require a two-judge majority vote.[23] None of the international criminal tribunals features a jury.

In the ICC, the Presidency of the Court constitutes a trial bench by choosing three judges from those in the 'Trial Division' after the pre-trial chamber has confirmed the charges against an accused, and transmitted the confirmation decision and case record; from that point forward the trial bench has primary control of the proceedings.[24] The rules in the *ad hoc* Tribunals are more fluid. Often, and especially in recent years, the chamber handling the pre-trial phase hears the trial as well, for reasons of efficiency.[25] If the Tribunal's President determines that the case management needs of the Tribunal or other factors warrant a different composition for trial,[26] he or she ascertains which of the three Trial Chambers in the Tribunal has judges available to hear the case; designates a permanent judge or judges from that Chamber to sit on the trial bench; and also

[20] ICTY Statute, Art. 12(2); ICTR Statute, Art. 11(2). On 'alternate' or 'reserve' judges and the narrow exception allowing a bench composed entirely of *ad litem* judges, see *infra* Section 7.1.4 and note 57.

[21] For example, if at the ICTY or ICTR the bench is composed of one permanent judge and two *ad litem* judges, the permanent judge presides. If the bench is composed of two permanent judges and one *ad litem* judge, the more senior permanent judge usually presides, though this is not always the case. For the rules on order of precedence, see ICTY Rule 17; ICTR Rule 17; ICC Court Regulation 10.

[22] SCSL Statute, Art. 12(3); ICC Court Regulation 13(2).

[23] ICTY Rule 87(A); ICTR Rule 87(A); SCSL Rule 87(A). The Rome Statute expresses a preference for unanimity, but ultimately does not require it. See Rome Statute, Art. 74(3). See also Chapter 10, Section 10.1.2 (discussing the requirement of majority concurrence in the verdict and the ICC's preference for unanimity).

[24] Rome Statute, Art. 61(11); ICC Rule 130; see also Rome Statute, Art. 39(1) (on divisions of Chambers). See also, e.g., *Prosecutor* v. *Lubanga*, No. ICC-01/04-01/06-842, Decision Constituting Trial Chamber I and Referring to It the Case of the Prosecutor v. Thomas Lubanga Dyilo, 6 March 2007. Confirmation of charges is discussed in Chapter 6, Section 6.1.

[25] On the transition from the pre-trial stage to the trial stage, see *infra* Section 7.6.1.

[26] For a former ICTY President's description of the factors that go into deciding how to assign cases, and of the working group that monitors caseload for this purpose, see Theodor Meron, 'Judicial Independence and Impartiality in International Criminal Tribunals', (2005) 99 *American Journal of International Law* 359, 364.

assigns any *ad litem* judges the UN Secretary-General has appointed to serve for that specific trial.[27] Sometimes the President leaves it to the presiding judge of the Trial Chamber to choose which of the permanent judges will sit, though the presiding judge must assign any *ad litem* judges the Secretary-General has appointed for the trial.[28]

7.1.3 Disqualification from sitting on the bench in a given case

The international criminal tribunals prohibit a judge from sitting on a trial bench in any case where his or her impartiality might reasonably be questioned.[29] Judges enjoy a presumption of impartiality,[30] and a party challenging a judge's impartiality bears a heavy burden when attempting to rebut this presumption by showing actual bias or a 'reasonable apprehension' of bias.[31] In a pre-trial decision in *Brđanin and Talić*, former ICTY judge David Hunt coined the 'apprehension of bias' standard repeated many times since: 'the reaction of the hypothetical fair-minded observer (with sufficient knowledge of the circumstances to make a reasonable judgment)' would be that the judge in question 'might not bring an impartial and unprejudiced mind' to the issue in question.[32]

The jurisprudence and rules elaborate some of the scenarios that might impair – or reasonably put into question – a judge's impartiality. Most fall into

[27] The Secretary-General makes this appointment upon the request of the Tribunal's President, and the President then issues an order formally assigning the appointed *ad litem* judge to one of the three Trial Chambers for a specific trial. ICTY Statute, Arts. 13 *ter*(2), 14(5); ICTR Statute, Arts. 12 *ter*(2), 13(5). See also, e.g., *Prosecutor* v. *Delić*, Case No. IT-04-83-PT, Order Assigning Judges to a Case Before a Trial Chamber, 2 July 2007 (President choosing one permanent judge of Trial Chamber I to sit on *Delić* trial bench, along with two *ad litem* judges appointed by Secretary-General for that trial); *Prosecutor* v. *Haradinaj, Balaj, and Brahimaj*, Case No. IT-04-84-PT, Order Reassigning a Case to a Trial Chamber, 15 January 2007 (transferring case from Trial Chamber II, which had presided over the pre-trial phase, to Trial Chamber I shortly before the start of trial); *Prosecutor* v. *Haradinaj, Balaj, and Brahimaj*, Case No. IT-04-84-PT, Order Assigning *Ad Litem* Judges to a Case Before the Trial Chamber, 19 January 2007 (Vice-President, acting for President, assigning two *ad litem* judges specifically to hear *Haradinaj* trial). The presiding judge of the *Haradinaj* Trial Chamber proceeded to trial with a bench composed of himself and these two *ad litem* judges.

[28] See, e.g., *Prosecutor* v. *Gotovina, Čermak, and Markač*, Case No. IT-06-90-PT, Order Composing a Trial Bench, 4 March 2008 (presiding judge of Trial Chamber I appointing himself from among the three permanent judges to sit on trial bench, along with the two *ad litem* judges appointed by the President specifically to hear *Gotovina* trial).

[29] Rome Statute, Art. 41(2)(a); ICTY Rule 15(A); ICTR Rule 15(A); SCSL Rule 15(A).

[30] *Prosecutor* v. *Galić*, Case No. IT-98-29-A, Judgement, 30 November 2006 ('*Galić* Appeal Judgement'), para. 41 (reaffirming *Prosecutor* v. *Furundžija*, Case No. IT-95-17/1-A, Judgement, 21 July 2000 ('*Furundžija* Appeal Judgement'), para. 197; *Prosecutor* v. *Akayesu*, Case No. ICTR-96-4-A, Judgement, 1 June 2001, para. 91)).

[31] *Galić* Appeal Judgement, *supra* note 30, para. 38 (reaffirming *Furundžija* Appeal Judgement, *supra* note 30, para. 189); *Prosecutor* v. *Sesay, Kallon, and Gbao* ('*RUF* Case'), Case No. SCSL-2004-15-AR15, Decision on Disqualification of Justice Robertson from Appeals Chamber, 13 March 2004 ('*RUF* Disqualification Appeal Decision'), para. 15; *Prosecutor* v. *Rutaganda*, Case No. ICTR-96-3-A, Judgement, 26 May 2003, para. 42.

[32] *Prosecutor* v. *Brđanin and Talić*, Case No. IT-99-36-PT, Decision on Application by Momir Talić for the Disqualification and Withdrawal of a Judge, 18 May 2000, para. 15. The Appeals Chamber later adopted this language in *Čelebići*. See *Prosecutor* v. *Delalić, Mucić, Delić, and Landžo*, Case No. IT-96-21-A, Judgement,

three categories: (1) a personal interest in the case, such as a political, financial, or other stake in the outcome;[33] (2) a personal connection – such as a close family relationship, friendship, or prior professional relationship – with a party or counsel;[34] and (3) the judge's public airing of an opinion relevant to an issue in the case that might reasonably be seen as prejudicing his or her thinking on that issue.[35] A judge's role in confirming the indictment or serving on the bench in the pre-trial phase of a case will not disqualify him or her from serving as a trial

20 February 2001 ('*Čelebići* Appeal Judgement'), para. 697; accord, e.g., *Prosecutor* v. *Hadžihasanović and Kubura*, Case No. IT-01-47-A, Judgement, 22 April 2008 ('*Hadžihasanović and Kubura* Appeal Judgement'), para. 78.

[33] ICC Rule 34(1)(a); ICTY Rule 15(A); ICTR Rule 15(A); *Furundžija* Appeal Judgement, *supra* note 30, para. 189. See also, e.g., *Prosecutor* v. *Šešelj*, Case No. IT-03-67-PT, Decision on Motion for Disqualification, 10 June 2003, paras. 3–4, 6 (dismissing challenge arguing that one judge's German nationality created bias because Germany had been traditionally hostile toward Serbia, and that the other judges' Catholic faith likewise created anti-Serb bias). The Rome Statute and ICC Rules list a similar scenario requiring disqualification: the judge 'has previously been involved in any capacity … in a related criminal case at the national level involving the person being investigated or prosecuted'. Rome Statute, Art. 41(2)(a); accord ICC Rule 34(1)(b). Another possible ground of disqualification could be a judge's active service as an official for his or her government. See, e.g., *Čelebići* Appeal Judgement, *supra* note 32, paras. 683–684 (judge elected Costa Rican Vice-President during trial not disqualified because she did not assume any government functions until after trial proceedings had ended).

[34] ICC Rule 34(1)(a). For example, in the *Karemera* case the presiding judge of the Trial Chamber, Judge Vaz, maintained a close personal friendship and lived in the same house as one of the prosecution attorneys during the pre-trial phase of proceedings. She chose not to divulge these facts until the accused filed motions challenging her impartiality several weeks into the trial. Before the remaining judges on the Bureau could decide the challenges, Judge Vaz recused herself, and the Bureau – composed of the President, Vice-President, and presiding judges of the three Trial Chambers – found it unnecessary to decide on the merits of the challenges. *Prosecutor* v. *Karemera, Rwamakuba, Ngirumpatse, and Nzirorera*, Case No. ICTR-98-44-T, Decision on Motions by Nzirorera and Rwamakuba for Disqualification of Judge Vaz, 17 May 2004 ('*Karemera et al.* May 2004 Bureau Decision'), para. 6; *infra* note 41 and accompanying text (at ICTR, Bureau may decide motion for disqualification). The ICTR Appeals Chamber subsequently determined that Judge Vaz's conduct 'gave rise to an appearance of bias'. Despite their knowledge of the relationship, the other two judges on the trial bench had remained silent when Judge Vaz dismissed an earlier oral motion to disqualify her. Consequently, the Appeals Chamber found further that the appearance of bias had tainted the entire bench. *Prosecutor* v. *Karemera, Ngirumpatse, Nzirorera, and Rwamakuba*, Case No. ICTR-98-44-AR15*bis*.2, Reasons for Decision on Interlocutory Appeals Regarding the Continuation of Proceedings with a Substitute Judge and on Nzirorera's Motion for Leave to Consider New Material, 22 October 2004 ('*Karemera et al.* October 2004 Appeal Decision'), paras. 67–68 (quotation at para. 67). As a result of the Appeals Chamber's ruling, a new trial panel was constituted to restart trial from the beginning. The resulting delays postponed trial for nearly a year, to 19 September 2005, and as of 1 December 2009 trial was still ongoing.

[35] ICC Rule 34(1)(d) ('[e]xpression of opinions, through the communications media, in writing or in public actions, that, objectively, could adversely affect the [judge's] required impartiality'). Such challenges usually fail. See, e.g., *Furundžija* Appeal Judgement, *supra* note 30, paras. 169–215 (in rape case, no reasonable appearance of bias arose from judge's previous status as member of UN Commission on the Status of Women, which called for the prosecution of mass rape at the ICTY); *Prosecutor* v. *Norman*, Case No. SCSL-04-14-PT, Decision on the Motion to Recuse Judge Winter from the Deliberation in the Preliminary Motion on the Recruitment of Child Soldiers, 28 May 2004, paras. 29–30 (in proceedings on whether child-soldier recruitment was a crime under international law, no reasonable appearance of bias where judge had previously reviewed and voiced support for UNICEF report favouring the prosecution of such a crime, but did not author the report). Occasionally, however, such challenges succeed. See, e.g., *RUF* Disqualification Appeal Decision, *supra* note 31, para. 18 (in case charging crimes against humanity against the leaders of a rebel group, reasonable appearance of bias where judge had previously expressed harsh negative opinions about the group in an academic work and opined that it had committed crimes against humanity). For more on *Norman* and *Sesay*, see James Cockayne, 'Special Court for Sierra Leone: Decisions on the Recusal of Judges Robertson and Winter', (2004) 2 *Journal of International Criminal Justice* 1154.

judge in the same case in the ICTY, ICTR, and SCSL,[36] but at the ICC such pre-trial involvement in a case does categorically disqualify a judge from sitting on the trial bench.[37]

Judges who have reason to question their own impartiality or the appearance thereof must withdraw, or ask the tribunal President or Presidency to excuse them.[38] Either party may also file a motion challenging a judge's impartiality and requesting disqualification.[39] The procedures governing such a challenge vary among the tribunals. The SCSL provides the simplest procedure: the party files the motion with the trial chamber, and the unchallenged judges decide whether to remove the challenged judge.[40] In the ICTR, the party files the motion with the presiding judge of the Trial Chamber, and 'if necessary' the Bureau – composed of the President, Vice-President, and presiding judges of the three Trial Chambers – decides whether to remove the judge.[41] In the ICTY, the presiding judge submits a report to the President who, 'if necessary', appoints a three-judge panel to determine the merits of the challenge.[42] In the ICC, all of the Court's judges, except the challenged judge, participate in deciding whether to grant the motion; an absolute majority is required to disqualify the challenged judge.[43]

[36] ICTY Rule 15(C); ICTR Rule 15(C); SCSL Rule 15(D). See also *Galić* Appeal Judgement, *supra* note 30, paras. 42, 44 (rejecting challenge to trial judge who confirmed the indictment in a different ICTY case, and giving rationale).

[37] Rome Statute Arts. 39(4), 41(2)(a). If faced with unresolved 'preliminary' issues, the trial chamber may refer the issues to a pre-trial chamber or pre-trial judge for decision, and thereby preserve the trial chamber's 'effective and fair functioning'. *Ibid.*, Art. 64(4).

[38] ICTY Rule 15(A) (judge may withdraw directly); Rome Statute, Art. 41(1) (judge asks Presidency to excuse him or her); ICC Rules 33, 35 (judge has duty to request to be excused where he or she has reason to believe that a ground for disqualification exists).

[39] ICTY Rule 15(B)(i); ICTR Rule 15(B); SCSL Rule 15(B); Rome Statute, Art. 41(2)(b); ICC Rule 34(2) (request for disqualification made in writing and addressed to challenged judge; challenged judge may present own views in writing).

[40] SCSL Rule 15(B).

[41] ICTR Rule 15(B). If the challenged judge is a member of the Bureau, the Bureau may decide the motion with fewer than all its members, see *Karemera et al.* May 2004 Bureau Decision, *supra* note 34, para. 2, or with a temporary substitute judge, see *Prosecutor* v. *Brđanin*, Case No. IT-99-36-R77, Decision on Application for Disqualification, 11 June 2004, para. 1. See also *Prosecutor* v. *Galić*, Case No. IT-98-29-AR54, Decision on Appeal from Refusal of Application for Disqualification and Withdrawal of Judge, 13 March 2003, para. 8 ('if necessary' means that if the petitioner challenges the decision of the presiding judge, the President refers the matter to the Bureau). *Brđanin* and *Galić* were decided under the previous version of the ICTY rule, where the President referred the matter to the Bureau. In *Karemera*, the challenged judge recused herself, and thus the ICTR Bureau found it unnecessary to decide the matter.

[42] ICTY Rule 15(B). The panel's decision is not subject to interlocutory appeal. *Ibid.* In the previous version of the ICTY rule, the President referred the matter to the Bureau, as in the ICTR. These decisions may be challenged on appeal at the end of trial. See, e.g., *Galić* Appeal Judgement, *supra* note 30, paras. 30–45.

[43] Rome Statute, Art. 41(2)(c) (challenged judge may present his or her views). See also Jules Dechênes, 'Excusing and Disqualification of Judges', in Otto Triffterer (ed.), *Commentary on the Rome Statute of the International Criminal Court: Observers' Notes, Article by Article* (1999), p. 626 (discussing Article 41(2)(c) and equating it with the 'absolute majority' standard in Article 40(4)); Jules Dechênes, 'Independence of the Judges', in Triffterer, *supra*, p. 623 (explaining, with respect to Article 40(4), that the exclusion of the challenged judge from the vote puts the total number of voting judges at seventeen, but opining that the 'absolute majority' required should be the absolute majority of the total number of the Court's judges – eighteen – and therefore ten votes are needed to disqualify the challenged judge).

While successful challenges at any of the tribunals are exceedingly rare,[44] in such cases the President or Presidency appoints another judge to sit in place of the disqualified judge.[45]

7.1.4 Temporary or permanent absence of a judge after trial has begun

The rules on judicial absence at the *ad hoc* Tribunals and the SCSL originated mainly as a practical reaction to dilemmas faced by those tribunals in practice. Because trials are usually very lengthy, there is a real prospect that one or more of the trial judges will, from time to time, not be available on a scheduled trial day. Not infrequently, moreover, judges on part-heard trials have died, become incapacitated by illness, have been recused from the case, or have failed to be re-elected to the tribunal. These tribunals – especially the ICTY and ICTR – have developed pragmatic mechanisms for dealing with short- and long-term judicial absences without necessarily having to postpone or restart the trial.[46] The ICC's procedures on judicial absence derive principally from the 1998 Statute and the 2002 Rules and thus predate much of the *ad hoc* Tribunals' important experience in this area; perhaps for that reason, these rules seem less accommodating. Reflecting this rigidity, the Rome Statute mandates that all three judges in a trial at the ICC be present for all trial hearings; when one cannot attend on a given day, it would appear that trial must be postponed.[47]

By contrast, the *ad hoc* Tribunals and SCSL allow two judges to continue with the trial if the third judge must be absent due to illness, urgent personal reasons, or 'authorised Tribunal business', provided they find it in the interests of justice to

[44] See, e.g., *In re Hartmann*, Case No. IT-02-54-R77.5, Report of Decision on Defence Motion for Disqualification of Two Members of the Trial Chamber and of Senior Legal Officer, 27 March 2009, para. 55 (disqualifying Judges Orie and Agius from serving on a bench specially appointed to hear contempt proceedings against former Office of the Prosecutor spokeswoman, and inviting the President to appoint other judges to replace them) (Judge Bonomy dissenting); *RUF* Disqualification Appeal Decision, *supra* note 31; *Karemera et al.* May 2004 Bureau Decision, *supra* note 34.

[45] ICC Rule 38(2); ICTY Rule 15(B)(iv); ICTR Rule 15(B); SCSL Rule 15(C); ICC Court Regulation 15(1).

[46] See Chapter 2, Section 2.1.4 (describing how judges at the *ad hoc* Tribunals are able to respond to unforeseen scenarios by rapidly amending the Rules to accommodate them).

[47] Rome Statute, Arts. 39(2), 74(1); *Prosecutor* v. *Lubanga*, Doc. No. ICC-01/04-01/06-1349, Decision on Whether Two Judges Alone May Hold a Hearing and Recommendations to the Presidency on Whether an Alternate Judge Should Be Assigned for Trial, 22 May 2008 ('*Lubanga* May 2008 Decision'), para. 15 (holding that all three judges must be present for each hearing, status conference, trial session, and deliberation, and 'any urgent issues that arise during the absence of a judge … will be dealt with solely on the basis of written representations'). Article 74(1) predates most of the *ad hoc* Tribunals' experience indicating that judges will frequently need to be absent for short periods of time due to illness, doctor's appointments, official trips, or other reasons. As discussed in Chapter 2, the ICC's rigid procedural framework makes it difficult to amend the Rules to respond to these sorts of problem that come to light only through practice, though the judges have often found ways to circumvent such rigidity through the promulgation of regulations. See Chapter 2, Sections 2.2.2–2.2.3.

continue, and the absence does not exceed five working days.[48] As pressure has mounted to speed up proceedings and trial sessions are often held simultaneously in different courtrooms, ICTY judges have frequently used this rule to avoid having to adjourn the proceedings, including when a judge must be absent from one trial session to be able to attend a simultaneous trial session in another case.[49] When it is necessary for the two remaining judges to rule on an objection or another matter, their decision must be unanimous.[50]

All the international criminal tribunals have mechanisms designed to avoid having to restart a part-heard trial where one of the judges becomes unavailable for the long term. In the ICC, SCSL, and ICTY, the President may assign an 'alternate' or 'reserve' judge who attends trial sessions from the beginning and attends the judges' deliberations, but does not have a vote.[51] If one of the original trial judges becomes unable to continue sitting, the President may then assign the alternate or reserve judge to sit in his or her place, and the trial continues, with the replacement judge now able to vote.[52] The ICTY has used a reserve judge in each of its three 'mega trials' involving six or seven political and military leaders, as well as in the high-profile trial of Radovan Karadžić, to avoid the disastrous consequences that

[48] ICTY Rule 15 *bis*(A); ICTR Rule 15 *bis*(A); accord SCSL Rule 16(A). ICTY judges have routinely invoked Rule 15 *bis*(A) without expressly stating why continuing without the other judge serves the interests of justice, and the parties seldom raise objections. See, e.g., *Prosecutor* v. *Gotovina, Čermak, and Markač*, Case No. IT-06-90-T, Transcript, 26 June 2009, p. 19365 (judge absent for 'urgent personal reasons'); *Prosecutor* v. *Popović, Beara, Nikolić, Miletić, Borovčanin, Gvero, and Pandurević*, Case No. IT-05-88-T, Transcript, 29 August 2007, p. 14422 (absent judge not feeling well); *ibid.*, 29 May 2007, p. 12131 (absent judge delayed in getting to Tribunal); *ibid.*, 23 March 2007, p. 9281 (judge absent 'for personal reasons'); 15 March 2007, p. 8985 (absent judge 'had to leave'). When the presiding judge is absent, the judge next in the line of precedence usually presides. See, e.g., *ibid.*, p. 9892 (Judge Kwon presiding where Judge Agius was 'indisposed'); *ibid.*, 16 May 2007, p. 11611 (same where Judge Agius away on official business).

[49] For example, while Judge Støle was sitting as the reserve judge on the *Popović* trial, the Secretary-General appointed him to also serve as a voting *ad litem* judge on the *Haradinaj* trial, which commenced several months after *Popović* and occasionally held hearings at the same time. When this happened, the other three *Popović* judges sat pursuant to Rule 15 *bis*(A). See *Prosecutor* v. *Popović, Beara, Nikolić, Miletić, Borovčanin, Gvero, and Pandurević*, Case No. IT-05-88-T, Transcript, 11 May 2007, p. 11348 (noting agreement among judges to proceed in this manner, and so proceeding). Despite the *Popović* Chamber's cautious invocation of Rule 15 *bis*(A), however, it is questionable whether such invocation is necessary merely because the reserve judge is absent, as the three voting judges are still present.

[50] In ICTY cases with a reserve judge, the two remaining voting judges must still reach unanimous agreement for rulings since, even though the reserve judge typically confers with the other judges as they deliberate on objections or other matters that require a contemporaneous ruling from the bench, such a judge has no formal vote. See, e.g., *ibid.*, 4 April 2007, p. 9957 (Chamber nullifying evidentiary ruling from previous day in which presiding judge made ruling with reserve judge's concurrence but over dissent of other voting judge).

[51] ICTY Statute, Art. 12(5) (Secretary-General appoints reserve judge from among available *ad litem* judges); ICTY Rules 15 *bis*(G), 15 *ter*; SCSL Statute, Art. 12(4) (Secretary-General or Sierra Leone government appoints one or more alternate judges); SCSL Rules 16(C), 16 *bis*; Rome Statute, Art. 74(1) (Presidency designates one or more alternate judges); ICC Rule 39; ICC Court Regulation 16; *Lubanga* May 2008 Decision, *supra* note 47, para. 17 (in deciding whether to designate alternate judge, Presidency should consider whether Court has resources for this purpose, anticipated length of trial, and personal circumstances of judges); see also *ibid.*, para. 23 (assessing these criteria and recommending that Presidency not designate alternate judge).

[52] ICC Rule 39; ICTY Rules 15 *bis*(G), 15 *ter*; SCSL Rules 16(C), 16 *bis*. Whether this judge can give his or her views on the issue being deliberated seems to differ in the ICC and ICTY. ICC Rule 39 and the *Lubanga*

could ensue from having to restart such lengthy and complex trials from the beginning.[53] In the SCSL, an alternate judge has sat with the bench in the Special Court's most important trial – that of former Liberian president Charles Taylor.[54] The ICC Presidency did not assign an alternate in the ICC's first trial, in the *Lubanga* case.[55]

Where a trial judge becomes permanently unavailable, and an alternate judge has not been appointed, it would appear the only option in the ICC is to restart the trial. In the SCSL, the two remaining judges may hear the rest of the trial if they are 'satisfied that it will not affect the decision either way'.[56] In the *ad hoc* Tribunals, the President may assign a 'substitute' judge and order the trial to begin anew, or to continue from that point.[57] If an accused does not consent to the trial continuing with a substitute judge, however, it can only proceed if the remaining two original trial judges unanimously decide that this course of action would serve the interests of justice.[58] Several ICTY and ICTR trials have proceeded with a substitute judge, both with and without the accused's consent.[59] The judges have considered the following factors, among others, as relevant: (1) whether the delay

Trial Chamber appear to have foreclosed this possibility. ICC Rule 39 (alternate judge 'shall sit through all the proceedings and deliberations of the case, but may not take part therein'); *Lubanga* May 2008 Decision, *supra* note 47, para. 15(c) (alternate judge cannot 'participate in the work of the Chamber' 'unless and until a member of the Chamber ceases permanently to function judicially during the trial'). No prohibition on reserve judges giving their opinion in deliberations exists in the ICTY. See, e.g., *supra* note 50.

[53] The mega trials were *Popović*, *Prlić*, and *Milutinović*. Since, as described below, the ICTY President can in some circumstances replace one judge who becomes permanently absent from trial with a substitute judge who has not been sitting with the chamber since the beginning of trial, the mega trials allowed for the possibility that two judges may step down from the trial bench without causing the trial to restart from the beginning. The first judge to become absent would presumably be replaced by the reserve judge, and the second by a substitute judge, though the Rules do not seem to express a preference as to the order of replacement. See ICTY Rule 15 *bis*(G). While the *Prlić* trial was ongoing as of 1 December 2009, none of the judges in *Popović* or *Milutinović* became permanently unavailable, and the reserve judges assigned to these cases never had to step in. On substitute judges, see *infra* text accompanying notes 57–62.

[54] Special Court for Sierra Leone, Press Release: Justice El Hadji Malick Sow of Senegal Sworn in as Alternate Judge, 9 May 2007, www.sc-sl.org/LinkClick.aspx?fileticket=SIQl4Ssen%2Bc%3D&tabid=110.

[55] See *supra* note 51.

[56] SCSL Statute, Art. 12(4); SCSL Rule 16(B)(i). This inartfully worded standard, which risks the impression that the two remaining judges must prejudge the outcome of the case in order to apply it, does not appear to have been tested, as in the three trials concluded in the SCSL as of 1 December 2009, no judge was unable to continue on a trial.

[57] ICTY Rule 15 *bis*(C); ICTR Rule 15 *bis*(C). In the interim, the President may authorise the two remaining judges to rule on 'routine matters'. ICTY Rule 15 *bis*(F); ICTR Rule 15 *bis*(F); on what 'routine matters' means, see *Prosecutor* v. *Karemera, Ngirumpatse, and Nzirorera*, Case No. ICTR-98-44-AR73.9, Decision on 'Joseph Nzirorera's Interlocutory Appeal of Decision on Obtaining Prior Statements of Prosecution Witnesses After They Have Testified', 31 May 2007, para. 10. Trial can continue even if the replacement results in bench composed entirely of *ad litem* judges. ICTY Statute, Art. 12(6); accord *Karemera et al.* October 2004 Appeal Decision, *supra* note 34, paras. 48–50.

[58] Either party may appeal this decision directly to the Appeals Chamber. ICTY Rule 15 *bis*(D), (F); ICTR Rule 15 *bis*(D). If neither party has given an opening statement or presented any evidence, however, the accused does not have standing to object to the assignment of a substitute judge. ICTY Rule 15 *bis*(C); ICTR Rule 15 *bis*(C).

[59] See, e.g., *Prosecutor* v. *Halilović*, Case No. IT-01-48-T, Judgement, 16 November 2005, Annex 2, para. 24 (noting 31 May 2005 substitution, with accused's consent, for ill judge who resigned); *Prosecutor* v. *Krajišnik*, Case No. IT-00-39 and 40, Decision Pursuant to Rule 15 *bis* (D), 16 December 2004 ('*Kraijišnik* December 2004 Decision') (no consent); *Prosecutor* v. *Milošević*, Case No. IT-02-54-T, Order Pursuant to Rule 15 *bis*(D), 29 March 2004 (no consent); *Prosecutor* v. *Nyiramasuhuko, Ntahobali, Nsabimana, Nteziryayo,*

caused by restarting the trial will infringe the accused's right to a speedy trial, or that of other accused waiting for available courtrooms to begin their own trials; (2) how far the parties' presentation of evidence has progressed; (3) whether and to what extent the substitute judge will be able to familiarise himself or herself with the evidence already presented and the demeanour of witnesses who have already testified; (4) whether re-calling witnesses to testify will put them at risk or cause them undue hardship; and (5) the extent to which the evidence already heard might now be unavailable.[60] The ICTR Appeals Chamber has emphasised that the judges must balance all the relevant factors in the totality of the circumstances.[61]

Where a substitute judge joins the bench, trial cannot resume until the new judge reviews the record and certifies his or her familiarity with it.[62] When the ICTY President assigned Judge Bonomy as a substitute on the *Milošević* bench after Judge May fell ill and had to resign,[63] Judge Bonomy spent several weeks reading transcripts of proceedings, watching video recordings, and examining evidence in order to bring himself up to speed.[64] While this process could be criticised on the basis that the substitute judge cannot be expected to satisfactorily review all the evidence already in the record while simultaneously attending trial sessions and deliberating on newly arising issues, as applied at the ICTY it does not seem that the parties have had a reasonable basis to argue that the overall fairness or administration of the trial has been adversely affected.

7.2 Location of trial

The trial is held at the seat of the tribunal unless otherwise decided. A decision to sit elsewhere must be made 'in the interests of justice'.[65] In 2007 and 2008, the ICTY for the first time held trial hearings away from The Hague, in

Kanyabashi, and Ndayambaye, Case No. ICTR-98-42-T, Decision in the Matter of Proceedings Under Rule 15 *bis*(D), 15 July 2003 ('*Butare* July 2003 Decision'), para. 34 (consent of only one of several accused); *Prosecutor* v. *Bagosora, Kabiligi, Ntabakuze, and Nsengiyumva*, Case No. ICTR-98-41-T, Decision on Continuation or Commencement *de Novo* of Trial, 11 June 2003 (where accused consented and prosecution preferred restarting trial, Trial Chamber deciding to continue without restarting).

60 *Kraijišnik* December 2004 Decision, *supra* note 59, paras. 14–17; *Butare* July 2003 Decision, *supra* note 59, para. 33, affirmed by *Prosecutor* v. *Nyiramasuhuko, Ntahobali, Nsabimana, Nteziryayo, Kanyabashi, and Ndayambaye*, Case No. ICTR-98-42-A15*bis*, Decision in the Matter of Proceedings Under Rule 15 *bis*(D), 24 September 2003 ('*Butare* September 2003 Appeal Decision'), paras. 22–36 (with Judge Hunt dissenting).

61 *Karemera et al.* October 2004 Appeal Decision, *supra* note 34, para. 54.

62 ICTY Rule 15 *bis*(D); ICTR Rule 15 *bis*(D).

63 *Prosecutor* v. *Milošević*, Case No. IT-02-54-T, Order Replacing Judge in a Case Before the Trial Chamber, 10 June 2004.

64 See *Prosecutor* v. *Milošević*, Case No. IT-02-54-T, Certification by Judge Bonomy of His Familiarity with the Record of the Proceedings, 10 June 2004.

65 ICC Rule 100(1); ICTY Rule 4; ICTR Rule 4; accord Rome Statute Art. 62 (trial at seat 'unless otherwise decided'). See also ICTY Statute, Art. 31 (ICTY seat in The Hague); Security Council Resolution 977, UN Doc. S/RES/977 (1995) (ICTR seat in Arusha, Tanzania); SCSL Rule 4 (SCSL seat in Freetown, Sierra Leone, but chamber may exercise functions away from Freetown 'if so authorized by the President', with no

facilities provided by the State Court of Bosnia and Herzegovina in Sarajevo.[66] The ICTR has held trial sessions in the Netherlands.[67] The Assembly of States Parties to the Rome Statute has contemplated that ICC trial hearings might likewise be held away from The Hague, as a means of increasing trial efficiency and exposing affected populations to the rule of law.[68] The SCSL has held the entire trial of Charles Taylor in The Hague in a courtroom borrowed from the ICC. Endorsing this arrangement, the Security Council determined that trying Taylor at the Special Court's seat in Freetown would disrupt peace and security in the region.[69]

7.3 Trial chamber control over the proceedings

The trial chamber must ensure that trial is fair, expeditious, and conducted in accordance with applicable procedural rules; it must also have due regard for the protection of victims and witnesses.[70] As Judge Hunt has acknowledged, a fair trial is one that is not only fair to the accused, but also to the prosecution, which acts on behalf of the international community.[71]

To aid it in discharging this duty, the trial chamber enjoys broad powers to control the conduct of proceedings, and to direct orders to the parties and other

express mention of 'interests of justice'). At the ICC, a two-thirds majority of the judges must approve the decision for the Court to sit in another state, and the state must consent. ICC Rule 100(3). At the ICTY, ICTR, and SCSL, the President makes the decision.

66 See *Prosecutor* v. *Delić*, Case No. IT-04-83-T, Order Concerning Hearing to Be Held in Sarajevo Pursuant to Rule 4 and Transfer of the Accused, 1 February 2008; International Criminal Tribunal for the former Yugoslavia, Press Release, 'Trial Chamber in Rasim Delić Case to Hold a Hearing in Sarajevo', 6 February 2008, www.icty.org/x/cases/delic/press/en/PR1214e%20Trial%20Chamber%20in%20Rasim%20Delic %20case%20to%20hold%20a%20hearing.pdf (noting that the February 2008 trial hearing in Sarajevo was 'at the request of the Prosecution, due to the specific circumstances of' prosecution witness Aiman Awad; that this hearing was the second *Delić* hearing in Sarajevo; and that the first hearing, in September 2007, had been the ICTY's first trial session outside The Hague).

67 See, e.g., *infra* note 141 (in June 2006, in the *Zigiranyirazo* case).

68 Assembly of States Parties to the Rome Statute of the International Criminal Court, Strategic Plan for the International Criminal Court, Doc. No. ICC-ASP/5/6, 4 August 2006, para. 34.

69 Security Council Resolution 1688, UN Doc. S/RES/1688 (2006), preambular para. 10 (noting that 'at present the trial of former President Taylor cannot be conducted within the subregion due to the security implications if he is held in Freetown at the Special Court'); *ibid.*, para 14 ('the continued presence of former President Taylor in the subregion is an impediment to stability and a threat to the peace of Liberia and of Sierra Leone and to international peace and security in the region'). The Security Council resolution ratified a previous arrangement among West African leaders that, if Nigeria agreed to surrender Taylor, who had been exiled there, they would push for him to be tried outside the region, for fear that his trial in Freetown would disrupt West African security. See Stephen J. Rapp, 'The Compact Model in International Criminal Justice: The Special Court for Sierra Leone', (2008) 57 *Drake Law Review* 11, 26–28. While the Resolution 1688 ratified this arrangement and served to override any conflicting domestic law that may have precluded it, the Special Court could have ordered that Taylor's trial be held outside Freetown on the basis of the SCSL's governing instruments alone. See SCSL Rule 4.

70 Rome Statute, Art. 64(2); ICTY Statute, Art. 20(1); ICTR Statute, Art. 19(1); SCSL Statute, Art. 17(2).

71 *Prosecutor* v. *Simić, Simić, Tadić, Todorović, and Zarić*, Case No. IT-95-9-PT, Separate Opinion of Judge David Hunt on Prosecutor's Motion for a Ruling Concerning the Testimony of a Witness, 27 July 1999, para. 27.

participants on a variety of matters.[72] In the words of the ICTR Appeals Chamber, '[d]ecisions relating to the general conduct of trial proceedings are matters within the discretion of the Trial Chamber'.[73] Trial judges' discretion in regulating trial proceedings is fitting in light of their 'organic familiarity with the day-to-day conduct of the parties and practical demands of the case'.[74] Some trial chambers have laid down written guidelines for the conduct of trial and the presentation of evidence, though most have not seen a need to do so.[75] A few of the more important features of the chamber's power to control the proceedings are discussed below.[76]

7.3.1 Orders on length of trial and evidence presentation

As discussed in Chapter 6, the chamber presiding over the pre-trial phase of proceedings makes decisions on the length of the prosecution's case-in-chief and the number of witnesses and exhibits it may lead at trial.[77] The chamber presiding over the trial generally enjoys the same sweeping powers.[78] When it takes over

[72] See Rome Statute, Art. 64(8)(b); ICTY Rule 54; ICTR Rule 54; SCSL Rule 54; accord *Prosecutor* v. *Stanišić and Simatović*, Case No. IT-03-69-AR73.2, Decision on Defence Appeal of the Decision on Future Course of Proceedings, 16 May 2008 ('*Stanišić and Simatović* May 2008 Appeal Decision'), para. 4.

[73] *Zigiranyirazo* v. *Prosecutor*, Case No. ICTR-2001-73-AR73, Decision on Interlocutory Appeal, 30 October 2006 ('*Zigiranyirazo* October 2006 Appeal Decision'), para. 9.

[74] *Milošević* v. *Prosecutor*, Case No. IT-02-54-AR73.7, Decision on Interlocutory Appeal of the Trial Chamber's Decision on the Assignment of Defense Counsel, 1 November 2004 ('*Milošević* November 2004 Appeal Decision'), para. 9. Despite this and several such acknowledgements by the *ad hoc* Tribunals' Appeals Chambers of the trial chambers' need for broad discretion, the Appeals Chambers have frequently dispensed with the principle. See Chapter 11, Sections 11.4.3, 11.5.2; see also, e.g., Chapter 10, note 248 and accompanying text (discussing Appeals Chamber interference in sentencing determinations).

[75] For examples of guidelines, see *Prosecutor* v. *Lubanga*, Doc. No. ICC-01/04-01/06-1140, Decision on Various Issues Related to Witnesses' Testimony During Trial, 29 January 2008; *Prosecutor* v. *Orić*, Case No. IT-03-68-T, Order Concerning Guidelines on Evidence and the Conduct of Parties During Trial Proceedings, 21 October 2004. See also Rome Statute, Art. 64(3)(a). But see *Prosecutor* v. *Taylor*, Case No. SCSL-03-1-T, Decision on Prosecution's Motion for an Order Establishing Guidelines for the Conduct of the Trial Proceedings, 16 July 2007, p. 2 (rejecting prosecution's proposed guidelines as unnecessary and potentially fettering the chamber's flexibility to deal with issues as they arise).

[76] Several other aspects of the trial chamber's control over the proceedings are discussed in other chapters of this volume. See *supra* note 7 (giving examples). The trial chamber's power to close the proceedings to the public, to issue and modify protective orders for witnesses, and to proceed in the accused's absence are discussed in Sections 7.4 and 7.5 of this chapter.

[77] This aspect of pre-trial proceedings is discussed in Chapter 6, Section 6.6.2.

[78] See ICTY Rules 65 *ter* (witness lists), 73 *bis* (power to limit number of prosecution witnesses and time available for examination and presentation of overall case), 73 *ter* (same for defence); ICTR Rules 73 *bis*–73 *ter* (similar); SCSL Rules 73 *bis*–73 *ter* (similar); Rome Statute, Art. 64(8)(b); ICC Rule 140; ICC Court Regulation 54. The ICTY Appeals Chamber has repeatedly sanctioned the broad employment of these powers. See, e.g., *Prosecutor* v. *Milošević*, Case No. IT-02-54-AR73, Reasons for Refusal of Leave to Appeal from Decision to Impose Time Limit, 16 May 2002, para. 13 (prosecution subject to chamber's power to manage proceedings); *ibid.*, para. 16 (trial chamber did not abuse its discretion in imposing time limits on prosecution case); *Prosecutor* v. *Galić*, Case No. IT-98-29-AR73, Decision on Application by Prosecution for Leave to Appeal, 14 December 2001, para. 7 (affirming trial chamber's oversight powers regarding how many witnesses prosecution may call); see also, e.g., *Prosecutor* v. *Lubanga*, Doc. No. ICC-01/04-01/06-1633, Decision on the 'Prosecution's Submission Pursuant to the Trial Chamber's "Decision on Prosecution's Request to Add Items to the Evidence to Be Relied on at Trial Filed on 21 April and 8 May 2008"' and the Prosecution's Related Application for Authorisation to Add One Item to the Evidence to Be Relied on at Trial, 20 January 2009, paras. 18–21 (allowing prosecution to add items to its evidence list and explaining reasons). Nevertheless, these powers are not unlimited, and must remain reasonable and respect equality of

the case, the chamber that will preside over the trial may adjust the case management framework as necessary during the remaining period of the pre-trial phase, and during trial depending on how the trial progresses. Following the close of the prosecution's case, the trial chamber makes decisions on the length of the defence's case-in-chief, and on the number of witnesses and exhibits it may call.[79] As the *ad hoc* Tribunals have matured, they have gained experience in managing cases where the prosecution often seeks to present evidence on thousands of criminal incidents involving scores of witnesses across broad geographical areas. Informing this experience is the unfortunate *Milošević* precedent, where the prosecution's overambitious case took far longer than anticipated despite the Trial Chamber's frequent intervention to limit its time and the number of witnesses it could call.[80] Facing increased pressure to speed up proceedings in light of the completion strategy, chambers have endeavoured – with varying success – to curtail the scope of the parties' cases, even applying innovative rules under which the prosecution may be ordered not to lead evidence on certain charges in the indictment.[81]

The trial chamber similarly maintains significant control over the manner in which the parties examine witnesses,[82] and may impose restrictions on counsel's contact with

arms between the parties. The ICTY Appeals Chamber has held, for example, that while equality of arms does not necessitate strict mathematical equality between the parties, the time available for the defence to present its case must be reasonably proportional to that given the prosecution. *Prosecutor* v. *Orić*, Case No. IT-03-68-AR73.2, Interlocutory Decision on Length of Defence Case, 20 July 2005, para. 7. See also *ibid.*, para. 9 (trial chamber's order allowing accused just thirty witnesses and twenty-seven days for case-in-chief not in reasonable proportion to prosecution's fifty witnesses and 100 days); *ibid.*, para. 6 (also unreasonable to prohibit accused from adducing evidence on military situation in Srebrenica, as such evidence would be key to supporting defence of military necessity).

[79] See Chapter 6, Section 6.6.2 (discussing *Prlić* Trial Chamber's adjustment of parties' overall time limits over the course of the trial); *infra* text accompanying notes 151, 166.

[80] For a detailed discussion of the Trial Chamber's attempts to manage the prosecution and defence cases in *Milošević*, including sweeping orders limiting the parties' time and the number of witnesses they could call, see Gideon Boas, *The Milošević Trial: Lessons for the Conduct of Complex International Criminal Proceedings* (2007), ch. 3; *ibid.*, p. 142 (discussing Chamber's order limiting prosecution's Kosovo case to ninety witnesses, and noting that prosecution ultimately led 133 Kosovo witnesses); *ibid.*, p. 143 (discussing order limiting prosecution to four witnesses per municipality to avoid cumulative evidence, and that the prosecution ignored that order and led more than four witnesses for some areas); *ibid.*, p. 154 (discussing how, despite Chamber's attempts to move defence case along, Milošević's evidence had focused almost entirely on Kosovo to the exclusion of Croatia and Bosnia by the time he died, 80 per cent of the way into the time allotted for his defence case); *ibid.* p. 197 n. 242 (citing case management orders in other ICTY cases).

[81] See Kwon, *supra* note 5, pp. 364, 372–376 and n. 42 (discussing the phenomenon of sprawling cases; some reasons behind it; how the judges amended Rule 73 *bis*(D) to allow chambers to order the prosecution not to present evidence on certain charges; and discussing the first decisions in which the rule was used for this purpose); see also, e.g., *Prosecutor* v. *Milutinović, Šainović, Ojdanić, Pavković, Lazarević, and Lukić*, Case No. IT-05-87-T, Decision on Application of Rule 73 *bis*, 11 July 2006; Chapter 6, Section 6.6.2 (discussing Rule 73 *bis*).

[82] See ICC Rule 140; ICTY Rule 90(F)–(H); ICTR Rule 90(F)–(G); SCSL Rule 90(F). See also *infra* notes 160–162 and accompanying text; see also, e.g., *Prosecutor* v. *Prlić, Stojić, Praljak, Petković, Ćorić, and Pušić*, Case No. IT-04-74-AR73.2, Decision on Joint Defence Interlocutory Appeal Against the Trial Chamber's Oral Decision of 8 May 2006 Relating to Cross-Examination by Defence and on Association of Defence Counsel's Request for Leave to File an *Amicus Curiae* Brief, 4 July 2006, p. 4 (upholding Trial Chamber's sweeping time limitations, including that the six accused, collectively, would be given the same amount of time to cross-examine a witness as the prosecution had to examine the witness).

witnesses,[83] including between defence counsel and the accused while the latter is testifying.[84] In addition, the judges may themselves pose questions to any witness at any time.[85] They may also call their own chamber witnesses or order the production of additional evidence.[86] All witnesses are required to testify under oath or a functionally equivalent affirmation.[87]

7.3.2 Sanctions for courtroom disruption and misconduct

Pursuant to the trial chamber's duty to maintain order at trial, if a person in the courtroom or the public gallery behaves disruptively, or in a manner detrimental to the fair-trial rights of the accused or the dignity of the proceedings, the chamber may expel that person.[88] Special rules, discussed below, apply where it is the accused who disrupts the proceedings.[89] The trial chamber may address more egregious conduct by ordering an investigation into whether the person committed an offence against the administration of justice.[90] Procedures for prosecuting offences against the administration of justice are examined later in this chapter.[91]

7.4 Public nature of trial and exceptions

The statutes of the international criminal tribunals recognise the accused's right to be tried in public.[92] As noted by the Trial Chamber in one of the ICTY's first written

[83] See, e.g., *infra* note 205 (ICC ban on contact between counsel and witness before witness's testimony).
[84] See, e.g., *Prosecutor* v. *Popović, Beara, Nikolić, Borovčanin, Miletić, Gvero, and Pandurević*, Case No. IT-05-88-T, Transcript, 26 January 2009, p. 30636–30638 (where Pandurević chose to testify during his case-in-chief, barring Pandurević and counsel from speaking to one another during cross-examination and re-examination about the content of Pandurević's testimony, unless specifically authorised to do so by the Trial Chamber); *Prosecutor* v. *Krajišnik*, Case No. IT-00-39-T, Finalized Procedure on Chamber Witnesses; Decisions and Orders on Several Evidentiary and Procedural Matters, 24 April 2006 ('*Krajišnik* Testimony Decision'), paras. 29–31 (where Krajišnik chose to testify during his case-in-chief, ordering Krajišnik, during the time period he was testifying, not to speak to anyone about his testimony, but allowing an exception for communicating with counsel about matters unrelated to his testimony).
[85] See *infra* notes 160–162 and accompanying text.
[86] For examples in the case law, see *infra* text accompanying note 180. The ICTY Rules also give an explicit power to the chamber to refuse to hear a witness called by a party who does not appear on the party's list of witnesses. ICTY Rule 90(G).
[87] Rome Statute, Art. 69(1); ICC Rule 66(1); ICTY Rule 90(A); ICTR Rule 90(B); SCSL Rule 90(B). But see, e.g., ICTY Rule 90(B) (no oath required for children not mature enough to understand the duty to tell the truth).
[88] Rome Statute, Art. 64(9)(b); ICC Rule 170 (also allowing permanent interdiction for repeated misconduct); ICTY Rule 80(A); ICTR Rule 80(A); SCSL Rule 80(A). For repeated offenders who fail to comply with trial chamber orders, in the ICC the trial chamber may prevent the person from attending the trial for a thirty-day period and issue a fine. ICC Rule 171 (if longer period needed, trial chamber must refer matter to Presidency).
[89] See *infra* text accompanying notes 129–130.
[90] See, e.g., ICC Rule 172.
[91] See *infra* Section 7.8.
[92] Rome Statute, Arts. 64(7), 67(1), 68(2); ICTY Statute, Arts. 20(4), 21(2); ICTR Statute, Arts. 19(4), 20(2); SCSL Statute, Art. 17(2); ICTY Rule 78; ICTR Rule 78; SCSL Rule 78; ICC Court Regulation 20(1). See also ICCPR, Art. 14(1) (also setting forth this right).

decisions, this right originates in the belief that public scrutiny of proceedings will help ensure that they remain fair.[93] Vindication of the right occurs not only through public trial hearings, but extends to all aspects of a case, including the parties' and other entities' written submissions, the chamber's decisions, and the trial record.[94] The tribunals accordingly allow members of the press and public to sit in the public gallery and view the trial directly through a wall of bulletproof glass; broadcast trial hearings over the Internet; and make transcripts, judicial and Registry decisions, and written submissions of the parties and other entities available on their websites.

Yet the statutes and rules also leave ample room for the trial chamber to impose measures to protect at-risk witnesses and sensitive documents from public exposure.[95] In determining such measures, the chamber must strike a balance between the rights of the accused to a fair trial; the rights of victims and witnesses to protection; and the right of the public to information about the case.[96] Due to the precarious security situation in the states of the former Yugoslavia, Rwanda, Sierra Leone, the Democratic Republic of the Congo, Sudan, and other countries that are the subject of ICC investigations and trials, protective measures have featured in virtually every trial at the international criminal tribunals. Despite such measures, several witnesses have been threatened, assaulted, or killed to prevent their testimony or in retribution for having testified.[97]

93 *Prosecutor* v. *Tadić*, Case No. IT-94-1-T, Decision on the Prosecutor's Motion Requesting Protective Measures for Victims and Witnesses, 10 August 1995 ('*Tadić* Protective Measures Decision'), para. 32.

94 *Prosecutor* v. *Brđanin and Talić*, Case No. IT-99-36-PT, Decision on Motion by Prosecution for Protective Measures, 3 July 2000 ('*Brđanin and Talić* Protective Measures Decision'), para. 55 ('[T]here is a public interest in the workings of courts generally ... not just in the hearings, but in everything to do with their working ... which should only be excluded if good cause is shown to the contrary.').

95 See Rome Statute, Arts. 64(6)(e), 64(7), 68; ICTY Statute, Art. 22; ICTR Statute, Art. 21; SCSL Statute, Art. 17(2); ICC Rules 85–88; ICTY Rule 75; ICTR Rule 75; SCSL Rule 75; ICC Court Regulation 20.

96 *Prosecutor* v. *Karadžić*, Case No. IT-95-5/18-PT, Decision on Motion for and Notifications of Protective Measures, 26 May 2009, para. 11; accord *Prosecutor* v. *Karadžić*, Case No. IT-95-5/18-PT, Decision on Prosecution's Motion for Delayed Disclosure for KDZ456, KDZ493, KDZ531 and KDZ 532, and Variation of Protective Measures for KDZ489, 5 June 2009 ('*Karadžić* Delayed Disclosure Decision'), para. 6; *Prosecutor* v. *Milošević*, Case No. IT-02-54-T, Decision on Prosecution Motion for Provisional Protective Measures Pursuant to Rule 69, 19 February 2002 ('*Milošević* Protective Measures Decision'), paras. 28, 32; *Brđanin and Talić* Protective Measures Decision, *supra* note 94, para. 7.

97 See, e.g., Bruce Zagaris, 'Law of War: A Bomb Kills Croatian Witness Who Was Cooperating with War Crimes Tribunal', (2000) 16 *International Enforcement Law Reporter* 977 (murder of prospective ICTY witness); Alan Zarembo, 'Rwanda's Genocide Witnesses are Killed as Wheels of Justice Slowly Begin Turning: More than 200 Rwandan Genocide Survivors Were Killed Last Year Before They Could Testify in Court', *Christian Science Monitor*, 23 January 1997, p. 7, available at www.csmonitor.com/1997/0123/012397.intl.intl.2.html; Andrew Purvis, 'Dead Witnesses Tell No Tales: Rwandan Genocide Survivors Are the Latest Targets of Hutu Killer Gangs', *Time* (International Edition), 23 September 1996, p. 35; Nasser Ega-Musa, 'Another Failure of Justice in Africa', *Washington Post*, 6 March 1997, p. A21 (witness murdered, along with family, after testifying at ICTR despite protective measures); Michael Farquhar, Global Policy Forum, 'Witness Intimidation Is a Serious Problem in Kosovo', 1 April 2005, www.globalpolicy.org/component/content/article/163/29346.html (intimidation of prospective ICTY witnesses in Kosovo); *Prosecutor* v. *Haradinaj, Balaj, and Brahimaj*, Case No. IT-04-84-T, Judgement, 3 April 2008 ('*Haradinaj et al.* Trial Judgement'), para. 6 (Trial Chamber noting 'significant difficulties in securing the testimony of a large number of witnesses'; that '[m]any witnesses cited fear as a prominent reason for not wishing to appear before the Trial Chamber to give evidence'; and that '[t]he Trial Chamber gained a strong impression that the trial was being held in an atmosphere where witnesses felt unsafe'); *Prosecutor* v. *Katanga and Ngudjolo*, Doc. No. ICC-01/04-01/07-T-81-Red-ENG, Transcript, 25 November 2009, p. 9

7.4.1 Trial in private or closed session

The chamber may hold hearings, or portions of a hearing, outside of public scrutiny if necessary to protect the safety or security of an at-risk victim or witness or the confidentiality of sensitive documents.[98] Because protective measures must be no more restrictive than necessary, however, chambers at the *ad hoc* Tribunals and SCSL have drawn a distinction between 'closed' session – expressly provided for in the Rules – and 'private' session, and utilise the latter much more frequently because it still allows the public to follow the trial to some degree. In closed session, blinds separate the public from the courtroom and no audiovisual transmission of the proceedings is broadcast into the gallery or over the Internet. In private session, no blinds are drawn; the audio is turned off, so spectators cannot hear what is said through the bulletproof glass, and if protective measures have been granted, a screen typically obscures the public's view of the witness.

7.4.2 Protective measures for witnesses and documents

The tribunals' statutes and rules entitle at-risk witnesses to protection, including the protection of their identities, as long as the measures ordered are consistent with the rights of the accused.[99] The onus is on the party seeking protective measures to demonstrate the existence of an objectively grounded risk to the security or welfare of the specific witness in question, or to his or her family, that would result from the knowledge that the witness will give or has given testimony.[100] In evaluating whether protective measures are warranted, the chamber must weigh the need for protection against the accused's right to have adequate time to prepare a defence.[101]

(investigator noting 'clear intimidation of our witnesses on the field' and 'foreseeable risk of also physical harm').

98 See Rome Statute, Arts. 64(7), 68(2); ICTY Statute, Arts. 20(4), 22; ICTR Statute, Arts. 19(4), 21; ICTY Rule 79 (closed session warranted to protect 'public order or morality'; the 'safety, security or non-disclosure of the identity of a victim or witness' where the chamber has ordered protective measures; or 'the interests of justice'); ICTR Rule 79 (same); SCSL Rule 79 (same); ICC Court Regulation 20.

99 Rome Statute, Arts. 64(6)(e), 68; ICTY Statute, Art. 20(1); ICTR Statute, Art. 19(1); ICC Rules 86–87; ICTY Rule 75(A); ICTR Rule 75(A); SCSL Rule 75(A).

100 *Prosecutor* v. *Martić*, Case No. IT-95-11-T, Decision on Prosecution's Motion for Variation of Protective Measures, 17 March 2006, p. 1; see also *ibid.*, p. 2 (allowing testimony in closed session due to objectively grounded risk to witness's security and welfare where witness had testified in past ICTY cases and experienced 'considerable adverse reactions from people in his place of residence'). Accord, e.g., *Prosecutor* v. *Serugendo*, Case No. ICTR-05-84-I, Decision on Motion for Protection of Witnesses, 1 June 2006, para. 2; see also *ibid.*, para. 3 (granting pseudonyms and other protected measures to certain defence witnesses with a 'close relationship to the Accused' and 'pre-existing vulnerabilities which have already created a need for their relocation to third countries and other well-founded fears of reprisals'). See also, e.g., *Prosecutor* v. *Haradinaj, Balaj, and Brahimaj*, Case No. IT-04-84-T, Decision on Prosecution's 30th and 31st Motions for Trial-Related Protective Measures, 6 November 2007, para. 4 (risk to witness justified maintaining his pseudonym and releasing only redacted version of his evidence).

101 See *supra* note 96 and sources cited therein.

This balance will almost never justify obscuring the witness's identity from the accused indefinitely. Indeed, only one witness before the *ad hoc* Tribunals ever testified anonymously: 'Witness L', whose real name was later revealed to be Dragan Opačić, in the *Tadić* case.[102] The Trial Chamber majority's decision to allow the prosecution to withhold the witness's identity from Tadić prompted a lengthy dissent and an intense academic debate about the practice.[103] Subsequent chambers denied motions requesting that a witness's name be withheld from the accused indefinitely,[104] and the Prosecutors abandoned the practice of seeking anonymity soon thereafter.[105]

Due to the severe adverse effect anonymity has on the accused's ability to prepare a defence, it is much more common for the trial chamber (or the pre-trial chamber before it) to grant the prosecution 'delayed disclosure' – that is, permission to refrain from disclosing information that would identify the witness to the accused until a certain number of days before the beginning of the trial or the witness's scheduled testimony, notwithstanding the normal rules on disclosure.[106] As discussed in more detail in Chapter 6,[107] in order for the trial chamber to grant delayed disclosure measures to a prosecution witness, the prosecution must show an objective likelihood of interference with the witness resulting from disclosure; as well as specific evidence of the risk, rather than an indeterminate risk to witnesses in general due, for example, to the poor security situation in the former Yugoslavia and Rwanda.[108] Witnesses whose testimony will more directly implicate the accused's own conduct may require greater protection.[109]

102 See Michael P. Scharf, *Balkan Justice* (1997), pp. 171–72. For the Trial Chamber's analysis, see *Tadić* Protective Measures Decision, *supra* note 93, paras. 53–86. This decision sparked an intense debate in 1996 and 1997.

103 See *Tadić* Protective Measures Decision, *supra* note 93, Separate Opinion of Judge Stephen on the Prosecutor's Motion Requesting Protective Measures for Victims and Witnesses. See also, e.g., Monroe Leigh, 'The Yugoslav Tribunal: Use of Unnamed Witnesses Against Accused', (1996) 90 *American Journal of International Law* 235; Christine M. Chinkin, 'Due Process and Witness Anonymity', (1997) 91 *American Journal of International Law* 75; Monroe Leigh, 'Witness Anonymity Is Inconsistent with Due Process', (1997) 91 *American Journal of International Law* 80.

104 See, e.g., *Prosecutor* v. *Blaškić*, Case No. IT-95-14-T, Decision on the Application of the Prosecutor Dated 17 October 1996 Requesting Protective Measures for Victims and Witnesses, 5 November 1996, para. 24 (beginning from 'a reasonable time before the start of the trial itself', 'the right of the accused to an equitable trial must take precedence and require that the veil of anonymity be lifted in his favour, even if the veil must continue to obstruct the view of the public and the media').

105 See Schabas, *supra* note 15, p. 474.

106 See ICTY Rule 69; ICTR Rule 69; SCSL Rule 69.

107 See Chapter 6, Section 6.5.1.5.

108 See *Karadžić* Delayed Disclosure Decision, *supra* note 96, paras. 9–12; *ibid.*, para. 12 (balance '"dictates clearly in favour of an accused's right to the identity of witnesses which the Prosecution intends to rely upon"') (quoting *Milošević* Protective Measures Decision, *supra* note 96, para. 32); *ibid.*, para. 15 (finding exceptional circumstances warranting delayed disclosure until thirty days prior to the witness's testimony). See also, e.g., *Prosecutor* v. *Taylor*, Case No. SCSL-03-1-PT, Decision on Confidential Prosecution Motion for Immediate Protective Measures for Witnesses, 5 May 2006 ('*Taylor* Protective Measures Decision'), p. 3 (allowing delayed disclosure of protected witnesses' identities until forty-two days before witness's testimony). On disclosure generally, see Chapter 6, Section 6.5.

109 See *Karadžić* Delayed Disclosure Decision, *supra* note 96, para. 11.

When a witness whose identity is protected testifies, the accused and the other courtroom participants can see the witness and vice versa, but the witness is separated from the public gallery by an opaque screen. The trial chamber (or the pre-trial chamber at an earlier stage of proceedings) assigns the witness a pseudonym to be used in any public proceedings, and orders that the witness's name and other identifying information be redacted from the public version of transcripts, filings, and other documents. Depending on the level of risk, the chamber may also order that the witness's image and voice be distorted on audiovisual transmissions.[110]

Documentary evidence may also be subject to protective measures.[111] The transcripts of portions of trial held in private or closed session are not accessible to the public, and chambers frequently order parts of transcripts redacted where a protected witness or other participant inadvertently states the witness's name or another piece of identifying information. Moreover, the parties typically file scores of confidential documents before the chamber, such documents containing sensitive medical or other information about the accused; national security information provided by a government or international organisation on condition that it remain confidential; or where the information would expose a vulnerable victim or witness.[112] Several persons have been tried for offences against the administration of justice for disclosing information about confidential documentary evidence.[113]

Protective measures ordered in one case remain in place in the future unless and until the chamber that imposed them, or another competent chamber, varies or rescinds them.[114] Parties in a subsequent case can move to vary the protective measures so that they may have full access to information such as confidential documents or the real name of a witness; they can also move to have the measures rescinded altogether, or to have them augmented. At the ICTY and ICTR, the motion goes to any chamber remaining seised of the case where the measures were originally

[110] ICC Rule 87(3); ICTY Rule 75(B); ICTR Rule 75(B); SCSL Rule 75(B). See also, e.g., *Prosecutor* v. *Abu Garda*, Doc. No. ICC-02/05-02/09-117-Red, Public Redacted Version of 'Decision on the Prosecutor's Application for Protective Measures Dated 22 September 2009', 9 October 2009, pp. 4–5 (ordering pseudonym, image and voice distortion in broadcasts, and expunging of witness's name from public court records; that any part of the proceedings requiring discussion of witness's name and identity be held in closed session; and prohibiting accused and other court participants from disclosing witness's name to public).

[111] See, e.g., *Brđanin and Talić* Protective Measures Decision, *supra* note 94, para. 65 (ordering prosecution to disclose unredacted version of indictment supporting material and other documents to the accused, and ordering the accused not to disclose the information to the public); *infra* note 115 (rules on access to confidential documents and other information from a previous case).

[112] For a discussion of the various tribunals' rules on the protection of national security information, see Chapter 6, Section 6.5.1.4.

[113] See, e.g., *In re Hartmann*, Case No. IT-02-54-R77.5, Judgement on Allegations of Contempt, 14 September 2009, paras. 89–90 (convicting former Office of the Prosecutor spokesperson of interfering with administration of justice for divulging in book and article information gleaned from confidential documents in *Milošević* trial). Offences against the administration of justice are discussed in Section 7.8, *infra*.

[114] ICTY Rule 75(F); ICTR Rule 75(F); SCSL Rule 75(F). See also, e.g., *Taylor* Protective Measures Decision, *supra* note 108, p. 2 and n. 1 (noting continuation in force of protective measures from prior SCSL trials, and citing several decisions from these cases).

ordered. If the earlier proceedings have concluded – as is often the case where the measures were ordered several years prior – the chamber seised of the current case decides the motion, in consultation with any judge of the original bench remaining at the tribunal.[115] If the earlier case is still on appeal, the Appeals Chamber has rare original jurisdiction to dispose of the motion at first instance, though trial chambers seem to have treated such appellate decisions as having the same binding, precedential force as second-instance Appeals Chamber decisions.[116] At the ICTY, the witness enjoying the protective measures must consent to the change, unless the moving party makes a 'compelling showing of exigent circumstances' or demonstrates that 'a miscarriage of justice would otherwise result'.[117] In a step that should facilitate trials in the courts of the former Yugoslavia of cases referred by the ICTY under Rule 11 *bis*, the ICTY's judges extended the rule on variation of protective measures to allow judges and parties in another jurisdiction to apply to have Tribunal-imposed protective measures varied or rescinded. The protected victim or witness himself or herself may also apply for variation of the measures.[118]

7.4.3 Testimony by video-link

In some circumstances, the trial chamber may allow the witness to testify from outside the courtroom via video-link. Video-link testimony may be warranted, for example, for especially sensitive witnesses such as children or victims of sexual violence who would be traumatised by being in the same room as the accused.[119] The chamber may also allow video-link testimony from other witnesses with valuable testimony who are unable or unwilling to travel to the seat of the tribunal where the testimony is so important to the party requesting the testimony that

[115] ICTY Rule 75(G), (I); ICTR Rule 75(G)–(H). See also SCSL Rule 75(G), (J) (motion always goes to chamber seised of current case, but alteration of measures only applies to current case and original measures remain in effect for all other purposes).

[116] See, e.g., *Prosecutor* v. *Haradinaj, Balaj, and Brahimaj*, Case No. IT-04-84-PT, Order on Motions for Access to Confidential Material, 27 September 2006, p. 3 (relying on several original-jurisdiction appeal decisions for the test: moving party must establish 'legitimate forensic purpose' justifying access to confidential material from other case; legitimate forensic purpose is established by showing existence of 'nexus' between movant's case and case from which confidential material is sought; nexus is established by showing a 'geographical, temporal or otherwise material overlap' between two proceedings, but respective charges need not be identical; and movant must show that material 'is likely to assist the applicant's case materially, or ... there is a good chance that it would') (footnotes and internal quotation marks omitted). See also Chapter 6, Section 6.5.4 (discussing access to confidential materials in other cases).

[117] ICTY Rule 75(J). See also, e.g., *Prosecutor* v. *Karadžić*, Case No. IT-95-5/18-T, Decision on Prosecution's Motion for Rescission of Protective Measures (KDZ546), 29 October 2009, paras. 5–6 (rescinding, with witness's consent, measures originally ordered in *Krstić* case).

[118] ICTY Rule 75(H). On Rule 11 *bis* referral, see Chapter 3, Section 3.1.3.

[119] See, e.g., Rome Statute, Art. 68(2); see also ICTY Rule 81 *bis*; SCSL Rule 85(D) (allowing evidence to be given by video-link); see also *Prosecutor* v. *Bagosora, Kabiligi, Ntabakuze, and Nsengiyumva*, Case No. ICTR-98-41-T, Decision on Prosecution Request for Testimony of Witness BT via Video-Link, 8 October 2004 ('*Military I* October 2004 Video-Link Decision'), paras. 7–8 (recognising that ICTR chambers can also hear video-link testimony despite the lack of a specific provision in the ICTR Rules).

it would be unfair to proceed without it, and allowing such testimony would not prejudice the accused's right of confrontation.[120]

7.5 Trial in accused's presence and exceptions

Trials *in absentia* are prohibited in the *ad hoc* Tribunals, SCSL, and ICC. Moreover, the accused has the right to be physically present in the courtroom for each trial session.[121] However, this right is not absolute,[122] and the rules and jurisprudence have recognised two main exceptions.[123]

[120] *Prosecutor* v. *Haradinaj, Balaj, and Brahimaj*, Case No. IT-04-84-T, Decision on Prosecution's Motion for Testimony Via Video-Link for Witness 54, 7 September 2007 ('*Haradinaj et al.* September 2007 Video-Link Decision'), para. 5; *Prosecutor* v. *Bagosora, Kabiligi, Ntabakuze, and Nsengiyumva*, Case No. ICTR-98-41-T, Decision on Testimony by Video-Conference, 20 December 2004 ('*Military I* December 2004 Video-Link Decision'), para. 4. See also, e.g., *Haradinaj et al.* September 2007 Video-Link Decision, *supra*, paras. 6–8 (finding that proposed teenage witness's young age and wish to remain close to his family support network constituted good reason for his unwillingness to travel to The Hague; that the witness's testimony was sufficiently important to the prosecution, as he was the only eyewitness to a certain charged crime; and that the accused would not be prejudiced by allowing this witness to appear by video-link); *Prosecutor* v. *Haradinaj, Balaj, and Brahimaj*, Case No. IT-04-84-T, Decision on Motion for Videolink (Witness 30), 14 September 2007, para. 6 (allowing video-link testimony for witness with post-traumatic stress disorder); *Prosecutor* v. *Popović, Beara, Nikolić, Borovčanin, Miletić, Gvero, and Pandurević*, Case No. IT-05-88-T, Decision on Popović's Motion Requesting Video-Conference Link Testimony of Two Witnesses, 28 May 2008, para. 14 (granting defence motion for video-link testimony of two witnesses where one did not want to travel and the other was ill); *Military I* December 2004 Video-Link Decision, *supra*, para. 7 (granting accused's motion to hear witness, a Canadian major, by video-link where the major's doctors had stated his health was too fragile to travel to Arusha); *Military I* October 2004 Video-Link Decision, *supra* note 119, paras. 11–16 (granting prosecution's motion to hear witness by video-link where anticipated testimony concerned 'an utterance by one of the Accused to another Accused which could be probative of several elements of the Prosecution case', and witness refused to travel to Arusha) (quotation at para. 11).

[121] Rome Statute, Art. 63(1); ICTY Statute, Art. 21(4)(d); ICTR Statute, Art. 20(4)(d); SCSL Statute, Art. 17(4)(d). Accord *Zigiranyirazo* October 2006 Appeal Decision, *supra* note 73, para. 13; ECCC Rule 81(1). See also ICCPR, Art. 14(3)(d) (also setting forth this right). By contrast, the Special Tribunal for Lebanon allows trials *in absentia*. See Statute of the Special Tribunal for Lebanon, UN Doc. S/RES/1757 (2007), Annex, Art. 22; Björn Elberling, 'The Next Step in History-Writing Through Criminal Law: Exactly How Tailor-Made Is the Special Tribunal for Lebanon?', (2008) 21 *Leiden Journal of International Law* 529, 535–538.

[122] *Prosecutor* v. *Nahimana, Barayagwiza, and Ngeze*, Case No. ICTR-99-52-A, Judgement, 28 November 2007 ('*Media* Appeal Judgement'), para. 99; *Zigiranyirazo* October 2006 Appeal Decision, *supra* note 73, para. 14; *Milošević* November 2004 Appeal Decision, *supra* note 74, para. 13.

[123] These and other exceptions also exist for certain types of pre-trial hearings, such as confirmation of charges proceedings in the ICC, which a pre-trial chamber may hold without the accused where he or she has waived the right to be present or cannot be found. Rome Statute, Art. 61(2); see also Chapter 6, Section 6.1 (discussing confirmation of charges); see also, e.g., Rome Statute, Art. 72(7)(a)(ii) (*ex parte* hearing for national security information). At the ICTY, another type of *in absentia* proceeding – only used in the early years when the judges had considerable time on their hands, as few accused had been apprehended, yet widely discussed in 1990s literature – allows a trial chamber to hear the prosecution's evidence against an at-large accused to determine if reasonable grounds exist for believing the accused responsible for the crimes charged. See ICTY Rule 61; see also, e.g., *Prosecutor* v. *Karadžić and Mladić*, Case Nos. IT-95-5-R61 and IT-95-18-R61, Review of the Indictments Pursuant to Rule 61 of the Rules of Procedure and Evidence, 11 July 1996 (extensive fifty-eight-page decision).

7.5.1 Waiver of right to presence

First, the accused may waive the right to be physically present at trial as long as the waiver is 'free and unequivocal (though it can be express or tacit) and done with full knowledge', and the accused continues to be represented by counsel.[124] The trial chamber may regard an accused who refuses to attend trial as impliedly waiving the right to be present.[125] The most extreme example may be that of ICTR accused Jean-Bosco Barayagwiza, who declared the proceedings a show trial and never attended a day of trial. The Trial Chamber proceeded in his absence but ordered counsel to continue representing him. On appeal the Appeals Chamber rejected Barayagwiza's challenge, finding that his refusal constituted a free, knowing, and unequivocal waiver.[126] In the ICTY, accused in joint trials have often given their written consent to trial continuing when they cannot attend trial on a given day.[127] In one ICTY case, moreover, a paraplegic accused consented to an arrangement by which he viewed his trial from the detention centre through closed-circuit video-link.[128]

7.5.2 Absence due to disruption

Second, trial may proceed in the accused's absence, and without a waiver, if insisting on physical presence would disrupt the trial or otherwise impair its expeditiousness beyond a permissible level. This may occur where the accused intentionally disrupts the trial by, for example, repeatedly speaking out of turn, shouting over the judges or prosecution attorneys, or berating witnesses. The trial chamber must give the accused a warning, and if he or she persists in 'substantial trial disruption' despite that warning, he or she forfeits the right to be present at trial and the chamber

[124] *Media* Appeal Judgement, *supra* note 122, para. 109 (accused must also be informed of right to be present and that presence is required at trial); accord, e.g., ECCC Rules, *supra* note 121, Rule 81(5).

[125] *Media* Appeal Judgement, *supra* note 122, paras. 99–107 (acknowledging that this principle also applies in the ICTY even though no express provision appears in ICTY Rules); ICTR Rule 82 *bis* (where accused refuses to attend, trial may proceed if accused has made initial appearance, Registrar has notified him or her of requirement to be present for trial, and 'the interests of the accused are represented by counsel'); SCSL Rule 60 (after accused has made initial appearance, he or she can expressly waive right to be present, or may impliedly do so by refusing to attend, but 'may be' represented by counsel of choosing or chamber-assigned counsel). See also, e.g., ECCC Rules, *supra* note 121, Rule 81(4).

[126] *Media* Appeal Judgement, *supra* note 122, paras. 94–116. Accord, e.g., *RUF* Case, Case No. SCSL-04-15-T, Ruling on the Issue of the Refusal of the Third Accused, Augustine Gbao, to Attend Hearing of the Special Court for Sierra Leone on 7 July 2004 and Succeeding Days, 12 July 2004, para. 12 (where accused declared that he did not recognise SCSL's legitimacy and therefore would not attend trial, trial chamber finding that he expressly waived his right to presence and ordering trial to proceed in his absence).

[127] See, e.g., *Prosecutor* v. *Popović, Beara, Nikolić, Miletić, Borovčanin, Gvero, and Pandurević*, Case No. IT-05-88-T, Transcript, 28 April 2009, p. 33312 (noting written consent of two accused to be absent from trial that day).

[128] See *Prosecutor* v. *Simić*, Case No. IT-95-9/2-S, Sentencing Judgement, 17 October 2002, para. 8 (accused filed twenty-five waivers of right to be present); *ibid.*, paras. 110–112 (accused pled guilty toward the end of the prosecution's case; Trial Chamber considered his cooperative attitude in agreeing to video-link arrangement as mitigating his sentence).

may order him or her removed from the courtroom.[129] The chamber should make provision for the accused to follow the proceedings via video-link or other electronic means, and exclude him or her for only as long as necessary.[130]

A more difficult scenario arises where the condition is unintentional, as where the accused suffers from a long-term illness that impairs his or her ability to attend trial. The *ad hoc* Tribunals have struggled to find the proper balance between the accused's right to be physically present and the requirement that trial be fair and expeditious. The proportionality test that the ICTY and ICTR have applied is essentially the same as that used to determine whether to impose counsel on a self-represented accused despite the latter's lack of consent: the disruption caused to the trial must be 'substantial',[131] and the accused's absence 'must be limited to the minimum extent necessary to protect the Tribunal's interest in assuring a reasonably expeditious trial' and 'remain in a reasonable relationship with the envisaged target'.[132] Before allowing trial to continue in the accused's absence, the trial chamber must exhaust other reasonable options, such as delaying the start of trial if the delay would be reasonable in the circumstances.[133]

As a general matter, trial chambers have used their power to order the accused's unconsenting attendance by video-link very sparingly, in part because the conditions justifying it are difficult to fulfil. The *Stanišić and Simatović* case in the ICTY demonstrates one chamber's struggle to correctly apply the test. Recalling that Stanišić's chronic ill health had already delayed trial by a month and a half and would likely continue to cause delays, thereby infringing co-accused Franko Simatović's right to an expeditious trial, the Trial Chamber ordered that Stanišić

[129] *Milošević* November 2004 Appeal Decision, *supra* note 74, para. 13; accord *Zigiranyirazo* October 2006 Appeal Decision, *supra* note 73, para. 14. See also Rome Statute, Art. 63(2); ICTY Rule 80(B); ICTR Rule 80(B); SCSL Rule 80(B); see also, e.g., *Prosecutor* v. *Šešelj*, Case No. IT-03-67-PT, Transcript, 1 November 2006, pp. 627–636 (removing accused under Rule 80(B) where accused labelled standby counsel a Tribunal 'spy', demanded counsel's expulsion from the courtroom, and repeatedly interrupted counsel and presiding judge when they attempted to speak despite presiding judge's warnings to cease disruptive behaviour). Cf. *Prosecutor* v. *Šešelj*, Case No. IT-03-67-AR73.3, Decision on Appeal Against the Trial Chamber's Decision on Assignment of Counsel, 20 October 2006 ('*Šešelj* October 2006 Appeal Decision'), para. 21 ('substantial and persistent obstruction to the proper and expeditious conduct of the trial' may similarly warrant restriction of accused's right to self-representation); *Prosecutor* v. *Orić*, Case No. IT-03-68-T, Transcript, 10 December 2004, pp. 2928–2929 (where accused stood up abruptly and started shouting at witness, presiding judge threatening to have him 'restrained' and ordering that his words not appear on the record). For more on the ICTY's problems in managing Vojislav Šešelj's disruptive behaviour and in attempting to impose counsel on him, see Chapter 5, Section 5.3.1.1.2.

[130] Rome Statute, Art. 63(2); SCSL Rule 80(B). See also, e.g., *Zigiranyirazo* October 2006 Appeal Decision, *supra* note 73, para. 12 (observing that the qualified right is one to *physical* presence, and participation via video-link falls short of physical presence).

[131] *Stanišić and Simatović* May 2008 Appeal Decision, *supra* note 72, para. 15.

[132] *Milošević* November 2004 Appeal Decision, *supra* note 74, para. 17 (internal quotation marks and citation omitted); accord, e.g., *Stanišić and Simatović* May 2008 Appeal Decision, *supra* note 72, paras. 16, 19; *Šešelj* October 2006 Appeal Decision, *supra* note 129, para. 20; *Zigiranyirazo* October 2006 Appeal Decision, *supra* note 73, para. 14. For a complete discussion of assignment of counsel in such circumstances, see Chapter 5, Section 5.3; see also *supra* note 129 and accompanying text.

[133] See *Stanišić and Simatović* May 2008 Appeal Decision, *supra* note 72, paras. 18–19.

follow the trial by video-link from the detention unit. The Appeals Chamber reversed, holding that the Trial Chamber had failed to give sufficient weight to Stanišić's right to be physically present in the courtroom – which the Appeals Chamber deemed 'fundamental' – and had given too much weight to a delay of just one-and-a-half months. At the same time, the Appeals Chamber left open the possibility that more substantial trial delays might warrant continuing with the accused participating by video-link. The Appeals Chamber also faulted the Trial Chamber for failing to examine whether Stanišić's mental state, which had allegedly been impaired by his physical illness, was sufficient to allow his effective participation by video-link.[134]

After a year of additional delays, the Trial Chamber found Stanišić fit to attend trial and ordered trial to proceed with relatively short and infrequent sessions, and the option for Stanišić to participate by video-link if necessary. According to an order issued by the Chamber entitled 'modalities for trial', on days that Stanišić claimed he was too ill to go to court, the Chamber would determine, in consultation with the detention unit's medical officer, whether Stanišić was truly too ill to attend. If the Chamber found him well enough, but Stanišić still refused to attend either in person or by video-link, the Chamber would deem him to have waived his right to be present and holds trial without him. If it found him too ill to attend, it would adjourn that day's proceedings.[135] On several occasions after the start of trial on 9 June 2009, Stanišić notified the Trial Chamber that he was too ill to attend, did not waive his right to be present, and did not wish to use the video-link. After considering the medical officer's report that Stanišić's condition had in fact remained unchanged, the Chamber invoked its modalities for trial – noting that neither party had attempted to appeal them – and continued in Stanišić's absence on those days.[136]

The ICTR's *Zigiranyirazo* case provides another instance, beyond the initial *Stanišić and Simatović* decision, in which the Trial Chamber's application of the proportionality test was later rejected by the Appeals Chamber. The prosecution proposed the testimony of a key insider witness, Zigiranyirazo's fellow ICTR accused Michel Bagaragaza, who was then in detention in The Hague. The Trial Chamber found that Bagaragaza would face a risk to his security if he were taken to Arusha to testify, and accordingly decided to hear his testimony in the Netherlands. When the Netherlands denied Zigiranyirazo permission to enter the country, the Trial

[134] See *ibid.*, paras. 12–22.

[135] See *Prosecutor* v. *Stanišić and Simatović*, Case No. IT-03-69-PT, Decision on Start of Trial and Modalities for Trial, 29 May 2009 ('*Stanišić and Simatović* May 2009 Decision'), para. 13; *ibid.*, Annex, paras. 1–8; *Prosecutor* v. *Stanišić and Simatović*, Case No. IT-03-69-T, Second Decision Amending Modalities for Trial, 1 September 2009, Annex A, paras. 1–8 (amending May 2009 modalities).

[136] See *Prosecutor* v. *Stanišić and Simatović*, Case No. IT-03-69-T, Reasons for Decision Denying the Stanišić Defence Request to Adjourn the Court Proceedings and for Decision to Proceed with the Court Session of 15 July 2009 in the Absence of the Accused, 15 October 2009 (recounting decisions of 30 June, 6 July, 7 July, and 15 July 2009).

Chamber maintained its decision to hold the trial hearings in The Hague, but with Zigiranyirazo following them along with counsel from Arusha through a video-link. To maintain equality of arms, examination and cross-examination were to be conducted mainly by prosecution and defence counsel from Arusha, with counsel for both parties also present in The Hague.[137]

After the Trial Chamber had heard Bagaragaza's testimony under this arrangement, the Appeals Chamber granted Zigiranyirazo's motion to exclude the testimony. While it acknowledged the Trial Chamber's concern for Bagaragaza's safety, the Appeals Chamber found no indication in the record that injury to Bagaragaza in Arusha could not be avoided through adequate security measures. Moreover, the Trial Chamber failed to explore other options for obtaining permission for Zigiranyirazo to enter the Netherlands, or for holding the trial sessions in a third country. The Appeals Chamber seemed to place special importance on the critical nature of Bagaragaza's evidence to proving Zigiranyirazo's criminal conduct, as well as Zigiranyirazo's inability to fully observe Bagaragaza's demeanour and assess his credibility through the video-link. Finding Zigiranyirazo's right to presence violated, the Appeals Chamber ordered Bagaragaza's evidence stricken from the record.[138]

If the trial chamber decides to continue in the accused's absence, it must take measures to ensure that the accused may still effectively participate in the trial. Effective participation requires, at a minimum, the ability to communicate freely with counsel, to address the court at any time, and to continually observe the witness and his or her demeanour.[139] Thus, the accused's counsel must be allowed to be present at trial and make submissions to the chamber, and the chamber must allow the accused to participate in the proceedings by video-link.[140] Nevertheless, as the Appeals Chamber suggested in *Stanišić and Simatović*, even these arrangements will be insufficient if the accused is still unable to effectively participate in his or her trial due, for example, to an impaired mental state.[141]

7.6 Stages of trial

Trial is held in a modern, technologically advanced courtroom in the presence of the three judges;[142] Registry officials, interpreters, court reporters, operators of

[137] See *Zigiranyirazo* October 2006 Appeal Decision, *supra* note 73, paras. 3–7.
[138] See *ibid.*, paras. 15–25.
[139] See *Stanišić and Simatović* May 2009 Decision, *supra* note 135, para. 13; *ibid.*, Annex, para. 5.
[140] Cf. *supra* note 130 and sources cited therein.
[141] See, e.g., *Stanišić and Simatović* May 2008 Appeal Decision, *supra* note 72, para. 20. In such circumstances, the trial chamber may find the accused unfit to stand trial. For a discussion of procedures on fitness to stand trial, see Chapter 6, note 206 and sources cited therein.
[142] Or four judges, if the President or Presidency has assigned an alternate or reserve judge. See *supra* Section 7.1.4.

sound and video equipment, and other technical support staff; prosecution and defence attorneys and their staff; and the accused. Also present are any members of the press or public who wish to attend, listening to the proceedings through speakers or headphones, with simultaneous interpretation into English and the language of the accused, along with French at the *ad hoc* Tribunals and the ICC. At the ICC, ICTY, ICTR, and SCSL, trial invariably lasts at least several months and, in some cases, even many years;[143] by contrast, trials at East Timor's Special Panels for Serious Crimes sometimes lasted just a few weeks.[144] This section looks at some of the more important events that occur during the course of the trial. While some portions of the discussion that follow touch upon rules of evidence, Chapter 9 contains a complete discussion of evidence at the international criminal tribunals, including rules governing the admission of written evidence in lieu of testimony; evidence in cases of sexual assault; judicial notice of adjudicated facts, facts of common knowledge, and agreed facts; and expert witnesses.

7.6.1 Transition from pre-trial phase

At a certain point during the pre-trial phase, the chamber that presided over pre-trial proceedings passes the case to the chamber that will hear the trial, in order for the latter to make the final preparations for the start of trial. The Rome Statute prescribes a specific event triggering the passage of the case at the ICC: the pre-trial chamber's confirmation of charges.[145] At the *ad hoc* Tribunals and the SCSL, the timing of the transition is more fluid and often depends on when judges, including *ad litem* judges, become available to constitute the bench that will hear the trial. As noted above, the former and latter benches often feature one or more of the same judges.[146]

Once constituted, the new trial chamber will often have to complete many items of business before trial can begin.[147] Common among these are rulings on disclosure;[148] judicial notice of adjudicated facts or facts of common knowledge;[149]

[143] See, e.g., *supra* notes 3–5 and accompanying text (discussing why trials typically last more than a year, and sometimes many years, especially at the ICTR); *supra* note 34 (discussing one of the many reasons why the ICTR's *Karemera* trial dragged on for many years); Boas, *supra* note 80, ch. 3 (discussing some of the reasons why the *Milošević* trial had gone on for four years at the time of the accused's death).

[144] See, e.g., *Prosecutor* v. *Damaio da Costa Nunes*, Case No. 1/2003, Judgement, 10 December 2003, para. 1 (trial from 29 October to 10 December 2003); *Prosecutor* v. *Joseph Leki*, Case No. 05/2000, Judgement, 11 June 2001, p. 1 (trial from 18 May to 11 June 2001); *Prosecutor* v. *João Fernández*, Case No. 01/00.G.C.2000, Judgement, 25 January 2001, Section I (trial from 10 January to 25 January 2001).

[145] Rome Statute, Art. 61(11); ICC Rule 130. See also *supra* note 24 and accompanying text.

[146] See *supra* text accompanying note 25.

[147] See generally Rome Statute, Art. 64(3); ICC Rules 132, 134; ICTY Rule 73 *bis*; ICTR Rule 73 *bis*; SCSL Rule 73 *bis*; ICC Court Regulation 54.

[148] See Chapter 6, Section 6.5. See also Rome Statute, Art. 64(3)(c) (expressly requiring trial chamber to 'provide for disclosure of documents or information not previously disclosed, sufficiently in advance of the commencement of the trial to enable adequate preparation for trial'); ICC Court Regulation 54(f), (*l*).

[149] See Chapter 9, Section 9.2.3.

protective measures for witnesses;[150] witness lists and the length of the prosecution's case;[151] and the charges on which the prosecution may proceed to adduce evidence.[152] The trial chamber may also require the parties to file pre-trial briefs if they have not already done so,[153] and set the date on which trial will begin.[154] Furthermore, at the ICC, where the pre-trial chamber has admitted evidence for purposes of the confirmation hearing, the trial chamber may, at its discretion, deem such evidence admitted for trial purposes as well.[155]

7.6.2 Opening statements and presentation of evidence

The ICTY, ICTR, and SCSL Rules express a preference regarding the order in which evidence is presented resembling that of common law jurisdictions: the prosecution presents its 'case-in-chief' first, followed by the defence. Yet these tribunals also allow the trial chamber to alter the order of presentation of evidence if it finds that doing so serves the interests of justice.[156] The ICC Statute and Rules leave it up to the parties to work out the order in which they present their respective cases-in-chief. Barring agreement, the trial chamber determines the order.[157] In practice at the *ad hoc* Tribunals and the SCSL, and in the ICC's first trial in *Lubanga*, the prosecution has presented its case first, followed by the defence.[158] For convenience, the present discussion assumes that the same order of presentation is adopted.

After giving an opening statement describing the alleged crimes of the accused and the evidence and arguments that will make up its case-in-chief,[159]

[150] See *supra* Section 7.4.2.

[151] See Chapter 6, Section 6.6.2; *supra* text accompanying notes 77–81. See also, e.g., ICC Court Regulation 54(a)–(g). At the *ad hoc* Tribunals and the SCSL, the trial chamber determines the length of the defence case at a pre-defence conference. See *infra* note 166 and accompanying text.

[152] See *supra* note 81 and accompanying text (discussing ICTY Rule 73 *bis*(D)); Chapter 6, Section 6.6.2.

[153] See, e.g., ICTY Rule 65 *ter*(E)–(F); ICTR Rule 73 *bis*(B), (F); SCSL Rule 73 *bis*(B), (F). As noted in Chapter 6, the defence's pre-trial brief is much less comprehensive than the prosecution's. See ICTY Rule 65 *ter*(F); ICTR Rule 73 *bis*(F); SCSL Rule 73 *bis*(F). Following the close of the prosecution's case-in-chief, the defence is required to file a second, more comprehensive pre-defence brief similar in content to the prosecution's pre-trial brief. See Chapter 6, Section 6.6.1. See also ICTY Rule 65 *ter*(G); ICTR Rule 73 *ter*(B); SCSL Rule 73 *ter*(B).

[154] See, e.g., ICC Rule 132(1).

[155] See, e.g., *Prosecutor* v. *Lubanga*, Doc. No. ICC-01/04-01/06-1084, Decision on the Status Before the Trial Chamber of the Evidence Heard by the Pre-Trial Chamber and the Decisions of the Pre-Trial Chamber in Trial Proceedings, and the Manner in Which Evidence Shall Be Submitted, 13 December 2007, para. 6 (noting that judicial comity supports such an exercise of discretion, unless admission would be inappropriate under the circumstances).

[156] ICTY Rule 85(A); ICTR Rule 85(A); SCSL Rule 85(A).

[157] Rome Statute, Art. 64(8); ICC Rule 140(1).

[158] See, e.g., *Prosecutor* v. *Lubanga*, Doc. No. ICC-01/04-01/06-T-110-ENG, Transcript, 28 January 2009, p. 20 (prosecution calling first witness in trial).

[159] ICTY Rule 84; ICTR Rule 84; SCSL Rule 84; ICC Court Regulation 54(a). The lawyer giving the statement is often the senior trial attorney assigned to the case, and the Prosecutor himself or herself often appears to give part of the argument, especially in the more important cases. See, e.g., *Prosecutor* v. *Popović, Beara, Nikolić, Miletić, Borovčanin, Gvero, and Pandurević*, Case No. IT-05-88-T, Transcript, 21 August 2006, p. 373 *et seq.* (opening statement given jointly by head prosecution trial attorney and Prosecutor herself); *Prosecutor* v. *Lubanga*, Doc. No. ICC-01/04-01/06-T-109-ENG, Transcript, 27 January 2009, pp. 2–3

the prosecution begins to call and examine witnesses one by one, and introduces documentary, physical, video, and other evidence. The defence may cross-examine the witnesses, and the prosecution may re-examine on matters raised during cross-examination. The judges may also pose questions to the witnesses at any time, and at the ICC they may allow questioning by the legal representatives of the victims.[160] As discussed above,[161] throughout trial the judges exercise broad powers to facilitate witness examination and ensure it remains within time limits and that counsel does not harass or intimidate the witness. They also make a myriad of oral rulings on contemporaneous motions and objections by the parties.[162]

At the close of the prosecution's case, the trial chamber at the *ad hoc* Tribunals and the SCSL may acquit the accused on some or all of the charges if it finds that the prosecution has failed to adduce evidence capable of supporting a conviction on the charge or charges in question.[163] If the chamber does not acquit on all charges, and the accused does not plead guilty at this point,[164] the defence puts on its case-in-chief, usually following a pause in the trial of some weeks in order to permit further preparation,[165] defence disclosure to the prosecution, the filing of a pre-defence brief, and a pre-defence conference at which the chamber may make orders with respect to the defence's witness list and the length of the defence case.[166]

Once trial resumes, the defence may choose to make an opening statement if it did not do so immediately after the prosecution's opening statement.[167] In the

(Prosecutor gave opening statement, but Deputy Prosecutor was to be head prosecution trial attorney during ordinary trial sessions).

[160] See ICTY Rules 85, 90(H) (judges in their discretion may allow cross-examination to go beyond scope of examination-in-chief, and re-examination to go beyond scope of cross-examination); ICTR Rules 85, 90(G) (same); SCSL Rule 85; ICC Rules 91 (governing when and how victim representatives may pose questions), 140 (governing parties' and judges' questioning). See also, e.g., *Prosecutor* v. *Lubanga*, Doc. No. ICC-01/04-01/06-T-209-ENG, Transcript, 14 July 2009, pp. 75–78 (judges questioning prosecution witness); *Prosecutor* v. *Prlić, Stojić, Praljak, Petković, Ćorić, and Pušić*, Case No. IT-04-74-T, Transcript, 14, 15, and 19 March 2007, pp. 15627–15633, 15825–15829, 15851–15866 (following closed-session episode where defence counsel made oral submissions to the chamber that defence counsel latter admitted were an unprofessional 'outburst', defence and prosecution presenting arguments on how and why the trial bench had overstepped its bounds in the quantity, quality, and timing of its questioning of party-called witnesses, and more generally on the proper role of a trial bench in conducting a trial). See also ICC Rule 140 (governing parties' and judges' questioning of witnesses); *Prosecutor* v. *Lubanga*, Doc. No. ICC-01/04-01/06-2127, Decision on the Manner of Questioning Witnesses by the Legal Representatives of Victims, 16 September 2009, para. 25 (quoting *Prosecutor* v. *Lubanga*, Doc. No. ICC-01/04-01/06-1432, Judgment on the Appeals of the Prosecutor and the Defence Against Trial Chamber I's Decision on Victims' Participation of 18 January 2008, 11 July 2008, para. 102) (victims may ask questions that go to accused's guilt or innocence). On victim participation in ICC proceedings generally, see Chapter 8.

[161] See *supra* Section 7.3.1.

[162] See, e.g., ICTY Rule 90(F); ICTR Rule 90(F); SCSL Rule 90(F). Chapter 9, on evidence, discusses some of these procedures.

[163] See Section 7.6.5, *infra*.

[164] Guilty plea proceedings are discussed in Chapter 6, Section 6.4.1.2. For an example of an ICTY accused pleading guilty mid-trial, see *infra* note 128 (Blagoje Simić).

[165] For a rare occasion where the defence put on no case-in-chief at all, see *infra* note 219.

[166] ICTY Rules 65 *ter*(G), 73 *ter*; ICTR Rule 73 *ter*; SCSL Rule 73 *ter*. On disclosure, see Chapter 6, Section 6.5. On the pre-defence brief, see *supra* note 153 and sources cited therein.

[167] ICTY Rule 84; ICTR Rule 84; SCSL Rule 84. By its terms, SCSL Rule 84 restricts the defence to making its opening statement at the opening of its case, and not immediately after the prosecution's opening statement.

ICTY and ICC, the accused person may also give an unsworn statement, and the trial chamber cannot compel the accused to submit to questioning about this statement.[168] The rules on examination, cross-examination, and re-examination are the same as those that apply to the prosecution described above.[169] As a corollary of the right against compelled self-incrimination, the accused may not be ordered to testify but may choose to do so.[170] The judges cannot use a decision not to testify as a factor in determining guilt.[171] If the accused opts to testify, however, he or she must do so under oath, and the trial chamber may require that any testimony occur via questions posed by defence counsel.[172] The prosecution and, in a multi-accused case, counsel for any co-accused may then cross-examine the accused.[173] Moreover, the trial chamber may determine when in the course of the defence case the accused may testify and impose other conditions that do not unreasonably

In *Lubanga*, defence counsel gave their opening statement immediately after the prosecution's and before the prosecution began calling evidence. See *Prosecutor* v. *Lubanga*, Doc. No. ICC-01/04-01/06-T-109-ENG, Transcript, 27 January 2009, pp. 3–33. In *Popović*, five defence teams chose to wait until the beginning of their respective cases to give opening statements, but two defence teams gave their statements at the beginning of trial. See *Prosecutor* v. *Popović, Beara, Nikolić, Miletić, Borovčanin, Gvero, and Pandurević*, Case No. IT-05-88-T, Transcript, 22 and 23 August 2006, pp. 535–544, 548–617.

168 Rome Statute, Art. 67(1)(h); ICTY Rule 84 *bis*; ICC Court Regulation 54(a). The chamber decides on the probative value, if any, to give to such a statement. See ICTY Rule 84 *bis*(B); *Prosecutor* v. *Limaj, Bala, and Musliu*, Case No. IT-03-66-A, Judgement, 27 September 2007, paras. 75, 78 (unsworn statement generally given less weight than testimony under oath). See also Giuliano Turone, 'The Denial of the Accused's Right to Make Unsworn Statements in *Delalić*', (2004) 2 *Journal of International Criminal Justice* 455; *Prosecutor* v. *Lubanga*, Doc. No. ICC-01/04-01/06-1346, Decision on Opening and Closing Statements, 22 May 2008, para. 16 (accused cannot be compelled to make opening or closing statement). For a three-and-a-half hour diatribe accusing the ICTY, among other sins, of 'falsify[ing] modern Serb history', see *Prosecutor* v. *Šešelj*, Case No. IT-03-67-T, Transcript, 8 November 2007, pp. 1857–1949 (quotation at p. 1858).

169 See *supra* note 160 and accompanying text.

170 Rome Statute, Art. 67(1)(g); ICTY Statute, Art. 21(4)(g); ICTR Statute, Art. 20(4)(g); SCSL Statute, Art. 17(4)(g); ICTY Rule 85(C); ICTR Rule 85(C); SCSL Rule 85(C); *Prosecutor* v. *Kvočka, Radić, Žigić, and Prcać*, Case No. IT-98-30/1-A, Judgement, 28 February 2005, paras. 125–127 (right of accused against self-incrimination allows certain exemptions from normal rules governing witnesses). See also *Prosecutor* v. *Prlić, Stojić, Praljak, Petković, Ćorić, and Pušić*, Case No. IT-04-74-T, Order on the Mode of Examining an Accused Pursuant to Rule 85(C) of the Rules, 1 July 2008 (giving examples of *Kvočka* principle, including that accused has right to be present during testimony of other witnesses despite normal rule against witnesses being present during each other's testimony, and accused has right to communicate with defence counsel throughout his or her own testimony).

171 Rome Statute, Art. 67(1)(g); *Čelebići* Appeal Judgement, *supra* note 32, para. 783. Accord, e.g., *Prosecutor* v. *Limaj, Bala, and Musliu*, Case No. IT-03-66-T, Judgement, 30 November 2005, para. 729; *Prosecutor* v. *Niyitegeka*, Case No. ICTR-96-14-T, Judgement and Sentence, 16 May 2003, para. 46.

172 *Prosecutor* v. *Blagojević and Jokić*, Case No. IT-02-60-A, Judgement, 9 May 2007 ('*Blagojević and Jokić* Appeal Judgement'), paras. 28–29, affirming *Prosecutor* v. *Blagojević and Jokić*, Case No. IT-02-60-T, Transcript, 17 June 2004, p. 10924. But see *Blagojević and Jokić* Appeal Judgement, *supra*, Partially Dissenting Opinion of Judge Shahabuddeen, paras. 1–10 (opining that trial chamber's refusal to allow Blagojević to testify other than through questioning by his counsel violated his fair-trial rights and necessitated retrial).

173 See, e.g., *Prosecutor* v. *Popović, Beara, Nikolić, Borovčanin, Miletić, Gvero, and Pandurević*, Case No. IT-05-88-T, Transcript, 23 February 2009, p. 32005 (where Pandurević chose to testify in his case-in-chief and counsel for his co-accused had already cross-examined him for approximately eight courtroom days, prosecution beginning its cross-examination of Pandurević); *Prosecutor* v. *Simba*, Case No. ICTR-01-76-T, Minutes of Proceedings, 25 March 2004, www.ictr.org/ENGLISH/cases/Simba/minutes/2005/53-050324.pdf (noting prosecution's cross-examination of Simba, after Simba had testified in his own case-in-chief).

interfere with the opportunity to testify.[174] The accused cannot insist on being the last witness to testify.[175]

At the *ad hoc* Tribunals and the SCSL, the prosecution may present evidence in rebuttal of evidence put forth for the first time by the defence during its case-in-chief,[176] provided such evidence (1) relates to a 'significant issue'; (2) arising 'directly out of' evidence presented in the defence's case-in-chief; (3) which 'could not reasonably have been anticipated' by the prosecution; and (4) which is not a 'fundamental part' of the case the prosecution needs to prove.[177] At the *ad hoc* Tribunals, the defence may then present evidence in 'rejoinder' to respond to the prosecution's rebuttal evidence.[178] A party cannot use rebuttal or rejoinder merely to put forward evidence available to it but not adduced during its case-in-chief. Thus, the prosecution may not introduce previously available rebuttal evidence to remedy a defect in its case brought to light during the defence's case-in-chief, and the defence may not introduce previously available rejoinder evidence to remedy a defect brought to light during the prosecution's rebuttal.[179]

In all the tribunals, the trial chamber may call witnesses on its own initiative, or order either party to produce additional evidence.[180] At the end of trial before the chamber retires to deliberate on the verdict, the parties may file written briefs and

[174] See, e.g., *Galić* Appeal Judgement, *supra* note 30, paras. 19–22.

[175] See, e.g., *Prosecutor* v. *Krajišnik*, Case No. IT-00-39-T, Reasons for Decision Denying Defence Motion for Time to Call Additional Witnesses, 16 August 2006, para. 49.

[176] ICTY Rules 85(A)(iii), 86(A); ICTR Rules 85(A)(iii), 86(A); SCSL Rule 85(A)(iii).

[177] *Prosecutor* v. *Milošević*, Case No. IT-02-54-T, Decision on Application for a Limited Re-Opening of the Bosnia and Kosovo Components of the Prosecution Case, 13 December 2005 ('*Milošević* Reopening Decision'), para. 10 (quoting *Čelebići* Appeal Judgement, *supra* note 32, paras. 273, 275); accord *Prosecutor* v. *Kordić and Čerkez*, Case No. IT-95-14/2-A, Judgement, 17 December 2004 ('*Kordić and Čerkez* Appeal Judgement'), paras. 220–221. See also, e.g., *Prosecutor* v. *Blagojević and Jokić*, Case No. IT-02-60-T, Decision on Prosecution's Motion to Admit Evidence in Rebuttal and Incorporated Motion to Admit Evidence Under Rule 92 *bis* in Its Case on Rebuttal and to Re-Open Its Case for a Limited Purpose, 13 September 2004 ('*Blagojević and Jokić* Reopening Decision'), para. 57 (proposed evidence on involvement of Bosnian Serb army in killings around city near Srebrenica implicated a fundamental part of the prosecution's case and thus could not be introduced in rebuttal); *Prosecutor* v. *Semanza*, Case No. ICTR-97-20-T, Decision on the Prosecutor's Motion for Leave to Call Rebuttal Evidence and the Prosecutor's Supplementary Motion for Leave to Call Rebuttal Evidence, 27 March 2002, paras. 9–10, 13 (granting prosecution's request to call seven witnesses to rebut evidence adduced during defence case-in-chief regarding key matters that prosecution could not reasonably have foreseen).

[178] ICTY Rules 85(A)(iv), 86(A); ICTR Rules 85(A)(iv), 86(A). The SCSL Rules make no provision for defence rejoinder.

[179] *Čelebići* Appeal Judgement, *supra* note 32, paras. 273, 275; *Blagojević and Jokić* Reopening Decision, *supra* note 177, para. 6; *Prosecutor* v. *Delalić, Mucić, Delić, and Landžo*, Case No. IT-96-21-T, Decision on the Prosecution's Alternative Request to Reopen the Prosecution's Case, 19 August 1998 ('*Čelebići* Reopening Decision'), para. 24.

[180] Rome Statute, Arts. 64(6)(d), 69(3); ICTY Rules 85(A)(v), 98; ICTR Rules 85(A)(v), 98; SCSL Rule 85(A)(iv). See also, e.g., *Prosecutor* v. *Krajišnik*, Case No. IT-00-39-T, Judgement, 27 September 2006, paras. 1204, 1255–1257 (noting that the chamber invoked Rule 98 to call several witnesses who had close contact with the accused, and had to subpoena several of them); *Krajišnik* Testimony Decision, *supra* note 84, Annex (appending detailed procedure on calling and examining chamber witnesses); *Prosecutor* v. *Stakić*, Case No. IT-97-24-T, Judgement, 31 July 2003, para. 551 and n. 1170 (trial chamber recounting its calling of several members of the local Bosnian Serb leadership under Rule 98 in order to explore whether the leadership had genocidal intent).

make oral closing arguments.[181] As discussed below, at the *ad hoc* Tribunals the parties must also present any sentencing evidence before the judges retire to deliberate on guilt or innocence.[182]

7.6.3 Reopening of a party's case

In addition to allowing rebuttal and rejoinder,[183] a trial chamber at the *ad hoc* Tribunals may allow a party to reopen its case to introduce 'fresh' evidence uncovered since the close of its case-in-chief that could not have been uncovered sooner through the exercise of reasonable diligence.[184] The Statutes and Rules make no provision for such a reopening, but the case law has recognised the practice since the Tribunals' early years. Rationalising a series of decisions attempting to distinguish reopening from rebuttal, the Trial Chamber in *Milošević* formulated a coherent three-pronged inquiry:

> i. Was the evidence obtained after the close of the [moving party's] case in chief ('newly obtained')? If not, then the test for re-opening is inapplicable, and the evidence is inadmissible for the purpose of a re-opened case in chief …
> ii. If the evidence was newly obtained, could this evidence have been identified and presented, through the exercise of reasonable diligence, during the [moving party's] case in chief? If so, then the evidence cannot be a basis for re-opening …
> iii. If the evidence could not have been identified and presented through the exercise of reasonable diligence, should the Trial Chamber nevertheless exercise its discretion under Rule 89(D) [providing that evidence may be excluded if its probative value is substantially outweighed by the need to ensure a fair trial] to deny re-opening?[185]

The burden of showing 'reasonable diligence' in obtaining the evidence rests on the party seeking to reopen its case, and a chamber is more likely to find such diligence where the party was ignorant of the very existence of the proposed item and such ignorance was reasonable, or the item was in the exclusive possession of an at-large accused.[186] Reasonable diligence 'must be understood with regard to the realities facing the parties, not measured by what a party with infinite time and limitless investigative resources might have discovered or understood'.[187]

181 ICC Rule 141(2); ICTY Rule 86; ICTR Rule 86; SCSL Rule 86.
182 See *infra* Section 7.6.6.
183 On rebuttal and rejoinder, see *supra* text accompanying notes 176–179.
184 *Kordić and Čerkez* Appeal Judgement, *supra* note 177, paras. 221–222; *Čelebići* Appeal Judgement, *supra* note 32, para. 276; *Blagojević and Jokić* Reopening Decision, *supra* note 177, para. 8; *Čelebići* Reopening Decision, *supra* note 179, para. 26.
185 *Milošević* Reopening Decision, *supra* note 177, para. 14 (relying, among other jurisprudence, on *Čelebići* Appeal Judgement, *supra* note 32, paras. 280, 288, 290).
186 *Milošević* Reopening Decision, *supra* note 177, paras. 24, 27.
187 *Prosecutor* v. *Popović, Beara, Nikolić, Borovčanin, Miletić, Gvero, and Pandurević*, Case No. IT-05-88-T, Decision on Motion to Reopen the Prosecution Case, 9 May 2008 ('*Popović et al.* Reopening Trial Decision'), para. 31 (finding that 'the Prosecution could not reasonably have understood that the direct

In determining the need to ensure a fair trial, the chamber weighs each item's probative value against the extent of any delay that would result from admitting the evidence, including the time the other party would need to prepare a response to it.[188]

Applying the test for reopening, the *Milošević* Trial Chamber determined that several items of evidence the prosecution sought to introduce did not provide a basis for reopening because they had been available to the prosecution during its case-in-chief.[189] For several other proposed items, the prosecution had not exercised reasonable diligence in obtaining the evidence.[190] The Chamber concluded that, in light of the significant amount of crime-based evidence already adduced in the case, none of the remaining items would be sufficiently probative of Milošević's own criminal conduct to outweigh the anticipated delay in trial, and denied the application in its entirety.[191]

In a subsequent decision, the *Popović* Trial Chamber expanded the category of evidence that could ground a successful motion for reopening. A few months after the close of its case-in-chief in February 2008, the prosecution moved to reopen so it could adduce several items of evidence relating to Popović's alleged involvement in the execution and burial of over thirty Muslim men in a mass grave at Bišina, in eastern Bosnia. These included seven items – two vehicle logs, an intercepted communication, two aerial photos of the grave, and two reports on the transfer of Muslim prisoners – that had been in the prosecution's possession during its case-in-chief.[192] In October 2007, a Bosnian official showed the previously unconfirmed Bišina grave to an ICTY investigator. After several months of investigative work, the investigator managed to piece together enough additional new evidence to figure out what had happened in Bišina; to rediscover the seven items among the prosecution's archives; and to ascertain that the seven items, together with the newly

involvement and direction of one of the Accused in an execution and burial ... would emerge from the exhumation of a relatively small number of bodies in an area previously unknown to the Prosecution'), affirmed by *Prosecutor* v. *Popović, Beara, Nikolić, Borovčanin, Miletić, Gvero, and Pandurević*, Case No. IT-05-88-AR73.5, Decision on Vujadin Popović's Interlocutory Appeal Against the Decision on the Prosecution's Motion to Reopen Its Case-in-Chief, 24 September 2008 ('*Popović et al.* Reopening Appeal Decision'), para. 19.

188 *Milošević* Reopening Decision, *supra* note 177, para. 36; accord *Blagojević and Jokić* Reopening Decision, *supra* note 177, paras. 10–11; *Čelebići* Reopening Decision, *supra* note 179, para. 27.

189 *Milošević* Reopening Decision, *supra* note 177, para. 23.

190 See *ibid.*, para. 25 (no reasonable diligence where prosecution only began to seek out certain items several months after the start of its case); paras. 29–30 (no reasonable diligence where government authorities were uncooperative in handing over evidence despite prosecution's repeated requests, and prosecution failed to seek court order compelling cooperation).

191 See *ibid.*, paras. 37–39. For an accused's failed attempt to reopen the defence case, see *Prosecutor* v. *Milutinović, Šainović, Ojdanić, Pavković, Lazarević, and Lukić*, Case No. IT-05-87-T, Decision on Lukić Motion for Reconsideration of Trial Chamber's Decision on Motion for Admission of Documents from Bar Table and Decision on Defence Request for Extension of Time for Filing of Final Trial Briefs, 2 July 2008, paras. 32–40.

192 See *Popović et al.* Reopening Trial Decision, *supra* note 187, paras. 5–9.

discovered evidence, showed that Popović was directly involved in the executions and burials.[193]

Modifying *Milošević*'s first prong, the *Popović* Trial Chamber held that, in order to constitute 'fresh' evidence capable of justifying reopening the moving party's case, an item need not necessarily be newly discovered.[194] It may also be 'evidence in a party's prior possession which becomes significant only in the light of other fresh evidence'.[195] The Chamber found that 'the Prosecution could not reasonably have understood the significance of the seven documents' because 'the significance of those documents became apparent only after the Prosecution discovered the specific relevance of the Bišina grave'.[196] The seven documents therefore qualified as fresh evidence.[197] Finding the other requirements for reopening satisfied for these documents and the newly discovered pieces of evidence, the Trial Chamber granted the prosecution's motion to reopen.[198] The Appeals Chamber rejected Popović's claim that the Trial Chamber erred in construing 'fresh evidence' so broadly.[199]

7.6.4 Witness proofing

Reflecting the practice in many common law jurisdictions, the ICTY, ICTR, and SCSL have since their earliest trials permitted prosecution and defence attorneys to conduct a trial-preparation exercise known as witness 'proofing',[200] defined as 'a meeting held between a party to the proceedings and a witness, usually shortly before the witness is to testify in court'.[201] The two chambers of the ICC that have addressed the question – the Pre-Trial and Trial Chambers in *Lubanga* – rejected

[193] *Ibid.*, para. 10. [194] *Ibid.*, para. 27.
[195] *Ibid.*, para. 28. [196] *Ibid.*, para. 29.
[197] *Ibid.* [198] See *ibid.*, paras. 29–40.
[199] *Popović et al.* Reopening Appeal Decision, *supra* note 187, para. 11 ('The Appeals Chamber is not persuaded that the Trial Chamber erred in making such a determination and is satisfied that, under the circumstances, the Trial Chamber's finding constituted a reasonable exercise of its discretion.').
[200] See *Prosecutor* v. *Karemera, Ngirumpatse, and Nzirorera*, Case No. ICTR-98-44-AR73.8, Decision on Interlocutory Appeal Regarding Witness Proofing, 11 May 2007 ('*Karemera et al.* Proofing Appeal Decision'), para. 9; *Prosecutor* v. *Karemera, Ngirumpatse, and Nzirorera*, Case No. ICTR-98-44-T, Decision on Defence Motions to Prohibit Witness Proofing, 15 December 2006 ('*Karemera et al.* Proofing Trial Decision'), paras. 9–10; *Prosecutor* v. *Milutinović, Šainović, Ojdanić, Pavković, Lazarević, and Lukić*, Case No. IT-05-87-T, Decision on Ojdanić Motion to Prohibit Witness Proofing, 12 December 2006 ('*Milutinović et al.* Proofing Decision'), para. 22; *RUF* Case, Decision on the Gbao and Sesay Joint Application for the Exclusion of the Testimony of Witness TF1-141, 26 October 2005 ('*RUF* Proofing Decision'), para. 33; *Prosecutor* v. *Limaj, Bala, and Musliu*, Case No. IT-03-66-T, Decision on Defence Motion on Prosecution Practice of 'Proofing' Witnesses, 10 December 2004 ('*Limaj et al.* Proofing Decision'), p. 2. The Statutes and Rules of these three tribunals, and of the ICC, are all silent on proofing.
[201] *Prosecutor* v. *Haradinaj, Balaj, and Brahimaj*, Case No. IT-04-84-T, Decision on Defence Request for Audio-Recording of Prosecution Witness Proofing Sessions, 23 May 2007 ('*Haradinaj et al.* Proofing Decision'), para. 8.

the practice well before any trial at that Court.[202] The resulting divergence between the law of the ICC and the other tribunals has generated some sharp exchanges among academic commentators over what had previously been an unremarkable practice.[203]

The ICTY Trial Chamber in *Haradinaj* identified the two objectives of proofing: 'to prepare and familiarize the witness with courtroom proceedings', and to 'review the witness's evidence'.[204] The first objective – witness familiarisation – aims at setting the witness at ease in the courtroom environment which is completely alien to most witnesses at international criminal trials. Though approaches vary, counsel will ordinarily explain the purpose of the trial; the layout of the courtroom; who the participants are, where they sit, and their roles; that the witness will have to swear to tell the truth; that the accused will be present in the courtroom; and the method of examination and cross-examination. Counsel may also warn the witness that questions on cross-examination can be stressful or aggressive, and that the experience in general can be traumatic. The *Lubanga* Pre-Trial and Trial Chambers have accepted that witness familiarisation is an important aspect of assuring an efficient trial, but have determined that the Victims and Witnesses Unit, rather than counsel, should be the entity that undertakes it.[205]

The second objective – reviewing the witness's evidence – has proven far more controversial. In most cases, a tribunal investigator will have interviewed the witness many years prior to his or her testimony, at a time much closer to the events in question, and taken a written statement. During proofing, counsel may show the

[202] *Prosecutor* v. *Lubanga*, Doc. No. ICC-01/04-01/06-1049, Decision Regarding the Practices Used to Prepare and Familiarise Witnesses for Giving Testimony at Trial, 30 November 2007 ('*Lubanga* Proofing Trial Decision'), para. 57; *Prosecutor* v. *Lubanga*, Doc. No. ICC-01/04-01/06-679, Decision on the Practices of Witness Familiarisation and Witness Proofing, 8 November 2006 ('*Lubanga* Proofing Pre-Trial Decision'), para. 42 (evidence review aspect of proofing 'not embraced by any general principle of law that can be derived from the national laws of the legal systems of the world').

[203] See, e.g., Ruben Karemaker, B. Don Taylor III, and Thomas Wayde Pittman, 'Witness Proofing in International Criminal Tribunals: A Critical Analysis of Widening Procedural Divergence', (2008) 21 *Leiden Journal of International Law* 683 ('Karemaker, Taylor, and Pittman, "Divergence"'); Ambos, *supra* note 17; Ruben Karemaker, B. Don Taylor III, and Thomas Wayde Pittman, 'Witness Proofing in International Criminal Tribunals: Response to Ambos', (2008) 21 *Leiden Journal of International Law* 917; Wayne Jordash, 'The Practice of "Witness Proofing" in International Criminal Tribunals: Why the International Criminal Court Should Prohibit the Practice', (2009) 22 *Leiden Journal of International Law* 501; Sergey Vasiliev, 'Proofing the Ban on "Witness Proofing": Did the ICC Get It Right?', (2009) 20 *Criminal Law Forum* 193. See also B. Don Taylor III, 'Witness Proofing in International Criminal Law: Is Widening Procedural Divergence in International Criminal Tribunals a Case for Concern?', paper submitted to the 22nd International Conference of the International Society for the Reform of Criminal Law, 11–15 July 2008, www.isrcl.org/Papers/ 2008/ Taylor.pdf, pp. 1–3 nn. 3 and 11 (citing many occurrences of proofing in ICTY and ICTR trials).

[204] *Haradinaj et al.* Proofing Decision, *supra* note 201, para. 8.

[205] *Lubanga* Proofing Trial Decision, *supra* note 202, paras. 30, 33, 53 (ultimately ordering Victims and Witnesses Unit to undertake witness familiarisation, and enumerating the items to be included in such familiarisation); *Lubanga* Proofing Pre-Trial Decision, *supra* note 202, paras. 19, 24; *ibid.*, para. 42 (ordering prosecution 'to refrain from all contact with the witness outside the courtroom from the moment the witness takes the stand'). Contra *Limaj et al.* Proofing Decision, *supra* note 200, p. 3 (witness familiarisation properly undertaken by counsel); *Karemera et al.* Proofing Trial Decision, *supra* note 200, para. 10 (same).

witness this statement in order to refresh the witness's memory and question the witness about inconsistencies between the statement and the witness's current recollection. Counsel may also show the witness the exhibits to be introduced during the testimony, and ask other questions likely to be asked at trial.[206] These aspects of proofing seek to streamline the testimony by focusing the witness on key issues relevant to the charges against the accused, and attempt to reduce the risk of meandering testimony.[207] Where new evidence emerges during proofing that is subject to the rules on disclosure, counsel will be obliged to disclose that evidence to the other party,[208] thereby reducing the risk that the latter will be unduly surprised by what the witness has to say at trial.[209]

Those opposed to proofing fear that the practice too closely resembles, or could easily devolve into, impermissible coaching or manipulation of evidence.[210] Proponents counter that opposing counsel is free to expose irregularities in witness preparation on cross-examination, and that the conduct of proofing sessions has often been the subject of cross-examination.[211] The judges can also examine the witness about the session.[212] Rules of professional conduct prohibit counsel from telling the witness what to say at trial, or asking the witness to conceal or

[206] See *Haradinaj et al.* Proofing Decision, *supra* note 201, para. 8 n. 20; *Limaj et al.* Proofing Decision, *supra* note 200, p. 2 (noting that the facts the investigator found relevant when interviewing the witness may differ somewhat from the facts trial counsel finds relevant to actual indictment, and that proofing helps draw out these differences and better focus the witness on what is relevant for trial). Acknowledging the concern about recollection, the *Lubanga* Trial Chamber ordered the Victims and Witnesses Unit to give each witness a copy of any past statements. See *Lubanga* Proofing Trial Decision, *supra* note 202, paras. 50, 55.

[207] *Milutinović et al.* Proofing Decision, *supra* note 200, para. 16; *Limaj et al.* Proofing Decision, *supra* note 200, p. 2.

[208] *RUF* Proofing Decision, *supra* note 200, para. 34. The rules on disclosure are discussed in Chapter 6, Section 6.5.

[209] *Milutinović et al.* Proofing Decision, *supra* note 200, para. 20 (citing *Limaj et al.* Proofing Decision, *supra* note 200, p. 2); *ibid.*, para. 23 (requesting the prosecution to conduct proofing sessions as early as possible, to give the accused sufficient time to prepare a response to any new evidence disclosed as a result of proofing).

[210] See, e.g., *Lubanga* Proofing Trial Decision, *supra* note 202, para. 52; Ambos, *supra* note 17, pp. 914–915. The *Lubanga* Trial Chamber further lamented that proofing 'may diminish what would otherwise be helpful spontaneity during the giving of evidence by a witness' and asserted, without elaboration, that '[t]he spontaneous nature of testimony can be of paramount importance to the Court's ability to find the truth'. *Lubanga* Proofing Trial Decision, *supra* note 202, para. 52. Yet ordinarily, courts strive to reduce the element of surprise in trials and indeed, as the ICTR Appeals Chamber has suggested, counsel might violate ethical duties owed to the client were counsel to 'force a witness to give evidence "cold" without first knowing what he will say'. *Karemera et al.* Proofing Appeal Decision, *supra* note 200, para. 10 (citing *Prosecutor* v. *Krstić*, Case No. IT-98-33-A, Decision on Application for Subpoenas, 1 July 2003, para. 8). Accord, e.g., Karemaker, Taylor, and Pittman, 'Reply', *supra* note 203, p. 921 (asserting that 'every crime-based witness … has in some way already told his or her factual version of events', and 'the surprise element of a witness's prospective testimony has already long been revealed by way of investigative statements and disclosure').

[211] See *Karemera et al.* Proofing Appeal Decision, *supra* note 200, para. 12; Karemaker, Taylor, and Pittman, 'Divergence', *supra* note 203, pp. 695–696 (cross-examination could focus on, among other things, the setting of the proofing session, the substance of the discussion, and the advice relayed). See also, e.g., *Karemera et al.* Proofing Trial Decision, *supra* note 200, para. 22 (noting that several witnesses in that trial had been cross-examined on the conduct of their proofing session).

[212] Karemaker, Taylor, and Pittman, 'Divergence', *supra* note 203, p. 696. On judicial questioning of witnesses, see *supra* note 160.

distort evidence.[213] Moreover, where misconduct during a proofing session occurs, the trial chamber has the means at its disposal for sanctioning the offending party.[214] Chambers at the trial and appellate levels of the ICTY, ICTR, and SCSL have uniformly rejected accused's attempts to wield the *Lubanga* decisions offensively to force a change in their longstanding practice.[215] The ICC Appeals Chamber has yet to opine on the matter.

7.6.5 Mid-trial proceedings for judgement of acquittal

After the prosecution has presented its case-in-chief and prior to the opening of the defence case, an accused at the *ad hoc* Tribunals or the SCSL may be acquitted of some or all of the charges.[216] This procedure – codified in SCSL Rule 98 and ICTY and ICTR Rule 98 *bis* – is often referred to in the common law tradition as 'no case to answer'.[217] If the chamber decides that the accused does have a case to answer on some or all of the charges, the accused may plead guilty to the remaining charges,[218] or proceed to put on his or her case-in-chief.[219] While mid-trial

[213] See, e.g., *Karemera et al.* Proofing Trial Decision, *supra* note 200, para. 16. At least one ICTY Trial Chamber has left open the possibility that irregularities in a party's proofing practices may justify an order that further proofing sessions be recorded. See *Haradinaj et al.* Proofing Decision, *supra* note 201, para. 22.

[214] Karemaker, Taylor, and Pittman, 'Divergence', *supra* note 203, p. 697. One such sanction may be a finding of contempt, or another offence against the administration of justice. See Section 7.8, *infra*.

[215] See *supra* note 200 and sources cited therein. The *RUF* and *Limaj* decisions predated both *Lubanga* decisions.

[216] See, e.g., *Prosecutor* v. *Orić*, Case No. IT-03-68-T, Transcript, 8 June 2005, pp. 9032–9033 ('*Orić* Rule 98 *bis* Decision') (acquitting the accused of plunder as a violation of the laws or customs of war as well as two other charges, but leaving all other charges intact); *Prosecutor* v. *Sikirica, Došen, and Kolundžija*, Case No. IT-95-8-T, Judgement on Defence Motions to Acquit, 3 September 2001, para. 172 (acquitting Sikirica and Došen on some charges, but leaving others intact for them and Kolundžija); *Prosecutor* v. *Kordić and Čerkez*, Case No. IT-95-14/2-T, Decision on Defence Motions for Judgement of Acquittal, 6 April 2000 ('*Kordić and Čerkez* Rule 98 *bis* Decision') (acquitting both accused with respect to a handful of charges, but leaving others intact). If acquitted of all charges, the accused walks free, provided judgement of acquittal is affirmed if the prosecution appeals. On the prosecution's right to appeal an acquittal in the international criminal tribunals, see Chapter 11, Section 11.5.

[217] See *Kordić and Čerkez* Rule 98 *bis* Decision, *supra* note 216, para. 9; see also *ibid.*, para. 10 (ICTY Rule 98 *bis* was adopted in March 1998); *ibid.*, para. 24 (observing that this procedure is unknown to civil law systems except Spain).

[218] See, e.g., *Prosecutor* v. *Sikirica, Došen, and Kolundžija*, Case No. IT-95-8-S, Sentencing Judgement, 13 November 2001, paras. 10–15 (recounting that, after an unsuccessful motion for acquittal under Rule 98 *bis* and following co-accused Sikirica's and Došen's presentation of their respective cases-in-chief but before beginning his own, Kolundžija entered into a plea deal with the prosecution, and Sikirica and Došen thereafter also pled guilty); *ibid.*, para. 245 (sentencing Sikirica to fifteen years, Došen to five years, and Kolundžija to three years).

[219] A rare third option is that the accused is not acquitted at the judgement-of-acquittal stage, but opts to put on no case-in-chief at all. In the single example of which we are aware, ICTY accused Ramush Haradinaj, Idriz Balaj, and Lahi Brahimaj – apparently believing the prosecution's case extremely weak – announced at the close of the prosecution case that they would not present respective cases-in-chief. The Trial Chamber accordingly bypassed the Rule 98 *bis* stage, ordered the presentation of final trial briefs and closing arguments, and proceeded to deliberations on the verdict and sentencing, ultimately acquitting Haradinaj and Brahimaj and giving Balaj a relatively light sentence. See *Haradinaj et al.* Trial Judgement, *supra* note 97, paras. 6, 502–505 and Appendix A para. 25. For explanations of the purposes behind mid-trial judgement-of-acquittal proceedings, see, e.g., *Prosecutor* v. *Norman, Fofana, and Kondewa* ('*CDF* Case'), Case No. SCSL-04-14-T, Decision on Motions for Judgment of Acquittal Pursuant to Rule 98, 21 October 2005 ('*CDF*

proceedings for judgement of acquittal are routine in ICTY, ICTR, and SCSL trials, the ICC's governing instruments contain no provision for such proceedings.

In an attempt to speed up Rule 98 *bis* proceedings in light of a practice that had developed whereby the parties filed written briefs and the trial chamber spent months composing a detailed written decision often approaching judgement length,[220] the ICTY's judges amended Rule 98 *bis* in December 2004 to require that the parties' submissions and the chamber's decision be done orally.[221] The SCSL's judges followed suit, but the ICTR still conducts written proceedings.[222]

The rule in each of these tribunals requires the trial chamber, after the prosecution has closed its case-in-chief, to analyse the sufficiency of the prosecution's evidence and acquit on any unsupported charges, regardless of whether the accused affirmatively moves for acquittal. Under the terms of ICTY Rule 98 *bis* and SCSL Rule 98, the chamber must acquit on a charge where 'there is no evidence capable of supporting a conviction' on that charge. ICTR Rule 98 *bis* provides slightly different wording – whether the 'evidence is insufficient to sustain a conviction' – but has been interpreted in the same manner as ICTY Rule 98 *bis*. The jurisprudence has clarified this standard. The ICTY Appeals Chamber in *Čelebići* framed the inquiry as 'whether there is evidence (if accepted) upon which a reasonable tribunal of fact could be satisfied beyond reasonable doubt of the guilt of the accused on the particular charge in question',[223] a holding it reaffirmed several months

Rule 98 Decision'), para. 39 (explaining purpose of procedure as 'not to determine the guilt of the accused, which should be made at the end of the case, but instead, to rule on "whether the Prosecution has put forward a case sufficient to warrant the defence being called to answer it"') (quoting *Kordić and Čerkez* Rule 98 *bis* Decision, *supra* note 216, para. 11); *Prosecutor* v. *Strugar*, Case No. IT-01-42-T, Decision on Defence Motion Requesting Judgement of Acquittal Pursuant to Rule 98 *bis*, 21 June 2004 ('*Strugar* Rule 98 *bis* Decision'), para. 20 (function of Rule 98 *bis* to 'separate out and bring to an end only those proceedings in respect of a charge for which there is no evidence on which a Chamber could convict, rather than to terminate prematurely cases where the evidence is merely weak').

220 See, e.g., *Prosecutor* v. *Milošević*, Case No. IT-02-54-T, Decision on Motion for Judgement of Acquittal, 16 June 2004 ('*Milošević* Rule 98 *bis* Decision') (136-page, 330-paragraph decision with two partially dissenting opinions); see also *Prosecutor* v. *Brima, Kamara, and Kanu* ('*AFRC* Case'), Case No. SCSL-04-16-T, Decision on Defence Motions for Judgement of Acquittal Pursuant to Rule 98, 31 March 2006 ('*AFRC* Rule 98 Decision') (ninety-eight-page, 332-paragraph decision); see also *Strugar* Rule 98 *bis* Decision, *supra* note 219, para. 20 (criticising the delay routinely caused).

221 ICTY Rule 98 *bis* ('At the close of the Prosecutor's case, the Trial Chamber shall, by oral decision and after hearing the oral submissions of the parties, enter a judgement of acquittal on any count if there is no evidence capable of supporting a conviction.'). The first case in which all Rule 98 *bis* proceedings were conducted orally was *Orić*. See *Orić* Rule 98 *bis* Decision, *supra* note 216, pp. 9035–9036 (noting that the parties' submissions and the Trial Chamber's ruling were completed in less than a week; estimating that two months of trial time were saved by the introduction of oral proceedings; and that the abbreviated proceedings, especially when multiplied across many cases, 'saved the Tribunal a lot of resources and money') (quotation at p. 9036).

222 SCSL Rule 98 is substantially similar to ICTY Rule 98 *bis*. In the ICTR, the accused must file the motion 'within seven days after the close of the Prosecutor's case-in-chief, unless the Chamber orders otherwise'. ICTR Rule 98 *bis*.

223 *Čelebići* Appeal Judgement, *supra* note 32, para. 434 (emphasis removed); accord *Kordić and Čerkez* Rule 98 *bis* Decision, *supra* note 216, para. 26 (test is 'not whether there is evidence which satisfies the Trial Chamber beyond a reasonable doubt of the guilt of the accused, but rather, whether there is evidence on which a reasonable Trial Chamber *could* convict') (emphasis added).

later in *Jelisić*.[224] The *Jelisić-Čelebići* standard has been consistently followed in judgement-of-acquittal decisions at the ICTY, ICTR, and SCSL.[225]

While the language of the rule in each tribunal refers to 'counts' instead of 'charges', this terminology exemplifies the confusion in the rules and jurisprudence over what those two terms mean and how they differ from one another. The more accurate term is that used by the *Čelebići* Appeals Chamber – 'charge'. As one of the authors has explained:

> A count will often consist of many, sometimes hundreds or thousands of, different charges that describe alleged criminal conduct in respect of a particular area or series of transactions. Hundreds of charges contained in a count could be dismissed without the count actually falling – so long as at least one charge is left.[226]

If the trial chamber acquits the accused of some, but not all, of the charges falling under a count in the indictment, the accused would likely then put on evidence in his or her case-in-chief attempting to refute the remaining charges.[227]

In general, the trial chamber should not examine questions of reliability of evidence or witness credibility when considering whether to acquit on a charge under SCSL Rule 98 or ICTY and ICTR Rule 98 *bis*. Instead, it should only discount the testimony of prosecution witnesses and other prosecution evidence if they are 'incapable of belief'[228] – as one Chamber put it, 'the Prosecution's case has completely

[224] *Prosecutor* v. *Jelisić*, Case No. IT-95-10-A, Judgement, 5 July 2001 ('*Jelisić* Appeal Judgement'), paras. 36–37 (also endorsing the holdings in *Kordić and Čerkez* Rule 98 *bis* Decision, *supra* note 216, para. 9, and *Prosecutor* v. *Kunarac, Kovač, and Vuković*, Case Nos. IT-96-23-T and IT-23-1-T, Decision on Motion for Acquittal, 3 July 2000, para. 3).

[225] See, e.g., *Prosecutor* v. *Muvunyi*, Case No. ICTR-00-55A-T, Decision on Motion for Judgement of Acquittal, 18 August 2009, para. 4; *Prosecutor* v. *Bikindi*, Case No. ICTR-2001-72-T, Decision on Defence Motion for Judgement of Acquittal, 26 June 2007 ('*Bikindi* Rule 98 *bis* Decision'), para. 10; *AFRC* Rule 98 Decision, *supra* note 220, para. 10; *Orić* Rule 98 *bis* Decision, *supra* note 216, p. 8983 (noting that the substance of the standard of review was not altered by the 2004 revamping of ICTY Rule 98 *bis* to mandate oral proceedings and implement certain other changes); *Milošević* Rule 98 *bis* Decision, *supra* note 220, para. 9.

[226] Boas, *supra* note 143, p. 127; see also Chapter 6, notes 54–55 and accompanying text (discussing the definition of a 'charge'). In the *Milošević* Rule 98 *bis* Decision, *supra* note 220, the Trial Chamber acquitted the accused on over 1,000 charges – including charges alleging responsibility for shelling and sniping in Sarajevo – but charges remained nonetheless under each of the sixty-six counts in the three indictments, and so none of the counts actually fell. Boas opines that the prosecution's failure to put on sufficient – or any – evidence to support these charges was a consequence of 'the strain of the breadth and scope' of the case it had attempted to put on. Boas, *supra* note 143, p. 127. For detailed discussions of the *Milošević* Rule 98 *bis* Decision – the closest thing that exists to a judgement in the *Milošević* case, as the Trial Chamber terminated proceedings before rendering final judgement due to the accused's untimely death – see especially *ibid*., pp. 121–128; Idi Gaparayi, 'The Milošević Trial at the Halfway Stage: Judgement on the Motion for Acquittal', (2004) 17 *Leiden Journal of International Law* 737.

[227] See, e.g., *Kordić and Čerkez* Rule 98 *bis* Decision, *supra* note 216, para. 35 (acquitting accused of plunder in some, but not all, locations alleged under Count 39). As explained in more detail in Chapter 6, '[i]t is each charge … that holds the potential of exposing the accused to individual criminal liability' while '[t]he counts in an indictment, by contrast, merely reflect the way in which the Prosecution chose to organise the charges in relation to the crimes allegedly committed'. *Prosecutor* v. *Haradinaj, Balaj, and Brahimaj*, Case No. IT-04-84-PT, Decision on Motion to Amend the Indictment and on Challenges to the Form of the Amended Indictment, 25 October 2006, para. 13; see also Chapter 6, notes 54–55 and accompanying text.

[228] *Prosecutor* v. *Bagosora, Kabiligi, Ntabakuze, and Nsengiyumva*, Case No. ICTR-98-41-T, Decision on Motion for Judgement of Acquittal, 2 February 2005 ('*Military I* Rule 98 *bis* Decision'), paras. 6 (quoting

broken down, either on its own presentation, or as a result of such fundamental questions being raised through cross examination as to the reliability and credibility of witnesses that the Prosecution is left without a case'.[229] The chamber looks at the prosecution's evidence as a whole in determining its sufficiency.[230]

A determination that the prosecution has adduced enough evidence on which the chamber, accepting the prosecution's evidence as true, *could* convict on a given charge does not predestine the chamber to ultimately enter a conviction at the end of trial, even if the accused calls no evidence to refute the prosecution's case during his or her case-in-chief. Instead, the chamber must make a fresh assessment of all the evidence – including its credibility and reliability – at the end of trial.[231] This fresh assessment is subject to a far more rigorous standard of proof than is applicable under ICTY and ICTR Rule 98 *bis* and SCSL Rule 98: a trial chamber may only convict with respect to a particular charge if convinced beyond a reasonable doubt that the accused is criminally liable for the conduct alleged. The 'beyond a reasonable doubt' standard is discussed in Chapter 10.[232]

7.6.6 Presentation of sentencing evidence

The manner in which the parties present sentencing evidence differs between the ICTY and ICTR, on one hand, and the ICC and SCSL on the other. Initially, the *ad hoc* Tribunals' Rules provided for a distinct 'pre-sentencing' procedure following conviction at which the parties presented sentencing evidence.[233] The ICTY's judges changed the relevant rules in 1998 to require the parties to adduce sentencing evidence at the end of trial itself, to be considered by the judges in their deliberations prior to rendering a verdict, and the ICTR's judges followed suit.[234] Since that change, ICTY and ICTR Trial Chambers issue a single judgement containing an analysis of the evidence and the accused's responsibility for

Jelisić Appeal Judgement, *supra* note 224, para. 55); accord *AFRC* Rule 98 Decision, *supra* note 220, para. 11; *CDF* Rule 98 Decision, *supra* note 219, para. 40.

229 *Kordić and Čerkez* Rule 98 *bis* Decision, *supra* note 216, para. 28.

230 *Bikindi* Rule 98 *bis* Decision, *supra* note 225, para. 13; *Military I* Rule 98 *bis* Decision, *supra* note 228, para. 11; *Milošević* Rule 98 *bis* Decision, *supra* note 220, para. 13(4).

231 *Bikindi* Rule 98 *bis* Decision, *supra* note 225, para. 13; *AFRC* Rule 98 Decision, *supra* note 220, para. 13; *Milošević* Rule 98 *bis* Decision, *supra* note 220, para. 13(6) (citing *Jelisić* Appeal Judgement, *supra* note 224, para. 37; *Kordić and Čerkez* Rule 98 *bis* Decision, *supra* note 216, para. 27).

232 See Chapter 10, Section 10.1.3.

233 See, e.g., International Tribunal for the Prosecution of Persons Responsible for Serious Violations of International Humanitarian Law Committed in the Territory of Former Yugoslavia Since 1991, Rules of Procedure and Evidence, UN Doc. IT/32/Rev. 12, 12 November 1997, Rule 100. See also, e.g., *Prosecutor* v. *Tadić*, Case No. IT-94-1-T, Sentencing Judgement, 14 July 1997, paras. 1, 3, 74 (noting conviction on 7 May 1997 and pre-sentencing hearing on 30 June 1997, and sentencing the accused to twenty years in prison).

234 ICTY Rule 85(A)(vi); ICTR Rule 85(A)(vi). See also ICTY Rule 87(C) (same judges who decide guilt must be the ones who determine sentence); ICTR Rule 87(C) (same). Rule 100 now provides for the pre-sentencing procedure only where the accused pleads guilty.

the charged crimes, along with a sentencing analysis if the Chamber finds the accused guilty.[235]

The ICC and SCSL still provide for a separate pre-sentencing procedure, in which the parties may submit additional evidence and arguments, though the chamber can also consider evidence put forward during the trial phase if relevant to determining the sentence.[236] The pre-sentencing procedure at the SCSL only takes place after the chamber has entered its guilty verdict.[237] The same may be the case for the ICC, though the ambiguous wording of the Statute and Rules appear to leave open the possibility that pre-sentencing proceedings, while separate from and subsequent to trial hearings relating to the guilt or innocence of the accused, could still be held prior to the verdict.[238] As of 1 December 2009, the ICC had yet to conclude its first trial, in *Lubanga*, in which it may resolve this question.

The *ad hoc* Tribunals' unified approach has drawn sharp criticism from defence counsel and many commentators. Their main argument is that the accused's right against self-incrimination is violated when he or she must choose between remaining silent and maintaining his or her innocence for the charged crimes and, at the same time, asserting that mitigating circumstances – such as the accused's regret – warrant a less harsh punishment. This dilemma could also arise in the ICC if, as discussed in the previous paragraph, the relevant provisions in the Statute and Rules are interpreted as allowing pre-sentencing proceedings prior to the verdict. When raised in court before chambers of the *ad hoc* Tribunals, such challenges have failed.[239]

[235] See Chapter 10, Section 10.1.6.

[236] Rome Statute, Art. 76(2) (trial chamber *may* make this a separate phase if it so desires, and *must* do so if prosecution or accused request); ICC Rule 143; SCSL Rule 100(A).

[237] SCSL Rule 100(A). See also, e.g., *CDF* Case, Case No. SCSL-04-14-T, Judgement on the Sentencing of Moinina Fofana and Allieu Kondewa, 9 October 2007, paras. 3, 9, p. 34 (noting 2 August 2007 conviction of accused on several counts and that a sentencing hearing was held on 19 September 2007, and sentencing Fofana to six years and Kondewa to eight years in prison).

[238] Neither the Statute nor the Rules compels the trial chamber to hold the separate pre-sentencing hearing only *after* it renders the verdict, leaving open the possibility that the hearing may be held prior to rendering the verdict. See Rome Statute, Art. 76(2) ('[B]efore the completion of the trial, the Trial Chamber may on its own motion and shall, at the request of the Prosecutor or the accused, hold a further hearing to hear any additional evidence or submissions relevant to the sentence.'); ICC Rule 143 ('[F]or the purpose of holding a further hearing on matters related to sentence … the Presiding Judge shall set the date of the further hearing.'). See also Alphons Orie, 'Accusatorial v. Inquisitorial Approach in International Criminal Proceedings Prior to the Establishment of the ICC and in the Proceedings Before the ICC', in Antonio Cassese, Paola Gaeta, and John R.W.D. Jones (eds.), *The Rome Statute of the International Criminal Court: A Commentary*, Vol. II (2002), pp. 1489–1490 (noting ambiguity in Statute and Rules over the timing of the sentencing phase, and the divergence in scholarly opinion on the matter).

[239] *Prosecutor* v. *Brđanin*, Case No. IT-99-36-T, Judgement, 1 September 2004, para. 1081 (citing *Prosecutor* v. *Vasiljević*, Case No. IT-98-32-A, Judgement, 25 February 2004, para. 177 ('an accused can express sincere regrets without admitting his participation in a crime'). For academic critique, see, e.g., Andrew N. Keller, 'Punishment for Violations of International Criminal Law: An Analysis of Sentencing at the ICTY and ICTR', (2001) 12 *Indiana International and Comparative Law Review* 53, 73 (2001) (arguing that exposing even 'professional' judges to inflammatory evidence relevant only to sentencing 'jeopardizes the perception of fairness at the Tribunals in return for mere marginal increases in operating efficiency', and praising the ICC's bifurcated approach).

7.6.7 *Deliberations on guilt and sentence*

After closing arguments, the trial chamber adjourns the proceedings and retires to chambers to deliberate on the evidence and determine the accused's guilt or innocence and, in the *ad hoc* Tribunals, any sentence to be imposed.[240] With extensive assistance from legal officers and other support staff, the chamber drafts a written judgement (called a 'decision' at the ICC) setting forth its legal conclusions and factual findings.[241] The deliberation and judgement-drafting process customarily takes several months. The chamber then reconvenes the trial in order to read out an oral summary of the judgement, its ultimate findings on guilt or innocence and, at the *ad hoc* Tribunals, the sentence.[242] Chapter 10 examines judgement and sentencing in detail.

7.7 Reconsideration of a chamber's own prior decision

The governing instruments of the ICTY, ICTR, SCSL, and ICC do not provide for a chamber's power to reconsider, and alter, one of its own prior decisions. Despite the lack of a specific provision, the *ad hoc* Tribunals and SCSL have recognised the power as inherent in their jurisdiction,[243] though the ICC appears thus far to have rejected the notion that it possesses such a power.[244]

[240] ICTY Rule 87; ICTR Rule 87; SCSL Rule 87; ICC Rule 142(1) (also requiring chamber, within a reasonable time, to 'inform all those who participated in the proceedings of the date on which [it] will pronounce its decision'). On whether the chamber determines the accused's sentence in the same deliberations in which it determines the verdict, see *supra* Section 7.6.6.

[241] Indeed, as former ICTY Judge Wald has acknowledged, the chamber's legal staff performs the bulk of the research, and typically drafts large portions of the trial judgement. See Patricia M. Wald, 'The International Criminal Tribunal for the Former Yugoslavia Comes of Age: Some Observations on Day-to-Day Dilemmas of an International Court', (2001) 5 *Washington University Journal of Law and Policy* 87, 93–94. The legal officers' drafts are, of course, subject to approval, revision, and rejection by the judges. The degree of judicial involvement in the drafting varies by judge and according to the importance each judge gives to a given issue or portion of the discussion.

[242] ICC Rule 44; ICTY Rule 98 *ter*.

[243] See, e.g., *Prosecutor* v. *Tolimir*, Case No. IT-05-88/2-AR73.1, Decision on Zdravko Tolimir's Request for Reconsideration of Appeals Chamber's Decision of 28 March 2008, 18 June 2008 ('*Tolimir* Reconsideration Appeal Decision'), para. 8; *Prosecutor* v. *Kajelijeli*, Case No. ICTR-98-44A-A, Judgement, 23 May 2005 ('*Kajelijeli* Appeal Judgement'), para. 203; *Prosecutor* v. *Šešelj*, Case No. IT-03-67-AR72.1, Decision on Motion for Reconsideration of the 'Decision on the Interlocutory Appeal Concerning Jurisdiction' Dated 31 August 2004, 15 June 2006 ('*Šešelj* Reconsideration Appeal Decision'), para. 9; *Nahimana, Ngeze, and Barayagwiza* v. *Prosecutor*, Case No. ICTR-99-52-A, Decision on Jean-Bosco Barayagwiza's Request for Reconsideration, 4 February 2005, p. 2; *Prosecutor* v. *Karemera, Ngirumpatse, and Nzirorera*, Case No. ICTR-98-44-T, Decision on Joseph Nzirorera's Motion for Reconsideration or Certification to Appeal, 11 October 2005, para. 8; *CDF Case*, Case No. SCSL-04-14-T, Decision on Urgent Motion for Reconsideration of the Orders for Compliance with the Order Concerning the Preparation and Presentation of the Defence Case, 7 December 2005 ('*CDF* Reconsideration Decision'), para. 12.

[244] See *Situation in Uganda*, Doc. No. ICC-02/04-01/05-60, Decision on the Prosecutor's Position on the Decision of Pre-Trial Chamber II to Redact Factual Descriptions of Crimes from the Warrants of Arrest, Motion for Reconsideration, and Motion for Clarification, 28 October 2005, paras. 18, 20, 23–24 (rejecting prosecution motion for reconsideration because the ICC's governing instruments make no provision for an 'unqualified' motion for reconsideration, and noting that the only general remedy for alleged errors is the appeals process). Accord, e.g., *Prosecutor* v. *Lubanga*, Doc. No. ICC-01/04-01/06-123, Decision on the Prosecution Motion for Reconsideration, 23 May 2006, pp. 3–4 (rejecting prosecution argument that a

While similar to the procedure known as 'revision', in that a successful motion for reconsideration or revision may result in the chamber altering a prior ruling, the two procedures differ in important ways explained in Chapter 11.[245] Like revision, both trial chambers and appeals chambers may reconsider prior decisions.[246]

The tribunals have articulated two bases on which a chamber may reconsider, and thus alter, a previous decision: the moving party has demonstrated 'a clear error of reasoning' in the prior decision or, more vaguely, that 'it is necessary [to reconsider and alter the decision] so [as] to prevent an injustice'.[247] The moving party must demonstrate how the chamber erred in the prior decision, or that particular circumstances exist or have arisen that would lead to an injustice if the decision were to remain unchanged.[248] The tribunals have emphasised that the remedy of reconsideration is both exceptional and discretionary.[249] Thus, the Appeals Chamber will not disturb a trial chamber's refusal to reconsider unless it finds an abuse of discretion, even if the Appeals Chamber would have exercised its discretion differently.[250]

single judge may reconsider her own prior decision); *Prosecutor* v. *Lubanga*, Doc. No. ICC-01/04-01/06-166, Decision on the Prosecution Motion for Reconsideration and, in the Alternative, Leave to Appeal, 23 June 2006, paras. 10–12 (reaffirming 23 May 2006 decision).

245 See Chapter 11 (Section 11.7.4 noting, for example, that revision is only available after the final decision terminating the proceedings in a given case, while reconsideration is, in principle, available for any decision). See also *Tolimir* Reconsideration Appeal Decision, *supra* note 243, para. 9 (distinguishing reconsideration from revision – deemed 'review' in the ICTY).

246 *Šešelj* Reconsideration Appeal Decision, *supra* note 243, para. 9 (Appeals Chamber); *Prosecutor* v. *Stanišić and Župljanin*, Case No. IT-08-91-T, Decision Denying the Prosecution Motion for Reconsideration of the Order Limiting the Number of Witnesses It May Call at Trial, 21 October 2009 ('*Stanišić and Župljanin* Reconsideration Decision'), para. 11 (trial chambers); see also *Prosecutor* v. *Krajišnik*, Case No. IT-00-39-A, Decision on Momčilo Krajišnik's Request for Reconsideration of the Pre-Appeal Judge's Decision of 11 June 2008, 4 July 2008 ('*Krajišnik* Reconsideration Pre-Appeal Decision'), p. 1 (pre-appeal judge has power to reconsider own prior decision). The ICTR Appeals Chamber provided a rationale for the Appeals Chamber possessing the power to reconsider: 'In a Tribunal with only one tier of appellate review, it is important to allow a meaningful opportunity for the Appeals Chamber to correct any mistakes it has made.' *Kajelijeli* Appeal Judgement, *supra* note 243, para. 203.

247 *Tolimir* Reconsideration Appeal Decision, *supra* note 243, para. 8. Accord, e.g., *Prosecutor* v. *Karadžić*, Case No. IT-95-5/18-T, Decision on Prosecution Request for Reconsideration of Decision on Second Prosecution Motion for Judicial Notice of Adjudicated Facts, 25 November 2009 ('*Karadžić* Reconsideration Decision'), para. 7; *CDF Case*, Case No. SCSL-04-14-T, Decision on Prosecution Appeal Against the Trial Chamber's Decision of 2 August 2004 Refusing Leave to File an Interlocutory Appeal, 17 January 2005, para. 35; *CDF* Reconsideration Decision, *supra* note 243, para. 13.

248 See *Karadžić* Reconsideration Decision, *supra* note 247, para. 7; *Prosecutor* v. *Perišić*, Case No. IT-04-81-T, Decision on Motion for Reconsideration of the Trial Chamber's Decision of 1 September 2008, 7 October 2008 ('*Perišić* Reconsideration Decision'), para. 7. Chambers also retain the authority to reconsider prior decisions on their own initiative. See, e.g., *infra* note 255 and accompanying text.

249 See, e.g., *Tolimir* Reconsideration Appeal Decision, *supra* note 243, para. 8; *Prosecutor* v. *Mucić, Delić, and Landžo*, Case No. IT-96-21A*bis*, Judgement on Sentence Appeal, 8 April 2003, para. 49; *CDF* Reconsideration Decision, *supra* note 243, para. 12.

250 See, e.g., *Prosecutor* v. *Bagosora, Kabiligi, Ntabakuze, and Nsengiyumva*, Case No. ICTR-98-41-A, Decision on Interlocutory Appeal from Refusal to Reconsider Decisions Relating to Protective Measures and Application for a Declaration of 'Lack of Jurisdiction', 2 May 2002, para. 10.

Motions for reconsideration by both parties are common. While, consonant with the exceptional nature of the remedy, most motions have been denied,[251] some have been granted, with the chamber altering its prior ruling in some respect.[252] In one of the many motions for reconsideration in *Milošević*, for example, the prosecution argued that the Trial Chamber should reconsider a prior decision refusing to admit several prosecution documents into evidence. Although the Chamber found that it had properly excluded most of the items,[253] it determined that the standard for admissibility had indeed been met for one document, and altered its decision by admitting the document into evidence.[254] The Trial Chamber also reconsidered, on its own initiative, its decision to admit two interviews proffered by the prosecution during its cross-examination of a defence witness, where the witness had not accepted the interviews as accurate. It determined that the standard for admissibility had not, in fact, been met for these interviews, and ordered them removed from evidence.[255]

7.8 Offences against the administration of justice

The governing instruments of the international criminal tribunals grant their judges the power to impose criminal penalties for conduct that impedes the administration

[251] See, e.g., *Tolimir* Reconsideration Appeal Decision, *supra* note 243, para. 12 (accused failed to demonstrate clear error or injustice from Appeals Chamber's prior decision that accused's right to receive materials in his own language did not require that they be rendered in Cyrillic, as opposed to Latin, script); *Kajelijeli* Appeal Judgement, *supra* note 243, paras. 204–207 (no clear error or injustice from declining to reconsider prior decisions on temporal and personal jurisdiction); *Krajišnik* Reconsideration Pre-Appeal Decision, *supra* note 246, p. 2 (no clear error or injustice from declining to reconsider decision barring accused from meeting with *amicus curiae*); *Stanišić and Župljanin* Reconsideration Decision, *supra* note 246, paras. 19–20 (no clear error or injustice from declining to reconsider decision limiting number of witnesses prosecution may call); *Karadžić* Reconsideration Decision, *supra* note 247, paras. 8–12 (finding no clear error in prior legal conclusion that the prosecution had not met the standard for judicial notice of adjudicated facts with respect to certain facts, and finding that no prejudice would result from the prior decision, as the prosecution could still tender this evidence at trial); *Prosecutor* v. *Popović, Beara, Nikolić, Miletić, Borovčanin, Gvero, and Pandurević*, Case No. IT-05-88-T, Decision on the Request for Reconsideration of the Decision on the Admissibility of the Expert Report and Proposed Expert Testimony of Professor Schabas, 30 July 2008 (no clear error or injustice from declining to reconsider decision excluding expert report of Professor William Schabas on crime of genocide).

[252] See, e.g., *Prosecutor* v. *Krajišnik*, Case No. IT-00-39-A, Decision on 'Motion by Momčilo Krajišnik for Reconsideration of the Appellate Chamber's Decision of September 11, 2007', 27 September 2007, p. 2 (granting motion to reconsider prior decision in which Appeals Chamber rejected accused's request to extend deadline to file appeals brief, as accused had been without translator for three weeks and injustice would result from denying him an extension); *Perišić* Reconsideration Decision, *supra* note 248, paras. 8, 11 (granting motion to reconsider prior decision in which Trial Chamber had erred in its reasoning when it found certain intercepts to be duplicates of others and thus inappropriate for judicial notice, and altering prior decision by taking judicial notice of these intercepts).

[253] See *Prosecutor* v. *Milošević*, Case No. IT-02-54-T, Decision on Prosecution Motion for Reconsideration Regarding Evidence of Defence Witnesses Mitar Balević, Vladislav Jovanović, Vukašin Andrić, and Dobre Aleksovski and Decision *Proprio Motu* Reconsidering Admission of Exhibits 837 and 838 Regarding Evidence of Defence Witness Barry Lituchy, 17 May 2005, paras. 20, 22–26.

[254] See *ibid.*, paras. 21, 30. [255] See *ibid.*, paras. 29–30.

of justice or threatens the integrity of the judicial process. At the ICTY, ICTR, and SCSL, this authority is not explicitly conferred by the respective Statute, but rather – in keeping with the largely adversarial procedural model followed in these tribunals – is viewed as grounded in the inherent power of judicial bodies to control and protect their proceedings.[256] To guide the exercise of this power, the judges of the ICTY in their quasi-legislative role adopted and repeatedly amended rules on contempt and perjury setting forth the basic elements of the offences, providing examples of qualifying conduct, and outlining the procedure to be followed for the investigation and prosecution of the offences.[257] As is typical, these rules were adopted by the ICTR and, with some modifications to reflect its unique characteristics and context, the SCSL.[258]

In contrast, the approach adopted at the ICC is an excellent illustration of the complexities of rule-making in that institution which are discussed in an earlier chapter.[259] In an apparent effort to cabin the discretion exercised by judges at the *ad hoc* Tribunals, the drafters of the Rome Statute and the ICC Rules included detailed and ostensibly exhaustive provisions[260] on misconduct affecting the proceedings that could give rise to criminal liability, as opposed to that which is subject only to administrative sanction; the applicable penalties and limitations periods; and the procedures to be followed both within and outside of the Court with regard to such offences.[261] Notwithstanding these provisions, the judges of the Court included an extremely broadly worded grant of discretionary authority in the Regulations of the Court, which state that '[i]n the event of non-compliance by a participant with the provisions of any regulation, or with an order of a Chamber made thereunder, the Chamber may issue any order that is deemed necessary in the

[256] See *Prosecutor* v. *Blaškić*, Case No. IT-95-14-AR108*bis*, Judgment on the Request of the Republic of Croatia for Review of the Decision of Trial Chamber II of 18 July 1997, 29 October 1997, para. 59 (upholding trial chamber's conclusion that Tribunal has inherent power to hold individuals in contempt for refusing to comply with ICTY subpoena); accord, e.g., *Prosecutor* v. *Tadić*, Case No. IT-94-1-A-R77, Judgment on Allegations of Contempt against Prior Counsel, Milan Vujin, 31 January 2000, para. 24; *Independent Counsel* v. *Brima, Jalloh, Kamara, and Kamara*, Case Nos. SCSL-2005-02 and SCSL-2005-03, Sentencing Judgment in Contempt Proceedings, 21 September 2005, para. 11; see also Göran Sluiter, 'The ICTY and Offences against the Administration of Justice', (2004) 2 *Journal of International Criminal Justice* 631–632 (2004) (comparing the flexible common law approach – characterised by lack of a statutory definition, judicial discretion in imposition of penalties, and summary proceedings – with the more restrictive civil law approach, which treats such offences like any other criminal offence and applies fixed definitions and penalties).

[257] See generally ICTY Rules 77, 91 (governing, respectively, contempt and false testimony under solemn declaration). See also Practice Direction on Procedure for the Investigation and Prosecution of Contempt before the International Tribunal, UN Doc. IT/227, 6 May 2004.

[258] See ICTR Rules 77, 91; SCSL Rules 77, 91.

[259] See Chapter 2, Section 2.2.

[260] See, e.g., Rome Statute, Art. 70 (providing that '[t]he Court shall have jurisdiction over the following offences against its administration of justice when committed intentionally', listing six offences, and including no residual category or other language indicating that the list is merely illustrative).

[261] See generally Rome Statute, Arts. 70, 71; ICC Rules, ch. 9 (Rules 163–172).

interests of justice'.[262] As of 1 December 2009, however, the Court had not yet had occasion to use its powers to sanction offences against the administration of justice, so it is not yet clear whether and how judges will take advantage of the apparently generous authority granted in the Regulations of the Court.

7.8.1 *Definition of the offences*

The conduct attracting penalties for interference with the administration of justice – deemed criminal offences at the *ad hoc* Tribunals and SCSL, and criminal and administrative violations at the ICC – is ostensibly defined in the text of the relevant Rules. In contrast to the law on the elements of the core crimes within the jurisdiction of these tribunals,[263] therefore, many of the decisions applying these provisions largely repeat the regulatory text with little elaboration.

Under Rule 77 of each of the ICTY, ICTR, and SCSL Rules, contempt is defined as one of five acts committed in order to 'knowingly and wilfully interfere with [the] administration of justice':[264] (1) 'contumacious' refusal or failure by a witness before a Chamber to answer a question,[265] where the otherwise circular term 'contumacious' is defined by the case law as 'persistent[]' refusal or failure to answer 'without reasonable excuse';[266] (2) disclosure of confidential information related to the tribunal's proceedings;[267] (3) unexcused failure to comply with an order to attend or produce documents before a Chamber;[268] (4) interference with a witness;[269] and

[262] ICC Court Regulation 29(1); see also ICC Court Regulation 29(2) ('This provision is without prejudice to the inherent powers of the Chamber.').

[263] See generally Gideon Boas, James L. Bischoff, and Natalie L. Reid, *Elements of Crimes Under International Law* (2008) (analysing the jurisprudence on the general requirements, specific requirements, and elements of underlying offences for the core categories of crimes against humanity, genocide, and war crimes).

[264] ICTY Rule 77(A); ICTR Rule 77(A); SCSL Rule 77(A). See also *Prosecutor* v. *Margetić*, Case No. IT-95-14-R77.6, Judgement on Allegations of Contempt, 7 February 2007 ('*Margetić* Contempt Judgment'), para. 37 (holding that this intent requirement applies to all forms of contempt within the jurisdiction of the tribunal); accord *Independent Counsel* v. *Samura*, Case No. SCSL-2005-01, Judgment in Contempt Proceedings, 26 October 2005 ('*Samura* Contempt Judgment'), para. 19.

[265] ICTY Rule 77(A)(i); ICTR Rule 77(A)(i); SCSL Rule 77(A)(i) (which replaces the term 'contumaciously' with 'subject to Rule 90(E)', a provision that grants a witness the right to refuse to make any statement which may incriminate him or her, subject to the Chamber's power to compel testimony that may not subsequently be used in any prosecution against the witness except for the offence of false testimony under solemn declaration). While neither the ICTY nor ICTR Rules expressly subject Rule 77 to the right granted in Rule 90(E), it is common practice for Chambers to read individual rules in light of the full panoply of procedural protections.

[266] *Prosecutor* v. *Jokić*, Case No. IT-05-88-R77.1, Judgement on Allegations of Contempt, 27 March 2009, para. 12 (adopting the reasoning of Judges Bonomy and Kwon in earlier contempt cases), upheld on appeal in *Prosecutor* v. *Jokić*, Case No. IT-05-88-R77.1-A, Judgement on Allegations of Contempt, 25 June 2009, paras. 28–30.

[267] ICTY Rule 77(A)(ii); ICTR Rule 77(A)(ii); SCSL Rule 77(A)(ii).

[268] ICTY Rule 77(A)(iii); ICTR Rule 77(A)(iii); SCSL Rule 77(A)(iii).

[269] ICTY Rule 77(A)(iv) (defining the *actus reus* of this form of contempt as committed by one who 'threatens, intimidates, causes any injury or offers a bribe to, or otherwise interferes with, a witness who is giving, has given, or is about to give evidence in proceedings before a Chamber, or a potential witness'); ICTR Rule 77(A)(iv) (same); SCSL Rule 77(A)(iv) (same). Under ICTY case law, the residual clause 'otherwise interferes with[] a witness … or a potential witness' has been defined as 'any conduct that is likely to dissuade

(5) coercion of a third party in order to prevent that person from complying with an obligation under a judicial order.[270] The SCSL Rules add a sixth form of contempt – knowing assistance of an accused in evading the jurisdiction of the Special Court.[271] While the jurisprudence of the ICTY and SCSL has confirmed that the list of qualifying acts in Rule 77 is not exhaustive,[272] it does not appear that either tribunal has ever convicted an individual of a form of contempt that is not expressly set forth in the sub-paragraphs of Rule 77. In addition to the general mental element requirement for all forms of contempt – that the contemnor intended to interfere with the administration of justice[273] – certain of the Rule 77 forms of contempt carry their own *mens rea*. Coercion of a third party, for example, must be done 'with the intention of preventing that other person from complying with an obligation under an order of a Judge or Chamber' in order to qualify as contempt.[274]

The second form of contempt set forth in the Rule – disclosure of confidential information, usually in breach of an order granting protective measures to witnesses – has received the most attention in ICTY jurisprudence as to both its *mens rea* and *actus reus*, as many of the contempt cases in that tribunal involve publication or dissemination of protected information. In order to be found guilty of contempt pursuant to this provision, the judicial order in question must apply to the alleged contemnor,[275] protect the specific information disclosed by the accused,

a witness or a potential witness from giving evidence, or to influence the nature of the witness'[s] or potential witness'[s] evidence', such as exposing him or her to threats, intimidation or injury by third parties. *Margetić* Contempt Judgment, *supra* note 264, para. 64 (citing *Prosecutor* v. *Brđanin*, Case No. IT-99-36-R77, Concerning Allegations against Milka Maglov, Decision on Motion for Acquittal Pursuant to Rule 98 *bis*, 19 March 2004 ('*Maglov* 98 *bis* Decision'), para. 27); *ibid.* paras. 64, 66 (noting that '[p]roof is not required that this conduct actually produced such a result', though the *mens rea* of intent to interfere with the administration of justice still applies).

270 ICTY Rule 77(A)(v) (defining the *actus reus* of this form of contempt as committed by one who 'threatens, intimidates, offers a bribe to, or otherwise seeks to coerce any other person, with the intention of preventing that other person from complying with an obligation under an order of a Judge or Chamber'); ICTR Rule 77(A)(v) (same); SCSL Rule 77(A)(v) (same). Incitement or attempt to commit any of the acts set forth in the subparagraphs of Rule 77 is also punishable as contempt. ICTY Rule 77(B); ICTR Rule 77(B); SCSL Rule 77(B).

271 SCSL Rule 77(A)(v)(i).

272 See *Samura* Contempt Judgment, *supra* note 264, para. 16 and n. 22; *Prosecutor* v. *Marijačić and Rebić*, Case No. IT-95-14-R77.2, Decision on Prosecution Motions to Amend the Indictment, 7 October 2005, para. 31: 'As indicated by ... paragraph (A) of Rule 77, individuals who knowingly and wilfully interfere with the administration of justice by the Tribunal may be found in contempt when they engage in conduct including those forms listed in sub-paragraphs (i) to (v), but these forms of commission do not constitute an exclusive list. It is therefore possible for a person to be charged with contempt of the Tribunal under the inherent power of the Tribunal articulated in Rule 77(A) where there is evidence of knowing and wilful interference with its administration of justice that does not fit within one of the categories articulated in sub-paragraphs (i) to (v).'

273 See *Maglov* 98 *bis* Decision, *supra* note 269, para. 16.

274 ICTY Rule 77(A)(v); ICTR Rule 77(A)(v); SCSL Rule 77(A)(v).

275 *Margetić* Contempt Judgment, *supra* note 264, para. 37. In a particularly expansive interpretation of its powers under the Statute (and indirectly the grant of power by the Security Council resolution that established the Tribunal), the ICTY has held that prosecution of contempt involving conduct out of court but directly related to the legal proceedings, like breach of a court order, is permissible because it is premised on broad and incidental jurisdiction over any person who may come into possession of information related to those proceedings. See, e.g., *Prosecutor* v. *Marijačić and Rebić*, Case No. IT-95-14-R77.2-A, Judgement, 27 September 2006, para. 24

and be in effect at the time of the alleged violation; and the alleged contemnor must have acted with actual knowledge, wilful blindness, or reckless indifference to the existence of the judicial order.[276]

False testimony under solemn declaration, referred to as perjury in common law jurisdictions, is the other principal offence against the administration of justice under the Rules of the *ad hoc* Tribunals and the SCSL. The regulatory provision and jurisprudence on this offence are even sparser than for contempt. The offence is defined simply (and only deductively, from reading the provision in light of its title) as the knowing and wilful giving of false testimony while under solemn declaration,[277] and there has been a single prosecution of this offence at the three tribunals – the proceedings against protected witness GAA at the ICTR.[278] In that case, the witness-contemnor pleaded guilty to falsely recanting his trial testimony in an evidentiary hearing before the Appeals Chamber in the *Kamuhanda* case, and was sentenced to nine months' imprisonment.[279]

7.8.2 Procedural steps

Under the current version of the Rules in effect at the ICTY and ICTR, contempt and false testimony proceedings are fairly similar. If a chamber has reason to believe an individual has committed the offence in question, it may (1) direct the prosecution to investigate the matter with a view to preparing an indictment; (2) instruct the Registrar to appoint an independent *amicus curiae* to investigate, if the prosecution has a conflict of interest; or (3) initiate proceedings itself, but only in cases of contempt.[280] Once the chamber is satisfied that there is a sufficient basis to proceed against the alleged contemnor, it may direct the prosecution or the *amicus curiae* to prosecute the matter, or prosecute the matter itself.[281] In the

(upholding the determination of the Trial Chamber in that case that personal jurisdiction extends to 'all persons coming into possession of the protected information, given that' the Rule regarding closed trial sessions 'is directed at the public in general'). As a result, under current ICTY law, this requirement will always be met.

276 *Margetić* Contempt Judgment, *supra* note 264, para. 37; see also *Prosecutor* v. *Aleksovski*, Case No. IT-95-14/1-AR77, Judgement on Appeal by Anto Nobilo Against Finding of Contempt, 30 May 2001 ('*Nobilo* Contempt Appeal Judgment'), paras. 45, 54 (holding that mere negligence would be insufficient to ground a contempt conviction, and that reckless indifference to the consequences of the act by which the order is violated, rather than to the existence of the order, was a sufficient mental state for contempt); *ibid*., para. 20 (defining the alternative mental state subsequent decisions term 'wilful blindness' as a 'deliberate failure to ascertain the circumstances under which a witness testified').

277 See ICTY Rule 91 (entitled 'False Testimony under Solemn Declaration' and including subparagraph (b), which sets forth the procedural steps a chamber may take '[i]f [it] has strong grounds for believing that a witness has knowingly and wilfully given false testimony'); ICTR Rule 91 (same); SCSL Rule 91 (same).

278 *Prosecutor* v. *GAA*, Case No. ICTR-07-90-R77-I, Judgment and Sentence, 4 December 2007. As a footnote on the cover page of the decision noted, '[t]he Accused is a protected witness who testified in different trial under the pseudonym GAA' so 'the real name of the Accused cannot be disclosed'.

279 *Ibid*., paras. 4, 5.

280 See ICTY Rules 77(C), 91(B); ICTR Rules 77(C), 91(B).

281 See ICTY Rules 77(D), 91(C); ICTR Rules 77(D), 91(C).

latter two options, the chamber may decide to proceed on the basis of a judicial order instead of an indictment,[282] and that order must set forth 'the nature of the charge with the precision expected of an indictment'.[283] Persons convicted of contempt or false testimony by a trial chamber have the right to automatic appeal of their conviction and/or sentence, while those convicted by the Appeals Chamber sitting as a court of first instance may appeal to the President of the tribunal, who will appoint a different panel of appellate judges to hear the appeal.[284]

The SCSL procedural provisions on contempt owe much to the common law jurisdiction in which that court has its seat: while the relevant provisions are somewhat similar to the *ad hoc* model described above, the procedure they describe is simpler, cognisant of the hybrid nature of the court, and even more reflective of the view that a court has the inherent power to punish contempt or perjury occurring before it. Instead of the options set forth above for proceeding when the chamber has reason to believe one of these offences has been committed, the SCSL Rules authorise the chamber to (1) deal with the matter itself in a summary proceeding; (2) refer the case to the Sierra Leonean authorities for investigation and prosecution; or (3) direct the appointment of an *amicus curiae* investigator.[285] If the last option is chosen, and the chamber determines that there is a sufficient basis to proceed to prosecution, the hearing may take place before a full trial chamber or a single judge.[286] The SCSL Rule regarding false testimony under solemn declaration tracks the equivalent provision in the ICTY and ICTR Rules.[287]

7.9 Conclusion

Ever since the ICTY's first trial, judges at the *ad hoc* Tribunals have struggled, with varying degrees of success, to develop procedures and case management strategies aimed at keeping trials to a reasonable length. In this endeavour, the judges frequently find themselves at odds with the respective Offices of the Prosecutor, which have shown reluctance to abandon their practice of issuing sweeping indictments

[282] See ICTY Rule 77(D)(ii); ICTR Rule 77(D)(ii).
[283] *Nobilo* Contempt Appeal Judgment, *supra* note 276, para. 56.
[284] See ICTY Rules 77(J), 77(K), 91(I); ICTR Rules 77(J), 77(K), 91(I).
[285] See SCSL Rule 77(C), 77(L) (providing for summary procedure before the Appeals Chamber with no right of appeal in the event of conviction).
[286] SCSL Rule 77(D). See also *Independent Counsel* v. *Brima, Jalloh, Kamara, and Kamara*, Case Nos. SCSL-2005-02, SCSL-2005-03, Sentencing Judgment in Contempt Proceedings, 21 September 2005 (decision by single judge on basis of trial prosecuted by *amicus curiae*).
[287] See generally SCSL Rule 91 (also providing that, where a chamber has strong grounds to believe a witness has given false testimony under solemn declaration, the procedure under Rule 77 shall be followed).

and putting on mammoth cases.[288] Many of the procedures discussed in this chapter did not appear in the original versions of the Rules of Procedure and Evidence, and were added later in an effort to expedite trials, often as codifications of principles developed in the jurisprudence.[289] The judges frequently invoke the accused's right to a speedy trial as the motivation behind these efforts, but the primary driving force has been the completion strategies. This reality has exposed the judges to charges of corner-cutting that ultimately undermine, rather than vindicate, the accused's rights.[290]

As a consequence of these rule changes, the judges have come to enjoy ever-increasing powers over the scope and shape of the case – in essence, over *how* the accused is prosecuted – though trial chambers continue to underutilise many of the powers available to them, especially in the area of case management.[291]

[288] See Kwon, *supra* note 5, p. 373 (referring to this practice as a 'hunting expedition', and citing as a 'prime example' the prosecution's fervent resistance to prosecuting Milošević on the Kosovo indictment first, and leaving the Croatia and Bosnia indictments for a later trial, as well as its opposition to severing the latter indictments when proposed by the Trial Chamber nearly four years into trial); *ibid.*, pp. 374–376 and n. 42 (citing several cases where the trial chamber invited the prosecution to cut charges from the indictment but the prosecution refused, claiming infringement of its independence). The practice of issuing sprawling indictments has existed since the earliest years of the ICTY. The prosecution's indictment in *Tadić* charged the accused, a physical perpetrator who would be considered of too little importance to warrant trial at the ICTY today, with a myriad of crimes, and the trial lasted for seventy-nine courtroom days. See International Tribunal for the Prosecution of Persons Responsible for Serious Violations of International Humanitarian Law Committed in the Territory of Former Yugoslavia Since 1991, Case Information Sheet: Duško Tadić, at www.icty.org/x/cases/tadic/cis/en/cis_tadic_en.pdf; *Prosecutor* v. *Tadić and Borovnica*, Case No. IT-94-1-I, Indictment (Amended), 14 December 1995 (thirty-four counts). On the Trial Chamber's largely unsuccessful struggle with the prosecution to keep the *Milošević* trial within reasonable time constraints, see generally Boas, *supra* note 143, ch. 3.

[289] See Boas, *supra* note 143, pp. 64–66, 189–193 (describing, among others, rules on pre-trial case management, witness lists, trimming indictments, and written testimony); Kwon, *supra* note 5, pp. 364–375 (describing rules on written testimony, judicial notice, and trimming indictments). For further discussion by ICTY practitioners and judges of rule changes designed to expedite proceedings, see generally Harmon, *supra* note 3; Theodor Meron, 'Procedural Evolution in the ICTY', (2004) 2 *Journal of International Criminal Justice* 520; Daryl A. Mundis, 'From "Common Law" Towards "Civil Law": The Evolution of the ICTY Rules of Procedure and Evidence', (2001) 14 *Leiden Journal of International Law* 367. For rules discussed in this chapter aimed at speeding up trials, see, e.g., *supra* Sections 7.1.4 (continuing with trial in a judge's absence), 7.3.1 (judicial control over length and manner of parties' presentation of evidence), 7.4.3 (hearing testimony by video-link), 7.5 (continuing with trial in accused's absence), 7.6.5 (acquitting accused of charges mid-trial), 7.6.6 (absence of separate pre-sentencing hearing at ICTY and ICTR). The Rome Statute and ICC Rules predate much of the *ad hoc* Tribunals' important experience in this area, and may therefore render the Court less well-equipped to deal effectively with difficult case management scenarios that may arise during trial. See, e.g., *supra* Section 7.1.4 (trial must apparently restart anew if judge becomes incapacitated and no alternate judge has been assigned).

[290] For criticism from within the Appeals Chamber, see *Prosecutor* v. *Milošević*, Case No. IT-02-54-AR73.4, Dissenting Opinion of Judge David Hunt on Admissibility of Evidence in Chief in the Form of Written Statements (Majority Decision Given 30 September 2003), 21 October 2003, paras. 20–22 (criticising expansive interpretation of rule on admission of written statements in lieu of oral testimony); *Butare* September 2003 Appeal Decision, *supra* note 60, Dissenting Opinion of Judge David Hunt, para. 17 (criticising ruling allowing trial to continue where one judge is unable to continue sitting, without the accused's consent to continue). For academic criticism, see, e.g., Gregory P. Lombardi, 'Legitimacy and the Expanding Power of the ICTY', (2003) 37 *New England Law Review* 887 (several rule changes motivated by completion strategy are *ultra vires*).

[291] See, e.g., Boas, *supra* note 143, pp. 201–204.

Observers have remarked that this increase in power brings procedures at the *ad hoc* Tribunals and the SCSL much closer to those of inquisitorial systems in civil law countries.[292] Others have made similar observations with respect to the ICC, dubbing it a 'mixed' system that is neither adversarial nor inquisitorial.[293] These views no doubt bear some truth. As a general matter, and especially in the pre-trial phase, the procedural frameworks of the international criminal tribunals are neither purely adversarial nor purely inquisitorial, but rather something new and *sui generis*, borrowing selectively from the two systems and adding to them many unique mechanisms not found in any national system.[294]

Yet this point should not be overstated, especially when it comes to the trial phase. The judges at the international criminal tribunals are certainly more interventionist than they would be in a common law courtroom. As noted above, this approach often brings them into tension with the prosecution, and sometimes even the defence.[295] But by and large, the process is still mostly party-driven, even at the ICC.[296] It is overwhelmingly the parties who seek out witnesses and compile documentary evidence, and who decide which witnesses to call and which documents to tender. For the prosecution, these decisions are based on what it discovered during an investigation in which the judges played little or no part, and on trial strategies devised within the Office of the Prosecutor. For the defence, these decisions are largely based on how best to expose inconsistencies and other weaknesses in the prosecution's evidence. While judges at all the tribunals may call witnesses of their own and question the parties' witnesses,[297] they tend to do so only to fill gaps in their knowledge or understanding that

[292] See, e.g., Kwon, *supra* note 5, pp. 363–364; Meron, *supra* note 289, pp. 522–523.

[293] See, e.g., Ambos, *supra* note 17, p. 912; Claus Kreß, 'The Procedural Law of the International Criminal Court in Outline: Anatomy of a Unique Compromise', (2003) 1 *Journal of International Criminal Justice* 603, 605.

[294] See Chapter 1, Section 1.2.

[295] See, e.g., *Hadžihasanović and Kubura* Appeal Judgement, *supra* note 32, paras. 77–107 (rejecting accused's allegations that judges exhibited pro-prosecution bias in the manner and extent to which they questioned certain defence witnesses); *Prosecutor* v. *Prlić, Stojić, Praljak, Petković, Ćorić, and Pušić*, Case No. IT-04-74-T, Transcript, 14, 15, and 19 March 2007, pp. 15627–15633, 15825–15829, 15851–15866 (prosecution and defence attorneys making extensive oral submissions on how the judges' interruption of the parties' examination of witnesses in order to interpose their own questions, along with the employment of other interventionist techniques, had improperly and unproductively interfered with the manner in which the parties chose to present their respective cases); see also *ibid.*, pp. 15630–15631 (defence counsel suggesting that trial bench consider disqualifying itself if it cannot conduct trial in the same largely adversarial way as other ICTY chambers); *ibid.*, p. 15829 (defence counsel lamenting elimination of element of surprise when judges interrupt cross-examination of 'difficult' witnesses to ask their own clarifying questions); *ibid.*, pp. 15855–15856 (prosecution attorney asserting that 'a party must be given a reasonable opportunity to conduct its examination according to his or her own plan', and arguing that confusion and wasted time result when the judges 'jump ahead and intervene') (quotation at p. 15856).

[296] See, e.g., Orie, *supra* note 238, p. 1477 (despite many civil law features, trial at ICC 'still very much common-law oriented'); accord *ibid.*, p. 1494.

[297] See *supra* notes 85–86, 160, 180 and accompanying text.

remain after the parties have put on their respective cases. For better or for worse, trial at the ICTY, ICTR, SCSL, and ICC remains, on balance, essentially adversarial.[298]

[298] See, e.g., *Prosecutor* v. *Prlić, Stojić, Praljak, Petković, Ćorić, and Pušić*, Case No. IT-04-74-T, Transcript, 19 March 2007, p. 15854 (prosecution attorney acknowledging hybrid nature of ICTY procedure but asserting that it is 'decidedly more adversarial than not, decidedly more common law than not'). See also Ambos, *supra* note 17, pp. 912–913 (unconvincingly arguing that *trial* at the ICC is not primarily adversarial, but is instead 'mixed').

8

The role and status of victims in international criminal procedure

CONTENTS

Although justice for the victims of mass atrocity – generally cast as retribution for the offender – has long been one of the central themes justifying international criminal trials, victims have not, until relatively recently, played a central role.[1] Often characterised as a direct result of the domination of the adversarial approach at the ICTY, ICTR, and SCSL, victims before those courts are essentially treated as witnesses. Their direct participation in the proceedings is strictly limited to giving evidence. Their input at other stages of the process is formally non-existent, their right to reparations is limited, and their practical influence negligible.

The Rome Statute transformed the role and status of victims in international criminal procedure. As a result, victims in proceedings before the ICC enjoy a panoply of participatory rights. Although their status at various stages of the proceedings falls just short of that of the parties, their direct participation is guaranteed. Their rights to orders for reparation are greatly expanded, as is at least the possibility of collecting such reparations. Their influence on the Court's first cases has already been important, and their role in the work of the ICC promises to be considerable.

While this seminal development in international criminal procedure has been lauded by many, several constituencies remain suspicious or conflicted. The Prosecutors are understandably wary of any perceived encroachment on their independence in deciding what cases to charge, or interference with their control of the case at trial. Simultaneously, to the extent that victims' interests more often align with those of the prosecution than with those of the accused, the prosecution may welcome victim involvement in the case. The accused have concerns with the fairness of proceedings in which victims play such a prominent role. When victims can introduce evidence at trial – which may or may not have been disclosed to the accused pre-trial – the accused will certainly feel that he or she faces multiple accusers, perhaps with competing agendas, but joined in a shared opposition to the defence.

Beyond the concerns of the parties – and quite separate from the legal issues involved in interpreting the Statute, Rules, and Regulations of the Court and the Registry – looms the spectre of efficiently managing direct victim participation.

[1] See, e.g., Mark A. Drumbl, *Atrocity, Punishment, and International Law* (2007), p. 86 (noting that '[r]etribution and general deterrence are the two most prominent punishment rationales in international criminal law').

The nature of the crimes within the Court's jurisdiction, coupled with its mandate to try only the most serious instances of these crimes, virtually guarantees that each case will encompass many hundreds – or thousands – of victims. Even if only a tiny fraction of these victims exercise their right to participate in the Court's work in the manner currently permitted by the Court's judges, managing that participation effectively so that it is meaningful while ensuring the fair and expeditious conduct of the proceedings will be a monumental task.

The ICC's procedural framework remains largely skeletal despite its large number of provisions.[2] This holds true with respect to the role and status of victims. Judicial interpretation of the Statute, Rules, and Regulations of the Court has begun to clothe that skeletal structure in flesh, with the Court's expansive decisions on participation being lauded by many in the NGO and victims' rights communities. Some of those early expansions have been rolled back by the Appeals Chamber. Yet much remains to be decided and the existing decisions have already worried many. It is too early to tell whether the Court's experiment in widespread victim participation will prove workable.

Chapter 8 begins with a brief description of the disparate roles and status of victims in national criminal proceedings, and the international law relevant to their treatment in national systems. We then describe the limited role of victims before the ICTY, ICTR, and SCSL in Section 8.2. Turning to the ICC, Section 8.3 describes the Court's turbulent first years, marked by internal disagreement over how best to implement its broad mandate. We describe the procedural framework within which victims participate directly in the Court's proceedings, and the rights which have been granted, expanded, and in some cases, limited by the Appeals Chamber. We discuss the modalities by which their participatory rights are implemented. Finally, Section 8.4 briefly discusses the role of victims before the ECCC, the first international(ised) criminal tribunal in which victims enjoy party status. Although it is a tribunal of a fundamentally different procedural character than the international criminal tribunals which preceded it, the ECCC's experience with victim participation may prove marginally instructive to the ICC's judges in The Hague.

8.1 Victims in national criminal proceedings

Much has been written about the role and status of victims in national criminal proceedings. As outlined in Chapter 1, little is to be gained by revisiting the systemic debates accompanying the early years of the *ad hoc* Tribunals' work. However, the broad differences between the role and status of victims in the adversarial and

[2] See Chapter 2, Section 2.2.1.

inquisitorial domestic criminal justice models explain much of the disparate roles accorded them before the *ad hoc* Tribunals, the ICC, and the ECCC.

8.1.1 Adversarial and inquisitorial domestic systems

In very general terms, in adversarial criminal proceedings the victim is a subject of the proceedings. While victims may have rights to notice of particular proceedings, to address the court on specific issues, and to request restitution for damage in the context of the prosecution, their role is essentially little different from that of any other witness.[3] They are not parties to the proceedings, have no authority to direct the investigation, affect the charging decision or procedure, or determine the conduct of the judicial proceedings. Because adversarial criminal proceedings are largely party-driven, the degree of victim participation in such proceedings is generally determined at the discretion of the prosecution and the accused. When victims appear before the court, it is generally *through* one of the parties, rather than in their own right or on their own terms. Claims for reparations, where available, are considered an adjunct of the criminal proceedings rather than an integral part of the proceedings.[4]

Conversely, and again in very general terms, in inquisitorial criminal proceedings victims have a much more central role.[5] Victims may play an important part in the prosecutor or court's decision to charge, or in forcing a review and reversal of the prosecutor or court's decision not to charge. In some inquisitorial systems, they are parties to the proceeding, with full participatory rights to examine witnesses, file written submissions, and request hearings. In others, they participate in their own right with full prosecutorial rights.[6] Reparation – usually compensation

[3] See William A. Schabas, *An Introduction to the International Criminal Court* (3rd edn 2007), pp. 323–324 (noting that under the common law, criminal prosecution is seen as essentially a matter of public policy in which victims have a role that is marginal at the best of times).

[4] It is a common perception that victim restitution is not available through criminal cases in common law countries. See, e.g., Salvatore Zappalà, *Human Rights in International Criminal Proceedings* (2003), p. 219 (noting that in the common law world civil litigation represents the 'only context in which victims can present their claims'). It is certainly true that civil litigation is the only context in which victims can fully present all claims against the accused they may have, and the only context in which they are in control of the form and content of such claims. Restitution for economic loss as an adjunct to the criminal proceeding, however, occurs quite frequently in common law jurisdictions. See, e.g., Kent Roach, 'Canada', in Craig M. Bradley (ed.), *Criminal Procedure: A Worldwide Study* (2nd edn 2007), p. 86 (noting that in Canada courts may require the accused to make restitution to the victim for readily ascertainable financial losses as part of the sentencing process); David J. Feldman, 'England and Wales', in Bradley, *supra*, p. 191 (noting that in England and Wales following a criminal conviction, courts have the power to order the convicted person to compensate the victim for personal injury, damage, or loss resulting from the offence).

[5] See Schabas, *supra* note 3, p. 323 (noting that 'civil law' or continental-type systems enable victims to participate directly in proceedings, and subsequently authorise them to use issues adjudicated during the criminal trial to resolve matters that are fundamentally private in nature).

[6] See Carsten Stahn, Héctor Olásolo, and Kate Gibson, 'Participation of Victims in Pre-Trial Proceedings of the ICC', (2006) 4 *Journal of International Criminal Justice* 219, 220 (noting a small number jurisdictions, such as Spain, in which victims have such rights).

from the convicted offender for the victim's loss[7] – is generally seen as an integral part of the criminal proceedings.[8] As inquisitorial proceedings are generally court-directed rather than party-driven, victims are logical participants with a stake in the proceedings different in kind from the parties or witnesses. Because the relationship between the parties is not adversarial, victim participation presumably does not create tensions between the accused's rights and the victim's interests.

8.1.2 Relevant international law on victim treatment in national systems

Until relatively recently, international law, and particularly international criminal law, had little to say regarding victims of crime, international or domestic. There was, for example, no role for victims – except as witnesses – before the international military tribunals at Nuremberg and Tokyo.[9] In 1985, the UN General Assembly unanimously adopted a Declaration of Basic Principles of Justice for Victims of Crime and Abuse of Power.[10] Minor aspects of the Declaration bear on international relations between states. The basic principles applicable to the treatment of crime victims, however, are directed at states in their domestic treatment of those victims. Thus, the Declaration calls upon states, among other things, to ensure that crime victims are treated with compassion and respect for their dignity, and to ensure that victims are entitled to access the mechanisms of justice and to prompt redress, as provided by national legislation, for the harm they have suffered.

The Declaration calls upon states to provide specific rights, including notification to victims of their role in the criminal justice process, and about the timing, progress, and disposition of their cases. States are to take care to minimise inconvenience to victims, protect their privacy, and ensure their safety and that of their family. Offenders should be required to make fair restitution to victims, and where compensation is not fully available from the offender, states should endeavour to provide financial compensation to victims.

[7] See *infra* note 14 for a description of reparation to victims of crime under the United Nations Basic Principles and Guidelines on the Right to a Remedy and Reparation for Victims of Gross Violations of International Human Rights Law and Serious Violations of International Humanitarian Law, General Assembly Resolution 60/147, UN GAOR 60th Sess., UN Doc. A/RES/60/147 (2006) ('2006 Basic Principles').

[8] See, e.g., Zappalà, *supra* note 4, p. 219 (noting that in civil law systems the right to participate as a *partie civile* accords victims the ability to obtain reparations and restitution in the context of criminal trials).

[9] See, e.g., Schabas, *supra* note 3, pp. 324–325 (noting that victims did not fare particularly well in the initial efforts at prosecution before those tribunals and that this was at least partially due to the marginalisation of crimes against humanity as a category of international crime, and arguing that the interests and sufferings of victims of the Nazis prior to September 1939 were ultimately betrayed by the Nuremberg judgement); Zappalà, *supra* note 4, p. 220 (noting that in Nuremberg and Tokyo, as well as at the *ad hoc* Tribunals, victims could be heard only as witnesses).

[10] See United Nations Declaration of Basic Principles of Justice for Victims of Crime and Abuse of Power, General Assembly Resolution 40/34, UN GAOR 40th Sess., 96th Plenary Mtg., Annex, UN Doc. A/RES/40/34 (1985).

Although not directly applicable to the work of international criminal tribunals, one aspect of the Declaration is particularly important to the present discussion. Paragraph 6(b) of the Declaration provides, in relevant part:

The responsiveness of judicial and administrative processes to the needs of victims should be facilitated by … (b) Allowing the views and concerns of victims to be presented and considered at appropriate stages of the proceedings where their personal interests are affected, without prejudice to the accused and consistent with the relevant national criminal justice system.

This paragraph informed the debate about the role and status of victims during the negotiation of the Rome Statute in 1998. It is in fact the basis of Article 68(3) of the Rome Statute, which lifts much of the operative language directly from the Declaration.[11] This language, and its origin in the Declaration, resurfaced as the ICC litigated its first cases analysing victims' participatory rights.[12]

In 2006, the UN General Assembly adopted the Basic Principles and Guidelines on the Right to a Remedy and Reparation for Victims of Gross Violations of International Human Rights Law and Serious Violations of International Humanitarian Law.[13] As with the 1985 Declaration, the 2006 Basic Principles are nominally directed at domestic implementation by states. The modalities of victims' participatory rights are little mentioned. However, the form and content of the reparations to which victims of gross human rights violations are entitled are rather comprehensively defined.[14] Although the 2006 Basic Principles postdate the Rome Statute, it is likely

[11] See, e.g., Claude Jorda and Jérôme de Hemptinne, 'The Status and Role of the Victim', in Antonio Cassese, Paola Gaeta, and John R.W.D. Jones (eds.), *The Rome Statute of the International Criminal Court: A Commentary*, Vol. II (2002), p. 1404 (noting that the wording of Article 68(3) relies heavily on the Declaration). See also War Crimes Research Office, 'Victim Participation Before the International Criminal Court', November 2007, pp. 10, 19, available at www.wcl.american.edu/warcrimes/icc/documents/WCROReportonVictimParticipationattheCaseStageofProceedingsFebruary2009.pdf?rd=1 (noting that the drafters of the Rome Statute were particularly influenced by the 1985 Declaration and that the language of Article 68(3) of the Rome Statute mirrors almost directly paragraph 6(6) of the 1985 Declaration).

[12] See, e.g., *Prosecutor* v. *Bemba*, Doc. No. ICC-01/05-01/08-320, Fourth Decision on Victims' Participation, 12 December 2008 ('*Bemba* Fourth Decision on Victims' Participation'), para. 16 (taking note of the 1985 Declaration and the 2006 Basic Principles as 'international instruments in particular with respect to rights of victims'); *Situation in the Democratic Republic of the Congo*, Doc. No. ICC-01/04-101-tEN-Corr, Decision on the Applications for Participation in the Proceedings of VPRS 1, VPRS 2, VPRS 3, VPRS 4, VPRS 5 and VPRS 6 (Public Redacted Version), 17 January 2006 ('*DRC* Decision on Victims' Participation'), para. 115 (noting that the 1985 Declaration recognises emotional suffering and economic loss as forms of harm).

[13] See 2006 Basic Principles, *supra* note 7.

[14] *Ibid.*, para. 15 ('Principle IX, Reparation for Harm Suffered') (providing that adequate, effective, and prompt reparation is intended to promote justice by redressing gross violations of international human rights law or serious violations of international humanitarian law, and that reparation should be proportional to the gravity of the violations and the harm suffered); *ibid.*, para. 18 (reparation under the Basic Principles includes: restitution, compensation, rehabilitation, satisfaction, and guarantees of non-repetition); *ibid.*, para. 19 (restitution should, whenever possible, restore the victim to the original situation before the violations occurred and includes, as appropriate, restitution of liberty, enjoyment of human rights, identity, family life and citizenship, return to one's place of residence, restoration of employment, and return of property); *ibid.*, para. 20 (compensation should be provided for any economically assessable damage, as appropriate and proportional to the gravity of the violation and the circumstances of each case, and includes physical or mental harm; lost opportunities, including employment, education, and social benefits; material damages and loss of earnings,

that when the ICC's reparations regime falls to be interpreted by its chambers, the 2006 Basic Principles will play a large interpretive role.[15]

8.2 Victims at the ICTY, ICTR and SCSL

8.2.1 Victims as witnesses

Although victims are defined specifically in the Rules of the ICTY, ICTR and SCSL,[16] delineation as a category of participant separate from witnesses is in most respects a distinction without a difference.[17] Victims have no formal input in the process by which the prosecution investigates, charges, or tries the case. Victims have no special rights of audience or address before chambers, including no right to address the chamber with regard to decisions on provisional release or issues relevant to sentencing.[18] Victims enjoy no greater access to protective measures than witnesses.[19] And although the ICTY, ICTR, and SCSL Registries all have victims and witnesses sections,[20] nothing in their mandates provides victims any greater participation in the proceedings.[21]

including earning potential; moral damage; and costs required for legal, medical, psychological and social services); *ibid.*, para. 21 (rehabilitation should include medical and psychological care as well as legal and social services); *ibid.*, para. 22 (satisfaction should include effective measures aimed at the cessation of continuing violations; verification of the facts and full and public disclosure of the truth; the search for the whereabouts of the disappeared; an official declaration or a judicial decision restoring the dignity, reputation, and rights of the victim; public apology; commemorations and tributes to the victims; and inclusion of an accurate account of the violations that occurred in training and in educational material at all levels); *ibid.*, para. 23 (guarantees of non-repetition should include measures which contribute to prevention).

15 See, e.g., *DRC* Decision on Victims' Participation, *supra* note 12, para. 115 (noting that in addition to the 1985 Declaration, the 2006 Basic Principles also recognised emotional suffering and economic loss as forms of harm).

16 ICTY Rule 2(A) (a 'person against whom a crime over which the Tribunal has jurisdiction has allegedly been committed'). Accord ICTR Rule 2(A). See also SCSL Rule 2(A) (a 'person against whom a crime over which the Special Court has jurisdiction has allegedly or has been found to have been committed').

17 See Schabas, *supra* note 3, p. 325 (noting that in practice, the role of victims in the work of the *ad hoc* Tribunals has not been important); Alexander Zahar and Göran Sluiter, *International Criminal Law: A Critical Introduction* (2008), p. 74 (stating categorically that the *ad hoc* Tribunals do not permit any participation by victims other than their role as witnesses).

18 See ICTY Rule 65; ICTR Rule 65; SCSL Rule 65.

19 See, e.g., ICTY Rule 75 ('Measures for the Protection of Victims and Witnesses'). Nothing in the text or application of Rule 75 differentiates either the test to be applied in granting protective measures or the appropriate protective measures for victims *qua* victims. For a full discussion of protective measures, see Chapter 7, Section 7.4.2.

20 See ICTY Rule 34 ('Victims and Witnesses Section'). The Victims and Witnesses Section recommends appropriate protective measures for victims and witnesses and 'provide[s] counselling and support for them, in particular in cases of rape and sexual assault'. ICTY Rule 34(A)(ii). To the extent such counselling and support are more often needed by victims than by witnesses this is a benefit, to be sure. It is not a benefit, however, with any direct relevance to the proceedings. Although having slightly more detailed support duties, nothing in the mandate of either the ICTR's Victims and Witnesses Support Unit or the SCSL's Witnesses and Victims Section provides victims any greater role in the proceedings. See ICTR Rule 34; SCSL Rule 34.

21 Indeed, the only substantive distinction between victims and witnesses with regard to the conduct of proceedings is tied directly to the victim's role *as* a witness. In cases involving sexual assault at the ICTY and the ICTR 'no corroboration of the victim's testimony shall be required'. ICTY Rule 96(i); ICTR Rule 96(i). The SCSL has no equivalent rule. Nor shall prior sexual conduct of the victim be admitted into evidence. ICTY Rule 96(iv); ICTR Rule 96(iv). Rule 96(iv) at the SCSL provides that '[c]redibility, character or predisposition

None of this is to suggest that victims in cases before the ICTY, ICTR, and SCSL are not treated with a degree of respect and sympathy appropriate to their experience. It is simply to acknowledge that they enjoy no formal role and are essentially endowed with no greater substantive 'rights' than any other witness.

8.2.2 Victims and reparation

8.2.2.1 The unlawful taking of property

The ICTY, ICTR, and SCSL are empowered to order one form of reparation – restitution to victims. By the terms of their Statutes, however, this restitution is limited to instances of the unlawful taking of property.[22] If the trial chamber concludes from the evidence that unlawful taking of property by the accused was associated with the crime for which it finds the accused guilty, it is required to make a specific finding to this effect in rendering judgement.[23]

Following such a finding, the trial chamber is empowered to hold a special hearing to determine the rightful owner of the property, even where the property is then held by a third party not otherwise connected with the crime for which the accused has been found guilty. If the trial chamber can determine the rightful owner – 'on the balance of probabilities', a fairly low evidentiary standard – it must order restitution of the property or the proceeds 'or make such other order as it may deem appropriate'.[24] If the rightful owner cannot be determined, the trial chamber must notify the competent national authorities, request them to make the determination, and issue appropriate orders following the national authorities' determination. Even this limited form of reparation available to the ICTY, ICTR, and SCSL has never been used.

8.2.2.2 Compensation for non-property injuries

Where injury to the victim involves damages not associated with the unlawful taking of property, the ICTY, ICTR, and SCSL's restorative powers are even more limited. The Registrar of each of the Tribunals is required to transmit to competent national authorities any judgements in which the accused is found guilty of a crime which has caused injury to a victim. To the extent permitted by the relevant

to sexual availability of a victim or witness cannot be inferred by reason of sexual nature of the prior or subsequent conduct of a victim or witness'. Here again, any protection afforded the victim is tied to his or her role as a witness. For a further explanation see Chapter 9, Section 9.1.4.

22 ICTY Statute, Art. 24(3) ('Penalties') ('In addition to imprisonment, the Trial Chambers may order the return of any property and proceeds acquired by criminal conduct, including by means of duress, to their rightful owners.'); ICTR Statute, Art. 23(3); SCSL Statute, Art. 19(3). See also Chapter 10, Section 10.3.2.

23 ICTY Rule 98 *ter*(B); ICTR Rule 88(B). No such finding is required at the SCSL. Instead, the trial chamber may order the forfeiture of the property, proceeds, and any assets acquired unlawfully or by criminal conduct. SCSL Rule 88(B).

24 ICTY Rule 105; ICTR Rule 105; SCSL Rule 104.

national jurisdiction, victims – or those claiming recovery on behalf of victims – may then bring an action in national court to claim compensation. The tribunals' Rules provide that the judgements transmitted by the Registrar shall be final and binding in such national proceedings as to the criminal responsibility of the convicted person for the injury.[25] Ultimately, to the extent that the tribunals have no formal role in such proceedings, and that such national proceedings are governed in all respects by national law, the actual restorative effect of the tribunals' judgements vis-à-vis non-property injuries is speculative at best.[26]

8.3 Victims at the ICC

Unlike their counterparts in cases before the ICTY, ICTR and SCSL, victims in proceedings before the ICC enjoy participatory rights 'in pursuance of their own personal interests'.[27] Indeed, direct victim participation in the Court's work has been trumpeted as one of the innovative achievements of the Rome Conference.[28] That achievement has given rise to two distinct regimes governing the role and status of victims before the ICC: participation and reparations. The complex participation regime has already generated considerable litigation, while the ICC's reparations regime is comparatively simple and largely awaits the Court's first convictions.[29]

8.3.1 Victim participation

8.3.1.1 Who is a victim?

Although named repeatedly in the Rome Statute, victims are nowhere therein defined. Instead, Rule 85(a) provides that victims are 'natural persons who have suffered harm as a result of the commission of any crime within the jurisdiction

25 ICTY Rule 106; ICTR Rule 106; SCSL Rule 105.

26 See Zappalà, *supra* note 4, p. 227 (noting that it is questionable whether this rule is really binding on states, as the Statute does not refer to compensation, and questioning whether the judges acted *ultra vires* in adopting the rule).

27 Robert Cryer, Håkan Friman, Darryl Robinson, and Elizabeth Wilmshurst, *An Introduction to International Criminal Law and Procedure* (2007), p. 361.

28 See, e.g., Schabas, *supra* note 3, p. 327 (characterising the attention given to the role and rights of victims in the Rome Statute as 'quite stunning when set aside the very secondary role they have been given historically by international criminal law and international humanitarian law'); International Bar Association, 'First Challenges: An Examination of Recent Landmark Developments at the International Criminal Court', June 2009, p. 32, available at www.ibanet.org (calling the participation of victims 'a fulfillment of one of the main goals of the Rome Statute').

29 See, e.g., Christine Chung, 'Victims' Participation at the International Criminal Court: Are Concessions of the Court Clouding the Promise?', (2008) 6 *Northwestern University Journal of International Human Rights* 459, 461 ('The record of the ICC's early years demonstrates that thousands of pages and thousands of hours (likely representing a substantial number of euro), have been expended in delivering actual participation in proceedings on behalf of very few victims').

of the Court'. Rule 85(b), however, states that victims may include 'organizations or institutions that have sustained direct harm to any of their property which is dedicated to religion, art or science or charitable purposes, and to their historic monuments, hospitals and other places and objects for humanitarian purposes'. Thus, victims are not only those individuals who have suffered qualifying personal harm, but also representatives of particular entities which have suffered qualifying property damage.

In the first instance in which the Court was faced with the issue of defining a victim, the Pre-Trial Chamber established the following four criteria for determining whether individuals may obtain the status of victim under Rule 85(a): the victim must be a natural person; he or she must have suffered harm; the crime from which the harm ensued must fall within the jurisdiction of the Court; and there must be a causal link between the crime and the harm suffered.[30]

8.3.1.2 The victim's general participatory right under Article 68(3)

The legal basis for most victim participation before the ICC is found in Article 68(3) of the Rome Statute, which provides:

> Where the personal interests of the victim are affected, the Court shall permit their views and concerns to be presented and considered at stages of the proceedings determined to be appropriate by the Court and in a manner which is not prejudicial to or inconsistent with the rights of the accused and a fair and impartial trial. Such views and concerns may be presented by the legal representatives of the victims where the Court considers it appropriate, in accordance with the Rules of Procedure and Evidence.

While certain narrow, direct participatory rights at specific proceedings are secured by other provisions – discussed below – it is Article 68(3) that has provided a generalised right of victim participation. As the Appeals Chamber noted, this article 'establishes the right for victim participation, for the first time, in international criminal proceedings'.[31] Yet Article 68(3) arguably raises far more questions than it answers. Who is to be considered a victim? What are the 'personal interests' that must be affected? What stages of the proceedings are 'appropriate' for victim participation? How, exactly, are the rights of the accused to be balanced against those of the victims? Answering but some of these questions has required extensive litigation.[32] Several others await future chambers.

[30] *DRC* Decision on Victims' Participation, *supra* note 12, para. 79. On the Appeals Chamber's interpretation of what constitutes harm, see *infra* text accompanying notes 116–117.

[31] *Prosecutor* v. *Lubanga*, Doc. No. ICC-01/04-01/06-1432, Judgment on the Appeals of the Prosecutor and the Defence Against Trial Chamber I's Decision on Victims' Participation of 18 January 2008 11 July 2008 ('*Lubanga* Appeal Judgement on Victims' Participation'), para. 96.

[32] See Sergey Vasiliev, 'Art. 68(3) and Personal Interests of Victims in the Emerging Practice of the ICC', in Carsten Stahn and Göran Sluiter (eds.), *The Emerging Practice of the International Criminal Court* (2009), pp. 637–638 n. 12 (noting over forty-five decisions dealing exclusively or partially with victim participation issues between January 2006 and November 2007).

Article 68(3) provides no specific limit on the stages of the proceedings in which victims may participate. Rather, it broadly secures a victim's right to participate at those stages 'determined to be appropriate by the Court'. Predictably, such broad governing language in the procedural framework has produced disparate results across the array of chambers dealing with victim participation requests in situations and cases before the Court. For almost three years, certain applicants enjoyed a 'procedural status' of victim during the investigation stages of situations,[33] until the Appeals Chamber clarified that no such status was contemplated in the Rome Statute or the Rules.[34] In defining victim participation at the case stage of proceedings, pre-trial chambers limited participation to victims of the actual crimes charged in the indictment. The first trial chamber to contemplate victim participation in trial proceedings, however, rejected the pre-trial chambers' approach and broadened the participatory right to victims of any crime within the jurisdiction of the Court, whether or not related to the charges in the case. Here again, the Appeals Chamber reversed the lower chamber and established the appropriate scope of victim participation.[35]

Even with the clarifications provided by the Appeals Chamber, however, the Court has not discovered any stage of the proceedings at which victims' participatory rights pursuant to Article 68(3) are *per se* inappropriate. Victims might still theoretically participate at the investigation stage of a situation.[36] They undoubtedly may participate throughout the pre-trial and trial phases of a case. Additionally, victims may participate in certain interlocutory appeals filed during any of these stages. Though no chamber has yet rendered judgement in any case, victim participation in appeals from judgements seems all but certain. This is not to suggest that direct participation in any specific proceeding within these stages is automatic. For example, chambers have often denied victim applications to participate in status conferences, at least where the chamber considered the subject matter of the conference to be of a technical nature unrelated to the victims' participation.[37] On balance, however, victim participation requests, at least in principle, have been granted more often than they have been rejected.

Victim participation at specific proceedings outside the ambit of Article 68(3) is discussed below and followed by a discussion of the general modalities of participation. Victim participation pursuant to Article 68(3) in the pre-trial stages of

[33] On the distinction between 'situations' and 'cases' under the Rome Statute, see Chapter 3, Section 3.2.1.

[34] See Section 8.3.1.7, *infra*. [35] See Section 8.3.1.9, *infra*.

[36] See *infra* note 87 and accompanying text.

[37] See, e.g., *Prosecutor* v. *Lubanga*, Doc. No. ICC-01/04-01/06-335, Decision on the Application for Participation of Victims a/0001/06 to a/0003/06 in the Status Conference of 24 August 2006, 17 August 2006, p. 3; *Prosecutor* v. *Lubanga*, Doc. No. ICC-01/04-01/06-380, Decision on the Application for Participation of Victims a/0001/06 to a/0003/06 in the Status Conference of 5 September 2006, 4 September 2006, p. 3.

situations and cases, trial proceedings, and interlocutory appellate proceedings will then be examined.

8.3.1.3 Participation under Article 15(3): proprio motu *investigations*

In the context of the Prosecutor's request to the Pre-Trial Chamber to authorise an investigation *proprio motu*,[38] victims have a direct statutory right to participate that does not depend upon Article 68(3). Where the Prosecutor seeks to open an investigation *proprio motu*, '[v]ictims may make representations to the Pre-Trial Chamber, in accordance with the Rules of Procedure and Evidence'.[39] Unlike participation pursuant to Article 68(3), victim participation in this context is not limited to the presentation of 'views and concerns'. There is no 'personal interests' requirement, and the text does not grant any special discretion to a pre-trial chamber to determine whether such participation is appropriate. The victim's participatory right in this instance seems absolute. The only precondition would appear to be that the victim must be 'known to the Court (either the Prosecutor or the Victims and Witnesses Unit)'.[40] This precondition is a logical one; victims cannot participate in proceedings of which they are not aware. Thus, the Rules require the Prosecutor to inform victims that he or she intends to seek the pre-trial chamber's authorisation to open an investigation *proprio motu*.[41]

On 26 November 2009, the ICC Prosecutor announced that he would formally seek the Pre-Trial Chamber's permission to open an investigation into the situation in Kenya.[42] As this represents the Prosecutor's first attempted use of the *proprio motu* investigative power, it will be the first opportunity for potential victims to participate in such a proceeding.

8.3.1.4 Participation under Article 19(3): jurisdiction or admissibility challenges

Victims are entitled to submit observations to the Court in proceedings with respect to jurisdiction or admissibility of cases.[43] As with victim participation in the context of the Prosecutor's request to open an investigation *proprio motu*, the victims' right

[38] On the pre-trial chamber's role in authorising investigations initiated by the prosecution *proprio motu*, see Chapter 3, Section 3.2.3.2.1.

[39] Rome Statute, Art. 15(3).

[40] *Situation in Uganda*, Doc No. ICC-02/04-01/5-101, Decision on Victims' Application for Participation a/0010/06, a/0064/06 to a/0070/06, a/0081/06 to a/0104/06 and a/0111/06 to a/0127/06, 10 August 2007 ('*Uganda* Decision on Victims' Participation'), para. 92.

[41] ICC Rule 50. The notification required extends to victims known to the Prosecutor or the Victims and Witnesses Unit, or the victims' legal representatives. Notification is not required if the Prosecutor decides that such notification would pose a danger to the integrity of the investigation or the life or well-being of victims and witnesses. ICC Rule 50(1). For other types of notice to which victims are entitled, see Section 8.3.1.6.5, *infra*.

[42] See *Situation in the Republic of Kenya*, Doc. No. ICC-01/09-3, Request for Authorisation of an Investigation Pursuant to Article 14, 26 November 2009. For more on the Prosecutor's request, see Chapter 3, Section 3.2.3.2.1.

[43] Rome Statute, Art. 19(3). Chapter 3, Section 3.2.3.2.3, discusses Article 19 proceedings generally.

to submit observations at this stage is not dependent upon Article 68(3), so their participation is similarly not subject to the 'personal interests' requirement, and the Court has no discretionary function in determining whether participation is appropriate. Once again, the participatory right is absolute, although limited to those victims 'who have already communicated to the Court in relation to that case'.[44]

For example, early in the *Lubanga* case, the Pre-Trial Chamber construed the accused's application for release as a challenge to the jurisdiction of the Court. Accordingly, the Chamber solicited submissions on the application from the three victims who had previously been granted the right to participate in the case stage of the proceedings pursuant to Article 68(3).[45] The victims opposed Lubanga's request in written submissions and the Chamber denied Lubanga's jurisdictional challenge.[46]

8.3.1.5 Participation under Rule 119(3): release pending or during trial and appeal

Yet another participatory right exists outside the ambit of Article 68(3), one created by the Rules rather than the Rome Statute. Before imposing or amending any conditions restricting liberty on a person whom the chamber is considering releasing from custody, the pre-trial chamber is required to seek the views of, among others, 'victims that have communicated with the Court in that case and whom the Chamber considers could be at risk as a result of a release or conditions imposed'.[47] This provision does not appear to be limited to those victims already granted the right to participate under Article 68(3), as victims may communicate with the Court without such status. Unlike participation in *proprio motu* investigation requests and jurisdiction or admissibility challenges, however, the right does not appear to be absolute. Communication with the Court is a necessary prerequisite, but the Court also appears to have discretion not to seek the views of victims whom it does not consider could be at risk.

In the *Lubanga* case, victims participated in the Pre-Trial Chamber's decisions on interim release from the very beginning, by filing written observations opposing the accused's application for release.[48] Lubanga was never granted interim release

[44] ICC Rule 59(1)(b).

[45] *Prosecutor* v. *Lubanga*, Doc. No. ICC-01/04-01/06-206, Decision Inviting the Democratic Republic of the Congo and the Victims in the Case to Comment on the Proceedings Pursuant to Article 19 of the Statute, 24 July 2006, pp. 3–4.

[46] *Prosecutor* v. *Lubanga*, Doc. No. ICC-01/04-01/06-512, Decision on the Defence Challenge to the Jurisdiction of the Court Pursuant to Article 19(2)(1) of the Statute, 3 October 2006, p. 4.

[47] ICC Rule 119(3). Regarding release pending or during trial and appeal see Chapter 4, Section 4.3.

[48] See *Prosecutor* v. *Lubanga*, Doc. No. ICC-01/04-01/06-530, Observations of Victims a/0001/06, a/0002/06 and a/0003/06 in Respect of the Application for Release Filed by the Defence, 9 October 2006; *Prosecutor* v. *Lubanga*, Doc. No. ICC-01/04-01/06-465, Decision Establishing a Deadline in Relation to the Defence Request for the Interim Release of Thomas Lubanga Dyilo, 22 September 2006 (noting Rule 119 and establishing a deadline for victims' submissions). See also Brianne N. McGonigle, 'Bridging the Divides in International Criminal Proceedings: An Examination into the Victim Participation Endeavor of the

by the Pre-Trial Chamber or by the Trial Chamber, which continued to note and consider the victims' initial submissions in subsequent reviews.[49] When a dispute over the prosecution's non-disclosure of exculpatory materials threatened to terminate the *Lubanga* case altogether in July 2008,[50] the Trial Chamber ordered Lubanga released, subject to the review of the Appeals Chamber. In its decision, the Trial Chamber outlined and considered at length the victims' submissions in opposition.[51]

8.3.1.6 General regulation of the modalities of victim participation

Where Article 68(3) permits victim participation, the Rules establish a procedural framework for the modalities of that participation.

8.3.1.6.1 Applications Any individual wishing to be granted victim status must make a written application to the Registry, which transmits the application to the relevant chamber.[52] The prosecution and defence may both reply to the application, and in response, or *proprio motu*, the chamber may reject the application where it appears that the individual does not meet the criteria of Article 68(3).[53]

8.3.1.6.2 Opening and closing statements Where it does not reject an application, the chamber is required to specify the proceedings and manner in which the victim's participation is considered appropriate.[54] In one of the limited number of instances in the procedural framework in which a specific type of participation is

International Criminal Court', (2009) 21 *Florida Journal of International Law* 93, 125 (noting that although the Pre-Trial Chamber almost certainly would have denied the application in any event, the victims' observations may have influenced the Chamber to deny the application).

[49] See, e.g., *Prosecutor* v. *Lubanga*, Doc. No. ICC-01/04-01/06-586, Decision on the Application for the Interim Release of Thomas Lubanga Dyilo, 18 October 2006, p. 2 (noting the victims' submissions in opposition to the requested release); *Prosecutor* v. *Lubanga*, Doc. No. ICC-01/04-01/06-826, Review of the 'Decision on the Application for the Interim Release of Thomas Lubanga Dyilo', 14 February 2007, p. 8; *Prosecutor* v. *Lubanga*, Doc. No. ICC-01/04-01/06-924, Second Review of the 'Decision on the Application for the Interim Release of Thomas Lubanga Dyilo', 11 June 2007, p. 8; *Prosecutor* v. *Lubanga*, Doc No. ICC-01/04-01/06-976, Decision Reviewing the 'Decision on the Application for the Interim Release of Thomas Lubanga Dyilo', 9 October 2007, paras. 2, 13; *Prosecutor* v. *Lubanga*, Doc. No. ICC-01/04-01/06-1151, Decision Reviewing the Trial Chamber's Ruling on the Detention of Thomas Lubanga Dyilo in Accordance with Rule 118(2), 1 February 2008, paras. 2, 13.

[50] For a detailed explanation of the nature of the dispute and its effects on the trial proceedings see Chapter 6, Section 6.5.1.4.

[51] See *Prosecutor* v. *Lubanga*, Doc. No. ICC-01/04-01/06-1418, Decision on the Release of Thomas Lubanga Dyilo, 2 July 2008, paras. 15–20.

[52] ICC Rule 89(1). The application forms are standardised by the Registry and are information intensive. See ICC Court Regulation 86. For an example of an application form, see www.icc-cpi.int/Menus/ICC/Structure+of+the+Court/Victims/Participation/Forms.htm.

[53] See also *Situation in Uganda*, Doc No. ICC-02/04-180, Decision on Victims' Application for Participation a/0192/07 to a/0194/07, a/0196/07, a/0200/07, a/0204/07, a/0206/07, a/ 0209/07, a/0212/07, a/0216/07, a/0217/07, a/0219/07 to a/0221/07, a/0228/07 to a/0230/07, a/0234/07, a/0235/07, a/0237/07, a/0324/07 and a/0326/07 Under Rule 89, 10 March 2009, p. 5.

[54] ICC Rule 89(1).

noted, the Rules provide that where the chamber finds it appropriate, victim participation 'may include making opening and closing statements'.[55] Such participation, however, is effected through the victim's legal representatives.[56]

8.3.1.6.3 Legal representatives Victims may be represented by a legal representative of their choice.[57] Where the interests of justice so require, a chamber may appoint a legal representative to a victim.[58] Where there are 'a number of victims', the chamber may request the victims to choose a common legal representative. If the victims cannot agree upon a common choice, the chamber may direct the Registrar to choose a common representative,[59] following which victims may request the relevant chamber to review the choice.[60] Victims who lack the resources to pay for a common legal representative may receive financial assistance from the Registry.[61] Similar to the requirements for defence counsel, legal representatives of victims may not withdraw from a case without leave of the relevant chamber.[62]

The victim's legal representative is entitled to attend and participate in the proceedings as permitted by the chamber. The chamber may allow the legal representative to make oral submissions in court, or may determine 'in the circumstances of the case' that the representative's intervention should be limited to written submissions.[63] The prosecution and defence are permitted to reply to any oral or written observations of the victim's representative.

Where the victim's legal representative wishes to question a witness, the chamber may require the representative to provide written notice of the questions with

[55] *Ibid.* See also *Prosecutor* v. *Lubanga*, Doc. No. ICC-01/04-01/06-462, Decision on the Arrangements for Participation of Victims a/0001/06, a/0002/06 and a/0003/06 at the Confirmation Hearing, 22 September 2006 ('*Lubanga* Pre-Trial Decision on Victims' Participation at Confirmation Hearing'), p. 6.

[56] In the *Lubanga* confirmation hearing, the participating victims' legal representatives made opening and closing statements. See *Prosecutor* v. *Lubanga*, Case No. ICC-01/04-01/06, Transcript, 9 November 2006, p. 75 (opening statements); *Prosecutor* v. *Lubanga*, Case No. ICC-01/04-01/06, Transcript, 28 November 2006, p. 45 (closing statements).

[57] ICC Rule 90. Rule 90(6) provides that a legal representative of a victim shall have the same minimum qualifications set forth in Rule 22(1) for defence counsel. On issues surrounding the appointment of counsel, see Chapter 5, Section 5.2.1.

[58] ICC Court Regulation 80(1).

[59] ICC Rule 90(2)–(3). Rule 90(4) also requires the chamber and the Registry to take all reasonable steps to ensure that conflicts of interest are avoided. See also *Prosecutor* v. *Bemba*, Doc. No. ICC-01/05-01/08-322, Fifth Decision on Victims' Issues Concerning Common Legal Representation of Victims, 16 December 2008 ('*Bemba* Decision Concerning Common Legal Representation'), paras. 5–7, 9 (noting that in appointing a common legal representative, criteria guiding such a choice might include: the language spoken by the victims, the links between the victims, the specific crimes alleged, and respect for local traditions).

[60] ICC Court Regulation 79(3). [61] ICC Rule 90(5).

[62] ICC Court Regulation 82. Regarding the professional conduct of defence counsel see Chapter 5, Section 5.2.2.

[63] ICC Rule 91(2).

the request, which shall be communicated to the prosecution and, 'where appropriate', the defence.[64] When such questions are requested and communicated, the prosecution and defence are permitted to make submissions on the questions. The chamber will then rule on the legal representative's request and, where granted, control how the representative questions the witness, including potentially putting the questions to the witness itself.[65]

8.3.1.6.4 The Office of Public Counsel for Victims The ICC's Regulations of the Court establish the Office of Public Counsel for Victims ('OPCV').[66] The OPCV's mandate is to provide support and assistance to victims and their legal representatives including, where appropriate, legal research and advice, and to appear before a chamber in respect of specific issues.[67] In some of the cases before the Court, the OPCV has also been assigned by a chamber to act as the legal representative of certain victims.[68]

With regard to the involvement of the OPCV during trial proceedings, the *Lubanga* Trial Chamber decided that the power to determine the OPCV's role was vested in the Chamber, because it was the Chamber which bore the responsibility to manage the proceedings and to ensure the fair and expeditious conduct of the trial. Noting that the OPCV was not a party to the case, the Chamber limited the OPCV's appearance in the case to the following instances: (1) where the Chamber requested the appearance; (2) where the OPCV appeared at the request of a victim or the victim's representative; (3) where the OPCV was formally the legal representative of a victim; and (4) in other instances if granted leave to appear.[69] As to access to the case record, the Chamber determined that where the OPCV was acting as a victim's formal legal representative, it would have the same access as

[64] ICC Rule 91(3)(a)–(b). See also *Prosecutor* v. *Lubanga*, Doc. No. ICC-01/04-01/06-2127, Decision on the Manner of Questioning Witnesses by the Legal Representatives of Victims, 16 September 2009 ('*Lubanga* Manner of Questioning Decision'), paras. 21–22 (noting that the questioning of witnesses by the victims' legal representatives pursuant to Rule 91(3) is one example of the ways in which the Rome Statute envisions the unequivocal right of victims to present their views and concerns).

[65] See, e.g., *Lubanga* Manner of Questioning Decision, *supra* note 64, para. 28 (holding that the legal representatives of the victims should follow a neutral approach in questioning witnesses because they are less likely than the parties to need to resort to the 'more combative technique of cross-examination', but noting that in certain instances, if approved by the chamber, it may be fully consistent with the legal representative's role to press, challenge, or discredit a witness).

[66] For a comprehensive overview of the OPCV and its mandate, see Paolina Massidda and Sarah Pellet, 'Role and Practice of the Office of Public Counsel for Victims', in Carsten Stahn and Göran Sluiter (eds.), *supra* note 32, pp. 691–706.

[67] ICC Court Regulation 81. See also ICC Registry Regulations 114–117; *Bemba* Decision Concerning Common Legal Representation, *supra* note 59, para. 8.

[68] See, e.g., *Bemba* Decision Concerning Common Legal Representation, *supra* note 59.

[69] *Prosecutor* v. *Lubanga*, Doc. No. ICC-01/04-01/06-1211, Decision on the Role of the Office for Public Counsel for Victims and Its Request for Access to Documents, 6 March 2008, paras. 30–35.

any other legal representative. Where the OPCV was not representing a victim, however, access would be denied.[70]

8.3.1.6.5 Notice In order to facilitate victim participation in *proprio motu* investigation requests, the Prosecutor is required to provide notice to victims known to the Prosecutor when he or she intends to seek the pre-trial chamber's authorisation to open such an investigation.[71] The Registry is required to inform victims of jurisdiction and admissibility challenges in order to facilitate victim participation in such proceedings.[72]

To facilitate victim applications for the right to participate in certain other proceedings for which neither the Rome Statute nor the Rules provides a direct participatory right, the Court is also required to provide notice of a decision of the Prosecutor not to initiate an investigation or not to prosecute,[73] and notice of a chamber's decision to hold a hearing to confirm charges.[74] Notice required of the Court in these instances must be provided to any victims or their legal representatives who have already participated in the proceedings, as well as – where possible – with those individuals who have communicated with the Court regarding the situation or case.

Finally, where victims have been granted the right to participate in a proceeding not specified in the Rome Statute (that is, *proprio motu* investigation requests and challenges to jurisdiction or admissibility, which have separate notification rules discussed above), such victims enjoy a generalised notification right. The Registry is required to notify such victims in a timely manner of any proceedings before the Court, as well as of any requests, submissions, motions, and any other documents relating to the requests, submissions, or motions.[75] The Registry is also required to notify victims of the decisions of the Court in any proceedings in which they have participated.[76]

[70] *Ibid.*, paras. 37–40.

[71] ICC Rule 50(1). The required notification extends to victims known to the Prosecutor or the Victims and Witnesses Unit, or the victims' legal representatives. Notification is not required if the Prosecutor decides that such notification would pose a danger to the integrity of the investigation or the life or well-being of victims and witnesses. *Ibid.*

[72] ICC Rule 59(1)(b). The required notification extends to victims who have already communicated with the Court in relation to the case, or their legal representatives.

[73] ICC Rule 92(2). The scope and manner of victim participation in such review proceedings remains unclear. See Stahn, Olásolo, and Gibson, *supra* note 6, p. 234 (noting that there is some confusion because the form of victim participation in such proceedings is not expressly determined in Rules 89 to 91, but reasoning that victims may make written submissions, and arguing that Rule 93 permits the chamber to seek the views of victims on any issue). The Prosecutor's decision not to prosecute is governed by Article 53. See Chapter 3, Section 3.2.3.2.1.

[74] ICC Rule 92(3). On the confirmation hearing, see Chapter 6, Section 6.1.1.

[75] ICC Rule 92(5). [76] ICC Rule 92(6).

8.3.1.6.6 Reviewing the record of the pre-trial proceedings The Registry is required to create and maintain a full and accurate record of all proceedings before the pre-trial chamber.[77] Victims or their legal representatives participating in the pre-trial proceedings are entitled to consult the record, subject to any restrictions concerning confidentiality and the protection of national security information.[78] As discussed below, the manner in which victims or their legal representatives may consult the record in the case is heavily regulated by the chambers, which assess victim requests to consult the record on a case-by-case basis during different proceedings.

8.3.1.6.7 Where the chamber desires input Where a victim is participating in proceedings, the chamber may seek the victim's views – or the victim's legal representative's views – 'on any issue'.[79] Additionally, the chamber may seek the views 'of other victims, as appropriate'. This would appear to vest a residual power in the chamber to solicit any victim's participation on any matter the chamber finds appropriate, and the relevant rule has been characterised as creating another 'regime for the involvement of victims', one that does not require the solicited victim to formally participate under the rubric of other applicable rules.[80]

8.3.1.7 Pre-trial participation in situations

In its earliest work, the Court had to grapple with whether victims could participate at the situation stage – that is, the investigative phase which precedes the formal identification of any specific individual accused of any particular offence.[81] In the *Situation in the Democratic Republic of the Congo* ('DRC'), the Pre-Trial Chamber construed 'proceedings' in Article 68(3) to include court proceedings that occur before the issuance of arrest warrants.[82] Over the Prosecutor's objection,

[77] ICC Rules 121(10), 131.

[78] At least with regard to victims, it should be noted that these rules appear to be unnecessarily duplicative. Rule 121 is captioned 'Proceedings Before the Confirmation Hearing' and appears in Chapter 5, Section V of the Rules, 'Proceedings with Regard to the Confirmation of Charges Under Art. 61'. Rule 131 is captioned 'Record of the Proceedings Transmitted by the Pre-Trial Chamber' and appears as the first rule in Chapter 6 titled 'Trial Procedure'. Yet Rule 131 refers specifically to the record required to be maintained under Rule 121(10), and provides victims no greater right of 'consultation'. See also *Prosecutor* v. *Lubanga*, Doc. No. ICC-01/04-01/06-1119, Decision on Victim's Participation, 18 January 2008 ('*Lubanga* First Trial Decision on Victims' Participation'), paras. 105–106 (noting the general right secured by Rule 131(2), but establishing a presumption that victims' legal representatives would have access only to the public filings in the record absent a specific finding by the Chamber).

[79] ICC Rule 93. Although the rule does not limit the issues upon which the Chamber may seek the views of the victim, it specifically lists Rules 107 ('Request for Review Under Art. 53, Paragraph 3(a)'), 109 ('Review by the Pre-Trial Chamber Under Art. 53, Paragraph 3(b)'), 125 ('Decision to Hold the Confirmation Hearing in the Absence of the Person Concerned'), 128 ('Amendment of the Charges'), 136 ('Joint and Separate Trials'), 139 ('Decision on Admission of Guilt'), and 191 ('Assurance Provided by the Court Under Art. 93, Paragraph 2').

[80] ICC Rule 93. See also Stahn, Olásolo, and Gibson, *supra* note 6, p. 237 (noting that Rule 93 was formulated as a compromise between those delegations that advocated for more extensive victim participation throughout the proceedings, and those that favoured a more restrictive approach).

[81] On the distinction between 'situations' and 'cases', see Chapter 3, Section 3.2.1.

[82] *DRC* Decision on Victims' Participation, *supra* note 12, para. 46.

the Chamber also found that the personal interests of victims are affected *in general* at the situation stage 'since the participation of victims at this stage can serve to clarify the facts, to punish the perpetrators of crimes and to request reparations for the harm suffered'.[83] Coupled with requiring only a distinctly *de minimis* causal link between the harm suffered and the commission of a crime within the jurisdiction of the Court, this liberal construction of the 'personal interests' requirement rendered the pool of qualified applicants quite large at the situation stage, and was the subject of substantial criticism.[84]

It took almost three years for the Appeals Chamber to determine that the decisions granting applicants the 'procedural status of victim' prior to the case phase were 'ill-founded and [had to] be set aside'.[85] The Appeals Chamber found that the prosecution's investigation did not qualify as judicial proceedings as contemplated by Article 68(3). Moreover, because authority to conduct investigations vests 'manifestly' in the prosecution, any acknowledgment by a pre-trial chamber of a right of victims to participate in the investigation would 'necessarily contravene the [Rome] Statute by reading into it a power outside its ambit and remit'.[86]

In the meantime, hundreds of applicants were granted an ultimately illusory participatory status in several situations. Although the Appeals Chamber clarified that Article 68(3) does not endow victims with a generalised right to participate in the investigative phase of a situation, it did not rule out the possibility of appropriate individualised victim participation at the situation phase *per se*; victims may apply to participate in judicial proceedings, including those 'affecting investigations'.[87]

[83] *Ibid.*, para. 63; *Uganda* Decision on Victims' Participation, *supra* note 40, para. 83; *Situation in Darfur, Sudan*, Doc. No. ICC-02/05-110, Decision on the Requests of the OPCD on the Production of Relevant Supporting Documentation Pursuant to Regulation 86(2)(e) of the Regulations of the Court and on the Disclosure of Exculpatory Materials by the Prosecutor, 3 December 2007, para. 2.

[84] See, e.g., Chung, *supra* note 29, pp. 526–529 (calling for the Court to disallow victim participation in the investigation stage based solely on a general interest in investigation); Jérôme de Hemptinne and Francesco Rindi, 'ICC Pre-Trial Chamber Allows Victims to Participate in the Investigation Phase of Proceedings', (2006) 4 *Journal of International Criminal Justice* 342; Vasiliev, *supra* note 32, p. 660 (arguing that such an overly generous approach obviates any meaningful legal effect of the 'personal interests' criterion).

[85] *Situation in the Democratic Republic of the Congo*, Doc. No. ICC-01/04-556, Judgment on Victim Participation in the Investigation Stage of the Proceedings in the Appeal of the OPCD Against the Decision of Pre-Trial Chamber I of 7 December 2007 and in the Appeals of the OPCD and the Prosecutor Against the Decision of Pre-Trial Chamber I of 24 December 2007, 19 December 2008 ('*DRC* Appeal Judgment on Victims' Participation in the Investigation Stage'), para. 59. See also *Situation in Darfur, Sudan*, Doc. No. ICC-02/05-177, Judgment on Victim Participation in the Investigation Stage of the Proceedings in the Appeal of the OPCD against the Decision of Pre-Trial Chamber I of 3 December 2007 and in the Appeals of the OPCD and the Prosecutor Against the Decision of Pre-Trial Chamber I of 6 December 2007, 2 February 2009, para. 7.

[86] *DRC* Appeal Judgment on Victims' Participation in the Investigation Stage, *supra* note 85, para. 52. See also *ibid.*, para. 56 (noting further that the Pre-Trial Chamber's acknowledgement of the 'procedural status' of victims in the situation stage extends Article 68(3) 'beyond its self-evident confines, to areas outside its ambit').

[87] *Ibid.*, para. 56 ('On the other hand, it must be clarified that victims are not precluded from seeking participation in any judicial proceedings, including proceedings affecting investigations, provided their personal interests are affected by the issues arising for resolution'); *ibid.*, para. 57 ('Having determined that the Pre-Trial Chamber cannot grant the procedural status of victim entailing a general right to participate in the investigation, the Appeals Chamber is not in a position to advise the Pre-Trial Chamber as to how

Although ultimately set aside, the Pre-Trial Chamber's approaches to determining the procedural rights of victims at the situation stage are illustrative of the thorny interpretive issues facing the Court in providing victims appropriate participatory rights within its broad mandate.[88]

The modalities of participation for victims previously granted the 'procedural status of victim' in the investigation phase were quite limited. Such victims were authorised to address the Pre-Trial Chamber in order to present their views and concerns, permitted to file documents pertaining to the situation, granted notification rights consistent with the Rome Statute and the Rules, and allowed to request that the Chamber order 'special' proceedings. They could not, however, access confidential filings in the record, nor attend confidential proceedings.[89] During the three-year period in which such generalised rights prevailed, they were of little practical effect, and are unlikely to be of significant substantive effect for any future victims granted the right to participate in situations before a case arises.

8.3.1.8 Pre-trial participation in cases

As discussed elsewhere in this book,[90] a case arises out of a situation once an arrest warrant or summons has been issued for an individual. Prior to the confirmation hearing, the case resides with the pre-trial chamber. Once charges are confirmed against the accused, the case passes to the trial chamber.[91]

During the pre-trial phase of a case, qualifying to participate as a victim is somewhat more difficult than qualifying to participate in a situation. This is because analysing the causal link between the crime and the harm suffered is more rigorous than for a situation. The victim applicant – or, upon review, the person previously granted victim status in the situation from which the case arises – must provide sufficient evidence to allow the chamber to establish that the victim has suffered harm directly linked to the crimes contained in the arrest warrant or that the victim suffered

applications for participation in judicial proceedings at the investigation stage of a situation should generally be dealt with in the future, in the absence of specific facts. It is for the Pre-Trial Chamber to determine how best to rule upon applications for participation, in compliance with the relevant provisions of the Court's texts. The Pre-Trial Chamber must do so bearing in mind that participatory rights can only be granted under Art. 68 (3) of the Statute once the requirements of that provision have been fulfilled').

88 At the time of writing, no pre-trial chamber had ruled on the participation of victims in a situation, as distinct from a particular case, subsequent to the Appeals Chamber's decision clarifying that no generalised participatory right exists. Accordingly, it remains to be seen what individualised showing pre-trial chambers will require of future applicants. It also remains unclear whether previously used analyses of harm, unrelated to the overturned generalised 'personal interests' question, will survive. Previously, being granted individualised participatory rights was anything but rigorous, at least vis-à-vis the analysis applicable to the causal link between the crime and the harm suffered. Harm was construed as resulting from the commission of the crime when the spatial and temporal circumstances surrounding the appearance of the harm and the occurrence of the crime seemed to overlap, or when they were at least compatible and not clearly inconsistent. See, e.g., *Uganda* Decision on Victims' Participation, *supra* note 40, para. 14.

89 *DRC* Decision on Victims' Participation, *supra* note 12, paras. 71, 75–76.

90 See Chapter 3, Section 3.2.1; Chapter 6, Section 6.3.1.

91 Rome Statute, Art. 61(11).

harm while intervening to help direct victims of the crimes alleged in the case, or to prevent others from becoming victims because of the commission of these crimes.[92] That the causality requirement in the context of a case is more stringent than for participation in a situation was amply illustrated in the *Lubanga* case, where six victims granted participant status in the *Situation in the DRC* failed to qualify for such status in the pre-trial phase of the case that arose out of that situation.[93] Four victims – from an applicant pool of over seventy – did meet the test.[94] The four applicants who qualified did so because they established that their sons had been conscripted or enlisted by Lubanga's armed group during the time period specified in the arrest warrant.[95]

As to the modalities of victim participation during the pre-trial phase of a case, there is no specific source to which victims can look to determine how or when they may play a role. The Rome Statute and the Rules provide only a framework, and the jurisprudence has provided little further guidance. As one Pre-Trial Chamber noted, Article 68(3) 'does not pre-establish a set of procedural rights (i.e. modalities of participation) that those granted the procedural status of victim at the pre-trial stage of a case may exercise, but rather leaves their determination to the discretion of the Chamber'.[96] In essence, each case is a blank page upon which victims' participatory rights have yet to be written. The scope of that participation is left to the discretion of the individual chamber. This fragmented approach resulted in disparate participatory rights for victims in the confirmation hearings held by different pre-trial chambers in the Court's first cases.

8.3.1.8.1 The confirmation hearing The hearing to confirm the charges against the accused is arguably the most important proceeding presided over by the pre-trial chamber.[97] In all three confirmation hearings held by the Court to date – in

[92] See *Prosecutor* v. *Lubanga*, Doc. No. ICC-01/04-01/06-172-tEN, Decision on the Applications for Participation in the Proceedings Submitted by VPRS 1 to VPRS 6 in the Case of The Prosecutor v. Thomas Lubanga Dyilo, 29 June 2006 ('*Lubanga* 29 June 2006 Decision on Victims' Participation'), pp. 6, 8. Accord *Bemba* Fourth Decision on Victims' Participation, *supra* note 12, paras. 74–78.

[93] *Lubanga* 29 June 2006 Decision on Victims' Participation, *supra* note 92, pp. 7–8. It is difficult to know exactly why the six victims earlier granted participatory status in the DRC situation failed the more stringent requirement for participation in the *Lubanga* case, as the details of each of the victims' statements were redacted from the public version of the Pre-Trial Chamber's decision. In rather conclusory language, the Pre-Trial Chamber simply considered that the six victims had not demonstrated 'any causal link between the harm they suffered and the crimes contained in the arrest warrant against Thomas Lubanga Dyilo'. *Ibid.*, p. 7.

[94] *Prosecutor* v. *Lubanga*, Doc No. ICC-01/04-01/06-601-tEN, Decision on Applications for Participation in Proceedings a/0004/06 to a/0009/06, a/0016/06 to a/0063/06, a/0071/06 to a/0080/06, and a/0105//06 in the Case of The Prosecutor v. Thomas Lubanga Dyilo, 20 October 2006, pp. 9–10 (granting only one out of sixty-five applicants participatory status without any reference to publicly available facts as to why the unsuccessful applicants failed to qualify). See also Chung, *supra* note 29, p. 470 n. 45 and accompanying text (describing this decision and others in which individuals filed applications to participate as victims in the case).

[95] Chung, *supra* note 29, p. 470.

[96] *Prosecutor* v. *Katanga and Ngudjolo*, Doc. No. ICC-01/04-01/07-474, Decision on the Set of Procedural Rights Attached to Procedural Status of Victim at the Pre-Trial Stage of the Case, 13 May 2008 ('*Katanga and Ngudjolo* Decision on Victims' Participation Pre-Trial'), para. 45(iv).

[97] For a detailed explanation of the Pre-Trial Chamber's role in the confirmation of charges, see Chapter 6, Section 6.1.1.

Lubanga, *Katanga and Ngudjolo*, and *Bemba* – victims have participated directly in the proceedings.

In the *Lubanga* case, the Pre-Trial Chamber characterised the confirmation hearing as an essential stage of the proceedings and held that the victims granted participant status in the case were entitled to participate in the confirmation hearing 'by presenting their views and concerns in order to help contribute to the prosecution of the crimes from which they allegedly have suffered and to, where relevant, subsequently be able to obtain reparations for harm suffered'.[98] Because the victims who sought participation in the confirmation hearing wished to remain anonymous, the Chamber had to determine the modalities of their participation in the context of that anonymity. While the Chamber granted the victims certain participatory rights, their anonymous status precluded them from being able to question witnesses at the confirmation hearing.[99] The victims' legal representatives, however, enjoyed the following participatory rights in the confirmation hearing: (1) notification and access to the public documents in the record; (2) attending public status conferences; (3) making opening and closing statements; and (4) the potential to intervene during public sessions of the hearing. The Chamber noted that it would rule on whether to permit such interventions on a case-by-case basis. Having limited participation to these four modalities, the Chamber did not foreclose the possibility that additional participation might become appropriate in (undefined) exceptional circumstances.[100] In addition to being active in filing written submissions, the legal representatives of four victims made opening and closing statements during the confirmation hearing.[101]

For the confirmation hearing in the *Katanga and Ngudjolo* case, the Pre-Trial Chamber established two sets of participatory rights for victims, based on whether the victim wished to remain anonymous. The victims who remained anonymous were granted the same rights accorded the anonymous victims in the *Lubanga* case, as described above. The participatory rights of the non-anonymous victims, however, were greatly expanded. These victims could (through their legal representatives): (1) access confidential (but not *ex parte*) records; (2) make submissions regarding the admissibility and probative value of the prosecution and defence evidence; (3) examine such evidence at the hearing; (4) examine witnesses; (5) attend all sessions in the confirmation process except those convened *ex parte*; (6) make

[98] *Lubanga* Pre-Trial Decision on Victims' Participation at Confirmation Hearing, *supra* note 55, p. 5.

[99] *Ibid.*, p. 7 (noting that the 'fundamental principle prohibiting anonymous accusations would be violated' if the victims were permitted to add any evidence to the prosecution's case file or to question the witnesses at the confirmation hearing).

[100] *Ibid.*, paras. 5–7. See also McGonigle, *supra* note 48, p. 127 (noting that upon the request of one of the victims' legal representatives, the Court put one question to the sole prosecution witness); *Prosecutor* v. *Lubanga*, Case No. ICC-01/04-01/09, Transcript, 21 November 2006.

[101] See *Prosecutor* v. *Lubanga*, Case No. ICC-01/04-01/09, Transcript, 9 November 2006; *Prosecutor* v. *Lubanga*, Case No. ICC-01/04-01/09, Transcript, 28 November 2006.

oral and written submissions on all issues or matters not specifically prohibited by the Rome Statute or the Rules; and (7) file written motions, responses, and replies on all matters not specifically prohibited by the Rome Statute or the Rules.[102] The legal representatives of the victims participated actively in the confirmation hearing, making opening and closing statements, arguing the admissibility of evidence, and making oral and written submissions on other matters, including on a variety of subjects following the close of the hearing.[103]

The victims who participated in the confirmation hearing in the *Bemba* case did not enjoy the expansive rights accorded the non-anonymous victims in *Katanga and Ngudjolo*. Deciding that no differentiation of participatory rights based on the accused's knowledge of the victims' identities was appropriate, the *Bemba* Pre-Trial Chamber limited all participating victims to the set of rights accorded the anonymous victims in previous confirmation hearings. The Chamber reasoned that such a differentiation would work to the detriment of those victims desiring protective measures.[104] Prior to the confirmation hearing, the OPCV, as the legal representative of certain of the participating victims, requested access to certain confidential materials in the record, as well as the right to attend certain confidential proceedings. In sharply rejecting the OPCV's request, the Pre-Trial Chamber noted that the request 'seem[ed] to be characterized by a tendency to disregard the letter, spirit and guidance' provided in the Pre-Trial Chamber's decision limiting victim participation 'with a view to securing further participatory rights during the confirmation hearing'.[105] As the victims in the *Lubanga* and *Katanga and Ngudjolo* cases had done before them, the victims in *Bemba* participated in the confirmation hearing to the full extent permitted by the Chamber, including filing written submissions following the hearing.[106]

8.3.1.9 Participation in trial proceedings

The Trial Chamber in *Lubanga* had the first opportunity to establish standards for the participatory rights of victims during trial. The victims who had been granted participant status in the *Lubanga* pre-trial proceedings sought to participate in the

[102] *Katanga and Ngudjolo* Decision on Victims' Participation Pre-Trial, *supra* note 96, paras. 124–142 (noting that under the Rome Statute and the ICC Rules, certain procedural remedies that can only be exercised by the prosecution, the defence, and certain other (undefined) parties – including the right to make challenges or raise issues with respect to the admissibility of the case or the jurisdiction of the Court – would be prohibited and unavailable).

[103] See War Crimes Research Office, 'Victim Participation at the Case Stage of Proceedings', February 2009, pp. 27–28, available at www.wcl.american.edu/warcrimes/icc/documents/WCROReportonVictimParticipationattheCase StageofProceedingsFebruary2009.pdf?rd=1.

[104] *Bemba* Fourth Decision on Victims' Participation, *supra* note 12, paras. 99–110.

[105] *Prosecutor* v. *Bemba*, Doc. No. ICC-01/05-01/08-349, Sixth Decision on Victims' Participation Relating to Certain Questions Raised by the Office of Public Counsel for Victims, 8 January 2009, para. 13.

[106] See, e.g., *Prosecutor* v. *Bemba*, Doc. No. ICC-01/05-01/08-424, Decision Pursuant to Art. 61(7)(1) and (b) of the Rome Statute on the Charges of the Prosecutor Against Jean-Pierre Bemba Gombo, 15 June 2009, paras.

trial. The Trial Chamber's first decision on the issue broadened the participatory right the Pre-Trial Chamber had narrowed when the *Lubanga* case arose from the *Situation in the DRC*. The Trial Chamber construed Rule 85 as not 'restricting the participation of victims to the crimes contained in the charges confirmed by [the] Pre-Trial Chamber'.[107] Thus, a victim of any crime falling within the jurisdiction of the Court could potentially participate, regardless of the specific charges confirmed in the *Lubanga* indictment.[108]

The Trial Chamber followed this pronouncement, however, by acknowledging that the interests of many victims of the *Situation in the DRC* would be unrelated to the substance of the specific case against the accused. Accordingly, granting such victims participatory rights at trial would serve no useful purpose.[109] Thus, the Trial Chamber decided that to participate in any particular aspect of the proceedings, the victim would be required to show, 'in a discrete written application, why his or her interests are affected by the evidence or issues then arising in the case and the nature and extent of the participation they seek'.[110] The Trial Chamber said it would examine such applications on a case-by-case basis, noting that involvement in or presence at a particular incident being considered, or the suffering of identifiable harm from such an incident, were examples of the factors the Chamber would be looking for prior to granting any participatory right. As to the standard of proof, the Chamber would assess the victim's application form and any available statements for whether they demonstrated '*prima facie*, credible grounds' to suggest the victim had suffered harm, without any substantive assessment of the credibility or reliability of the application.[111]

As to the modalities of victim participation at trial, the Trial Chamber established a presumption that participating victims would be permitted to make opening and closing statements during trial, through their legal representatives.[112] Additionally,

14, 18 (noting victims' participation in the confirmation hearing, particularly two different sets of written submissions that the legal representatives of the victims were permitted to file following the close of the confirmation hearing).

107 *Lubanga* First Trial Decision on Victims' Participation, *supra* note 78, para. 93.

108 *Ibid.*, para. 95 (an applicant need only establish either (1) an evidentiary link between the victim and the evidence that would be presented in the course of the trial; or (2) that the victim was affected by an issue arising during trial because the victim's personal interests were 'in a real sense engaged by it'). Judge Blattmann dissented from this broadening of the potential participant pool, noting that not requiring a link between the victim's harm and the actual charges before the chamber would upset the balance between the interests of the victim and the rights of the accused to a fair and expeditious trial. *Prosecutor* v. *Lubanga*, Doc. No. ICC-01/04-01/06-1119, Decision on Victim's Participation, 18 January 2008, Separate and Dissenting Opinion of Judge René Blattmann.

109 *Lubanga* First Trial Decision on Victims' Participation, *supra* note 78, para. 93.

110 *Ibid.*, para. 96. Giving some further detail, the Trial Chamber noted that it would assess whether the interests of the victims related to the prosecution's 'summary of presentation of evidence', and would be aided by the report on the applications provided by the Registry's Victims Participation and Reparation Section. *Ibid.*, para. 102.

111 *Ibid.*, para. 99.

112 *Ibid.*, para. 117; *Prosecutor* v. *Lubanga*, Doc. No. ICC-01/04-01/06-1556, Decision on the Applications by Victims to Participate in the Proceedings, 15 December 2008 ('*Lubanga* Second Trial Decision on Victims' Participation'), para. 135.

where the Chamber granted a general participatory right, victims would be entitled at any stage of the trial to seek leave of the Chamber to: (1) access confidential filings in the case; (2) introduce evidence and challenge the admissibility and relevance of the parties' evidence; (3) express their views and concerns through statements, examination of witnesses, or filing written submissions; and (4) participate in hearings and status conferences.[113] None of this was to be automatic, however, because the Chamber would determine on a case-by-case basis whether the specifically requested participation was appropriate and consistent with the rights of the accused to a fair and expeditious trial.

The Trial Chamber granted both the prosecution and the accused leave to appeal its decision on victim participation. The parties challenged, among other things, the Trial Chamber's expansion of the participatory right to victims unconnected to the crimes charged; the Trial Chamber's decision permitting victims to lead evidence pertaining to the guilt or innocence of the accused at trial; and the Chamber's decision allowing victims to challenge the admissibility of evidence proffered by the parties. The Appeals Chamber reversed the Trial Chamber's holding which had decoupled the victim applicant's right to participate from the actual charges in the trial. Here, the Appeals Chamber looked at the narrow purpose of trial – the determination of guilt or innocence of the accused for the crimes charged – and reasoned that only victims of the crimes charged would be able to demonstrate that the trial, as such, affected their personal interests.[114] Thus, 'for the purposes of participation in the trial proceedings, the harm alleged by a victim and the concept of personal interests under article 68(3) of the Statute must be linked with the charges confirmed against the accused'.[115]

The Appeals Chamber also clarified the notion of 'personal' harm qualifying for victim status under Rule 85(a). It noted that material, physical, and psychological harm were all forms of harm that fell within the rule, so long as that harm was suffered personally by the victim. Rejecting what it characterised as the Trial Chamber's 'preoccupation with the interpretation of Rule 85 … in the context of "direct and indirect harm"', the Appeals Chamber clarified that the only appropriate inquiry is whether the harm is personal to the victim.[116] If the claimed harm is personal to the individual, it can attach to both 'direct and indirect victims'. This was of particular relevance to the crimes with which Lubanga was charged – the recruitment of child soldiers – as the parents of some of the child soldier victims sought to participate in their own right as victims. Following the appeal, the Trial Chamber found that some of those parent victim applicants qualified in their own

[113] See *Lubanga* First Trial Decision on Victims' Participation, *supra* note 78, paras. 105–109, 112–118.

[114] *Lubanga* Appeal Judgement on Victims' Participation, *supra* note 31, para. 62.

[115] *Ibid.*, para. 65. [116] *Ibid.*, para. 37.

right to participate, as the psychological harm they suffered was personal, albeit indirect.[117]

The Appeals Chamber upheld the Trial Chamber's decision potentially permitting victims to lead evidence at trial and challenge the admissibility of the evidence proffered by the parties. In doing so, the Appeals Chamber acknowledged that the Rome Statute and the Court's procedural framework charge the parties – that is, the prosecution and the defence – with leading evidence.[118] However, the Appeals Chamber accepted the Trial Chamber's reasoning that the Rome Statute gives a trial chamber the power to request the submission 'of all evidence that it considers necessary for the determination of the truth'.[119] Thus, this residual power of the chamber permits victims to 'request' the chamber to, in turn, request the submission of evidence from the parties.

In a strongly worded dissent, Judge Pikis parted with the Appeals Chamber's decision, noting that the admissibility of evidence at trial is not 'the victims' concern', and that it would be inappropriate for victims to be accorded the right to challenge the admissibility of the evidence proffered by the parties.[120] As to whether victims could lead their own evidence, Judge Pikis noted that it is the prosecution that bears the exclusive responsibility to investigate the case and prove the charges at trial. Moreover, he opined that the accused's right to a fair and expeditious trial could well be undermined by the victims presenting evidence which they had not been required to disclose to the defence pre-trial. Additionally, permitting victims to lead evidence puts the accused in the position of having multiple accusers.[121] The Appeals Chamber majority did not directly address Judge Pikis's concerns. Presumably, the majority is satisfied that the Trial Chamber's tight control over victim participation will suffice to ensure that the accused's rights to a fair and expeditious trial are not jeopardised.

Ultimately, over 100 victims were granted participatory rights in the *Lubanga* trial. As of 1 December 2009, the Court's second trial, *Katanga and Ngudjolo*, was in its first days. Following the lead of the *Lubanga* Trial and Appeals Chambers, the *Katanga and Ngudjolo* Trial Chamber had decided to permit 359 victims to participate in the trial proceedings.[122] Thus, a victim's right to participate in trial proceedings before the ICC remains potentially expansive, yet tightly constrained.

[117] See *Lubanga* Second Trial Decision on Victims' Participation, *supra* note 112, para. 120.

[118] *Lubanga* Appeal Judgement on Victims' Participation, *supra* note 31, para. 93.

[119] *Ibid.*, paras. 86–88.

[120] *Prosecutor* v. *Lubanga*, Doc. No. ICC-01/04-01/06-1432, Judgment on the Appeals of The Prosecutor and The Defence Against Trial Chamber I's Decision on Victims' Participation of 18 January 2008, 11 July 2008, Partly Dissenting Opinion of Judge G.M. Pikis, para. 19.

[121] See *ibid.*, paras. 6–14.

[122] See *Prosecutor* v. *Katanga and Ngudjolo*, Case No. ICC-01/04-01/07, 'Case Information Sheet No. ICC-PIDS-CIS-DRC2-03-004/09_Eng. Updated 25 November 2009', www.icc-cpi.int/NR/rdonlyres/EB9A6468-C81F-403F-86A1-BB01A002199F/281311/Katanga_Chui_ENG1.pdf.

Victims may potentially participate directly at trial in a manner as yet unknown in international criminal proceedings. Yet, in virtually every instance, that participation will have to be discretely sought, individually considered by the chamber with reaction from the parties, and, if approved, conducted within the potentially narrow limits applied by the trial chamber. The substantive extent of such participation remains largely to be seen.

8.3.1.10 Participation in interlocutory appeals

Where victims have already been granted participatory rights by the pre-trial chamber (or the trial chamber), they do not need to prove to the Appeals Chamber that they are victims within the meaning of Rule 85 in order to participate in interlocutory appeals arising from a decision of the inferior chamber.[123] Thus, the victim does not have to demonstrate again that he or she is a victim – that is, that he or she suffered harm, that the crime from which the harm ensued falls within the jurisdiction of the Court, or that there is a causal link between the crime and the harm suffered. Instead, the Appeals Chamber will proceed directly to a determination of whether the participating victim's personal interests are affected by the specific interlocutory appeal at issue.

In contrast to the expansive construction of the personal interests criterion in Article 68(3) recognised by the Pre-Trial Chambers for victim participation in the situation stage, the Appeals Chamber has substantially narrowed the pool of victims that may participate in interlocutory appeals. To participate in such an appeal, the victim must show how his or her personal interests are affected 'by the particular appeal' at issue.[124] Thus, the following four criteria must be analysed: (1) whether the individuals seeking participation are victims in the situation phase of the proceedings; (2) whether they have personal interests that are affected by the issues on appeal; (3) whether their participation is appropriate; and (4) whether the manner of participation is not prejudicial to or inconsistent with the rights of the accused and a fair and impartial trial.[125] Additionally, once a victim has met these criteria, and been granted leave to participate in the appeal, that participation will

[123] *Situation in Darfur, Sudan*, Doc. No. ICC-02/05-138, Decision on Victim Participation in the Appeal of the Office of Public Counsel for the Defence Against Pre-Trial Chamber I's Decision of 3 December 2007 and in the Appeals of the Prosecutor and the Office of Public Counsel for the Defence Against Pre-Trial Chamber I's Decision of 6 December 2007, 18 June 2008 ('*Darfur* Appeal Decision on Victims' Participation'), para. 53; *Prosecutor* v. *Lubanga*, Doc. No. ICC-01/04-01/06-824, Judgment on the Appeal of Mr. Thomas Lubanga Dyilo Against the Decision of Pre-Trial Chamber I Entitled 'Decision sur la demande de mise and liberté provisoire de Thomas Lubanga Dyilo', 13 February 2007 ('*Lubanga* Appeal Judgement on Provisional Release'), para. 45.

[124] *Lubanga* Appeal Judgement on Provisional Release, *supra* note 123, para. 38.

[125] *Darfur* Appeal Decision on Victims' Participation, *supra* note 123, para. 51. As to the last of these criteria, the Appeals Chamber is mindful that at the situation stage, suspects have yet to be identified by the Prosecutor. Accordingly, any analysis of the fourth criterion is with a view to safeguarding the rights of *future* suspects. *Ibid.*, para. 52.

also be narrowly construed. As the Appeals Chamber itself has stated, it 'will limit the victims to presenting their views and concerns respecting their personal interests solely to the issues raised on appeal. Observations to be received by the victims must be specifically relevant to the issues arising in the appeal and to the extent that their personal interests are affected by the proceedings'.[126]

8.3.1.11 Participation in appeals from a conviction or acquittal

Neither the Rome Statute nor the Rules explicitly permits victims to participate in appeals from convictions or acquittals. Although the Court has yet to deliver a judgement in any case, whether any victims are permitted to participate in the appeal would appear to be governed by the generalised participatory right secured by Article 68(3). There is little reason to suppose that the Appeals Chamber would need to revise the criteria it has developed for victim participation in interlocutory appeals. Accordingly, victims will need to demonstrate that their personal interests are affected by the issues on appeal. Where a conviction or acquittal is concerned, this should prove easier than in interlocutory appeals where the issues are separate and discrete.

8.3.2 Victim reparations

Compared to the reparations regimes of the *ad hoc* Tribunals, the Rome Statute has been hailed as a major step forward.[127] The powers of the Court to determine and award reparations are considerable.[128] Additionally, the Rome Statute established a Trust Fund 'for the benefit of victims of crimes within the jurisdiction of the Court, and of the families of such victims'.[129] Although the reparations regime lies fallow at the moment, awaiting the Court's first convictions, it should provide a robust engine of victim compensation.[130]

[126] *Prosecutor* v. *Lubanga*, Doc. No. ICC-01/04-01/06-2205, Judgment on the Appeals of Mr. Lubanga Dyilo and the Prosecutor Against the Decision of Trial Chamber I of 14 July 2009 Entitled 'Decision Giving Notice to the Parties and Participants that the Legal Characterisation of the Facts May Be Subject to Change in Accordance with Regulation 55(2) of the Regulations of the Court', 8 December 2009, para. 34; see also *ibid.*, para. 36 (finding that twenty-seven victims met the test and were permitted to participate in the appeal).

[127] See, e.g., Zappalà, *supra* note 4, p. 228 (characterising Article 75 of the Rome Statute as a 'commendable attempt to strengthen the guarantees for victims'); *ibid.*, p. 229 (noting that the Rome Statute generally offers much stronger protection to victims in this regard than the reparation regime of the *ad hoc* Tribunals); Cryer, Friman, Robinson, and Wilmshurst, *supra* note 27, p. 400 ('The ICC reparations regime is an unprecedented and often hailed restorative justice element in international criminal law'); Linda M. Keller, 'Seeking Justice at the International Criminal Court: Victim's Reparations', (2007) 29 *Thomas Jefferson Law Review* 189, 189 (characterising the ICC as a major achievement in international criminal justice for victims, with particular regard to the reparations regime).

[128] See Rome Statute, Art. 75. [129] *Ibid.*, Art. 79(1).

[130] But see Cryer, Friman, Robinson, and Wilmshurst, *supra* note 27, p. 400 (noting that the reparations regime is not yet fully developed and requires further elaboration).

The Rome Statute provides:

> The Court shall establish principles relating to reparations to, or in respect of, victims, including restitution, compensation and rehabilitation. On this basis, in its decision the Court may, either upon request or on its own motion in exceptional circumstances, determine the scope and extent of any damage, loss and injury to, or in respect of, victims and will state the principles on which it is acting.[131]

A reparations order may be entered directly by a trial chamber against a convicted person.[132] States parties are required to give effect to any such orders.[133] Where the Court finds it appropriate, the Court may order the reparations paid through the Trust Fund.[134]

Before making any reparations order, the Court may invite representations on behalf of the convicted person, victims, 'other interested persons', or interested states.[135] Additionally, the Court may seek the cooperation of states parties, if the Court determines that such cooperation is necessary to give effect to any reparation order.[136]

While the Rome Statute provides a broad outline of the reparations regime, the procedural details are found in the Rules and the Regulations. The Court may, *proprio motu*, decide to pursue a reparations order. In that instance, the Registrar is required to provide notification of the Court's intent to victims. If a victim requests the Court not to pursue such an order on the victim's behalf, the Court may not proceed to make such an order.[137] Where a reparations request initiates with a victim, the victim must apply in writing to the Registrar.[138] The Registrar is also required to provide 'adequate publicity' of reparation proceedings.[139]

In assessing the appropriate reparations, the Court is required to take into account the scope and extent of any damage, loss, or injury to the victim. Individual awards may be made to victims, but the Court may also award reparations on a collective basis where it finds that to be more appropriate. The Court may appoint experts to aid it in assessing the scope and extent of any damage, loss, or injury to victims, and to 'suggest various options concerning the appropriate types and modalities of

[131] See Rome Statute, Art. 75(1). [132] *Ibid.*, Art. 75(2).

[133] *Ibid.*, Art. 75(5). The state party is required to give effect to the reparations order just as it would to fines or forfeitures ordered by the Court pursuant to Rule 109.

[134] *Ibid.*, Art. 75(2). [135] *Ibid.*, Art. 75(3).

[136] *Ibid.*, Art. 75(4). The cooperation of states parties in this regard is governed by the Rules. See ICC Rule 93(1). On general cooperation obligations of states parties, see Chapter 3, Section 3.2.6.

[137] ICC Rule 95. Where the victim decides to make a specific reparations request in response to the Court's intention, the Court will proceed as if the victim had initiated the request under Rule 94.

[138] ICC Rule 94(1). When trial commences, the Registrar is to be directed by the Court to provide notification of the victim's request – subject to any protective measures – to the accused and, to the extent possible, to 'any interested persons or any interested States'. ICC Rule 94(2).

[139] ICC Rule 96.

reparations'.[140] Pursuant to the Regulations of the Registry, the Chamber may also request the Registrar to provide similar information or recommendations.[141]

8.4 Victims at the ECCC

With the Extraordinary Chambers in the Courts of Cambodia, the victims' rights pendulum has swung through its widest arc. Unlike victims even at the ICC, victims before the ECCC may become civil parties to the case with full participatory rights. Interestingly, this was established by the ECCC's judges in their promulgation of its Internal Rules ('ECCC Rules') as victims are absent from the ECCC Statute.[142]

8.4.1 Victim participation as a civil party

Pursuant to the ECCC Rules, the 'right to take civil action' may be exercised by victims of any crime coming within the jurisdiction of the chamber.[143] The purpose of civil party status for victims before the ECCC is to permit victims to 'participate in criminal proceedings against those responsible for crimes within the jurisdiction of the ECCC by supporting the prosecution', and to allow victims 'to seek collective and moral reparations'.[144] In order for civil party action to be 'admissible', the alleged injury to the victim must be: 'physical, material or psychological … the direct consequence of the offence, personal and have actually come into being'.[145]

Any victim participating before the ECCC as a civil party becomes a party to the criminal proceedings. Once joined as a civil party to the criminal proceedings, the victim may not be questioned as a simple witness in the case, but may only be interviewed under the same conditions applicable to the accused.[146] Civil-party victims have the right to be represented before the chamber by counsel, and a group of civil-party victims may choose to be represented by common counsel.[147] Although parties to the criminal proceedings, civil-party victims may still be granted appropriate protective measures.[148] Since beginning its operations in earnest, the ECCC's chambers have expansively defined and permitted civil-party participation.[149]

[140] ICC Rule 97(2). The Court is also required – where appropriate – to invite observations on the expert report or reports from victims, the convicted person, other interested persons and interested states.

[141] ICC Registry Regulation 110(2).

[142] See Law on the Establishment of the Extraordinary Chambers in the Courts of Cambodia for the Prosecution of Crimes Committed During the Period of Democratic Kampuchea, as amended on 27 October 2004, Doc. No. NS/RKM/1004/006, unofficial translation by the Council of Jurists and the Secretariat of the Task Force, revised on 26 August 2007 ('ECCC Statute'). See also Chapter 2, Section 2.1.4 (discussing whether this sort of expansive judicial quasi-legislation is appropriate).

[143] ECCC Rule 23. [144] ECCC Rule 23(1)(a)–(b). [145] ECCC Rule 23(2).

[146] ECCC Rule 23(6)(a). See also ECCC Rule 59 (entitled 'Interview of a Civil Party', establishing a formal regime for the questioning of civil party victims by the Co-Investigating Judges).

[147] ECCC Rule 23(7)–(8). [148] ECCC Rules 23(6)(c), 29.

[149] See, e.g., *Co-Prosecutors* v. *Nuon*, Case No. 002/19-09-2007-ECCC/OCIJ (PTC01), Decision on Civil Party Participation in Provisional Detention Appeals, 20 March 2008 (holding that victims who had been

8.4.2 Victims and reparations

The ECCC Statute does not mention victims, nor does it seem to envisage reparations. The Statute provides that in addition to imprisonment, the chamber 'may order the confiscation of personal property, money, and real property acquired unlawfully or by criminal conduct'.[150] The Statute further provides that the confiscated property 'shall be returned to the State'.[151]

The ECCC's judges, however, substantially modified the Statute by adopting a rule which provides that '[s]ubject to [the ECCC Statute], the Chamber may award only collective and moral reparations to Civil Parties'.[152] Such reparations are to be awarded against convicted persons, and may take the following forms: (1) an order to publish the judgement in any appropriate news or other media at the convicted person's expense; (2) an order to fund a non-profit activity or service that is intended for the benefit of victims; or (3) other appropriate and comparable forms of reparation.[153]

Like the ICC, the ECCC's reparations regime awaits the Extraordinary Chambers' first conviction. Given the expansive reparation rights provided in the Rules, however, and the judges' liberal construction of the participation regime, the potential reparations to victims may be considerable.

8.5 Conclusion

The ICTY, ICTR, and SCSL will all soon be at an end, and their approach to the role and status of victims in their proceedings has provided little substance to the core concerns which animate the ICC on this issue. On the other end of the spectrum, the ECCC, while proving to be even more expansive in its approach to victim participation than the ICC, is an outlier in the world of international criminal trials, owing its approach to the issue more to Cambodian law and history than to the progressive development of international criminal procedure. The real measure of the role and status of victims in international criminal procedure must be taken at the ICC.

Whether the ICC's grand experiment in victim participation will ultimately prove workable remains to be seen. The ICC's reparations regime – while promising much – lies dormant; its victim participation regime has developed sporadically and seemingly without a coherent theme. Some of its early decisions have also

admitted as civil parties in the case against Nuon Chea were entitled to participate in appeals of provisional detention orders); see also Jenia Iontcheva Turner, 'International Decision', (2009) 103 *American Journal of International Law* 116, 116 (characterising this decision as providing 'the most expansive interpretation to date by an international criminal court of victim participation at the pretrial stage').

150 ECCC Statute, *supra* note 142, Art. 39.

151 *Ibid.* 152 ECCC Rule 23(12). 153 *Ibid.*

raised serious practical concerns. Merely managing the paper flow is an enormous task, and the Court has been heavily criticised for its seeming inability to govern that flow in a timely manner. Litigating the issues surrounding victim participation has consumed thousands of hours of the Court's time and the parties' resources. Ultimately, the victim participation rights gained in that struggle have been largely potential rights, in some cases wholly illusory.

Perhaps in no instance is victim participation more fraught with practical and theoretical difficulty than with direct intervention at trial. Even with trial participation limited to a small number of common legal representatives, one cannot help but wonder, for example, how 359 victims will meaningfully participate in the *Katanga and Ngudjolo* trial. Moreover, meaningful participation at trial is itself problematic, as Judge Pikis pointed out in his dissent to the Appeals Chamber's decision permitting such participation.[154] Although the accused will face only a limited number of counsel in court, those few counsel represent hundreds of voices, something that is not lost on the accused or on any other participant in the trial, including the judges.[155]

Finally, Article 68(3)'s prohibition on victim participation that infringes on the accused's right to a fair and impartial trial has undergone little meaningful analysis by the Court. But this balance is probably the most important one found in Article 68(3). So long as the victim's right to participate remains largely marginal, there seems little difficulty balancing that participation fairly against the rights of the accused. As the victim's participatory right becomes more meaningful, however, something understandably coveted and fought for by the victims and their constituencies, that participation implicates the accused's rights more directly. This is the Court's great challenge, one it has so far avoided. It cannot do so forever.

[154] See *supra* text accompanying notes 120–121.

[155] See, e.g., Schabas, *supra* note 3, p. 324 (noting that those on the 'defence side', in particular, are suspicious of efforts to promote victim participation, seeing it as a threat which further distorts the equality of arms balance between the prosecution and the accused).

9

Evidence

CONTENTS

From the very first version issued at the ICTY in 1994, proceedings at each of the major international criminal tribunals have been governed in part by a body of rules termed the 'Rules of Procedure and Evidence'. Although this title may suggest that evidentiary law is given roughly equal treatment in these provisions as other areas of procedure, this is far from the case. The ICTY Rules contain 164 rules with multiple paragraphs and subparagraphs, but only seventeen pertain to the manner in which proposed evidence becomes part of the trial record and the factual basis on which the final judgement rests. The 157 provisions in the ICTR Rules include only fourteen such provisions; the 225 provisions in the ICC Rules list only thirteen, with fewer than a handful of additional relevant provisions in the Rome Statute and Court Regulations; and of the SCSL Rules' 141 provisions, a mere fourteen relate to the law of evidence. As the jurisprudence interpreting these provisions amply demonstrates, their sparseness is no accident. To the contrary, the rules are drafted and applied to ensure maximum flexibility for chambers in their efforts to run fair and expeditious trials.

This chapter examines the law governing the presentation, admission, and evaluation of evidence in trials at the ICC, ICTY, ICTR, and SCSL.[1] Section 9.1 reviews the guidelines established by the governing instruments and case law of these tribunals to cabin the broad discretion granted to chambers to admit evidence and weigh that evidence in the course of deliberations.[2] Section 9.2 examines the various ways in which evidence is presented, and compares the different approaches in the tribunals to the use of witnesses, documents,[3] and other methods of proving facts. Finally, Section 9.3 discusses the privileges that have been recognised at the tribunals, which exempt limited categories of potential evidence from compelled production or presentation at trial.

9.1 Admission and assessment of evidence

The governing instruments of the international criminal tribunals 'establish a regime for the admission of evidence which is wide and liberal'.[4] Unlike criminal trials in common law jurisdictions – where, in an effort to ensure the integrity and reliability of verdicts, the rules of evidence employ a host of prophylactic measures to restrict the proof on which lay juries may rely – evidentiary law in international criminal trials relies heavily on the presumption that the finders of fact are

[1] Other aspects of trial procedure that relate to evidence are discussed in Chapter 7, including questioning of witnesses; the solemn undertaking that precedes testimony; the power of the trial chamber to order additional evidence; and judicial orders to the parties on the manner and scope of evidence presentation.

[2] ICC pre-trial chambers also admit and consider evidence for purposes of the confirmation of charges hearing. See Chapter 6, Section 6.1.1.1.2. The rules and standards discussed in this chapter apply equally to this stage of the proceedings.

[3] For purposes of this chapter, the terms 'documents' and 'documentary evidence' are defined broadly to include not just writings, but demonstrative exhibits such as maps, charts, and photographs, as well as other forms of visual and auditory materials, such as video recordings and recorded communications.

[4] *Prosecutor* v. *Simić*, Case No. IT-95-9-PT, Decision on the Prosecution Motion Under Rule 73 for a Ruling Concerning the Testimony of a Witness, 27 July 1999 ('*Simić* Pre-Trial Privilege Decision'), para. 40 (referring to the ICTY Rules). See also Gideon Boas, 'Admissibility of Evidence Under the Rules of Procedure and Evidence of the ICTY: Development of the "Flexibility Principle"', *in* Richard May *et al.* (eds.), *Essays on ICTY Procedure and Evidence in Honour of Gabrielle Kirk McDonald* (2001), p. 263; Richard May and Marieke Wierda, 'Trends in International Criminal Evidence: Nuremberg, Tokyo, The Hague, and Arusha', (1999) 37 *Columbia Journal of Transnational Law* 725, 727 (explaining that '[t]he approach to evidence' in past and present tribunals 'has been to use elements from both the common law and civil law systems', in which 'the rules governing the admissibility of evidence may be seen as more akin to the "inquisitorial" model and leave wide discretion to the judges').

professional judges, who are expected 'by virtue of their training and experience, to hear the evidence in the context in which it was obtained and accord it appropriate weight'.[5] It is not at all clear, however, that this presumption of the professional expertise of the international criminal judiciary is well founded, as a significant proportion of the judges that have served at these tribunals have had limited or no prior experience as judges or practising criminal attorneys in their home jurisdictions. One former ICTY appellate judge has spoken publicly of these concerns, noting that '[t]oo many of the judges elected by the UN General Assembly reflect the non-legal culture of those who elect them', and 'have no more than the basic legal qualification required', and concluding that '[m]any have absolutely no idea of judicial independence, and some – mainly judges who had had no experience of courts prior to their election – have no idea of the need for a judge to approach the task of determining guilt impartially and without pre-existing conclusions in relation to that guilt'.[6]

Be that as it may, trial judges enjoy significant discretion under the respective statutes, rules, and regulations of each tribunal in determining what evidence may be admitted, what should be excluded, and how much weight should be given to the evidence in the course of their deliberations on the merits,[7] and they are not bound

[5] *Prosecutor* v. *Tadić*, Case No. IT-94-1-T, Decision on Defence Motion on Hearsay, 5 August 1996, para. 17. See also O-Gon Kwon, 'The Challenge of An International Criminal Trial as Seen from the Bench', (2007) 5 *Journal of International Criminal Justice* 360, 363–364 (noting that while 'in practice, the common-law adversarial model has predominated most aspects of the [ICTY]'s procedure … as time has progressed the Tribunal has also adopted a number of essentially civil-law mechanisms for tendering and admitting evidence'); Antonio Cassese, 'Statement by the President at a Briefing to Members of Diplomatic Missions Concerning the Adoption of the Rules of Procedure and Evidence of the ICTY', UN Doc. IT/29, 11 February 1994 ('There will be no jury sitting at the Tribunal, needing to be shielded from irrelevancies or given guidance as to the weight of the evidence they have heard.'); *Prosecutor* v. *Norman, Fofana, and Kondewa* ('*CDF* Case'), Case No. SCSL-04-14-AR65, Fofana – Appeal Against Decision Refusing Bail, 11 March 2005 ('*CDF* Bail Interlocutory Appeal'), para. 26 (referring to one of the key evidentiary provisions in the SCSL Rules, and explaining that this less restrictive approach 'ensures that the administration of justice will not be brought into disrepute by artificial or technical rules, often devised for jury trial, which prevent judges from having access to information which is relevant' and 'is designed to avoid sterile legal debate over admissibility so the court can concentrate on the pragmatic issue').

[6] David Hunt, Address at the Conference of the Australian and New Zealand Society International Law, Canberra, 19 June 2004 (on file with authors).

[7] See, e.g., *Prosecutor* v. *Gatete*, Case No. ICTR-2000-61-T, Decision on Defence Motion on Admissibility of Allegations Outside the Temporal Jurisdiction of the Tribunal, 3 November 2009 ('*Gatete* Admissibility Decision'), para. 3; *Prosecutor* v. *Lubanga*, Doc. No. ICC-01/04-01/06-1084, Decision on the Status Before the Trial Chamber of the Evidence Heard by the Pre-Trial Chamber and the Decisions of the Pre-Trial Chamber in Trial Proceedings, and the Manner in Which Evidence Shall Be Submitted, 13 December 2007, para. 5 (the ICC's 'statutory and regulatory framework undoubtedly establishes the unfettered authority of the Trial Chamber to rule on procedural matters and the admissibility and relevance of evidence, subject always to any contrary decision of the Appeals Chamber'); *Simba* v. *Prosecutor*, Case No. ICTR-01-76-A, Judgement, 27 November 2007, para. 19 (decision to admit or exclude evidence is within the discretion of the trial chamber and warrants appellate intervention only in limited circumstances); accord *Prosecutor* v. *Naletilić and Martinović*, Case No. IT-98-34-A, Judgement, 3 May 2006, para. 257 (appellate intervention to exclude evidence appropriate only if trial chamber 'committed a discernible error in the exercise of its discretion [which] resulted in unfair prejudice to the appellant'); *Prosecutor* v. *Brima, Kamara, and Kanu*

by domestic evidentiary rules.[8] At the *ad hoc* Tribunals and the SCSL in particular, chambers are expressly authorised to fill lacunae in the Rules and 'apply rules of evidence which will best favour a fair determination of the matter before [them] and are consonant with the spirit of the Statute and the general principles of law'.[9] This section of the chapter reviews the basic principles that have been set forth in the governing instruments or developed in the case law to guide the exercise of this judicial discretion.

9.1.1 Admissibility of evidence

While the tribunals' governing instruments contain several provisions regulating how evidence is presented, admitted, and assessed, each institution's Rules contain a key provision – frequently referred to as the 'general rule' – that forms the core of its evidence law. At the *ad hoc* Tribunals, this provision states simply that '[a] Chamber may admit any relevant evidence which it deems to have probative value'.[10] The corresponding provision in the SCSL Rules is even briefer and to the point: 'A Chamber may admit any relevant evidence.'[11] As with much else in the ICC's instruments, the general rule regarding the admission of evidence is wordier and peppered with cross-references, but is equally liberal, and provides in relevant part that '[a] Chamber shall have the authority … to assess freely all evidence submitted in order to determine its relevance or admissibility' in accordance with principles outlined in the Rome Statute, including consideration of the probative value of the proffered evidence.[12]

('*AFRC* Case'), Case No. SCSL-04-16-T, Judgement, 20 June 2007, para. 100. Despite this and several such acknowledgements by the *ad hoc* Tribunals' Appeals Chambers of the trial chambers' need for broad discretion, the Appeals Chambers have frequently dispensed with the principle. See Chapter 11, Sections 11.4.3, 11.5.2; see also, e.g., Chapter 10, note 248 and accompanying text (discussing Appeals Chamber interference in sentencing determinations).

8 ICC Rule 63(5) (except to the extent that resort to general principles of law reflected in national approaches is necessary); ICTY Rule 89(A); ICTR Rule 89(A); SCSL Rule 89(A). See also *Prosecutor* v. *Brđanin*, Case No. IT-99-36-T, Decision on the Defence Objection to Intercept Evidence, 3 October 2003 ('*Brđanin* Intercept Decision'), para. 63(7) (adopting the earlier holding of the *Čelebići* Trial Chamber that '[i]t would constitute a dangerous obstacle to the administration of justice if evidence which is relevant and of probative value could not be admitted merely because of a minor breach of procedural rules which the Trial Chamber is not bound to apply'); accord *Prosecutor* v. *Lubanga*, Doc. No. ICC-01/04-01/06-1981, Decision on the Admission of Material from the 'Bar Table', 24 June 2009 ('*Lubanga* Bar Table Decision'), para. 36 ('[E]vidence obtained in breach of national procedural laws, even though those rules may implement national standards protecting human rights, does not automatically trigger the application of Article 69(7) of the Statute', which mandates exclusion in certain limited circumstances).

9 ICTY Rule 89(B); ICTR Rule 89(B); SCSL Rule 89(B).

10 ICTY Rule 89(C); ICTR Rule 89(C).

11 SCSL Rule 89(C).

12 ICC Rule 63(2); see also Rome Statute, Art. 69(4).

9.1.1.1 A low threshold

The burden of establishing admissibility is on the tendering party,[13] but the standards applied are concededly permissive.[14] At the ICTY, ICTR, and ICC, chambers apply a nominally two-pronged test of admissibility to determine whether proposed proof offered by a party may become part of the record in the case. First, any testimony, document, or other potential evidence must be relevant, in that there must be a connection between the proposed evidence and one or more allegations against the accused.[15] Second, the proposed evidence cannot be devoid of probative value; that is, if credited, the evidence must be capable of tending to prove or disprove one or more allegations against the accused.[16] In practice, judges effectively collapse the two steps, so the determination by a chamber at these tribunals that a proposed item of evidence is relevant generally reflects a conclusion that, as tendered, it has

[13] See, e.g., *Prosecutor* v. *Stanišić and Župljanin*, Case No. IT-08-91-T, Decision Denying the Stanišić Motion for Exclusion of Recorded Intercepts, 16 December 2009 ('*Stanišić and Župljanin* Admissibility Decision'), para. 18; *Prosecutor* v. *Lubanga*, Doc. No. ICC-01/04-01/06-1399, Decision on the Admissibility of Four Documents, 13 June 2008 ('*Lubanga* Pre-Trial Admissibility Decision'), para. 25 ('If a challenge is made to the admissibility of evidence, it appears logical that the burden rests with the party seeking to introduce the evidence – in this case the prosecution. This has been the practice of the ICTY and there seems no reason to disturb this self-evidently sensible requirement.'); *Prosecutor* v. *Nyiramasuhuko*, Case No. ICTR-98-42-AR73.2, Decision on Pauline Nyiramasuhuko's Appeal on the Admissibility of Evidence, 4 October 2004, para. 7; *Prosecutor* v. *Taylor*, Case No. SCSL-03-01-AR73, Decision on Prosecution Notice of Appeal and Submissions Concerning the Decision Regarding the Tender of Documents, 6 February 2009 ('*Taylor* Admissibility Interlocutory Appeal'), paras. 38–42.

[14] See, e.g., *Prosecutor* v. *Perišić*, Case No. IT-04-81-T, Order for Guidelines on the Admission and Presentation of Evidence and Conduct of Counsel in Court, 29 October 2008, para. 32 ('[T]he threshold standard for the admission of evidence ... should not be set excessively high, as often documents are sought to be admitted into evidence, not as ultimate proof of guilt or innocence, but to provide a context and complete the picture presented by the evidence in general') (quoting *Prosecutor* v. *Delalić, Mucić, Delić, and Landžo*, Case No. IT-96-21-T, Decision on the Motion of Prosecution for the Admissibility of Evidence, 19 January 1998, para. 20).

[15] *Gatete* Admissibility Decision, *supra* note 7, para. 3; *Lubanga* Pre-Trial Admissibility Decision, *supra* note 13, para. 27 (proposed evidence is relevant if it 'relates to the matters that are properly to be considered by the Chamber in its investigation of the charges against the accused and its consideration of the views and concerns of participating victims'); *Prosecutor* v. *Hadžihasanović and Kubura*, Case No. IT-01-47-T, Decision on the Admissibility of Documents of the Defence of Enver Hadžihasanović, 22 June 2005, para. 17 ('[F]or one fact to be relevant to another there must be a connection or nexus between the two which makes it possible to infer the existence of one from the existence of the other') (internal citation omitted); *Prosecutor* v. *Milutinović, Šainović, Ojdanić, Pavković, Lazarević, and Lukić*, Case No. IT-05-87-T, Decision on Prosecution Motion to Admit Documentary Evidence, 10 October 2006, para. 32 (defining relevance simply as 'how the evidence relates to the indictment').

[16] *Prosecutor* v. *Katanga and Ngudjolo*, Doc. No. ICC-01/04-01/07-717, Decision on the Confirmation of Charges, 30 September 2008 ('*Katanga and Ngudjolo* Confirmation Decision'), para. 77 ('[P]robative value is one of the factors to be taken into consideration when assessing the admissibility of a piece of evidence' and a chamber 'must look at the intrinsic coherence of any item of evidence, and ... declare inadmissible those items of evidence of which probative value is deemed *prima facie* absent after such an analysis'); *Lubanga* Pre-Trial Admissibility Decision, *supra* note 13, paras. 28, 32 (noting that 'this will always be a fact-sensitive decision, and the court is free to assess any evidence that is relevant to, and probative of, the issues in the case, so long as it is fair for the evidence to be introduced'); *Prosecutor* v. *Karemera, Ngirumpatse, and Nzirorera*, Case No. ICTR-98-44-T, Decision on Joseph Nzirorera's Motion to Admit Documents Authored by Enoch Ruhigira, 26 March 2008 ('*Karemera et al.* Admissibility Decision'), para. 3 ('It is sufficient for the

at least some probative value.[17] At the SCSL, however, chambers have been adamant that the general rule prescribes a single criterion for admissibility, and that the party advocating admission need only establish that the proposed evidence is relevant.[18] In any event, at all of these tribunals, the conclusion as to how much probative value should be ascribed is a matter for determination at the end of the trial.[19] In certain circumstances, and particularly where necessary to resolve a dispute regarding admissibility of a proposed item of evidence, trial chambers will admit evidence – and consider it at the end of trial – for a limited purpose.[20]

Another distinction between the evidentiary regimes applied at the tribunals is the manner in which each evaluates the reliability of proposed evidence. At the

moving party to establish the *prima facie* relevance and probative value of the evidence for admission under Rule 89(C)'); accord *Prosecutor* v. *Milutinović, Šainović, Ojdanić, Pavković, Lazarević, and Lukić*, Case No. IT-05-87-T, Judgement, 26 February 2009 ('*Milutinović et al.* Trial Judgement'), Vol. I, para. 36.

[17] See, e.g., *Milutinović et al.* Trial Judgement, *supra* note 16, Vol. I, para. 36 (defining relevance as the tendency 'to make the existence of any fact that is of consequence to the determination of an issue in a case more or less probable than it would be without the evidence'); *Prosecutor* v. *Galić*, Case No. IT-98-29-AR73.2, Decision on Interlocutory Appeal Concerning Rule 92 *bis*(C), 7 June 2002, para. 35 (holding that 'evidence is admissible only if it is relevant and it is relevant only if it has probative value'); *Prosecutor* v. *Delalić, Mucić, Delić, and Landžo*, Case No. IT-96-21-T, Decision on Prosecutor's Oral Requests for the Admission of Exhibit 155 into Evidence and for an Order to Compel the Accused, Zdravko Mucić, to Provide a Handwriting Sample, 19 January 1998 ('*Čelebići* Admissibility Decision'), para. 32 (noting that 'it seems that there is implicit in "relevancy" an element of "probative value"'); *Karemera et al.* Admissibility Decision, *supra* note 16, paras. 4–10 (nominally applying the two-pronged test, but reviewing aspects of the proposed item that relate to probative value in order to determine relevance).

[18] See, e.g., *Taylor* Admissibility Interlocutory Appeal, *supra* note 13, para. 37 ('At the admissibility stage, the only test is that of relevance.'); *AFRC* Case, Case No. SCSL-04-16-PT, Decision on Joint Defence Motion to Exclude All Evidence from Witness TF1–277 Pursuant to Rule 89(C) and/or Rule 95, 24 May 2005, para. 13 ('[SCSL] Rule 89(C), under which evidence need only be relevant to be admissible, is in broader terms than the equivalent provisions of the ICTY and ICTR Rules, which require that evidence be both relevant and probative'). But see *Taylor* Admissibility Interlocutory Appeal, *supra* note 13, para. 40 (upholding Trial Chamber's determination that a document could not be adduced through a witness who had no personal knowledge of it, and holding that '[w]hen determining the relevance of a document, the Trial Chamber must require the tendering party to lay a foundation of the witness's competence to give evidence in relation to that document').

[19] See *infra* Section 9.1.2. The breadth of evidence that is deemed admissible under the relevance-probative value inquiry is complemented by other notable features of, or omissions from, the Rules. For example, at the *ad hoc* Tribunals and the SCSL, '[e]vidence of a consistent pattern of conduct' that is 'relevant to' crimes within the jurisdiction of each tribunal 'may be admissible in the interests of justice'. ICTY Rule 93; ICTR Rule 93; SCSL Rule 93. Although each rule refers to 'serious violations of international humanitarian law under the Statute', this phrase should be read as referring to the full extent of crimes punishable by these tribunals. See, e.g., Gideon Boas, James L. Bischoff, and Natalie L. Reid, *Elements of Crimes in International Criminal Law* (2008) ('Boas, Bischoff, and Reid, *Elements of Crimes*'), p. 4 (explaining that this phrase is 'understood in those instruments to cover not only war crimes, but also crimes against humanity and genocide'). In addition, unlike most common law jurisdictions, there is no 'best evidence' rule requiring that originals of documents be submitted whenever possible. See, e.g., *CDF* Bail Interlocutory Appeal, *supra* note 5, paras. 24–25 (overturning a trial judge's decision to deny admission to unsigned documents on the basis that they were not the 'best evidence' and were thus unreliable, and holding instead that the 'best evidence' rule is 'an anachronism … developed in a pre-industrial age').

[20] See, e.g., *Prosecutor* v. *Popović, Beara, Nikolić, Borovčanin, Miletić, Gvero, and Pandurević*, Case No. IT-05-88-T, Decision on Exhibits Tendered by the Prosecution in the Cross-Examination of Witnesses Called by Gvero, 30 July 2009, p. 4 (holding that document put to witness 'in connection with an earlier response that he had made' was 'used for a very limited purpose and as such causes no prejudice to the Defence'); *Prosecutor* v. *Boškoski and Tarčulovski*, Case No. IT-04-82-T, Decision on Prosecution's Motion for Admission of Exhibits from the Bar Table with Confidential Annexes A to E, 14 May 2007, para. 28

ad hoc Tribunals, trial chambers have treated reliability as inherent in the admissibility inquiry; that is, the assessment of whether the evidence can appropriately be taken as proof of the matter asserted is the 'invisible golden thread' running through the factors of relevance and probative value.[21] At the ICC and the SCSL, however, evaluation of the reliability of evidence is not a factor in determining whether it should be admitted, but rather goes to the weight given to the evidence by the trial chamber in its deliberations on the merits.[22]

Nevertheless, even where reliability is considered at the admissibility stage, the burden placed on the party seeking admission is far from onerous. As one trial chamber explained when setting forth its evidentiary guidelines, '[t]he implicit requirement of reliability means no more than that there must be sufficient indicia of reliability to make out a *prima facie* case for the admission' of the item of evidence.[23] For documentary evidence, this assessment of *prima facie* reliability frequently includes an evaluation of its apparent authenticity;[24] the credibility of witness testimony, by contrast, is generally not assessed until the end of the trial,

(admitting documents for the 'limited and specific purpose' of establishing 'the nature and functioning of a reporting system', and rejecting defence arguments that they were inadmissible because referenced attachments were missing).

[21] *Čelebići* Admissibility Decision, *supra* note 17, para. 32; accord, e.g., *Prosecutor* v. *Popović, Beara, Nikolić, Borovčanin, Miletić, Gvero, and Pandurević*, Case No. IT-05-88-AR73.2, Decision on Joint Defence Interlocutory Appeal Concerning the Status of Richard Butler as an Expert Witness, 30 January 2008, para. 22 (consideration given to reliability of proposed evidence in order to determine relevance and probative value); *Stanišić and Župljanin* Admissibility Decision, *supra* note 13, para. 14 ('The intercepts' tendered as evidence 'will be found to have probative value if the Trial Chamber finds they are sufficiently reliable, authentic and relevant to the issues in this case'); *Rutaganda* v. *Prosecutor*, Case No. ICTR-96-3-A, Judgement, 26 May 2003, paras. 33, 266.

[22] See *Katanga and Ngudjolo* Confirmation Decision, *supra* note 16, para. 78 ('Despite the controversies which have arisen at the international tribunals … as to whether reliability is a separate or inherent component of the admissibility of a particular item of evidence, the Chamber prefers … to consider reliability as a component of the evidence when determining its weight') (internal quotation marks and footnote omitted); *CDF* Bail Interlocutory Appeal, *supra* note 5, para. 8 ('Evidence is admissible once it is shown to be relevant: the question of its reliability is determined thereafter, and is not a condition for its admission').

[23] *Prosecutor* v. *Brđanin*, Case No. IT-99-36-T, Order on the Standards Governing the Admission of Evidence, 15 February 2002 ('*Brđanin* Evidence Order'), para. 18. See also *Prosecutor* v. *Prlić, Stojić, Praljak, Petković, Ćorić, and Pušić*, Case No. IT-04-74-AR73.16, Decision on Jadranko Prlić's Interlocutory Appeal Against the Decision on Prlić Defence Motion for Reconsideration of the Decision on Admission of Documentary Evidence, 3 November 2009 ('*Prlić et al.* Interlocutory Appeal on Document Admission'), para. 27 (rejecting accused's appeal of decision denying admission to tendered newspaper articles for failure to establish *prima facie* relevance, and holding that trial chamber did not abuse discretion by requiring 'such basic information as the sources and dates of the documents in question').

[24] See *Prlić et al.* Interlocutory Appeal on Document Admission, *supra* note 23, para. 34 (distinguishing between 'prima facie proof' and 'definite proof' of authenticity, and holding that the former 'is appropriate at the admissibility stage'); *Prosecutor* v. *Muvunyi*, Case No. ICTR-2000-55A-T, Decision on Motion to Strike or Exclude Portion of Prosecutor's Exhibit No. 34, Alternatively Defense Objections to Prosecutor's Exhibit N[o]. 34, 30 May 2006, para. 15 (ordering previously admitted exhibits, and all evidence associated with those exhibits, to be excluded on grounds of lack of reliability or authenticity, where the original Kinyarwanda document and its purported English translation did not match). See also ICTY Rule 89(E) ('A Chamber may request verification of the authenticity of evidence obtained out of court'); ICTR Rule 89(D) (same). There is no corresponding rule at the SCSL – a purposeful omission, given how closely the SCSL Rules follow the ICTR Rules, which in turn largely reflect the ICTY Rules.

though warnings for perjury may be given during testimony if warranted.[25] As with probative value, a definitive assessment of the reliability of admitted evidence in the *ad hoc* Tribunals is made at a later stage in the proceedings.[26]

9.1.1.2 Few exclusions

Notwithstanding the generally permissive approach to the admission of evidence, all the tribunals are required to exclude evidence obtained through means or methods that raise significant questions as to its reliability, or when the admission of the evidence would undermine the integrity of the proceedings.[27] At the *ad hoc* Tribunals, this exclusionary provision is supplemented by a rule – in writing at the ICTY, as a matter of case law at the ICTR – permitting judges to exclude evidence 'if its probative value is substantially outweighed by the need to ensure a fair trial'.[28] The Rome Statute also permits ICC judges to consider potential prejudice when assessing admissibility.[29] The purpose of these rules, in particular the *ad hoc* Tribunals' discretionary provision, is to ensure that 'the correct balance [is] maintained between the fundamental rights of the accused and the essential interests of the international community in the prosecution of persons charged with serious violations of international humanitarian law'.[30]

In practice, however, these rules are not applied strictly. For example, the fact that evidence was obtained in violation of domestic laws does not necessarily mean that it must be excluded. Trial chambers have thus admitted intercepted communications, regardless of whether prior legal authorisation was obtained,[31] and

[25] See *infra* Section 9.1.2 (discussing credibility determinations); ICTY Rule 91(A) (authorising chambers to 'warn a witness of the duty to tell the truth and the consequences that may result from a failure to do so', namely prosecution for false testimony); ICTR Rule 91(A) (same); SCSL Rule 91(A) (same).

[26] See *Prlić et al.* Interlocutory Appeal on Document Admission, *supra* note 23, paras. 33, 34; see also *infra* Section 9.1.2.

[27] Rome Statute, Art. 69(7) (specifying that exclusionary rule applies to evidence obtained in violation of the Statute or international human rights law, if (1) it 'casts substantial doubt' on its reliability, or (2) 'admission would be antithetical to and would seriously damage the integrity of the proceedings'); ICTY Rule 95 (requiring exclusion if evidence 'obtained by methods which cast substantial doubt on its reliability or if its admission is antithetical to, and would seriously damage, the integrity of the proceedings'); ICTR Rule 95 (same); SCSL Rule 95 (requiring exclusion if admission 'would bring the administration of justice into serious disrepute').

[28] ICTY Rule 89(D). At the ICTR, see, e.g., *Nahimana, Barayagwiza, and Ngeze* v. *Prosecutor*, Case No. ICTR-99-52-A, Judgement, 28 November 2007 ('*Media* Appeal Judgement'), para. 319 & n. 764 (holding that '[a] Trial Chamber can also exclude evidence whose admission could affect the fairness of the proceedings' and so it may 'refuse to admit evidence whose probative value is significantly inferior to its prejudicial effect for the Defence').

[29] Rome Statute. Art. 69(4) ('The Court may rule on the relevance or admissibility of any evidence, taking into account, *inter alia*, the probative value of the evidence and any prejudice that such evidence may cause to a fair trial or to a fair evaluation of the testimony of a witness'); *Lubanga* Bar Table Decision, *supra* note 8, para. 33 (apparently paraphrasing this provision as requiring consideration of 'the probative value of the evidence as against its prejudicial effect').

[30] *Prosecutor* v. *Nikolić*, Case No. IT-94-2-AR73, Decision on Interlocutory Appeal Concerning Legality of Arrest, 5 June 2003, para. 30 (cited in *Brđanin* Intercept Decision, *supra* note 8, para. 61).

[31] See, e.g., *Brđanin* Intercept Decision, *supra* note 8, para. 53 (holding that 'evidence obtained by eavesdropping on an enemy's telephone calls during the course of a war is certainly not … antithetical to and certainly would not seriously damage the integrity of the proceedings' so such intercepts 'are not as such subject to

documentary evidence obtained in a search of the accused's residence, regardless of whether local procedural requirements were satisfied.[32] While relatively rare, chambers have occasionally excluded evidence pursuant to these rules, including statements of an accused obtained in violation of the right to counsel,[33] or in circumstances where it was not clear that the statements were given voluntarily.[34]

9.1.2 Evaluation of evidence

Although trial chambers confer and rule on a host of oral and written motions in the course of the trial, including evidentiary matters, the tribunals' governing instruments specify that final deliberations shall take place after all the evidence has been submitted.[35] For each charge in the indictment, the chamber must review the entire body of evidence adduced at trial to determine whether the prosecution has met its burden of proof beyond a reasonable doubt.[36] Inherent in those

exclusion under Rule 95 and should therefore be admitted'); accord *Stanišić and Župljanin* Admissibility Decision, *supra* note 13, paras. 14, 21 (collecting decisions and concluding that 'even if the intercepts were obtained illegally, the illegality would not rise to the level that it would seriously damage the integrity of the proceedings such that they must be excluded').

32 See, e.g., *Lubanga* Bar Table Decision, *supra* note 8, paras. 38–41, 48 (concluding, as did the Pre-Trial Chamber in the same case, that even a clear violation of the right to privacy does not require exclusion of the documents seized); *Prosecutor* v. *Delalić, Mucić, Delić, and Landžo*, Case No. IT-96-21-T, Decision on the Tendering of Prosecution Exhibits 104–108, 9 February 1998, paras. 18–20 (rejecting argument that alleged procedural irregularities in a search of the accused Mucić's residence warranted exclusion).

33 See *Prosecutor* v. *Karemera, Ngirumpatse, and Nzirorera*, Case No. ICTR-98-44-T, Decision on the Prosecution Motion for Admission into Evidence of Post-Arrest Interviews with Joseph Nzirorera and Mathieu Ngirumpatse, 2 November 2007, paras. 23–32; see also *Prosecutor* v. *Delalić, Mucić, Delić, and Landžo*, Case No. IT-96-21-T, Decision on Zdravko Mucić's Motion for the Exclusion of Evidence, 2 September 1997 ('*Čelebići* Trial Decision on Evidence Exclusion'), para. 43 (concluding that statements taken in violation of this right would likely trigger mandatory exclusion under ICTY Rule 95).

34 See *Prosecutor* v. *Delalić, Mucić, Delić, and Landžo*, Case No. IT-96-21-A, Judgement, 20 February 2001, para. 555 ('There is no doubt that statements obtained from suspects which are not voluntary, or which seem to be voluntary but are obtained by oppressive conduct, cannot pass the test under [ICTY] Rule 95.'); *Prosecutor* v. *Halilović*, Case No. IT-01-48-AR73.2, Decision on Interlocutory Appeal Concerning Admission of Record of Interview of the Accused from the Bar Table, 19 August 2005, p. 23 (excluding the record of accused's interview under ICTY Rule 89(D) where the Trial Chamber ignored (1) the effect that the prosecution's inducement of provisional release may have had on the accused's interview; (2) the reasonable possibility that the accused wrongly believed the indictment could have been withdrawn if he cooperated; and (3) inadequate representation by counsel); *Prosecutor* v. *Sesay, Kallon and Gbao* ('*RUF* Case'), Case No. SCSL-04-15-T, Oral Ruling on the Admissibility of Alleged Confessional Statements Obtained by Investigators of the Office of the Prosecutor from the First Accused, Issa Hassan Sesay, 5 July 2007, para. 4 (excluding certain statements made by the accused during interviews by the Prosecution, under SCSL Rule 95, as they 'were not voluntary in that they were obtained by fear of prejudice and hope of advantage held out by persons in authority'). See also *Čelebići* Trial Decision on Evidence Exclusion, *supra* note 33, paras. 63–70 (considering whether statements obtained from a suspect by allegedly oppressive conduct are inadmissible under ICTY Rule 95, and concluding that there was no evidence that the interview was oppressive).

35 See ICC Rules 141, 142; ICTY Rule 87; ICTR Rule 87; SCSL Rule 87. Deliberations are discussed briefly in Chapter 7, Section 7.6.7, and judgements are examined in detail in Chapter 10.

36 See, e.g., *Prosecutor* v. *Lubanga*, Doc. No. ICC-01/04-01/06-803-tEN, Decision on the Confirmation of Charges, 29 January 2007 ('*Lubanga* Confirmation Decision'), para. 116 ('In addition, the Chamber considers that the probative value of these attestations must be determined as part of the assessment of the totality of the evidence admitted for the purpose of the confirmation hearing.'); *Brđanin* Evidence Order, *supra* note 23, para. 19 (noting that ICTY practice is 'to admit documents and video recordings and then decide what weight to give them in the context of the trial record as a whole.'); *Prosecutor* v. *Kajelijeli*, Case No.

determinations are decisions about what was actually established at trial, and the extent to which the judges can rely on what they saw, heard, and read in formulating the factual findings that ground the judgement on the merits. In evidentiary terms, if decisions on admissibility reflect preliminary conclusions on whether proposed evidence has any probative value at all, deliberations are the final assessment of how much probative value that evidence has.[37] As a general matter, many of the objections typically raised to the admissibility of evidence in common law jurisdictions are considered only at this stage of international criminal proceedings.[38] Moreover, because they are subsumed into the judgement, a chamber's conclusions as to any particular item of evidence are rarely discussed at any length, but instead are typically only implicit in the final factual finding.[39]

For witnesses, the evaluation of probative value revolves around credibility.[40] As in domestic jurisdictions, the reliability of witness evidence may be challenged by the opposing party in several different ways, including pointing out inconsistencies between prior statements and current testimony, identifying discrepancies among the accounts offered by different witnesses, and questioning the accuracy of a witness's

ICTR-98-44A-T, Judgement and Sentence, 1 December 2003, para. 156 ('In considering what weight should be given to a specific witness testimony, the totality of the testimony (demeanour, corroboration, credibility, etc.) of the witnesses is taken into account by the Chamber'); *ibid.*, para. 453 ('The Chamber will, in its legal findings, assess the Charge of Conspiracy to Commit Genocide based upon the totality of evidence in the case.'); *Prosecutor* v. *Sesay*, Case No. SCSL-04-15-T, Decision on Prosecution Motion To Admit into Evidence a Document Referred to in Cross-Examination, 2 August 2006, p. 3 ('[T]he Rules favour a flexible approach to the issue of admissibility of evidence, leaving the issue of weight to be determined when assessing probative value of the totality of the evidence.') (internal quotation marks and citation omitted). The 'beyond a reasonable doubt' standard is discussed in detail in Chapter 10, Section 10.1.3. The definition of 'charge' is discussed in Chapter 6, notes 60, 106 and accompanying text; and Chapter 7, notes 226–227 and accompanying text.

37 See, e.g., *Gatete* Admissibility Decision, *supra* note 7, para. 4 (explaining that admissibility 'requires some relevance and probative value', and determination of weight given to evidence 'is an assessment made by the Chamber at the end of the case'); accord *Milutinović et al.* Trial Judgement, *supra* note 16, Vol. I, para. 36; *Prosecutor* v. *Taylor*, Case No. SCSL-03-01-PT, Prosecutor's Motion for an Order Establishing Guidelines for the Conduct of Trial Proceedings, 22 May 2007, para. 14.

38 See *infra* Section 9.1.3 (discussing hearsay); see also *Katanga and Ngudjolo* Confirmation Decision, *supra* note 16, para. 109 ('[T]he parties' inability to cross-examine a prosecution source [the deceased author of a manuscript offered as evidence] is simply one factor in the Chamber's determination of the probative value accorded to the evidence in question.'); *ibid.*, para. 165 ('[W]here authentication of documentary evidence can be derived from other sources … photographic evidence … will be accorded probative value in proportion to (i) the level of authentication provided by the witness who introduces the evidence, and (ii) the reliability of the accompanying witness statement.'); *Prosecutor* v. *Popović, Beara, Nikolić, Borovčanin, Miletić, Gvero, and Pandurević*, Case No. IT-05-88-T, Decision on Admissibility of Intercepted Communications, 7 December 2007, para. 73 (discussing best-evidence rule); *Prosecutor* v. *Kordić and Čerkez*, Case No. IT-95-14/2-A, Decision on Prosecutor's Submissions Concerning Zagreb Exhibits and Presidential Transcripts, 1 December 2000, paras. 27, 44 (discussing authentication); *ibid.*, paras. 36, 38 (discussing prohibition on cumulative evidence).

39 As discussed in Chapter 10, however, the requirement of a reasoned judgement sometimes mandates that the chamber detail its assessment of particular pieces of evidence. See Chapter 10, Section 10.1.1.

40 *Milutinović et al.* Trial Judgement, *supra* note 16, Vol. I, paras. 60–61 (noting that 'credibility is essentially a factor of reliability' and explaining that '[t]hroughout its consideration of the evidence', Chamber had 'regard to demeanour, conduct, and circumstances of each individual witness', and 'had the advantage, in the case of almost every witness, of being able to observe that witness giving evidence in its presence, to study the

recollection.[41] Given the nature of the conflicts that are the background to international criminal proceedings, it is unsurprising that allegations of political, ethnic, or national bias are also frequently levelled at witnesses, particularly those called by the prosecution.[42] Trial chambers have emphasized, however, that while cultural or social factors may be taken into account,[43] determinations as to the reliability of witnesses must be made in light of the circumstances of each individual.[44] Moreover, in light of the passage of time – in some cases, up to a decade or more – between the underlying events, the initial witness interviews and statements, and eventual testimony at trial, minor inconsistencies between prior statements and testimony (or between different witnesses's accounts) do not necessarily affect the reliability of the witness's evidence.[45] For some witnesses, however, their credibility may be so undermined that the chamber gives their evidence no weight at all;[46] for most, the

demeanour and conduct of the witness in court, and to form an impression of whether the witness appeared to be trying to give a reliable account').

41 See, e.g., *Prosecutor* v. *Gotovina, Čermak, and Markač*, Case No. IT-06-90-T, Decision on the Admission of Statements of Four Witnesses Pursuant to Rule 92 Quater, 24 July 2008, para. 6 ('When examining the reliability of the evidence of an unavailable witness, the Chamber will consider ... inconsistencies in the statement.'); *Lubanga* Confirmation Decision, *supra* note 36, para. 122 n. 127 ('[I]nconsistencies or inaccuracies between the prior statements and oral testimony of a witness, or between different witnesses, are relevant factors in judging weight.'); *Niyitegeka* v. *Prosecutor*, Case No. ICTR-96-14-A, Judgement, 9 July 2004, para. 96 ('[A] Trial Chamber is bound to take into account inconsistencies and any explanations offered in respect of them when weighing the probative value of the evidence.'); *RUF* Case, Case No. SCSL-04-15-T, Decision on Sesay Defense Motion to Direct the Prosecutor to Investigate the Matter of False Testimony by Witness TF1–366, 25 July 2006, para. 29 ('[I]nconsistencies, inaccuracies or contradictions in the evidence of a witness ... are issues to be considered by the Court in its assessment of the credibility and the reliability of the witness'[s] evidence.').

42 See, e.g., *Nahimana, Barayagwiza, and Ngeze* v. *Prosecutor*, Case No. ICTR-99-52-A, Decision on Appellant Jean-Bosco Barayagwiza's Motions for Leave to Submit Additional Grounds of Appeal, to Amend the Notice of Appeal and to Correct His Appellant's Brief, 17 August 2006, para. 27 (discussing allegation of 'Error in Failing to Consider the Question of Credibility of Witnesses as Being Likely to be Affected by their Ethnicity, Political and or Ideological Motives'); *Prosecutor* v. *Strugar*, Case No. IT-01-42-PT, Decision on the Defence Motions to Oppose Admission of Prosecution Expert Reports Pursuant to Rule 94 *Bis*, 1 April 2004 (discussing challenge to witness testimony on grounds of political bias); *Prosecutor* v. *Ntakirutimana and Ntakirutimana*, Case No. ICTR-96-10-A, Judgement, 13 December 2004 ('*Ntakirutimana and Ntakirutimana* Appeal Judgement'), para. 256 (rejecting challenge to witness's testimony as politically motivated).

43 See, e.g., *Prosecutor* v. *Limaj, Musliu, and Bala*, Case No. IT-03-66-T, Judgement, 30 November 2005, para. 15 (Trial Chamber noting its awareness 'that many victim-witnesses with Albanian roots had family links in varying degrees to each other' or lived close to other witnesses, and that 'cultural factors of loyalty and honour may also have affected their evidence').

44 See, e.g., *Prosecutor* v. *Tadić*, Case No. IT-94-1-T, Opinion and Judgement, 7 May 1997, para. 541 ('It is neither appropriate, nor correct, to conclude that a witness is deemed to be inherently unreliable solely because he was the victim of a crime committed by a person' sharing ethnic, religious, or other group affiliation with the accused).

45 See, e.g., *Rutaganda* v. *Prosecutor*, Case No. ICTR-96-3-A, Judgement, 25 May 2003, para. 427 ('[S]uch minor inconsistencies, as those identified by the Appellant, certainly cannot suffice to render Witness H's entire testimony unreliable'); *Milutinović et al.* Trial Judgement, *supra* note 16, Vol. I, para. 49 (also considering 'the difference in questions put to the witnesses at different stages of the investigation and in court, and the traumatic situations in which the witnesses found themselves during the events' in question); accord *RUF* Case, Case No. SCSL-04-15-T, Judgement, 2 March 2009 ('*RUF* Trial Judgement'), para. 489 ('[T]he mere existence of inconsistencies in the testimony of a witness does not undermine the witness's credibility .... [S]ince the events in question took place many years ago, some details may be confused and some may be forgotten.').

46 See, e.g., *Milutinović et al.* Trial Judgement, *supra* note 16, Vol. I, para. 61 (noting that '[s]ome witnesses displayed such a lack of candour toward the Chamber that their evidence was essentially rejected'); *Prosecutor* v. *Nahimana, Barayagwiza, and Ngeze*, Case No. ICTR-99-52-T, Judgement and Sentence, 3 December 2003,

assessment of reliability is more nuanced, and their testimony may be credited on some issues, but not others.[47]

For documents, determinations of probative value at this stage of the trial process typically involve consideration of challenges to authenticity,[48] but may also overlap with assessments of witness credibility if the document is tendered through a witness.[49] Moreover, the reliance a trial chamber places on a particular document is often not a decision taken in isolation, but rather reflects the extent to which the document's contents are consistent with or corroborated by other evidence in the record.[50] This cautious approach to documentary evidence is often used where

para. 551 ('In her testimony, [the witness] lied repeatedly, denying that she made many statements, including her own broadcast, until confronted with them. Evasive to the point of squirming, her voice often reaching the feverish pitch of her broadcasts, which have been played in the courtroom, this witness made a deplorable impression on the Chamber. For these reasons, the Chamber rejects Bemeriki's testimony in its entirety.'); *Prosecutor* v. *Musema*, Case No. ICTR-96-13-T, Judgement and Sentence, 27 January 2000 ('*Musema* Trial Judgement'), Separate Opinion of Judge Pillay, paras. 25, 30 ('I note the numerous inconsistencies between the testimony of the Accused, the Defence exhibits and prior statements made by the Accused … For th[is] reason', among others, 'I reject the testimony of the Accused as inherently unreliable in its entirety.').

[47] See, e.g., *Milutinović et al.* Trial Judgement, *supra* note 16, Vol. I, para. 61 ('[W]here the Chamber found a witness to be not credible upon one issue, it did not automatically discard all of his or her evidence, but rather assessed the witness's credibility upon each issue in light of the evidence in the trial as a whole.'); *Prosecutor* v. *Haradinaj, Balaj, and Brahimaj*, Case No. IT-04-84-T, Judgement, 3 April 2008, para. 13 (concluding that even though '[s]ome of the witnesses that were former members of the warring factions were evasive or not entirely truthful regarding the roles they played', the Trial Chamber 'sometimes relied on other aspects' of their testimony, as required by ICTY Appeals Chamber precedent); *Lubanga* Confirmation Decision, *supra* note 36, para. 119 n. 124 ('[T]he Chamber holds that the examples … pertaining to [alleged] serious contradictions, chronic uncertainty, severe memory lapses, serious mistakes, as well as an alarming lack of knowledge of her working environment and the general background in Ituri, do not necessarily affect the truthfulness of [the witness's] testimony as a whole.'); *Ndindabahizi* v. *Prosecutor*, Case No. ICTR-01-71-A, Judgement, 16 January 2007, para. 82 (upholding Trial Chamber's decision to accept one witness's testimony as to statements made by accused, but to reject his speculation as to why the accused made those statements, and to reject his testimony on another issue because it 'appeared evasive and uncertain'); *Ntakirutimana and Ntakirutimana* Appeal, Judgement, *supra* note 42, para. 215 ('[I]t is settled jurisprudence of the Tribunal that a Trial Chamber may find some portions of a witness's testimony credible, and rely upon them in imposing a conviction, while rejecting other portions of the same witness's testimony as not credible.'); *RUF* Trial Judgement, *supra* note 45, para. 490 ('Even if some aspects of a witness's testimony are not believed by the Chamber, the Chamber may still accept other portions as presented provided they are credible in their context and particularly where they are corroborated.').

[48] See, e.g., *Prosecutor* v. *Brđanin*, Case No. IT-99-36-A, Judgement, 3 April 2007, para. 38 (citing with approval the *Brđanin* Trial Chamber's observation that 'in order to assess the authenticity of documents' it 'considered them in light of evidence as to their source and custody and other documentary evidence and witness testimony') (alteration omitted).

[49] See, e.g., *Katanga and Ngudjolo* Confirmation Decision, *supra* note 16, para. 165; see also *Prosecutor* v. *Boškoski and Tarčulovski*, Case No. IT-04-82-T, Decision on Tarčulovski Second Motion for Admission of Exhibits from the Bar Table with Annex A, 7 April 2008, para. 5 ('In the particular case of a document which is to be relied on to challenge or test the credibility of a witness, the failure … to put the document to the witness in court, in order to give the witness the opportunity to comment on it, will normally preclude the admission of the document.').

[50] See, e.g., *Milutinović et al.* Trial Judgement, *supra* note 16, Vol. III, paras. 591–594 (reviewing defence challenges to reports establishing the accused Ojdanić's knowledge of subordinates' crimes in Kosovo and concluding that 'the various other reports and communications received … show that' one in particular 'was not an isolated document of unique significance' but rather was 'consistent with other information received by Ojdanić at the time'; and that '[n]one of the challenges to the authenticity and receipt of these reports' by the accused 'has been adequately established').

the documents were not put to any testifying witness, or were subject to challenges by the opposing party that could not be definitively resolved.[51]

9.1.3 Treatment of hearsay

The practice of the international tribunals with regard to hearsay[52] is perhaps the best illustration of their expansive approach to admissibility, and how chambers actually exercise their discretion in the evaluation of evidence. Hearsay is generally excluded in common law jurisdictions because of concerns about reliability.[53] Although there are several exceptions to the rule excluding this type of evidence, they are usually limited to certain well-established circumstances in which courts have traditionally concluded that the context in which the statement was made renders it sufficiently reliable that it may be admitted.[54]

Consideration of hearsay in common law jurisdictions typically involves a somewhat complicated analysis of admissibility: does the statement even qualify as hearsay; does it fall within an exception; and even if not a traditional exception to the exclusionary rule, is the statement nevertheless sufficiently reliable to be admitted? In contrast, the international criminal tribunals' approach is deceptively simple. Hearsay is admissible, like any other proposed evidence, on a showing of relevance

[51] See, e.g., *Prosecutor* v. *Orić*, Case No. IT-03-68-T, Judgement, 30 June 2006, paras. 32–47 (Trial Chamber explaining that it either determined that the documents were authentic or used the challenged documents 'with some caution and only in as far as they corroborate, or are corroborated by, other acceptable evidence, and never as a sole basis for a finding of guilt') (quotation at paras. 33, 47). The Appeals Chamber eventually overturned Naser Orić's conviction because the Trial Chamber had 'made no findings … on either of … two fundamental elements' of superior responsibility, the sole form of responsibility charged in the indictment. *Prosecutor* v. *Orić*, Case No. IT-03-68-A, Judgement, 3 July 2008, para. 189 (explaining that the Trial Chamber had failed to consider whether the accused's 'subordinate[s] bore criminal responsibility and [whether] he knew or had reason to know of … their criminal conduct'). See also Gideon Boas, James L. Bischoff, and Natalie L. Reid, *Forms of Responsibility in International Criminal Law* (2007) ('Boas, Bischoff, and Reid, *Forms of Responsibility*'), pp. 247–252 (noting this and other flaws of the *Orić* Trial Judgement).

[52] Hearsay is often defined as an out-of-court statement offered to prove the truth of the matter asserted, with the classic example being a fact witness testifying to something that someone else has said, not what she herself observed. Kenneth S. Broun *et al.*, *McCormick on Evidence*, Vol. II (6th edn 2006) ('*McCormick*') § 246 (a leading American treatise explaining that when 'witness W reports on the stand that declarant D has stated that X was driving a car at a given time and place[, and the] proponent is trying with this evidence to prove that X did so act', D's out-of-court statement 'is being offered to prove the truth of the matter asserted, and by definition, it is hearsay').

[53] See, e.g., *McCormick*, *supra* note 52, § 245 (explaining that '[i]n order … to expose inaccuracies that might be present with respect to' a witness's perception, memory, terminology, and sincerity, 'the Anglo-American tradition evolved three conditions under which witnesses ordinarily are required to testify: oath, personal presence at the trial, and cross-examination', and that '[t]he rule against hearsay is designed to insure compliance with these ideal conditions, and when one of them is absent, the hearsay objection becomes pertinent').

[54] These include, but certainly are not limited to, a 'dying declaration' or statement made by someone in apprehension of his or her imminent death, which common law courts have admitted for centuries on the theory that a person about to die has no reason to deceive; an 'excited utterance', or statement made by someone upon or soon after the occurrence of a startling event, admitted on the theory that the declarant did not have an opportunity to reflect and fabricate an account; and records kept in the ordinary course of business or execution of professional duties. See *McCormick*, *supra* note 52, chs. 25–34.

and probative value.[55] As a result, instead of determining in an abstract and preliminary manner that certain categories of evidence are inherently so (un)reliable that their admissibility is assessed as a matter of law, the emphasis in international criminal proceedings is on the free and full evaluation of all the evidence by the trial chamber. While there are rare occasions in which a chamber will conclude that a proposed item of hearsay evidence is so evidently unreliable that it should not be admitted,[56] most hearsay challenges to evidence are resolved by reminding the party opposing admission that the fact '[t]hat a Trial Chamber admits a hearsay statement, does not necessarily imply that it accepts it as [definitively] reliable and probative'; those decisions are made 'at the end of trial when weighing and evaluating the evidence as a whole, in light of the context and of the nature of the evidence itself, including the credibility and reliability of the relevant witness'.[57]

In the course of that final assessment – and though 'as a matter of law, it is permissible to base a conviction on hearsay'[58] – several chambers have decided to give relatively little weight to hearsay evidence,[59] and to rely on it only if corroborated. For example, the *Lubanga* Pre-Trial Chamber at the ICC decided to admit anonymous hearsay for purposes of the confirmation hearing, but concluded that in light of 'the difficulties that such evidence may present to the Defence in relation to the possibility of ascertaining its truthfulness and authenticity', it would as a general

[55] See, e.g., *Prosecutor* v. *Stanišić and Župljanin*, Case No. IT-08-91-T, Order on Revised Guidelines on the Admission and Presentation of Evidence, 2 October 2009, Annex A, para. 5 (stating that 'circumstantial evidence including hearsay is admissible', but the probative value eventually assigned at the end of the trial 'will in general be less than the direct evidence of a witness'); *Lubanga* Confirmation Decision, *supra* note 36, para. 103; *Prosecutor* v. *Rutaganda*, Case No. ICTR-96-3-T, Judgement and Sentence, 6 December 1999, para. 18; *AFRC* Case, Case No. SCSL-04-16-PT, Decision on Joint Defence Motion to Exclude All Evidence from Witness TF1–277 Pursuant to Rule 89(C) and/or Rule 95, 24 May 2005, para. 24.

[56] See, e.g., *Prosecutor* v. *Kordić and Čerkez*, Case No. IT-95-14/2-AR73.5, Decision on Appeal Regarding Statement of a Deceased Witness, 21 July 2000, paras. 24–28 (finding an uncorroborated, unsworn, out-of-court statement that had been translated multiple times so unreliable as to be excluded by ICTY Rule 89(C), because '[a] piece of evidence may be so lacking in terms of the indicia of reliability that it is not "probative" and is therefore inadmissible'). See also generally *Prosecutor* v. *Aleksovski*, Case No. IT-95-14/1-AR73, Decision on Prosecutor's Appeal on Admissibility of Evidence, 16 February 1999 ('*Aleksovski* Admissibility Interlocutory Appeal'), para. 15 ('Since such evidence is admitted to prove the truth of its contents, a Trial Chamber must be satisfied that it is reliable for that purpose, in the sense of being voluntary, truthful and trustworthy, as appropriate; and for this purpose may consider both the content of the hearsay statement and the circumstances under which the evidence arose.').

[57] *Prosecutor* v. *Akayesu*, Case No. ICTR-96-4-A, Judgement, 1 June 2001 ('*Akayesu* Appeal Judgement'), para. 292; accord *Prosecutor* v. *Haraqija and Morina*, Case No. IT-04-84-R77.4-A, Judgement, 23 July 2009 ('*Haraqija and Morina* Contempt Judgement'), para. 62 ('[I]t follows from jurisprudence that not all evidence characterized as hearsay can be considered untested or unreliable.'); *Prosecutor* v. *Taylor*, Case No. SCSL-03-01-T, Decision on Prosecution Motion for Admission of Documents of Certain Intergovernmental Organisations and of Certain Governments, 26 February 2009, para. 15 ('Simply admitting a document into evidence does not amount to a finding that the evidence is credible.').

[58] *Haraqija and Morina* Contempt Judgement, *supra* note 57, para. 63 & n. 187 (citing *Prosecutor* v. *Kordić and Čerkez*, Case No. IT-95-14/2-A, Judgement, 17 December 2004, para. 294, which affirmed a conviction 'based on hearsay and circumstantial evidence where [the] Trial Chamber exhaustively considered credibility issues and surrounding circumstances', but noting nevertheless that 'caution is warranted' when reaching such verdicts).

[59] See, e.g., *Aleksovski* Admissibility Interlocutory Appeal, *supra* note 56, para. 15 ('[T]he weight or probative value to be afforded to [hearsay] evidence will usually be less than that given to the testimony of a witness who has given it under a form of oath and who has been cross-examined, although even this will depend upon

rule use the hearsay 'only to corroborate other evidence'.[60] Similarly, in assessing whether trial chambers have appropriately exercised their discretion in the evaluation of evidence, the ICTR Appeals Chamber has held that the hearsay testimony of a particular witness in the *Media* case was acceptable only 'to the extent that it [was] corroborated';[61] and concluded that 'vague and unverifiable hearsay' evidence of a witness in the *Ndindabahizi* trial was given excessive weight because he never explained how he learned of an alleged killing at a roadblock, nor even the basis for his belief that the killing occurred.[62] Finally, in a recent decision in a contempt proceeding, the ICTY Appeals Chamber overturned the conviction of Astrit Haraqija, former Minister of Culture, Youth, and Sports of Kosovo, because it concluded that the Trial Chamber had 'erred in placing decisive weight ... on the untested [hearsay] evidence emanating from' his co-accused, and had given insufficient consideration to flaws in that hearsay evidence, including its vagueness and lack of corroboration.[63] Notwithstanding these examples of careful consideration of the appropriate weight to be given to hearsay evidence, and despite the justification offered for the permissive approach to admissibility of such evidence, it is unlikely that most chambers actually expend a great deal of time assessing the reliability of each item of hearsay at the end of a lengthy trial, during which hundreds (or sometimes thousands) of individual exhibits are admitted, and hundreds of witnesses give evidence.[64]

In addition to corroboration, the factors chambers consider in determining how much weight may be placed on hearsay evidence include the 'source and precise character' of the information;[65] whether the opposing party had an opportunity

the infinitely variable circumstances which surround hearsay evidence.'); accord *Karera* v. *Prosecutor*, Case No. ICTR-01-74-A, Judgement, 2 February 2009 ('*Karera* Appeal Judgement'), para. 36.

60 *Lubanga* Confirmation Decision, *supra* note 36, para. 106.

61 *Media* Appeal Judgement, *supra* note 28, para. 473.

62 *Ndindabahizi* v. *Prosecutor*, Case No. ICTR-01-71-A, Judgement, 16 January 2007, para. 115. See also *Muvunyi* v. *Prosecutor*, Case No. ICTR-2000-55A-A, Judgement, 29 August 2008, para. 70 (overturning conviction based on vague hearsay). Compare *Rutaganda* v. *Prosecutor*, Case No. ICTR-96-3-A, Judgement, 26 May 2003, para. 154 (hearsay evidence had probative value because witness directly observed the scene and heard the statement in question firsthand).

63 *Haraqija and Morina* Contempt Judgement, *supra* note 57, paras. 63–69 (quotation at para. 69). The Appeals Chamber also explained that while untested evidence should be corroborated before it may be relied upon in reaching a verdict, not all hearsay is necessarily untested. See *ibid.*, paras. 63, 64 (affirming the Trial Chamber's ruling that 'the requirement of sufficient corroboration' applies 'to all untested evidence underpinning a conviction'). For another decision regarding admission of an accused's statement, see *Prosecutor* v. *Popović, Beara, Nikolić, Borovčanin, Miletić, Gvero, and Pandurević*, Case No. IT-05-88-T, Decision on the Admissibility of the Borovčanin Interview and the Amendment of the Rule 65 *ter* Exhibit List, 25 October 2007 ('*Popović et al.* Accused Interview Decision'), paras. 28–39, 51–80 (discussing appellate jurisprudence on the issue, and admitting accused Borovčanin's statement in evidence against him, but declining to consider the statement against any of his co-accused unless he testified).

64 See Steven R. Ratner, Jason S. Abrams, and James L. Bischoff, *Accountability for Human Rights Atrocities in International Law: Beyond the Nuremberg Legacy* (3rd edn 2009), p. 294 (noting that 'the liberal admission of evidence over the course of a long trial results in a massive trial record, including thousands of pages of transcript', and cautioning '[j]udges [not to] overestimate their ability at the end of trial to sort through this huge quantum of material and properly evaluate each discrete item').

65 *Media* Appeal Judgement, *supra* note 28, para. 831 (hearsay evidence had probative value because source was diplomat who was present at meetings in question, had a documentary record of the interaction, and considered the information reliable); accord *Karera* Appeal Judgement, *supra* note 59, para. 39.

to cross-examine the declarant;[66] and whether the hearsay is 'firsthand' or more removed.[67]

9.1.4 Evidence in cases involving sexual violence

If the treatment of hearsay is an illustration of how evidentiary rules work at the international criminal tribunals, the statutory and regulatory provisions regarding evidence in sex crime cases offer a particularly clear example of how and why those rules are made. In the middle of the few and general evidentiary provisions in each tribunal's Rules are one or two provisions that deal specifically and exclusively with the admission and evaluation of victim testimony and other kinds of evidence regarding allegations of sexual violence.[68] As many commentators have noted, the very existence of these rules and their progressive nature owe a significant debt to the concerted efforts of human rights groups, especially those focused on women's rights.[69] In particular, these rules are designed to prevent the application of 'standards of evidence which have traditionally discriminated against women and impeded their access to criminal justice systems domestically' through, for example, gender stereotypes regarding virtue, promiscuity, or truthfulness.[70]

In contrast to the generally flexible and permissive approach to admission of evidence at the tribunals, therefore, the salient feature of these particular rules is the limitation or elimination of a trial chamber's discretion as to certain types of evidence.[71]

[66] *Aleksovski* Admissibility Interlocutory Appeal, *supra* note 56, para. 15; *Akayesu* Appeal Judgement, *supra* note 57, para. 287.

[67] *Aleksovski* Admissibility Interlocutory Appeal, *supra* note 56, para. 15.

[68] See ICC Rules 70, 71; ICTY Rule 96; ICTR Rule 96; SCSL Rule 96.

[69] See, e.g., Janet Halley, 'Rape at Rome: Feminist Interventions in the Criminalization of Sex-Related Violence in Positive International Criminal Law', (2008) 30 *Michigan Journal of International Law* 1; Jennifer Green, Rhonda Copelon, Patrick Cotter, and Beth Stephens, 'Affecting the Rules for the Prosecution of Rape and Other Gender-Based Violence Before the International Criminal Tribunal for the Former Yugoslavia: A Feminist Proposal and Critique', (1994) 5 *Hastings Women's Law Journal* 171 (including 'a brief history of the international efforts by women's groups and their supporters to ensure that the [ICTY] addresses crimes of gender, thus exemplifying the ways in which women can affect and make international law') (quotation at p. 171).

[70] Kate Fitzgerald, 'Problems of Prosecution and Adjudication of Rape and Other Sexual Assaults Under International Law', (1997) 8 *European Journal of International Law* 638, 639. See also Donald K. Piragoff, 'Evidence', in Roy S. Lee (ed.), *The International Criminal Court: Elements of Crimes and Rules of Procedure and Evidence* (2001), p. 355 (also explaining that those in favour of specific prohibitive provisions in the ICC Rules, as already existed in the *ad hoc* Tribunals' Rules, were concerned that general rules allowing judicial discretion would be applied in a discriminatory fashion to require corroboration in sexual violence cases); *Prosecutor* v. *Šešelj*, Case No. IT-03-67-PT, Decision on Prosecution's Motion for Non-Disclosure of Names and Other Identifying Information, 27 May 2005, p. 4 n. 10 (explaining that the relevant provision in the ICTY Rules, discussed below, was adopted 'in consideration of the unique concerns of victims of sexual assault').

[71] See Robert Cryer, Håkan Friman, Darryl Robinson, and Elizabeth Wilmshurst, *An Introduction to International Criminal Law and Procedure* (2007), pp. 384–385 (describing the general approach as 'a

Although expressed slightly differently in the *ad hoc* Tribunals' Rules on one hand, and the ICC and SCSL Rules on the other, the provisions are focused on the same two basic issues – consent, and potential challenges to the credibility of the victim-witness.

At the ICTY and ICTR, a trial chamber cannot require corroboration as a condition for admitting the testimony of a victim of sexual violence, and cannot hear evidence relating to the victim's prior sexual conduct.[72] Evidence of consent cannot be offered unless the defence first satisfies the trial chamber, *in camera*, that the evidence is both relevant and probative;[73] and consent cannot be allowed as a defence if there is evidence that it was not freely given.[74] The ICC and SCSL also impose restrictions intended to protect victims and limit the discretion of trial chambers in this area, though they are styled as 'principles of evidence' rather than presumptions against admission. First, consent cannot be inferred from the victim's words or conduct where he or she was unable, because of coercion, threats, or lack of capacity, to give genuine consent;[75] second, consent cannot be inferred from lack of resistance or silence on the part of the victim;[76] and third, a trial chamber can draw no inferences as to '[c]redibility, character or predisposition to sexual availability of a victim or witness' based on prior or subsequent conduct.[77] In addition, as a result of the negotiations leading to the adoption of the ICC Rules,[78] one of the general provisions on evidence reflects marked concern for cases alleging sexual violence, and states that 'a Chamber shall not impose a legal requirement that corroboration is required in order to prove any crime within the jurisdiction of the Court, in particular, crimes of sexual violence'.[79]

presumption in favour of admission of evidence' that is reversed, or 'the evidence is banned altogether', in cases of sexual assault). See also *Prosecutor* v. *Halilović*, Case No. IT-0-48-A, Judgement, 16 October 2007, Declaration of Judge Shahabuddeen, para. 11 (noting that Rule 96(iv), discussed below, 'mandates exclusion of the evidence' it covers and 'nothing is left to the judgment of the court, except to find that' the circumstance requiring application of the rule exists).

[72] ICTY Rule 96(i), (iv); ICTR Rule 96(i), (iv). See also *Musema* Trial Judgement *supra* note 46, para. 45 (noting that the rule regarding corroboration merely 'accords to the testimony of a victim of sexual assault the same basis of evaluation of reliability as the testimony of victims of other crimes').

[73] ICTY Rule 96(iii); ICTR Rule 96(iii).

[74] ICTY Rule 96(ii) ('[C]onsent shall not be allowed as a defence if the victim (a) has been subjected to or threatened with or has had reason to fear violence, duress, detention or psychological oppression, or (b) reasonably believed that if the victim did not submit, another might be so subjected, threatened or put in fear.'); ICTR Rule 96(ii) (same). See also *Gacumbitsi* v. *Prosecutor*, Case No. ICTR-2001-64-A, Judgement, 7 July 2006, paras. 154, 156 (adopting the reasoning of an ICTY trial chamber and concluding that Rule 96 'must be read simply to define the circumstances under which evidence of consent will be admissible' to raise reasonable doubt, and does not refer to an element of or affirmative defence to the crime).

[75] ICC Rule 70(a), (b) (providing that such an inference cannot be made 'where force, threat of force, coercion or taking advantage of a coercive environment undermined the victim's ability to give voluntary and genuine consent' or where he or she was simply 'incapable of giving genuine consent'); SCSL Rule 96(i), (ii) (same).

[76] ICC Rule 70(c); SCSL Rule 96(iii).

[77] ICC Rule 70(d); SCSL Rule 96(iv).

[78] See Piragoff, *supra* note 70, pp. 355–357.

[79] ICC Rule 63(4).

Applying these rules, the Appeals Chamber in the *Kunarac* case – one of two at the ICTY to focus on crimes of sexual violence[80] – rejected one of the accused's challenges to the trial judgement and held that the Trial Chamber was 'entitled not to require corroboration for the testimony of rape victims' and thus did not err in accepting such evidence, but noted that the lower chamber 'at the same time was aware of the inherent problems of a decision based solely on the testimony of the victims'.[81] The Appeals Chamber affirmed the convictions and sentences imposed on all three accused in the case for the rape and enslavement of the victim-witnesses.[82]

9.2 Methods of adducing evidence

9.2.1 Witnesses

Witnesses are crucial to contemporary international criminal trials. Unlike the trials in the period immediately following the Second World War, current proceedings in international tribunals do not have the benefit of detailed documentation of the facts and conduct underlying the charges.[83] As a result, the information provided by individuals who personally experienced the events in question,[84] or who have particular knowledge of the context of the alleged crimes, or of connections between the alleged conduct of the accused and the commission of offences,[85] forms a significant part of evidence on which a trial chamber will base its judgement.[86]

9.2.1.1 Live testimony and witness statements

In their original form, the governing instruments for each of the *ad hoc* Tribunals, the SCSL, and the ICC expressed a preference for *viva voce*, or live, testimony, where the witness appears before the trial chamber to answer questions posed by

[80] See generally Boas, Bischoff, and Reid, *Elements of Crimes*, *supra* note 19, pp. 66–68, 86–88 (discussing the *Kunarac* and *Furundžija* cases and their elaboration and application of the crimes of rape and enslavement as crimes against humanity).

[81] *Prosecutor* v. *Kunarac, Kovač, and Vuković*, Case Nos. IT-96-23-A and IT-96-23/1-A, Judgement, 12 June 2002, para. 281.

[82] *Ibid.*, pp. 131–133 (affirming convictions and sentences of Dragoljub Kunarac, Radomir Kovač, and Zoran Vuković).

[83] See Patricia M. Wald, 'To "Establish Incredible Events by Credible Evidence": The Use of Affidavit Testimony in Yugoslavia War Crimes Tribunal Proceedings', (2001) 42 *Harvard International Law Journal* 535, 537–538.

[84] These percipient witnesses are generally referred to as 'crime base' witnesses, as they tend to give evidence in relation to a specific location or geographic unit where crimes were allegedly committed.

[85] Generally referred to as 'linkage' witnesses, as their evidence goes to the crucial question of whether the accused is sufficiently connected to the offences charged to be held criminally responsible for them. The substantive law governing this aspect of international criminal liability is the focus of Volume I of this series. See generally Boas, Bischoff, and Reid, *Forms of Responsibility*, *supra* note 51.

[86] For specific rules regarding statements and evidence presented through an accused, see Chapter 7, Section 7.6.2.

the parties or the bench.[87] As the *ad hoc* Tribunals hit their stride in the early 2000s, the rules expressing this preference were qualified, amended, and supplemented through a series of amendments adopted in recognition of the increasing pressures of multiple trials, each with a large number of witnesses, many of whom would give evidence that was not directly related to the question of the individual criminal responsibility of the accused standing trial.[88] In their current form, the rules applicable at the *ad hoc* Tribunals – and especially the ICTY – permit certain kinds of witness evidence to be given in writing, and reflect the conclusion of an extended process of jurisprudential development of the law on acceptable forms of evidence.[89] As with other aspects of the Rules of each tribunal, these rules also reflect the pressures of the completion strategies geared towards bringing the work of these temporary tribunals to a close.[90]

At the ICTY and SCSL, three rules govern the admission of witness evidence through means other than live testimony. First, Rule 92 *bis* authorises trial chambers to 'dispense with the attendance of a witness … and instead admit' that evidence, 'in whole or in part … in the form of a written statement or transcript' that complies with the strict conditions laid out in the rule,[91] as long as the evidence 'goes to proof of a matter other than the acts and conduct of the accused charged in the indictment'.[92]

Second, Rule 92 *ter*[93] provides for the admission of witness evidence in the form of a written statement or transcript, even if it goes to proof of the acts and conduct of the accused, if three conditions are met: the witness must (1) be present in court, (2) be available for cross-examination and questioning by the bench, and (3) attest to the accuracy of the written statement or transcript.[94] In essence, Rule 92 *ter*

[87] See Rome Statute, Art. 69 ('The testimony of a witness at trial shall be given in person', except as provided elsewhere in the Statute or in the ICC Rules); ICTY Rule 90(A) (providing, as of 11 February 1994, that '[w]itnesses shall, in principle, be heard directly by the Chambers', but may give evidence by deposition 'where it is not possible to secure the [witness's] presence'); ICTR Rule 90(A) ('Witnesses shall, in principle, be heard directly by the Chambers unless a Chamber has ordered that the witness be heard by means of a deposition'); SCSL Rule 90(A) ('Witnesses may give evidence directly', or by deposition or communications media, as provided elsewhere in the Rules).

[88] See Wald, *supra* note 83, pp. 545–548 (noting that these revisions were adopted 'not without some dissent').

[89] See Kwon, *supra* note 5, pp. 364–368 (discussing, in particular, the extensive decisional law in the *Milošević* case on these points); Eugene O'Sullivan and Deirdre Montgomery, 'The Erosion of the Right to Confrontation under the Cloak of Fairness at the ICTY', (2010) 8 *Journal of International Criminal Justice* 511, 516–520. As noted elsewhere in this volume, these rule changes have sometimes resolved conflicts in the jurisprudence or reversed decisions taken by trial or appellate chambers. See Chapter 2, Section 2.1.4.

[90] See Kwon, *supra* note 5, p. 364; Ratner, Abrams, and Bischoff, *supra* note 64, p. 290.

[91] ICTY Rule 92 *bis*(B) (requiring, among other things, that the statement be accompanied by a declaration by the person making the statement, which must be, in turn, witnessed by 'a person authorised to witness such a declaration in accordance with the law and procedure of a State' or an ICTY official).

[92] ICTY Rule 92 *bis*(A); see also SCSL Rule 92 *bis*(A) (providing more simply that 'a Chamber may, in lieu of oral testimony, admit as evidence in whole or in part, information including written statements and transcripts, that do not go to proof of the acts and conduct of the accused'). See also *infra* text accompanying notes 99–104.

[93] Rule 92 *ter* also governs situations where an ICTY trial chamber determines that a Rule 92 *bis* witness should be present for cross-examination. See ICTY Rule 92 *bis*(C).

[94] ICTY Rule 92 *ter*; SCSL Rule 92 *ter*.

permits written evidence to substitute for the witness's examination-in-chief, but not for the witness's cross-examination, and allows the proffering party to dispense with Rule 92 *bis* requirements while ensuring that evidence going directly to the alleged criminal responsibility of accused is subject to cross-examination.[95]

Finally, Rule 92 *quater* governs the evidence of an unavailable witness, defined as someone 'who has subsequently died [after giving the statement], or who can no longer with reasonable diligence be traced, or who is by reason of bodily or mental condition unable to testify orally'.[96] The Rule authorises the admission of the written statement or transcript, regardless of its form, if the chamber is satisfied that the witness is truly unavailable and the proposed evidence is reliable.[97] For Rule 92 *quater* witnesses, the fact that the evidence is relevant to the 'acts and conduct of the accused as charged in the indictment' is not a *per se* bar, but rather only a factor that weighs against admission.[98]

The ICTR Rules include only Rule 92 *bis*. Like the ICTY version, however, ICTR Rule 92 *bis* lists a number of factors that chambers should consider in determining whether evidence may be admitted in written form, and divides them into factors counselling in favour of, and factors weighing against, admission in that form. The former include 'circumstances in which the evidence':

(a) is of a cumulative nature, in that other witnesses will give or have given oral testimony of similar facts;
(b) relates to relevant historical, political or military background;
(c) consists of a general or statistical analysis of the ethnic composition of the population in the places to which the indictment relates;
(d) concerns the impact of crimes upon victims;

95 See Kwon, *supra* note 5, pp. 364–368 (explaining this rationale of the jurisprudence codified in Rule 92 *ter*, and observing that Judge Kwon's 'common-law colleagues on the bench eventually came to agree with [him] that admitting written statements with cross-examination was an appropriate and fair way to expedite the proceedings') (quotation at p. 367). The decisions eventually codified in Rule 92 *ter* interpreted and applied Rule 89(F) of the ICTY Rules, which provides that '[a] Chamber may receive the evidence of a witness orally or, where the interests of justice allow, in written form'. See Kwon, *supra* note 5, pp. 364–368.

96 ICTY Rule 92 *quater*(A); SCSL Rule 92 *quater*(A).

97 ICTY Rule 92 *quater*(A); SCSL Rule 92 *quater*(A).

98 ICTY Rule 92 *quater*(B); SCSL Rule 92 *quater*(B). For an example of a decision admitting Rule 92 *quater* evidence going to 'acts and conduct', see *Prosecutor* v. *Popović, Beara, Nikolić, Borovčanin, Miletić, Gvero, and Pandurević*, Case No. IT-05-88-T, Decision on Prosecution Motion for Admission of Evidence Pursuant to Rule 92 *quater*, 21 April 2008, paras. 42, 45, 48, 57, 64 (admitting the prior testimony of four deceased witnesses whose evidence went to the conduct and mental states of some of the accused). The ICTY judges have also recently added Rule 92 *quinquies* to that Tribunal's Rules. See Rules of Procedure and Evidence of the International Criminal Tribunal for the former Yugoslavia, UN Doc. IT/32/Rev.44, as amended 10 December 2009, available at www.icty.org/x/file/Legal%20Library/Rules_procedure_evidence/IT032_rev44_en.pdf. Apparently motivated by difficulties in securing witness testimony in the *Šešelj* and *Haradinaj* cases, see, e.g., Steve Czajkowski, 'ICTY Delays Seselj Trial over Witness Intimidation Concerns', *Jurist*, 12 February 2009, http://jurist.law.pitt.edu/paperchase/2009/02/icty-delays-seselj-trial-over-witness.php (describing the *Šešelj* Trial Chamber's grant of the prosecution's motion to adjourn the trial in order to protect the integrity of the proceedings); Alexander Zahar, 'International Court and Private Citizen', (2009) 12 *New Criminal Law Review* 569, 570–572, Rule 92 *quinquies* outlines the circumstances and conditions under which a chamber may 'admit the evidence of a person in the form of a written statement or a transcript of evidence given by the person in proceedings before the [ICTY]', even if it does not satisfy the criteria of Rule 92 *bis* as to form,

(e) relates to issues of the character of the accused; or
(f) relates to factors to be taken into account in determining sentence.[99]

In contrast to the oddly particular provisions in this list – reflecting the codification of accreted case law – the factors weighing against admission include common sense considerations grounded in the concern that procedural innovation not detract from the overall fairness of the trial. Chambers at both *ad hoc* Tribunals are directed to consider whether '(a) there is an overriding public interest in the evidence in question being presented orally; (b) a party objecting can demonstrate that its nature and source render[] it unreliable, or that its prejudicial effect outweighs its probative value; or (c) there are any other factors which make it appropriate for the witness to attend for cross-examination'.[100]

The explicit prohibition in Rule 92 *bis* against admitting written witness evidence relating to the acts and conduct of the accused arises out of concerns that permitting such evidence, which typically goes directly to the ultimate issue of the accused's criminal responsibility, would breach the fundamental right of confrontation,[101] and deprive the judges of a crucial tool for assessing the credibility of such key witnesses.[102] For these reasons, the restriction does not apply to the conduct or mental state of other individuals who commit the crimes for which the accused is allegedly responsible.[103] Rather, it operates to prevent the presentation of evidence in written form that goes to the conduct or mental state of the accused that purports to satisfy the elements of the forms of responsibility charged in the indictment, such as joint criminal enterprise, superior responsibility, aiding and abetting, or instigation.[104] For example, the *Popović* Trial Chamber admitted

and even if it goes to the acts and conduct of the accused. Chief among these conditions is that the trial chamber be satisfied that 'the failure of the person to attend or to give evidence has been materially influenced by improper interference, including threats, intimidation, injury, bribery, or coercion'.

99 ICTR Rule 92 *bis*(A)(i); ICTY Rule 92 *bis*(A)(i)

100 ICTY Rule 92 *bis*(A)(ii); ICTR Rule 92 *bis*(A)(ii).

101 See ICCPR, Art. 14(3)(e) (listing as a minimum fair trial guarantee the accused's right '[t]o examine, or have examined, the witnesses against' him or her); Rome Statute, Art. 67(1)(e) (same); ICTY Statute, Art. 21(4)(e) (same); ICTR Statute, Art. 20(4)(e) (same); SCSL Statute, Art. 17(4)(e) (same). See also *Prosecutor* v. *Kordić and Čerkez*, Case No. IT-95-14/2-AR73.5, Decision on Appeal Regarding Statement of a Deceased Witness, 21 July 2000, para. 23 (overturning Trial Chamber's admission of a witness statement, the only evidence of the accused's presence at a particular location, because among other things, its admission was 'in marked tension with the guarantee in Article 21(4) that the accused has the right to examine the witnesses against him').

102 See O'Sullivan and Montgomery, *supra* note 89, p. 513 (noting importance of live testimony to credibility determinations); Wald, *supra* note 83, p. 551 (former ICTY judge asking '[h]ow does one assess the credibility of a piece of paper?' and opining that 'a very different aura surrounds' live testimony in court before judges, and which is subject to cross-examination); see also *ibid.* (noting her suspicion of statements produced by 'a witness speaking one language to an interrogator speaking another who writes it down in the [latter] language and has it read back to the witness in the [former language] by a third party').

103 *Prosecutor* v. *Galić*, Case No. IT-98-29-AR73.2, Decision on Interlocutory Appeal Concerning Rule 92*bis*(C), 7 June 2002 ('*Galić* Interlocutory Appeal Decision'), para. 9; see also *Prosecutor* v. *Slobodan Milošević*, Case No. IT-02-54-PT, Decision on Prosecution's Request to Have Written Statements Admitted Under Rule 92 *bis*, 21 March 2002, para. 22 ('The phrase "acts and conduct of the accused" … is a plain expression and should be given its ordinary meaning: deeds and behaviour of the accused.').

104 *Galić* Interlocutory Appeal Decision, *supra* note 103, paras. 10–11; accord *Prosecutor* v. *Popović, Beara, Nikolić, Borovčanin, Miletić, Gvero, and Pandurević*, Case No. IT-05-88-T, Decision on Prosecution's

statements from thirteen Bosnian Muslim witnesses which did not 'mention any of the Accused by name[,] … describe acts or conduct of unidentified persons who could be the Accused[, or] … appear to describe specific individual events at which the Prosecution alleges any of the Accused was personally present';[105] but refused to admit the prior testimony of a fourteenth witness that described a meeting which apparently 'play[ed] a prominent role in the Prosecution's theory of this case', and which had allegedly been attended by one of the accused.[106]

At the ICC, perhaps because that court is still very much in its infancy, there has been little softening of the preference expressed in the Rome Statute and ICC Rules for live testimony at trial, whether in court or by other means of communication such as audio or video link,[107] though judges have permitted the use of witness evidence in written form for the confirmation hearing at the pre-trial stage.[108] In addition, the Rules specifically authorise the introduction of 'previously recorded audio or video testimony of a witness' before the Court, 'or the transcript or other documented evidence of such testimony', so long as the parties had (or will have) an opportunity to examine the witness.[109]

Notwithstanding the absence of strict exclusionary rules on admissibility, and despite the provisions for written witness evidence discussed in this section, the process of adducing evidence at the international criminal tribunals is still predominantly adversarial, in that the parties bear the primary responsibility for development of the factual record on which the chambers' judgements or decisions are

Confidential Motion for Admission of Written Evidence in Lieu of *Viva Voce* Testimony Pursuant to Rule 92 *bis*, 12 September 2006 ('*Popović et al.* Rule 92 *bis* Decision'), paras. 57, 75. For more on the forms of responsibility that have been recognised and applied at the international criminal tribunals, see generally Boas, Bischoff, and Reid, *Forms of Responsibility*, *supra* note 51.

105 *Popović et al.* Rule 92 *bis* Decision, *supra* note 104, para. 77.

106 *Ibid.*, para. 76. See also *ibid.*, para. 28 (refusing to admit portions of an exhibit discussed in the proffered transcript from another trial, which included intercepted communications that referred directly to the accused in the case before it, even though it was offered merely to prove 'the process involved in corroborating the information contained in the communications in order to determine their authenticity').

107 See, e.g., *Prosecutor* v. *Lubanga*, Doc. No. ICC-01/04-01/06-1140, Decision on Various Issues Related to Witnesses' Testimony During Trial, 29 January 2008, para. 41 ('The Chamber accepts the submissions of the parties that the presumption is that witnesses will give evidence by way of live in-court testimony, in accordance with Article 69(2) of the Statute', but 'will authorise the use of audio or video-link whenever necessary' according to the requirements of the ICC Rules.). For more on the use of video-link testimony for sensitive witnesses, see Chapter 7, Section 7.4.3.

108 See, e.g., *Prosecutor* v. *Lubanga*, Doc. No. ICC-01/04-01/06-517, Decision Concerning the Prosecution Proposed Summary Evidence, 4 October 2006, pp. 3–4 (authorising the prosecution to rely on summary evidence, instead of witness statements or interview notes and transcripts, 'given the exceptional circumstances faced in the present case as a result of the recent deterioration of the security situation in certain parts of the Democratic Republic of the Congo and [its] impact … on the range of available and feasible protective measures' for witnesses).

109 See ICC Rule 68 (providing in subparagraph (a) that such evidence is admissible '[i]f the witness who gave the previously recorded testimony is not present before the Trial Chamber', provided that 'both the Prosecutor and the defence had the opportunity to examine the witness during the recording'; and in subparagraph (b) that it may be introduced even for a testifying witness in the instant case if 'he or she does not object to the submission of the previously recorded testimony and the Prosecutor, the defence and the Chamber have the opportunity to examine the witness during the proceedings').

based.[110] In this context, cross-examination of the opposing party's witnesses can play a crucial role in exposing flaws in proposed evidence and increasing the accuracy and reliability of the record.[111] Excessive reliance on written evidence – as may increasingly be the case for tribunal prosecutors pushed to shorten trials[112] – therefore poses significant concerns for equality of arms (between the prosecution and the defence) and accuracy of factual findings, and thus ultimately the overall fairness of the trial.[113]

9.2.1.2 Experts

In addition to testimony by percipient witnesses, international criminal prosecutions frequently rely on the live testimony or written reports of experts in several subject areas – including history,[114] linguistics,[115] forensics,[116] and military

[110] See, e.g., Kwon, *supra* note 5, p. 363 ('[I]n practice, the common-law adversarial model has predominated most aspects of the [ICTY]'s procedure: the production of witnesses and evidence is predominantly party-driven and ... most witnesses are still heard live'). For more on common law and civil law influences on international criminal procedure, see Chapter 1, Section 1.2; Chapter 12, Section 12.2; see also Mirjan Damaška, 'The Uncertain Fate of Evidentiary Transplants: Anglo-American and Contemporary Experiments', (1997) 45 *American Journal of Comparative Law* 839.

[111] See, e.g., O'Sullivan and Montgomery, *supra* note 89, p. 513 ('Cross-examination is the ultimate means of demonstrating truth and of testing veracity and credibility, for the cross-examination with the most honest witness also can provide the means to explore the frailties of the testimony.').

[112] See, e.g., *Prosecutor* v. *Karadžić*, Case No. IT-95-5/18-PT, Transcript, 8 September 2009, p. 445 (Judge Kwon explaining that the Prosecution sought in its submission to have all but two witnesses' evidence, in one of the most important ICTY cases, adduced in whole or in part through written statements or transcripts of prior testimony, pursuant to ICTY Rules 92 *bis*, *ter*, and *quater*) (referring to *Prosecutor* v. *Karadžić*, Case No. IT-95-5/18-PT, Prosecution Submission Pursuant to Rule 73 *bis*(D), 31 August 2009).

[113] See Ratner, Abrams, and Bischoff, *supra* note 64, p. 294 (noting that '[i]n the ad hoc tribunals, the prosecution – with its greater resources, institutional memory, and large banks of evidence from previous trials – relies much more heavily on' the flexible approach offered by the evidentiary rules, and recommending that chambers consider 'the burden on the accused in attempting to rebut it, and the trial-time consumed in this attempt'); see also Steven Kay, 'The Move from Oral Evidence to Written Evidence', (2004) 2 *Journal of International Criminal Justice* 495, 496 ('Although these rules may be used by both parties, they are primarily designed to be employed by the Prosecution'); *ibid*., p. 501 ('Can an accused in such a position be validly bound by a time limit applied to the Prosecution in his trial, when he is in fact dealing with a body of evidence that would have been accumulated outside the temporal frame of his proceedings?').

[114] See, e.g., *Prosecutor* v. *Nahimana, Ngeze, and Barayagwiza*, Case No. ICTR-99-52-T, Oral Decision on Qualification of Expert – Alison Des Forges, 20 May 2002 (concluding that Des Forges, an academic and human rights researcher who had published extensively on the causes of the Rwandan genocide, was an expert in human rights and Rwandan political and social history, and could therefore testify as an expert witness); *Prosecutor* v. *Stanišić and Župljanin*, Case No. IT-08-91-T, Written Reasons for the Trial Chamber's Oral Decision Accepting Dorothea Hanson as an Expert Witness, 5 November 2009 ('*Stanišić and Župljanin* Expert Decision') (permitting Hanson, a specialist in East European Area Studies and Modern Balkan History, to appear as an expert witness).

[115] See, e.g., *Prosecutor* v. *Akayesu*, Case No. ICTR-96-4-T, Judgement, 2 September 1998, para. 146 (stating that the Trial Chamber 'relied substantially on the testimony of Dr. Mathias Ruzindana, an expert witness on linguistics, for its understanding' of several key terms in Kinyarwanda, including the expressions used to describe rape and words used to refer to the perpetrators and victims of the crimes charged); *Prosecutor* v. *Popović, Beara, Nikolić, Borovčanin, Miletić, Gvero, and Pandurević*, Case No. IT-05-88-T, Transcript, 25 August 2008 (expert testimony of Slobodan Remetić on linguistic analysis of intercepts connected to one of the accused).

[116] See, e.g., *Prosecutor* v. *Perišić*, Case No. IT-04-81-T, Decision on Uncontested Srebrenica Expert Reports, 26 August 2009 (admitting several expert reports in different subfields of forensic science, including forensic anthropology, forensic pathology, forensic chemistry, and forensic investigation); *Prosecutor* v. *Nyiramasuhuko, Kanyabashi, Ndayambaje, Nsabimana, Ntahobali, and Nteziryayo*, Case No. ICTR-98-42-T, Decision on Prosecutor's Motion for Leave to Add a Handwriting Expert to His Witness List, 14 October 2004 (admitting report of Antipas Nyanjwa, a forensic document expert); *CDF* Case, Case No.

analysis[117] – to provide context, clarification, or additional support for facts adduced by other means. Explicit authority for the use of expert witnesses appears in the Rules of the ICTY, ICTR, and SCSL,[118] and is implicitly recognised in the ICC Rules and Court Regulations.[119] Each of these tribunals permits expert witnesses to be present during the testimony of other witnesses.[120] However, in the *ad hoc* Tribunals and the SCSL, if the other party accepts the proffered witness statement or expert report, does not challenge the qualifications of the expert, and does not wish to cross-examine the expert witness, the chamber may admit the statement or report without calling the witness to testify.[121] If the other party wishes to question the expert, the report or statement is generally admitted in place of the direct examination by the moving party, and the witness will appear for cross-examination.[122]

In proceedings at the ICC to date, the *Lubanga* Trial Chamber has expressed a preference for joint instruction of experts by the parties, though the parties

SCSL-04-14-T, Decision on Prosecution Request for Leave to Call Additional Expert Witness Dr. William Haglund, 1 October 2004 (admitting Haglund's report on forensic assessment and investigations of two grave sites relevant to the case).

[117] See, e.g., *Prosecutor* v. *Popović, Beara, Nikolić, Borovčanin, Miletić, Gvero, and Pandurević*, Case No. IT-05-88-T, Decision on Defense Rule 94 *bis* Notice Regarding Prosecution Expert Witness Richard Butler, 19 September 2007 (*'Popović et al.* Expert Decision'); *Prosecutor* v. *Gotovina, Čermak, and Markač*, Case No. IT-06-90-T, Decision on Admission of Expert Report of Geoffrey Corn, 22 September 2009, para. 6 (admitting an expert report on 'practical applications of the laws of war in military operations' into evidence and refusing to separate the technical parts of the report from the otherwise inadmissible legal sections); *Prosecutor* v. *Ndindiliyimana, Bizimungu, Nzuwonemeye, and Sagahutu*, Case No. ICTR-00-56-T, Decision on the Prosecution's Objections to Expert Witnesses Lugan and Strizek, 23 October 2008, para. 16 (permitting Bernard Lugan to testify as a military expert and ordering that his testimony be limited to the 'historical and military context in which the events alleged in the Indictment occurred'); *CDF* Case, Case No. SCSL-04-14-T, Decision on Fofana Submissions Regarding Proposed Expert Witness Daniel J. Hoffman Ph.D., 1 October 2004, p. 3 (permitting Hoffman, a 'socio-cultural anthropologist with particular knowledge of the anthropology of armed conflicts and irregular combatants', to testify as an expert because his testimony 'is likely to assist the Chamber in understanding and determining issues relating to the structure and organization of the CDF, in particular the relationships between and among Kamajor fighters and commanders and the distribution and delegation of power within Sierra Leone's civil militia').

[118] ICTY Rule 94 *bis*; ICTR Rule 94 *bis*; SCSL Rule 94 *bis*.

[119] See, e.g., ICC Rules 91, 140(3), 191 (referring to expert witnesses); ICC Court Regulation 44 (providing, *inter alia*, for the maintenance of a list of experts who may be instructed by the parties or the chamber, and outlining the powers of the chamber with regard to evidence adduced through experts); ICC Court Regulation 54 (referring to joint or separate instruction of expert witnesses by participants).

[120] ICC Rule 140(3); ICTY Rule 90(C); ICTR Rule 90(D); SCSL Rule 90(D).

[121] ICTY Rule 94 *bis*(C); ICTR Rule 94 *bis*(C); SCSL Rule 94 *bis*(C).

[122] See, e.g., *AFRC* Case, Case No SCSL-2004-16-T, Decision on Prosecution Request for Leave to Call an Additional Witness (Zainab Hawa Bangura) pursuant to Rule 73 *bis*(E), and on Joint Defence Notice to Inform the Trial Chamber of Its Position vis-à-vis the Proposed Expert Witness (Mrs. Bangura) Pursuant to Rule 94 *bis*, 5 August 2005 ('*AFRC* Expert Decision'), para. 30 (holding that the non-moving party has only two options under the rule on expert witnesses: '(a) to notify the Trial Chamber that it accepts the expert witness statement, in which case the Trial Chamber may admit the statement without necessarily calling the witness to testify; or (b) to notify the Trial Chamber that it wishes to cross-examine the expert witness, in which case the witness will necessarily appear in court for purposes of cross-examination').

may still seek leave to retain and instruct separate experts on the same issue.[123] The Chamber has also designated and instructed its own experts to provide reports and testimony on several different topics relevant to the allegations in that case.[124]

Regardless of the method by which it is presented, the threshold test for admission of expert evidence in these tribunals is whether the expert witness can impartially offer specialised knowledge that will assist the chamber in understanding the evidence before it.[125] As the ICTR Appeals Chamber explained:

> Expert witnesses are ordinarily afforded wide latitude to offer opinions within their expertise; their views need not be based upon firsthand knowledge or experience. Indeed, in the ordinary case the expert witness lacks personal familiarity with the particular case, but instead offers a view based on his or her specialized knowledge regarding a technical, scientific, or otherwise discrete set of ideas or concepts that is expected to lie outside the lay person's ken.[126]

To be admissible, the report, statement, or anticipated testimony must fall within the witness's area of expertise.[127] In addition, ICTY chambers generally require

[123] See, e.g., *Prosecutor* v. *Lubanga*, Doc. No. ICC-01/04-01/06-1069, Decision on the Procedures to Be Adopted for Instructing Expert Witnesses, 10 December 2007, paras. 16–17.

[124] See, e.g., *Prosecutor* v. *Lubanga*, Doc. No. ICC-01/04-01/06-1934, Instructions to the Court's Expert on Names and Other Social Conventions in the Democratic Republic of Congo, 5 June 2009; *Prosecutor* v. *Lubanga*, Doc. No. ICC-01/04-01/06-1671, Instructions to the Court's Expert on Child Soldiers and Trauma, 6 February 2009; *Prosecutor* v. *Lubanga*, Doc. No. ICC-01/04-01/06-1558, Instructions to the Court's Expert on Background and Context, 17 December 2008. In an unusual move, the *Katanga and Ngudjolo* Trial Chamber also appointed two experts to assist it in determining whether the accused Katanga 'fully understands and speaks French', so as to permit the discontinuance of translation into Lingala. *Prosecutor* v. *Katanga and Ngudjolo*, Doc. No. ICC-01/04-01/07-1300, Order Instructing Experts Pursuant to Regulation 44 of the Regulations of the Court, 14 July 2009, para. 1.

[125] See, e.g., *Popović et al.* Expert Decision, *supra* note 117, para. 23 (defining 'expert witness' as one who has 'the special knowledge, experience, or skills needed to potentially assist the Trial Chamber in its understanding or determination of issues in dispute', who due to his or her qualifications 'can give opinions and draw conclusions, within the confines of his or her expertise' that is 'intended to enlighten the Judges on specific issues of a technical nature'); *Stanišić and Župljanin* Expert Decision, *supra* note 114, para. 9 ('An expert is expected to make statements and draw conclusions independently and impartially'); *Prosecutor* v. *Galić*, Case No. IT-98-29-T, Decision Concerning the Expert Witnesses Ewa Tabeau and Richard Philips, 3 July 2002, p. 2; *Prosecutor* v. *Akayesu*, Case No. ICTR-96-4-T, Decision on a Defence Motion for the Appearance of an Accused as an Expert Witness, 9 March 1998, p. 2 ('[I]n order to be entitled to appear, an expert witness must not only be recognized expert in his field, but must also be impartial in the case'); accord *Media* Appeal Judgement, *supra* note 28, para. 198; *AFRC* Expert Decision, *supra* note 122, paras. 23, 31 (citing the Headquarters Agreement between Sierra Leone and the United Nations and *ad hoc* Tribunal jurisprudence, and defining expert as 'a person … appearing at the instance of the Special Court, a suspect or an accused to present testimony based on special knowledge, skills, experience or training' who can 'assist the Chamber to understand or determine an issue in dispute and the context in which the events took place').

[126] *Prosecutor* v. *Semanza*, Case No. ICTR-97-20-A, Judgement, 20 May 2005 ('*Semanza* Appeal Judgement'), para. 303.

[127] See, e.g., *Prosecutor* v. *Dragomir Milošević*, Case No. IT-98-29/1-T, Decision on Admission of Expert Report of Robert Donia, 15 February 2007, para. 6; *Prosecutor* v. *Karemera, Ngirumpatse, and Nzirorera*, Case No. ICTR-98-44-T, Decision on Edouard Karemera's Motion for the Admission of an Expert Witness, 22 May 2009 ('*Karemera et al.* Expert Decision'), para. 5; *AFRC* Expert Decision, *supra* note 122, para. 31.

that the proposed expert evidence meet 'minimum standards of reliability',[128] and have also considered whether 'there is transparency in the methods and sources used by the expert witness, including the established or assumed facts on which the expert witness relied'.[129]

9.2.2 Other documentary evidence

Notwithstanding the importance of witness testimony, international criminal trials are too complex, and the circumstances giving rise to the proceedings too extensive in terms of geography, time periods, and number of alleged criminal transactions, for all evidence to be adduced through witnesses.[130] At the ICTY, ICTR, and ICC, both the prosecution and defence rely extensively on contemporaneous documents that are offered for admission directly by counsel – generally referred to as offered 'from the bar table' – and which are evaluated during deliberations solely on the strength of their contents, albeit in the context of all the evidence submitted in the case.[131] As one ICTY Trial Chamber noted, however, submission of evidence in this fashion may be expeditious, but would likely adversely affect the weight placed on the evidence:

> It is desirable that documents are tendered for admission through witnesses who are able to comment on them. A party is not necessarily precluded from seeking the admission of a document even though it was not put to a witness with knowledge of the document (or its content) when that witness gave testimony in court. However, the failure to put the

[128] *Stanišić and Župljanin* Expert Decision, *supra* note 114, para. 8; see *supra* Section 9.1.1.1 (discussing reliability as a factor in weighing the admissibility of evidence at the *ad hoc* Tribunals). See also *Karemera et al.* Expert Decision, *supra* note 127, para. 5 (similar requirement applied at the ICTR). But see *Popović et al.* Expert Decision, *supra* note 117, para. 26 (holding that the admissibility determination is simply 'whether the witness has sufficient expertise in a relevant subject area such that the Trial Chamber may benefit from hearing his or her opinion' and that 'the questions of objectivity, impartiality and independence become relevant to assess the weight to be accorded to that opinion evidence').

[129] *Popović et al.* Expert Decision, *supra* note 117, para. 30 (collecting decisions).

[130] See Wald, *supra* note 83, p. 549 (noting that, even in 2001, before the later 'mega-trials', 'ICTY trials, on average, involve[d] a hundred witnesses or more, and each witness, on average, takes up a full trial day'). Indeed, this scope and complexity, combined with the pressures of the completion strategies at the ICTY and ICTR, drive the increasing reliance on written witness evidence. See *supra* Sections 9.2.1.1, 9.2.1.2.

[131] See, e.g., *Lubanga* Bar Table Decision, *supra* note 8, para. 50(b) (admitting, with limited exceptions, a number of documents tendered 'from the bar table' by the prosecution); *ibid.*, para. 1 (explaining that this phrase 'describes the situation when documents or other material are submitted directly by counsel, rather than introduced via a witness as part of his or her testimony'); *Prosecutor* v. *Lukić and Lukić*, Case No. IT-98-32/1-T, Decision on Milan Lukić's Fourth Bar Table Motion, 5 May 2009 (largely granting accused's motion for admission of documents not adduced through witnesses); *Prosecutor* v. *Karemera, Ngirumpatse, and Nzirorera*, Case No. ICTR-98-44-T, Decision on Joseph Nzirorera's Motion to Admit Documents from the Bar Table: Public Statements and Minutes, 14 April 2009 (largely granting accused's motion, and admitting part or all of nine interviews of alleged co-participants in joint criminal enterprise). But see *Prosecutor* v. *Karadžić*, Case No. IT-95-5/18-PT, Order on the Procedure for the Conduct of Trial, 8 October 2009, para. R (directing the parties to keep use of bar table motions 'to a minimum'); *Taylor* Admissibility Interlocutory Appeal, *supra* note 13, paras. 30, 42, & p. 15 (holding that 'documentary evidence, by its very nature, is tendered *in lieu* of oral testimony', so a document tendered without a witness must satisfy the requirements of SCSL Rule 92 *bis*); see also *supra* Section 9.2.1.1 (discussing this rule).

document to such a witness is [not only] relevant to the exercise of the Chamber's discretion to admit the document [but is also] likely to limit the value of the document in evidence.[132]

In addition, documents that support or are cited in witness statements submitted in lieu of oral testimony are routinely admitted into evidence.[133]

9.2.3 Judicial notice and uncontested facts

Judges at each tribunal must take judicial notice – that is, cannot require proof – of 'facts of common knowledge'.[134] As in many domestic jurisdictions, this rule promotes judicial efficiency by avoiding time-consuming efforts by the parties to prove 'notorious' and undisputed facts, such as basic scientific precepts, or geographic or historical facts,[135] which are 'so ... clearly established or susceptible to determination by reference to readily obtainable and authoritative sources that evidence of their existence is unnecessary'.[136] The ICC Rules go one step further, and expressly authorise chambers to consider a factual allegation contained in a charging document, an item of documentary evidence, or anticipated witness testimony as proved, if the prosecution and defence agree that the fact is uncontested.[137] As of 1 December 2009, however, it appears that no ICC chamber had yet taken judicial notice of any fact.

[132] *Prosecutor* v. *Đorđević*, Case No. IT-05-87/1-T, Decision on Prosecution's Motion to Re-Open the Case and Exceed the Word Limit and Second Motion to Admit Exhibits from the Bar Table, 7 December 2009, para. 5.

[133] See, e.g., *Prosecutor* v. *Stanišić and Simatović*, Case No. IT-03-69-T, Decision on Prosecution's Motion for the Admission of Written Evidence of Witness Slobodan Lazarević Pursuant to Rule 92 *ter* with Confidential Annex, 16 May 2008, para. 24 (exhibits that accompany a witness statement, and which 'form an inseparable and indispensable part of the evidence of the witness', may be admitted). Submission of written witness evidence in lieu of oral testimony is discussed in Section 9.2.1.1, *supra*.

[134] Rome Statute, Art. 69(6); ICTY Rule 94(A); ICTR Rule 94(A); SCSL Rule 94(A). On the mandatory nature of this direction in the governing instruments, see, e.g., *Prosecutor* v. *Karemera, Ngirumpatse, and Nzirorera*, Case No. ICTR-98-44-AR73(C), Decision on Prosecutor's Interlocutory Appeal of Decision on Judicial Notice, 16 June 2006 ('*Karemera et al.* Judicial Notice Appeal Decision'), para. 23 (holding that if trial chamber has determined that fact is common knowledge, it has no discretion to nevertheless require that proof be led).

[135] *Prosecutor* v. *Slobodan Milošević*, Case No. IT-02-54-AR73.5, Decision on the Prosecution's Interlocutory Appeal Against the Trial Chamber's 10 April 2003 Decision on Prosecution Motion for Judicial Notice of Adjudicated Facts, 28 October 2003 ('*Milošević* Judicial Notice Decision'), p. 4; accord *Semanza* Appeal Judgement, *supra* note 126, para. 194 (describing these facts as 'not only widely known but also beyond reasonable dispute').

[136] *Prosecutor* v. *Semanza*, Case No. ICTR-97-20-T, Decision on the Prosecutor's Motion for Judicial Notice and Presumption of Facts Pursuant to Rules 94 and 54, 3 May 2000 ('*Semanza* Judicial Notice Decision'), para. 4; accord *Prosecutor* v. *Popović, Beara, Nikolić, Borovčanin, Miletić, Gvero, and Pandurević*, Case No. IT-05-88-T, Decision on Prosecution Motion for Judicial Notice of Facts of Common Knowledge Pursuant to Rule 94(A), 26 September 2006, para. 13. See also *ibid.*, para. 15 (holding that, to be judicially noticed, facts of common knowledge must be 'sufficiently well defined ... that the accuracy of their application to the described situation is not reasonably in doubt') (quoting *Karemera et al.* Judicial Notice Appeal Decision, *supra* note 134, para. 29).

[137] ICC Rule 69 (noting, however, that the chamber need not accept the fact as proved if it 'is of the opinion that a more complete presentation of the alleged facts is required in the interests of justice, in particular the interests of the victims'). Although not featured in their Rules, *ad hoc* Tribunal chambers may also accept facts that are uncontested. See, e.g., *Milutinović et al.* Trial Judgement, *supra* note 16, Vol. I, para. 61.

After nine years of fact-finding by chambers at both the trial and appellate level, the ICTR took judicial notice of the commonly known fact that genocide against the Tutsi population in Rwanda occurred in 1994.[138] At the SCSL, the determination that an armed conflict took place in Sierra Leone was reached by the Appeals Chamber less than a year after the first trial began,[139] because as that Chamber noted, the existence of an armed conflict as brutal as that in Sierra Leone is 'a notorious fact of history' that 'cannot be subject to reasonable dispute' in a court seated in that country.[140] It is less clear, however, that the ICTR's conclusion on genocide was an appropriate exercise of the power to judicially notice *facts*, as the occurrence of genocide requires a quintessentially legal inquiry into the mental states of those involved in the commission of the underlying offences.[141]

The ICTY, ICTR, and SCSL Rules also permit chambers to take judicial notice of 'adjudicated facts or documentary evidence from other proceedings' of the respective tribunal 'relating to the matter at issue in the current proceedings'.[142] The *ad hoc* Tribunals' Appeals Chambers have concluded, however, that taking judicial notice of such facts merely 'establishes a well-founded presumption for the accuracy of this fact', which need not then be proved at trial, but which may nevertheless be challenged by the opposing party.[143] As a result, these Tribunals have asserted that judicial notice of an adjudicated fact will lift the prosecution's initial burden of production – that is, its responsibility to adduce evidence in support of a factual allegation – but will not affect its ultimate burden of persuasion of guilt beyond a reasonable doubt, and the defence may challenge the noticed fact 'by introducing reliable and credible evidence to the contrary'.[144]

[138] *Karemera et al.* Judicial Notice Appeal Decision, *supra* note 134, para. 35 ('The fact of the Rwandan genocide is a part of world history, a fact as certain as any other, a classic instance of a "fact of common knowledge."'). The first case to be tried by the ICTR, *Prosecutor* v. *Akayesu*, began hearings in 1997.

[139] *CDF* Case, Case No. SCSL-2004-14-AR73, Fofana – Decision on Appeal Against 'Decision on Prosecution's Motion for Judicial Notice and Admission of Evidence', 16 May 2005 ('*CDF* Judicial Notice Appeal Decision'), paras. 36–40. See also Second Annual Report of the President of the Special Court for Sierra Leone, www.sc-sl.org/LinkClick.aspx?fileticket=pmp4ckQZ098%3d&tabid=176, p. 5 (reporting that this case was the first trial before the SCSL, and began in June 2004).

[140] *CDF* Judicial Notice Appeal Decision, *supra* note 139, para. 37 (relying on ICTR case law holding that common knowledge may include facts that are generally known within a tribunal's territorial jurisdiction) (citing *Semanza* Judicial Notice Decision, *supra* note 136, para. 24).

[141] See generally Boas, Bischoff, and Reid, *Elements of Crimes*, *supra* note 19, ch. 3, Section 3.2.1 (reviewing the general requirements that qualify an underlying offence as genocide, including the specific intent to partially or totally destroy a distinct group that is objectively defined on the basis of nationality, ethnicity, race, or religion).

[142] ICTY Rule 94(B); ICTR Rule 94(B); SCSL Rule 94(B).

[143] *Prosecutor* v. *Momir Nikolić*, Case No. IT-02-60/1-A, Decision on Appellant's Motion for Judicial Notice, 1 April 2005, para. 11 (citing *Milošević* Judicial Notice Decision, *supra* note 135, p. 4); *Karemera, Ngirumpatse, and Nzirorera* v. *Prosecutor*, Case No. ICTR-98-44-AR73.17, Decision on Joseph Nzirorera's Appeal of Decision on Admission of Evidence Rebutting Adjudicated Facts, 29 May 2009, para. 13.

[144] *Karemera et al.* Judicial Notice Appeal Decision, *supra* note 134, para. 42. But see *infra* text accompanying notes 161–165 (questioning whether this test in fact imposes a burden of persuasion on the accused).

The test for judicial notice of adjudicated facts at the ICTY involves consideration of several factors developed in the case law of that Tribunal, and is comprised of two stages.[145] First, the chamber determines whether the proffered fact is potentially admissible: it must be (1) discrete, concrete, and identifiable;[146] (2) relevant to the case before the chamber considering the motion; (3) actually a fact, in that it cannot include legal conclusions or characterisations; (4) actually adjudicated, in that it cannot be based on a plea agreement or agreement between the parties in the previous proceeding; and (5) finally adjudicated, in that it was either not contested on appeal, or was finally established on appeal.[147] Moreover, the fact as formulated in the moving party's application cannot (6) relate to the accused's conduct or mental state; or (7) differ in any significant respect from the manner in which the fact was expressed as adjudicated in the previous proceeding.[148] Second, even if the putative adjudicated fact satisfies these criteria, chambers retain discretion to deny the motion if granting judicial notice would be contrary to the interests of justice, such as when it infringes an accused's right to a fair trial.[149] ICTR decisions on adjudicated facts apply some or all of these factors, and similarly emphasise the trial chamber's discretion.[150] It is unclear whether and to what extent the *ad hoc* Tribunals' case law on adjudicated facts will influence ICC proceedings, as the governing instruments of that Court do not make explicit provision for this form of judicial notice.

In explaining its decision to exercise its discretion not to notice several facts, even though they satisfied the criteria for admission, the *Popović* Trial Chamber

[145] *Prosecutor* v. *Popović, Beara, Nikolić, Borovčanin, Miletić, Gvero, and Pandurević*, Case No. IT-05-88-T, Decision on Prosecution Motion for Judicial Notice of Adjudicated Facts, 26 September 2006 ('*Popović et al.* Adjudicated Facts Decision'), para. 4.

[146] See *Prosecutor* v. *Stanišić and Simatović*, Case No. IT-03-69-T, Decision on Prosecution's Motion for Judicial Notice of Adjudicated Facts, 25 November 2009 ('*Stanišić and Simatović* Adjudicated Facts Decision'), paras. 26, 32 (noting that to satisfy this criterion, the proffered fact cannot be vague or unclear, but must be comprehensible in the context in which it is offered); *Popović et al.* Adjudicated Facts Decision, *supra* note 145, para. 6 (holding that a chamber 'must deny judicial notice where a purported [adjudicated] fact is inextricably commingled either with other facts that do not themselves fulfil the requirements for judicial notice … or with other accessory facts that serve to obscure the principal fact'); *ibid.*, para. 9 (the fact must be identified with sufficient precision by the moving party).

[147] *Stanišić and Simatović* Adjudicated Facts Decision, *supra* note 146, para. 27 (collecting decisions, including *Popović et al.* Adjudicated Facts Decision, *supra* note 145).

[148] *Popović et al.* Adjudicated Facts Decision, *supra* note 145, para. 7 (considering that minor inaccuracies or ambiguities may be corrected by a chamber on its own initiative).

[149] *Ibid.*, para. 4; accord, e.g., *Prosecutor* v. *Krajišnik*, Case No. IT-00-39-T, Decision on Third and Fourth Prosecution Motion for Judicial Notice of Adjudicated Facts, 24 March 2005, para. 12; *Karemera et al.* Judicial Notice Appeal Decision, *supra* note 134, para. 39.

[150] See, e.g., *Prosecutor* v. *Bizimungu, Mugenzi, Bicamumpaka, and Mugiraneza*, Case No. ICTR-99-50-T, Decision on the Prosecutor's Motion and Notice of Adjudicated Facts, 10 December 2004, paras. 10–14 (citing factors and noting ICTR precedents); *Prosecutor* v. *Karemera, Ngirumpatse, and Nzirorera*, Case No. ICTR-98-44-T, Decision on Joseph Nziorera's Motion for Judicial Notice of Adjudicated Facts: Bagosora Judgement, 20 May 2009, para. 3 (noting that both *ad hoc* Tribunals require that the fact not be subject to, or have been reversed on, appeal; and deciding the motion on that basis alone).

highlighted three additional considerations that have informed prior and subsequent decisions.[151] First, the Chamber considered whether judicial notice would actually promote judicial economy, and denied the prosecution's request to notice facts that were 'unduly broad, vague, tendentious, or conclusory', because of the possibility that attempts at rebuttal by the accused could consume excessive time and resources.[152] Second, the Trial Chamber denied judicial notice to proposed adjudicated facts where different trial judgements reached fundamentally inconsistent conclusions on the same subject, and considered an inconsistency as fundamental 'where the respective factual findings in the relevant original judgements cannot both be reasonably regarded as true'.[153] Third, the Chamber assessed whether the proposed adjudicated fact went to 'issues which are at the core of this case', and thus could not be judicially noticed without adversely affecting the accused's right to a fair and public trial.[154]

At the ICTY, where several cases arise out of the same conflicts or alleged criminal transactions, it is relatively rare for parties to seek judicial notice on the ground that a particular fact constitutes common knowledge, but chambers have frequently taken judicial notice of facts found in previous trials and appeals. For example, the *Stanišić and Simatović* Trial Chamber took judicial notice of hundreds of facts regarding the conflict in Bosnia and Herzegovina, including scores of facts relevant to the specific crime-base sites of Bosanski Šamac and Srebrenica, which had been established in the *Blagojević and Jokić*, *Brđanin*, *Čelebići*, *Krstić*, *Kvočka*, *Stakić*, *Strugar*, *Simić*, and *Tadić* trials;[155] and the *Perišić* Trial Chamber accepted hundreds of facts from the Trial Judgement in the *Galić* case, which had also focused on crimes committed during the siege of Sarajevo.[156]

[151] See, e.g., *Prosecutor* v. *Tolimir*, Case No. IT-05-88/2-PT, Decision on Prosecution Motion for Judicial Notice of Adjudicated Facts Pursuant to Rule 94(B), 17 December 2009, paras. 32–33; *Prosecutor* v. *Karadžić*, Case No. IT-95-5/18-PT, Decision on First Prosecution Motion for Judicial Notice of Adjudicated Facts, 5 June 2009, para. 35.

[152] *Popović et al.* Adjudicated Facts Decision, *supra* note 145, para. 16.

[153] *Ibid.*, para. 17 & n. 61 (explaining that 'a discrepancy between a specified number of victims listed in the factual findings of two or more judgements' is just such 'a fundamental inconsistency justifying the denial of judicial notice'; and citing inconsistent findings on the number of victims in a particular location in the *Krstić* and *Blagojević and Jokić* Trial Judgements, respectively).

[154] *Ibid.*, para. 19 & n. 64 (declining to notice dozens of facts on this basis, including previous chambers' findings relating to the conduct of forces under the alleged command and control of the accused, such as conduct of the Zvornik Brigade, and the responsibility of the Drina Corps command for the conduct of other forces in their area of operations).

[155] *Stanišić and Simatović* Adjudicated Facts Decision, *supra* note 146, para. 92 (referring to facts set out in the annex to the prosecution's motion).

[156] See, e.g., *Prosecutor* v. *Perišić*, Case No. IT-04-81-PT, Decision on Prosecution's Motion for Judicial Notice of Adjudicated Facts Concerning Sarajevo, 26 June 2008, p. 14 (referring to facts set out in the annex to the prosecution's motion, and taking judicial notice of facts relating to historical background, presence and activities of armed forces in Sarajevo between 1992 and 1994, sniping and shelling incidents during the same period, and injuries and deaths caused by such sniping and shelling).

As in the context of witness testimony, the prohibition on taking judicial notice of facts relating to the conduct and mental state of the accused is grounded in the right of confrontation.[157] In addition, as the *Popović* Trial Chamber noted, factual findings from other trials 'bearing on the acts, conduct, and mental state of a person not on trial before it' may not be reliable evidence for the purpose of ascertaining guilt or innocence, because the interests of the accused in the different trials may not be aligned, or may in fact be adverse to each other.[158] Here too, the ICTY exclusion is narrowly tailored, and focuses on 'the conduct of the accused fulfilling the physical and mental elements of the form [or forms] of responsibility through which he or she is charged with responsibility'; it does not include the conduct of others for whom the accused is alleged to be responsible, such as subordinates, co-participants in a joint criminal enterprise, or those whom the prosecution contends the accused aided and abetted in their criminal conduct.[159]

The practice of the *ad hoc* Tribunals – particularly the ICTY – in respect of adjudicated facts illustrates how a focus on expeditiousness, and an inattention to possible consequences of developments in the jurisprudence, may impose undue burdens on the defence.[160] Consonant with its purpose of promoting judicial economy, the Rule was first interpreted and applied as permitting only the admission of facts that were not subject to reasonable dispute, and thus need not be proved or disproved at trial.[161] By approving and adopting the 'rebuttable presumption' approach discussed above,[162] however, the majority of the ICTY Appeals Chamber in the *Milošević* decision effectively shifted the burden of persuasion to the accused, by requiring the defence to adduce evidence to disprove the 'presumed' fact offered by the prosecution.[163] Combined with the recent practice of imposing time limits on the parties for the presentation of evidence and argument,[164] this approach to

157 See *supra* Section 9.2.1.1, note 101 and accompanying text (discussing 'acts and conduct' of the accused). Decisions in the contexts of written witness evidence and judicial notice of adjudicated facts generally apply the same standards when determining which alleged acts, omissions, or mental states qualify as 'acts and conduct' of the accused. See *Popović et al.* Accused Interview Decision, *supra* note 63, para. 71.

158 *Popović et al.* Adjudicated Facts Decision, *supra* note 145, para. 12 (observing that the accused in the earlier trial 'may have had significantly less incentive to contest those facts, or may indeed have expressed agreement with them in an attempt to allow the blame to fall on someone else').

159 *Ibid.*, para. 13 & nn. 45–47 (rejecting accused's arguments that the facts in question related to conduct and mental state of subordinates and an alleged fellow participant in a joint criminal enterprise, and finding that Bosnian Muslim refugees' subjection to a terror campaign 'upon the arrival of Serb forces in Potočari' should be admitted as an adjudicated fact).

160 See generally O'Sullivan and Montgomery, *supra* note 89. See also *supra* note 113 (citing commentators noting that although the rule is facially neutral and available to both sides, the prosecution is far more likely to invoke it to relieve part of its burden of production).

161 See Gideon Boas, *The Milošević Trial: Lessons for the Conduct of Complex International Criminal Proceedings* (2007), p. 50 (explaining that this approach prevailed until February 2003).

162 See *supra* text accompanying notes 143–144.

163 See *Milošević* Judicial Notice Decision, *supra* note 135, Dissenting Opinion of Judge David Hunt, paras. 7–9.

164 See Chapter 6, Section 6.6.2.

adjudicated facts means that the defence must weigh using its limited time and resources for rebuttal against the certainty that failure to challenge possibly crucial facts will result in acceptance of their accuracy and reliability by the trial chamber. It is regrettable that more trial chambers have not exercised their discretion ina manner that could moderate these potential adverse consequences, such as the *Popović* Trial Chamber's refusal to notice facts that relate to the core issues in the case, or which would require extensive and time-consuming rebuttal efforts by the accused.[165]

9.3 Privileges

The governing instruments and jurisprudence of the international criminal tribunals recognise several evidentiary privileges. As in domestic jurisdictions, these rights or exemptions from disclosure of information in legal proceedings can apply to verbal and written communications as well as other documents. In the context of international criminal practice, however, certain of these privileges are largely or exclusively invoked when an individual is called to testify as a live witness, so the law governing whether they can resist disclosure of the information sought by a party or the court is typically framed as a matter of testimonial privilege.

9.3.1 Professional privileges

All the international criminal tribunals confer specific protection on communications or other information disclosed in the context of certain professional relationships. The ICC Rules go the furthest, and not only expressly recognise a privilege for communications between attorneys and clients, but also strongly encourage chambers to accord privileges for communications 'between a person and his or her medical doctor, psychiatrist, psychologist or counsellor', and 'between a person and a member of a religious clergy … made in the context of a sacred confession where it is an integral part of the practice of that religion'.[166] Moreover, the Rules empower ICC chambers to extend the protection of professional privilege to communications made in other contexts if a three-part test is met: (1) the communication must be made 'in the course of a confidential relationship producing a reasonable expectation of privacy and non-disclosure'; (2) '[c]onfidentiality' must be 'essential to the nature and type of relationship

[165] See *supra* text accompanying notes 151–154.

[166] ICC Rule 73(3) (directing chambers to 'give particular regard to recognizing [such communications] as privileged'); see also *Prosecutor* v. *Lubanga*, Doc. No. ICC-01/04-01/06-2165, Prosecution's Submission on the Production of Medical Records, 15 October 2009, para. 4 (noting that '[t]he Rules do not *definitively* declare that any other specified professional or confidential relationships create privileges') (emphasis added).

between the person and the confidant'; and (3) '[r]ecognition of the privilege would further the objectives of the Statute and the Rules'.[167] As of 1 December 2009, no chamber of the ICC had yet exercised its authority to recognise other professional privileges.

While the corresponding provisions in the respective Rules of the ICTY, ICTR, and SCSL are not as extensive, each of those tribunals' Rules – like those of the ICC – explicitly provide that communications between attorneys and their clients are privileged and exempt from disclosure, unless the client consents to such disclosure, or the witness through whom the communication is offered as evidence is a third party to whom the communication was disclosed.[168] This privilege is in keeping with the right of an accused, grounded in international human rights law and enshrined in all of the tribunals' statutes, 'to communicate with counsel of his or her choosing'[169] – a link that is made manifest in the relevant provision in the Rome Statute, which frames the right as one of 'communicati[ng] freely' and 'in confidence' with counsel of the accused's choice.[170] In addition to the specified exceptions that are common to the tribunals' respective rules, which all provide that the privilege is waived by the client's consent or disclosure to and by a third party, the SCSL Rules also explicitly note that an allegation of ineffective assistance of counsel by the accused waives the privilege as to all communications relevant to that allegation.[171]

Unlike the law on privilege in certain domestic jurisdictions, which may require that the communication be made for the purpose of seeking or providing legal advice to be shielded from disclosure,[172] both the terms of the relevant rules and the

[167] ICC Rule 73(2).

[168] See generally ICC Rule 73(1) (requiring written consent by a client for the first form of waiver); ICTY Rule 97; ICTR Rule 97; SCSL Rule 97. Neither the plain text of the rule at the *ad hoc* Tribunals and SCSL, nor subsequent practice, requires that the client's consent to disclosure be in writing. See, e.g., *Prosecutor* v. *Krajišnik*, Case No. IT-00-39-A, Decision on Momćilo Krajišnik's Motion to Present Additional Evidence and to Call Additional Witnesses Pursuant to Rule 115 and to Reconsider Decision Not to Call Former Counsel, 6 November 2008 ('*Krajišnik* Counsel Appeal Decision'), para. 28 (noting that, if former counsel were called to testify, accused would be present in court to waive privilege during the hearing). The tribunals' rules on disclosure also provide protection for attorney work product. See Chapter 6, Section 6.5.1.4.

[169] ICTY Statute, Art. 21(4)(b); ICTR Statute, Art. 17; SCSL Statute, Art. 17(4)(b).

[170] Rome Statute, Art. 67(1)(b); see also *Prosecutor* v. *Gotovina, Čermak, and Markač*, Case No. IT-06-90-T, Decision on Requests for Temporary Restraining Orders Directed to the Republic of Croatia and Reasons for the Chamber's Order of 11 December 2009, 18 December 2009 ('*Gotovina et al.* TRO Decision'), para. 16 (observing that '[t]his privilege is central to the functioning of the defence of an accused').

[171] SCSL Rule 97(iii). But see *Krajišnik* Counsel Appeal Decision, *supra* note 168, para. 28 (in the absence of similar provision in ICTY Rules, ICTY Appeals Chamber rejecting prosecution argument that accused had waived privilege by asserting ineffective assistance of counsel). The relevant ICTR rule also varies slightly from the provisions in the instruments of other tribunals. In the wake of several instances of fee-splitting between appointed counsel and accused – where counsel funnelled a portion of the remuneration provided by the Registry to the accused – ICTR Rule 97 was amended to expressly provide that the confidentiality of attorney-client communications cannot be used to shield this practice. See, e.g., Statement by the Registrar, Mr. Adama Dieng, on Allegations of Fee Splitting Between a Detainee of the ICTR and His Defence Counsel, UN Doc. ICTR/INFO-9-3-06.EN, 29 October 2001 (discussing allegations arising in *Prosecutor* v. *Nzirorera*). On fee-splitting, see Chapter 5, Section 5.2.6.

[172] See, e.g., *Restatement (Third) of the Law Governing Lawyers* § 68(4) (2009) (reflecting the law in most U.S. jurisdictions and requiring that communication be made 'for the purpose of obtaining or providing legal

manner in which they have been applied suggest that the attorney–client privilege at the tribunals attaches by virtue of the context in which the communication is made or information provided, and does not depend on the nature or specific content of the communication or information.[173]

9.3.2 Testimonial privileges

There are generally three circumstances in which the international criminal tribunals permit an individual to invoke a legal right not to disclose information in the course of examination by a party or the court at trial, or not to appear as a witness at all. The tribunals have recognised (1) a privilege against compelled self-incrimination (and, at the ICC, incrimination of family members); (2) a qualified privilege against disclosure of the work product of war correspondents (and, at the SCSL, identities of those who facilitate the correspondents' work); and (3) a privilege specifically accorded to the International Committee of the Red Cross ('ICRC').[174] Each of these privileges is discussed below.

9.3.2.1 Compelled incrimination

The Rules of each of the tribunals provide that an individual testifying before a chamber may decline to answer a question if the testimony might incriminate the witness.[175] Though these provisions also authorise chambers to require the witness to answer, testimony thus compelled may not be used against the witness in a

assistance for the client'); Bankim Thanki, *The Law of Privilege* (2006), p. 34 ('[L]egal advice privilege' under English law 'attaches to "all communications made in confidence between solicitors and their clients for the purpose of giving or obtaining legal advice even at a stage where litigation is not in contemplation"') (quoting *Three Rivers District Council* v. *Governor and Company of the Bank of England*, [2004] UKHL 48 at para. 50 (per Lord Roger)); Evidence Act 1995 (Australia), Section 118 (Australian federal law requiring that the communication be made 'for the dominant purpose of … providing legal advice to the client').

[173] See, e.g., *Gotovina et al.* TRO Decision, *supra* note 170, para. 16 (holding that ICTY Rule 97 'enshrines the principle that *all* communications between lawyer and client are privileged') (emphasis added); ICC Rule 73 (referring repeatedly to the context in which the communication is made). See also Piragoff, *supra* note 70, p. 360 (noting that during the negotiation and drafting of the Rome Statute, a proposal to include an explicit limitation of the privilege to communications made for the purpose of legal advice was rejected in favour of the phrase 'communications made in the context of the professional relationship', in an effort to 'subtly enable the Court not to recognize a privilege if the communication was outside [these] bounds', that is, 'not made for the purpose of giving or receiving legal advice').

[174] In addition to these privileges, the tribunals have also held that an interpreter employed by a tribunal could not be compelled to testify on behalf of a party, and that a human rights worker could withhold the names of confidential sources. See, respectively, *Prosecutor* v. *Delalić, Mucić, Delić, and Landžo*, Case No. IT-96-21-T, Decision on the Motion Ex Parte by the Defence of Zdravko Mucić Concerning the Issue of a Subpoena to an Interpreter, 8 July 1997; *AFRC* Case, Case No. SCSL-04-16-AR73, Decision on Prosecution Appeal Against Decision on Oral Application for Witness TF1–150 to Testify Without Being Compelled to Answer Questions on Grounds of Confidentiality, 26 May 2006.

[175] ICC Rule 74(3)(a) ('A witness may object to making any statement that might tend to incriminate him or her.'); ICTY Rule 90(E) (same, except replacing the phrase 'him or her' with 'the witness'); ICTR Rule 90(E) (similar, but noting that the witness 'may refuse' to make any potentially incriminating statement); SCSL Rule 90(E) (identical to ICTR provision). See also Chapter 7, text accompanying notes 167–171 (discussing this privilege with regard to the accused).

prosecution for any offence other than false testimony.[176] Of course, the chamber may conclude, after hearing the party seeking to lead the evidence, that it is not necessary to compel the witness to answer.[177]

The ICC procedure with regard to this privilege is especially detailed. The witness, the prosecution, or the defence can inform the chamber that the witness's testimony may raise an issue of self-incrimination.[178] Before a chamber may compel a witness to provide the testimony, it must consider '(a) [t]he importance of the anticipated evidence; (b) [w]hether the witness would be providing unique evidence; (c) [t]he nature of the possible incrimination, if known; and (d) [t]he sufficiency of the protections for the witness, in the particular circumstances';[179] and may require the witness to answer only if it assures him or her that the testimony will be kept confidential and will not be used in a subsequent prosecution by the Court.[180] Before the chamber offers those assurances, however, it must seek the views of the prosecution in an *ex parte* consultation.[181] Finally, to give effect to the assurances, the chamber must order a series of protective measures such as *in camera* proceedings, sealing orders, and the use of a pseudonym.[182]

In addition to these explicit procedural safeguards for the privilege against compelled self-incrimination, the ICC Rules also recognise a privilege against incrimination of an accused by a close relative, and provide that a witness 'who is a spouse, child or parent of an accused person, shall not be required by a Chamber to make any statement that might tend to incriminate that accused person'.[183] The Rules limit the potential benefit of this privilege, however, by apparently authorising the chamber to draw an adverse inference from the witness's testimony – the chamber 'may take into account that the witness ... objected to reply to a question which was intended to contradict a previous statement made by the witness, or the witness was selective in choosing which questions to answer'.[184]

9.3.2.2 War correspondents

Much of what the general public knows about the conflicts that have given rise to the cases brought before these international tribunals, including the allegations of criminal conduct that ground the prosecution's charges, is due to the work of local and foreign journalists reporting from conflict zones. In certain cases, therefore,

[176] See ICC Rule 74(3)(c)(ii); ICTY Rule 90(E); ICTR Rule 90(E); SCSL Rule 90(E).

[177] See, e.g., *Prosecutor* v. *Perišić*, Case No. IT-04-81-T, Transcript, 30 June 2009, pp. 7654–7660 (permitting the witness to invoke Rule 90(E) and refuse to answer a question on the ground that it may incriminate him).

[178] ICC Rule 74(8), (9).

[179] ICC Rule 74(5). [180] ICC Rule 74(2), (3). [181] ICC Rule 74(4).

[182] ICC Rule 74(7). Protective measures are discussed in Chapter 7, Section 7.4.2.

[183] ICC Rule 75. [184] *Ibid.*

these war correspondents – who were on the ground and talking to victims, witnesses, and alleged perpetrators well in advance of any tribunal investigators – may have information that the parties to the eventual criminal case do not. Frequently, the more sensitive the information, the more likely it was provided to the correspondent in confidence, on the understanding that its source would not be publicly disclosed. As in domestic jurisdictions, the question of whether journalists can be compelled to disclose their sources (or the unpublished information provided by such sources) in international proceedings lays bare tensions between the rights to information and freedom of the press, the unique role of the media in uncovering and publicising matters of great concern, and the truth-seeking function of a criminal trial.

This question has arisen at least twice in the international criminal tribunals, and has twice been resolved by recognising a qualified privilege that affords significant protection to those who provide information and other support to war correspondents. In 2002, the ICTY Appeals Chamber held, in an interlocutory appeal in the *Brđanin* case, that a trial chamber could issue a subpoena to a war correspondent only if a two-part test were satisfied: the evidence sought by the subpoena (1) must be of 'direct and important value in determining a core issue in the case', and (2) must not be reasonably obtainable elsewhere.[185] In short, compelling production or testimony from a war correspondent must be the last resort, and should only be used when the potential value of the facts thus adduced merits the risk that the disclosure will have a chilling effect on the ability of such journalists to obtain information and inform the public.[186] The Appeals Chamber placed particular emphasis on the unique position of war correspondents – as distinct from other journalists – and concluded that the need for protection was 'particularly clear and weighty in the case of war correspondents' because of their role in 'keeping the international public informed about matters of life and death'.[187]

Seven years later, the SCSL was confronted with a slightly different question, which arose in the context of testimony by a Liberian war correspondent in the *Taylor* case: should any privilege be recognised that would permit the witness to withhold the name or other identifying information of an individual who did not provide him with information, but rather facilitated his work by helping him enter Sierra Leone? The *Taylor* Trial Chamber adopted the reasoning and test set forth in the *Brđanin* decision, and concluded that the privilege was not limited

[185] *Prosecutor* v. *Brđanin*, Case No. IT-99-36-AR73.9, Decision on Interlocutory Appeal, 11 December 2002 ('*Brđanin* Privilege Appeal Decision'), para. 50. The journalist in question was Jonathan Randal, a correspondent for the *Washington Post*.

[186] See *ibid*., paras. 45–50.

[187] *Ibid*., para. 36. See also *ibid*., paras. 29, 36, 39–40 (noting the impact of images of detainees in Bosnian camps 'in awakening the international community to the seriousness of the human rights situation during the conflict in Bosnia Herzegovina').

to sources, but extended to facilitators, because no principled distinction can be drawn 'between a "facilitator" and a "source"[;] both types of persons assist journalists in producing information which might otherwise remain uncovered', that is, unknown.[188]

Contrary to domestic approaches to journalistic privilege, which tend to restrict the scope of any protection to information for which confidentiality was expressly promised,[189] neither the *Brđanin* nor *Taylor* decisions placed any weight on whether the information or assistance was provided in confidence.[190] In fact, the information at issue in *Brđanin* was an interview between the correspondent and the accused, in the presence of another journalist, and for the purpose of obtaining 'on the record' statements for an article that was later published.[191] In practice, therefore, the international criminal tribunals likely provide greater protection for journalistic sources and work product – at least for war correspondents – than is presently afforded in most national jurisdictions.

9.3.2.3 International Committee of the Red Cross

By virtue of the ICRC's unparalleled access to conflict zones and detention facilities, its representatives frequently have uncommon knowledge of the facts underlying the charges in international criminal proceedings. Unlike the qualified privilege conferred upon war correspondents, however, the ICTY and the drafters of the Rome Statute concluded that an absolute privilege against testimony or production of documentary evidence is necessary to protect the ability of the ICRC to carry out its mandate.[192]

188 *Prosecutor* v. *Taylor*, Case No. SCSL-2003-01-T, Decision on the Defence Motion for the Disclosure of the Identity of a Confidential 'Source' Raised During Cross-Examination of TF1–355, 6 March 2009, para. 25.

189 See, e.g., Privacy International, 'Silencing Sources: An International Survey of Protections and Threats to Journalists' Sources', November 2007, www.privacyinternational.org/article.shtml?cmd%5B347%5D=x-347–558384 (noting that over 100 countries have adopted laws protecting journalists' confidential sources); Committee of Ministers of the Council of Europe, 'Recommendation No. R (2000) 7 of the Committee of Ministers to Member States on the Right of Journalists Not to Disclose Their Sources of Information', 8 March 2000, available at https://wcd.coe.int/ViewDoc.jsp?id=342907&Site=CM (relevant to disclosure of identifying information of sources).

190 See Erik Bierbauer and Rebecca Jenkin, 'A Growing Distance Between The Hague and Strasbourg? An International Criminal Tribunal and the European Court of Human Rights Reach Different Results in Two Reporter's Privilege Cases', *MLRC MediaLawLetter*, September 2009 (on file with authors), pp. 135–136, 139.

191 See *Brđanin* Privilege Appeal Decision, *supra* note 185, paras. 3–9.

192 See, e.g., Gabor Rona, 'The ICRC Privilege Not to Testify: Confidentiality in Action', 28 February 2004, available at www.icrc.org/web/eng/siteeng0.nsf/html/5WSD9Q ('No other organizations, whether non-governmental, like Médecins sans Frontières (MSF), or intergovernmental, like UNHCR, were granted this privilege [by the ICC Rules]. The extraordinary treatment accorded to the ICRC reflects the appreciation of States for its unique status and role in the world.'). See also *Prosecutor* v. *Muvunyi*, Case No. ICTR-2000-55A-T, Reasons for the Chamber's Decision on the Accused's Motion to Exclude Witness TQ, 15 July 2005, para. 16 ('While international law grants the ICRC the exceptional privilege of non-disclosure of information which is in the possession of its employees and which relates to [its] activities … such privilege is *not* granted to national Red Cross societies.') (emphasis in original).

This privilege was first recognised by judicial decision at the ICTY, when a majority of the *Simić* Pre-Trial Chamber ruled in 1999 that the ICRC had a right under customary international law to non-disclosure of information relating to activities undertaken by its officials and employees in the execution of its mandate to promote the application of international humanitarian law and protect and assist the victims of armed conflict.[193] In concluding that the privilege was both necessary to ensure the fulfilment of this mandate and cognisable as a limitation on the chamber's otherwise broad discretion to admit evidence,[194] the *Simić* majority placed particular emphasis on three factors: (1) the unique role and status of the ICRC as an independent humanitarian organisation with a mandate conferred upon it by the international community;[195] (2) the ICRC's consistent position of not testifying before courts 'as a consequence of the principles of … neutrality, impartiality and independence' that underlie its work;[196] and (3) the Chamber's acceptance of the ICRC's submissions that requiring ICRC representatives to testify about information gained in the course of their work 'would destroy the relationship of trust on which it relies to carry out its mandate'.[197] This single decision by the majority of a pre-trial bench has had an outsize influence on international criminal procedure: it appears to be the only decision at the *ad hoc* Tribunals or SCSL with any detailed assessment of the asserted ICRC privilege, and is therefore by default the leading authority on the question. Moreover, it arguably paved the way for recognition of a similar privilege in the ICC Rules adopted three years later.[198]

The ICC Rules that expressly confer the ICRC's evidentiary privilege provide that, unless the information is already publicly available or the ICRC waives its right to non-disclosure,

> [t]he Court shall regard as privileged … including by way of testimony of any present or past official or employee of the International Committee of the Red Cross (ICRC), any information, documents or other evidence which it came into the possession of in

[193] *Simić* Pre-Trial Privilege Decision, *supra* note 4, paras. 73–74 (concluding that the Geneva Conventions and the general practice of states under those treaties with regard to the ICRC established a customary international legal right against disclosure of such information); see also *ibid.*, paras. 46–47 (describing the ICRC's mandate); but see *ibid.*, Separate Opinion of Judge David Hunt (dissenting and arguing that the Chamber should have recognised only a qualified privilege). In his dissent, Judge Hunt questioned the majority's conclusion that customary international law requires recognition of an absolute privilege, and noted sceptically (and accurately) that 'it is an enormous step to assume' that states had ever contemplated an absolute immunity of the ICRC from giving evidence in international courts, particularly in light of the role of such courts in enforcing the Geneva Conventions. See *ibid.*, Separate Opinion of Judge David Hunt, paras. 20–23 (quotation at para. 23).

[194] See, e.g., *ibid.*, paras. 42, 73.

[195] See, e.g., *ibid.*, paras. 46, 72 & n. 56.

[196] *Ibid.*, para. 64. [197] *Ibid.*, para. 65.

[198] See Stéphane Jeannet, 'Testimony of ICRC Delegates Before the International Criminal Court', *International Review of the Red Cross*, No. 840, December 2000, available at www.icrc.org/web/eng/siteeng0.nsf/html/57JQTE (explaining that *Simić* 'set in motion a broader reflection within the ICRC regarding the confidentiality of information before international tribunals, and in particular the future International Criminal Court'; and outlining 'the ICRC's endeavours within the framework of the Preparatory Commission for the

the course, or as a consequence, of the performance by ICRC of its functions under the Statutes of the International Red Cross and Red Crescent Movement.[199]

Apparently recognising that there are circumstances in which the ICRC may have the best (or the only) evidence of criminal activity, the ICC Rules also outline a process whereby the Court may formally seek the consent of the ICRC to disclosure of the information.[200] A waiver of privilege by the ICRC need not, however, be express or written: although the Court must open consultations with the ICRC 'in order to seek to resolve the matter by cooperative means',[201] the onus then shifts to the ICRC, which must 'object in writing' to prevent disclosure of the information.[202] If the ICRC so objects, the plain terms of the Rule apply, and the privilege bars disclosure of the information, by testimony or otherwise.[203]

9.4 Conclusion

As created by the governing instruments of the international tribunals and developed by judicial decisions, the evidentiary regime in international criminal procedure comprises three basic precepts. First, trial judges have a broad and frequently exercised discretion to admit almost any evidence that they believe will assist them in reaching a fair and accurate verdict. Second, the very few restrictions that are imposed on this discretion reflect either attempts to protect the integrity of the proceedings, or the determination that particular individuals, activities, or relationships – such as victims of sexual violence, the work of war correspondents or the ICRC, or the attorney-client relationship – are especially deserving of legal protection that can outweigh even the interests that animate criminal trials. Third, to counteract the permissive approach to admissibility, trial judges are expected to critically assess all evidence in the record in the course of their deliberations on the merits, and to ensure that their conclusions as to whether the prosecution has met its burden of proof are fully supported by reliable evidence.

This area of the law is not free from controversy. First, the pressures of managing massive, high-profile trials under intense scrutiny from international bodies,

Establishment of an International Criminal Court ... to secure a provision protecting the confidentiality of the organization's information, and the results of those steps').

199 ICC Rule 73(4). See also ICC Rule 73(4)(b) (clarifying that the privilege is inapplicable if the 'information, documents or other evidence' have already been disclosed 'in public statements and documents of [the] ICRC'); ICC Rule 73(5) (clarifying that the privilege does not bar admission of the same evidence from another source if acquired 'independently of ICRC and its officials or employees').

200 ICC Rule 73(6) (providing that the chamber must first determine 'that ICRC information, documents or other evidence are of great importance for a particular case', and directing it to consider 'the circumstances of the case, the relevance of the evidence sought, whether the evidence could be obtained from a source other than ICRC, the interests of justice and of victims, and the performance of the Court's and ICRC's functions').

201 *Ibid.* 202 ICC Rule 73(4)(a).

203 See Rona, *supra* note 192 ('The ICRC ... retains the final say on release of its information.').

national governments, and the media have at times led to shortcuts focused on shortening the length of the proceedings – for example, through judicial decisions and regulatory amendments permitting the greatly expanded use of written witness evidence and adjudicated facts at the ICTY and ICTR. Second, the emphasis placed on ensuring the greatest flexibility for the trial chamber in determining what evidence may become part of the trial record, and potentially the basis for a finding of guilt, has caused some frustration among defence teams, who must trust that their objections and challenges will be considered during the *in camera* deliberations at the end of trial. As noted above, however, it is unlikely that chambers will consistently and exhaustively evaluate the varying levels of probative value and reliability of the thousands of exhibits and hundreds of witnesses through which evidence was adduced in the course of the trial. Finally, the procedural innovations that distinguish international criminal proceedings can also heighten the tension between the goals of fairness and expeditiousness in such trials, particularly where the modifications relax requirements that were originally intended to protect the rights of the accused. As with other procedural regimes discussed in this volume, the evidentiary law of the international criminal tribunals attempts to strike an appropriate balance between the demands of trial management and the goal of producing reasoned, persuasive, and well-founded judgements. It is not always successful.

10

Judgement and sentencing

CONTENTS

Trial chambers at the international criminal tribunals must accompany their verdict with a written judgement setting forth the judges' reasoning. Due to many factors, judgements at the international criminal tribunals have been notoriously lengthy.[1] These include, among others, the chamber's need to articulate factual findings in detail; the sprawling nature of the crime base in many cases; the accused's senior status and the consequent need to set forth analyses of large quantities of linkage evidence; the joinder of several accused into the same trial; and a tradition of lengthy judgements dating from the earliest ICTY and ICTR trials.[2] If the chamber convicts the accused and decides to impose a penalty of imprisonment, the judges also must set forth the reasons supporting the sentence in the same or a subsequent written judgement. For reasons discussed below, sentencing decisions at the international criminal tribunals, though guided by a large and detailed body of jurisprudence, have been unpredictable and sentences have been often astonishingly lenient considering the extreme gravity of the crimes.[3]

This chapter looks at judgement, sentences of imprisonment and other penalties, and post-conviction and post-acquittal procedures at the international criminal tribunals. Though occasional reference is made to internationalised tribunals other than the SCSL, the chapter's main focus is the ICTY, the ICTR, and the SCSL as the most influential internationalised tribunal; these three tribunals have handed down many judgements and sentences and have contributed the bulk of the law on judgement and sentencing. ICC procedures are also discussed, although as of 1 December 2009, no ICC chamber had yet rendered a final verdict in any case. In this chapter, since the relevant rules across the various tribunals are substantially similar in nature, we discuss them in tandem, rather than dedicating separate sections to each tribunal.[4] For convenience, as we have done elsewhere in this book,[5] we use the term 'judgement' throughout the chapter to refer to the trial chamber's final decision on guilt or innocence, even though the ICC uses the term

[1] Most judgements number between 200 and 400 pages. For a judgement whose extreme length was arguably justified by the Trial Chamber's need to address charges against six leaders, see *Prosecutor* v. *Milutinović, Šainović, Ojdanić, Pavković, Lazarević, and Lukić*, Case No. IT-05-87-T, Judgement, 26 February 2009 ('*Milutinović et al.* Trial Judgement') (four volumes; 1,743 pages with annexes). For another judgement whose remarkable length was arguably not justified, see *Prosecutor* v. *Hadžihasanović and Kubura*, Case No. IT-01-47-T, Judgement, 15 March 2006 ('*Hadžihasanović and Kubura* Trial Judgement') (two accused; 676 pages with annexes).

[2] See, e.g., *Prosecutor* v. *Delalić, Mucić, Delić, and Landžo*, Case No. IT-96-21-T, Judgement, 16 November 1998 ('*Čelebići* Trial Judgement') (452-page, 1291-paragraph judgement convicting three of four low-level accused of war crimes at a single prison camp during several months in 1992).

[3] See Gideon Boas, James L. Bischoff, and Natalie L. Reid, *Elements of Crimes Under International Law* (2008) ('Boas, Bischoff, and Reid, *Elements of Crimes*'), pp. 357–363; see also *infra* Section 10.2.4; text accompanying note 250.

[4] See Chapter 1, Section 1.3 (noting that some chapters discuss the tribunals in tandem, while others discuss them in separate subsections, mainly depending on whether their respective procedures differ significantly from one another).

[5] See Chapter 1, Section 1.3 (describing terminology used in this book).

'decision' for this document and reserves the term 'judgement' for written judicial pronouncements of the ICC Appeals Chamber.[6]

The chapter begins in Section 10.1 by examining the requirements for the judgement, including that the chamber give the reasons behind its findings and that any finding of guilt be supported by evidence satisfying a majority of the judges beyond a reasonable doubt. The section notes the law on concurrent and cumulative convictions, discussed in detail in Volumes I and II of this series, as well as separate and dissenting opinions and sentencing judgements. Section 10.2 explores sentencing at the international criminal tribunals, along with the factors chambers have used to arrive at the number of years the convicted person must spend in prison. It also recalls Volume II's discussion of the many criticisms of the tribunals' sentencing practice. Section 10.3 lists the additional punishments and penalties available to the chamber, including the imposition of a fine and reparations to victims, a topic explored more thoroughly in Chapter 8. Section 10.4 looks at the procedures that apply when an accused is convicted and must be transferred to a state to serve the sentence, or when an accused is acquitted and must be released or held pending appeal. Section 10.5 examines the rules on enforcement of the sentence in a national prison and possible release of the prisoner before the full term has elapsed, and Section 10.6 offers some concluding remarks on judgement and sentencing practice at the tribunals.

10.1 Judgement

The bulk of the jurisprudence on the requirements for the judgement relates to two matters: the obligation that the trial chamber explain the reasons for its factual findings and legal conclusions, and the requirement that the chamber be convinced of the accused's guilt beyond a reasonable doubt before entering a conviction. The subsections that follow address these and the other key aspects of the judgement and related procedures, and include a brief review of the law on concurrent and cumulative convictions.

10.1.1 Requirement of a reasoned, written judgement

The governing instruments of the international criminal tribunals direct the trial chamber, after deciding the verdict in private deliberations and pronouncing it in

[6] The Rome Statute confusingly uses the term 'decision' to refer both to the trial chamber's interlocutory decisions (on jurisdiction, evidence, and so forth), and to the document explaining the final verdict. See Rome Statute, Arts. 74, 81–82, 83(4). See also William A. Schabas, *An Introduction to the International Criminal Court* (3rd edn 2007), p. 301 (describing rejection of term 'judgement' at drafting conference in favour of more generic term 'decision', possibly to avoid association with particular national systems of criminal procedure).

public,[7] to issue a written judgement providing a statement of the chamber's factual finding and the reasoning supporting its legal holdings.[8] The requirement that the judgement be written serves at least two objectives: first, to make the judgement more accessible to the public and thus subject to more effective scrutiny;[9] and second, so that the parties and the Appeals Chamber may better follow the trial chamber's characterisation of the parties' arguments, evaluation of the evidence, reasoning, and legal conclusions, and better discern any error.[10] The judges draft the judgement in one of the tribunal's working languages: English or French for the ICTY, ICTR, and ICC; and English for the SCSL. At the ICTY and ICC, if the accused does not understand this language, the tribunal must translate the judgement into a language the accused understands.[11] In practice, the ICTY and ICTR also translate the judgement into the Tribunal's other working language, as the ICC likely will as well.

Unlike a common-law jury, the trial chamber as finder of fact must explain how it arrived at its factual findings.[12] In effecting this requirement, chambers have dedicated large segments of the judgement to factual analysis, typically with citations in the footnotes to the evidence containing the fact in question – such as the name or pseudonym of a witness and the transcript page containing her testimony; the exhibit number of a document; and an agreed or adjudicated fact.[13] The judges cannot venture beyond the facts and circumstances alleged in the indictment, and may only base their findings on the testimony and other materials previously admitted into evidence.[14]

The requirement of a reasoned judgement mandates that the trial chamber identify all the elements of the crimes and forms of responsibility charged in the

[7] On these procedures, see Chapter 7, Section 7.6.7; Chapter 10, Section 10.1.7.

[8] Rome Statute, Art. 74(5); ICTY Statute, Art. 23(2); ICTR Statute, Art. 22(2); SCSL Statute, Art. 18; ICTY Rule 98 *ter*(C); ICTR Rule 88(C); SCSL Rule 88(C). See also *Prosecutor* v. *Kvočka, Radić, Žigić, and Prcać*, Case No. IT-98-30/1-A, Judgement, 28 February 2005 ('*Kvočka et al.* Appeal Judgement'), para. 23 (accused has *right* to reasoned opinion). As of 1 December 2009, no ICC trial chamber had yet issued a final judgement in any case. For views on what Article 74(5) of the Rome Statute requires, see Otto Triffterer, 'Requirements for the Decision', in Otto Triffterer (ed.), *Commentary on the Rome Statute of the International Criminal Court: Observers' Notes, Article by Article* (1999), pp. 693–694.

[9] On this objective in international criminal trials generally, see Chapter 7, Section 7.4.

[10] *Prosecutor* v. *Naletlić and Martinović*, Case No. IT-98-34-A, Judgement, 3 May 2006 ('*Naletilić and Martinović* Appeal Judgement'), para. 603; Triffterer, *supra* note 8, p. 964.

[11] Rome Statute, Art. 67(1)(f); ICC Rule 144; ICTY Rule 98 *ter*(B). The translations typically take many months. At the ICTR, some trial judgements have been translated into Kinyarwanda, including those in the *Akayesu*, *Kambanda*, *Kamuhanda*, *Musema*, *Ndindabahizi*, *Ntakirutimana and Ntakirutimana*, *Seromba*, and *Serushago* cases. In an effort to further outreach efforts in the former Yugoslavia, the ICTY sometimes translates its judgements into Serbo-Croatian, or 'BCS' – the acronym the Tribunal uses to describe the common language spoken in Bosnia, Croatia, Montenegro, Serbia, and parts of Kosovo – even where the accused's primary language is not BCS. For example, the Trial Judgement in *Limaj*, a case concerning three Kosovo Albanian accused, was written in English and translated into French, Albanian, and BCS.

[12] See *Prosecutor* v. *Ntagerura, Bagambiki, and Imanishimwe*, Case No. ICTR-99-46-A, Judgement, 7 July 2006 ('*Cyangugu* Appeal Judgement'), para. 169.

[13] Agreed and adjudicated facts are discussed in Chapter 9, Section 9.2.3.

[14] See, e.g., Rome Statute, Art. 74(2).

indictment, and assess the evidence supporting its factual and legal conclusions on those elements and its ultimate finding of guilt or innocence on each charge.[15] An appellant claiming the trial chamber breached the requirement of a reasoned judgement must point to specific issues, factual findings, or arguments the chamber allegedly ignored, and explain why the omission is so significant as to invalidate the finding or conclusion in question or otherwise constitute a miscarriage of justice.[16] On appeal, 'it is not enough to allege a general deficiency throughout the Trial Judgement and request review of unspecified findings of the Trial Chamber – lest the appeal procedure effectively become[] a trial *de novo*'.[17] Because '[e]vidence before a Trial Chamber is notoriously voluminous' and 'a Trial Chamber cannot be expected to refer to it all',[18] trial chambers are presumed to have evaluated all evidence in the record as long as nothing indicates that the chamber disregarded a particular piece of evidence.[19]

The *Krajišnik* case provides an application of this rather vague standard. On appeal, the *amici curiae* representing the interests of the accused argued that the Trial Chamber's 'illustrative approach' to discussing the evidence ran afoul of the reasoned judgement requirement. In its Judgement, the Trial Chamber had

[15] *Prosecutor* v. *Kordić and Čerkez*, Case No. IT-95-14/2-A, Judgement, 17 December 2004 ('*Kordić and Čerkez* Appeal Judgement'), para. 383. Accord *Prosecutor* v. *Kajelijeli*, Case No. ICTR-98-44A-A, Judgement, 23 May 2005 ('*Kajelijeli* Appeal Judgement'), para. 60; *Kvočka et al.* Appeal Judgement, *supra* note 8, para. 23; *Prosecutor* v. *Sesay, Kallon, and Gbao* ('*RUF* Case'), Case No. SCSL-04-15-A, Judgement, 26 October 2009 ('*RUF* Appeal Judgement'), paras. 345, 415; see also, e.g., *ibid.*, para. 695 (rejecting accused Sesay's contention that Trial Chamber failed to provide sufficient reasoning in section describing mining at a certain locale, where Sesay was actually convicted of crimes in relation to mining at a different locale, and for this latter locale Sesay failed to challenge the Trial Chamber's factual findings); *ibid.*, paras. 710–712 (reversing conviction of Sesay for enslavement as a crime against humanity where Trial Chamber failed to explain how its factual findings satisfied the legal elements of enslavement). For the ICTY Appeals Chamber's response to one Trial Chamber's failure to assess the evidence satisfying each element of the charged crimes and forms of responsibility, see *infra* note 245 (*Kordić and Čerkez* case).

[16] *Prosecutor* v. *Strugar*, Case No. IT-01-42-A, Judgement, 17 July 2008 ('*Strugar* Appeal Judgement'), para. 24; *Prosecutor* v. *Brđanin*, Case No. IT-99-36-A, Judgement, 3 April 2007 ('*Brđanin* Appeal Judgement'), para. 9. Accord, e.g., *RUF* Appeal Judgement, *supra* note 15, paras. 345, 412; *Prosecutor* v. *Galić*, Case No. IT-98-28-A, Judgement, 30 November 2006 ('*Galić* Appeal Judgement'), paras. 256–257; *Kvočka et al.* Appeal Judgement, *supra* note 8, paras. 23, 368; *Musema* v. *Prosecutor*, Case No. ICTR-96-13-A, Judgement, 16 November 2001 ('*Musema* Appeal Judgement'), para. 21. See also, e.g., *Prosecutor* v. *Gacumbitsi*, Case No. ICTR-2001-64-A, Judgement, 7 July 2006 ('*Gacumbitsi* Appeal Judgement'), para. 74 (rejecting accused's challenge to Trial Chamber's reliance on insider witness's testimony, where accused provided no explanation as to why witness had a motive to lie); *Prosecutor* v. *Semanza*, Case No. ICTR-97-20-A, Judgement, 20 May 2005 ('*Semanza* Appeal Judgement'), paras. 130–131 (rejecting accused's contention that Trial Chamber failed to consider evidence showing that he left his house on 8 April 1994 to flee from the advancing Rwandan Patriotic Front, where accused failed to show how Trial Chamber disregarded that evidence); *infra* text accompanying note 60 (illustration of this principle in *Halilović* case); *infra* note 248 (prosecution's failure to explain impact of error in *Orić* appeal).

[17] *Prosecutor* v. *Krajišnik*, Case No. IT-00-39-A, Judgement, 17 March 2009 ('*Krajišnik* Appeal Judgement'), para. 142.

[18] *Brđanin* Appeal Judgement, *supra* note 16, para. 11.

[19] *Kvočka et al.* Appeal Judgement, *supra* note 8, para. 23; accord, e.g., *RUF* Appeal Judgement, *supra* note 15, para. 39; *Strugar* Appeal Judgement, *supra* note 16, para. 24; *Brđanin* Appeal Judgement, *supra* note 16, para. 11. See also, e.g., *Galić* Appeal Judgement, *supra* note 16, paras. 259–263 (rejecting several assertions that Trial Chamber completely ignored certain evidence favourable to accused); *Naletilić and Martinović* Appeal Judgement, *supra* note 10, para. 138 (rejecting prosecution contention that Trial Chamber failed to

stated: '[T]here is no practical way of presenting in detail all the evidence it has heard and received during the trial. The Chamber has been able to present only the most relevant parts of the evidence in detail, but generally has had to confine itself to presenting evidence in a summarized form'.[20] The Appeals Chamber held that this approach did not mean that the Trial Chamber failed to examine the evidence bearing on its legal conclusions or its findings of guilt. Since the *amici* did not explain precisely how the Trial Chamber's illustrative approach invalidated specific findings of guilt, the Appeals Chamber deemed the challenge meritless.[21]

A more troubling example appears in *Halilović*. There, the prosecution claimed the Trial Chamber had ignored a key piece of evidence in finding that the prosecution had failed to prove Halilović's superior responsibility for failing to punish troops under his command. Specifically, the Chamber was unconvinced that Halilović had effective control over Bosnian Muslim Army troops who killed Bosnian Croat civilians during an operation to break Bosnian Croat forces' blockade of the city of Mostar.[22] The evidence in question was a letter written by Halilović himself to Bosnian president Alija Izetbegović relating that he had led the team that carried out this operation. The Appeals Chamber agreed with the prosecution that the Trial Judgement made no mention of the letter; that the omission might signal that the Trial Chamber disregarded relevant evidence; and that the letter, if believed, would have corroborated exhibits and testimony the Trial Chamber found unreliable and could have led it to convict Halilović.[23] Nonetheless, the Appeals Chamber considered that 'the Trial Chamber might legitimately have looked with extreme caution at a document written many months after the events by an accused who chose not to testify', and thus '[i]t cannot be said that, even considering this piece of evidence, no reasonable trier of fact could have reached the conclusions that the Trial Chamber reached'.[24] Given the seeming importance of the letter in establishing Halilović's presence during the operation, the Trial Chamber's failure to even

consider certain victim-witnesses' testimony that Martinović used derogatory terms to refer to them, as the Chamber relied on their testimony in other respects and nothing in the Judgement suggested that it completely disregarded the evidence that Martinović used derogatory terms); contra, e.g., *ibid.*, para. 604–607 (agreeing with Martinović that Trial Chamber violated reasoned judgement requirement by failing to acknowledge or discuss his assistance to Bosnian Muslim prisoners in its discussion of mitigating factors in sentencing, even though the Trial Chamber had considered such assistance earlier in the Judgement; but ultimately finding that such assistance was minimal and did not require reducing Martinović's sentence).

[20] *Prosecutor* v. *Krajišnik*, Case No. IT-00-39-T, Judgement, 27 September 2006, para. 292; see also *ibid.*, para. 889 (Trial Chamber explaining that it could not 'possibly discuss here all the evidence relevant to the Accused's responsibility which it received in the course of two-and-a-half years of trial and subsequently analysed. Having carefully deliberated on this vast amount of evidence, what the Chamber can (and must) do is to illustrate the types of fact that underlie its conclusions').

[21] See *Krajišnik* Appeal Judgement, *supra* note 17, paras. 140–144.

[22] *Prosecutor* v. *Halilović*, Case No. IT-01-48-T, Judgement, 16 November 2005 ('*Halilović* Trial Judgement'), paras. 372, 743–747, 752.

[23] *Prosecutor* v. *Halilović*, Case No. IT-01-48-A, Judgement, 16 October 2007 ('*Halilović* Appeal Judgement'), para. 124.

[24] *Ibid.*

acknowledge the letter's existence certainly seems like the type of omission that could constitute a breach of the reasoned judgement requirement, regardless of whether the Trial Chamber would ultimately have reached the same conclusion upon considering the letter together with the other evidence.

As these two cases demonstrate, the trial chamber need not discuss or refer to the testimony of every witness, every piece of evidence, or every legal argument made by a party,[25] or articulate every step of its reasoning.[26] Instead, the chamber has the discretion to choose which legal arguments to address.[27] Likewise, the chamber need not explain its assessment of every witness's credibility,[28] or evaluate every inconsistency in a witness's testimony[29] or in an item of documentary evidence.[30]

In some circumstances, however, the chamber must assess the credibility of certain witnesses, including 'where there is a genuine and significant dispute surrounding a witness's credibility and the witness's testimony is truly central to the question whether a particular element is proven'.[31] This principle was tested in the *Muvunyi* case. At trial, two prosecution witnesses testified that Muvunyi gave a speech at a meeting in which he called for the Tutsis to be killed. On appeal from his conviction for direct and public incitement to commit genocide, Muvunyi argued that the witnesses's respective accounts differed as to who else was at the meeting, when it

[25] *Strugar* Appeal Judgement, *supra* note 16, para. 24. Accord, e.g., *Gacumbitsi* Appeal Judgement, *supra* note 16, para. 74; *Kajelijeli* Appeal Judgement, *supra* note 15, para. 60 (citing *Musema* Appeal Judgement, *supra* note 16, para. 20); *Kvočka et al.* Appeal Judgement, *supra* note 8, para. 23; *Prosecutor* v. *Kupreškić, Kupreškić, Kupreškić, Josipović, and Šantić*, Case No. IT-95-16-A, Appeal Judgement, 23 October 2001 ('*Kupreškić et al.* Appeal Judgement'), para. 39.

[26] *RUF* Appeal Judgement, *supra* note 15, para. 345 (quoting *Krajišnik* Appeal Judgement, *supra* note 17, para. 139). See also, e.g., *Cyangugu* Appeal Judgement, *supra* note 12, para. 206 (rejecting prosecution challenge to Trial Chamber's finding that certain prosecution witnesses were 'alleged accomplices' of the accused, and thus should be viewed with suspicion, even though Trial Chamber did not elaborate on the nature of the alleged complicity or analyse why they might have had a motive to give false testimony); *ibid.*, para. 240 (similar holding, where prosecution challenged Trial Chamber's reliance on defence witness who had been charged with crimes in Rwanda); *Kvočka et al.* Appeal Judgement, *supra* note 8, para. 398 (rejecting accused Radić's argument that Trial Chamber failed to sufficiently explain its findings relating to his involvement in sexual violence).

[27] *Kvočka et al.* Appeal Judgement, *supra* note 8, para. 23. See also, e.g., *ibid.*, paras. 21–25 (rejecting accused Žigić's challenge to the Trial Judgement as insufficiently reasoned based on his contention that the Trial Chamber 'ignored more than 75 percent of the evidence', 'selected only evidence in favour of conviction', and 'questions and objections raised by him were not addressed') (quotations at para. 21).

[28] *Kajelijeli* Appeal Judgement, *supra* note 15, para. 60; *Kvočka et al.* Appeal Judgement, *supra* note 8, para. 23 ('If the Trial Chamber did not refer to the evidence given by a witness, even if it is in contradiction to the Trial Chamber's finding, it is to be presumed that the Trial Chamber assessed and weighed the evidence, but found the evidence did not prevent it from arriving at its actual findings.').

[29] *Brđanin* Appeal Judgement, *supra* note 16, para. 28 ('Mere assertions that the testimony of one witness is inconsistent with the conclusions of the Trial Chamber are insufficient.'). See also, e.g., *ibid.*, paras. 55, 106, 210, 301 (summarily dismissing several challenges of this nature); *Prosecutor* v. *Delalić, Mucić, Delić, and Landžo*, Case No. IT-96-21-A, Judgement, 20 February 2001 ('*Čelebići* Appeal Judgement'), para. 498 (accused Delić failed to show that the Trial Chamber erred in apparently disregarding small inconsistencies in a particular witness's testimony, and in finding the testimony credible and basing a conviction on it).

[30] *Milutinović et al.* Trial Judgement, *supra* note 1, Vol. I, para. 64.

[31] *Kajelijeli* Appeal Judgement, *supra* note 15, para. 61.

was held, and precisely what Muvunyi had said that might be taken as an exhortation to kill Tutsis. Nevertheless, the Trial Chamber found the testimonies credible and, indeed, 'strikingly similar'.[32] The ICTR Appeals Chamber determined that the Trial Chamber had breached the reasoned judgement requirement because it did not address discrepancies in 'core details' of the respective testimonies. The Appeals Chamber also found that the Trial Chamber had erred in not explaining why it chose not to credit the testimony of a third witness that Muvunyi spoke only on security issues, and did not denigrate Tutsis. In an extremely rare move, the Appeals Chamber quashed Muvunyi's incitement conviction and remanded the case for retrial on these charges.[33]

The Appeals Chambers have identified a second, arguably more common example where a trial chamber needs to detail its credibility assessment: where a finding that the accused was present at the crime scene, or some other relevant identification of the accused, depends on the testimony of a single eyewitness, and the evidence reveals stress or other conditions likely to undermine the accuracy of that witness's identification.[34] Even here, however, the trial chamber 'is only expected to identify the *relevant* factors, and to address the *significant* negative factors'.[35] Thus, where a party puts on several witnesses who are unable to make a meaningful contribution to the relevant facts in question, the trial chamber may base its finding on the testimony of another witness without expressly stating that it found each of the other witnesses' evidence irrelevant, or why.[36]

The ICTY Appeals Chamber has stated that '[i]t is … not possible to draw any inferences about the quality of a judgement from the length of particular parts of the judgement in relation to other judgements or parts of the same judgement'.[37] While it is preferable that the trial chamber make factual findings in relation to each incident and victim described in the indictment, the Appeals Chamber has not

[32] *Prosecutor* v. *Muvunyi*, Case No. ICTR-2000-55A-T, Judgement and Sentence, 12 September 2006, paras. 206–211 (quotation at para. 209).

[33] See *Prosecutor* v. *Muvunyi*, Case No. ICTR-2000-55A-A, Judgement, 29 August 2008 ('*Muvunyi* Appeal Judgement'), paras. 142–148, p. 67. The Appeals Chamber later clarified that the prosecution could present new evidence relating to this incident in the new trial. See *Prosecutor* v. *Muvunyi*, Case No. ICTR-2000-55A-AR73, Decision on the Prosecutor's Appeal Concerning the Scope of Evidence to Be Adduced in the Retrial, 24 March 2009 (Judges Shahabuddeen and Meron, dissenting). As of 1 December 2009, retrial in *Muvunyi* continued, with the defence preparing to present its case.

[34] See, e.g., *Kajelijeli* Appeal Judgement, *supra* note 15, para. 61; *Kupreškić et al.* Appeal Judgement, *supra* note 25, para. 39. See also *Kajelijeli* Appeal Judgement, *supra* note 15, para. 62 (holding that the Trial Chamber did not err in failing to include in the judgement a credibility assessment of a particular defence witness, who testified that the accused was not at the crime scene at the relevant time, because several other witnesses attested to the accused's presence at the crime scene).

[35] *Kvočka et al.* Appeal Judgement, *supra* note 8, para. 24 (emphasis in original).

[36] *Ibid.*

[37] *Kvočka et al.* Appeal Judgement, *supra* note 8, para. 23. Accord, e.g., *RUF* Appeal Judgement, *supra* note 15, para. 346 (rejecting accused Gbao's challenge to the trial judgement as insufficiently reasoned because, in Gbao's submission, parts of it were too short compared to analogous parts of other trial judgements).

insisted on this sort of 'systematic' approach.[38] It has instead upheld guilty verdicts on a given count in the indictment where the trial chamber articulated its findings in relation to at least one incident involving at least one victim organised under that count.[39]

10.1.2 Majority concurrence in the verdict and separate opinions

Unlike the rule pertaining to criminal jury verdicts in most US jurisdictions as well as jurisdictions in some other countries, the judges' decision on guilt or innocence need not be unanimous; instead, only two of the three judges must agree in order to convict or acquit an accused on any charge.[40] The Rome Statute encourages a unanimous verdict, nevertheless, it does not demand unanimity, and ultimately only two out of three judges must concur.[41]

The tribunals' governing instruments allow judges of the trial chamber to append separate and dissenting opinions to the judgement.[42] In a practice probably inspired by the ICJ, many international criminal judgements have featured separate opinions – sometimes termed 'declarations' – with the authoring judge's own thoughts on a given issue or issues in the case, which often entail concurrence with the majority's conclusion but not with its reasoning.[43] Equally common are dissenting opinions, including some in which the dissenting judge states that he or she would have acquitted the accused.[44]

Some have argued that the publication of dissenting views may weaken the verdict's (and, by extension, the tribunal's) authority, and more broadly the

[38] *Kvočka et al.* Appeal Judgement, *supra* note 8, paras. 73–74 (quotation at para. 73).

[39] See, e.g., *ibid.*; accord *Halilović* Appeal Judgement, *supra* note 23, para. 123. When the Appeals Chamber overturns some of the trial chamber's guilty findings under a given count but upholds the conviction itself, it should consider reducing the convicted person's sentence. Sentencing is discussed in Section 10.2 *infra*.

[40] ICTY Statute, Art. 23(2); ICTR Statute, Art. 22(2); SCSL Statute, Art. 18; ICTY Rule 98 *ter*(C); ICTR Rule 88(C); SCSL Rule 88(C).

[41] Rome Statute, Art. 74(3) ('The judges shall attempt to achieve unanimity in their decision, failing which the decision shall be taken by a majority of the judges.'). See also, e.g., *Apodaca* v. *Oregon*, 406 U.S. 404 (1972) (U.S. Supreme Court holding that non-unanimous guilty verdict does not violate accused's constitutional rights).

[42] ICTY Statute, Art. 23(2); ICTR Statute, Art. 22(2); SCSL Statute, Art. 18; ICTY Rule 98 *ter*(C); ICTR Rule 88(C); SCSL Rule 88(C).

[43] See, e.g., *Prosecutor* v. *Fofana and Kondewa* ('*CDF* Case'), Case No. SCSL-04-14-J, Judgement, 2 August 2007 ('*CDF* Trial Judgement'), Separate and Concurring Opinion of Justice Boutet (agreeing with majority on all points, but opining that it gave too much prominence to the role of Sierra Leone president in possibly mitigating accused's guilt); *Prosecutor* v. *Galić*, Case. No. IT-98-29-T, Judgement and Opinion, 5 December 2003, Separate and Partially Dissenting Opinion of Judge Nieto-Navia (agreeing with decision to convict but disagreeing with several conclusions and the sentence).

[44] See, e.g., *CDF* Trial Judgement, *supra* note 43, Separate Concurring and Partially Dissenting Opinion of Hon. Justice Bankole Thompson Filed Pursuant to Article 18 of the Statute (explaining why he would have acquitted both accused); *CDF* Case, Case No. SCSL-04-14-T, Judgement on the Sentencing of Moinina Fofana and Allieu Kondewa, 9 October 2007 ('*CDF* Sentencing Judgement'), Dissenting Opinion of Hon. Justice Bankole Thompson from Sentencing Judgement Filed Pursuant to Article 18 of the Statute, p. A-2 (taking no

administration of justice itself, especially where the disagreement concerns factual findings critical to the guilt of the accused; and that signing the dissent may also violate the principle of confidential deliberations.[45] The Rome Statute's provisions on separate and dissenting opinions may reflect unease at allowing the judges to voice independent views: 'The Trial Chamber shall issue one decision. When there is no unanimity, the Trial Chamber's decision shall contain the views of the majority and the minority.'[46] Otto Triffterer has suggested that 'this means [that] different findings on the evidence and/or different conclusions ought to be mentioned within the decision of the majority, without, however, indicating any assignment to a specific judge'.[47] While Triffterer's reading is not the only one possible from the Statute's language,[48] disallowing signed dissents may help ameliorate some of the concerns noted above. It certainly seems in some judgements that the outvoted judge, perhaps disgruntled that his or her arguments in deliberations did not win the day, issues a dissent merely as a means to air this dissatisfaction.[49] Despite these potential problems, however, it seems inherent in the principle of judicial independence that a judge should be able to express a dissenting view when he or she believes the majority is incorrect and sign the dissent, leaving it to future chambers, jurists, and the public to determine the weight to be attributed to it on the basis of the force and coherence of the judge's reasoning.

view on sentence due to belief that both accused should have been acquitted); *Prosecutor* v. *Simić, Tadić, and Zarić*, Case No. IT-95-9-T, Judgement, 17 October 2003, Separate and Partially Dissenting Opinion of Judge Per-Johan Lindholm (explaining why he would have acquitted Tadić and Zarić outright, and given Simić a lighter sentence). Certainly the most prolific publisher of separate and dissenting opinions at the ICTY was former appeals judge Mohamed Shahabuddeen, also formerly of the ICJ, who resigned from the ICC in 2009 shortly after his election as a judge of that Court.

45 See, e.g., Frank Terrier, 'The Procedure Before the Trial Chamber', in Antonio Cassese, Paola Gaeta, and John R.W.D. Jones (eds.), *The Rome Statute of the International Criminal Court: A Commentary*, Vol. II (2002), pp. 1314–1315.

46 Rome Statute, Art. 74(5).

47 Triffterer, *supra* note 8, p. 964.

48 For example, the provision could instead mean that the majority's opinion and any dissenting opinions need only appear *seriatim* in the same document, and nothing in the language states that the dissenting views may not be signed. Both of these aspects have routinely characterised judgements at the ICTY, ICTR, and SCSL. ICC chambers have permitted signed dissents in interlocutory decisions, both in the same document as the majority opinion and in a separate document. See, e.g., *Prosecutor* v. *Lubanga*, Doc. No. ICC-01/04-01/06-1432, Judgment on the Appeals of the Prosecutor and the Defence Against Trial Chamber I's Decision on Victims' Participation of 18 January 2008, 11 July 2008, Partly Dissenting Opinion of Judge G.M. Pikis (beginning immediately after the majority opinion on page 37); *Prosecutor* v. *Lubanga*, Doc. No. ICC-01/04-01/06-1432-Anx, Judgment on the Appeals of the Prosecutor and the Defence Against Trial Chamber I's Decision on Victims' Participation of 18 January 2008, 23 July 2008, Partly Dissenting Opinion of Judge Philippe Kirsch (filed twelve days later; appended to the majority opinion and styled as an 'annex').

49 See, e.g., Gideon Boas, 'The Case for a New Appellate Jurisdiction for International Criminal Law', in Göran Sluiter and Sergey Vasiliev (eds.), *International Criminal Procedure: Towards a Coherent Body of Law* (2009), p. 441 n. 137 (discussing a sharp exchange between Judges Hunt and Shahabuddeen about whether the ICTY has sacrificed fair-trial rights in favour of the completion strategy; opining that the exchange 'exemplifies an odd (and unfortunate) practice that has arisen in the Appeals Chambers'; that '[i]t appears that Appeals Judges feel, and are, free to engage in argument and counter-argument ... which at times descends into something like an exchange of thinly disguised abuse'; and concluding that this practice 'does little to imbue the external reader (let alone the parties) with confidence in such an important institution as an appellate court').

10.1.3 Proof beyond a reasonable doubt

In order to convict on a particular charge,[50] the governing instruments of all the international criminal tribunals require the trial chamber to be convinced of the accused's guilt beyond a reasonable doubt.[51] The ICTR Appeals Chamber has explained that this requirement is a corollary of the presumption of innocence enjoyed by the accused.[52] While a precise definition in the case law of what constitutes a 'reasonable' doubt has proven elusive,[53] the ICTY Appeals Chamber has clarified that the mere existence of some possibility, however slight, that a given event could have happened in another way does not by itself give rise to a reasonable doubt.[54] At the other end of the spectrum, another ICTY Chamber has cautioned that '[n]ot even the gravest of suspicions can establish proof beyond reasonable doubt'.[55]

The prosecution need not establish every fact alleged in the indictment beyond a reasonable doubt, but need only do so for those facts necessary for a finding of guilt.[56] The standard of proof therefore requires that the chamber be satisfied beyond a reasonable doubt that the evidence establishes: (1) each general requirement of a core category of crime under which the charge in question appears in the indictment; (2) the elements of at least one underlying offence alleged under

[50] On the definition of 'charge' and how this differs from 'counts' in the indictment, see Chapter 6, notes 56, 102 and accompanying text; Chapter 7, text accompanying note 226; *Milutinović et al.* Trial Judgement, *supra* note 1, Vol. I, para. 70.

[51] Rome Statute, Art. 66(3); ICTY Rule 87(A); ICTR Rule 87(A); SCSL Rule 87(A). Other standards of proof apply at other stages of the proceedings. See, e.g., Chapter 3, Section 3.2.3.2.1 (ICC prosecution needs reasonable basis to launch an investigation); Chapter 4, Section 4.1.1 (*ad hoc* Tribunals' Prosecutors need sufficient basis to initiate an investigation); Chapter 6, Section 6.1.1.1.1 (prosecution must establish a '*prima facie*' case for an indictment to be confirmed); Chapter 7, Section 7.6.4 (accused may be acquitted midway through trial where no evidence exists capable of supporting a conviction); *infra* note 61 (accused need only show mitigating circumstances in sentencing on a balance of the probabilities).

[52] *Cyangugu* Appeal Judgement, *supra* note 12, paras. 170, 175.

[53] See William A. Schabas, 'Presumption of Innocence', in Triffterer, *supra* note 8, p. 842 (citing case law from common-law jurisdictions holding that reasonable doubt is not 'any doubt, beyond a shadow of a doubt, absolute certainty, or moral certainty', but it also does not imply 'such doubt as would give rise to a grave uncertainty') (internal quotation marks and citations omitted). See also, e.g., *Prosecutor* v. *Jelisić*, Case No. IT-95-10-T, Judgement, 14 December 1999, paras. 92–93 (Trial Chamber unable to find beyond reasonable doubt that accused based choice of who to kill, among Muslim detainees, on an intention to destroy representative members of Muslim community, where one victim-witness testified to having seen a list of names entitled 'people to execute', but another witness testified that the accused picked persons from the list at random to be killed, and a third witness testified that he picked persons without regard to the list).

[54] *Galić* Appeal Judgement, *supra* note 16, para. 259 (rejecting accused's challenge to Trial Chamber's finding that the Sarajevo Romanija Corps committed most of the shelling and sniping of civilians in Sarajevo, as accused had only proffered the mere possibility that it was actually Bosnian Muslim Army forces who, in an effort to gain international sympathy, fired on the civilians). Accord, e.g., *Halilović* Appeal Judgement, *supra* note 23, para. 109.

[55] *Prosecutor* v. *Simić, Simić, Simić, Todorović, and Zarić*, Case No. IT-95-9-R77, Judgement in the Matter of Contempt Allegations Against an Accused and His Counsel, 30 June 2006, para. 99.

[56] *Cyangugu* Appeal Judgement, *supra* note 12, paras. 174–175; *Milutinović et al.* Trial Judgement, *supra* note 1, Vol. I, para. 63. See also, e.g., *RUF* Appeal Judgement, *supra* note 15, para. 117 (holding that the trial chamber's findings on the identities of the participants in a joint criminal enterprise ('JCE'), other than the accused, need not be made beyond a reasonable doubt, because the identities of other JCE participants is not

that category (including the specific requirements of persecution as a crime against humanity if applicable to the charge); and (3) the elements of at least one form of responsibility alleged in relation to that underlying offence.[57] The evidence must also establish beyond a reasonable doubt any other fact that, in the circumstances of the case, is indispensable for the conviction.[58]

The ICTY and ICTR Appeals Chambers have held that a trial chamber may not use a 'piecemeal' approach in applying the standard of proof. Instead, it must analyse individual items of evidence in light of the entire body of evidence before drawing conclusions on whether the prosecution has proven a given fact, critical to a finding of guilt, beyond a reasonable doubt:

> The task of a trier of fact is that of assessing all the relevant evidence presented with a holistic approach; this is all the more necessary in cases as complex as the ones before the International Tribunal. According to the Statute and the Rules, the trier of fact should render a reasoned opinion on the basis of the entire body of evidence without applying the standard of proof 'beyond reasonable doubt' with a piecemeal approach.[59]

On appeal in *Halilović*, the prosecution argued that the Trial Chamber erred in using a piecemeal approach to evaluate several constituent items of evidence that, according to the prosecution, in the aggregate demonstrated Halilović's effective control over troops that perpetrated offences during an operation to break Bosnian Croat forces' blockade of Mostar. The Appeals Chamber rejected the challenge, finding that the prosecution had not adequately explained how the Trial Chamber's erroneous application of the standard of proof to each item of evidence in isolation

an element that must be proven in order convict the accused of a crime through participation in a JCE). As the *Milutinović* Trial Chamber stressed, '"[m]aterial facts" that have to be pleaded in an indictment to provide the accused with the information necessary to prepare his defence are not always necessarily facts that have to be proved beyond a reasonable doubt'. *Milutinović et al.* Trial Judgement, *supra* note 1, Vol. I, para. 63 (citing *Cyangugu* Appeal Judgement, *supra* note 12, para. 175 n. 356); accord, e.g., *RUF* Appeal Judgement, *supra* note 15, para. 117. On pleading principles for the indictment, see Chapter 6, Section 6.1.2.1.

57 See *Milutinović et al.* Trial Judgement, *supra* note 1, Vol. I, para. 62. Accord, e.g., *RUF* Appeal Judgement, *supra* note 15, para. 117; *Halilović* Appeal Judgement, *supra* note 23, paras. 125, 129; *Brđanin* Appeal Judgement, *supra* note 16, para. 12; *Cyangugu* Appeal Judgement, *supra* note 12, paras. 174–175. See also, e.g., *ibid*, paras. 186–187 (holding that the killing of the victims in question – the *actus reus* of the underlying offence – was a material fact that had to be proven beyond a reasonable doubt). On the meaning of the terms 'general requirement', 'specific requirement', 'core category', and 'underlying offence', see Boas, Bischoff, and Reid, *Elements of Crimes*, *supra* note 3, pp. 9–13.

58 *Halilović* Appeal Judgement, *supra* note 23, paras. 125, 129; *Cyangugu* Appeal Judgement, *supra* note 12, para. 174. See also, e.g., *Kupreškić et al.* Appeal Judgement, *supra* note 25, para. 226 (rejecting prosecution argument that Trial Chamber erred in applying 'beyond reasonable doubt' standard to the testimony of Witness H that the accused participated in an attack on her house, because the testimony in question was not merely one of many pieces of evidence tending to show discriminatory intent; instead, '[t]he persecution conviction of Zoran and Mirjan Kupreškić hinged upon their participation in the attack on Witness H's house').

59 *Halilović* Appeal Judgement, *supra* note 23, para. 128. Accord *ibid*., paras. 119, 125; *Cyangugu* Appeal Judgement, *supra* note 12, para. 174 ('Only after the analysis of all the relevant evidence, can the Trial Chamber determine whether the evidence upon which the Prosecution relies should be accepted as establishing the existence of the facts alleged … At this fact-finding stage, the standard of proof beyond a reasonable doubt is applied to establish the facts forming the elements of the crime or the form of responsibility alleged against the accused, as well as with respect to the facts which are indispensable for entering a conviction.').

contributed to the Trial Chamber's ultimate conclusion that the prosecution had not proven Halilović's effective control over the troops.[60]

The prosecution must also prove aggravating factors in sentencing beyond a reasonable doubt. While the accused bears the burden of proving mitigating circumstances, he or she need only do so on a balance of the probabilities – that is, that the fact in question is more likely true than not.[61]

10.1.4 Structure of the judgement

Beyond the requirements of a reasoned written judgement reached by a majority of judges, and that the trial chamber find the accused's guilt beyond a reasonable doubt,[62] the tribunals' governing instruments leave how to structure the judgement largely in the chamber's hands. The way in which each chamber has chosen to structure its judgement has varied, but most judgements at the ICTY, ICTR, and SCSL share certain elements:[63] an introduction identifying the accused and the charges against her; a section setting forth the chamber's considerations regarding the evaluation of evidence, including its methodology in weighing the evidence and applying the 'beyond a reasonable doubt' standard; a historical background; the law on the elements of the statutory crimes and underlying offences charged in the indictment; the law on the forms of responsibility charged in the indictment; factual findings on the major incidents charged in the indictment, often organised by locale; application of the substantive law on crimes to these facts, and conclusions as to which, if any, crimes were committed; application of the law on the forms of responsibility to these conclusions with respect to each accused; findings

[60] See *Halilović* Appeal Judgement, *supra* note 23, paras. 126–132. See also *supra* notes 16–17 and accompanying text (appellant bears the burden of showing how the trial chamber's alleged shortcoming breached the reasoned judgement requirement).

[61] *Kajelijeli* Appeal Judgement, *supra* note 15, para. 294; *Prosecutor* v. *Blaškić*, Case No. IT-95-14-A, Judgement, 29 July 2004 ('*Blaškić* Appeal Judgement'), paras. 686, 697; *Čelebići* Appeal Judgement, *supra* note 29, paras. 590, 763; *RUF* Case, Case No. SCSL-04-15-T, Sentencing Judgement, 8 April 2009 ('*RUF* Sentencing Judgement'), paras. 24, 28; *Prosecutor* v. *Limaj, Bala, and Musliu*, Case No. IT-03-66-T, Judgement, 30 November 2005 ('*Limaj et al.* Trial Judgement'), para. 729. It remains to be seen whether the chambers of the ICC will adopt this dichotomy between the respective standards of proof for aggravating and mitigating factors. Aggravating and mitigating circumstances in sentencing are discussed in Section 10.2.2, *infra*.

[62] See *supra* Sections 10.1.1, 10.1.3.

[63] By comparison, judgement formats at East Timor's Special Panels for Serious Crimes varied. At times the judges attempted to mimic the structure of ICTY and ICTR judgements, and these judgements tend to be those that are better reasoned. See, e.g., *Prosecutor* v. *Joni Marques, Manuel da Costa, João da Costa, Paulo da Costa, Amélio da Costa, Hilário da Silva, Gonsalo dos Santos, Alarico Fernandes, Mautersa Monis, Gilberto Fernandes, and Syaful Anwar*, Case No. 09/2000, Judgment, 11 December 2001 ('*Los Palos* case'). Other judgements are far more cursory. See, e.g., *Prosecutor* v. *Victor Manuel Alves*, Case No. 1/2002, Judgement, 8 July 2004; *Prosecutor* v. *Carlos Soares*, Case No. 9/2002, Judgement, 8 December 2003; *Prosecutor* v. *Anastacio Martins and Domingos Gonçalves*, Case No. 11/2001, Judgement, 13 November 2003. On problems with the Special Panels' legal analyses in judgements generally, see Boas, Bischoff, and Reid, *Elements of Crimes*, *supra* note 3, pp. 121–128.

on the individual responsibility of each accused; and analysis and conclusions on concurrent and cumulative convictions.[64]

Subsequent to the elimination of separate sentencing proceedings at the ICTY and the ICTR in 1998, judgements in those Tribunals also contain the chamber's evaluation and application of sentencing factors. At the SCSL, this analysis appears in a separate sentencing judgement, as it presumably will for the ICC.[65] In all the tribunals, the judgement concludes with a disposition setting forth the trial chamber's verdict for each of the accused on each count of the indictment. Separate and dissenting opinions follow the disposition,[66] and annexes at the end set forth the case's procedural history, maps, photos, and tables defining abbreviations and acronyms.

10.1.5 Concurrent and cumulative convictions

In Volumes I and II we examined 'concurrent' and 'cumulative' convictions, two discrete sets of legal principles developed by the *ad hoc* Tribunals and since endorsed by the SCSL, though apparently not without some confusion between the two concepts.[67] As of 1 December 2009, no ICC chamber had yet rendered final judgement, and it remains to be seen to what extent that Court will import these principles, if at all. We briefly restate the main features of this law, and direct the reader to the previous two volumes for the full discussion.

The law on *concurrent convictions* determines when a trial chamber may convict an accused under more than one form of responsibility for the same crime. If the trial chamber decides to convict for a given crime for which the prosecution has charged several forms of responsibility at once, it may choose the form it feels comes closest to describing the accused's contributory conduct,[68] or it may concurrently

[64] Concurrent and cumulative convictions are discussed in Section 10.1.5, *infra*. Most judgements are comprised of a single volume. For a unique approach, see *Milutinović et al.* Trial Judgement, *supra* note 1 (four volumes, the first setting forth the law on crimes and forms of responsibility, and the Chamber's general findings on the armed conflict; the second setting forth the chamber's findings on the crimes committed in the various municipalities; the third setting forth the chamber's analysis of the individual responsibility of the six accused and sentencing; and the fourth containing an analysis of evidence in relation to more than 800 named victims, a table of short forms, and a list of witnesses).

[65] On the divergence between the ICTY and ICTR on one hand, and the SCSL and the ICC on the other, with respect to separate sentencing procedures, see Chapter 7, Section 7.6.5.

[66] On separate and dissenting opinions, see *supra* Section 10.1.2.

[67] See *infra* note 70.

[68] The *Milutinović* Trial Judgement provides the best illustration of this principle. The prosecution charged the six accused through all the forms of responsibility. The Trial Chamber ultimately chose to characterise Ojdanić and Lazarević as aiders and abettors of the crimes in Counts 1 and 2 of the indictment, through both acts and omissions. See *Milutinović et al.* Trial Judgement, *supra* note 1, Vol. III, paras. 628–630, 927–930. It exercised its discretion not to examine their liability for planning, instigating, or ordering, *ibid.*, Vol. III, paras. 619, 920, and dismissed JCE and superior responsibility upon finding that the prosecution had failed to prove certain of their elements, *ibid.*, Vol. III, paras. 618, 632–633, 919, 933. For Šainović, Pavković, and Lukić, the Chamber chose JCE as the most appropriate form of responsibility and convicted them under it for several crimes, and opted not to examine their responsibility under any other form. See *ibid.*, Vol. III, paras.

convict the accused under two or several of the forms.[69] Nevertheless, appellate case law prohibits trial chambers from concurrently convicting an accused under physical commission, joint criminal enterprise, planning, instigating, or ordering, on the one hand, and superior responsibility, on the other.[70]

The law on *cumulative convictions*, by contrast, determines when the chamber may or must convict an accused for more than one crime on the basis of the same acts or omissions. Where the prosecution has proven two (or more) crimes arising out of the same conduct involving the same victims, the chamber may only convict the accused of both (or all) crimes if each has a materially

474–475, 787–788, 1137–1140. As for Milutinović, the Chamber found that the evidence failed to satisfy the elements of any form of responsibility, and acquitted him outright. See *ibid.*, Vol. III, paras. 271–284. But see *infra* note 70 (SCSL Appeals Chamber apparently holding, contrary to ICTY and ICTR appellate jurisprudence, that concurrent convictions are mandatory). See also Gideon Boas, James L. Bischoff, and Natalie L. Reid, *Forms of Responsibility in International Criminal Law* (2007) ('Boas, Bischoff, and Reid, *Forms of Responsibility*'), p. 383 (prosecution routinely charges multiple forms of responsibility for same crime); *ibid.*, pp. 384–385 (examples in indictments).

69 Boas, Bischoff, and Reid, *Forms of Responsibility*, *supra* note 68, p. 388. In Volume I, we reached the conclusion that the ICTR Appeals Chamber had sanctioned such concurrent convictions by examining the separate opinions appended to the 2005 *Kamuhanda* Appeal Judgement and counting the votes. See *ibid.*, pp. 389–391. Subsequently, the ICTR Appeals Chamber ruled definitively that concurrent convictions are permissible. See *Ndindabahizi* v. *Prosecutor*, Case No. ICTR-01-71-A, Judgement, 16 January 2007 ('*Ndindabahizi* Appeal Judgement'), para. 122. At the same time, the *Ndindabahizi* Appeals Chamber also held that 'alternative' convictions under more than one form of responsibility should be avoided because they are 'incompatible with the principle that a judgement has to express unambiguously the scope of the convicted person's criminal responsibility'. *Ndindabahizi* Appeal Judgement, *supra*, para. 122. See *Prosecutor* v. *Ndindabahizi*, Case No. ICTR-2001-71-I, Judgement and Sentence, 15 July 2004 ('*Ndindabahizi* Trial Judgement'), para. 485 ('[T]he Accused himself committed the crime of extermination [as a crime against humanity]. He participated in creating, and contributed to, the conditions for the mass killing of Tutsi on Gitwa Hill on 26 April 1994, by distributing weapons, transporting attackers, and speaking words of encouragement that would have reasonably appeared to give official approval for an attack. Alternatively … by [his] words and deeds, the Accused directly and substantially contributed to the crime of extermination committed by the attackers … and is thereby guilty of both instigating, and of aiding and abetting, that crime.'). Yet the Appeals Chamber interpreted this passage not as imposing alternative convictions on Ndindabahizi, but as imposing concurrent convictions on him, and accordingly allowed the convictions to stand. *Ndindabahizi* Appeal Judgement, *supra*, para. 123. Judge Güney dissented from this ruling, not because he disagreed that concurrent convictions were permissible, but because he believed that an accused cannot be convicted of physically committing extermination by merely 'distributing weapons, transporting attackers, and speaking words of encouragement'. See *Ndindabahizi* Appeal Judgment, *supra*, Partially Dissenting Opinion of Judge Güney. Judge Güney likened the majority's expansion of the definition of 'commission' to the unfortunate and poorly reasoned precedent set by the ICTR Appeals Chamber majority in *Gacumbitsi*, from which Judge Güney had also dissented as creating a new form of responsibility without any evident support. See *ibid.*, para. 4; see also Boas, Bischoff, and Reid, *Forms of Responsibility*, *supra* note 68, p. 121 (discussing Judge Güney's *Gacumbitsi* dissent). We have similarly lamented this broadening of the scope of 'commission' liability and chambers' seeming obsession with labelling the accused a 'committer' of the crime in question, rather than characterising conduct such as Ndindabahizi's and Gacumbitsi's solely, and appropriately, as aiding and abetting or another form of accomplice liability. *Ibid.*, pp. 422–423; see also *infra* text accompanying note 124.

70 The SCSL Appeals Chamber has since endorsed this prohibition for the Special Court, see *Prosecutor* v. *Brima, Kamara, and Kanu* ('*AFRC* Case'), Case No. SCSL-2004-16-A, Judgement, 22 February 2008 ('*AFRC* Appeal Judgement'), para. 214, as did some panels of the now-defunct Special Panels for Serious Crimes in East Timor, see, e.g., *Prosecutor* v. *Marcelino Soares*, Case No. 11/2003, Judgement, 11 December 2003 ('*Soares* Trial Judgement'), para. 23(a). The SCSL Appeals Chamber seems to have gone on, however, to hold that a trial chamber must concurrently convict an accused pursuant to all charged forms of responsibility when their elements are satisfied on the evidence. See *ibid.*, para. 215. This holding apparently resulted from the Appeals Chamber confusing concurrent convictions, which are optional, and cumulative convictions,

distinct element. Where one of the two crimes lacks a materially distinct element, the chamber may convict only for the crime with the additional element, and must acquit on the lesser included offence.[71] Cumulative convictions are possible where the crimes in question have a mutually distinct general requirement, or where the prosecution has charged the same crime through two or more underlying offences that between themselves have mutually distinct elements.[72] When the elements of two or more crimes are satisfied on the trial chamber's factual findings and none subsumes the other, the chamber is obliged to convict cumulatively for both or all of them.[73]

10.1.6 Sentencing judgements

Prior to the elimination of a separate 'pre-sentencing procedure' at the *ad hoc* Tribunals in 1998, trial chambers rendered their judgements on the accused's guilt or innocence first.[74] Where they found the accused guilty on at least one charge, they then received written and oral submissions on sentencing, and rendered a 'sentencing judgement'. As noted above,[75] subsequent to the 1998 rule amendment, the chambers' analyses of guilt or innocence and sentence appear in the same judgement. The SCSL retains the bifurcated procedure, as does the

which are mandatory. See *infra* note 73 and accompanying text. If the trial chamber finds on the facts that the elements of one or more of the former forms of responsibility are satisfied and the elements of superior responsibility are also satisfied, the chamber must enter a conviction under one or more of those forms of responsibility to the exclusion of superior responsibility. Boas, Bischoff, and Reid, *Forms of Responsibility*, *supra* note 68, p. 398. In Volume I, we argued that this rule is fundamentally inconsistent with the deference traditionally accorded to trial chambers as the finders of fact, and at the very least should not operate to force the trial chamber to choose a form of responsibility effected through omission – such as instigating by omission or aiding and abetting by omission, two forms invented from whole cloth by trial chambers in *dicta* – where superior responsibility has also been charged and its elements satisfied on the evidence. *Ibid.*, pp. 401–404, 424. Subsequently, at least one ICTY Trial Chamber interpreted the rule, in *dicta*, in the manner we have urged. See *Milutinović et al.* Trial Judgement, *supra* note 1, Vol. I, paras. 78–79; *ibid.*, Vol. III, para. 622. The Chamber did not apply this interpretation to the facts, however, and instead chose to convict two of the accused as aiders and abettors, including by omission, to the exclusion of superior responsibility. See *supra* note 68.

71 Boas, Bischoff, and Reid, *Elements of Crimes*, *supra* note 3, pp. 326–327, 331. The SCSL Appeals Chamber has since endorsed this test for the Special Court. See *CDF* Case, Case No. SCSL-04-14-A, Judgement, 28 May 2008 ('*CDF* Appeal Judgement'), para. 220; *RUF* Appeal Judgement, *supra* note 15, paras. 1190–1200; see also *ibid.*, paras. 1192–1199 (finding the Trial Chamber correctly applied the test in entering some cumulative convictions, but misapplied it in entering others, and vacating those convictions).

72 See Boas, Bischoff, and Reid, *Elements of Crimes*, *supra* note 3, pp. 331–354 (including a discussion of the complicated and flawed body of jurisprudence addressing these 'intra-article' cumulative convictions). On the meaning of the terms 'general requirement' and 'underlying offence', see *ibid.*, pp. 9–13.

73 *Ibid.*, pp. 354–355. Subsequent to the submission of Volume II's manuscript to the publisher, the ICTY Appeals Chamber in *Strugar* reaffirmed that trial chambers do not have the discretion to choose. As we predicted, *ibid.*, p. 349, the Appeals Chamber ruled that the Trial Chamber erred in considering the particular circumstances of the case before it in convicting Strugar for fewer than all the crimes available on the facts and under the jurisprudence on cumulative convictions. See *Strugar* Appeal Judgement, *supra* note 16, para. 324. The Appeals Chamber went on to enter the additional convictions itself, but did not increase Strugar's sentence. *Ibid.*, paras. 332, 388.

74 On the pre-sentencing procedure, see Chapter 7, Section 7.6.5.

75 See *supra* text accompanying note 65.

ICC, and the SCSL's trial chambers have rendered separate sentencing judgements in the three trials that have concluded.[76] The bifurcated procedure is more coherent and better protects the right against self-incrimination: it spares accused from having to assert, on the one hand, their innocence, but argue alternatively that even if they are guilty, mitigating circumstances dictate a reduced sentence.[77] While bifurcation may lead to longer and consequently more expensive proceedings, this potential administrative and financial burden is justified by the legal principles at stake.

The *ad hoc* Tribunals still render sentencing judgements in the event the accused pleads guilty, in which the trial chamber sets forth its written analysis of whether the accused made the plea voluntarily, knowingly, and unequivocally; whether, in the chamber's view, the admitted facts satisfy the elements of the charged crimes and forms of responsibility; and if so, the sentence that should be imposed, taking into account the sentencing factors recognised in the jurisprudence and the sentencing recommendations provided by the parties.[78] The SCSL and ICC would presumably also issue a sentencing judgement upon acceptance of a plea agreement, but no accused has yet pled guilty at either court.[79]

10.1.7 Delivery of judgement and notice of appeal

As noted in Chapter 7, the judges of the trial chamber typically spend several weeks or months deliberating on and drafting the judgement.[80] The judges must then reconvene the trial to render the verdict and read out a summary of the judgement in public and in the presence of both parties.[81] Either party may file a notice of appeal from the judgement, or a portion thereof, setting forth the grounds of appeal.[82] Appellate proceedings are discussed in Chapter 11. Section 10.4 describes what happens to a convicted or acquitted person in the time period between the verdict and the conclusion of any appeals.

[76] See *RUF* Sentencing Judgement, *supra* note 61 (ninety-nine pages); *CDF* Sentencing Judgement, *supra* note 44 (thirty-five pages); *AFRC* Case, Case No. SCSL-04-16-T, Sentencing Judgement, 19 July 2007 (thirty-six pages).

[77] As noted in Chapter 7, this compelling argument has routinely failed to sway completion-strategy-oriented chambers at the *ad hoc* Tribunals. See Chapter 7, Section 7.6.5.

[78] See ICTY Rules 62 *bis*, 62 *ter*, 100; ICTR Rules 62(B), 62 *bis*, 100. For examples of sentencing judgements, see *Prosecutor* v. *Nzabirinda*, Case No. ICTR-2001-77-T, Sentencing Judgement, 23 February 2007 ('*Nzabirinda* Sentencing Judgement'); *Prosecutor* v. *Momir Nikolić*, Case No. IT-02-60/1-S, Sentencing Judgement, 2 December 2003 ('*Momir Nikolić* Sentencing Judgement').

[79] See Chapter 6, Section 6.4. See also Rome Statute, Art. 65; ICC Rule 139; SCSL Rules 62, 100(B).

[80] See Chapter 7, Section 7.6.7.

[81] Rome Statute, Art. 74(5); ICTY Statute, Art. 23(2); ICTR Statute, Art. 23(2); SCSL Statute, Art. 18; ICC Rule 144(1); ICTY Rule 98 *ter*(A); ICTR Rule 88(A); SCSL Rule 88(A).

[82] Rome Statute, Art. 81; ICTY Statute, Art. 25(1); ICTR Statute, Art. 24(1); SCSL Statute, Art. 20(1); ICC Rule 150; ICTY Rule 108 (party has thirty days from judgement to file notice of appeal); ICTR Rule 108 (same); SCSL Rule 108(A) (fourteen days); ICC Court Regulation 57.

10.2 Sentencing

International criminal trials culminate with the trial chamber rendering a verdict and, if the verdict is conviction, the pronouncement of the penalty. Penalties available at the international criminal tribunals include, principally, sentencing to prison for a term of years, and also fines, forfeiture of ill-gotten gains, restitution, and other forms of reparations to victims.[83] Unlike the Tribunals at Nuremberg and Tokyo, none of the modern international criminal tribunals permits the death penalty, though life sentences are possible (except at the SCSL) and have been handed down.[84] They also make no provision for corporal punishment, penitentiary servitude, or community service.

Due in large part to the widely varying range of approaches in domestic criminal systems, states have been unable to reach consensus on a uniform set of criteria relevant to the sentencing decision and how such criteria should be applied.[85] The result is a surprising dearth of provisions in the tribunals' governing instruments to cabin – or at least guide – the hands of the judges as they determine the convicted person's sentence. The broad discretion afforded trial chambers has generated an unpredictability that makes sentencing one of the most criticised areas of international criminal law. Indeed, as one ICTY Trial Chamber frankly acknowledged, 'it is difficult to detect any pattern or guidance in the sentencing "practice" of the Tribunal'.[86]

In this section, we touch upon the main purposes of sentencing and the sentencing factors most often identified in the jurisprudence. We have set forth our major

[83] See Rome Statute, Art. 77; ICTY Statute, Art. 24; ICTR Statute, Art. 23; SCSL Statute, Art. 19; ICC Rules 146–147; ICTY Rules 77(G), 91(G), 77 *bis*, 101(A), 105; ICTR Rules 77(G), 91(G), 101(A), 105; SCSL Rules 77(G), 91(C), 101(A), 104. On fines, forfeiture, reparations, and restitution, see *infra* Section 10.3.

[84] Rome Statute, Art. 77(1)(b); ICTY Rule 101(A); ICTR Rule 101(A); SCSL Rule 101(A). See also, e.g., Report of the Secretary-General Pursuant to Paragraph 2 of Security Council Resolution 808 (1993), 3 May 1993, UN Doc. S/25704, paras. 111–112 (recommending that ICTY be empowered to impose life sentences, but not death penalty). The Rome Statute prohibits a trial chamber from imposing a sentence in excess of thirty years, except 'when justified by the extreme gravity of the crime and the individual circumstances of the convicted person'. Rome Statute, Art. 77(1); see also ICC Rule 145(3); *infra* note 193 and accompanying text. The SCSL Statute and Rules require the chamber to specify the number of years the convicted person must spend in prison. SCSL Statute, Art. 19(1); SCSL Rule 101(A). Due to the extreme gravity of the crimes and the relatively senior status of most accused at the ICTR, several chambers of that Tribunal have imposed life sentences. See generally Robert D. Sloane, 'Sentencing for the "Crime of Crimes": The Evolving "Common Law" of Sentencing of the International Criminal Tribunal for Rwanda', (2007) 5 *Journal of International Criminal Justice* 713. See also, e.g., *Gacumbitsi* Appeal Judgement, *supra* note 16, paras. 204–206 (quashing Trial Chamber's thirty-year sentence and imposing life sentence); *Prosecutor* v. *Kamuhanda*, Case No. ICTR-99-54A-A, Judgement, 19 September 2005, para. 126 (affirming Trial Chamber's life sentence). Life sentences at the ICTY have been much rarer. See, e.g., *Galić* Appeal Judgement, *supra* note 16, p. 191 (2006 Appeal Judgement quashing Trial Chamber's twenty-year sentence and imposing a life sentence, the first ever at the ICTY).

[85] For the difficult debates leading up to the sparse imprisonment and sentencing provisions in the Rome Statute, see, e.g., William A. Schabas, 'Penalties', in Cassese, Gaeta, and Jones, *supra* note 45, pp. 1507–1512; Rolf Einar Fife, 'Applicable Penalties', in Triffterer, *supra* note 8, p. 989.

[86] *Milutinović et al.* Trial Judgement, *supra* note 1, Vol. III, para. 1143.

criticisms of the tribunals' sentencing practice in Volume II of this series,[87] and confine Section 10.2.4 of this chapter to a brief summary of them. We discuss fines, restitution and other reparations, and forfeiture in Section 10.3.

10.2.1 Purposes of sentencing

Following the lead of national courts, the international criminal tribunals have acknowledged four main rationales underlying sentencing: deterrence, retribution, incapacitation, and reconciliation,[88] with deterrence and retribution singled out as the most important.[89] Chambers have explained that the sentence they impose should deter the accused from committing crimes in the future and deter others contemplating criminal conduct,[90] though the deterrent effect of international criminal trials is debatable.[91] They have likewise emphasised the retributive purpose of sentencing, hastening to add that the severity of a convicted person's sentence should not be seen as a form of revenge on behalf of the victims, but rather a reflection of the indignation of the international community at the accused's conduct.[92]

[87] See Boas, Bischoff, and Reid, *Elements of Crimes*, *supra* note 3, pp. 356–369, 383–384.

[88] See especially *Prosecutor* v. *Erdemović*, Case No. IT-96-22-T, Sentencing Judgement, 29 November 1996 ('*Erdemović* November 1996 Sentencing Judgement'), paras. 57–66. Accord, e.g., *Limaj et al.* Trial Judgement, *supra* note 61, para. 723; *Prosecutor* v. *Ntakirutimana and Ntakirutimana*, Case Nos. ICTR-96-10-T and ICTR-96-17-T, Judgement and Sentence, 21 February 2003 ('*Ntakirutimana and Ntakirutimana* Trial Judgement'), para. 882. For the East Timor Special Panels' recognition of these purposes, see, e.g., *Prosecutor* v. *Cloe, Cab, Fuli, and Lelan*, Case No. 4/2003, Judgement, 16 November 2004 ('*Cloe et al.* Trial Judgement'), para. 22; *Soares* Trial Judgement, *supra* note 70, para. 28.

[89] See, e.g., *Prosecutor* v. *Aleksovski*, Case No. IT-95-14/1-A, Judgement, 24 March 2000, para. 185.

[90] See, e.g., *Kordić and Čerkez* Appeal Judgement, *supra* note 15, paras. 1073, 1076–1078 (discussing 'individual' and 'general' deterrence); *Čelebići* Appeal Judgement, *supra* note 29, para. 801 (also cautioning that deterrence should not be given 'undue prominence' in the sentencing determination) (quoting *Prosecutor* v. *Tadić*, Case Nos. IT-94-1-A and IT-94-1-A *bis*, Judgement in Sentencing Appeals, 26 January 2000 ('*Tadić* Judgement on Sentencing Appeal'), para. 48). For the East Timor Special Panels, see, e.g., *Soares* Trial Judgement, *supra* note 70, para. 29 ('In East Timor there is an additional requirement for deterrence because just across the border there are thousands of recalcitrant ex-militia men with the capability of once again destabilizing this country by means of murder.'); *Prosecutor* v. *Damaio da Costa Nunes*, Case No. 1/2003, Judgement, 10 December 2003 ('*da Costa Nunes* Trial Judgement'), para. 84.

[91] For example, although Rwanda has not experienced a significant episode of mass violence since 1994, this relative peace is more likely due to the policies of the current Rwandan Patriotic Front government than to fear of prosecution in the ICTR, the ICC, or another international court. Moreover, the ICTY's 1993 creation failed to curtail the abuses of the Bosnian wars, or deter the Srebrenica massacres, or the abuses in Kosovo and Macedonia even after the ICTY had handed down several convictions. And internal armed conflict continues in eastern Congo despite the ICC's prosecution of Thomas Lubanga, Germain Katanga, and Mathieu Ngudjolo. On this issue generally, see Michael L. Smidt, 'The International Criminal Court: An Effective Means of Deterrence?', (2001) 167 *Military Law Review* 156 (at pages 185–196, specifically discussing the questionable deterrent effect of international criminal trials); see also Mark B. Harmon and Fergal Gaynor, 'Ordinary Sentences for Extraordinary Crimes', (2007) 5 *Journal of International Criminal Justice* 683, 694–696.

[92] See, e.g., *Kordić and Čerkez* Appeal Judgement, *supra* note 15, para. 1075 (endorsing *Erdemović* November 1996 Sentencing Judgement, *supra* note 88, para. 65). Accord, e.g., *AFRC* Case, Case No. SCSL-04-16-T, Sentencing Judgement, 19 July 2007 ('*AFRC* Sentencing Judgement'), para. 15; *Prosecutor* v. *Jokić*, Case

Incapacitation refers to the removal of the convicted person from society through imprisonment so that he or she cannot do further harm or provoke further conflict. Incapacitation takes on special importance in the international criminal tribunals, especially in recent years, as most of the accused were important political, military, or paramilitary leaders who proved themselves very adept at exploiting ethnic and internecine animosities. The removal of these persons has arguably fostered a degree of peace and security in the former Yugoslavia, Rwanda, Sierra Leone, and elsewhere.[93] Chambers have also recognised the rehabilitation of the convicted person that could occur in prison as an appropriate consideration in sentencing.[94] Beyond these four purposes, some chambers have recognised a fifth: 'individual and general affirmative prevention aimed at influencing the legal awareness of the accused, the victims, their relatives, the witnesses, and the general public in order to reassure them that the legal system is being implemented and enforced'.[95]

10.2.2 Factors for determining the sentence

Unlike most domestic penal codes, none of the international criminal tribunals has sentencing tariffs establishing maximum and minimum penalties for the different crimes in its jurisdiction. Moreover, none has a set of sentencing guidelines to aid trial chambers in the difficult task of determining the number of years the convicted person is to spend in prison. The delegates negotiating the Rome Statute could not reach consensus on a sentencing tariff or guidelines for the ICC,[96] and the ICTY Appeals Chamber has expressly rejected calls to adopt guidelines, emphasising the discretionary nature of the sentencing decision: 'The sentence must always be

No. IT-01-42/1-S, Sentencing Judgement, 18 March 2004 ('*Jokić* Sentencing Judgement'), para. 31 ('As a form of retribution, punishment expresses society's condemnation of the criminal act and of the person who committed it and should be proportional to the seriousness of the crimes.'); *da Costa Nunes* Trial Judgement, *supra* note 90, para. 84.

93 See, e.g., *Erdemović* November 1996 Sentencing Judgement, *supra* note 88, para. 65. Accord, e.g., *Ntakirutimana and Ntakirutimana* Trial Judgement, *supra* note 88, para. 882. See also, e.g., *da Costa Nunes* Trial Judgement, *supra* note 90, para. 85 ('[T]he objective of punishing the perpetrators of the serious crimes committed in East Timor in 1999 is to avoid impunity and thereby to promote national reconciliation and the restoration of peace.'). The East Timor Special Panels prosecuted only low-level perpetrators; all the important leaders remained safely at large for the duration of the Panels' existence. On the Panels' regrettable track record, see Boas, Bischoff, and Reid, *Elements of Crimes*, *supra* note 3, pp. 120–128.

94 See, e.g., *Kordić and Čerkez* Appeal Judgement, *supra* note 15, para. 1079 (adding, however, that '[i]t would violate the principle of proportionality and endanger the pursuit of other sentencing purposes if rehabilitative considerations were given undue prominence in the sentencing process'). Accord, e.g., *Čelebići* Appeal Judgement, *supra* note 29, para. 806; *AFRC* Sentencing Judgement, *supra* note 92, paras. 14, 17; *Prosecutor v. Babić*, Case No. IT-03-72-S, Sentencing Judgement, 29 June 2004, para. 46 (loss of freedom 'provides the context for the convicted person's reflection on the wrongfulness of his acts … [t]his process contributes to the reintegration of the convicted person into society').

95 *Kordić and Čerkez* Appeal Judgement, *supra* note 15, para. 1073; see also *ibid.*, paras. 1080–1182 (elaborating on this concept); Accord, e.g., *AFRC* Sentencing Judgement, *supra* note 92, para. 16; *Limaj et al.* Trial Judgement, *supra* note 61, para. 723 n. 2420.

96 See Schabas, *supra* note 85, pp. 1508–1509.

decided according to the facts of each particular case and the individual guilt of the perpetrator'.[97] The Appeals Chambers have repeatedly reaffirmed the discretionary and individualised nature of sentencing decisions, and the need to base them on the totality of the circumstances.[98] Even though it has acknowledged the individualised nature of the exercise, however, the ICTY Appeals Chamber has also indicated that 'sentences of like individuals in like cases should be comparable': 'While similar cases do not provide a legally binding tariff of sentences, they can be of assistance in sentencing if they involve the commission of the same offences in substantially similar circumstances'.[99]

Despite the absence of tariffs or guidelines, the governing instruments of the various tribunals do lay down some basic sentencing parameters, including illustrative lists of aggravating and mitigating factors. These factors guide trial chambers in determining the convicted person's sentence after it accepts the person's guilty plea or convicts the person following a trial. They also guide the Appeals Chambers in reviewing the trial chamber's sentence, modifying it, or imposing a new one. For the ICTY, ICTR, and SCSL, the factors include: (1) the gravity of the offence; (2) the individual circumstances of the convicted person; (3) substantial cooperation with the Prosecutor; (4) any aggravating circumstances; (5) any mitigating circumstances; (6) the general sentencing practice of the former Yugoslavia, Rwanda, and Sierra Leone, respectively; and (7) the extent to which the person has already served time for the same conduct.[100] The ICC's list is substantially similar.[101] The sentencing decisions of these tribunals, and of the East Timor Special Panels for Serious Crimes, have helpfully elaborated on the criteria and posited several aggravating and mitigating circumstances.[102] Still, precisely how the chambers

[97] *Blaškić* Appeal Judgement, *supra* note 61, para. 680. Accord, e.g., *Prosecutor* v. *Krstić*, Case No. IT-98-33-A, Judgement, 19 April 2004 ('*Krstić* Appeal Judgement'), para. 242; *Čelebići* Appeal Judgement, *supra* note 29, para. 715; *Prosecutor* v. *Furundžija*, Case No. IT-95-17/1-A, Judgement, 21 July 2000 ('*Furundžija* Appeal Judgement'), para. 238.

[98] See, e.g., *Strugar* Appeal Judgement, *supra* note 16, para. 336; *Blaškić* Appeal Judgement, *supra* note 61, para. 680; *Prosecutor* v. *Akayesu*, Case No. ICTR-96-4-A, Judgement, 1 June 2001 ('*Akayesu* Appeal Judgement'), para. 407.

[99] *Strugar* Appeal Judgement, *supra* note 16, para. 348. Accord *RUF* Appeal Judgement, *supra* note 15, paras. 1317–1318. See also *Strugar* Appeal Judgement, *supra* note 16, para. 349 (clarifying that 'previous sentencing practice is but one factor among a host of others which must be taken into account when determining the sentence'); *ibid.*, paras. 350–352 (Trial Chamber acted properly in comparing Strugar's sentence to that of his subordinate Jokić, because the comparison was just one factor in the Chamber's overall analysis).

[100] See ICTY Statute, Art. 24(1)–(2); ICTR Statute, Art. 23(1)–(2); SCSL Statute, Art. 19(1)–(2); ICTY Rule 101; ICTR Rule 101; SCSL Rule 101. Accord, e.g., *Prosecutor* v. *Hadžihasanović and Kubura*, Case No. IT-01-47-A, Judgement, 22 April 2008 ('*Hadžihasanović and Kubura* Appeal Judgement'), para. 302.

[101] See Rome Statute, Art. 78(1)–(2); ICC Rule 145.

[102] See generally, e.g., James Meernik and Kimi King, 'The Sentencing Determinants of the International Criminal Tribunal for the Former Yugoslavia: An Empirical and Doctrinal Analysis', (2003) 16 *Leiden Journal of International Law* 717. As of 1 December 2009, the ICC had not sentenced an accused and thus had not contributed to the jurisprudential development of these factors, though the ICC Rules provide significantly more guidance than the Rules of the ICTY, ICTR, and SCSL, and will be cited below where relevant.

ultimately use these factors to arrive at the most important conclusion – the specific number of years for the sentence – remains largely a mystery.[103] The subsections that follow highlight the main holdings of the case law on the factors relevant to sentencing.

10.2.2.1 Gravity of the crime

The tribunals have recognised gravity of the crime as the most important factor – the 'litmus test' – for determining the appropriate sentence.[104] They have accorded the gravity factor an expansive scope, sometimes referring to it as 'totality of the culpable conduct'.[105] Relying on ICTY and ICTR precedent, the SCSL Trial Chamber in the *AFRC* case encapsulated what the inquiry entails:

> The determination of the gravity of the crime must be individually assessed. In making such an assessment, the Trial Chamber may examine, *inter alia*, the general nature of the underlying criminal conduct; the form and degree of participation of the Accused or the specific role played by the Accused in the commission of the crime; the degree of suffering, impact or consequences of the crime for the immediate victim in terms of physical, emotional and psychological effects; the effects of the crime on relatives of the immediate victims and/or the broader targeted group; the vulnerability of the victims; and the number of victims.[106]

Drawing from this and many chambers' formulations, gravity of the crime could be said to contain four sub-components: inherent gravity of the crime; gravity of

[103] See *supra* note 86 and accompanying text (noting *Milutinović* Trial Chamber's acknowledgment that 'it is difficult to detect any pattern or guidance in the sentencing "practice" of the Tribunal'). Indeed, the *Milutinović* case provides a good example in which the determination of the ultimate number of years is exceedingly difficult to discern. After engaging in an extensive analysis of the various sentencing factors (much of which is noted in the footnotes of the subsections below), and repeatedly acknowledging the extreme gravity of each convicted person's criminal conduct, the Trial Chamber handed down sentences of twenty-two, fifteen, twenty-two, fifteen, and twenty-two years, respectively, for Šainović, Ojdanić, Pavković, Lazarević, and Lukić. See *Milutinović et al.* Trial Judgement, *supra* note 1, Vol. III, paras. 1208–1212. Following the lead of virtually every chamber of the ICTY, ICTR, and SCSL before it, the Chamber chose not to explain the math that led it to these precise numbers. For more on the perception that chambers are simply 'pulling numbers out of the air', see *infra* notes 250–253 and accompanying text.

[104] *Akayesu* Appeal Judgement, *supra* note 98, para. 413 (quoting *Čelebići* Trial Judgement, *supra* note 2, para. 1225). Accord, e.g., *Čelebići* Appeal Judgement, *supra* note 29, para. 731; *Prosecutor* v. *Plavšić*, Case No. IT-00-39 and 40/1-S, Sentencing Judgement, 27 February 2003 ('*Plavšić* Sentencing Judgement'), para. 25 (gravity the 'cardinal feature').

[105] *Strugar* Appeal Judgement, *supra* note 16, para. 335. Accord, e.g., *RUF* Appeal Judgement, *supra* note 15, para. 1229.

[106] *AFRC* Sentencing Judgement, *supra* note 92, para. 19 (footnotes omitted) (citing, among others, *Blaškić* Appeal Judgement, *supra* note 61, para. 683; *Prosecutor* v. *Blagojević and Jokić*, Case No. IT-02-60-T, Judgement, 17 January 2005, para. 833). Accord, e.g., *RUF* Appeal Judgement, *supra* note 15, para. 1229; *Gacumbitsi* Appeal Judgement, *supra* note 16, para. 204; *Čelebići* Appeal Judgement, *supra* note 29, para. 731 ('The determination of the gravity of the crime requires a consideration of the particular circumstances of the case, as well as the form and degree of the participation of the accused in the crime.') (quoting *Prosecutor* v. *Kupreškić, Kupreškić, Kupreškić, Josipović, Papić, and Šantić*, Case No. IT-95-16-T, Judgement, 14 January 2000, para. 852).

the crime as committed; role of the accused; and impact on the victims. We briefly address each in a separate subsection.

10.2.2.1.1 Inherent gravity of the crime Some decisions at the *ad hoc* Tribunals held that genocide is inherently more grave than crimes against humanity, and that crimes against humanity are inherently more grave than war crimes,[107] a position with which some judges and commentators have agreed.[108] Nevertheless, the ICTY and ICTR Appeals Chambers have rejected an abstract ranking of the core categories of crime, and held that no inherent ranking or hierarchy exists among them.[109] Thus, a sentence for genocide need not necessarily be harsher than a sentence for a crime against humanity based on the same underlying conduct, and a sentence for crimes against humanity need not necessarily be harsher than a sentence for a war crime, though in practice the Tribunals have tended to hand down harsher sentences for genocide.

Some chambers have also held that inherent characteristics of certain underlying offences render them graver, in the abstract, than underlying offences that lack such elements. These have included offences other than genocide that have discriminatory intent as an element – especially persecution as a crime against humanity[110] – and sexual offences.[111] This jurisprudence would appear to be inconsistent with the Appeals Chambers' declarations that there exists no hierarchy among core categories of crime.

10.2.2.1.2 Gravity of the crime as committed Chambers have routinely had regard in sentencing to the gravity of the conduct in which the physical perpetrators actually engaged. A chamber is likely to find a crime graver, and thus deserving of a harsher sentence, where it was committed through especially violent or heinous

[107] See, e.g., *Prosecutor* v. *Niyitegeka*, Case No. ICTR-96-14-A, Judgement, 9 July 2004, para. 53; *Prosecutor* v. *Kambanda*, Case No. ICTR-97-23-S, Judgement and Sentence, 4 September 1998 ('*Kambanda* Sentencing Judgement'), para. 16; *Prosecutor* v. *Tadić*, Case No. IT-94-1-T*bis*-R117, Sentencing Judgement, 11 November 1999, paras. 28–29.

[108] See, e.g., *Tadić* Judgement on Sentencing Appeal, *supra* note 90, Separate Opinion of Judge Cassese, para. 16; Boas, Bischoff, and Reid, *Elements of Crimes*, *supra* note 3, pp. 143, 363–367; Allison Marston Danner, 'Constructing a Hierarchy of Crimes in International Criminal Law Sentencing', (2001) 87 *Virginia Law Review* 415, 420, 477.

[109] See, e.g., *Prosecutor* v. *Stakić*, Case No. IT-97-24-A, Judgement, 22 March 2006, para. 375; *Rutaganda* v. *Prosecutor*, Case No. ICTR-96-3-A, Judgement, 26 May 2003, para. 590.

[110] See, e.g., *Prosecutor* v. *Banović*, Case No. IT-02-65/1-S, Sentencing Judgement, 28 October 2003, para. 91; *Prosecutor* v. *Sikirica, Došen, and Kolundžija*, Case No. IT-95-8-S, Sentencing Judgement, 13 November 2001 ('*Sikirica et al.* Sentencing Judgement'), para. 232; *Prosecutor* v. *Todorović*, Case No. IT-95-9/1-S, Sentencing Judgement, 31 July 2001, para. 113 ('[T]he crime of persecution is inherently very serious. It is the only crime against humanity which requires that the perpetrator act with a discriminatory intent and, by its nature, it incorporates other crimes. On account of its distinctive features, the crime of persecution justifies a more severe penalty.') (citing *Prosecutor* v. *Blaškić*, Case No. IT-95-14-T, Judgement, 3 March 2000, para. 785).

[111] See, e.g., *Blaškić* Appeal Judgement, *supra* note 61, para. 686; *Prosecutor* v. *Kunarac, Kovač, and Vuković*, Case No. IT-96-23 and IT-96–23/1-A, Judgement, 12 June 2002 ('*Kunarac et al.* Appeal Judgement'), para. 352.

means.[112] That the crimes in question were committed in places of civilian sanctuary, such as churches, mosques, schools, and hospitals, will typically serve to render them more grave.[113] Crimes will likely also be considered graver where their duration extends over a longer period of time.[114]

The *Blaškić* Appeals Chamber considered a number of key facts as establishing the gravity of the crimes in that case:

> The crimes of which the Appellant has been convicted are serious violations of international humanitarian law, directed almost exclusively against Bosnian Muslims. Their arbitrary detention in pitiful conditions, and in a climate of fear, combined with their employment for forced labour or as human shields, establishes the gravity of the offences in this case.[115]

The *Milutinović* Trial Chamber made a similar assessment:

> [T]he Accused have all, save Milan Milutinović, been found guilty of committing or aiding and abetting the forcible displacement of hundreds of thousands of Kosovo Albanians. These crimes were not isolated instances, but rather part of a widespread and systematic campaign of terror and violence over a period of just over two months. Some of the victims were of a particularly vulnerable nature, such as young women, elderly people, and children. The Trial Chamber therefore finds that the crimes for which each of the Accused has been found to incur criminal liability are of a high level of gravity.[116]

10.2.2.1.3 Form of participation of the accused In assessing the gravity of the crime, chambers take into consideration the form and degree of participation of the convicted person in the crime's commission.[117] We have discussed the jurisprudence relating to this factor – including its flaws – in Volume I, and refer the reader to that discussion for elaboration on the points below and examples of their operation in practice.[118]

Many chambers have found that the accused's personal involvement in the crime(s) as a physical perpetrator makes the criminal conduct graver and thus has an aggravating effect on the sentence. The aggravating effect of personal involvement

[112] See, e.g., *Hadžihasanović and Kubura* Appeal Judgement, *supra* note 100, para. 317 (aggravation where victim decapitated); *Blaškić* Appeal Judgement, *supra* note 61, para. 686; *Cloe et al.* Trial Judgement, *supra* note 88, para. 20 (finding 'brutality and callousness' of murders to be aggravating factors).

[113] See, e.g., *RUF* Appeal Judgement, *supra* note 15, para. 1275; *Prosecutor* v. *Muhimana*, Case No. ICTR-95-1B-T, Judgement and Sentence, 28 April 2005 ('*Muhimana* Trial Judgement'), para. 605 (finding aggravation on this basis).

[114] See, e.g., *Hadžihasanović and Kubura* Appeal Judgement, *supra* note 100, para. 317; *Blaškić* Appeal Judgement, *supra* note 61, para. 686; *Kunarac et al.* Appeal Judgement, *supra* note 111, para. 356 (Trial Chamber did not err in finding that a two-month duration of enslavement was sufficient to constitute an aggravating factor).

[115] *Blaškić* Appeal Judgement, *supra* note 61, para. 684.

[116] *Milutinović et al.* Trial Judgement, *supra* note 1, Vol. III, paras. 1173, 1174. Gravity based on the crimes' impact on the victims is discussed text accompanying notes 128–133, *infra*.

[117] See, e.g., *Milutinović et al.* Trial Judgement, *supra* note 1, Vol. III, para. 1147.

[118] See Boas, Bischoff, and Reid, *Forms of Responsibility*, *supra* note 68, pp. 406–414, 419–423.

is higher when the accused holds a position of authority and shows support for or acquiescence in subordinate crimes through his or her actions.[119] Where an accused has aided and abetted another in committing the crime, the generally laxer mental elements have led most sentencing chambers to consider such conduct less grave than participation through physical commission, participation in a joint criminal enterprise (JCE), planning, instigating, or ordering.[120]

Indirect involvement has generally been considered as lessening the gravity of the crime.[121] If the accused's responsibility is engaged through a failure to act, the chamber is likely to consider this conduct less grave in sentencing than that of a similarly situated person who played a direct role in ordering or otherwise coordinating the physical perpetrators in their commission of crimes.[122] Consequently, the indirect nature of superior responsibility – that is, responsibility for the omission of failing to prevent, stop, or punish subordinate crimes – has tended to place it even below aiding and abetting on the gravity continuum in chambers' sentencing decisions.[123] As we have argued, despite jurisprudence placing physical commission at the 'more grave' end of a continuum and relegating aiding and abetting and superior responsibility to the 'less grave' end, a high-level accomplice or superior may well make a greater contribution to the commission of mass atrocities than a physical perpetrator, because the former's position of influence or authority has a legitimising effect on the actions of the physical perpetrator, or because he or she makes available the means necessary for a multitude of perpetrators to bring a massive crime to fruition.[124] On balance, the jurisprudence has yet to take this reality into account.

Where the trial chamber finds the accused responsible as a superior, it must assess both the gravity of the crime, and the gravity of the accused's failure to prevent or stop it or to punish the perpetrators afterwards.[125] The chamber cannot regard the accused's lack of direct involvement in the crime as a mitigating circumstance, as superior responsibility, by definition, entails an omission.[126] By a

[119] See, e.g., *Hadžihasanović and Kubura* Appeal Judgement, *supra* note 100, para. 320; *Blaškić* Appeal Judgement, *supra* note 61, para. 686; *Milutinović et al.* Trial Judgement, *supra* note 1, Vol. III, para. 1151; *Soares* Trial Judgement, *supra* note 70, para. 25 (finding aggravation where convicted person, a village level commander of the Indonesian Armed Forces, 'savagely us[ed] a stick and a solid iron bar [to beat the victim], thereby setting a bad example for his subordinates and inciting them to further violence').

[120] See Boas, Bischoff, and Reid, *Forms of Responsibility*, *supra* note 68, pp. 406–412. See also, e.g., *Cloe et al.* Trial Judgement, *supra* note 88, para. 20 (considering as mitigating the severity of accused Cloe's conduct the fact that he did not himself inflict wounds on the victims, but instead led the physical perpetrators to the victims' location).

[121] See, e.g., *Blaškić* Appeal Judgement, *supra* note 61, para. 696.

[122] See, e.g., *Strugar* Appeal Judgement, *supra* note 16, paras. 353–356.

[123] See Boas, Bischoff, and Reid, *Forms of Responsibility*, *supra* note 68, pp. 412–413.

[124] See *ibid.*, pp. 419–423. See also *supra* text accompanying note 69.

[125] See *Strugar* Appeal Judgement, *supra* note 16, para. 386.

[126] See, e.g., *ibid.*, para. 381 (Trial Chamber did not err in refusing to accept Strugar's indirect participation as a mitigating factor, as it found him responsible as a superior for failing to prevent and punish the crimes in question).

similar token, it cannot regard the accused's position of authority as an aggravating circumstance.[127]

10.2.2.1.4 Impact on victims In assessing the gravity of the crime, chambers also take into account the effect or impact of the crime on the victims, including the extent of any physical, psychological, or emotional suffering.[128] A chamber will likely consider a crime graver the larger the number of victims;[129] where the victims are especially vulnerable, such as pregnant women, children, or elderly people;[130] or where the perpetrators humiliate the victim.[131] Crimes will also be regarded as graver where the victims' suffering is prolonged or can be expected to extend into the future.[132] Chambers have also considered the effect of the crime on the victim's surviving relatives when assessing the crime's gravity.[133]

10.2.2.2 Individual circumstances of the convicted person

The Statutes of the international criminal tribunals expressly list the individual circumstances of the convicted person as a factor for determining the sentence.[134] In the jurisprudence, this requirement has entailed an inquiry into a number of facts personal to the convicted person which, if accepted by the chamber, usually

[127] *Hadžihasanović and Kubura* Appeal Judgement, *supra* note 100, para. 320.

[128] See, e.g., *Blaškić* Appeal Judgement, *supra* note 61, para. 683; *Milutinović et al.* Trial Judgement, *supra* note 1, Vol. III, para. 1147.

[129] See, e.g., *Hadžihasanović and Kubura* Appeal Judgement, *supra* note 100, para. 317; *Blaškić* Appeal Judgement, *supra* note 61, para. 684 ('[T]he abuse of the sizeable number of 247 human beings as human shields and – in doing so – endangering their lives at least *in abstracto* has to be seen as a serious aggravating factor.'); *Milutinović et al.* Trial Judgement, *supra* note 1, Vol. III, para. 1151. Accord ICC Rule 145(2)(b)(iv).

[130] See, e.g., *Blaškić* Appeal Judgement, *supra* note 61, paras. 683, 686; *Kunarac et al.* Appeal Judgement, *supra* note 111, para. 352 (Trial Chamber did not err in considering, as an aggravating factor, that the crimes were committed against 'particularly vulnerable and defenceless women') (internal quotation marks and citation omitted); *ibid.*, paras. 355, 405 (Trial Chamber did not err in considering victims' youth as an aggravating factor); *Milutinović et al.* Trial Judgement, *supra* note 1, Vol. III, para. 1151; *ibid.*, paras. 1173–1174 (in concluding that the crimes were 'of a high level of gravity', noting that '[s]ome of the victims were of a particularly vulnerable nature, such as young women, elderly people, and children'); *Muhimana* Trial Judgement, *supra* note 113, para. 607 (finding aggravation where victim of accused's rape was only fifteen years old); *ibid.*, para. 612 (finding aggravation where accused cut pregnant woman's baby out of her womb, and where assailants under the direction of accused cut off her arms and stuck sharpened sticks into the sockets); *Soares* Trial Judgement, *supra* note 70, para. 25 (aggravating sentence after finding that 'all victims were helpless civilians who could expect protection during their custody, instead of barbarous treatment'); *da Costa Nunes* Trial Judgement, *supra* note 90, para. 81 (similar). Accord ICC Rule 145(2)(b)(iii).

[131] See, e.g., *Muhimana* Trial Judgement, *supra* note 113, para. 609 (conducting rapes in front of onlookers constituted an aggravating factor); *ibid.*, para. 611 (parading recently raped women naked in public constituted an aggravating factor).

[132] See, e.g., *Kunarac et al.* Appeal Judgement, *supra* note 111, para. 409; *Milutinović et al.* Trial Judgement, *supra* note 1, Vol. III, para. 1147.

[133] See, e.g., *Blaškić* Appeal Judgement, *supra* note 61, para. 683; *Milutinović et al.* Trial Judgement, *supra* note 1, Vol. III, para. 1147; *Prosecutor* v. *Mrđa*, Case No. IT-02-59-S, Sentencing Judgement, 31 March 2004, para. 40 (considering that the victims' surviving relatives suffered emotional pain, and that this fact contributed to the seriousness of the crimes).

[134] Rome Statute, Art. 78(1); ICTY Statute, Art. 24(2); ICTR Statute, Art. 23(2); SCSL Statute, Art. 19(2).

tend to have a mitigating effect on the sentence. Chambers have found the convicted person's youth and immaturity at the time of the crimes to have a mitigating effect.[135] The person's advanced age, and consequent short life expectancy, could also reduce the time the chamber considers it just or appropriate for him or her to remain in prison.[136] A person's diminished mental capacity could also operate to mitigate the sentence,[137] as could the fact that the convicted person has a spouse or children that will be deprived of support during his or her imprisonment.[138] In addition, chambers have found, in exceptional cases, that the person's ill or deteriorating health serves to mitigate the sentence.[139]

10.2.2.3 Cooperation with the prosecution

The ICTY, ICTR, and SCSL Rules each list 'substantial cooperation' with the prosecution, before or after conviction, as a circumstance the trial chamber should take into account as possibly mitigating the convicted person's sentence.[140] The ICC Rules' formulation is broader, noting that 'any cooperation with the Court' may be

[135] See, e.g., *Čelebići* Appeal Judgement, *supra* note 29, para. 590; *Erdemović* November 1996 Sentencing Judgement, *supra* note 88, para. 95 (Erdemović was twenty-three at the time of the crimes). Accord ICC Rule 145(1)(c).

[136] See, e.g., *Blaškić* Appeal Judgement, *supra* note 61, para. 696; *Milutinović et al.* Trial Judgement, *supra* note 1, Vol. III, para. 1152; *ibid.*, para. 1188 (accused Ojdanić's age not advanced enough to constitute a mitigating factor); *Jokić* Sentencing Judgement, *supra* note 92, para. 100 (considering in mitigation accused's advanced age, but noting that this factor is shared by many accused and thus has limited importance); *Prosecutor* v. *Strugar*, Case No. IT-01-42-T, Judgement, 31 January 2005 ('*Strugar* Trial Judgement'), para. 469 (considering in mitigation that accused was seventy-one years old); *Plavšić* Sentencing Judgement, *supra* note 104, paras. 105–106 (considering in mitigation accused's age of seventy-two because 'physical deterioration associated with advanced years makes serving the same sentence harder for an older than a younger accused', and 'an offender of advanced years may have little worthwhile life left upon release') (quotation at para. 105).

[137] See, e.g., *Blaškić* Appeal Judgement, *supra* note 61, para. 696; *Milutinović et al.* Trial Judgement, *supra* note 1, Vol. III, para. 1152. Cf., e.g., *Cloe et al.* Trial Judgement, *supra* note 88, para. 20 ('Further mitigating is, that [the convicted persons] were illiterate farmers who must be considered as victims of circumstances themselves, as they would not have committed the crimes without the despicable system of the Indonesian Armed Forces … to pit one part of the local population against another.').

[138] See, e.g., *Kunarac et al.* Appeal Judgement, *supra* note 111, para. 362 (Trial Chamber erred in failing to consider, in mitigation, that accused Kunarac had three young children, but due to the number and severity of the crimes, this error did not require a revision of the sentence); *Strugar* Trial Judgement, *supra* note 136, para. 469 (considering in mitigation that accused's imprisonment would leave his elderly and infirm wife without his daily support, and accused's concern for his wife would make serving his sentence particularly difficult); *Cloe et al.* Trial Judgement, *supra* note 88, para. 20 (considering as a mitigating factor that 'each accused has to provide by farming for a wife, several children and other dependants, so that a prison term is particularly harsh for him'). But see, e.g., *da Costa Nunes* Trial Judgement, *supra* note 90, para. 78 (even though convicted person had a wife and children, 'this may be said of many accused persons, and cannot be given any significant weight in a case of this gravity').

[139] See, e.g., *Strugar* Appeal Judgement, *supra* note 16, para. 392 and p. 146 (accepting that Strugar's health had deteriorated since trial and, though finding him responsible for additional crimes, reducing his sentence from eight to seven-and-a-half years); *Strugar* Trial Judgement, *supra* note 136, para. 469 (considering in mitigation accused's poor health, including vascular dementia and depression); see also, e.g., *Blaškić* Appeal Judgement, *supra* note 61, para. 696; *Milutinović et al.* Trial Judgement, *supra* note 1, Vol. III, para. 1152 ('Poor health is to be considered only in exceptional or rare cases.'); *ibid.*, paras. 1188, 1193, 1203 (health of accused Ojdanić, Pavković, and Lukić not poor enough to constitute a mitigating factor); *ibid.*, para. 1199 (accused Lazarević's health problems serious enough to constitute a mitigating factor).

[140] ICTY Rule 101(B)(ii); ICTR Rule 101(B)(ii); SCSL Rule 101(B)(iii).

considered in mitigation.[141] This mitigating circumstance most often arises in the context of plea bargaining, where the prosecution agrees to recommend a lighter sentence in exchange for the accused's plea of guilty and cooperation in other cases, such as aiding in an investigation or testifying at another accused's trial.[142] Several chambers have acknowledged cooperation with the prosecution as a mitigating circumstance in the case at hand,[143] while others have found that the convicted person did not cooperate and thus should not be entitled to mitigation on that basis.[144] Even where the prosecution asserts that the convicted person has provided substantial cooperation, it is ultimately for the trial chamber to decide whether the person has indeed substantially cooperated.[145]

Where the trial chamber decides that the convicted person's cooperation was less substantial than the prosecution submits, the reasoned judgement requirement mandates that it thoroughly explain the reasons for the deviation.[146] For example, in *Momir Nikolić*, the Trial Chamber noted and regarded as a mitigating factor prosecution submissions that Nikolić had already provided substantial assistance in locating mass graves, had testified in a previous trial, and had agreed to testify in future trials concerning the events in and around Srebrenica. But the Trial Chamber also noted Nikolić's 'numerous instances' of evasiveness when testifying in the *Blagojević and Jokić* trial, that such testimony had suffered from a lack of detail and openness, and his admission that he had previously lied to the

[141] ICC Rule 145(2)(a)(ii).

[142] Plea bargaining is discussed in Chapter 6, Section 6.4.2.

[143] See, e.g., *Milutinović et al.* Trial Judgement, *supra* note 1, Vol. III, para. 1183 (acknowledging accused Šainović's post-indictment interview with the prosecution as a mitigating factor, though not rising to the level of 'substantial cooperation'); *ibid.*, para. 1198 (accused Lazarević provided substantial cooperation to the prosecution in giving it an extensive interview and several new documents just days after his initial appearance); *Prosecutor* v. *Deronjić*, Case No. IT-02-61-S, Sentencing Judgement, 30 March 2004, paras. 244–255, 280 and p. 78 (accepting parties' submissions that the cooperation provided by Deronjić – through, among other things, testifying in several previous cases, providing new documents to the prosecution, and identifying new crimes and perpetrators previously unknown to the prosecution – was substantial; declining to assess for itself the forensic quality of the prior testimony; and ultimately sentencing Deronjić to ten years in light of this and other mitigating circumstances); *Momir Nikolić* Sentencing Judgement, *supra* note 78, paras. 154–156, 171 (as described at note 146, *infra*, conducting its own assessment despite prosecution's assurances); but see *Kambanda* Sentencing Judgement, *supra* note 107, paras. 47, 61–62 (acknowledging former Rwandan Prime Minister's cooperation with prosecution but still imposing life sentence for genocide and other crimes). The Trial Chamber's imposition of a life sentence on Kambanda, despite his plea of guilty, some ninety hours of interviews, and agreement to testify in future trials, led Kambanda to refuse further cooperation and proved a significant disincentive for other ICTR accused to plead guilty. See Chapter 6, Section 6.4.2; see also Steven R. Ratner, Jason S. Abrams, and James L. Bischoff, *Accountability for Human Rights Atrocities in International Law: Beyond the Nuremberg Legacy* (3rd edn 2009), pp. 227–228.

[144] See, e.g., *Blaškić* Appeal Judgement, *supra* note 61, para. 701 (affirming Trial Chamber's refusal to mitigate based on cooperation); *Nzabirinda* Sentencing Judgement, *supra* note 78, para. 74 (noting accused's guilty plea and promise to cooperate with prosecution in future, but finding that 'this offer cannot be considered as a mitigating circumstance in and of itself' because accused had not yet demonstrated substantial cooperation).

[145] *Prosecutor* v. *Momir Nikolić*, Case No. IT-02-60/1-A, Judgement on Sentencing Appeal, 8 March 2006 ('*Momir Nikolić* Judgement on Sentencing Appeal'), para. 93.

[146] On the reasoned judgement requirement generally, see *supra* Section 10.1.1.

prosecution.[147] The Appeals Chamber found that the Trial Chamber had breached the reasoned judgement requirement in only explaining one instance of evasiveness in the *Blagojević and Jokić* testimony and no instances of lack of detail or openness; and in not acknowledging that, after having lied to the prosecution, Nikolić voluntarily re-approached the prosecution, apologised, and corrected his untruthful statements. The Appeals Chamber noted that it would consider the Trial Chamber's underestimation of the degree of Nikolić's cooperation in revising Nikolić's sentence.[148] Noting this and another error, it ultimately reduced his sentence from twenty-three to twenty years.[149]

10.2.2.4 Other aggravating circumstances

Beyond the others mentioned above, the tribunals have considered several factors as potentially aggravating the convicted person's sentence. These include, among others: (1) the person has relevant prior convictions for international crimes or crimes of a similar nature;[150] (2) the person engaged in the conduct with discriminatory intent, where discriminatory intent is not already an element of the crime for which he or she was convicted;[151] (3) the person had reprehensible motives;[152] (4) the person held a leadership position, a position of authority, or was otherwise a person of influence;[153] (5) the person abused his or her powers or position of authority to help

[147] See *Momir Nikolić* Sentencing Judgement, *supra* note 78, paras. 154–156, 171.

[148] See *Momir Nikolić* Judgement on Sentencing Appeal, *supra* note 145, paras. 98–115.

[149] *Ibid.*, para. 135 and p. 51. See also Chapter 6, note 247 and sources cited therein (discussing how the prosecution dropped Nikolić from its witness list in at least one subsequent case).

[150] See, e.g., ICC Rule 145(2)(b)(i).

[151] See, e.g., *Blaškić* Appeal Judgement, *supra* note 61, paras. 686, 693, 695; *Milutinović et al.* Trial Judgement, *supra* note 1, Vol. III, para. 1151. Accord, e.g., *RUF* Appeal Judgement, *supra* note 15, paras. 1236–1237 (finding that Trial Chamber erred in considering, as an aggravating factor, the specific intent Sesay had when he participated in acts of terrorism and collective punishments as war crimes, since specific intent is already an element of each offence); *Prosecutor* v. *Vasiljević*, Case No. IT-98-32-T, Judgement, 29 November 2002, para. 278 (considering in aggravation accused's discriminatory intent, and remarking that 'crimes based upon ethnic grounds are particularly reprehensible, and the existence of such a state of mind is relevant to the sentence to be imposed either as an ingredient of that crime or as a matter of aggravation where it is not such an ingredient'). Accord ICC Rule 145(2)(b)(v).

[152] See, e.g., *Blaškić* Appeal Judgement, *supra* note 61, para. 686; *Milutinović et al.* Trial Judgement, *supra* note 1, Vol. III, para. 1151.

[153] See *Strugar* Appeal Judgement, *supra* note 16, paras. 353–354 (Trial Chamber did not err in considering that 'the Accused's position as a commander at a very high level in the [Yugoslav National Army] command structure, reporting directly to the Federal Secretariat of Defence, serves to emphasize the seriousness of his failure to prevent the shelling and to punish the perpetrators' and consequently aggravates his sentence) (at para. 353, quoting *Strugar* Trial Judgement, *supra* note 136, para. 464); *Kambanda* v. *Prosecutor*, Case No. ICTR-97-23-A, Judgement, 19 October 2000, para. 126 (upholding Trial Chamber's consideration of accused's high position as Rwandan Prime Minister as an aggravating factor); *da Costa Nunes* Trial Judgement, *supra* note 90, para. 82 (considering as an aggravating factor that the convicted person, a platoon commander of a pro-Indonesia militia, 'held a position of responsibility within his militia group, and therefore was in a position to avoid unnecessary bloodshed'). Accord, e.g., ICC Rule 145(2)(b)(ii). This aggravating circumstance is unavailable where the chamber has held the accused responsible for failing to prevent or punish the crimes under superior responsibility. See *supra* note 127 and accompanying text.

commit crimes;[154] (6) the person, far from expressing regret or remorse, is pleased with or proud of his or her actions;[155] and (7) the person engaged in the criminal conduct with zeal.[156] A chamber cannot regard the accused's exercise of the right to remain silent as an aggravating circumstance,[157] and cannot 'double count' as an aggravating circumstance any factor or element that the chamber also considered as relevant in the analysis of the crime's gravity.[158] As noted above, the prosecution must prove the existence of aggravating factors beyond a reasonable doubt.[159]

10.2.2.5 Other mitigating circumstances

Beyond cooperation with the prosecution and others mentioned above and below, the tribunals have considered several factors as potentially mitigating the convicted person's sentence. These include, among others: (1) the person opted to plead guilty, thereby obviating the need for trial;[160] (2) the person voluntarily surrendered to the tribunal upon his indictment becoming public;[161] (3) the person was

[154] See, e.g., *RUF* Appeal Judgement, *supra* note 15, para. 1315 (Trial Chamber did not err in finding that accused Gbao abused his position of authority, and in considering this abuse an aggravating factor); *Hadžihasanović and Kubura* Appeal Judgement, *supra* note 100, para. 320; *Milutinović et al.* Trial Judgement, *supra* note 1, Vol. III, para. 1151; *ibid.*, para. 1180 ('Although the Chamber acknowledges that Šainović was acting in the midst of a complicated situation, including the defence of the country against NATO bombing and some combat operations against the [Kosovo Liberation Army], the Chamber nevertheless finds that he abused his position of authority and that this aggravates his sentence.'); *ibid.*, para. 1185 (aggravating the sentence of the accused Ojdanić where, despite having received a letter from the ICTY Prosecutor warning him of crimes being committed by his subordinates, his Tribunal indictment a month later, and an awareness of previous crimes by his subordinates, continued to issue orders 'in his official capacity as the highest ranking officer of the [Yugoslav Army]', thereby abusing his superior position); *Muhimana* Trial Judgement, *supra* note 113, para. 604 (finding aggravation in sentence where accused, a high-level political official in the locale where the crimes were committed, 'instead of using, or attempting to use, his position within the community to promote peace and reconciliation ... actively participated in the atrocities'); *Sikirica et al.* Sentencing Judgement, *supra* note 110, para. 172 (finding aggravation in sentence where accused Došen abused position of trust and authority). Accord ICC Rule 145(2)(b)(ii).

[155] See, e.g., *Soares* Trial Judgement, *supra* note 70, para. 25.

[156] See, e.g., *Simba* v. *Prosecutor*, Case No. ICTR-01-76-A, Judgement, 27 November 2007, para. 320 (holding that 'zeal and sadism are factors to be considered, where appropriate, as aggravating factors rather than in the assessment of the gravity of an offence'); *Blaškić* Appeal Judgement, *supra* note 61, para. 686; *Milutinović et al.* Trial Judgement, *supra* note 1, Vol. III, para. 1151.

[157] See, e.g., *Blaškić* Appeal Judgement, *supra* note 61, para. 686.

[158] See, e.g., *RUF* Appeal Judgement, *supra* note 15, paras. 1236–1237; *Milutinović et al.* Trial Judgement, *supra* note 1, Vol. III, para. 1149.

[159] See *supra* text accompanying note 61.

[160] See, e.g., *Blaškić* Appeal Judgement, *supra* note 61, paras. 686, 714; *Prosecutor* v. *Jelisić*, Case No. IT-95-10-A, Judgement, 5 July 2001, para. 122 (while Trial Chamber considered accused's guilty plea in mitigation, it did not accord it much weight, and did not thereby abuse its discretion); *Milutinović et al.* Trial Judgement, *supra* note 1, Vol. III, para. 1152; *Cloe et al.* Trial Judgement, *supra* note 88, para. 20 (mitigating sentences where '[e]ach accused pleaded guilty to the charges at an early stage of the trial, thus enabling the Court to turn its resources to other cases'); *Plavšić* Sentencing Judgement, *supra* note 104, paras. 80–81 (opining that 'acknowledgement and full disclosure of serious crimes are very important in establishing the truth in relation to such crimes'; '[t]his together with acceptance of responsibility for the committed wrongs will promote reconciliation'; and giving 'significant weight' to Plavšić's plea of guilty which, 'particularly in light of her former position as President of Republika Srpska, should promote reconciliation in Bosnia and Herzegovina').

[161] See, e.g., *Blaškić* Appeal Judgement, *supra* note 61, para. 696; *Milutinović et al.* Trial Judgement, *supra* note 1, Vol. III, para. 1152; *ibid.*, para. 1200 (accused Lazarević's voluntary surrender constitutes a

of good character prior to the crimes;[162] (4) the person exhibited good behaviour in the tribunal's detention unit or during trial proceedings;[163] (5) the person aided or showed compassion toward some detainees or victims;[164] (6) the person committed the offences in question under duress or out of necessity;[165] (7) the person acted on the basis of a superior order,[166] unless the order was manifestly unlawful;[167] (8) the

mitigating factor); *Plavšić* Sentencing Judgement, *supra* note 104, para. 84 (same for Plavšić). See also Harmon and Gaynor, *supra* note 91, p. 705 (explaining why voluntary surrender is especially valuable to international criminal tribunals, including that the tribunal is dependent on states to make arrests, which are often delayed, and that accused involved in the same transaction have often been arrested at different times and tried separately instead of in one joined trial, thereby consuming additional time and resources).

162 See, e.g., *RUF* Appeal Judgement, *supra* note 15, paras. 1241–1242 (upholding Trial Chamber's rejection of defence witnesses' testimony regarding accused Sesay's good character). Considering the high rank or other position of responsibility held by many accused before international criminal tribunals, chambers may be more likely to find them to have been of good character prior to the crimes than would be the case in most domestic prosecutions. See, e.g., *Blaškić* Appeal Judgement, *supra* note 61, paras. 696, 706, 728 (finding that Blaškić, a colonel, was of good character and that this fact should serve to mitigate his sentence); *Milutinović et al.* Trial Judgement, *supra* note 1, Vol. III, para. 1152; *ibid.*, para. 1179 (acknowledging that prior to the events in question, each accused was 'of apparent good character'); *ibid.*, para. 1181 (acknowledging accused Šainović's good character prior to the events, but giving such character no credit in mitigation because Šainović received a letter from the ICTY Prosecutor warning of the crimes and his potential liability, yet still persisted in criminal conduct); *Ntakirutimana and Ntakirutimana* Trial Judgement, *supra* note 88, para. 895 (considering in mitigation that pastor 'Elizaphan Ntakirutimana was essentially a person of good moral character until the events of April to July 1994 during which he was swept along with many Rwandans into criminal conduct').

163 See, e.g., *Hadžihasanović and Kubura* Appeal Judgement, *supra* note 100, para. 325 (Trial Chamber acted within discretion in considering Hadžihasanović's good behaviour in the detention unit and during trial as a mitigating circumstance); *Blaškić* Appeal Judgement, *supra* note 61, para. 696; *Milutinović et al.* Trial Judgement, *supra* note 1, Vol. III, para. 1152; *ibid.*, para. 1178 (crediting the accused for their good behaviour during trial and in the detention unit, which 'enhanced the ability of the Chamber to discharge its duty ... to ensure that the trial was conducted in a fair and expeditious manner'); *Jokić* Sentencing Judgement, *supra* note 92, para. 100.

164 See, e.g., *Blaškić* Appeal Judgement, *supra* note 61, para. 696; *Milutinović et al.* Trial Judgement, *supra* note 1, Vol. III, para. 1152; *Prosecutor* v. *Niyitegeka*, Case No. ICTR-96-14-T, Judgement, 16 May 2003, para. 494 ('In mitigation of the Accused's sentence, the Chamber has considered evidence that the Accused intervened and saved a group of refugees from Interahamwe [and] thus saved these refugees' lives.'); *Sikirica et al.* Sentencing Judgement, *supra* note 110, para. 195 (considering in mitigation that 'Došen, as shift leader, often acted to ameliorate the terrible conditions that prevailed in the Keraterm camp, in relation to particular detainees'); *ibid.*, para. 229 ('The Chamber has heard ample evidence of Dragan Kolundžija's efforts to ease the harsh conditions in the Keraterm camp for many of the detainees ...[O]n the basis of the testimony as to his benevolent attitude towards the detainees, Dragan Kolundžija should receive a significant reduction in his sentence').

165 See, e.g., *Blaškić* Appeal Judgement, *supra* note 61, para. 696; *Milutinović et al.* Trial Judgement, *supra* note 1, Vol. III, para. 1152; *Prosecutor* v. *Erdemović*, Case No. IT-96-22-T*bis*, Sentencing Judgement, 5 March 1998, para. 17 (considering in mitigation that accused credibly felt compelled to kill Bosnian Muslim victims on threat that he would himself be killed if he did not). Accord ICC Rule 145(a)(i).

166 See, e.g., *RUF* Appeal Judgement, *supra* note 15, paras. 1280–1281 (rejecting accused Kallon's assertion that the Trial Chamber should have reduced his sentence because he was acting on orders of his superior Foday Sankoh); *Cloe et al.* Trial Judgement, *supra* note 88, para. 20 (regarding as a mitigating factor that the accused 'felt compelled to follow orders by [militia leader Anton Lelan Sufa], whom they considered as their commander'). Accord ICTY Statute, Art. 7(4); ICTR Statute, Art. 6(4); SCSL Statute, Art. 6(4).

167 An ICTY case illustrating this caveat is that of Darko Mrđa. Mrđa was a Bosnian Serb policeman who pled guilty to participating, under orders, in the separation and killing of some 200 military-aged men from a bus convoy of non-Serb civilians. *Mrđa* Sentencing Judgment, *supra* note 133, para. 10. He argued for leniency in sentencing because, 'against the backdrop of hatred prevailing at the material time, a person as young and of such low rank as [he] could not have opposed the orders he received'. *Ibid.*, para. 66. The Trial Chamber rejected this argument: '[T]he orders were so manifestly unlawful that Darko Mrđa must have been well

person had a very low or no rank in the military hierarchy;[168] (9) the person has expressed remorse – that is, 'acceptance of some measure of moral blameworthiness for personal wrongdoing'[169] – which the trial chamber finds sincere;[170] (10) the person has otherwise expressed sympathy, compassion, or sorrow for the victims of the crime;[171] (11) the person worked to foster reconciliation after the conflict;[172] (12) the person has no prior criminal record;[173] and (13) the person complied with the conditions of his provisional release.[174] As noted above, the accused must prove

aware that they violated the most elementary laws of war and the basic dictates of humanity. The fact that he obeyed such orders, as opposed to acting on his own initiative, does not merit mitigation of punishment.' *Ibid.*, para. 67; see also *ibid.*, para. 129 (handing down a twenty-seven-year sentence). Accord Rome Statute, Art. 33. See also Ratner, Abrams, and Bischoff, *supra* note 143, pp. 150–152 (discussing the defence of superior orders in international law generally and remarking that, 'for offences that do not entail a flagrant assault on the human person (most obviously property offences, but perhaps deportation and other crimes), superior orders might represent a valid defense for some personnel') (quotation at p. 152).

[168] See, e.g., *Erdemović* November 1996 Sentencing Judgement, *supra* note 88, paras. 92–95 (considering in mitigation that Erdemović held no rank in the military hierarchy).

[169] *Strugar* Appeal Judgement, *supra* note 16, para. 365.

[170] See, e.g., *ibid.*, paras. 365, 377–378 (upholding Trial Chamber's decision not to regard a letter written by Strugar to a Croatian minister the day after the shelling of Dubrovnik, in which he expressed regret for the crimes, as a sincere expression of remorse, since Strugar then failed to punish the troops responsible for the shelling despite his effective control over them); *Blaškić* Appeal Judgement, *supra* note 61, paras. 696, 705 (disagreeing with Trial Chamber's finding that Blaškić's remorse was not sincere, and considering such remorse in mitigation of his sentence); *Sikirica et al.* Sentencing Judgement, *supra* note 110, para. 152 (finding the following statement by accused Sikirica to be sincere and to constitute a mitigating factor: 'I deeply regret everything that happened in Keraterm while I was there. I feel only regret for all the lives that have been lost and the lives that were damaged in Prijedor, in Keraterm, and unfortunately, I contributed to the destruction of these lives.'); *ibid.*, paras. 194, 230 (also considering accused Došen's and Kolundžija's statements of remorse to be sincere).

[171] See, e.g., *Strugar* Appeal Judgement, *supra* note 16, para. 366; *Milutinović et al.* Trial Judgement, *supra* note 1, Vol. III, para. 1152; *Prosecutor* v. *Brđanin*, Case No. IT-99-36-T, Judgement, 1 September 2004, para. 1139 (accepting accused's expressions of sorrow as sincere and considering them as a mitigating circumstance). The mitigating impact of expressions of sorrow and regret can be expected to be somewhat less than expressions of remorse. See, e.g., *RUF* Appeal Judgement, *supra* note 15, paras. 1248–1249 (noting that rarely will expressions of regret or empathy be regarded as mitigating factors, and upholding the Trial Chamber's decision not to take this factor into account for accused Sesay); *Strugar* Appeal Judgement, *supra* note 16, para. 380 (upholding Trial Chamber's decision not to regard expressions of sorrow by Strugar's counsel on his behalf as a mitigating circumstance).

[172] See, e.g., *Milutinović et al.* Trial Judgement, *supra* note 1, Vol. III, para. 1152; *Jokić* Sentencing Judgement, *supra* note 92, paras. 90–91, 103 (finding mitigation upon noting evidence that, after the crimes in question, 'Jokić was instrumental in ensuring that a comprehensive ceasefire was agreed upon and implemented', and 'participated in political activities programmatically aimed at promoting a peaceful solution to the conflicts in the region') (quotations at paras. 90 and 91, respectively); *Plavšić* Sentencing Judgement, *supra* note 104, paras. 87–94 (considering in mitigation Plavšić's important role in securing acceptance for the Dayton Peace Accords in Republika Srpska).

[173] See, e.g., *Blaškić* Appeal Judgement, *supra* note 61, para. 696. Like the mitigating circumstance of good moral character, the status of many accused at international criminal tribunals as military professionals or high-ranking politicians makes it more likely that they will have no prior criminal record. See, e.g., *Milutinović et al.* Trial Judgement, *supra* note 1, Vol. III, para. 1152; *ibid.*, para. 1179 (considering as a mitigating factor that, prior to the events in question, none of the accused had a criminal record). See also, e.g., *Soares* Trial Judgement, *supra* note 70, para. 26; *da Costa Nunes* Trial Judgement, *supra* note 90, paras. 79–80 (acknowledging this factor and its applicability to da Costa Nunes, but ultimately giving it no weight in mitigation).

[174] See, e.g., *Hadžihasanović and Kubura* Appeal Judgement, *supra* note 100, para. 325 (Trial Chamber acted within discretion in considering Hadžihasanović's compliance with his conditions of provisional release as a mitigating circumstance); *Milutinović et al.* Trial Judgement, *supra* note 1, Vol. III, para. 1152.

mitigating factors on a balance of the probabilities.[175] The chamber has the discretion to determine the weight to attach to a mitigating factor, and even where the accused proves the existence of one or more factors, he or she is not thereby automatically entitled to a sentencing discount.[176]

10.2.2.6 Sentencing practice in a national system

The Statutes of the ICTY, ICTR, and SCSL direct the trial chamber to 'have recourse to the general practice regarding prison sentences' in the national courts of the state where the crimes were committed: respectively, the former Yugoslavia, Rwanda, and Sierra Leone.[177] The SCSL Statute adds the caveat 'as appropriate'; while the SCSL Rules originally repeated the mandate that Sierra Leonean sentencing practice be examined, the judges of the Special Court later deleted this provision. The delegates at Rome rejected proposals to include a similar provision allowing an ICC chamber to consider sentencing practice in the state of which the convicted person is a national or the state where the crimes were committed.[178]

In analysing this factor, chambers have had regard to the criminal codes in force at the time of the crimes' commission, as well as any relevant national case law.[179] Yet in practice, this factor has not proven significant in the sentences of the tribunals. The SCSL Appeals Chamber has held that the 'as appropriate' qualifier unique to the SCSL Statute obviates any need for SCSL chambers to consider Sierra Leonean sentencing practice unless the accused stands convicted of one of the Sierra Leonean domestic crimes in the Statute, and no accused was ever tried for one of those crimes.[180] For their part, the ICTY and ICTR Appeals Chambers have held that while trial chambers must consider the sentencing practice of the national system in question, they are not obliged to conform their sentences to national practice, although they are required to explain any divergence.[181] Hence,

[175] See *supra* text accompanying note 61.

[176] See, e.g., *RUF* Appeal Judgement, *supra* note 15, para. 1239; *Milutinović et al.* Trial Judgement, *supra* note 1, Vol. III, para. 1150.

[177] ICTY Statute, Art. 24(1) (containing quoted language); ICTR Statute, Art. 23(1); SCSL Statute, Art. 19(1) (also expressly directing the trial chamber to have recourse to ICTR sentencing practice). The ICTY and ICTR Rules repeat this consideration. ICTY Rule 101(B)(iii); ICTR Rule 101(B)(iii).

[178] See Schabas, *supra* note 85, p. 1504 (noting states' inability to reach consensus on proposal to allow ICC to consider penalties in the national law of the convicted person's state of nationality, the territorial state, and the state with jurisdiction over the person).

[179] See, e.g., *Milutinović et al.* Trial Judgement, *supra* note 1, Vol. III, paras. 1154–1160 (in case regarding events in Kosovo in 1999, examining the relevant statutes of Serbia, of which Kosovo formed part in 1999, as well as the Serbian Constitution, and Serbian court rulings relating to sentencing).

[180] *CDF* Appeal Judgement, *supra* note 71, paras. 476–477; accord, e.g., *AFRC* Appeal Judgement, *supra* note 70, para. 311; *AFRC* Sentencing Judgement, *supra* note 92, para. 32 (finding that 'it is not appropriate to adopt [Sierra Leonean] practice in the present case since none of the Accused was indicted for, nor convicted of', the national crimes listed in the SCSL Statute).

[181] See, e.g., *Prosecutor* v. *Dragan Nikolić*, Case No. IT-94-2-A, Judgement on Sentencing Appeal, 4 February 2005, para. 69 (in case of divergence, 'care should be taken to explain the sentence to be imposed with

the chamber is ultimately free to impose a sentence in excess of, or lighter than, what national law would dictate.[182] The *Kunarac* Trial Chamber offered a rationale: '[V]ery important underlying differences often exist between national prosecutions and prosecutions in this jurisdiction[;] the nature, scope and the scale of the offences tried before the International Tribunal do not allow for an automatic application of the sentencing practices of the former Yugoslavia'.[183] Despite the Appeals Chambers' admonition that deviations from national sentencing practice must be explained, most judgements contain only a summary reference to such practice.[184]

10.2.2.7 Time served

The international criminal tribunals' governing instruments direct the trial chamber to deduct from the convicted person's sentence any time served pursuant to an order of the tribunal: that is, time spent in detention awaiting trial at the tribunal and during trial – and, where the Appeals Chamber revises the sentence or hands down a new one, during appeals proceedings.[185] Chambers have routinely applied this principle,[186] sometimes specifying in the trial or sentencing judgement how much time the convicted person has already served.[187] The governing instruments also allow, but do not require, the trial chamber to deduct any time already spent

reference to the sentencing practice of the former Yugoslavia, especially where international law provides no guidance for a particular sentencing practice') (quoting and endorsing *Prosecutor* v. *Kunarac, Kovač, and Vuković*, Case Nos. IT-96-23-T & IT-96-23/1-T, Judgement, 22 February 2001 ('*Kunarac et al.* Trial Judgement'), para. 829); *Semanza* Appeal Judgement, *supra* note 16, para. 377; *Krstić* Appeal Judgement, *supra* note 97, para. 260; see also, e.g., *Hadžihasanović and Kubura* Appeal Judgement, *supra* note 100, paras. 335, 346 (holding that Trial Chamber erred in failing to 'adequately articulate the applicable sentencing practices of the former Yugoslavia in its sentencing determination', but that the error did not require adjustment of the sentence in this case).

182 See, e.g., *Blaškić* Appeal Judgement, *supra* note 61, para. 681; *Momir Nikolić* Sentencing Judgement, *supra* note 78, para. 96.

183 *Kunarac et al.* Trial Judgement, *supra* note 181, para. 829. The ICTY Appeals Chamber has repeatedly endorsed this rationale. See, e.g., *Blaškić* Appeal Judgement, *supra* note 61, para. 682; *Krstić* Appeal Judgement, *supra* note 97, para. 260.

184 A particularly egregious example is the one-sentence paragraph in *Ndindabahizi* Trial Judgement, *supra* note 69, para. 501: 'The Chamber has also found guidance in the practice of sentencing in Rwanda, as referred to in previous judgements of the Tribunal.'

185 Rome Statute, Art. 78(2); ICTY Rule 101(C); ICTR Rule 101(C); SCSL Rule 101(D).

186 See, e.g., *RUF* Appeal Judgement, *supra* note 15, p. 480 (sentencing Sesay, Kallon, and Gbao to fifty-two, forty, and twenty-five years, respectively, 'subject to credit being given under Rule 101(D) … for the period for which [each] has already been in detention'); *AFRC* Sentencing Judgement, *supra* note 92, p. 36.

187 See, e.g., *Prosecutor* v. *Orić*, Case No. IT-03-68-T, Judgement, 30 June 2006 ('*Orić* Trial Judgement'), paras. 782–784 (sentencing Orić to two years; noting that he had already been in custody for three years, two months, and twenty-one days; and accordingly ordering his immediate release); *Hadžihasanović and Kubura* Trial Judgement, *supra* note 1, pp. 625, 627 (sentencing Hadžihasanović and Kubura to five and two-and-a-half years, respectively, and ordering that each be given credit for the 828 days they had already been detained); *Milutinović et al.* Trial Judgement, *supra* note 1, Vol. III, paras. 1208–1212 (sentencing five of the six accused to terms longer than the time already served; noting the date each was brought into the Tribunal's custody; and ordering that credit be given for time served); *da Costa Nunes* Trial Judgement, *supra* note 90, p. 21 (sentencing da Costa Nunes to ten-and-a-half years, but deducting the '1 year 3 months and 20 days' he had already served in detention pursuant to orders of the East Timor Special Panels).

in prison serving a penalty imposed by a national court 'for the same act'.[188] The Rome Statute's formulation is potentially broader, allowing a deduction for any detention 'in connection with conduct underlying the crime', which presumably could include detention by order of a national or other international court, and time spent in pre-trial detention, during trial, or serving a sentence imposed by that court.[189]

10.2.3 Consecutive or concurrent sentencing

At the *ad hoc* Tribunals and the SCSL, when the trial chamber convicts the accused of more than one crime, it may impose a global sentence or a sentence for each conviction; in the latter case, it may order these to run consecutively or concurrently.[190] In practice, most chambers have ordered sentences to run concurrently,[191] a factor which no doubt contributes to the perception that sentences handed down by international criminal tribunals are too lenient in light of the severity of the conduct.[192] At the ICC, the chamber must pronounce a separate sentence for each crime, and then a joint sentence specifying the total period of imprisonment. The total must not exceed thirty years, but life sentences are possible 'when justified by the extreme gravity of the crime and the individual circumstances of the convicted person'.[193]

10.2.4 Problems in the application of sentencing factors

We are among the many who have criticised the *ad hoc* Tribunals – and especially the ICTY – for chronic shortcomings in applying the factors described above in a consistent and predictable manner. This incoherent sentencing practice has resulted in sentences that are often inconsistent across similar cases and, at the ICTY, far too lenient given the seriousness of the conduct, all the more so when compared to harsh sentences many national courts impose for crimes of far lesser

188 ICTY Statute, Art. 10(3); ICTR Statute, Art. 9(3); SCSL Statute, Art. 9(3); accord ICTY Rule 101(B)(iv); ICTR Rule 101(B)(iv); SCSL Rule 101(B)(iii).

189 Rome Statute, Art. 78(2).

190 ICTY Rule 87(C); ICTR Rule 87(C); SCSL Rule 101(C). See also, e.g., *Čelebići* Appeal Judgement, *supra* note 29, para. 430; *Blaškić* Appeal Judgement, *supra* note 61, para. 718 (holding that the competence to enter a global sentence 'does not entitle the International Tribunal to impose a single sentence arbitrarily' and that 'due consideration must be given to each particular offence in order for its gravity to be determined').

191 See, e.g., *RUF* Appeal Judgement, *supra* note 15, para. 1210 (noting Trial Chamber's concurrent fifty-two-year term of imprisonment for Sesay, composed of sixteen separate sentences of fifty-two, forty-five, thirty-three, forty, forty, forty-five, forty-five, forty, thirty-five, fifty, forty, fifty, fifty, twenty, fifty-one, and forty-five years, respectively).

192 See *infra* text accompanying notes 194–195, 251. See also *infra* note 238 and accompanying text (ICTY's tendency to allow early release after two-thirds of sentence served).

193 Rome Statute, Arts. 77(1), 78(3) (quotation at Art. 77(1)(b)); ICC Rule 145(3). See also *supra* note 84.

gravity. Moreover, the Appeals Chamber has also declined to recognise a hierarchy among the categories of crimes within the Tribunal's jurisdiction, despite elements rendering genocide inherently more grave than crimes against humanity, and crimes against humanity inherently more grave than war crimes, provided the underlying conduct is the same. Instead, the Appeals Chamber has maintained that no difference in sentence can be inferred from the category – genocide, crimes against humanity, or war crimes – into which a particular underlying offence falls. And the Appeals Chamber has shown little hesitation to interfere with the trial chamber's sentencing determinations, including by substituting its own assessment when it simply disagrees with that of the trial chamber, despite its recognition that the trial chamber is best placed to ascertain the appropriate punishment based on all the circumstances. We elaborate on these points in Volume II of this series.[194] Regrettably, an examination of other tribunals' sentences reveals that these criticisms are not confined to the ICTY and ICTR.[195]

10.3 Other penalties

In addition to or in lieu of a sentence of imprisonment, the governing instruments of the international criminal tribunals also allow the trial chamber to impose other penalties on the accused. This section provides a brief review of the other available penalties.

10.3.1 Fines

In the ICTY, ICTR, and SCSL, trial chambers may impose a fine on the accused only in cases where the latter is convicted of contempt or of giving false testimony,

[194] See Boas, Bischoff, and Reid, *Elements of Crimes*, *supra* note 3, pp. 356–369, 383–384.

[195] See, e.g., *CDF* Appeal Judgement, *supra* note 71, paras. 554–567 (acknowledging that Trial Chamber was excessively lenient in sentencing Fofana to six years and Kondewa to eight years despite the heinousness of their crimes, and opining that, '[i]n assessing the appropriate sentence, the obligation of the Appeals Chamber is … to impose sentences that reflect the revulsion of the international community to such crimes as those for which the accused persons have been convicted'; but then raising their respective sentences to just fifteen and twenty years, respectively) (quotation at para. 565); *AFRC* Appeal Judgement, *supra* note 70, paras. 326–330 (Appeals Chamber affirming Trial Chamber's many concurrent sentences on each of the accused, the longest of which were fifty, forty-five, and fifty years respectively for Brima, Kamara, and Kanu; and affirming total sentences of fifty, forty-five, and fifty years respectively, instead of ordering the sentences to run consecutively, despite Appeals Chamber's endorsement of Trial Chamber's finding that 'Brima, Kamara and Kanu have been found responsible for some of the most heinous, brutal and atrocious crimes ever recorded in human history') (quotation at para. 328); *ibid.*, para. 328 (quote from Trial Judgement summarising the ghastly, conscience-shocking atrocities for which Brima, Kamara, and Kanu were found responsible); *Cloe et al.* Trial Judgement, *supra* note 88, paras. 25–29 (convicting the accused of murder as a crime against humanity, and sentencing three of them to just five years' imprisonment each for personally and intentionally inflicting wounds on the victim and thereby causing his death); *Soares* Trial Judgement, *supra* note 70, pp. 4, 13 (finding Soares guilty of murder as a crime against humanity where he savagely beat a victim and failed to intervene when others beat him, and the victim later died from the wounds, but sentencing him to just nine years for the murder); *da Costa Nunes* Trial Judgement, *supra* note 90, p. 20 (imposing sentence of ten-and-a-half years for two murders and one instance of persecution as crimes against humanity). See also *infra* note 238 and accompanying text (ICTY's tendency to allow early release after two-thirds of sentence served).

both offences against the administration of justice.[196] While sentencing to prison is another available punishment in contempt cases, most contempt cases have resulted in only a fine.[197]

By contrast, the Rome Statute does not restrict the availability of fines solely to convictions for offences against the administration of justice.[198] Instead, it provides that the trial chamber may also impose a fine on an accused convicted of genocide, war crimes, or crimes against humanity, but only '[i]n addition to imprisonment'.[199] In determining whether to impose a fine in addition to imprisonment, the chamber must consider, together with the normal sentencing factors, the financial capacity of the convicted person; the extent to which his or her criminal conduct was motivated by personal financial gain; the 'proportionate gains' actually derived from the crime; and the damages and injuries caused. In no event may the fine exceed 75 per cent of the convicted person's total assets.[200] The chamber may order the fine deposited into the Court's trust fund, to be used to help the victims of crimes within the Court's jurisdiction and their families.[201]

10.3.2 Restitution, forfeiture, and reparations

In the *ad hoc* Tribunals, if the trial chamber finds the accused guilty of a crime involving the unlawful taking of property, it 'may order the return of any property and proceeds acquired by criminal conduct, including by means of duress, to their rightful owners'.[202] The Rome Statute similarly provides for restitution as a form of reparation to victims.[203] Chapter 8 discusses restitution and reparations in greater detail.[204]

[196] ICTY Rules 77(G), 77 *bis*, 91(G); ICTR Rules 77(G), 91(G); SCSL Rule 77(G). Offences against the administration of justice are discussed in Chapter 7, Section 7.7.

[197] Compare, e.g., *Prosecutor* v. *Margetić*, Case No. IT-95-14-R77.6, Judgement on Allegations of Contempt, 7 February 2007, para. 94 (sentencing accused to three months' imprisonment and imposing a fine of 10,000 euros), with *In re Hartmann*, Case No. IT-02-54-R77.5, Judgement on Allegations of Contempt, 14 September 2009, para. 90 (imposing fine of 7,000 euros but no imprisonment).

[198] Rome Statute, Art. 70(3) ('In the event of conviction [for an offence against the administration of justice], the Court may impose a term of imprisonment not exceeding five years, or a fine in accordance with the Rules … or both.').

[199] Rome Statute, Art. 77(2)(a). See also Schabas, *supra* note 85, pp. 1514–1515 (discussing how the drafters of the Rome Statute arrived at the conclusion that fines should be only a secondary penalty when the accused is convicted of genocide, crimes against humanity, or war crimes).

[200] ICC Rule 146(1)–(2). See also ICC Rule 146(5) (procedure in the event of non-payment). See also Rolf Einar Fife, 'Penalties', in Roy S. Lee (ed.), *The International Criminal Court: Elements of Crimes and Rules of Procedure and Evidence* (2001), pp. 566–569 (describing the negotiations leading up to these criteria).

[201] Rome Statute, Art. 79(2); ICC Rule 148.

[202] ICTY Statute, Art. 24(3). Accord ICTR Statute, Art. 23(3); ICTY Rule 105; ICTR Rule 105. If the trial chamber determines that the accused unlawfully took property, it must make a particularised finding to this effect in the judgement. ICTY Rule 98 *ter*(B); ICTR Rule 88(B).

[203] Rome Statute, Art. 75. See also ICC Rule 218(3)–(4).

[204] See Chapter 8, Sections 8.2.2, 8.3.2.

The ICC and SCSL additionally provide for forfeiture.[205] A chamber at the ICC may order 'forfeiture of proceeds, property and assets derived directly or indirectly from that crime, without prejudice to the rights of bona fide third parties'.[206] The 'property' referred to in this provision excludes the instrumentalities of the crime – that is, property used or intended to be used to commit the crime – as the drafters could not reach consensus on forfeiture of instrumentalities.[207] If the chamber becomes aware of a 'bona fide third party' who has an interest in the proceeds at issue, it must give notice to that party, and the prosecution, convicted person, and third party may then present evidence relevant to forfeiture. If, after considering the evidence, the chamber finds that the convicted person derived the proceeds directly or indirectly from the crime – and, presumably, that the third party does not have a right to the proceeds[208] – it may order forfeiture.[209] It may then order the proceeds deposited into the Court's trust fund for use in helping victims and their families.[210] The SCSL's forfeiture provision is similar: where a chamber of the Special Court finds forfeiture warranted, it may order the proceeds returned to their rightful owner or their transfer to the government of Sierra Leone.[211]

10.4 Procedures upon conviction or acquittal

As noted elsewhere in this volume,[212] trial proceedings end when the chamber reconvenes the trial and delivers its verdict upon the accused, with one of three possible outcomes: (1) the accused is acquitted of all charges in the indictment; (2) the accused is acquitted of some charges but convicted of others; or (3) the accused is convicted of all charges. Where the accused is convicted of at least some of the charges, three further outcomes are possible: (1) the chamber sentences the accused to a term of years equal to or less than the time already served during the pre-trial and trial phases, with or without non-prison penalties such as a fine or restitution;[213] (2) the chamber sentences the accused to a term of years longer than that already

[205] Rome Statute, Art. 77(2)(b); SCSL Statute, Art. 19(3); ICC Rule 147; SCSL Rule 104.

[206] Rome Statute, Art. 77(2)(b). See also ICC Rules 147, 218. While the Statute and Rules do not define the term 'forfeiture', the chair of the Rome Conference working group on penalties has characterised it as 'the divestiture or permanent deprivation from the convicted person of specific property without compensation'. Fife, *supra* note 85, p. 997.

[207] See Schabas, *supra* note 85, p. 1516; Fife, *supra* note 85, pp. 996–997.

[208] See Fife, *supra* note 85, pp. 997–998 (suggesting that, in the context of armed conflict or other situations of massive crime, third parties may rarely have a good-faith interest in the proceeds of the crime). See also generally Fife, *supra* note 200, pp. 569–572 (discussing negotiations leading to forfeiture provisions in ICC Rules).

[209] ICC Rule 147. See also ICC Rule 218(1)–(2) (providing further directions relating to forfeiture orders); Rome Statute, Art. 109 (procedure for when state party is unable to give effect to forfeiture order).

[210] Rome Statute, Art. 79(2); ICC Rule 148.

[211] SCSL Statute, Art. 19(3); SCSL Rule 104.

[212] See Chapter 7, Section 7.6.7.

[213] As noted above, the tribunals must give credit for time served. See *supra* Section 10.2.2.7.

served, with or without non-prison penalties; or (3) the chamber imposes only a non-prison penalty.

If the trial chamber convicts the accused and imposes a term of imprisonment, the tribunal continues to hold the convicted person pending any appeals. If there are no appeals, or if the Appeals Chamber affirms the conviction and the person has not yet served the entire sentence in the tribunal's detention unit, the tribunal must transfer the accused to a willing state to serve the sentence, as none of the international criminal tribunals has its own long-term prison. Section 10.4.1 discusses these procedures. If, on the other hand, the trial chamber convicts the accused and sentences him or her to time served or imposes a penalty not entailing imprisonment, or acquits the accused outright, the tribunal must release the accused from its custody, with certain exceptions pending a prosecution appeal. Section 10.4.2 examines these procedures. Section 10.5 examines enforcement of the sentence and the rules on evaluating petitions for early release.

10.4.1 Status of the convicted person and transfer to national prison

Where the trial chamber convicts the accused and sentences him or her to a term of imprisonment, the sentence begins to run from the day the chamber pronounces it.[214] As noted above, chambers must give credit for time served in custody pursuant to an order of the tribunal. Time served consists, for the most part, of time spent in the tribunal's detention unit during the pre-trial and trial phases.[215] Notice of appeal by either party stays enforcement of the sentence until the Appeals Chamber resolves the appeal, but the convicted person remains in the tribunal's detention unit.[216]

If all appeals have been exhausted and the person remains convicted and sentenced to a term of years longer than the time already served, the tribunal must transfer the person to one of the countries that have agreed to house, in their national prisons, persons convicted by the tribunal. These countries appear in a list maintained by the tribunal.[217] The SCSL Statute mandates imprisonment in Sierra Leone, 'unless circumstances require otherwise'; in such circumstances, the convicted person may serve the sentence in any state that has an agreement with the

[214] ICTY Rule 102(A); ICTR Rule 102(A); SCSL Rule 102(A). If the accused is on provisional release or otherwise outside the tribunal's custody at the time the judgement is pronounced, the trial chamber must issue a warrant for his or her arrest. ICTY Rule 102(A); ICTR Rule 102(A); SCSL Rule 102(A).

[215] See *supra* note 185 and accompanying text.

[216] Rome Statute, Art. 81(3)(a); ICTY Rule 102(A); ICTR Rule 102(A); SCSL Rule 102(A). See also Chapter 4, note 169 and accompanying text (discussing detention on acquittal).

[217] See Rome Statute, Art. 103(1)(a); ICTY Statute, Art. 27; ICTR Statute, Art. 26 (also providing that imprisonment may be served in Rwanda, though no ICTR convicted person has yet been sent there to serve imprisonment); SCSL Statute, Art. 22; ICTY Rule 103(A); ICTR Rule 103(A) (President must notify Rwanda prior to decision); SCSL Rule 103(B). For agreements between states and the ICTY, see www.icty.org/sections/LegalLibrary/MemberStatesCooperation (Albania, Austria, Belgium, Denmark, Estonia, Finland, France, Italy, Norway, Poland, Portugal, Slovakia, Spain, Sweden, Ukraine, and United Kingdom); for an

SCSL, or that has an agreement with the ICTY or ICTR and has indicated to the SCSL Registrar its willingness to accept persons convicted by the Special Court.[218] In practice, the Special Court has transferred all eight persons whose convictions have been affirmed on appeal to Rwanda's Mpanga Prison, to serve their sentences in a part of the facility originally built to house ICTR convicted persons.[219] Perhaps ironically, the ICTR itself has yet to send a convicted person to Rwanda to serve his or her sentence.

At the *ad hoc* Tribunals and the SCSL, the tribunal President picks the state of enforcement from the list.[220] A practice direction provides guidance for this decision, with criteria such as the person's personal circumstances; his or her linguistic skills; whether he or she is expected to appear as a witness in other tribunal cases; and the proximity of his or her family and other close relations to the state of enforcement.[221] The ICC Rules also assign this decision to the Presidency, which must take into account, among other things, '[t]he principle that States Parties should share the responsibility for enforcing sentences'; the convicted person's views; and the person's nationality.[222] Pending the finalisation of arrangements for

example of a transfer to the state of enforcement, see, e.g., International Criminal Tribunal for the former Yugoslavia, Press Release: Radoslav Brđanin Transferred to Denmark to Serve Sentence, 4 March 2008, www.icty.org/x/cases/brdanin/press/en/PR1222e%20Brdanin%20Transferred%20to%20Denmark%20to%20Serve%20Sentence.pdf. For agreements between states and the ICTR, see www.ictr.org/ENGLISH/agreements/index.htm (Benin, France, Italy, Mali, Rwanda, Swaziland, and Sweden). For agreements between states and the SCSL, see www.sc-sl.org/DOCUMENTS/tabid/176/Default.aspx (Finland, Rwanda, Sweden, and United Kingdom).

218 SCSL Statute, Art. 22(1); accord SCSL Rule 103(A). The security risk of the accused's detention in Sierra Leone might justify detention in another state. Report of the Secretary-General on the Establishment of a Special Court for Sierra Leone, UN Doc. S/2000/915, 4 October 2000, para. 49.

219 See Special Court for Sierra Leone, Press Release: Special Court Prisoners Transferred to Rwanda to Serve Their Sentences, 31 October 2009, www.sc-sl.org/LinkClick.aspx?fileticket=YiPY3dNd%2fiI%3d&tabid=53. The transfer occurred on 31 October 2009, a mere five days after the Appeals Chamber affirmed the convictions in the *RUF* case. See generally *RUF* Appeal Judgement, *supra* note 15.

220 See, e.g., *Prosecutor* v. *Imanishimwe*, Case No. ICTR-99-46, Decision on the Enforcement of Sentence, 3 November 2008 (ICTR President noting that he had consulted Mali, which is on the ICTR's list of states, and received its consent to imprison Imanishimwe; noting that he had notified Rwanda of his intention to send Imanishimwe to Mali; and inviting the Registrar 'to request officially the Government of the Republic of Mali to enforce the sentence of Samuel Imanishimwe and, should the Government of the Republic of Mali grant the request, notify the President and take all the necessary measures to facilitate the transfer of Samuel Imanishimwe to Mali').

221 See Practice Direction on the Procedure for the International Tribunal's Designation of the State in Which a Convicted Person Is to Serve His/Her Sentence of Imprisonment, UN Doc. IT/137/Rev. 1, 1 September 2009, paras. 4–5 (ICTY); Practice Direction on the Procedure for Designation of the State in Which a Convicted Person Is to Serve His/Her Sentence of Imprisonment, 23 September 2008, www.ictr.org/ENGLISH/basicdocs/pracdirections/designation_state_08.pdf, paras. 3–4 (ICTR); Practice Direction for Designation of State of Enforcement of Sentence, 10 July 2009, www.sc-sl.org/LinkClick.aspx?fileticket=imjLbjWP%2fkY%3d&tabid=176, paras. 4–5 (SCSL).

222 Rome Statute, Art. 103(3); ICC Rule 199 (Presidency makes decision). The Rome Statute and ICC Rules flesh out several other details concerning how the Presidency chooses the state of enforcement. For example, if no state is willing to accept the convicted person, the Netherlands, as host state, must house him in one of its prisons. Rome Statute, Art. 103(4). At any time, the Court may transfer the convicted person from the state of enforcement to another state. *Ibid.*, Art. 104. See also, e.g., ICC Rule 200 (concerning maintenance of list of states of enforcement); ICC Rule 201 (elaborating on principle of equitable distribution); ICC Rule 203 (sentenced person may submit to President views on state of enforcement); ICC Rule 205 (chosen state

the convicted person's transfer to the state of enforcement, the tribunal continues to house the person in its detention unit.[223]

10.4.2 Procedure upon acquittal or conviction to time served

If a trial chamber acquits the accused or hands down a sentence equal to or lesser than the time already served, the chamber must release the accused, unless the prosecutor notifies the chamber of its intent to file a notice of appeal. The chamber must then decide whether to order the accused's continued detention, or whether to release him or her, pending the appeal.[224] In making this decision, the *Cyangugu* Trial Chamber at the ICTR gave weight to the substantial number of years acquitted persons Ntagerura and Bagambiki had already been detained, and ordered that they be released pending appeal.[225] The Rome Statute provides further guidance: a trial chamber shall have regard, among other things, 'to the concrete risk of flight, the seriousness of the offence charged and the probability of success on appeal'.[226] Oddly, this latter criterion presumably requires the trial chamber to assess the soundness of its own factual findings and legal conclusions.

Release of an acquitted person into freedom is not always easy. For those few ICTR accused who have been acquitted, returning home to Rwanda has proven unfeasible. Most fear retaliation by the government, led since 1994 by the Rwandan Patriotic Front, the political successor to the Tutsi rebel group that defeated the *génocidaire* government and stopped the genocide. They also fear a backlash from the public. Moreover, as persons who have been accused (even though not convicted) of genocide and other heinous crimes, most third

may reject designation, in which case President designates another state); ICC Rule 210 (procedure for changing designation of state of enforcement).

223 ICTY Rule 103(C). The ICTR and SCSL have no such explicit provision in their Rules, but in practice both continue to house the convicted person until his transfer. See, e.g., *RUF* Appeal Judgement, *supra* note 15, p. 480 (ordering that the three accused 'remain in the custody of the Special Court … pending the finalization of arrangements to serve their sentences'). See also *ibid.* text accompanying note 219 (all three accused were transferred to Rwanda five days later to serve their sentences).

224 Rome Statute, Art. 81(3)(b)–(c); ICTY Rule 99; ICTR Rule 99; SCSL Rule 99. See also, e.g., *Halilović* Trial Judgement, *supra* note 22, paras. 753–754 (acquitting Halilović of all charges and ordering his immediate release); *Orić* Trial Judgement, *supra* note 187, paras. 782–784 (sentencing Orić to a period less than the time he had already been in detention, and ordering his immediate release); *Prosecutor* v. *Ntagerura, Bagambiki, and Imanishimwe*, Case No. ICTR-99-46-T, Judgement, 25 February 2004, paras. 829–830 (ordering acquitted accused Ntagerura and Bagambiki immediately released, subject to any further order the Trial Chamber may make under Rule 99(B)). For more on Ntagerura and Bagambiki, see *infra* notes 225, 227.

225 *Prosecutor* v. *Ntagerura, Bagambiki, and Imanishimwe*, Case No. ICTR-99-46-T, Decision on the Prosecutor's Request Pursuant to Rule 99(B), 26 February 2004 (denying prosecution's motion that Ntagerura and Bagambiki continue in detention pending appeal judgement, as the two accused had 'already been subject to many years of detention', but granting prosecution alternative motion that they be granted interim release). In reality, Ntagerura and Bagambiki remained detained at an ICTR safe house, as they were neither able to return home to Rwanda, nor move around freely in Tanzania, nor relocate to a third state. See *infra* note 227 and accompanying text. On interim release, see Chapter 4, Section 4.3.3.

226 Rome Statute, Art. 81(3)(c)(i).

states – including Tanzania, where the Tribunal sits – have been unwilling to grant them refuge, and the Tribunal has no power to order states to admit them. As a result, most of these persons remain confined to an ICTR-controlled safe house in Arusha, practically unable to leave.[227] Ntagerura and Bagambiki, whose acquittals were affirmed on appeal, are among those living in the safe house.[228]

10.5 Enforcement of sentence and procedures for early release

In a manifestation of primacy, including at the ICC,[229] the tribunal's sentence is binding on the state of enforcement, and the state may not modify the sentence or release the prisoner early without the tribunal's consent.[230] The manner in which the prisoner serves the sentence and the conditions of imprisonment are determined by the law of the state of enforcement,[231] but the tribunal maintains the authority and duty to supervise enforcement.[232]

If a prisoner convicted by the ICTY, ICTR, or SCSL becomes eligible for pardon or commutation of sentence under the law of the state of enforcement, the state must notify the tribunal.[233] The tribunal's President then decides, in consultation with other judges, whether to grant early release.[234] The prisoner

[227] On this conundrum, see Kevin Jon Heller, 'What Happens to the Acquitted?', (2008) 21 *Leiden Journal of International Law* 663; Benoit Henry, 'The Acquitted Accused, a Forgotten Party of the ICTR', (2005) 12 *New England Journal of International and Comparative Law* 81.

[228] See *supra* notes 224–225 and accompanying text.

[229] On the *ad hoc* Tribunals' primacy and the primacy of the ICC with respect to certain issues, see generally Chapter 3.

[230] See, e.g., Rome Statute, Arts. 105(1), 110(1); SCSL Statute, Art. 22(2).

[231] Rome Statute, Art. 106(2); ICTY Statute, Art. 27; ICTR Statute, Art. 26; SCSL Statute, Art. 22(2). The Rome Statute expressly provides that the state of enforcement may not treat the convicted person any better, or any worse, than other prisoners convicted of similar crimes in that state. Rome Statute, Art. 106(2).

[232] Rome Statute, Art. 106(1) (enforcement of sentence must also 'be consistent with widely accepted international treaty standards governing treatment of prisoners'); *ibid.*, Art. 110(2); ICTY Statute, Art. 27; ICTR Statute, Art. 26; SCSL Statute, Art. 22(2); ICC Rule 211(1) (guidelines to aid the Court in its supervisory role); ICTY Rule 104; ICTR Rule 104. See also, e.g., Guénaël Mettraux, *International Crimes and the* Ad Hoc *Tribunals* (2005), p. 359 n. 5 (describing an Italian court's decision to reduce ICTY accused Goran Jelisić's forty-year sentence to thirty years without first consulting the ICTY President, in contravention of the ICTY Statute and Rules). The state of enforcement is also obliged to enforce the tribunal's fines, forfeiture, and reparation orders. See, e.g., Rome Statute, Arts. 75(5), 109; ICC Rules 212, 217–222; ICC Court Regulation 116.

[233] ICTY Rule 123; ICTR Rule 124; SCSL Rule 123. See also Practice Direction for the Determination of Applications for Pardon, Commutation of Sentence, and Early Release of Persons Convicted by the International Tribunal, UN Doc. IT/146/Rev.2, 1 September 2009 ('ICTY Practice Direction on Early Release'), para. 1. In the ICTY, the Registrar then informs the prisoner that he or she may be eligible for pardon, commutation, or early release; requests reports from the ICTY Prosecutor and the state; and forwards the information to the President and the prisoner. *Ibid.*, paras. 3–4.

[234] ICTY Statute, Art. 28; ICTR Statute, Art. 27; SCSL Statute, Art. 23; ICTY Rule 124 (President makes decision in consultation with members of the Bureau 'and any permanent Judges of the sentencing Chamber who remain Judges of the Tribunal'); ICTR Rule 125 (same, but President must also notify the Rwandan government). See also ICTY Practice Direction on Early Release, *supra* note 233, para. 6 (President forwards

may also directly petition the President for early release.[235] The ICTY and ICTR Rules set forth the criteria the President considers, including the gravity of the crimes of conviction, the degree to which the prisoner has demonstrated rehabilitation, and any substantial cooperation with the Prosecutor.[236] The decision is public unless the President decides otherwise, and is not subject to appeal.[237] The ICTY President has granted early release to many convicted persons, particularly where the person has served two-thirds of the sentence, including in cases where the person was originally given a very light sentence despite being convicted of heinous crimes.[238] The ICTY and ICTR, and possibly the SCSL, will eventually establish legacy bodies to perform the sentence-review function in lieu

information received from Prosecutor and state, as well as President's own comments, to Bureau and sentencing judges, and then consults with them).

[235] See, e.g., ICTY Practice Direction on Early Release, *supra* note 233, para. 2. Though not provided for explicitly in the Rules, the *ad hoc* Tribunals have also entertained petitions for early release by convicted persons who have not yet been transferred to the state of enforcement. See, e.g., *Prosecutor* v. *Zarić*, Case No. IT-95-9, Order of the President on the Application for Early Release of Simo Zarić, 21 January 2004, p. 3 (considering that 'the conditions for eligibility regarding early release applications should be applied equally' whether the prisoner has been transferred to the state of enforcement or continues in the Tribunal's detention unit); see also *ibid*., p. 5 (granting early release).

[236] ICTY Rule 125; ICTR Rule 126. See also SCSL Rule 124 (mimicking the SCSL Statute in expressly listing only 'the interests of justice' and 'the general principles of law' as criteria).

[237] ICTY Practice Direction on Early Release, *supra* note 233, paras. 8, 10.

[238] See, e.g., *Prosecutor* v. *Furundžija*, Case No. IT-95-17/1, Order of the President on the Application for the Early Release of Anto Furundžija, 29 July 2004 (ICTY President granting early release where state of enforcement notified him that Furundžija would soon be eligible for release upon serving two-thirds of his ten-year sentence; considering the state's report detailing his impeccable behaviour in prison and his expressions of remorse; considering that the information provided 'establishe[d] the strong likelihood that Mr. Furundžija will successfully reintegrate himself into the community upon release'; and notwithstanding the prosecution's submission that Furundžija had not cooperated with it); *Prosecutor* v. *Plavšić*, Case Nos. IT-00-39 & 40/1-ES, Decision of the President on the Application for Pardon or Commutation of Sentence of Mrs. Biljana Plavšić, 14 September 2009, paras. 8–14 (despite one Bureau judge's disagreement, ICTY President granting early release after two-thirds of sentence, in accordance with Swedish law, where Plavšić exhibited substantial evidence of rehabilitation, remorse, good behaviour in prison, and was of an advanced age); *Prosecutor* v. *Krnojelac*, Case No. IT-97-25-ES, Decision of the President on the Application for Pardon or Commutation of Sentence of Milorad Krnojelac, 9 July 2009, paras. 20–24 (granting commutation after two-thirds of sentence where, among other things, Krnojelac exhibited 'substantial evidence of rehabilitation'; behaved well in the Italian prison; and suffered from a prolonged illness causing him severe pain) (quotation at para. 20); *Prosecutor* v. *Banović*, Case No. IT-02-65/1-ES, Decision of the President on Commutation of Sentence, 3 September 2008, paras. 13–15, 18 (granting commutation after two-thirds of sentence where, among other things, Banović had expressed 'substantial remorse'; exhibited good behaviour in the French prison; made a 'substantial effort to return to being a productive member of society by arranging in advance for employment upon deportation to Serbia' from France upon release; had volunteered to provide testimony in an ICTY trial; and provided a statement for the prosecution in a trial at the State Court of Bosnia and Herzegovina) (quotations at para. 13); *Prosecutor* v. *Hazim Delić*, Case No. IT-96-21-ES, Decision on Hazim Delić's Motion for Commutation of Sentence, 24 June 2008, paras. 19–22 (granting commutation after two-thirds of sentence despite President's own acknowledgement that Delić's crimes 'were committed with particular brutality', including by using 'an electric shock device on his victims'; because 'a substantial period of time had passed since he committed those crimes' and there was, in President's and consulted judges' view, 'sufficient evidence of rehabilitation to warrant granting' the request for commutation; and Delić behaved well in prison); *supra* note 235 (early release of Simo Zarić). On the astonishing leniency of ICTY sentences, see *supra* text accompanying notes 192, 194–195; *infra* text accompanying note 251.

of the President, as some prisoner's sentences will run until decades after these Tribunals cease to exist.[239]

The ICC must review, on its own motion, any sentence after the prisoner has served two-thirds of it, or after twenty-five years where the prisoner was sentenced to life, to determine whether the prisoner should be released early.[240] If the three-judge bench of the Appeals Chamber assigned to this task decides not to order the prisoner's release, it must review this decision every three years thereafter.[241] The criteria to be applied are similar to those for early release in the ICTY and ICTR.[242]

10.6 Conclusion

In 2001 Patricia Wald, a former federal appeals judge in the United States and serving at the time as a trial judge at the ICTY, gave a frank assessment of ICTY judgements:

> Reading some of the several-hundred-pages-long, format-stylized judgments of the ICTY, one can guess that many of the judgments are the work of a committee rather than an individual judge or judges ... In my U.S. experience the emphasis is on telling the parties and the public why the judges came to a particular result in light of relevant facts and law. In the culture of some of my new colleagues, the format appears to be more ritualistic, requiring a formal recitation of what the parties argued; what the abstract legal theory is; what the factual findings of the court are; and then, finally and not always predictably, the ultimate result. There seems to be less premium on making transparent the judges' reasoning as to how the law applies to the facts, except where dissenting or concurring judges file separate statements. In my opinion, there is less emphasis on style and readability ... For these reasons ICTY judgments sometimes seem stilted, bureaucratic, and insufficiently reasoned, making them largely inaccessible to the reader and frustrating to the press and even legal scholars who try to analyze them.[243]

[239] See ICTY Rule 104 (providing for supervision by the Tribunal 'or a body designated by it'); ICTR Rule 104 (same).

[240] Rome Statute, Art. 110(3). The review is conducted by three judges of the Appeals Chamber, appointed by that Chamber. For the details of the procedure, see ICC Rules 223–224.

[241] Rome Statute, Art. 110(5); ICC Rule 224(3) (every three years unless the three-judge bench of the Appeals Chamber 'establishes a shorter interval').

[242] The factors in the Rome Statute are the prisoner's 'early and continuing willingness' to cooperate with ICC investigations and prosecutions; assistance in locating assets subject to a fine, forfeiture, or reparation; and any other factor 'establishing a clear and significant change of circumstances sufficient to justify the reduction of sentence'. Rome Statute, Art. 110(4). The factors in the ICC Rules are the prisoner's conduct in detention; prospects for 'resocialisation'; whether early release would give rise to 'significant social instability'; actions by the prisoner to aid victims; the impact on victims of the prisoner's early release; and the prisoner's individual circumstances, including poor health and advanced age. ICC Rule 223. For the ICC's provisions on the transfer of the convicted person from the state of enforcement to the state of enforcement upon completion of the sentence, see Rome Statute, Art. 107; ICC Rule 213.

[243] Patricia M. Wald, 'The International Criminal Tribunal for the Former Yugoslavia Comes of Age: Some Observations on Day-to-Day Dilemmas of an International Court', (2001) 5 *Washington University Journal of Law and Policy* 87, 93–94.

These words are still true today, and the other tribunals have perpetuated the cumbersome drafting style begun in the ICTY's first case. Chambers expend considerable energy 'ticking off the boxes' of the established ritual. They often describe the facts witness by witness, municipality by municipality, and dedicate large swathes of the judgement to recounting the parties' arguments before finally turning to what is often a cursory analysis of the law and application of the facts to that law.[244]

Nonetheless, while many appellants have attacked the trial chamber's shoddy reasoning or failure to consider certain evidence, the Appeals Chambers have been reluctant to reverse on this ground or even rebuke the chamber for the lack of clarity. While often finding breaches of the reasoned judgement requirement, the Appeals Chambers have gone to great lengths to rationalise and explain away the shortcomings, or acknowledge the errors but then proceed to make the legal and factual corrections themselves,[245] instead of identifying the errors, stating the correct legal principle, and remanding for the trial chamber to make a proper factual determination in light of the correct law. This practice may be motivated, at least in part, by an extreme aversion to the inevitable delay of months or years in the resolution of the case that would result from vacating the verdict and ordering a retrial or resentencing.[246] In the aggregate, such an outcome might seriously hinder the Tribunals' completion-strategy goals.

[244] This exercise frequently involves a perfunctory comparative survey of national law on a given subject. Among the many stylistic habits that lend an air of stiltedness to judgements (and other decisions) are the judges' routine reference to themselves in the third person as 'the Trial Chamber', instead of the much simpler 'we', and their tendency to preface many sentences with an unnecessary 'The Trial Chamber notes that' instead of simply stating the proposition. In addition, many judges make frequent use of Latin, and refer to the accused formalistically by first and last name in every instance. See, e.g., *Halilović* Trial Judgement, *supra* note 22 (repeatedly using the full given and surname of each witness and other persons discussed in the judgement, including the accused Sefer Halilović). Some trial chambers see the need to preface the accused's name, on each instance, with 'Mr.', 'Ms.', 'Gen.', 'Col.' and the like. Much of this stylistic awkwardness seems to stem from a belief by some judges and legal staff that inaccessible language is still stylistically valued in legal writing in the English language. On this issue generally, see Bryan A. Garner, *Legal Writing in Plain English* (2001).

[245] See generally *supra* Section 10.1.1 and sources cited therein. See also generally, e.g., *Kvočka et al.* Appeal Judgement, *supra* note 8 (shortcomings throughout judgement); *Blaškić* Appeal Judgement, *supra* note 61 (same); *supra* notes 20–24, 60 (shortcomings in *Halilović* and *Krajišnik*). A rare, if implicit, rebuke came in *Kordić and Čerkez*, where the Appeals Chamber exhibited palpable frustration at the Trial Chamber's failure to make findings on each element of the crimes for which it convicted the accused. Yet instead of vacating the judgement and acquitting or remanding for further proceedings, the Appeals Chamber took up the tedious (and dubious, given the normal limits of appellate jurisdiction) task of performing its own *de novo* assessment of much of the evidence. See *Kordić and Čerkez* Appeal Judgement, *supra* note 15, paras. 379–388 (explaining Trial Chamber's error and Appeals Chamber's plan to reassess all the relevant evidence itself); *ibid.*, paras. 389–724 (performing this task). This exercise added significant length to the Appeal Judgement.

[246] For example, in *Erdemović*, the ICTY Appeals Chamber found, by majority, that Erdemović's guilty plea was not informed and famously held, by majority, that duress did not constitute an absolute defence to his crimes. It refused Erdemović's request that the Appeals Chamber revise the Trial Chamber's ten-year sentence itself, and instead remitted the case to a different Trial Chamber. See *Prosecutor* v. *Erdemović*, Case No. IT-96-22-A, Judgement, 7 October 1997, pp. 17–18. In *Muvunyi*, the ICTR Appeals Chamber found several factual and legal errors in the Trial Chamber's judgement and reversed all but one of Muvunyi's

On the other hand, considering that the international criminal tribunals lack a third instance, the Appeals Chamber's practice of making its own factual findings, entering new convictions itself, and revising the sentence may violate the parties' right to appeal those determinations, as the Appeals Chamber's word will be the last.[247] It is also highly questionable whether the Appeals Chamber, separated from the day-to-day conduct of the trial and not having observed the demeanour of the witnesses or the accused, is in a good position to make such determinations in the first place – realities the Appeals Chamber itself has candidly acknowledged, though too rarely.[248] Chapter 11 discusses concerns about the appellate practice of the international criminal tribunals.

A fundamental requirement of a fair trial is that the sentence be well explained, proportionate to the conduct, and consistent, and therefore predictable.[249] Chambers of the *ad hoc* Tribunals and the SCSL have not had much difficulty explaining the factors that have gone into their sentencing determinations, and in fact the body of jurisprudence on sentencing criteria, and aggravating and mitigating circumstances, is quite substantial, as Section 10.2.2 above illustrates. While the judges are usually careful to analyse the gravity of the crime, the personal circumstances of the convicted person, and to note which facts they regard as aggravating or mitigating circumstances, few judgements are clear on how the judges weighed the circumstances to arrive at a precise number of years. Indeed, as discussed above,[250] it often seems as though the trial chamber has simply pulled the number

convictions. The Appeals Chamber quashed this conviction, for direct and public incitement to commit genocide, which stemmed from a speech he gave at the Gikore Trade Centre, and ordered retrial under Rule 118(C) of the ICTR Rules only on those charges. *Muvunyi* Appeal Judgement, *supra* note 33, paras. 142–148, p. 67 (discussed at text accompanying notes 32–33, *supra*).

247 A narrow exception is revision proceedings, discussed in Chapter 11, Section 11.7.

248 In the *Orić* case, the ICTY Appeals Chamber invoked these concerns apparently out of expediency to acquit the accused – who had only been sentenced to time served in any event, and was no longer in detention – rather than re-evaluate the entire trial record. It found that the Trial Chamber had failed to substantiate how two legal elements of superior responsibility, pursuant to which the Trial Chamber had convicted Orić, had been met on the evidence adduced at trial. The Appeals Chamber held that 'an appeal is not a trial de novo and the Appeals Chamber cannot be expected to act as a primary trier of fact. Not only is the Appeals Chamber not in the best position to assess the reliability and credibility of the evidence, but doing so would also deprive the Parties of their fundamental right to appeal factual findings. In the present case, the re-evaluation of the trial record would affect the vast majority of the findings necessary to establish all the three elements of criminal responsibility pursuant to Article 7(3) of the Statute and would, in effect, require the Appeals Chamber to decide the case anew. The Appeals Chamber does not consider that such task lies within its functions'. *Prosecutor* v. *Orić*, Case No. IT-03-68-A, Judgement, 3 July 2008, para. 186. The Appeals Chamber decided not to order a retrial, because the parties had not asked for one, and because the prosecution had failed to point to evidence already in the record, or present new evidence on appeal, that would remedy the Trial Judgement's identified shortcomings. *Ibid.*, para. 187; see also *ibid.*, para. 188 (acquitting Orić outright). On the appellant's need to point to such evidence, see *supra* note 16 and accompanying text.

249 See, e.g., *Čelebići* Appeal Judgement, *supra* note 29, para. 756 ('One of the fundamental elements in any rational and fair system of criminal justice is consistency of punishment.').

250 See *supra* note 103 and accompanying text.

out of the air, probably influenced by the general severity (or lack thereof) of sentences handed down in previous cases at the tribunal.[251] The lack of sentencing tariffs or guidelines, the broad discretion afforded chambers in sentencing, and the Appeals Chambers' practice of modifying sentences when they make new factual findings or simply disagree with the trial chamber's weighing of factors,[252] have all contributed to the sentencing unpredictability in the international criminal tribunals.[253]

The same phenomenon will likely plague the ICC for decades to come if tariffs or guidelines, or both, are not adopted. As Robert Sloane has noted,[254] the ICTY Appeals Chamber's acknowledgment in one of its earliest judgements remains true today despite a decade of ensuing sentencing jurisprudence: 'It is ... premature to speak of an emerging "penal regime", and the coherence in sentencing practice that this denotes'.[255] Unfortunately, most of the current debate on revamping the law applied in the ICC focuses on defining the crime of aggression and allowing prosecutions for it, to the exclusion of resolving

[251] See *supra* note 99 and accompanying text (permissibility of looking at prior tribunal sentences as an aid in determining the sentence). This phenomenon of pulling the ultimate number out of the air may help account for the remarkable levity in ICTY sentences. A troubling aspect of the ICTY's practice, especially for observers from states where life sentences are routinely given for single murders, is the frequent disconnect between the heinousness of the accused's conduct and the sentence imposed on him. Too many ICTY judges appear to have taken guidance from the early *Furundžija* Trial Chamber's dubious assertion that '[i]t is the infallibility of punishment, rather than the severity of the sanction, which is the tool for retribution, stigmatisation, and deterrence'. *Prosecutor* v. *Furundžija*, Case No. IT-95-17/1-T, Judgement, 10 December 1998, para. 290 (also opining that '[t]his is particularly the case for the International Tribunal; penalties are made more onerous by its international stature, moral authority and impact upon world public opinion, and this punitive effect must be borne in mind when assessing the suitable length of the sentence'); see also Iain Bonomy, 'The Reality of Conducting a War Crimes Trial', (2007) 5 *Journal of International Criminal Justice* 348, 351 (former ICTY judge remarking on the relative levity of ICTY sentences compared to 'those imposed in an equivalent domestic context'). Another reason for the levity of sentences is chambers' tendency to impose concurrent, rather than consecutive, convictions for multiple crimes. See *supra* note 191 and accompanying text. For a comprehensive analysis of why sentences at the ICTY are so relatively light, see generally Harmon and Gaynor, *supra* note 91; see also, e.g., *ibid*., p. 688 (discussing the guilty-plea case of Miroslav Bralo, who admitted to murdering several persons himself; raping a woman, detaining her for several weeks, and allowing his comrades to serially rape her; and a number of other vicious atrocities; and was given a twenty-year sentence). Further compounding the sense that the ICTY's punishments are too light is the tendency of the ICTY President to allow early release of convicted persons after serving two-thirds of their sentence, despite the heinousness of their crimes. See *supra* note 238 and accompanying text. On balance, the East Timor SPSC's sentences were also astonishingly lenient. See, e.g., *supra* note 195 and SPSC sources cited therein.

[252] See, e.g., Boas, Bischoff, and Reid, *Forms of Responsibility*, *supra* note 68, pp. 411–412 (discussing the ICTR Appeals Chamber's imposition of a harsher sentence on Laurent Semanza); Boas, Bischoff, and Reid, *Elements of Crimes*, *supra* note 3, pp. 367–369 (discussing the ICTY Appeals Chamber's imposition of a harsher sentence on Stanislav Galić, and the ICTR Appeals Chamber's imposition of a harsher sentence on Sylvestre Gacumbitsi).

[253] As noted above, even chambers of the tribunals have on occasion acknowledged this unpredictability. See, e.g., *Milutinović et al.* Trial Judgement, *supra* note 1, Vol. III, para. 1143 ('[I]t is difficult to detect any pattern or guidance in the sentencing "practice" of the [ICTY]').

[254] Sloane, *supra* note 84, p. 715.

[255] *Furundžija* Appeal Judgement, *supra* note 97, para. 237 (footnote omitted).

many more critical gaps and shortcomings.[256] There appears to be no viable plan to amend the Rome Statute or Rules to incorporate sentencing tariffs or guidelines.[257] Difficult as they may be, negotiations on this subject and ultimate agreement will be necessary for a fair and well-regarded sentencing practice at the ICC.

[256] See Boas, Bischoff, and Reid, *Elements of Crimes*, *supra* note 3, pp. 379–383 (noting some of these shortcomings); *ibid.*, p. 384 (urging ICC to adopt guidelines and to eschew the ICTY's practice of handing down excessively lenient sentences).

[257] For a pre-ICC study comparing sentences for international crimes in a number of national jurisdictions, see Daniel B. Pickard, 'Proposed Sentencing Guidelines for the International Criminal Court', (1997) 20 *Loyola of Los Angeles International and Comparative Law Journal* 123.

11

Appeal and revision

CONTENTS

The right to appeal a conviction in international criminal law, ostensibly founded on the *jus cogens* norm of a right to a fair trial,[1] is embodied in several international instruments, including the statutes of the international criminal tribunals, and today likely forms part of customary international law.[2] The right finds its origins in various sources, including international human rights law and the right to appeal a criminal conviction in national jurisdictions. The statutes of the international criminal tribunals also provide for a process known as 'review' at the *ad hoc* Tribunals and 'revision' at the ICC, in which a party may seek to have the decision that terminated the proceedings altered.[3] For convenience, as we have done elsewhere in this book,[4] we use the term 'revision' throughout the chapter to refer to this procedure.

Like many areas of international criminal procedure discussed in this volume, the appeal and revision processes at the international criminal tribunals reflect elements of both the common law and civil law traditions. On balance, however, they maintain more of a common law character, evidenced by the operation, at least at certain tribunals, of a system of binding precedent, and the requirement that an appeal be confined to the lower chamber's errors of law and fact and is not a *de novo* proceeding.[5] As noted elsewhere in this volume, however, the unusual procedural structure of international criminal law – which, in the case of appeal and revision, varies somewhat across the tribunals – must be considered in its own right, and not through the lens of any national legal system or tradition, to be properly understood.[6]

Broadly speaking, the right of appeal allows either party to challenge a trial chamber's decision, judgement, or sentence on the grounds of alleged error of law or fact leading to a miscarriage of justice,[7] and the Appeals Chamber can affirm, reverse, or revise the lower chamber's decision.[8] Where a new and decisive fact has been discovered after the final decision which terminated proceedings, the right to request revision allows the convicted person – and, at the *ad hoc* Tribunals, the

[1] See Antonio Cassese, *International Criminal Law* (2nd edn 2008), p. 424. For the status of the right to a fair trial in international law, see Chapter 1, Section 1.1.5.

[2] For a discussion of the customary international law foundation for the right of appeal, see *infra* Section 11.2.

[3] This procedure is referred to by the word '*révision*' in the French versions of the ICC, ICTY, ICTR, and SCSL Statutes. In the English, however, the Rome Statute uses the term 'revision' while the ICTY, ICTR, and SCSL Statutes use the term 'review'. See Rome Statute, Art. 84; ICTY Statute, Art. 26; ICTR Statute, Art. 25; SCSL Statute, Art. 21.

[4] See Chapter 1, Section 1.3 (describing terminology used in this book).

[5] See *infra* Section 11.5.2 (especially text accompanying notes 143–144); see also *infra* text accompanying notes 158–159. For a discussion of the differences in the approach to appeal in the civil and common law legal systems, see Cassese, *supra* note 1, pp. 424–425. But see *ibid.*, p. 425 (asserting incorrectly that a prosecutor in a common law system cannot appeal against sentence).

[6] See Chapter 1, Section 1.2; Chapter 12, Section 12.2.

[7] Rome Statute, Art. 81; ICTY Statute, Art. 25(1); ICTR Statute, Art. 24(1); SCSL Statute, Art. 20(2). See also *infra* Sections 11.4–11.5.

[8] Rome Statute, Art. 83; ICTY Statute, Art. 25(2); ICTR Statute, Art. 24(2); SCSL Statute, Art. 20(2). See also *infra* Section 11.5.

prosecution – to present this fact to the relevant chamber in an effort to have the chamber modify the decision.[9] As with most procedures, the law governing appeal and revision proceedings is essentially the same across the two *ad hoc* Tribunals and the SCSL.[10] The Rome Statute grants appeal and revision rights that are broadly similar to those of the *ad hoc* Tribunals and the SCSL but also differ in certain ways, and it allows victims to appeal through their legal representatives.[11]

This chapter discusses appeal and revision in the international criminal tribunals. It first briefly considers, in Section 11.1, the structure of appellate chambers in international criminal tribunals. Sections 11.2 and 11.3 focus on two broader issues related to appeal and revision: respectively, the legal framework for the right of appeal in international criminal law, and the operation of the doctrine of precedent in the various tribunals. The next two sections then examine appeals procedures in detail: Section 11.4 focuses on interlocutory appeals, while Section 11.5 considers appeals from judgements of acquittal and conviction, and appeals against the sentence. The law relating to admission of additional evidence post-trial is then outlined in Section 11.6, and post-final judgement revision procedures are considered in Section 11.7. Finally, Section 11.8 provides some concluding thoughts on appeal and revision in international criminal law.

11.1 Structure of chambers in the international criminal tribunals

The chambers of the international criminal tribunals reflect the same general structure, although they vary in some important details. The ICTY, ICTR, and SCSL Statutes establish a two-tiered hierarchy, with the trial chambers presiding over pre-trial and trial proceedings, and the Appeals Chambers hearing interlocutory appeals from decisions taken by the trial chamber prior to final judgement; appeals from judgement and sentence; and applications for revision.[12] These Appeals Chambers also have original jurisdiction over some matters, such as certain requests for access to confidential materials,[13] and at the SCSL but not at the *ad hoc* Tribunals, any challenge to the Special Court's jurisdiction.[14] The Rome Statute establishes

[9] Rome Statute, Art. 84; ICTY Statute, Art. 26; ICTR Statute, Art. 25; SCSL Statute, Art. 21. See also *infra* Section 11.7.

[10] See *infra* Section 11.7.

[11] See generally Rome Statute, Arts. 81–82. See also *infra* Sections 11.3.2, 11.7.3.

[12] See Rome Statute, Art. 39; ICTY Statute, Art. 12; ICTR Statute, Art. 11; SCSL Statute, Art. 12.

[13] See Chapter 7, Section 7.4.2.

[14] See SCSL Rule 72; see also *infra* Section 11.4. Two other internationalised criminal tribunals, the Special Panels for Serious Crimes (SPSC) and the ECCC, have a similar structure. For the now-defunct SPSC, the United Nations Transitional Administration of East Timor (UNTAET) established panels composed of Timorese and international judges within the Dili District Court to hear trials, and a mixed panel in the Court of Appeal to hear interlocutory appeals and appeals from final judgement. See UNTAET Regulation 2000/11 on the Organisation of Courts in East Timor, as amended by Regulation 2001/25, 14 September 2001, Sections 10.3, 14, 15; UNTAET Regulation 2000/30 on the Transitional Rules of Criminal Procedure, 25 September 2000, Sections 23, 27, 40, 41. In Cambodia, the ECCC consists of mixed benches of Cambodian

a three-tiered structure for the ICC of pre-trial chambers, trial chambers, and the Appeals Chamber.[15] Pre-trial and trial chambers are on equal hierarchical footing. The Appeals Chamber enjoys hierarchical superiority and hears interlocutory appeals from pre-trial and trial decisions, appeals from judgement and sentence, and requests for revision.[16]

11.2 Evolution of the right of appeal under international law

While some manifestation of a right to request revision of a judgement has been recognised in international treaties dating back to 1899 and 1907,[17] and appeared in the Statutes of the Permanent Court of International Justice and the International Court of Justice (ICJ),[18] no rights relating to appeal or revision were provided for at the International Military Tribunals at Nuremberg and Tokyo.[19] Between the Second World War and the early 1950s, negotiations for the creation of an international criminal court led to the view that the future court should, like the Nuremberg and Tokyo Tribunals, be composed of only one tier of chambers and that no right of appeal was necessary.[20] Yet the negotiators also decided that such a court should have the power to revise its judgements on the basis of new evidence.[21] The Cold War paralysis halted these discussions, making the creation of an international criminal court politically unrealistic for several decades.

In the intervening period between those discussions and the creation of the *ad hoc* Tribunals in the early 1990s, a right for a criminal defendant to appeal his or her conviction and sentence was included in various international human rights

and international judges within the trial courts and the Supreme Court. ECCC Statute, Arts. 2 *new*, Art. 36 *new*.

15 See Rome Statute, Art. 39.

16 See *ibid*., Art. 82.

17 See Hague Convention (I) with Respect to the Pacific Settlement of Disputes, 29 July 1899, entered into force 4 September 1900, 26 *Martens Nouveau Recueil* (ser. 2) 949, 187 Consol. T.S. 429, Art. 55; Hague Convention (I) with Respect to the Pacific Settlement of Disputes, 18 October 1907, entered into force 26 January 1910, 1 Bevans 577, 205 Consol. T.S. 233, Art. 83. A right of revision arose with the discovery of a new fact unknown at the time of the decision which would have had a decisive influence on the decision.

18 Statute of the Permanent Court of International Justice, 6 LNTS 390, 114 BFSP 860, 16 December 1920, entered into force 20 August 1921, Art. 61(1) (with the additional element that the lack of knowledge of the fact at the original proceedings must not have been through negligence of the party applying for revision); Statute of the International Court of Justice, 26 June 1945, entered into force 24 October 1945, 3 Bevans 1179, T.S. 993 ('ICJ Statute'), Art. 61(1) (same). For further discussion, see Ann-Marie La Rosa, 'Revision Procedure under the Rome Statute', in Antonio Cassese, Paola Gaeta, and John R.W.D. Jones (eds.), *The Rome Statute of the International Criminal Court: A Commentary* (2002), Vol. II, pp. 1560–1561.

19 Charter of the International Military Tribunal, 8 August 1945, 82 UNTS 279 ('IMT Charter'), Art. 26; Charter of the International Military Tribunal of the Far East, 19 January 1946, Art. 17, available at www.alhaq.org/etemplate.php?id=81. At the Nuremberg Tribunal, however, the Prosecutor had the power to examine fresh evidence after a conviction or sentence and bring fresh charges against the convicted person based on this evidence. See IMT Charter, *supra* note 18, Art. 29.

20 Report of the 1951 Committee on International Criminal Jurisdiction, UN Doc. A/2136 ('1951 UN Committee Report'), para. 159; Report of the 1953 Committee on International Criminal Jurisdiction, UN Doc. A/2645/Supp, para. 139.

21 1951 UN Committee Report, *supra* note 20, para. 164.

treaties, including the 1948 Universal Declaration of Human Rights,[22] the 1984 Protocol No. 7 to the ECHR,[23] the 1966 ICCPR, and the 1969 ACHR. Thus, when the discussions relating to the creation of an international criminal court began again in the 1990s, the International Law Commission (ILC) was in a position to assert that the court should incorporate a right of appeal and have an appeals chamber to hear such appeals.[24] The Report of the Secretary-General for the drafting of the ICTY Statute also stated the right of appeal is 'a fundamental element of individual civil and political rights and has, *inter alia*, been incorporated in the [ICCPR]'.[25] The Security Council's passage of resolutions creating the ICTY and ICTR and implementing their Statutes, which provide for rights of appeal and to request revision, suggests that body's endorsement of the Secretary-General's conclusion.[26] Following the lead of the *ad hoc* Tribunals and on the ILC's recommendation, the drafters at Rome included within the ICC's Statute robust rights of appeal and to request revision.[27] Other internationalised tribunals have followed suit by incorporating the right of appeal in their governing instruments.[28]

In subsequently interpreting the appeals provisions of the ICTY Statute, the Appeals Chamber affirmed that the Statute 'stands in conformity with the [ICCPR] which insists upon a right of appeal'[29] and considers the right of appeal an 'imperative norm of international law'.[30] In another case, the Appeals Chamber remarked that '[t]he right of appeal is a component of the fair trial requirement', which is in turn, 'of course, a requirement of international customary law'.[31] Later chambers

[22] Universal Declaration of Human Rights, UN Doc. A/810, 10 December 1948, Art. 8.

[23] Protocol No. 7 to the Convention for the Protection of Human Rights and Fundamental Freedoms, 22 November 1984, entered into force 1 November 1988, ETS 117 ('Protocol No. 7'). See Chapter 1, Section 1.1.5; Chapter 12, Section 12.1 (considering the relevance of the human rights regime to the identification and interpretation of international criminal procedure more generally). The regulatory framework giving effect to rights and obligations in respect of the right of an accused to appeal and revision in international criminal trials reflects a close adherence to such a right in human rights law.

[24] Report of the International Law Commission on the Work of Its Forty-Sixth Session, UN Doc. A/CN.4/ SER.A/ 1994/Add.1 (1994).

[25] Report of the Secretary-General Pursuant to Paragraph 2 of Security Council Resolution 808 (1993), UN Doc. S/25704, 3 May 1993, para. 116.

[26] ICTR Statute, Art. 24(2); ICTY Statute, Art. 25(2).

[27] Rome Statute, Part VIII (including Arts. 81–83).

[28] See, e.g., SCSL Statute, Art. 20; ECCC Statute, Art. 36 *new*.

[29] *Prosecutor* v. *Tadić*, Case No. IT-94-1-T, Decision on the Defence Motion for Interlocutory Appeal on Jurisdiction, 2 October 1995, para. 4.

[30] *Prosecutor* v. *Tadić*, Case No. IT-94-1-A-AR77, Appeal Judgement on Allegations of Contempt Against Prior Counsel, Milan Vujin, 27 February 2001, p. 3 (citing Article 14 of the ICCPR, addressing the right of appeal and the right of revision).

[31] *Prosecutor* v. *Aleksovski*, Case No. IT-95-14/1-A, Judgement, 24 March 2000 ('*Aleksovski* Appeal Judgement'), para. 104 (citing Shabtai Rosenne, *The Law and Practice of the International Court* (1985), p. 613). Other evidence includes reference to a right of appeal in international humanitarian law treaties as early as the Geneva Convention Relative to the Treatment of Prisoners of War, 12 August 1949, entered into force 21 October 1950, 75 UNTS 135, Art. 106. Furthermore, the large number of parties to Rome Statute, which enshrines rights of appeal and revision, may provide *opinio juris* that these rights exist. See *supra* note 27 and accompanying text.

of the *ad hoc* Tribunals have similarly held that the right to request revision constitutes a general principle of international law.[32] Notwithstanding the absence of a right of appeal at Nuremberg and Tokyo, the right of appeal and the right to request revision can both be regarded today as fundamental components of international criminal law.

11.3 *Stare decisis* at the international criminal tribunals

The doctrine of *stare decisis* embodies the principle that the *ratio decidendi*[33] of a judgement in dealing with an issue of law – referred to in some jurisdictions as the holding of the court – is binding on later courts, at least where the facts of a subsequent case are, in relevant part, substantially the same.[34] As Lord Denning succinctly put it: 'International law knows no rule of *stare decisis*.'[35] Nevertheless, the ICJ and the European Court of Human Rights – examples of international law jurisdictions analogous, in some ways, to the international criminal tribunals – both give normative authority to previous decisions, even though they do not follow a formal rule of precedent.[36] National judicial decisions are also a 'subsidiary means for the determination of the rules of law'.[37] As discussed below, the *ad hoc* Tribunals' Appeals Chambers have invoked the doctrine of precedent to hold that

[32] See, e.g., *Prosecutor* v. *Orić*, Case No. IT-03-68-A, Judgment, 3 July 2008, Partially Dissenting Opinion and Declaration of Judge Liu, para. 8 (noting that 'judicial integrity' and 'respect for the correct principles of international law' require that the Appeals Chamber revise 'material errors in its reasoning'); see also *Barayagwiza* v. *Prosecutor*, Case No. ICTR-97-19-AR72, Decision (Prosecutor's Request for Review or Reconsideration), 31 March 2000 ('*Barayagwiza* Review Decision'), paras. 37–40 (discussing international and national precedent for the Appeals Chamber's power of revision). For reference to the right of revision as a principle of customary international law, see Effects of Awards of Compensation Made by the United Nations Administrative Tribunal, Advisory Opinion of 13 July 1954 ('Effects of Awards Decision'), (1954) ICJ Rep. 47, 55 (holding that, although the UN Administrative Tribunal's Statute stated its decisions were 'final and without appeal', such provisions need not 'be considered as excluding the Tribunal from itself revising a judgement in special circumstances when new facts of decisive importance have been discovered', and distinguishing such a situation from an 'appeal'). But see Rome Statute, Art. 84(1) (permitting a convicted person to apply for revision of a decision, and authorising the Prosecutor to seek revision, but solely on behalf of the convicted). See also La Rosa, *supra* note 18, p. 1563 ('Although the Draft Statute discussed at Rome included a provision enabling the Prosecutor to apply for revision of an acquittal' within five years, 'States quickly reached the conclusion that because of the technical and legal problems which would arise, it was better to exclude this option') (footnotes omitted).

[33] The Latin phrase means literally 'the reason for deciding'. The *ratio decidendi* of a higher court in a common law jurisdiction is binding on the lower courts by the operation of the doctrine of precedent. See, e.g., *Deakin* v. *Webb* (1904) 1 CLR 585 (High Court of Australia) (defining the term as any indispensable factor in the process of reasoning that leads to a judicial decision).

[34] See Bryan A. Garner (ed.), *Black's Law Dictionary* (7th edn 1999) ('*Black's Law Dictionary*'), p. 1414.

[35] *Trendtex Trading Corporation* v. *Central Bank of Nigeria*, [1977] QB 529, 524.

[36] The persuasive authority of prior ICJ decisions arises notwithstanding the ICJ Statute, which provides that '[t]he decision of the Court has no binding force except between the parties and in respect of that particular case'. ICJ Statute, *supra* note 18, Art. 59. See also Mohammed Shahabuddeen, *Precedent in the World Court* (1996), p. 239. For discussion of the European Court of Human Rights, see Karen Reid, *A Practitioner's Guide to the European Convention on Human Rights* (1998).

[37] ICJ Statute, *supra* note 18, Art. 38(1)(d).

lower chambers are bound by appellate rulings, not only in the case at hand, but in future cases.[38]

At the national level, common and civil law systems generally reflect different positions on whether previous decisions are a binding source of law. The idea of 'judge-made law' can be seen, and generally is seen, by civil law systems as a violation of the separation of powers.[39] The issue is more complex than a simple dichotomy between the two systems, however, in that almost all jurisdictions – either as a matter of legal prescription or practice – give previous decisions some degree of normative force.[40] Moreover, despite the civil law aversion to judge-made law, judges at the *ad hoc* Tribunals and the SCSL operate not only as jurisprudential lawmakers, but also as quasi-legislators through their drafting and amendment of the tribunals' Rules, an issue explored more thoroughly in Chapter 2.[41] Antonio Cassese explains that the judges are, 'in a sense, both rule-makers and decision-makers', as they created 'the first international criminal procedural and evidentiary codes ever adopted [which] had to be amended gradually to deal with a panoply of contingencies which were not anticipated by the framers of their Statutes'.[42]

At the core of criminal law, both national and international, is the principle of legality – that is, the accused's right not to be punished for an act that was not criminal when it was performed.[43] In theory, the doctrine of precedent acts to limit incursions on this right by limiting the creation of new law or the amendment of existing law, so that an accused is not tried for conduct that was not criminal at the time of its commission.[44] In the process, it provides certainty and consistency in law. Yet even in a national system that recognises binding precedents, judges' attempts to 'distinguish' prior decisions, in order to avoid the effects of their holdings, may ultimately circumvent the principle of legality.[45] This result could occur,

[38] See *infra* Section 11.3.1; see also Xavier Tracol, 'The Precedent of Appeals Chambers Decisions in the International Criminal Tribunals', (2004) 17 *Leiden Journal of International Law* 67, 68; Mark A. Drumbl and Kenneth S. Gallant, 'Appeals in the *Ad hoc* International Criminal Tribunals: Structure, Procedure, and Recent Cases', (2001) 3 *The Journal of Appellate Practice and Process* 589, 632.

[39] See, e.g., John Bell, *French Legal Cultures* (2001), p. vii.

[40] For more detailed discussion of these issues, see generally Gideon Boas, 'The Case for a New Appellate Jurisdiction for International Criminal Law', in Göran Sluiter and Sergey Vasiliev (eds.), *International Criminal Procedure: Towards A Coherent Body of Law* (2008), pp. 417–455.

[41] On judges as rule-makers and associated problems, see Chapter 2, Section 2.1.4.

[42] Antonio Cassese, 'The Statute of the International Criminal Court: Some Preliminary Reflections', (1999) 10 *European Journal of International Law* 144, 163.

[43] See, e.g., ICCPR, Art. 15(1); see also Gideon Boas, James L. Bischoff, and Natalie L. Reid, *Forms of Responsibility in International Criminal Law* (2007) ('Boas, Bischoff, and Reid, *Forms of Responsibility*'), p. 8.

[44] See ICCPR, Art. 15(1) (embodying the principle of *nullum crimen, nulla poena sine praevia lege poenali*, often abbreviated to *nullum crimen sine lege*, or *nullum poena sine lege*); *Black's Law Dictionary*, *supra* note 34, p. 1095 (defining the term as the principle prohibiting punishment without a law authorising it).

[45] The practice of 'distinguishing' the current case from a precedent allows a court to reach a different conclusion from the result in the previous case, by determining that the unique facts of the current case render the reasoning of the precedent inapplicable. This allows a lower court bound by precedent to reach a just outcome. Even in a court where the precedent may be overruled, distinguishing the previous decision

for example, when a chamber, through the jurisprudence, expands an offence or form of responsibility,[46] or limits a defence. These judicial expansions and limitations of the law can pose an even greater threat to the principle of legality when they are effected by an appellate chamber of last instance, as that body will have the final say and the accused will have no opportunity to seek a second opinion.

With these problems in mind, the subsections that follow focus on one specific aspect of *stare decisis* relevant to the subject matter of this chapter: how the doctrine operates in the international criminal tribunals to render the decisions of the appeals chamber binding on lower courts and persuasive for future appeals chambers.

11.3.1 Status of appellate precedent at the ad hoc *Tribunals*

The *ad hoc* Tribunals' Statutes do not directly deal with the issue of precedent.[47] In its first ruling on the question of whether the doctrine of precedent applied to the ICTY, the Appeals Chamber resorted to a creative reading of Article 25 of the ICTY Statute, a provision which outlines the right of appeal but says nothing about the binding force of appeal decisions.[48] Relying on a purposive interpretation of how best to fulfil the Tribunal's mandate of prosecuting serious crimes, the Appeals Chamber concluded that a doctrine of *stare decisis* applies in that jurisdiction, and that ICTY trial chambers are bound by the *ratio decidendi* of previous Appeals Chamber decisions.[49] According to the Chamber, this conclusion reflects the hierarchical structure of the Tribunal, the need for certainty and predictability, and the need to ensure fair trials through the consistent application of principles across the chambers of the Tribunal.[50] The trial chambers of the ICTY and ICTR

may be preferred to directly overruling a previous decision; for example, the UK House of Lords prefers to distinguish its own previous decisions rather than explicitly overrule them. See Boas, *supra* note 40, p. 425.

46 See, e.g., Boas, Bischoff, and Reid, *Forms of Responsibility*, *supra* note 43, ch. 2 (discussing the jurisprudential creation of joint criminal enterprise, and the judges' extensive reliance upon it to find accused responsible for crimes).

47 Because no significant variation emerges from the practice of the internationalised tribunals, we will not discuss these tribunals separately in this subsection, except to note that Article 20(3) of the SCSL Statute directs the judges of its Appeals Chamber to be guided by the decisions of the Appeals Chamber of the ICTY and ICTR. See also SCSL Statute, Art. 14 (stating that in the interpretation and application of the laws of Sierra Leone, the judges shall be guided by the decisions of the Supreme Court of Sierra Leone). The Statute provides further that the ICTR's Rules of Procedure and Evidence shall apply at the Special Court, though they may be and have been amended by the judges of the Special Court. See *ibid.*, Art. 14; see also, e.g., Chapter 7, Section 7.6.6 (discussing the SCSL's divergent rules on pre-sentencing proceedings). Given its similarity in structure and principles, the SCSL has generally followed the jurisprudence of the *ad hoc* Tribunals, for example, in relation to 'witness proofing'. See *Prosecutor* v. *Sesay, Kallon and Gbao* ('*RUF* Case'), Case No. SCSL-04-15-T, Decision on the Gbao and Sesay Joint Application for the Exclusion of the Testimony of Witness TF1-141, 26 October 2005, para. 33. On proofing, see Chapter 7, Section 7.6.4.

48 *Aleksovski* Appeal Judgment, *supra* note 31, para. 113; accord *Prosecutor* v. *Delalić, Mucić, Delić, and Landžo*, Case No. IT-96-21-A*bis*, Judgement, 20 February 2001, para. 8.

49 *Aleksovski* Appeal Judgement, *supra* note 31, para. 113.

50 See *ibid.*

regard the decisions of both their Appeals Chambers as equally authoritative and, indeed, binding on them.[51]

Consistent with the principle of binding precedent, ICTY and ICTR trial chambers have followed prior appellate holdings even where they expressly disagree with the Appeals Chamber's reasoning. For example, in the *Orić* case, the Trial Chamber took the view that superior responsibility should attach to an accused who takes up a position of command after his new subordinates have engaged in criminal conduct, if he failed thereafter to punish such conduct. Notwithstanding this view, the Trial Chamber stated that '[s]ince the Appeals Chamber … has taken a different view for reasons which will not be questioned here, the Trial Chamber finds itself bound' to apply the Appeals Chamber's holding that such an accused does not incur superior responsibility.[52] Another example concerned a specially composed ICTY Trial Chamber considering a prosecution motion to join three cases that were geographically and temporally very different. Despite some evident uneasiness, the Chamber felt itself bound by an expansive definition of joinder established in Appeals Chamber precedent: '[T]he Appeals Chamber decision makes it very difficult for any Trial Chamber seized of a joinder request alleging that the accused had a "common purpose" to conclude that such a requirement has not been met, even if the common purpose is a very broad and long-term one.'[53] Nonetheless, the Trial Chamber ultimately denied the motion for joinder, finding that while the Appeals Chamber's test was easily met, other discretionary factors in reaching a decision on joinder were not satisfied.[54]

As concerns the binding or persuasive nature of appellate decisions on future benches of the Appeals Chamber, the ICTY Appeals Chamber noted that the highest courts of both civil and common law jurisdictions normally follow their own previous decisions and will only depart from them 'in exceptional circumstances'.[55] While recognising the benefits of 'certainty, stability, and predictability', the Appeals Chamber stated that 'there may be instances in which the strict, absolute application of that principle may lead to injustice'.[56] As such, it 'should

[51] See Boas, Bischoff, and Reid, *Forms of Responsibility*, *supra* note 43, p. 26 n. 94 (noting that the trial chambers often refer to the two Appeals Chambers as if they were a single entity).

[52] *Prosecutor* v. *Orić*, Case No. IT-03-68-T, Judgement, 30 June 2006, para. 335 (applying *Prosecutor* v. *Hadžihasanović, Alagić, and Kubura*, Case No. IT-01-47-AR72, Decision on Interlocutory Appeal Challenging Jurisdiction in Relation to Command Responsibility, 16 July 2003, para. 51). See also *Prosecutor* v. *Hadžihasanović and Kubura*, Case No. IT-01-47-T, Judgement, 15 March 2006, para. 198 (also disagreeing with the Appeals Chamber's holding, but accepting it as binding authority). For more on the three decisions, including a discussion of the flaws in the Appeals Chamber's analysis, see Boas, Bischoff, and Reid, *Forms of Responsibility*, *supra* note 43, pp. 233–237.

[53] *Prosecutor* v. *Martić*, *Prosecutor* v. *Stanišić and Simatović*, and *Prosecutor* v. *Šešelj*, Case Nos. IT-95-11-PT, IT-03-69-PT and IT-03-67-PT, Decision on Prosecution Motion for Joinder, 10 November 2005, para. 32.

[54] *Ibid.*, para. 57.

[55] *Aleksovski* Appeal Judgement, *supra* note 31, para. 97.

[56] *Ibid.*, para. 101.

follow its previous decisions, but should be free to depart from them for cogent reasons in the interests of justice',[57] such as where the previous decision was wrongly decided because the judges were ill informed about the relevant law.[58] The ICTR Appeals Chamber has endorsed this holding.[59] The Appeals Chambers have found cogent reasons to depart from a previous legal holding only rarely.[60] Each Appeals Chamber has tended to treat the decisions of the other as highly persuasive.[61] Trial Chambers have likewise treated each other's decisions as persuasive, including from the ICTY to the ICTR and vice versa.[62]

11.3.2 Status of appellate precedent at the ICC

While the Rome Statute establishes a hierarchy among the sources of law the Court is to apply,[63] the ICC's governing instruments do not give any indication of a hierarchy among the three layers of chambers – pre-trial, trial, and appeals. With respect to the persuasive or binding force of the Court's own precedent, Article 21(2) of the Rome Statute states that '[t]he Court may apply principles and rules of law as interpreted in its previous decisions'. The word 'may' suggests the absence of a formal doctrine of binding precedent. While decisions of the Appeals Chamber in a particular case or situation would naturally be followed by the chamber whose decision was under appeal, the Statute does not stipulate whether such decisions must be followed by lower chambers in different cases. The ICC Appeals Chamber has not yet ruled on whether its precedent absolutely binds lower chambers, or itself, in other cases, but the practice of the pre-trial

[57] *Ibid.*, para. 107. [58] *Ibid.*, para. 108.

[59] *Semanza* v. *Prosecutor*, Case No. ICTR-97-20-A, Decision, 31 May 2000 ('*Semanza* Precedent Appeal Decision'), para. 92.

[60] See, e.g., Gideon Boas, James L. Bischoff, and Natalie L. Reid, *Elements of Crimes Under International Law* (2008) ('Boas, Bischoff, and Reid, *Elements of Crimes*'), pp. 344–348 (discussing the small handful of cases where the Appeals Chambers have departed from their own previous holdings).

[61] See, e.g., *Prosecutor* v. *Zelenović*, Case No. IT-96-23/2-A, Judgement, 31 October 2007, para. 10. (ICTY Appeals Chamber stating that criteria for sentencing appeals are well established in both the ICTY and the ICTR, and citing four ICTR cases in support); *Simba* v. *Prosecutor*, Case No. ICTR-01-76-A, Judgement, 27 November 2007, para. 260 (ICTR Appeals Chamber relying on ICTY precedent); *Prosecutor* v. *Bagaragaza*, Case No. ICTR-05-86-AR11*bis*, Decision on Rule 11*bis* Appeal, 30 August 2006, para. 9 (ICTR Appeals Chamber holding that the ICTY Appeals Chamber's case law on referral of cases to national jurisdictions 'is largely applicable in the context of this Tribunal as well'); *Prosecutor* v. *Naletilić and Martinović*, Case No. IT-98-34-A, Decision on Naletilic's Amended Second Rule 115 Motion and Third Rule 115 Motion to Present Additional Evidence, 7 July 2005, para. 20 (ICTY Appeals Chamber 'endors[ing] the position of the ICTR Appeals Chamber that "the Appeals Chamber ordinarily treats its prior interlocutory decisions as binding in continued proceedings"').

[62] See, e.g., *Prosecutor* v. *Stakić*, Case No. IT-97-24-A, Judgement, 22 March 2006 ('*Stakić* Appeal Judgement'), para. 416 (accepting, in principle, the use of ICTR trial chamber decisions as persuasive authority on ICTY trial chambers, but concluding that the decisions in question were not appropriate authority for the Trial Chamber in the case below).

[63] Rome Statute, Art. 21(1).

and trial chambers so far seems to have been to accept and apply decisions of the Appeals Chamber.[64]

As for lateral relationships, the various pre-trial and trial chambers have in practice cited one another as persuasive precedent,[65] and the Appeals Chamber has tended to follow on its own previous decisions.[66] At the same time, the composition of the Appeals Chamber changes at regular intervals as judges' terms expire, as they die or resign, and as other judges are elected.[67] It is still unclear what impact, if any, this relatively frequent turnover may have on how future Appeals Chambers regard prior appellate decisions.

The ICC does not consider itself bound by the jurisprudence of the *ad hoc* Tribunals. Some differences between the ICC and the *ad hoc* Tribunals result from special procedures established in their respective governing instruments, such as the system of victim participation established by the Rome Statute.[68] However, the ICC has effected other significant departures from *ad hoc* Tribunal practice through its jurisprudence, including by rejecting the practice of witness 'proofing'[69]

[64] See, e.g., *Prosecutor* v. *Bemba*, Doc. No. ICC-01/05-01/08-424, Decision on the Evidence Disclosure System and Setting a Timetable for Disclosure Between the Parties, 31 July 2008, para. 14 & n. 5 (Pre-Trial Chamber applying an Appeals Chamber decision from a different case). The Appeals Chamber has stated that '[t]he Pre-Trial and Trial Chambers of the ICC are in no way inferior courts in the sense that inferior courts are perceived and classified in England and Wales'. *Situation in the Democratic Republic of the Congo*, Doc. No. ICC-01/04-168, Judgement on the Prosecutor's Application for Extraordinary Review of Pre-Trial Chamber I's 31 March 2006 Decision Denying Leave to Appeal, 13 July 2006, para. 30. In one decision, the *Katanga and Ngudjolo* Pre-Trial Chamber seems to have taken this statement to heart, referencing its own case law, the case law of the Appeals Chamber, and that of a different Pre-Trial Chamber without giving superior weight to the case law of the Appeals Chamber. See *Prosecutor* v. *Katanga and Ngudjolo*, Doc. No. ICC-01/04-01/07-384, Decision on Application for Leave to Appeal by the Defence of Mathieu Ngudjolo Chui Against the Decision on Joinder, 9 April 2008. In a different decision, however, the same Pre-Trial Chamber appears to have deferred to the Appeals Chamber, discussing its own case law but affirming that it was consistent with what the Appeals Chamber had held. See *Prosecutor* v. *Katanga and Ngudjolo*, Doc. No. ICC-01/04-01/07-357, Decision on the Applications for Participation in the Proceedings of Applicants a/0327/07 to a/0337/07 and a/0001/08, 2 April 2008.

[65] See e.g., *Prosecutor* v. *Kony, Otti, Odhiambo, and Ongwen*, Doc. No. ICC-02/04-01/05-252, Decision on Victims' Applications for Participation, a/0010/06, a/0064/06 to a/0070/06, a/0081/06 to a/0104/06 and a/0111/06 to a/0127/06, 10 August 2007, para 5 ('[T]he Single Judge will, whenever appropriate, take into account the principles established and the practice followed so far by the Court in the area of victims' participation, with particular focus on the jurisprudence of Pre-Trial Chamber I in the situation in the Democratic Republic of the Congo'); *Prosecutor* v. *Lubanga*, Doc. No. ICC-01/04-01/06-1084, Decision on the Status Before the Trial Chamber of the Evidence Heard by the Pre-Trial Chamber and the Decisions of the Pre-Trial Chamber in Trial Proceedings, and the Manner in Which Evidence Shall Be Submitted, 13 December 2007, paras. 4–8 (noting in relation to the admission of evidence that 'the Trial Chamber should only disturb the Pre-Trial Chamber's Decisions if it is necessary to do so' and if it 'would be an inappropriate approach').

[66] See, e.g., *Prosecutor* v. *Katanga and Ngudjolo*, Doc. No. ICC-01/04-01/07-1497, Judgment on the Appeal of Mr. Germain Katanga Against the Oral Decision of Trial Chamber II of 12 June 2009 on the Admissibility of the Case, 25 September 2009, para. 37 (relying on *Situation in the Democratic Republic of the Congo*, Doc. No. ICC-01/04-169, Judgment on the Prosecutor's Appeal Against the Decision of Pre-Trial Chamber I Entitled 'Decision on the Prosecutor's Application for Warrants of Arrest, Article 58', 13 July 2006 ('*Congo* Appeal Decision on Warrants'), para. 84, for the test for determining whether an error of law has materially affected a lower chamber's decision).

[67] See Rome Statute, Art. 36(9)(b) (one third of judges elected every three years).

[68] On victims generally, see Chapter 8.

[69] See Chapter 7, Section 7.6.4.

and the procedure known as 'reconsideration'[70] – both of which are common at the *ad hoc* Tribunals. In *Lubanga*, the Trial Chamber stated the ICTY and ICTR precedents on proofing are 'in no sense binding on the Trial Chamber at this Court … [T]he Chamber does not consider the procedural rules and jurisdiction of the ad hoc Tribunals to be automatically applicable to the ICC without detailed analysis'.[71] Nevertheless, in that same decision the Trial Chamber acknowledged 'the importance of considering the practice and jurisprudence at the ad hoc [T]ribunals'.[72] Chambers of the ICC have allowed parties to submit arguments based on *ad hoc* Tribunal jurisprudence,[73] and have cited *ad hoc* Tribunal jurisprudence on numerous occasions to support their decisions. Among these are decisions on admissibility of evidence,[74] disclosure of exculpatory materials,[75] leave for interlocutory appeals,[76] and disclosure of witness identities.[77]

Despite the ICC's apparent reliance on prior decisions as persuasive but not binding authority, there are areas of the Court's procedural makeup that might benefit from binding precedent. For example, the ICC framework reserves for the Assembly of States Parties (ASP) the role of making and amending rules of procedure and evidence.[78] The judges could use a system of binding precedent as a means of solidifying the interpretations they give the Rome Statute and ICC Rules in the case law. It appears, however, that they have chosen a different

[70] See *ibid*., Section 7.7.

[71] *Prosecutor* v. *Lubanga*, Doc. No. ICC-01/04-01/06-1049, Decision Regarding the Practices Used to Prepare and Familiarise Witnesses for Giving Testimony at Trial, 30 November 2007, para. 44.

[72] *Ibid*., para. 45.

[73] See, e.g., *Prosecutor* v. *Katanga and Ngudjolo*, Doc. No. ICC-01/04-01/07-522, Judgment on the Appeal of Mr. Germain Katanga Against the Decision of the Pre-Trial Chamber I Entitled 'Decision on the Defence Request Concerning Languages', 27 May 2008, paras. 15–16 (allowing submissions on ICTY precedent on a given issue as potentially helpful to the Appeals Chamber in the case at hand); *Prosecutor* v. *Lubanga*, Doc. No. ICC-01/04-01/06-1399, Decision on the Admissibility of Four Documents, 13 June 2008 ('*Lubanga* Pre-Trial Admissibility Decision'), para. 12 (noting prosecution's argument that *ad hoc* Tribunal precedents on the issue in question should be considered persuasive authority).

[74] See, e.g., *Prosecutor* v. *Lubanga*, Doc. No. ICC-01/04-01/06-803-tEN, Decision on the Confirmation of Charges, 29 January 2007 ('*Lubanga* Confirmation Decision'), paras. 87–89 (relying on ICTY decision on admitting intercepted communications into evidence); *Lubanga* Pre-Trial Admissibility Decision, *supra* note 73, para. 25 ('If a challenge is made to the admissibility of evidence, it appears logical that the burden rests with the party seeking to introduce the evidence – in this case the prosecution. This has been the practice of the ICTY and there seems no reason to disturb this self-evidently sensible requirement.').

[75] See, e.g., *Prosecutor* v. *Lubanga*, Doc. No. ICC-01/04-01/06-1401, Decision on the Consequences of Non-Disclosure of Exculpatory Materials Covered by Article 54(3)(e) Agreements and the Application to Stay the Prosecution of the Accused, Together with Certain Other Issues Raised at the Status Conference on 10 June 2008, 13 June 2008, paras. 77–78, 80–81 (discussing various ICTY cases supporting the Chamber's decision on disclosure of exculpatory materials).

[76] See, e.g., *Situation in Uganda*, Doc. No. ICC-02/04-01/05-US-EXP, Decision on Prosecutor's Application for Leave to Appeal in Part Pre-Trial Chamber II's Decision on the Prosecutor's Applications for Warrants of Arrest Under Article 58, 19 August 2005, paras. 16–21 (relying on ICTR and SCSL authority on the test for granting leave to file an interlocutory appeal).

[77] See, e.g., *Prosecutor* v. *Lubanga*, Doc. No. ICC-01/04-01/06-773, Judgement on the Appeal of Mr. Thomas Lubanga Dyilo Against the Decision of Pre-Trial Chamber I Entitled 'First Decision on the Prosecution Requests and Amended Requests for Redactions under Rule 81', 14 December 2006, para. 20 (relying on ICTY precedent on disclosure of witness identities to the other party).

[78] See Chapter 2, Section 2.2.2.

avenue for achieving a greater say in the development of the law through the judge-made Regulations, a process that entails only passive participation by the ASP. This particular expansion of judicial power is examined elsewhere in this volume.[79]

11.4 Interlocutory appeals

Unlike the rights of appeal and revision from final judgements, the right of interlocutory appeal cannot be regarded as a fundamental component of international criminal law – at least in the sense of being a requirement established by universally recognised human rights norms.[80] To varying degrees, however, all of the international criminal tribunals permit the parties to file interlocutory appeals in the Appeals Chamber against decisions by lower chambers or single judges. Interlocutory appeals of some types of decisions are as of right, and the appellant may thus file the appeal directly with the Appeals Chamber. All other interlocutory appeals are discretionary, and leave to file the appeal must be obtained from the judge or chamber that issued the impugned decision. In this way, the lower chamber serves as gatekeeper to the Appeals Chamber. The standards by which discretionary interlocutory appeals are permitted by chambers are largely similar across the tribunals, as is the standard of review applied by the Appeals Chambers in their examination of the appeal.

11.4.1 Interlocutory appeals as of right

For some types of decisions, the appellant does not need leave of the chamber that issued the impugned decision in order to file an appeal. In the *ad hoc* Tribunals, the parties may appeal as of right from (1) decisions on preliminary motions challenging the jurisdiction of the Tribunal;[81] (2) a decision of the Tribunal's referring chamber whether or not to refer a case to a national jurisdiction;[82] (3) a decision in which two judges of a trial chamber decide to continue with the proceedings in

[79] See Chapter 2, Section 2.2.3; Chapter 12, Section 12.3.

[80] See, e.g., *Prosecutor* v. *Lubanga*, Doc. No. ICC-01/04-168, Judgment on the Prosecutor's Application for Extraordinary Review of Pre-Trial Chamber I's 31 March 2006 Decision Denying Leave to Appeal, 13 July 2006 ('*Lubanga* July 2006 Appeal Decision'), para. 38 ('Is a right to appeal against every decision of a hierarchically subordinate court to a court of appeal, or specifically an interlocutory decision of a criminal court to the court of appeal acknowledged by universally recognized human rights norms? The answer is in the negative. Only final decisions of a criminal court determinative of its verdict or decisions pertaining to the punishment meted out to the convict are assured as an indispensable right of man.').

[81] ICTY Rule 72(B)(i); ICTR Rule 72(B)(i). On challenges to the jurisdiction of the tribunal, see Chapter 6, text accompanying notes 71–74.

[82] ICTY Rule 11 *bis*(I); ICTR Rule 11 *bis*(H). On referral of cases from the *ad hoc* Tribunals to national jurisdictions, see Chapter 3, Section 3.1.3.

a partly heard trial using a substitute judge;[83] (4) decisions on provisional release from detention pending or during trial or appeal;[84] (5) decisions rendered during contempt proceedings by a Trial Chamber;[85] and (6) at the ICTY, decisions on applications requesting that a state be ordered to produce documents or information.[86] Appeals from any other decision may proceed only with leave. In contrast, there are no interlocutory appeals as of right at the SCSL; instead, the SCSL Appeals Chamber has original jurisdiction to hear challenges to the Special Court's jurisdiction, while interlocutory appeals are discretionary.[87]

At the ICC, interlocutory appeals as of right may be filed against (1) decisions with respect to jurisdiction or admissibility;[88] (2) decisions on release from detention pending or during trial or appeal;[89] (3) decisions by the pre-trial chamber *proprio motu* in relation to a 'unique investigative opportunity';[90] and (4) orders for reparations.[91] For any other decision, leave to appeal must be obtained from the chamber that issued the impugned decision.

11.4.2 Interlocutory appeals at the lower chamber's discretion

Whether a party may file an interlocutory appeal on an issue for which interlocutory appeal does not lie as of right is wholly within the discretion of the chamber that issued the impugned decision. At the *ad hoc* Tribunals and the ICC, the standard governing the exercise of that discretion is the same: leave to pursue such an

[83] ICTY Rule 15 *bis*(D); ICTR Rule 15 *bis*(D). On the ability of chambers to conduct proceedings with less than a full complement of judges, and to continue trial with a substitute or alternate judge when one judge can no longer continue sitting, see Chapter 7, Section 7.1.4.

[84] ICTY Rule 65(D); ICTR Rule 65(D). On release from detention pending or during trial or appeal, see Chapter 4, Section 4.3.

[85] ICTY Rule 77(J); ICTR Rule 77(J). On contempt proceedings generally, see Chapter 7, Section 7.8 (discussing offences against the administration of justice).

[86] ICTY Rule 54 *bis*(C). On the tribunals' authority to issue orders or requests to states, see Chapter 3, Sections 3.1.4, 3.2.6; Chapter 6, Section 6.3.2.

[87] This is true even for similar types of decisions for which an appeal as of right is available in the *ad hoc* Tribunals. For example, decisions on release from detention pending or during trial (termed 'bail' at the SCSL) are only subject to appeal in cases where leave is granted by a judge of the Appeals Chamber 'upon good cause being shown'. SCSL Rule 65(E). Preliminary motions challenging the Special Court's jurisdiction made in the trial chamber prior to the prosecution's opening statement 'which raise a serious issue relating to jurisdiction' are automatically referred to a bench of at least three judges of the Appeals Chamber. SCSL Rule 72(E). These are not appeals as such, because the trial chamber does not rule on the motion, and the appellate bench becomes the chamber of first instance. For more on the SCSL Appeals Chamber's original jurisdiction over certain matters, see *supra* text accompanying note 13; *infra* text accompanying notes 102–103.

[88] Rome Statute, Art. 82(1)(a). On jurisdiction and admissibility of cases before the ICC, see Chapter 3, Section 3.2.3.

[89] Rome Statute, Art. 82(1)(b). In early drafts of the Statute, no right of appeal against interim or custody decisions was included, and this was not amended until the Rome Conference itself. See Robert Roth and Marc Henzelin, 'The Appeal Procedure of the ICC', in Cassese, Gaeta, and Jones, *supra* note 18, p. 1537. On release from detention pending or during trial or appeal generally, see Chapter 4, Section 4.3.

[90] Rome Statute, Arts. 56(3), 82(1)(c). On these procedures, see Chapter 4, Section 4.1.

[91] Rome Statute, Art. 82(4).

appeal may be granted by a pre-trial or trial chamber where the decision 'involves an issue that would significantly affect the fair and expeditious conduct of the proceedings or the outcome of the trial, and for which, in the opinion of [the chamber] an immediate resolution by the Appeals Chamber may materially advance the proceedings'.[92]

Thus, the party seeking leave to appeal must satisfy the chamber with regard to two different conditions, the first directed at the impact of the impugned decision on the fairness of the proceedings, and the second involving more practical considerations about the benefit of the Appeals Chamber's intervention in the proceedings.[93] The party seeking leave to appeal must satisfy the lower chamber as to both conditions, no matter the importance of the point of law being challenged.[94] Additionally, chambers at the *ad hoc* Tribunals have held that permission to file a discretionary interlocutory appeal 'is not concerned with whether a decision was correctly reasoned or not'.[95] Accordingly, whether to permit a discretionary

[92] *Ibid.*, Art. 82(1)(d). Accord ICTY Rules 72(B)(ii), 73(B) (trial chamber may grant certification to appeal 'if the decision involves an issue that would significantly affect the fair and expeditious conduct of the proceedings or the outcome of the trial, and for which, in the opinion of the Trial Chamber, an immediate resolution by the Appeals Chamber may materially advance the proceedings'); ICTR Rules 72(B)(ii), 73(B) (same).

[93] See, e.g., *Lubanga* July 2006 Appeal Decision, *supra* note 80, para. 8 (concluding that Article 82(1)(d) of the Rome Statute has two components, the first describing the prerequisites for the definition of an appealable issue, and the second the criteria by reference to which the pre-trial or trial chamber may state such an issue for the Appeals Chamber).

[94] See, e.g., *ibid.*, para. 14 (identification of an issue qualifying as significantly affecting the fair and expeditious conduct of the proceedings or the outcome of the trial is not sufficient; the issue must still be one for which, in the opinion of the pre-trial or trial chamber, an immediate resolution by the Appeals Chamber may materially advance the proceedings); *Prosecutor* v. *Karadžić*, Case No. IT-95-5/18-T, Decision on Accused's Application for Certification to Appeal Decision on Appointment of Counsel and Order on Further Trial Proceedings, 23 November 2009 ('*Karadžić* November 2009 Certification Decision'), para. 6 (quoting *Prosecutor* v. *Halilović*, Case No. IT-05-87-PT, Decision on Prosecution Request for Certification for Interlocutory Appeal of 'Decision on Prosecutor's Motion Seeking Leave to Amend the Indictment', 12 January 2005, p. 1) ('even when an important point of law is raised … the effect of Rule 73(B) is to preclude certification unless the party seeking certification establishes that both conditions are satisfied'); *Prosecutor* v. *Karemera, Ngirumpatse, and Nzirorera*, Case No. ICTR-98-44-T, Decision on Joseph Nzirorera's Application for Certification to Appeal Oral Decision on 26th Notice of Rule 66 Violation and 17th Notice of Rule 68 Violation, 25 November 2009, para. 2 (denying a request for certification based on the prosecution's alleged violation of its continuing disclosure obligations, and noting that the moving party must demonstrate that both requirements of Rule 73(B) are satisfied, and even then, certification to appeal must remain exceptional).

[95] See, e.g., *Karadžić* November 2009 Certification Decision, *supra* note 94, para. 6 (quoting *Prosecutor* v. *Milutinović, Šainović, Ojdanić, Pavković, Lazarević, and Lukić*, Case No. IT-05-87-T, Decision on Lukić Motion for Reconsideration of Trial Chamber's Decision on Motion for Admission of Documents from Bar Table and Decision on Defence Request for Extension of Time for Filing of Final Trial Briefs, 2 July 2008, para. 42); accord *Prosecutor* v. *Bizimungu, Mugenzi, Bicamumpaka, and Mugiraneza*, Case No. ICTR-99-50-T, Decision on Mugiraneza's Request for Certification to Appeal and Mugenzi's and Bizimungu's Requests for Reconsideration of the Decision on the Objections of Mugiraneza and Bicamumpaka to the Engagement of Mr. Everard O'Donnel as a Chambers Consultant Dated 29 August 2009, 23 September 2009, para. 13 (in deciding whether to grant leave to appeal, trial chambers do not consider the merits of the challenged decision; rather, the inquiry involves only a consideration of whether the criteria outlined in Rule 73(B) have been satisfied); *Prosecutor* v. *Ntahobali*, Case No. ICTR-97-21-T, Case No. ICTR-98-42-T, Decision on Ntahobali's Motion for Certification to Appeal the Decision on Ntahobali's Motion for Admission of Two Rwandan Judgements Involving Prosecution Witness TQ, 14 January 2009, paras. 11–12 (denying the motion for certification while noting that the requirements of Rule 73(B) are not met through a general reference to the submission on which the impugned decision was rendered; and that the accused's

interlocutory appeal is a question of fairness and procedural appropriateness, and is not directly related to whether the chamber that issued the impugned decision committed any error.

Leave to appeal is termed 'certification' in the parlance of the *ad hoc* Tribunals' Rules, and has been characterised as such in the jurisprudence of the ICC.[96] Hundreds of applications for certification of discretionary interlocutory appeals have been litigated at the *ad hoc* Tribunals. The ICC has also dealt with a number of such applications. Even a cursory review of the voluminous jurisprudence reveals that the applicable standard is a malleable one that provides significant discretion to chambers. In some instances, it is difficult to accept that the impugned decision does not constitute an issue that would affect the fair and expeditious conduct of the proceedings or the outcome of the trial.[97] To give one example, in confirming the charges against Thomas Lubanga, the ICC Pre-Trial Chamber added certain charges not included in the prosecution's proposed charging document.[98] The prosecution sought leave to appeal, noting that the decision forced it to proceed on a charge it had already determined should not go forward. This critical question of prosecutorial independence and judicial control would seem to implicate directly the type of exceptional issue for which interlocutory appeals are appropriate. Yet the Pre-Trial Chamber, perhaps out of expedience, simply concluded that the prosecution had not raised an issue 'that would affect the fair and expeditious conduct of the proceedings or the outcome of the trial'.[99]

At the SCSL, by contrast, interlocutory appeals may be granted only 'in exceptional circumstances and to avoid irreparable prejudice to a party'.[100] SCSL trial chambers have consistently held that these criteria establish a high threshold; that both the 'exceptional circumstances' and 'irreparable prejudice' criteria must be met; and that interlocutory appeals are the exception, not the rule.[101] Although they

application generally revisited the thrust of his previous arguments that led to the impugned decision, rather than demonstrating the conditions required for the Trial Chamber to grant certification).

96 See, e.g., *Lubanga* July 2006 Appeal Decision, *supra* note 80, para. 20 ('In essence, the Pre-Trial or Trial Chamber is vested with the power to state, or more accurately still, to certify the existence of an appealable issue.').

97 See, e.g., *Prosecutor* v. *Milutinović, Šainović, Ojdanić, Pavković, Lazarević, and Lukić*, Case No. IT-05-87-T, Decision on Defence Application for Certification of Interlocutory Appeal of Rule 98 *bis* Decision, 14 June 2007, paras. 13–16 (holding that Trial Chamber's decision that an omission can qualify as participation in a joint criminal enterprise implicated neither the fair and expeditious conduct of the accused's trial nor its outcome); *Prosecutor* v. *Bagosora, Kabiligi, Ntabakuze, and Nsengiyumua*, Case No. ICTR-98-41-T, Decision on the Defense Requests for Certification of the 'Decision on the Defense Motions for the Reinstatement of Jeal Yaovi Degli as Lead Counsel for Gratien Kabiligi', 2 January 2005, paras. 9–10 (holding that the accused's lack of consent to newly assigned defence counsel did not implicate the fair and expeditious conduct of his trial or its outcome).

98 *Lubanga* Confirmation Decision, *supra* note 74, para. 204.

99 *Prosecutor* v. *Lubanga*, Doc. No. ICC-01/04-01/06-915, Decision on the Prosecution and Defence Applications for Leave to Appeal the Decision on the Confirmation of Charges, 24 May 2007, para. 45.

100 SCSL Rule 73(B).

101 See, e.g., *Prosecutor* v. *Taylor*, Case No. SCSL-03-1-T, Decision on Defence Application for Leave to Appeal the 4 May 2009 Oral Decision Requiring the Defence to Commence Its Case on 29 June 2009, 28 May

are not appeals, certain preliminary motions[102] filed in the trial chamber prior to the prosecution's opening statement are heard in the first instance by a three-judge bench of the Appeals Chamber. This occurs when the motion raises 'an issue that would significantly affect the fair and expeditious conduct of the proceedings or the outcome of a trial'.[103]

11.4.3 Standard of review on interlocutory appeals

To succeed on an interlocutory appeal – regardless of whether the interlocutory appeal lies as of right, or finds its way to the Appeals Chamber upon certification by the lower chamber – the appellant must persuade the Appeals Chamber that the lower chamber erred. In principle, the Appeals Chambers of the *ad hoc* Tribunals and the SCSL afford deference to the trial chamber's discretionary decisions regarding the conduct of trial and to its trial management rulings.[104] This deference is not absolute, however, and the Appeals Chambers will examine whether the trial chamber has fallen into error or has abused its discretionary power,[105] or 'whether the Trial Chamber has correctly exercised its discretion in reaching [its] decision'.[106]

2009, p. 3 (leave to appeal may be granted by the SCSL Trial Chamber pursuant to Rule 73(B) only in cases where the conjunctive conditions of exceptional circumstances and irreparable prejudice are both satisfied); *Prosecutor* v. *Norman, Fofana, and Kondewa* ('*CDF* Case'), Case No. SCSL-04-14-T, Decision on Application by First Accused for Leave to Appeal Against the Decision on Their Motion for Extension of Time to Submit Documents Pursuant to Rule 92 bis, 17 July 2006, pp. 3–4 (noting that, as a general rule, interlocutory decisions are not subject to appeal; Rule 73(B) involves a high threshold that must be met before the trial chamber can exercise its discretion to grant leave to appeal; the rule specifically requires that an application for leave to appeal must show exceptional circumstances and irreparable prejudice; and the two-pronged test is conjunctive and so both prongs must be satisfied).

102 At the SCSL, preliminary motions are (1) objections based on lack of jurisdiction; (2) objections based on defects in the form of the indictment; (3) applications for severance of crimes joined in one indictment or for separate trials; (4) objections based on the denial of a request for the assignment of counsel; and (5) objections based on abuse of process. SCSL Rule 72(B).

103 SCSL Rule 72(F).

104 See, e.g., *Prosecutor* v. *Tolimir, Miletić, and Gvero*, Case No. IT-04-80-AR73.1, Decision on Radivoje Miletić's Interlocutory Appeal Against the Trial Chamber's Decision on Joinder of Accused, 27 January 2006, para. 4 ('Deference is afforded to the Trial Chamber's discretion in these decisions because they "draw on the Trial Chamber's organic familiarity with the day-to-day conduct of the parties and the practical demands of the case, and require a complex balancing of intangibles in crafting a case-specific order to properly regulate a highly variable set of trial proceedings."') (quoting *Prosecutor* v. *Slobodan Milošević*, Case No. IT-02-54-T, Reasons for Decision on Assignment of Defence Counsel, 22 September 2004, para. 9); *Prosecutor* v. *Prlić, Stojić, Praljak, Petković, Ćorić, and Pušić*, Case No. IT-04-74-AR73.2, Decision on Joint Defence Interlocutory Appeal Against the Trial Chamber's Oral Decision of 8 May 2006 Relating to Cross-Examination by Defence and on Association of Defence Counsel's Request for Leave to File an Amicus Curiae Brief, 4 July 2006, p. 4 n. 13.

105 See *Prosecutor* v. *Milošević*, Case Nos. IT-99-37-AR73, IT-01-50-AR73, and IT-01-51-AR73, Reasons for Decision on Prosecution Interlocutory Appeal from Refusal to Order Joinder, 18 April 2002, paras. 4–6 ('Where an appeal is brought from a discretionary decision of a Trial Chamber, the issue in that appeal is not whether the decision was correct, in the sense that the Appeals Chamber agrees with that decision, but rather whether the Trial Chamber has correctly exercised its discretion in reaching that decision.') (quotation at para. 4).

106 *Prosecutor* v. *Popović, Beara, Nikolić, Miletić, Borovčanin, Gvero, and Pandurević*, Case No. IT-05–88-AR65.10, Decision on Radivoje Miletić's Appeal Against Decision on Miletić's Motion for Provisional Release, 19 November 2009 ('*Popović et al.* November 2009 Appeal Decision'), para. 4.

Under the applicable standard of review – articulated identically at the *ad hoc* Tribunals and the SCSL – the Appeals Chamber will only overturn a trial chamber's discretionary decision where it finds it to be: (1) based on an incorrect interpretation of governing law; (2) based on a patently incorrect conclusion of fact; or (3) so unfair or unreasonable as to constitute an abuse of the trial chamber's discretion.[107] In its review, the Appeals Chamber will consider whether the trial chamber has misdirected itself as to the legal principle or law to be applied,[108] or has given weight to extraneous or irrelevant considerations, or has failed to give (sufficient) weight to relevant considerations in reaching its decision.[109] The scope of the Appeals Chamber's review of the trial chamber's discretion is thus very limited; even where the Appeals Chamber would not itself have arrived at the same outcome, the trial chamber's decision will stand unless it is so unreasonable as to force the conclusion that the trial chamber failed to exercise its discretion judiciously.[110]

Despite the seemingly high level of deference accorded trial chambers in their decisions on the general conduct of trial, the Appeals Chambers have at times overturned trial chamber decisions in a manner which seems to have involved the Appeals Chamber substituting its judgement for that of the trial chamber.[111] As discussed elsewhere in this volume, the Appeals Chambers have injected themselves into trial chambers' management of their cases to overturn decisions regarding, among many others, release from detention pending or during trial;[112] the length of time given to the parties to present their evidence;[113] joinder of indictments;[114] self-representation;[115] whether to proceed with trial with an ill accused participating from outside the courtroom via video-link;[116] and whether the evidence of certain witnesses may be given in writing.[117]

[107] *Ibid.*, para. 5. Accord, e.g., *Prosecutor* v. *Taylor*, Case No. SCSL-03-1-T, Decision on 'Defence Notice of Appeal and Submissions Regarding the 4 May 2009 Oral Decision Requiring the Defence to Commence Its Case on 29 June 2009', 23 June 2009 ('*Taylor* June 2009 Appeal Decision'), para. 13; *Prosecutor* v. *Karemera, Ngirumpatse, and Nzirorera*, Case No. ICTR-98-44-AR73.16, Decision on Appeal Concerning the Severance of Mathieu Ngirumpatse, 19 June 2009, para. 16.

[108] See, e.g., *Taylor* June 2009 Appeal Decision, *supra* note 107, para. 13.

[109] See, e.g., *Popović et al.* November 2009 Appeal Decision, *supra* note 106, para. 5; *CDF Case*, Case No. SCSL-04-14-A, Judgment, 28 May 2008 ('*CDF* Appeal Judgment'), para. 36 (a trial chamber commits a discernible error when it misdirects itself as to the legal principle to be applied; takes irrelevant factors into consideration; fails to consider relevant factors or to give them sufficient weight; or makes an error as to the facts upon which it has exercised its discretion).

[110] See, e.g., *Popović et al.* November 2009 Appeal Decision, *supra* note 106, para. 4 (the relevant inquiry is not whether the Appeals Chamber agrees with the trial chamber's discretionary decision, but rather whether the trial chamber has correctly exercised its discretion in reaching that decision); *Taylor* June 2009 Appeal Decision, *supra* note 107, para. 13.

[111] See Boas, *supra* note 40, pp. 27–30 (discussing several cases of Appeals Chamber interference in trial chamber decisions).

[112] See Chapter 4, Section 4.3.

[113] See Chapter 6, Section 6.6.2.

[114] See Chapter 6, Section 6.2.3.

[115] See Chapter 5, Section 5.3.1.

[116] See Chapter 7, Section 7.5.2.

[117] See Chapter 9, p. 353, notes 88–90 (listing sources discussing the case law leading to the creation of Rules 92 *bis* and 92 *ter* at the ICTY); see also Gideon Boas, *The Milošević Trial: Lessons for the Conduct of Complex International Criminal Proceedings* (2007), p. 44 (discussing the principal appellate decisions in question).

The ICC Appeals Chamber has yet to articulate any formalised standard of review applicable to interlocutory appeals in a manner similar to the *ad hoc* Tribunals and the SCSL. Nevertheless, the Rome Statute seems to provide some guidance by listing what actions the Appeals Chamber may take on appeals from decisions of acquittal or conviction. In such appeals, if the Chamber finds that the proceedings appealed from 'were unfair in a way that affected the reliability of the decision … or that the decision … appealed from was materially affected by error of fact or law or procedural error', it may reverse or amend the decision.[118] The Appeals Chamber may well be amenable to concluding that these provisions are equally applicable to discretionary interlocutory appeals.

In the *Situation in the Democratic Republic of the Congo*, the prosecution appealed from a pre-trial decision denying its application for an arrest warrant for Bosco Ntaganda.[119] The Pre-Trial Chamber declared the case inadmissible, a decision for which the prosecution enjoyed an interlocutory appeal as of right. In its appeal, the prosecution noted that the Rome Statute specifies no grounds of appeal for interlocutory appeals against decisions on admissibility, and argued that the Appeals Chamber should import the categories of error applicable to appeals against decisions on acquittal and conviction in the Rome Statute – namely, procedural error, error of fact, and error of law.[120] The Appeals Chamber accepted the prosecution's argument,[121] and further noted that in the absence of any specific listed grounds of appeal 'the parties are at liberty to raise any relevant ground of appeal including the grounds' applicable to decisions on acquittal and conviction.[122]

11.5 Appeals against acquittal, conviction, or sentence

Each of the international criminal tribunals accords a statutory right of appeal to both parties against a final judgement of acquittal or conviction. While the ICC Appeals Chamber has yet to entertain any appeals against final judgements of acquittal or conviction, the Appeals Chambers of the *ad hoc* Tribunals and the SCSL have heard them in almost every case. In many appeals before the latter chambers, both parties have alleged error with respect to various aspects of the trial chamber's judgement.

11.5.1 Bases for appeal

At the *ad hoc* Tribunals and the SCSL, the Appeals Chambers are empowered to hear appeals from persons convicted by a trial chamber or from the prosecution

[118] Rome Statute, Art. 83(2).
[119] *Congo* Appeal Decision on Warrants, *supra* note 66, paras. 4–17.
[120] *Ibid.*, para. 34. [121] *Ibid.*, para. 35.
[122] *Ibid.*, para. 34. For a discussion of the Appeals Chamber's holding on the substantive issue in this decision, see Chapter 3, Section 3.2.3.1.5.

on the following grounds: (1) an error on a question of law invalidating the decision; or (2) an error of fact that has occasioned a miscarriage of justice.[123] The SCSL Statute lists procedural error as an additional ground.[124] In their reviews, the Appeals Chambers may affirm, reverse, or revise the decisions taken by the trial chamber.[125] Moreover, the SCSL Appeals Chamber is statutorily required to be 'guided by the decisions of the Appeals Chamber[s] of the International Tribunals for the former Yugoslavia and for Rwanda'.[126]

The parties before the ICC have similar substantive rights to appeal. The prosecution, the convicted person, or the prosecution on behalf of the convicted person may appeal from a decision on acquittal or conviction based on the following grounds: (1) procedural error; (2) error of fact; or (3) error of law.[127] Additionally, the convicted person, or the prosecution on the convicted person's behalf, may appeal on '[a]ny other ground that affects the fairness or reliability of the proceedings or decision'.[128] In any appeal, the Appeals Chamber may reverse or amend the decision, remand a factual issue back to the original chamber, or order a new trial to take place before a different trial chamber.[129] Since the ICC had yet to render any decisions on acquittal or conviction as of 1 December 2009, there has been no jurisprudence on which to assess how the Appeals Chamber will review such decisions.

11.5.2 Standard of review

In their jurisprudence, the Appeals Chambers of the *ad hoc* Tribunals and the SCSL have articulated the various standards of review for appeals from final judgements. These standards are generally stated concisely, and in identical terms, in a discrete section of each appeal judgement. Limited by the criteria established in each of their Statutes, the Appeals Chambers will only hear arguments from the parties on errors of law that invalidate the decision of the trial chamber, and errors of fact that resulted in a miscarriage of justice.[130] The Appeals Chambers have held

[123] ICTY Statute, Art. 25(1); ICTR Statute, Art. 25(1); SCSL Statute, Art. 20(1).

[124] SCSL Statute, Art. 20(1)(a).

[125] ICTY Statute, Art. 25(2); ICTR Statute, Art. 25(2); SCSL Statute, Art. 20(2). In rare instances, the Appeals Chambers have also remanded a case back to the trial chamber for further action. See Chapter 10, text accompanying notes 33, 246, pp. 382, 419–420.

[126] SCSL Statute, Art. 20(3).

[127] Rome Statute, Art. 81(1)(a)–(b).

[128] *Ibid.*, Art. 81(1)(b)(iv).

[129] *Ibid.*, Art. 83(2).

[130] See, e.g., *Prosecutor* v. *Dragomir Milošević*, Case No. IT-98-29/1-A, Judgement, 12 November 2009 ('*Dragomir Milošević* Appeal Judgement'), para. 12; *Prosecutor* v. *Zigiranyirazo*, Case No. ICTR-01-73-A, Judgement, 16 November 2009 ('*Zigiranyirazo* Appeal Judgement'), para. 8 (Appeals Chamber reviews only errors of law that invalidate the decision of the trial chamber and errors of fact that occasioned a miscarriage of justice); *Prosecutor* v. *Ntagerura, Bagambiki, and Imanishimwe*, Case No. ICTR-99-46-A, Judgement, 7 July 2006 ('*Cyangugu* Appeal Judgement'), para. 11 (Article 24 of the ICTR Statute addresses errors of law that invalidate the decision and errors of fact which occasion a miscarriage of justice); *CDF* Appeal

that only in exceptional circumstances will they also hear appeals where a party has raised a legal issue that would not lead to the invalidation of the judgement, but that is of general significance to the tribunal's jurisprudence.[131]

11.5.2.1 Errors of law

The Appeals Chamber reviews claims alleging an error of law *de novo.* Any party alleging an error of law must precisely identify the alleged error, must present arguments in support of its claim, and must explain how the error invalidates the trial chamber's decision.[132] If a party alleges an error of law that would have no effect on the outcome of the trial chamber's decision, the Appeals Chamber will reject the claim.[133] Even if the party's arguments are insufficient to support the contention of an error, however, the Appeals Chamber may still find, for other reasons, that the lower chamber committed an error of law.[134]

The Appeals Chamber reviews the trial chamber's impugned conclusions of law to determine whether or not they are correct.[135] Unlike factual findings, described below, the Appeals Chamber does not treat the trial chamber's legal conclusions deferentially, and the Appeals Chamber gives the trial chamber no measure of discretion. Where the Appeals Chamber finds an error of law in the trial judgement arising from the application of an incorrect legal standard, it articulates the correct

Judgment, *supra* note 109, para. 32 (under the SCSL Statute and Rules, only arguments relating to errors of law that invalidate the decision of the trial chamber will merit consideration).

131 See, e.g., *Dragomir Milošević* Appeal Judgement, *supra* note 130, para. 12; *Zigiranyirazo* Appeal Judgement, *supra* note 130, para. 9 (noting that, even if the appellant's arguments do not support the contention that the trial chamber's error invalidates its decision, the Appeals Chamber may still step in and, for other reasons, conclude that the trial chamber committed legal error); *CDF* Appeal Judgment, *supra* note 109, para. 32 (noting that some international criminal tribunals hold the view that in exceptional circumstances, the Appeals Chamber may consider legal issues raised by a party or *proprio motu*, even where the issue would not lead to the invalidation of the judgement, if it is of general significance to the tribunal's jurisprudence, and citing several appeal judgements from the ICTY, including *Prosecutor* v. *Galić*, Case No. IT-98-29-A, Judgement, 30 November 2006 ('*Galić* Appeal Judgement'), para. 6).

132 See, e.g., *Dragomir Milošević* Appeal Judgement, *supra* note 130, para. 13; *Zigiranyirazo* Appeal Judgement, *supra* note 130, para. 10; *Cyangugu* Appeal Judgement, *supra* note 130, para. 11. Although it nominally holds the parties to a standard of precision in their pleading practices, see *infra* text accompanying note 167, the ICTY Appeals Chamber has also held that it has inherent discretion to determine which of the parties' submissions merit a reasoned opinion in writing, and that it may dismiss arguments that are manifestly unfounded without providing its own detailed reasoning. Moreover, it has held that submissions will be dismissed without detailed reasoning where the appealing party's argument does not have the potential to cause the impugned decision to be reversed or revised. See, e.g., *Prosecutor* v. *Hadžihasanović and Kubura*, Case No. IT-01-47-A, Appeal Judgement, 22 April 2008 ('*Hadžihasanović and Kubura* Appeal Judgement'), paras. 14, 16. See also *infra* text accompanying note 167.

133 See, e.g., *Dragomir Milošević* Appeal Judgement, *supra* note 130, para. 13; *Hadžihasanović and Kubura* Appeal Judgement, *supra* note 132, para. 8; *Prosecutor* v. *Kupreškić, Kupreškić, Kupreškić, Josipović, and Šantić*, Case No. IT-95-16-A, Appeal Judgement, 23 October 2001 ('*Kupreškić et al.* Appeal Judgement'), para. 22; *CDF* Appeal Judgment, *supra* note 109, para. 32.

134 See, e.g., *Dragomir Milošević* Appeal Judgement, *supra* note 130, para. 13; *Hadžihasanović and Kubura* Appeal Judgement, *supra* note 132, para. 8; *Zigiranyirazo* Appeal Judgement, *supra* note 130, para. 9; *Cyangugu* Appeal Judgement, *supra* note 130, para. 11.

135 See, e.g., *Dragomir Milošević* Appeal Judgement, *supra* note 130, para. 14; *Hadžihasanović and Kubura* Appeal Judgement, *supra* note 132, para. 9.

legal interpretation and reviews the relevant factual findings of the trial chamber against that interpretation.[136] In so doing, the Appeals Chamber determines whether it is itself convinced beyond reasonable doubt as to the challenged factual finding, under the correct legal standard, before it will confirm that finding on appeal.[137] Where the appellant claims the trial chamber's lack of a reasoned opinion constitutes an error of law, the appellant must identify the specific issues, factual findings, or arguments that the trial chamber omitted to address and explain why the trial chamber's omission invalidates its decision.[138] The Appeals Chambers on several occasions have identified errors of law and invalidated portions of trial chamber judgements.[139]

11.5.2.2 Errors of fact

The Appeals Chambers have stated that they apply a standard of reasonableness to alleged errors of fact, and that only an error of fact resulting in a miscarriage of justice will cause them to overturn a decision by the trial chamber.[140] Thus, in principle, the Appeals Chamber will only substitute its own finding for that of the trial chamber when no reasonable trial chamber could have reached the original decision or where the finding is 'wholly erroneous'.[141]

[136] See, e.g., *Dragomir Milošević* Appeal Judgement, *supra* note 130, para. 14; *Zigiranyirazo* Appeal Judgement, *supra* note 130, para. 10; *Hadžihasanović and Kubura* Appeal Judgement, *supra* note 132, para. 9; *Prosecutor* v. *Kordić and Čerkez*, Case No. IT-95-14/2-A, Judgement, 17 December 2004, para. 17.

[137] See, e.g., *Dragomir Milošević* Appeal Judgement, *supra* note 130, para. 14; *Zigiranyirazo* Appeal Judgement, *supra* note 130, para. 10; *Hadžihasanović and Kubura* Appeal Judgement, *supra* note 132, para. 9.

[138] See, e.g., *Dragomir Milošević* Appeal Judgement, *supra* note 130, para. 13. This standard is discussed in detail in Chapter 10, Section 10.1.1.

[139] See, e.g., *Prosecutor* v. *Brđanin*, Case. No. IT-99-36-A, Judgement, 3 April 2007, para. 414 (finding that the Trial Chamber erred in its understanding of the doctrine of joint criminal enterprise); *Stakić* Appeal Judgement, *supra* note 62, para. 63 (finding that the Trial Chamber 'erred in conducting its analysis of the responsibility of the Appellant within the framework of "co-perpetratorship"'); *Prosecutor* v. *Kajelijeli*, Case No. ICTR 98-44A-A, Judgement, 23 May 2005, para. 81 (finding that 'concurrent conviction[s] for individual and superior liability in relation to the same count based on the same facts constitutes a legal error invalidating the Trial Judgement'); *Prosecutor* v. *Blaškić*, Case No. IT-95-14-A, Judgement, 29 July 2004 ('*Blaškić* Appeal Judgement'), para. 62 (identifying an error in the Trial Chamber's interpretation of the 'had reason to know' prong of the superior responsibility test); *Prosecutor* v. *Bagilishema*, Case No. ICTR-95-1A-A, Judgement, 7 June 2001, para. 55 (overruling the Trial Chamber's holding on the doctrine of effective control as applied to civilians, but finding that the error did not affect the verdict as the accused lacked the required *mens rea*).

[140] See, e.g., *Dragomir Milošević* Appeal Judgement, *supra* note 130, para. 15; *Zigiranyirazo* Appeal Judgement, *supra* note 130, para. 11; *CDF* Appeal Judgment, *supra* note 109, para. 33 (the Appeals Chamber will not lightly overturn findings of fact reached by a trial chamber); *Hadžihasanović and Kubura* Appeal Judgement, *supra* note 132, para. 10.

[141] *Dragomir Milošević* Appeal Judgement, *supra* note 130, para. 15. Accord, e.g., *Zigiranyirazo* Appeal Judgement, *supra* note 130, para. 11; *CDF* Appeal Judgment, *supra* note 109, para. 33; *Hadžihasanović and Kubura* Appeal Judgement, *supra* note 132, para. 10; *Kupreškić et al.* Appeal Judgement, *supra* note 133, para. 41 (where the Appeals Chamber is satisfied that the trial chamber returned a conviction on the basis of evidence that could not have been accepted by a reasonable tribunal, or where the evaluation of the evidence was 'wholly erroneous', it will overturn the conviction, because under such circumstances no reasonable tribunal of fact could be satisfied beyond a reasonable doubt that the accused had participated in the criminal conduct).

In this regard, the Appeals Chambers have said that they 'will not lightly disturb findings of fact by a Trial Chamber'.[142] Indeed, they have taken great pains to stress that they are deferential to the fact-finding function of the trial chambers, and often reiterate that appeals are not trials *de novo*.[143] As the *Kupreškić* Appeals Chamber noted:

> [T]he task of hearing, assessing and weighing the evidence presented at trial is left primarily to the Trial Chamber. Thus, the Appeals Chamber must give a margin of deference to a finding of fact reached by a Trial Chamber. Only where the evidence relied on by the Trial Chamber could not have been accepted by any reasonable tribunal of fact or where the evaluation of the evidence is 'wholly erroneous' may the Appeals Chamber substitute its own finding for that of the Trial Chamber.[144]

The ICTY Appeals Chamber has held that identical standards of reasonableness and deference to the trial chamber's factual findings apply when the prosecution appeals against an acquittal as when the accused appeals a conviction.[145] At the same time, however, the Appeals Chamber stated that because the prosecution bears the burden of proving the guilt of the accused beyond a reasonable doubt, the significance of an error of fact occasioning a miscarriage of justice is somewhat different for a prosecution appeal against acquittal than for a defence appeal against conviction.[146] While the accused must show that the trial chamber's factual errors create a reasonable doubt as to guilt, the prosecution must show that that the trial record permits no reasonable doubt of the accused's guilt.[147]

As with interlocutory appeals, described above, the deferential language employed by the Appeals Chambers has not precluded them from overturning trial chambers' findings and substituting their own judgement. In *Krstić*, the Trial Chamber convicted the accused for participating in a joint criminal enterprise to commit genocide at Srebrenica. The Appeals Chamber overturned Krstić's conviction because, in its view, the evidence upon which the Trial Chamber relied did not establish that Krstić or his corps of the Bosnian Serb Army had perpetrated

[142] *Dragomir Milošević* Appeal Judgement, *supra* note 130, para. 15. Accord, e.g., *Zigiranyirazo* Appeal Judgement, *supra* note 130, para. 11; *CDF* Appeal Judgment, *supra* note 109, para. 33; *Hadžihasanović and Kubura* Appeal Judgement, *supra* note 132, para. 11; *Cyangugu* Appeal Judgement, *supra* note 130, para. 12 (where an erroneous finding of fact is alleged, the Appeals Chamber will give deference to the trial chamber that received the evidence at trial, as the trial chamber is best placed to assess the evidence, including the demeanour of witnesses).

[143] See, e.g., *Dragomir Milošević* Appeal Judgement, *supra* note 130, para. 14; *Hadžihasanović and Kubura* Appeal Judgement, *supra* note 132, para. 9; *Kupreškić et al.* Appeal Judgement, *supra* note 133, para. 22 (stating that, as has been held by the Appeals Chamber on numerous occasions, an appeal is not an opportunity for the parties to reargue their cases; it does not involve a trial *de novo*).

[144] *Kupreškić et al.* Appeal Judgement, *supra* note 133, para. 30. See also *CDF* Appeal Judgment, *supra* note 109, para. 34 (quoting the same language from the *Kupreškić* Appeal Judgement and adopting it as a statement of general principle).

[145] *Prosecutor* v. *Mrkšić and Šljivančin*, Case No. IT-95-13/1-A, Judgement, 5 May 2009 ('*Mrkšić and Šljivančin* Appeal Judgement'), para. 15.

[146] See *ibid.* [147] *Ibid.*

any crimes; rather, the Appeals Chamber's view of the trial record was that the evidence demonstrated only that Krstić knowingly permitted corps resources to be used in support of a genocidal plan devised by others.[148] Accordingly, the Appeals Chamber overturned the Trial Chamber's conviction for genocide, and entered a conviction for aiding and abetting genocide.[149]

In the *Kupreškić* case, the Appeals Chamber similarly substituted its view of the facts for the Trial Chamber's findings. There, the Trial Chamber relied heavily upon the testimony of an eyewitness who testified that two of the accused were present at the scene of an attack during which her father was killed. In accepting the witness's testimony, the Trial Chamber noted that any doubts about her credibility were outweighed by 'the impression made by the witness upon the Trial Chamber while she was giving evidence', and further noted that her 'evidence concerning the identification of the accused was unshaken'.[150] Accordingly, the Trial Chamber had 'no doubt that she was a truthful and accurate witness' of the events.[151] While nominally conceding that it was required to be deferential to the Trial Chamber's assessment of the witness's credibility, the Appeals Chamber disagreed with that assessment based upon its own review of the factual record. Among other reasons, the Appeals Chamber believed that the Trial Chamber had given too much weight to the witness's confident demeanour during testimony. Although it had not seen the witness, nor heard her testify, the Appeals Chamber considered that the Trial Chamber committed factual error because, according to the Appeals Chamber, there were 'several strong indications on the trial record that her absolute conviction in her identification evidence was very much a reflection of her personality and not necessarily an indicator of her reliability'.[152] According to the Appeals Chamber, the Trial Chamber had failed to appropriately assess what it had seen and heard.

11.5.2.3 Procedural error

As noted above, both the SCSL and the ICC also permit appeals from final judgement on the ground of procedural error. Although the ICC has yet to articulate what this might mean under the Rome Statute, the SCSL Appeals Chamber has described procedural errors that will 'vitiate the proceedings'.[153] While not all

[148] *Prosecutor* v. *Krstić*, Case No. IT-98-30-A, Judgement, 19 April 2004, para. 137.

[149] *Ibid.*, para. 143 ('The Trial Chamber's conviction of Krstić as a participant in a joint criminal enterprise to commit genocide is set aside and a conviction for aiding and abetting genocide is entered instead'). For a detailed analysis of the Appeals Chamber's discussion of what it believed to be the appropriate form of responsibility to describe Krstić's criminal responsibility, see Boas, Bischoff, and Reid, *Forms of Responsibility*, *supra* note 43, pp. 296–298.

[150] *Prosecutor* v. *Kupreškić, Kupreškić, Kupreškić, Josipović, and Šantić*, Case No. IT-95-16-T, Judgement, 14 January 2000, para. 425.

[151] *Ibid.* [152] *Ibid.*, para. 154.

[153] *CDF* Appeal Judgment, *supra* note 109, para. 35.

procedural errors have such a dramatic effect, errors that affect the fairness of trial will undoubtedly satisfy this standard.[154] Procedural errors that can be corrected, waived, or ignored as immaterial or inconsequential, without injustice to the parties, will not constitute reversible error.[155]

11.5.3 Appeals against the sentence

The Rome Statute provides that either the prosecution or the convicted person may appeal against the sentence on the grounds that it is disproportionate to the crime.[156] Although the Statutes of the *ad hoc* Tribunals make no specific provision for appeals against the sentence imposed by the trial chamber, the Appeals Chamber has always entertained such challenges.[157]

As the ICTY Appeals Chamber has noted, appeals against the sentence 'as appeals from a trial judgement, are appeals *stricto sensu*; they are of a corrective nature and are not trials *de novo*'.[158] Accordingly, the Appeals Chambers at the *ad hoc* Tribunals and SCSL apply the same standard of review to appeals against sentence as to appeals against the judgement.[159] Trial chambers are vested with a broad discretion in determining an appropriate sentence because they must tailor penalties to fit the circumstances of the accused and the gravity of the crime.[160] This means that the Appeals Chamber will not revise a sentence unless the trial chamber has committed a discernible error in exercising its discretion or has failed to follow the applicable law on the several different factors that go into determining the sentence, as discussed in detail in Chapter 10.[161] As with appeals from

154 *Ibid.* 155 *Ibid.* 156 Rome Statute., Art. 81(2)(a).

157 This section is concerned with appeals against the sentence imposed by the trial chamber on the grounds that the trial chamber committed a discernible error in sentencing, not with cases in which the Appeals Chamber revises a sentence because it has entered a new conviction or acquitted the convicted person of one or more (but not all) of the charges.

158 *Prosecutor* v. *Momir Nikolić*, Case No. IT-02-60/1-A, Judgement on Sentencing Appeal, 8 March 2006 ('*Momir Nikolić* Judgement on Sentencing Appeal'), para. 7. See also *ibid.*, para. 6 (both Article 24 of the ICTY Statute and Rule 101 of the ICTY Rules contain general guidelines for a trial chamber that amount to an obligation to take in account certain factors at sentencing). Accord *Semanza* v. *Prosecutor*, Case No. ICTR-97-20-A, Judgement, 20 May 2005 ('*Semanza* Appeal Judgement'), para. 312. On sentencing, see Chapter 10, Section 10.2.

159 See, e.g., *Momir Nikolić* Judgement on Sentencing Appeal, *supra* note 158, para. 7 (pursuant to the ICTY Statute, the role of the Appeals Chamber is limited to correcting errors of law that invalidate a decision and errors of fact which have occasioned a miscarriage of justice, the criteria for which are well established in the jurisprudence of the ICTY and the ICTR). See also, e.g., *Semanza* Appeal Judgement, *supra* note 158, para. 312 (as a general rule, the Appeals Chamber will not revise a sentence unless the trial chamber has committed a discernible error in exercising its discretion).

160 See, e.g., *Momir Nikolić* Judgement on Sentencing Appeal, *supra* note 158, para. 8; *Semanza* Appeal Judgement, *supra* note 158, para. 312.

161 See, e.g., *Momir Nikolić* Judgement on Sentencing Appeal, *supra* note 158, para. 8; *Semanza* Appeal Judgement, *supra* note 158, para. 312 (a trial chamber's sentencing decision may only be disturbed on appeal if the appellant shows that the trial chamber erred in the weighing process either by taking into account what it ought not to have considered or by failing to take into account what it ought to have considered). See also Chapter 10, Section 10.2.2 (on the sentencing factors).

judgement, the appellant bears the burden of demonstrating how the trial chamber 'ventured outside its discretionary framework in imposing [the] sentence'.[162]

As with appeals from judgements, the deference that the Appeals Chamber gives trial chambers in sentencing decisions often exists more in principle than in reality. As discussed in Chapter 10, the Appeals Chamber has intervened in the trial chamber's sentence determination where it believed that the trial chamber misapplied a sentencing factor as a matter of law.[163] At times, however, such intervention occurs with regard to precisely the types of factual assessments that the trial chamber is, in principle, in the best position to measure. The Appeals Chamber quashed the twenty-year sentence imposed on Stanislav Galić and substituted a life term after finding that the Trial Chamber had failed to appreciate the gravity of Galić's crimes, even though it was the Trial Chamber that had heard voluminous amounts of evidence on those very crimes and directly observed the witnesses's demeanour.[164] Similarly, the Appeals Chamber reduced Momir Nikolić's sentence from twenty-three to twenty years after finding that, among other things, the Trial Chamber had failed to properly appreciate whether Nikolić was evasive during testimony in the *Blagojević and Jokić* trial.[165]

11.5.4 Submissions on appeal

Appellants before the tribunals face an uphill battle. As discussed above, the Appeals Chamber will, in principle, pay great deference to the trial chamber's factual findings, and thus place a heavy burden of persuasion on appellants. Additionally, if appellants are to have the Appeals Chamber review the merits of their challenges, they must be careful to present detailed arguments supported with extensive citations to the trial record, as the Appeals Chambers have held that deficient submissions may be summarily dismissed.[166]

162 *Momir Nikolić* Judgement on Sentencing Appeal, *supra* note 158, para. 8. Accord, e.g., *Semanza* Appeal Judgement, *supra* note 158, para. 312.

163 See Chapter 10, Section 10.2.2.3. See also Boas, Bischoff, and Reid, *Elements of Crimes*, *supra* note 60, ch. 5, Section 5.3.3. (discussing several instances where the Appeals Chamber interfered with the trial chamber's sentence determination).

164 *Galić* Appeal Judgement, *supra* note 131, para. 456, p. 204; see also *ibid*., para. 455 ('The sentence rendered [by the Trial Chamber] was taken from the wrong shelf. Galić's crimes were characterized by exceptional brutality and cruelty, his participation was systematic, prolonged and premeditated and he abused his senior position of VRS Corps commander. In the Appeals Chamber's view, the sentence imposed on Galić by the Trial Chamber falls outside the range of sentences available to it in the circumstances of this case. The Appeals Chamber considers that the sentence of only 20 years was so unreasonable and plainly unjust, in that it underestimated the gravity of Galić's criminal conduct, that it is able to infer that the Trial Chamber failed to exercise its discretion properly.').

165 See Chapter 10, Section 10.2.2.3 (discussing the *Nikolić* Trial and Appeal Judgements).

166 See, e.g., *Mrkšić and Šljivančin* Appeal Judgement, *supra* note 145, para. 17 (arguments that do not have the potential to cause the impugned decision to be reversed or revised may be immediately dismissed by the Appeals Chamber and need not be considered on the merits); *Zigiranyirazo* Appeal Judgement, *supra* note 130, para. 12 (same); *Cyangugu* Appeal Judgement, *supra* note 130, para. 13 (Appeals Chamber cannot be

In articulating the general standard of appellate practice, the Appeals Chambers have identified particular types of submissions which will be dismissed without any detailed analysis. Such deficient submissions include (1) arguments that fail to identify the challenged factual findings, that misrepresent the factual findings or evidence, or that ignore other relevant factual findings; (2) mere assertions that the trial chamber must have failed to consider relevant evidence, with no attempt to show that no reasonable trier of fact could have reached the same conclusion on the same evidence; (3) challenges to factual findings on which a conviction does not rely, and arguments that are clearly irrelevant, that lend support to, or that are not inconsistent with the challenged finding; (4) arguments that challenge a trial chamber's reliance or failure to rely on one item of evidence, without explaining why the conviction should not stand on the basis of the remaining evidence; (5) arguments contrary to common sense; (6) challenges to factual findings where the relevance of the factual finding is unclear and has not been explained by the appellant; (7) mere repetition of arguments that were unsuccessful at trial, with no demonstration that they were erroneously rejected by the trial chamber; (8) allegations based on material not in the record; (9) unsupported or undeveloped assertions, or a failure to articulate error; and (10) mere assertions that the trial chamber failed to give sufficient weight to evidence or failed to interpret evidence in a particular manner.[167]

As the *ad hoc* Tribunals' Appeals Chambers have grown busier, they have become more aggressive in dismissing claims on the ground of deficient submissions. The *Galić* case represents one of the more serious examples of deficient appellate submissions. The Trial Chamber convicted Galić for his role as the commander in charge of the infamous sniping campaign conducted against civilians during the siege of Sarajevo, and sentenced him to twenty years in prison. On appeal, the Appeals Chamber summarily dismissed several of Galić's submissions. In one ground, Galić alleged numerous instances of factual error in the judgement. In its review, the Appeals Chamber noted with regard to the submissions that 'for the most part they consist of bare assertions that are dismissed without substantial reasoning as they do not meet the requirements for appeal'.[168] With regard to another ground of alleged error in the trial judgement, the Appeals Chamber said that because Galić had failed to point 'to any specific findings that were insufficiently supported by corroborating evidence, and the Trial Judgement is replete with factual findings based on a substantial volume of corroborating evidence, the

expected to consider a party's submissions in detail if they are obscure, contradictory, vague, or suffer from other formal and obvious insufficiencies).

[167] *Dragomir Milošević* Appeal Judgement, *supra* note 130, para. 17. See also, e.g., *Cyangugu* Appeal Judgement, *supra* note 130, para. 14 (Appeals Chamber has inherent discretion in selecting which submissions merit a detailed, reasoned opinion in writing and will dismiss arguments which are evidently unfounded without providing detailed reasoning).

[168] *Galić* Appeal Judgement, *supra* note 131, para. 228.

Appeals Chamber declines to engage in an exhaustive, undirected review of the Trial Judgement'.[169] The Appeals Chamber dismissed Galić's grounds of appeal and upheld the prosecution's appeal against his sentence. As noted above, the Appeals Chamber imposed a life sentence.[170]

11.6 Additional evidence on appeal

The international criminal tribunals allow additional evidence on appeal under certain conditions.[171] At the *ad hoc* Tribunals and the SCSL, a party may lead additional evidence on appeal if the Appeals Chamber finds that the evidence was not available at trial, is relevant and credible, and could have been a decisive factor in reaching the decision at trial.[172]

To satisfy the requirement that the evidence was not available at trial, the moving party must show that it was not available 'in any form whatsoever',[173] and that it could not have discovered it through the exercise of due diligence.[174] While evidence may also be deemed 'unavailable' for these purposes in the event of gross negligence in the conduct of trial counsel, a strategic decision by counsel not to present evidence does not equate to gross negligence, even if that determination turns out to be incorrect.[175] The Appeals Chamber will presume due diligence unless the moving party can show gross negligence.[176]

For the Appeals Chamber to find the additional evidence relevant, it must pertain to 'findings material to the conviction or sentence'.[177] The evidence need only be such that it 'could have had an impact on the verdict', not that it would necessarily have done so.[178] Furthermore, even where the additional evidence sought to be adduced was available at trial, or could have been discovered through the exercise of due diligence, the Appeals Chamber may still allow it to be admitted on appeal if the moving party can establish that the evidence *would* have had an impact on

[169] *Ibid.*, para. 223. [170] *Ibid.*, para. 456.

[171] See ICTY Rule 115; ICTR Rule 115; SCSL Rule 115; ICC Court Regulation 62.

[172] ICTY Rule 115(B); ICTR Rule 115(B); SCSL Rule 115(B).

[173] *Nahimana, Barayagwiza, and Ngeze* v. *Prosecutor*, Case No. ICTR-99-52-A, Decision on Appellant Jean-Bosco Barayagwiza's Motions for Leave to Present Additional Evidence Pursuant to Rule 115 of the Rules of Procedure and Evidence, 8 December 2006 ('*Media* Additional Evidence Appeal Decision'), para. 40.

[174] See *Kupreškić et al.* Appeal Judgement, *supra* note 133, para. 50; *Prosecutor* v. *Tadić*, Case No. IT-94-1-A, Decision on Appellant's Motion for the Extension of the Time-Limit and Admission of Additional Evidence, 15 October 1998 ('*Tadić* Additional Evidence Appeal Decision'), paras. 36, 47. See also, e.g., *Kajelijeli* v. *Prosecutor*, Case No. ICTR-98-44A-A, Decision on Defence Motion for the Admission of Additional Evidence Pursuant to Rule 115 of the Rules of Procedure and Evidence, 28 October 2004, para. 15 (moving party must provide details on its due diligence and the unavailability of the evidence during trial); *Prosecutor* v. *Mejakić, Gruban, Dušan and Knežević*, Case No. IT-02-65-AR11*bis*.1, Decision on Joint Defense Motion To Admit Additional Evidence Before the Appeals Chamber Pursuant to Rule 115, 16 November 2005, paras. 19–20, 33–34, 43 (denying motion for failure to provide such details).

[175] See *Tadić* Additional Evidence Appeal Decision, *supra* note 174, paras. 48–50.

[176] *Ibid.*, para. 48.

[177] *Kupreškić et al.* Appeal Judgement, *supra* note 133, para. 62.

[178] *Ibid.*, para. 66. Accord *Media* Additional Evidence Appeal Decision, *supra* note 173, para. 6.

the verdict if admitted at trial, and its exclusion on appeal would amount to a miscarriage of justice.[179] Applying this standard, the ICTR Appeals Chamber rejected the accused Barayagwiza's motion seeking to admit certain recently declassified documents on appeal because unclassified versions of the documents had existed during trial, Barayagwiza may have been able to obtain the classified documents in any event through a U.S. Freedom of Information Act request, and he had failed to convince the Appeals Chamber that their admission at trial would have had a decisive effect on the Trial Chamber's decision.[180]

The motion must clearly identify the trial chamber's specific factual finding to which the additional evidence allegedly relates.[181] Where the Appeals Chamber admits the additional evidence, it considers it in conjunction with the trial record to determine if the trial judgement can be sustained, or if it must be vacated or amended.[182] It may also allow the opposing party to admit rebuttal evidence.[183] The Appeals Chambers have admitted additional evidence on appeal regarding, for example, witness statements[184] and a letter from an academic professor.[185]

ICC Court Regulation 62 refers to the presentation of additional evidence before the ICC Appeals Chamber, thought it does not set forth any test to be applied for determining whether to admit such evidence. No practice yet exists regarding this regulation, and it is unclear whether the Court will follow the precedent of the other international criminal tribunals.

11.7 Revision

The governing instruments of the ICTY, ICTR, SCSL, and ICC incorporate some version of the right to have a final judgement reviewed and potentially revised.[186] The

[179] See *Prosecutor* v. *Haradinaj, Balaj, and Brahimaj*, Case No. IT-04-84-AR65.2, Decision on Lahi Brahimaj's Request to Present Additional Evidence Under Rule 115, 3 March 2006 ('*Haradinaj et al.* Additional Evidence Appeal Decision'), para. 11 and n. 28 (collecting ICTY cases on this standard); accord *Media* Additional Evidence Appeal Decision, *supra* note 173, para. 6.

[180] *Media* Additional Evidence Appeal Decision, *supra* note 173, paras. 40–44. See also, e.g., *RUF* Case, Case No. SCSL-04-15-A, Decision on Gbao Motion to Admit Additional Evidence Pursuant to Rule 115, 5 August 2009 (relying on *ad hoc* Tribunal jurisprudence on the standard for admission of evidence on appeal, and denying motion).

[181] ICTY Rule 115(A); ICTR Rule 115(A); SCSL Rule 115(A).

[182] ICTY Rule 115(B); ICTR Rule 115(B); SCSL Rule 115(B). See also, e.g., *Media* Additional Evidence Appeal Decision, *supra* note 173, para. 7 ('[W]hether the additional evidence was or was not available at trial, the additional evidence must always be assessed in the context of the evidence presented at trial, and not in isolation.').

[183] ICTY Rule 115(A), (B); ICTR Rule 115(A), (B); SCSL Rule 115(A), (B). See also *Haradinaj et al.* Additional Evidence Appeal Decision, *supra* note 179, para. 44 (stating that 'rebuttal material is admissible if it directly affects the substance of the additional evidence admitted by the Appeals Chamber'; finding that the prosecution's proposed rebuttal evidence had such an effect; and admitting the accused's additional evidence and the prosecution's rebuttal evidence on appeal) (internal quotation marks omitted).

[184] *Nahimana, Barayagwiza, and Ngeze* v. *Prosecutor*, Case No. ICTR-99-52-A, Decision on Motions Relating to the Appellant Hassan Ngeze's and the Prosecution's Requests for Leave to Present Additional Evidence of Witnesses ABC1 and EB, 27 November 2006, paras. 3, 38–39.

[185] *Haradinaj et al.* Additional Evidence Appeal Decision, *supra* note 179, paras. 12, 32–39.

[186] See Rome Statute, Art. 84; ICTY Statute, Art. 26; ICTR Statute, Art. 25; SCSL Statute, Art. 21. As noted above, see *supra* text accompanying note 3, the latter three instruments use the term 'review' in English,

right to request revision is well established in international criminal law, is similarly found in other international jurisdictions[187] and in most domestic jurisdictions,[188] and operates as a safeguard against factual errors that may have occurred during the original proceedings. The right arises if new facts come to light once proceedings have terminated. For the international criminal tribunals, this most often means once the Appeals Chamber has rendered its judgement on the merits.

The requirement of new facts reflects a reticence to disturb a final judgement for which all other remedies have been exhausted, and incorporates principles of *res judicata* and *non bis in idem*.[189] There are strong interests in ensuring that the judicial pronouncement is final and conclusive of rights and duties, and in avoiding *ad infinitum* litigation. Nevertheless, there is an equally strong countervailing interest in preventing a miscarriage of justice if circumstances, such as a new fact, arise or become known subsequent to a final judgement that throw an important aspect of the judgement substantially into question. In attempting to strike a balance between these competing interests, international courts have imposed strict limits on the granting of revision. While the ICTR has granted at least one application for revision,[190] the ICTY has entertained but has never granted such an application.[191] The ICC has yet to produce jurisprudence on this subject because no chamber of that Court has rendered a final judgement in any case. As for other international courts, as far as can be determined, the ICJ has heard one application for revision and rejected it,[192] and the European Court of Human Rights considered at least one such application but then ruled after hearing the merits that the decision in question did not need to be revised.[193] These courts' experience shows revision to be an exceptional remedy in international law.

while the former uses the term 'revision'. For convenience, we have chosen to use the term 'revision' in this chapter.

187 See, e.g., ICJ Statute, supra note 18, Art. 61; Protocol No. 7, *supra* note 23, Art. 4.

188 ICTY Manual on Developed Practices (2009), available at www.icty.org/x/file/About/Reports%20and 20Publications/manual_developed_practices/icty_manual_on_developed_practices.pdf, p. 145 (noting that, '[a]s in most domestic jurisdictions, the ICTY Statute and Rules provide for a review procedure distinct from the ordinary appellate process').

189 Peter Butt (ed.), *Butterworths Concise Australian Legal Dictionary* (2nd edn 2001) (defining *res judicata* as '[a]n issue that has been definitively settled by judicial decision'). On *non bis in idem*, see Chapter 3, Sections 3.1.1, 3.2.3.1.4.

190 See *Barayagwiza* Review Decision, *supra* note 32, para. 75 (granting prosecution's request for revision and reversing an earlier Appeals Chamber decision terminating the proceedings).

191 ICTY Manual on Developed Practices, *supra* note 188, p. 145. See also, e.g., *Prosecutor* v. *Blaškić*, Case No. IT-95-14-R, Decision on Prosecutor's Request for Review or Reconsideration, 23 November 2006 ('*Blaškić* Review Decision') (denying prosecution's application for revision because all of the alleged new facts were merely additional evidence of facts already considered at earlier stages of the proceedings); *Naletilić* v. *Prosecutor*, Case No. IT-98-34-R, Decision on Mladen Naletilić's Request for Review, 19 March 2009 (similarly denying Naletilić's application for revision).

192 See Application for Revision and Interpretation of the Judgment of 24 February 1982 in the Case Concerning the Continental Shelf (*Tunisia* v. *Libyan Arab Jamahiriya*), Judgement, (1985) ICJ Rep. 192.

193 *Pardo* v. *France*, Eur. Ct. H.R. App. No. 13416/87, 10 July 1996, available at http://cmiskp.echr.coe.int/tkp197/iew.asp?item=2&portal=hbkm&action=html&highlight=pardo%20l%20france&sessionid=47756062&skin=hudoc-en (revising judgement of 20 September 1993).

Even where a court's founding instruments do not grant it express powers of revision, as when its statute stipulates that decisions are 'final and without appeal', the court may nevertheless have an inherent power to recognise a right of revision on the basis of new facts.[194] Thus, while applications for revision are rarely successful, the right to request revision seems to be an inherent part of the judicial function.

The discussion that follows first explores the meaning and scope of the requirement that the party seeking revision point to new facts that have arisen since the final judgement. It then outlines the other legal criteria for assessing an application for revision and making a decision. Because the criteria and procedures differ somewhat between the *ad hoc* Tribunals and the SCSL, on one hand, and the ICC, on the other, separate subsections describe the standard for revision in each.

11.7.1 New facts

At the *ad hoc* Tribunals and the SCSL, either party may seek revision of a final judgement if a new fact comes to light subsequent to the entry of a final judgement that, if known in the original proceedings, would have resulted in a different verdict.[195] At the ICC, a convicted person has a right to request revision of the 'final judgment of conviction or sentence' where a new fact has been discovered that would likely have resulted in a different verdict, and its unavailability at trial was not attributable to the convicted person or the party making the application on his or her behalf.[196] The right also arises where decisive evidence used at the trial and upon which the conviction depends was 'false, forged, or falsified';[197] and if a judge in the original proceedings committed serious misconduct sufficient to justify removal from office[198] – an issue not expressly addressed in the *ad hoc* Tribunals' governing instruments.

[194] See, e.g., Effects of Awards Decision, *supra* note 32, p. 55 (notwithstanding UN Administrative Tribunal Statute's provision that decisions were final and without appeal, holding that such provisions 'need not be considered as excluding the [UN Administrative] Tribunal from itself revising a judgment in special circumstances when new facts of decisive importance have been discovered').

[195] ICTY Statute, Art. 26; ICTR Statute, Art. 25; SCSL Statute, Art. 21; ICTY Rule 119; ICTR Rule 120; SCSL Rule 120. See also, e.g., *Prosecutor* v. *Ntagerura, Bagambiki, and Imanishimwe*, Case No. ICTR-99-46-T, Decision on the Coalition for Women's Human Rights in Conflict Situation[s'] Motion for Reconsideration of the Decision on the Application to File an Amicus Curiae Brief, 24 September 2001, para. 9 (noting that 'review is an exceptional measure that may be invoked *where a new and potentially decisive fact has been discovered*', and denying application for failure to raise a new fact).

[196] Rome Statute, Art. 84(1)(a) (quotation at Art. 84(1)). The English version of the Rome Statute actually uses the term 'new evidence', instead of 'new fact'. Rome Statute, Art. 84(1)(a). On this terminology, see *infra* text accompanying notes 204–206.

[197] *Ibid.*, Art. 84(1)(b). [198] *Ibid.*, Art. 84(1)(c).

Drawing on earlier jurisprudence, the ICTY Appeals Chamber in *Blaškić* provided a summary of what constitutes a new fact:

A new fact refers to new information of an evidentiary nature of a fact that was not in issue during the trial or appeal proceedings. This means that it must not have been among the factors that the deciding body could have taken into account in reaching its verdict. In other words, what is relevant is whether the deciding body knew about the fact or not in arriving at its decision.[199]

New facts can come to light in a variety of ways. As discussed in Chapter 3, the collection of evidence for international criminal trials often requires state cooperation, which is not always forthcoming.[200] Belated state cooperation – for example, by more recent, moderate governments in the former Yugoslavia – has often led to new facts emerging after a final judgement has been rendered.[201]

The admission of additional evidence on appeal and the revision requirement of a new fact differ fundamentally.[202] For the latter, the fact must literally be new, and cannot simply be newly discovered evidence relating to a fact which was already considered during the prior stages of the proceedings.[203] The ICC has yet to consider an application for revision. When it does, some confusion may arise from the use of the words 'new evidence' in the English version of the Rome Statute.[204] The French version uses the words '*fait nouveau*', which translates literally to 'new fact'. The use of this term aligns with the words chosen by the drafters of the ICTY and ICTR Statutes: *fait nouveau* in French, and 'new fact' in English.[205] The distinction between the words 'fact' and 'evidence' is critical in light of the jurisprudence of the *ad hoc* Tribunals which, as noted above, draws a distinction between a new fact on which revision may be grounded, and newly discovered evidence related to a fact already considered in the original proceedings.[206] In the *ad hoc* Tribunals'

199 *Blaškić* Review Decision, *supra* note 191, para. 14 (footnotes, internal quotation marks, and alterations omitted). Accord, e.g., *Niyitegeka* v. *Prosecutor*, Case No. ICTR-96-14-R, Decision on Request for Review, 30 June 2006 ('*Niyitegeka* Review Decision'), para. 6; *Prosecutor* v. *Tadić*, Case No. IT-94-1-R, Decision on Motion for Review, 30 July 2002 ('*Tadić* Review Decision'), para. 25; *Prosecutor* v. *Jelisić*, Case No. IT-95-10-R, Decision on Motion for Review, 2 May 2002 ('*Jelisić* Review Decision'), p. 3.

200 See Chapter 3, Section 3.1.

201 See, e.g., *Blaškić* Appeal Judgement, *supra* note 139, para. 4.

202 See, e.g., *Niyitegeka* Review Decision, *supra* note 199, paras. 47–48; *Prosecutor* v. *Josipović*, Case No. IT-95-16-R2, Decision on Motion for Review, 7 March 2003 ('*Josipović* 2003 Review Decision'), paras. 18–19; *Tadić* Review Decision, *supra* note 199, para. 25.

203 See, e.g., *Niyitegeka* Review Decision, *supra* note 199, para. 47; *Barayagwiza* Review Decision, *supra* note 32, para. 42; *Tadić* Additional Evidence Appeal Decision, *supra* note 174, para. 32 ('The mere subsequent discovery of evidence of a fact which was known at trial is not itself a new fact within the meaning of Rule 119 of the [ICTY] Rules. In the view of the Appeals Chamber, the alleged new fact evidence submitted by the Appellant is not evidence of a new fact; it is additional evidence of facts put in issue at the trial.').

204 Rome Statute, Art. 84(1)(a).

205 By contrast, the words chosen for additional evidence on appeal in the French version of the Rules are *preuves supplémentaires*. See, e.g., ICTR Rule 115 (French version); compare, e.g., ICTR Rule 120 (French version) (using *fait nouveau* for revision proceedings, where the English version uses 'new facts').

206 See *infra* text accompanying note 203.

jurisprudence, neither a change in the Rules nor the case law can constitute a new fact justifying revision.[207]

11.7.2 Standard for revision at the **ad hoc** *Tribunals and SCSL*

The Statutes of the *ad hoc* Tribunals and the SCSL specify the right of revision where a new fact has been discovered that was not known during the proceedings.[208] While such proceedings would normally follow a final appeal judgement, where neither party filed an appeal and the time for filing has expired, a party may file an application for revision before the chamber that issued the trial judgement or other order terminating the proceedings.[209] Both the convicted person and the prosecution may apply for revision,[210] but the Rules restrict the prosecution's right to apply to within one year of the final decision in question.[211] It is unclear what could happen if a convicted person attempts to file an application for revision several years from now, after the Tribunals have closed their doors. The Tribunals may create a legacy body to address these and similar issues that may arise, such as requests for early release from prison, or requests by courts or parties in national proceedings for access to confidential materials in an ICTY or ICTR case.[212]

The chamber seised of an application for revision conducts a preliminary examination of the application to decide whether to grant revision, considering whether a final decision has been issued and if the party can satisfy the cumulative criteria established in the jurisprudence. If it finds these requirements satisfied, the chamber will revise the final judgement to take account of the new facts.

11.7.2.1 Final decision

The ICTY and ICTR Rules provide only for a 'final judgement' to be revised.[213] Most parties applying for revision have sought to revise final judgements of the Appeals Chamber.[214] Despite the plain terms of the Rules, chambers have broadly construed

[207] See, e.g., *Prosecutor* v. *Semanza*, Case No. ICTR-97-20-I, Decision on the Prosecutor's Urgent Motion for Review, 7 February 2001, para. 6.

[208] ICTY Statute, Art. 26; ICTR Statute, Art. 25; SCSL Statute, Art. 21.

[209] See *Blaškić* Review Decision, *supra* note 191, para. 22 ('[T]he proper forum for the filing of a request for review is the judicial body which rendered the final judgement. This body may be either the Trial Chamber (when the parties have not lodged an appeal) or the Appeals Chamber, when the judgement has been appealed.').

[210] ICTY Statute, Art. 26; ICTR Statute, Art. 25; SCSL Statute, Art. 21.

[211] ICTY Rule 119(A); ICTR Rule 120(A); SCSL Rule 120.

[212] On legacy issues generally, see Open Society Justice Initiative, 'Briefing Paper: Residual Functions of the UN International Criminal Tribunals for the Former Yugoslavia and Rwanda and the Special Court for Sierra Leone and Potential Mechanisms to Address Them', January 2008, available at www.iclsfoundation.org/wp-content/uploads/2009/05/icls-rfbriefingpaper-update4osji-feb2008-website.pdf.

[213] ICTY Rule 120(A); ICTR Rule 119(A). The *ad hoc* Tribunals' Statutes make reference only to 'decision', ICTY Statute, Art. 26; ICTR Statute, Art. 25, as do the Statute and Rules of the SCSL, SCSL Statute, Art. 21(1); SCSL Rule 120.

[214] See, e.g., *Blaškić* Review Decision, *supra* note 191 (prosecution request); *Prosecutor* v. *Radić*, Case No. IT-98-30/1-R.1, Decision on Defence Request for Review, 31 October 2006 (Public Redacted Version) ('*Radić* Review Decision').

the phrase 'final judgement' to also include any decision that terminated the original proceedings.[215] In the ICTR's *Media* case, for instance, the prosecution sought revision of an Appeals Chamber decision to dismiss the indictment against Jean-Bosco Barayagwiza. Although the decision was not a conviction or acquittal, the Appeals Chamber held that it gave rise to a right of revision because it terminated the proceedings against that accused.[216] Similarly, the ICTY Appeals Chamber has ruled that a decision to accept a withdrawal of an appeal qualifies as a final judgement for purposes of revision.[217] Chambers have routinely rejected applications to review and revise decisions other than those terminating the proceedings.[218]

The finality of a decision is a prerequisite to the exercise of the power of revision.[219] Without a 'final judgement' – that is, a decision terminating the proceedings – no right to apply for revision exists, nor does the tribunal have any power to actually implement a revision. Alteration of the decision may be possible, however, through a similar procedure known as 'reconsideration', discussed in Chapter 7.[220]

11.7.2.2 Criteria

In evaluating whether revision is appropriate, chambers of the *ad hoc* Tribunals have applied the test outlined by the ICTR Appeals Chamber in *Barayagwiza*.[221] The Appeals Chamber set forth four criteria which must, absent exceptional circumstances,[222] be cumulatively satisfied for a revision to take place:

(1) There must be a new fact;
(2) this fact must not have been known by the moving party at the time of the original proceedings;
(3) the lack of discovery of the new fact must not have been through the lack of due diligence on the part of the moving party; and
(4) it must be shown that the new fact could have been a decisive factor in reaching the original decision.[223]

[215] See, e.g., *Barayagwiza* Review Decision, *supra* note 32, para. 49; *Prosecutor* v. *Tadić*, Case No. IT-94-1-R, Order of the President Assigning Judges to the Appeals Chamber, 29 October 2001, p. 2.

[216] *Barayagwiza* Review Decision, *supra* note 32, para. 49.

[217] See *Prosecutor* v. *Strugar*, Case No. IT-01-42-Misc.1, Decision on Strugar's Request to Reopen Appeal Proceedings, 7 June 2007, para. 21.

[218] See, e.g., *Prosecutor* v. *Semanza*, Case No. ICTR-97-20-A, Decision (Request for Review of the Appeals Chamber's Decision of 31 May 2000), 4 May 2001 ('*Semanza* Review Decision'); *Prosecutor* v. *Kanyabashi*, Case No. ICTR-96-15-AR72, Decision (Motion for Review or Reconsideration), 12 September 2000; *Prosecutor* v. *Nyiramasuhuko*, Case No. ICTR-97-21-AR72, Decision (Request for Review), 16 June 2000. A chamber might instead entertain such motions as motions for reconsideration. See *infra* Section 11.7.4.

[219] See, e.g., *Tadić* Review Decision, *supra* note 199, para. 24; *Semanza* Review Decision, *supra* note 218, p. 2.

[220] See *infra* Section 11.7.4; Chapter 7, Section 7.7.

[221] See *Barayagwiza* March 2000 Decision, *supra* note 32, para. 41. See also, e.g., *Blaškić* Review Decision, *supra* note 191, para. 7; *Radić* Review Decision, *supra* note 214, para. 10; *Prosecutor* v. *Žigić*, Case No. IT-98-30/1-R.2, Decision on Zoran Žigić's Request for Review under Rule 119, 25 August 2006, para. 8; *Prosecutor* v. *Josipović*, Case No. IT-95-16-R.3, Decision on Motion for Review, 2 April 2004, p. 3; *Josipović* 2003 Review Decision, *supra* note 202, para. 12; *Tadić* Review Decision, *supra* note 199, para. 20; *Jelisić* Review Decision, *supra* note 199, pp. 2–3.

[222] On these exceptional circumstances, see *infra* text accompanying notes 228–229.

[223] *Barayagwiza* Review Decision, *supra* note 32, para. 41.

If the chamber finds that all four criteria have been satisfied, it will then revise the final judgement to take account of the new fact, and alter the original disposition accordingly. It should specify generally which findings remain unchanged and which have been revised. For example, in *Barayagwiza*, the Appeals Chamber originally had found a violation of Barayagwiza's rights, dismissed the indictment against him, and ordered his release. Upon revision, the Appeals Chamber reaffirmed that Barayagwiza's rights had been violated but, on the basis of new facts submitted by the prosecution, found the violation to be less serious than the Appeals Chamber had originally considered it to be, and that its original remedy had consequently been disproportionate. The Appeals Chamber revised the disposition, rejecting Barayagwiza's request for release, but providing him with more limited remedies: financial compensation if later found not guilty, or a reduction in sentence if found guilty.[224] Ultimately, the Trial Chamber found Barayagwiza guilty after a trial, and gave him a reduction in sentence in accordance with the Appeals Chamber's directive.[225] The Appeals Chamber affirmed the conviction, and reduced his sentence even further.[226]

Chambers have applied these four criteria in a restrictive manner. Indeed, despite many applications for revision, the ICTY has not yet granted revision.[227] The Appeals Chambers have recognised a narrow exception to the requirement that all four criteria be fulfilled: 'wholly exceptional circumstances', in which a new fact is so crucial to the impugned decision that the second and third criteria can be dispensed with in order to prevent a miscarriage of justice.[228] Hence, the reviewing chamber may allow revision on the basis of a new fact even if it was known to the moving party during the original proceedings or could have been discovered through the party's due diligence, but only if the party can show that a miscarriage of justice would otherwise result.[229]

224 *Ibid.*, paras. 74–75.

225 See *Prosecutor* v. *Nahimana, Barayagwiza, and Ngeze*, Case No. ICTR-99-52-T, Judgement and Sentence, 3 December 2003, para. 1107.

226 See *Prosecutor* v. *Nahimana, Barayagwiza, and Ngeze*, Case No. ITCR-99-52-A, Judgement, 28 November 2007, para. 1097.

227 ICTY Manual on Developed Practices, *supra* note 188, p. 145.

228 *Barayagwiza* Review Decision, *supra* note 32, para. 65.

229 In finding this limited exception to the second and third criteria, the *Barayagwiza* Appeals Chamber noted that these criteria are based on the ICTR Rules, which introduce additional conditions not listed in the Statute. *Ibid.*, paras. 63, 65. The ICTR Statute refers to a new fact 'which was not known'. ICTR Statute, Art. 25; accord ICTY Statute, Art. 26 (same); SCSL Statute, Art. 21(1) (same). The ICTR Rules, on the other hand, refer to a new fact 'which was not known by the moving party'. ICTR Rule 120(A); accord ICTY Rule 119(A). Compare SCSL Rule 120 (not containing 'by the moving party'). The ICTR Appeals Chamber interpreted the 'lack of knowledge' reference in the Statute to be the knowledge of the chamber when it made its original decision, and the Rules as being merely 'directory in nature', when confronted with these exceptional circumstances. *Barayagwiza* Review Decision, *supra* note 32, paras. 52, 63–69 (quotation at para. 65).

Finally, the ICTY Appeals Chamber has stressed that '[t]he appeal process of the International Tribunal is not designed for the purpose of allowing parties to remedy their own failings or oversights during trial or sentencing'.[230] Underscoring the exceptional nature of the remedy of revision, the ICTR Appeals Chamber has extended this principle to applications for revision.[231]

11.7.3 Standard for revision at the ICC

The Rome Statute outlines a right to apply to the Appeals Chamber for revision of a 'final judgement of conviction or sentence' on the basis of 'new evidence'.[232] Only the person convicted or, after death, his or her representative, can lodge such an application, though the prosecution may lodge it on behalf of the convicted person.[233] This latter restriction severely limits the prosecutorial right to revision and is a departure from the *ad hoc* Tribunals and SCSL which, as described above, allow the prosecution to apply for revision even though the revised judgement may put the person in a worse position.[234] In another deviation from ICTY and ICTR practice, the plain terms of the Rome Statute suggest that an interlocutory decision that terminates proceedings cannot be revised, as such a decision would not constitute a 'final judgement of conviction or sentence'. And while the *ad hoc* Tribunals may allow a trial chamber to hear an application for revision if it was the trial chamber that rendered the final decision in the case,[235] at the ICC only the Appeals Chamber hears such applications.

11.7.3.1 Criteria

The Rome Statute sets forth a non-cumulative list of three scenarios which may justify revision: (1) where new evidence has been discovered that may have resulted in a different verdict, provided that the evidence was not available at trial and its unavailability was not wholly or partially attributable to the convicted person or the party making the application on his or her behalf;[236] (2) where 'decisive evidence' used at the trial and upon which the conviction depends was 'false, forged, or falsified';[237] and (3) where one or more of the judges at the trial committed

[230] *Prosecutor* v. *Erdemović*, Case No. IT-96-22-A, Judgement, 7 October 1997, para. 15.

[231] *Barayagwiza* Review Decision, *supra* note 32, para. 43.

[232] Rome Statute, Art. 84(1).

[233] *Ibid.* (listing 'spouses, children, parents or one person alive at the time of the accused's death who has been given express written instructions from the accused to bring such a claim').

[234] For a discussion of the merits of the restriction, and the debate over a draft version of the Rome Statute that included a provision enabling the Prosecutor to apply for revision of an acquittal, see La Rosa, *supra* note 18, p. 1563.

[235] See *supra* Section 11.7.2.1.

[236] Rome Statute, Art. 84(1)(a).

[237] *Ibid.*, Art. 84(1)(b).

misconduct serious enough to justify his or her removal from office.[238] The Appeals Chamber may reject any application it deems unfounded.[239] If it accepts an application as meritorious, the Chamber may either reconvene the original trial chamber, constitute a new trial chamber, or retain jurisdiction over the case, 'with a view to, after hearing the parties … arriving at a determination on whether the judgement should be revised'.[240] The chamber that hears the merits of the application holds a hearing to aid it in determining whether the conviction or sentence should be revised; if it decides that revision is warranted, it implements the necessary revision to the judgement.[241]

Where revision proceedings lead to a determination that the person's conviction was in error, the Rome Statute outlines a right to compensation with provisions that closely reflect those of the ICCPR.[242] Such a right was not included in the Statutes of the *ad hoc* Tribunals or the SCSL. The Rome Statute also expands on the provisions in the ICCPR by expressly creating an additional category which, in language at least, is consistent with *ad hoc* Tribunal jurisprudence on the criteria for revision. The Rome Statute allows for compensation not only where the failure to discover the new evidence is not attributable to the person,[243] but also 'in exceptional circumstances' even where it is attributable to him or her, provided 'conclusive facts show[] that there has been a grave and manifest miscarriage of justice'.[244] This remedy would follow logically to ensure compensation for wrongful punishment in such a situation.

11.7.4 Revision versus reconsideration

While a party submitting a motion to alter a prior ruling will often include motions for both revision and 'reconsideration', the two procedures differ in important ways. As noted above, revision is only applicable to final judgements or other decisions terminating the proceedings, and where new facts can be shown. It is expressly included among the statutory powers of the *ad hoc* Tribunals, the SCSL and the

[238] *Ibid.*, Art. 84(1)(c).

[239] *Ibid.*, Art. 84(2); see also ICC Rule 159 ('An application for revision … shall be in writing and shall set out the grounds on which the revision is sought. It shall as far as possible be accompanied by supporting material.').

[240] Rome Statute, Art. 84(2). For example, the Appeals Chamber might remand a case to the trial chamber where significant new facts must be assessed, or may remain seised of the matter itself to avoid unnecessary delays. See La Rosa, *supra* note 18, p. 1572.

[241] Rome Statute, Art. 84(2); ICC Rule 161.

[242] Compare ICCPR, Art. 14(6) with Rome Statute, Art. 85(2) (same, except using 'him or her' instead of 'him', and omitting reference to pardon).

[243] Rome Statute, Art. 85(2).

[244] *Ibid.*, Art. 85(3). See also *supra* Section 11.7.2.2 (discussing ICTR Appeals Chamber's relaxing of revision criteria in exceptional circumstances where ignoring a critical fact would lead to a miscarriage of justice, even if the fact's non-discovery is attributable to the moving party).

ICC. By contrast, a party may seek reconsideration at any stage of the proceedings, and need not show new facts. Although such a procedure does not appear in the governing instruments of the tribunals, the ICTY, ICTR, and SCSL have found a right of reconsideration inherent in their jurisdiction. Chambers of the ICC have thus far rejected such a notion. Reconsideration is discussed in greater detail in Chapter 7.[245]

11.8 Conclusion

Neil MacCormick and Robert Summers have argued that applying lessons of the past 'to solve problems of the present and future is a basic part of human practical reason'.[246] Notwithstanding this simple truth, the binding nature of previous appellate decisions on trial chambers may cause problems for international criminal justice. The ICTY and ICTR Appeals Chambers already allow themselves the right to not be bound by their own previous decisions 'for cogent reasons in the interest of justice', though admittedly the Appeals Chambers have only actually found cogent reasons to depart from a prior holding in a small number of cases.[247]

There are a number of reasons why the trial chambers, in the interests of justice and armed with cogent reasons, should arguably be afforded a similar right to depart from appellate rulings. Examples abound of past and present ICTY and ICTR judges expressing concerns at the decision-making of the Appeals Chambers, noting that the Appeals Chamber misapplies its own tests;[248] that it sometimes determines matters out of apprehension of the Tribunals' completion strategies, with insufficient regard for the right of the accused to a fair trial;[249] that it unduly interferes in the domain of the Trial Chamber;[250] or that it simply gets the law quite wrong.[251] Add to this inherent structural oddities of the tribunals – for example,

[245] See Chapter 7, Section 7.7.

[246] D. Neil MacCormick and Robert S. Summers, 'Introduction', in D. Neil MacCormick and Robert S. Summers (eds.), *Interpreting Precedents: A Comparative Study* (1997), p. 1.

[247] See *supra* text accompanying note 60.

[248] See Boas, *supra* note 40, pp. 436–439. See also, e.g., *Blaškić* Appeal Judgement, *supra* note 139, Partial Dissenting Opinion of Judge Weinberg de Roca, para. 2.

[249] See Boas, *supra* note 40, pp. 439–442. See also, e.g., *Prosecutor* v. *Milošević*, Case No. IT-02-54-AR73.4, Dissenting Opinion of Judge David Hunt on Admissibility of Evidence in Chief in the Form of Written Statements (Majority Decision Given 30 September 2003), 21 October 2003, paras. 20–22; *Prosecutor* v. *Nyiramasuhuko*, Case No. ICTR-98-42-A15*bis*, Decision in the Matter of Proceedings Under Rule 15*bis* (D), Dissenting Opinion of Judge David Hunt, 24 September 2003, para. 17.

[250] See Boas, *supra* note 40, pp. 442–445. See also, e.g., *Galić* Appeal Judgement, *supra* note 131, Separate and Partially Dissenting Opinion of Judge Meron, para. 4.

[251] See Boas, *supra* note 40, pp. 445–449. See also, e.g., *Prosecutor* v. *Milošević*, Case No. IT-02-54-T, Decision on Prosecution Motion for the Admission of Transcripts in Lieu of Viva Voce Testimony Pursuant to Rule 92*bis*(D) – Foča Transcripts, Dissenting Opinion of Judge Patrick Robinson, 30 June 2003; *Prosecutor* v. *Milošević*, Case No. IT-02-54-AR73.5, Decision on Prosecution's Interlocutory Appeal Against the Trial Chamber's 10 April 2003 Decision on Prosecution Motion for Judicial Notice of Adjudicated Facts, 28 October 2003, Dissenting Opinion of Judge David Hunt, para 7.

that the President both presides over the Appeals Chamber, and is responsible for the administrative and political functioning of the Tribunal, or that judges are often appointed to the Appeals Chamber with no appellate or even judicial experience[252] – and an argument begins to emerge for a reconsideration of the strict operation of the doctrine of precedent in international criminal law.[253]

252 On the problem of election of judges to the tribunals notwithstanding their lack of judicial or even legal experience, see Chapter 7, Section 7.1.1.

253 See Boas, *supra* note 40, pp. 451–455.

12

Conclusion

CONTENTS

This volume examines the tangible body of rules and practices applied in the international criminal tribunals during the various steps of an international criminal prosecution: investigation; arrest; detention; charging; disclosure and other pretrial preparation; guilty pleas; trial; appeal and other post-conviction relief; punishment; and imprisonment. It also reviews other procedures essential to conducting effective investigations and fair and expeditious trials, including rules and practices on admissibility of cases, evidence, and case management; and rules relating to the issuing of orders to states and private individuals; to the assignment of defence counsel and self-representation; the election, appointment, and recusal of judges; victim participation; and reparations.

In considering this vast array of issues, we have endeavoured, first and foremost, to explain the rules of procedure and give examples of how they function in practice. At the same time, we have sought to grapple with some of the more fundamental themes that are intertwined in the legal framework of international criminal procedure, including the ways in which international criminal tribunals and their creators constructed this area of law; how they have shaped its evolution to meet new challenges and changing circumstances; whether this effort has been successful; and whether it has adversely affected other important interests. Many of the rules of international criminal procedure seek a balance between two interests that are frequently in opposition. The international community, and especially victims, demand swift and effective justice for those who are responsible for mass atrocities. Yet the vehicle the international community has chosen for holding these individuals accountable is a criminal trial, with its myriad concomitant safeguards protecting the rights of the accused. The international criminal tribunals have been broadly successful in crafting and applying rules of procedure that strike an appropriate balance, though in some areas their solutions may have gone too far in one direction or the other.[1] This tension among the right of the accused to a fair trial, the right of victims to justice, and the legitimate expectations of the international community to see these trials conducted both fairly and efficiently, emerges in many ways throughout the chapters of this volume.

Three issues that resonate for the future development of international criminal procedure are worthy of note in concluding our appraisal of this body of law. First is the very foundation of international criminal procedure, that is, the legitimacy and coherence of a framework that underpins this dynamic area of international law. Second is the evolution of this body of law, from a creature of compromise between the common law and civil law systems, into a *sui generis* regime that reflects the unique challenges of international criminal proceedings – a development driven largely by the need to manage and expedite complex trials. Third is the trend in the tribunals' rules and jurisprudence toward ever expanding judicial power.

12.1 International criminal procedure: a coherent body of international law

When determining whether an emerging set of legal rules and practices may legitimately be deemed a discrete body of law, two basic considerations are its coherence and the sources upon which it is based. Like several other areas of international law, international criminal law is a relatively new field, but one that has grown extremely rapidly since the end of the Cold War, thanks in large part to the activity of the international criminal tribunals. In Volumes I and II of this series, it was unnecessary – beyond identifying the legal framework and the relevant aspects of the law as applied – to engage in an examination of the legitimacy of substantive international criminal law. After two decades of prolific practice at the international criminal tribunals, combined with a myriad of other progressive developments at the international and national levels since the Second World War, the forms of international criminal responsibility and the elements of the core

[1] See, e.g., Chapter 4, Section 4.3.2 (tribunals' application of rules on detention results in accused spending many years in detention before trial); Chapter 5, Section 5.3 (tribunals' application of rules on self-representation results in self-represented accused being able to substantially disrupt proceedings); Chapter 7, Section 7.5.2 (tribunals' application of rules making it very difficult to hold trial in the absence of an accused suffering from prolonged illness, even one capable of following the trial by video-link from a remote location); Chapter 8, Section 8.3.1 (ICC's changing analysis of appropriate victim participation in the Court's proceedings); Chapter 10, Sections 10.2.4, 10.5 (tribunals' imposition of lenient sentences and release of convicted persons after two-thirds of sentence).

categories of international crime have become broadly accepted as forming part of the regime of international criminal law, just as international criminal law has gained acceptance as part of the regime of international law.[2]

The same cannot yet be said of international criminal procedure, the content and legitimacy of which remains under intense scrutiny. While it appears that initially international criminal procedure was largely ignored in scholarship beyond describing and critiquing certain aspects of the operation of the international criminal tribunals, scholars have begun to pose questions about the foundation for this body of law in the traditional sources of international law, and have expressed doubts about whether one can really talk about international criminal procedure as a body of international law.[3]

As we have argued in Chapter 1, the provisions in the governing instruments of the international criminal tribunals are a form of subsidiary treaty law. While each tribunal was created under different circumstances and was given a different mandate, jurisdictional parameters, and procedural structures, they all trace their roots to a bilateral or multilateral treaty.[4] These roots in a traditional source of international law, however, do not alone provide the legal principles that give a philosophical foundation for this body of law. Instead, the development and application of the procedural instruments of the international criminal tribunals have been guided by the fundamental principle of an individual's right to a fair trial – itself a *jus cogens* norm of international human rights law embodied in many treaties. These human rights principles are the glue that binds together the entire body of international criminal procedure, and the central component that imbues it with legitimacy.[5]

Scholars have also suggested that international criminal procedure lacks sufficient coherence to be considered an established and discrete body of law.[6] There

[2] This is not to say, of course, that significant differences of opinion have ceased to exist with respect to particular crimes, underlying offences, and forms of responsibility. The form of responsibility known as 'joint criminal enterprise', for example, has come under intense scrutiny, and many doubt its purported customary pedigree. See generally Gideon Boas, James L. Bischoff, and Natalie L. Reid, *Forms of Responsibility in International Criminal Law* (2007), p. 9 n. 5.

[3] See, e.g., Antonio Cassese, *International Criminal Law* (2nd edn 2008), p. 378; Göran Sluiter, 'The Law of International Criminal Procedure and Domestic War Crimes Trials', (2006) 6 *International Criminal Law Review* 605, 606.

[4] See Chapter 1, Section 1.1.2. As noted in Chapter 1, the Security Council created the *ad hoc* Tribunals pursuant to Chapter VII of the UN Charter, and they thereby derive their constitutional legitimacy from their status as subsidiary bodies of the United Nations, an organisation that was itself created by a treaty (the UN Charter) with almost universal membership. Several of the internationalised tribunals, such as the SCSL and the ECCC, were developed under agreements between the relevant host state and the United Nations (though others, such as the SPSC, were set up by a UN body with transitional authority over the affected area). The Rome Statute and the ICC Rules are products of a traditional multilateral treaty-making process. In these ways, the structural legitimising foundation of international criminal procedure is rooted in treaty law, a primary source of international law identified in Article 38(1)(a) of the Statute of the International Court of Justice.

[5] See Chapter 1, Section 1.1.5.

[6] See *supra* note 4 and sources cited therein.

are certainly examples of different tribunals applying different rules in similar circumstances, or applying similar but not identical rules, or indeed construing and applying the same or analogous rules differently from one another. The content of this volume reveals many important examples of such divergent practice, including the varying procedures at the ICC and *ad hoc* Tribunals for the bringing of indictments and the confirmation of charges;[7] statutory differences in the Prosecutors' powers of investigation across the tribunals;[8] the distinct relationship between the *ad hoc* Tribunals and states, on the one hand, and the ICC and states, on the other, deriving from the primacy of the *ad hoc* Tribunals[9] and complementarity provisions in the Rome Statute;[10] and dramatic philosophical and regulatory differences in how victims participate in proceedings at the tribunals, and are compensated for their losses.[11] Other examples of divergence include the availability of judgement-of-acquittal proceedings at the ICTY, ICTR, and SCSL, but not at the ICC;[12] the lack of a mechanism at the ICC to proceed with trial hearings on a given day where one judge is absent;[13] different methods of determining the disqualification of judges;[14] and the absence of a distinct pre-sentencing procedure at the *ad hoc* Tribunals where one exists before the ICC and SCSL.[15]

Nevertheless, the fact that different tribunals apply procedural rules differently is hardly remarkable. In domestic criminal justice systems, one can see jurisdictions within a single country (for example, different jurisdictions within federated states such as the United States or Australia) articulating in legislation or applying procedural rules differently. Such procedural divergence does not undermine the coherence, nor the legitimacy, of domestic criminal procedure, particularly where a constitutional foundation secures fair trial protections rooted in a governing source and from which none of the divergent procedures may derogate. That differences exist within a broadly coherent body of procedural rules is a common and healthy feature of a functioning legal system.

The same holds true for rules and practices of international criminal procedure which, as we have discussed, are themselves rooted in a common foundation. Importantly, none of the above examples of divergent procedural practice derogates from the fundamental principle of an individual's right to a fair trial. While variations exist, a critical review of international criminal procedure across the international criminal tribunals suggests a far greater cohesion than it does incoherence or fragmentation. Even these examples, while revealing dissimilarities in rules and practice across the tribunals, suggest a singularity of purpose and betray a coherence far more profound than a superficial examination

[7] See Chapter 6, Section 6.1. [8] See Chapter 4, Section 4.1.2. [9] See Chapter 3, Section 3.1.
[10] See Chapter 3, Section 3.2. [11] See Chapter 8, Sections 8.2, 8.3.
[12] See Chapter 7, Section 7.6.5. [13] See Chapter 7, Section 7.1.4.
[14] See Chapter 7, Section 7.1.3. [15] See Chapter 7, Section 7.6.6.

might suggest. For example, despite substantive differences between accusation procedures between the ICC and the other tribunals, all of them require and practice judicial supervision of charging in order to ensure that there is a reasonable basis to detain and try someone.[16] Suspects are accorded a series of rights that are broadly consistent across the international criminal tribunals.[17] These include, among others, the right against self-incrimination;[18] the right to assistance of counsel during interviews;[19] and the right of accused to know the charges against them, a right protected in practice by permitting challenges to the form of indictment at the *ad hoc* Tribunals and SCSL, and by the confirmation process at ICC.[20] Other examples include the requirement that convictions only be entered on proof beyond a reasonable doubt;[21] that the accused has a right to give evidence;[22] that the accused has a near-absolute right to be present at his or her trial;[23] that the accused has a right of confrontation;[24] and the right to a public trial.[25] Furthermore, notwithstanding the permissive approach to admissibility of evidence in their proceedings,[26] all the tribunals have provisions requiring exclusion of evidence if its admission would undermine the integrity of proceedings or breach fundamental human rights guarantees.[27]

These procedures demonstrate that the coherence of international criminal procedure derives from its compliance with human rights principles, which are a foundational part of the construct of international criminal law. Yet this does not mean that these rules are always interpreted and applied in a manner consistent with human rights law or international law more broadly. The regime of international criminal procedure applies rules that, while broadly consistent with the right to a fair trial, can vary or modify the application of what are described in the tribunals' statutes as 'minimum guarantees'. Examples of this phenomenon include the flexible rules of evidence that modify the accused's right to cross-examine witnesses;[28] that the right to a public trial is subject to the protection of victims and witnesses;[29] the circumstances under which indicted persons in custody will be granted release pending or during trial or appeal,[30] and some limits on the presumptive right to self-representation.[31] These variations do not undermine the legitimacy and coherence given to international criminal procedure by human rights principles. Quite the contrary, they show that this body of law holds together despite differences in application.

[16] See Chapter 6, Section 6.1. [17] See Chapter 4, Section 4.2.
[18] See Chapter 4, Section 4.2.1. [19] See Chapter 4, Section 4.2.2.
[20] See Chapter 6, Sections 6.1.1, 6.1.2.1. [21] See Chapter 10, Section 10.1.3.
[22] See Chapter 7, Section 7.6.2. [23] See Chapter 7, Section 7.5.
[24] See Chapter 9, Section 9.2.1.1. [25] See Chapter 7, Section 7.4.
[26] See Chapter 9, Section 9.1.1. [27] See Chapter 9, Section 9.1.1.2.
[28] See Chapter 9, Section 9.1. [29] See Chapter 7, Section 7.4.2.
[30] See Chapter 4, Section 4.3. [31] See Chapter 5, Section 5.3.

12.2 Innovation and the *sui generis* nature of international criminal procedure

Newcomers to the tribunals are frequently baffled or vexed when they encounter procedures that reflect practices in domestic jurisdictions different from their own. For example, the fact that the parties are primarily responsible for developing the trial record,[32] and thus the expectation that they will examine witnesses with little or no intervention from the bench, may be entirely foreign to practitioners more familiar with inquisitorial systems. Similarly, counsel from adversarial systems can be confounded by the participation rights offered to victims at the ICC and ECCC,[33] the broad discretion afforded to chambers to consider evidence that would never be admitted in their home jurisdictions,[34] or judicial powers that appear to encroach on prosecutorial discretion.[35] At other times, resistance to a particular practice – such as witness proofing[36] – may stem not from the fact that it comes from a common law or civil law tradition, but because it seems inconsistent with notions of the professional obligations of attorneys that are not unique to a particular legal system.[37]

As noted throughout this volume, the procedural framework within which all the tribunals operate is fundamentally adversarial, but also incorporates inquisitorial features to varying degrees.[38] Parties drive every phase of the proceedings. At almost all the tribunals surveyed, the decision to launch an investigation rests with the prosecution,[39] which must then determine whether and which of the underlying facts indicate that crimes within the jurisdiction of the respective tribunal have been committed.[40] At the *ad hoc* Tribunals and the SCSL, where judicial review of the resulting indictment is generally limited to ensuring a sufficient factual basis

[32] See generally Chapter 7, Sections 7.6.2, 7.9; Chapter 9, text accompanying notes 110–111.

[33] See Chapter 8, Sections 8.3.1, 8.4.1. [34] See Chapter 9, Sections 9.1.1, 9.1.3.

[35] See Chapter 6, text accompanying notes 66–70 (discussing judicial authority to alter the legal characterisation of facts confirmed in the indictment); Chapter 6, Section 6.6.2 (examining chambers' powers to restrict the scope of trials by ordering that evidence not be led on certain charges in the indictment); Chapter 3, Section 3.1.2 (ICTY Bureau's ability to veto an indictment).

[36] See Chapter 7, Section 7.6.4.

[37] See Code of Conduct of the Bar of England and Wales (8th edn 2004), Rule 705(a) ('A barrister must not … rehearse, practise or coach a witness in relation to his evidence'). But see William T. Pizzi and Walter Perron, 'Crime Victims in German Courtrooms: A Comparative Perspective on American Problems', (1996) *32 Stanford Journal of International Law* 37, 64 (noting, critically, that such 'pretrial witness preparation … is standard practice in serious American criminal cases').

[38] See Chapter 1, Section 1.2; Chapter 6, text accompanying notes 66–70; Chapter 7, Section 7.9; Chapter 9, text accompanying notes 110–111.

[39] See generally Chapter 4, Section 4.1. The notable exception is the ECCC, which has Co-Investigating Judges. See Chapter 1, Section 1.2. Even at the ICC, the Prosecutor retains discretion to decide whether to initiate an investigation in response to a referral from a state or the Security Council. See Chapter 3, Section 3.2.2.

[40] See Chapter 6, Section 6.1; see also *ibid.*, text accompanying notes 66–70 (discussing ICC jurisprudence clarifying that, notwithstanding regulatory authority to alter the legal characterisation of facts, only facts alleged by the prosecution and confirmed by the pre-trial chamber may form the basis of the subsequent trial).

for the detention and trial of the accused, the onus is on the defence to challenge any legal inadequacies of the charging instrument.[41] At all the tribunals, it is the parties that propose witnesses and indicate the preferred form and extent of their potential evidence;[42] who seek subpoenas and other orders from the chambers to aid their preparation for trial;[43] who move for reconsideration of judicial orders or leave to file interlocutory appeals of trial chamber decisions;[44] or in the case of the defence, move for a judgement of acquittal at the end of the prosecution's case.[45]

On the other hand, provisions in the governing instruments of all the tribunals confer a great deal of discretionary authority on the judges that is more akin to the broader role of courts in inquisitorial systems. Pre-trial or trial chambers may alter the legal characterisation of the charges;[46] direct that certain charges will be excluded from the trial;[47] and appoint their own experts or *amici curiae*;[48] trial chambers may call their own witnesses and question the parties' witnesses;[49] and appellate chambers may admit new evidence and revise factual findings, convictions, and sentences, rather than simply remanding the case to the trial level.[50]

What the preceding chapters' review of the various procedural regimes demonstrates most clearly, however, is that those responsible for crafting that framework have increasingly adopted new tools and techniques to tackle the problems of managing trials that may involve several co-accused, hundreds of witnesses, and thousands of items of evidence. In doing so, the judges have created procedures without identical counterparts in any of the national systems from which they were derived. Moving beyond their own previous experience, judges have promulgated and made frequent use of rules that facilitate the admission of written evidence in lieu of testimony to the extent that a witness's appearance at trial may be shortened or, in certain instances, dispensed with completely;[51] liberally permitted the joining of cases;[52] struggled with effectively managing self-represented accused;[53] empowered themselves to intervene in the parties' presentation of their respective cases by limiting the number of witnesses that may be called or the total amount of time a party may be allocated;[54] and

[41] See Chapter 6, Section 6.1.2.1. But see *ibid.*, text accompanying notes 39–44 (noting approvingly that ICC chambers typically review both the legal and factual bases for the charges before issuing arrest warrants).
[42] See Chapter 7, Sections 7.3.1, 7.6.2, 7.9; Chapter 9, Section 9.2.
[43] See Chapter 3, Sections 3.1.4, 3.2.6; Chapter 6, Section 6.3.2.
[44] See Chapter 7, Section 7.7; Chapter 11, Section 11.4.
[45] See Chapter 7, Section 7.6.5.
[46] See Chapter 6, text accompanying notes 66–70 (discussing this practice at the ICC).
[47] See Chapter 6, Section 6.6.2.
[48] See Chapter 9, Section 9.2.1.2 (on experts); Chapter 5, Section 5.6 (on *amici curiae*).
[49] See Chapter 7, Section 7.6.2.
[50] See Chapter 11, Sections 11.6, 11.7.
[51] See O-Gon Kwon, 'The Challenge of an International Criminal Trial as Seen from the Bench', (2007) 5 *Journal of International Criminal Justice* 360, 364–368 (discussing the extensive decisional law in the *Milošević* case on the admission of written evidence in lieu of oral testimony, and opining that it constitutes a blend of common law and civil law mechanisms). See also Chapter 9, Section 9.2.1.1.
[52] See Chapter 6, Section 6.2.
[53] See Chapter 5, Section 5.3.
[54] See Chapter 6, Section 6.6.2.

given themselves the authority to limit the scope of the prosecution's case against the accused.[55] As described in the preceding chapters and in the following section, the judges' creation and application of these procedural tools has not always been uncontroversial.

Beyond the difficulties associated with the nature of the cases before the tribunals, their trials are further complicated by the international character of the various actors who participate in the proceedings, as well as by lingering security concerns in the states whose conflicts spawned the tribunals. Victims and witnesses often face risks at home because of their participation in the tribunals' trials, which has given rise to extensive and elaborate protective measures regimes.[56] In a further effort to protect individuals placed at risk by their participation, the judges have recognised a unique testimonial privilege for war correspondents.[57] States and international organisations such as the ICRC are similarly concerned about the disclosure of sensitive security information, and the tribunals have developed tools for protecting these entities' legitimate interests.[58] Where witnesses are unable to travel the often great distances to the tribunals to participate, the judges have developed procedures permitting international audio- or video-link testimony.[59] Each of these developments has required the judges to balance the concerns of various constituents against the fair trial rights of the accused on an individual basis.

Furthermore, the nature of the international context in which the tribunals operate has required them to develop unique procedural tools for managing their relationships with states and international organisations in an effective manner. Most of these tools have no analogue in any domestic system. Interacting with the host state; facilitating the cooperation of other states in the investigation, arrest, and surrender of suspects and accused;[60] ordering the deferral of cases in national proceedings;[61] referring indicted cases back to national courts and continuing to monitor those cases;[62] consulting with states on applications for temporary release of accused from detention;[63] managing relationships with the states in which convicted persons serve their sentences;[64] and interacting effectively with international organisations, particularly the Security Council,[65] all illustrate the multi-dimensional complexity of the tribunals' work and the unique procedural difficulties with which they have had to contend.

At the infancy of the *ad hoc* Tribunals, the melding of procedures drawn from across the adversarial/inquisitorial divide produced a new creature with an uncertain pedigree which was viewed with some scepticism. In the face of that scepticism,

[55] See Chapter 6, Section 6.6.2. [56] See Chapter 7, Sections 7.4.1, 7.4.2.
[57] See Chapter 9, Section 9.3.2.2. [58] See Chapter 6, Sections 6.3.2, 6.5.1.4.
[59] See Chapter 7, Section 7.4.3. [60] See Chapter 4, Sections 4.1, 4.2.
[61] See Chapter 3, Section 3.1.1. [62] See Chapter 3, Section 3.1.3.
[63] See Chapter 4, Section 4.3. [64] See Chapter 10, Sections 10.4, 10.5.
[65] See, e.g., Chapter 3, Section 3.2.5.

and dealing with the unique issues discussed repeatedly in the previous chapters, the tribunals have been forced to adapt and innovate in order to fulfil the difficult mandates bestowed upon them by the international community. Those unique challenges can no longer be solved – if, indeed, they ever could – solely by looking to national approaches, a lesson which the tribunals seem to have learned, if not without some growing pains. Sixteen years after the creation of the ICTY, what has emerged for it and its successors is a truly *sui generis* body of international criminal procedure.

12.3 Judicial appropriation of power at the international criminal tribunals

Many of the procedural innovations discussed in the previous section and throughout this volume form part of a broader trend at the international criminal tribunals of judicial expansion of power. As international criminal procedure has evolved, the judges at these tribunals have effected a gradual but steady appropriation of authority, not only in dealing with the parties before them, but also with entities such as states and private individuals. In most cases, this process has not been expressly sanctioned by the bodies responsible for amending the tribunals' constitutions – the Security Council for the *ad hoc* Tribunals and the Assembly of States Parties (ASP) for the ICC. These bodies' inaction in the face of such developments could signal tacit approval or at least acquiescence,[66] though it may also be the result of an inability of the various stakeholders within these bodies to agree on a single course of action.

The manner in which the Security Council originally delegated the ICTY and ICTR rule-making role to the judges laid the foundation for a sweeping exercise of judicial power.[67] With sparse procedural guidance in the Statutes, the judge-made Rules govern almost every aspect of the investigation, pre-trial, trial, sentencing, and appeals phases.[68] Many of these procedures have no obvious statutory basis, and yet have become critical to the Tribunals' functioning; examples include the ability to hear interlocutory appeals;[69] powers of subpoena and contempt;[70] procedures for guilty pleas and plea bargaining;[71] and the power to refer indicted cases

[66] See, e.g., Allison Marston Danner, 'When Courts Make Law: How the International Criminal Tribunals Recast the Laws of War', (2006) 59 *Vanderbilt Law Review* 1, 43 ('If the lawmaking undertaken by the Tribunals ran contrary to the wishes of the Security Council we would, in theory, expect to see the members of the Council taking steps to rein in their wayward creation. The relationship of the Security Council to the Tribunals, however, does not demonstrate this pattern.'); Chapter 2, Section 2.2.3 (ASP's lack of objection over the manner in which the ICC judges have employed their regulation-making power may suggest willingness to allow the judges greater control over shaping the Court's procedure).

[67] See Chapter 2, Section 2.1.1.

[68] See Chapter 2, Section 2.1.3.

[69] See Chapter 11, Section 11.4.

[70] See Chapter 6, Section 6.3.2; Chapter 7, Section 7.8.

[71] See Chapter 6, Section 6.4.

to national authorities for prosecution.[72] The judges have robustly asserted their power to compel the cooperation of national authorities by, for example, demanding deferral of cases from state authorities in virtually any circumstance,[73] and ruling states' conditions on the surrender of suspects null and void.[74] Chambers have extended this authority through the case law to find the inherent power to issue binding orders for the production of testimony and documents to states and international organisations, and to issue subpoenas to individuals under threat of contempt.[75] The judges have also conferred upon themselves significant license to manage the scope and presentation of cases and to intervene – in theory if not often in practice – in the parties' strategic decisions.[76] Thus, for instance, judges at the ICTY could veto indictments if they found the suspect insufficiently senior;[77] may order the prosecution not to present evidence on certain charges in the indictment;[78] and may place strict limits on the number of witnesses the parties may call at trial, and the time available to the parties to question witnesses and lead other evidence at trial.[79] In another example of the broad exercise of their granted powers, ICTY judges in plenary have sometimes acted as quasi-legislators to amend certain rules in order to overrule decisions of the Appeals Chamber.[80]

The architects of the ICC intended to circumscribe the judges' authority to a far greater extent.[81] In sharp contrast to the ICTY and ICTR Statutes, the Rome Statute contains scores of lengthy procedural rules – as one former ICTY judge put it, 'a fortress of restrictions'[82] – that can only be amended by a two-thirds majority vote

[72] See Chapter 3, Section 3.1.3. For criticism of the ICTY's recognition and employment of powers not listed in the Statute, see generally Gregory P. Lombardi, 'Legitimacy and the Expanding Power of the ICTY', (2003) 37 *New England Law Review* 887.

[73] See Chapter 3, Section 3.1.1 (discussing the broad nature of the criteria for deferral under ICTY and ICTR Rule 9).

[74] See Chapter 3, Section 3.1.4.

[75] See Chapter 3, Section 3.1.4; Chapter 6, Section 6.3.2. For a particularly broad rule, see Rule 54 of the ICTY and ICTR: 'At the request of either party or *proprio motu*, a Judge or a Trial Chamber may issue such orders, summonses, subpoenas, warrants and transfer orders as may be necessary for the purposes of an investigation or for the preparation or conduct of the trial.' Alexander Zahar characterises Rule 54 as 'remarkable not only as a bold act of judicial self-aggrandizement, but for begging the question about the limits of its application'. Alexander Zahar, 'International Court and Private Citizen', (2009) 12 *New Criminal Law Review* 569, 576 (footnote omitted).

[76] See Chapter 6, Sections 6.6.1, 6.6.2; Chapter 7, Sections 7.3.1, 7.9.

[77] See Chapter 3, Section 3.1.2.

[78] See Chapter 6, Section 6.6.2 (discussing ICTY Rule 73 *bis*).

[79] See Chapter 6, Sections 6.6.1, 6.6.2; Chapter 7, Sections 7.3.1, 7.9.

[80] See Chapter 2, Section 2.1.4.

[81] See, e.g., William W. Burke-White, 'The International Criminal Court and the Future of Legal Accountability', (2003) *ILSA Journal of International and Comparative Law* 195, 196 (arguing that, as a result of the architects' fears of creating a powerful court, '[t]here is probably no weaker court in the world – including the local traffic court down the street – than the International Criminal Court'); David Hunt, 'The International Criminal Court: High Hopes, "Creative Ambiguity" and an Unfortunate Mistrust in International Judges', (2004) 2 *Journal of International Criminal Justice* 56, 61 (arguing that the Rome Statute 'evinces a deep suspicion of the Court's judges').

[82] Hunt, *supra* note 81, p. 61.

in the ASP.[83] The ASP likewise creates and amends, by two-thirds majority, the ICC Rules.[84] Alterations to the procedural framework thus require slow and cumbersome multilateral negotiations, limiting the judges' ability to adapt the framework to respond to novel situations that arise in practice. Through the Statute's complementarity provisions, moreover, states sought to reserve for themselves considerable prerogatives, including the ability to curtail many of the Court's efforts to take action with respect to them or individuals within their territory. A prime example is the complicated system for determining the admissibility of a case, replete with opportunities for states to keep cases off the Court's docket and challenge any finding of admissibility.[85] Other examples include the absence of a subpoena power and the existence of several grounds on which a state may permissibly decline to surrender an ICC suspect or may otherwise refuse requests for cooperation.[86] Commentators have remarked that the Rome Statute and ICC Rules serve in many respects as a straightjacket that unduly stifles judges' flexibility and adaptability.[87]

In spite of these restrictions, the ICC's judges have, like their ICTY and ICTR counterparts, managed to expand the scope of their powers significantly by liberally interpreting provisions of the respective Statutes and Rules. They have also made aggressive use of judge-made Regulations, notwithstanding the Regulations' ostensible restriction to matters of 'routine functioning'.[88] Judges have given themselves the power to change the legal characterisation of the facts against the accused at any time during the trial, with the result that the accused may be called to answer additional alleged crimes, as long as these do not exceed the facts described in the charging document.[89] Moreover, one Pre-Trial Chamber added new charges against an accused without the Prosecutor's consent, despite statutory language expressly conferring on the Prosecutor the decision whether to add new charges, and thereby effectively compelled the Prosecutor to lead evidence on those charges.[90] The absence of any notion of 'self-referral' in the governing instruments

83 See Chapter 2, Sections 2.2.1, 2.2.2. 84 See Chapter 2, Section 2.2.2.

85 See Chapter 3, Section 3.2.3.2. See also Burke-White, *supra* note 81, p. 197 (arguing that, as a result of the complementarity provisions, 'all a national court has to do to block the ICC from prosecuting is to conduct a good faith investigation and determine that no crime was committed'; and '[e]ven if an individual is within the ICC's jurisdiction and the prosecutor wants to pursue the case, if a national court – any national court – investigates or prosecutes, the ICC is effectively stopped in its tracks').

86 See Chapter 3, Section 3.2.6; Hunt, *supra* note 81, pp. 69–70.

87 See, e.g., Hunt, *supra* note 82, pp. 62–63; Burke-White, *supra* note 81, pp. 197–198; Mohamed M. El Zeidy, 'The Principle of Complementarity: A New Machinery to Implement International Criminal Law', (2002) 23 *Michigan Journal of International Law* 869, 909–910, 918, 969–970; Giuliano Turone, 'Powers and Duties of the Prosecutor', in Antonio Cassese, Paola Gaeta, and John R.W.D. Jones (eds.), *The Rome Statute of the International Criminal Court: A Commentary*, Vol. I (2002), p. 1163.

88 See Chapter 2, Section 2.2.3.

89 See ICC Court Regulation 55(2); see also Chapter 2, Section 2.2.3; Chapter 6, Section 6.1.2.

90 See Gideon Boas, James L. Bischoff, and Natalie L. Reid, *Elements of Crimes Under International Law* (2008), pp. 302–303 (discussing *Prosecutor* v. *Lubanga*, Doc. No. ICC-01/04-01/06-803-tEN, Decision on the Confirmation of Charges, 29 January 2007, para. 204, and concluding that '[t]his course of action would appear to contradict the unambiguous mandate set forth in the Rome Statute'); Chapter 11, Section 11.4.2 (discussing the Pre-Trial Chamber's refusal to grant leave to appeal this decision). See also Matthew Happold,

has not deterred chambers at all levels from giving the practice their stamp of approval through inventive interpretations of the complementarity provisions.[91] As a consequence, a self-referring state need only stop its investigations to render a case admissible before the ICC, and the Court will not really scrutinise the state's reasons or examine its true capacity to investigate and prosecute.[92] The resulting laxity of the complementarity regime was almost certainly not contemplated by the Statute's drafters, who declared it 'the duty of every State to exercise its criminal jurisdiction over those responsible for international crimes'.[93]

In some respects, the ICC's judges exercise their powers even more expansively than *ad hoc* Tribunal chambers – a paradoxical development, given the formal restrictions on the former and the relative freedom accorded the latter in their respective Statutes. For example, despite granting themselves the regulatory authority to do so, ICTY judges have been generally reluctant to intervene extensively in the parties' decisions on case management or to restrict the scope of indictments.[94] Meanwhile, the ICC's judges have already engineered several ways to 'escape from the shackles by which they have been confined by suspicious states'.[95] The degree of judicial activism exhibited at the international criminal tribunals must be alarming to many states, especially with regard to the ICC, whose jurisdictional reach is not confined to a limited geographical area or temporal scope. While the Rome Statute has already enjoyed a surprisingly large number of ratifications, more than eighty states have yet to ratify it – including some of the most influential, such as the United States, Russia, China, and India – and many are watching the judges' performance with a close and wary eye.[96]

'Prosecutor v. Thomas Lubanga, Decision of Pre-Trial Chamber I of the International Criminal Court, 29 January 2007', (2007) 56 *International and Comparative Law Quarterly* 713, 724 (characterising decision as part of an ongoing struggle between the Prosecutor and Chambers over who determines the shape and scope of the case).

[91] See Chapter 3, Sections 3.2.3.1.1, 3.2.3.1.2. See also William A. Schabas, 'Prosecutorial Discretion v. Judicial Activism at the International Criminal Court', (2008) 6 *Journal of International Criminal Justice* 731, 757 (characterising the *Lubanga* Pre-Trial Chamber's admissibility decision as an exercise of judicial activism); *ibid.*, pp. 760–761 ('Our concern must be that opportunistic constructions of the ICC Statute driven by the need to generate activity will linger in the future, distorting the proper role of the ICC in the campaign against impunity and the protection of human rights').

[92] See Chapter 3, Sections 3.2.4, 3.3.

[93] Rome Statute, preambular para. 6.

[94] See Chapter 6, Section 6.6; Chapter 7, Section 7.9.

[95] Hunt, *supra* note 81, p. 70.

[96] See, e.g., David J. Scheffer, 'The United States and the International Criminal Court', (1999) 93 *American Journal of International Law* 12, 19 (head of U.S. delegation at Rome expressing U.S. concerns that the ICC's judges might too easily find cases admissible); Gerhard Hafner, Kristen Boon, Anne Rübesame, and Jonathan Huston, 'A Response to the American View as Presented by Ruth Wedgwood', (1999) 10 *European Journal of International Law* 108, 116–120 (attempting to assuage U.S. anxieties about the manner in which ICC judges might interpret and employ the complementarity provisions); Lombardi, *supra* note 73, p. 901 (noting U.S. fears about the ICC; that '[t]he standard response to those fears has been that the powers of the Court and of the prosecutor are carefully circumscribed by the Rome Statute'; but arguing that 'if the ICTY has gone beyond its Statute, it seems equally possible that the ICC may do the same'). See also generally (2005) 3 *Journal of International Criminal Justice* 608 *et seq.* (articles on the attitudes of China, Russia, India, and Iran towards the ICC).

This third volume of the *International Criminal Law Practitioner Library Series* completes our review of international criminal law. The first two volumes considered the forms of responsibility and the elements of the core categories of international crimes, which together form the substantive law. This third volume has addressed international criminal procedure, an equally crucial and, at least until recently, less critically reviewed component of international criminal law. The procedural rules of international criminal law supply the framework within which the substantive law operates, and are vital to the law's functioning. Our overarching goal has been to assist practitioners in the investigation, development, and presentation of cases; to support chambers in the application of an accurate and appropriately flexible approach to their many duties; and to provide scholars and others with a more precise and nuanced understanding of the corpus of international criminal law – substantive and procedural – as practised at the various tribunals.

Index